"Philosophers Tommy L. Lott and John P. Pittmar
that captures the existential urgency, vibrancy
Africana philosophical thought. This philosopł
knowledge production, critique, and clarification that is mgmy ....
emancipationist world-making of a people whose theories must prove actionable, in the
form of concrete liberation."

George Yancy, Duquesne University, editor of *Cornel West: A Critical Reader*

"Authoritative, compendious, and detailed, this landmark publication sets a standard
against which every other reference work in the field must be judged."

Wilson J. Moses, The Pennsylvania State University

"*A Companion to African-American Philosophy* is an indispensable and elegant guide to a
constellation of inquiries into and about African-American thought and the production of
that thought."

Wahneema Lubiano, Duke University

"A new convergence of reflections on the African-American experience by some of the
most active philosophers in the United States. An important reference work for scholars
and a useful tool in the classroom."

Emmanuel Chukwudi Eze, DePaul University

"This is the most thorough compilation of contemporary African-American philosophy I
have yet seen. The inclusion of a selection of essays on cultural issues is a great addition.
From racism to reparations to rap, these essays show how philosophers can illuminate
current debates and eliminate persistent confusions in the mainstream discussions of
these topics."

Linda Martín Alcoff, Syracuse University

"*A Companion to African-American Philosophy* is a valuable reference source. The editors
have done an excellent job of representing the essential themes of African-American
philosophical thought as well as notable individuals from the field. Libraries that support
black history/studies, philosophy, American studies, and contemporary American
thought should definitely purchase the *Companion*: it is well worth the cost. The novice
will especially gain a wealth of information."

Reference Reviews

Blackwell Companions to Philosophy

This outstanding student reference series offers a comprehensive and authoritative survey of philosophy as a whole. Written by today's leading philosophers, each volume provides lucid and engaging coverage of the key figures, terms, topics, and problems of the field. Taken together, the volumes provide the ideal basis for course use, representing an unparalleled work of reference for students and specialists alike.

Already published in the series:

1. The Blackwell Companion to Philosophy, Second Edition
   Edited by Nicholas Bunnin and Eric Tsui-James

2. A Companion to Ethics
   Edited by Peter Singer

3. A Companion to Aesthetics
   Edited by David Cooper

4. A Companion to Epistemology
   Edited by Jonathan Dancy and Ernest Sosa

5. A Companion to Contemporary Political Philosophy
   Edited by Robert E. Goodin and Philip Pettit

6. A Companion to Philosophy of Mind
   Edited by Samuel Guttenplan

7. A Companion to Metaphysics
   Edited by Jaegwon Kim and Ernest Sosa

8. A Companion to Philosophy of Law and Legal Theory
   Edited by Dennis Patterson

9. A Companion to Philosophy of Religion
   Edited by Philip L. Quinn and Charles Taliaferro

10. A Companion to the Philosophy of Language
    Edited by Bob Hale and Crispin Wright

11. A Companion to World Philosophies
    Edited by Eliot Deutsch and Ron Bontekoe

12. A Companion to Continental Philosophy
    Edited by Simon Critchley and William Schroeder

13. A Companion to Feminist Philosophy
    Edited by Alison M. Jaggar and Iris Marion Young

14. A Companion to Cognitive Science
    Edited by William Bechtel and George Graham

15. A Companion to Bioethics
    Edited by Helga Kuhse and Peter Singer

16. A Companion to the Philosophers
    Edited by Robert L. Arrington

17. A Companion to Business Ethics
    Edited by Robert E. Frederick

18. A Companion to the Philosophy of Science
    Edited by W. H. Newton-Smith

19. A Companion to Environmental Philosophy
    Edited by Dale Jamieson

20. A Companion to Analytic Philosophy
    Edited by A. P. Martinich and David Sosa

21. A Companion to Genethics
    Edited by Justine Burley and John Harris

22. A Companion to Philosophical Logic
    Edited by Dale Jacquette

23. A Companion to Early Modern Philosophy
    Edited by Steven Nadler

24. A Companion to Philosophy in the Middle Ages
    Edited by Jorge J. E. Gracia and Timothy B. Noone

25. A Companion to African-American Philosophy
    Edited by Tommy L. Lott and John P. Pittman

26. A Companion to Applied Ethics
    Edited by R. G. Frey and Christopher Heath Wellman

27. A Companion to the Philosophy of Education
    Edited by Randall Curren

28. A Companion to African Philosophy
    Edited by Kwasi Wiredu

29. A Companion to Heidegger
    Edited by Hubert L. Dreyfus and Mark A. Wrathall

30. A Companion to Rationalism
    Edited by Alan Nelson

31. A Companion to Ancient Philosophy
    Edited by Mary Louise Gill and Pierre Pellegrin

32. A Companion to Pragmatism
    Edited by John R. Shook and Joseph Margolis

33. A Companion to Nietzsche
    Edited by Keith Ansell Pearson

34. A Companion to Socrates
    Edited by Sara Ahbel-Rappe and Rachanar Kamtekar

35. A Companion to Phenomenology and Existentialism
    Edited by Hubert L Dreyfus and Mark A Wrathall

*Blackwell
Companions to
Philosophy*

A Companion to African-American Philosophy

Edited by

Tommy L. Lott
and
John P. Pittman

Blackwell
Publishing

BLACKWELL PUBLISHING
350 Main Street, Malden, MA 02148-5020, USA
9600 Garsington Road, Oxford OX4 2DQ, UK
550 Swanston Street, Carlton, Victoria 3053, Australia

First published 2003 by Blackwell Publishing Ltd
First published in paperback 2006

1   2006

Library of Congress Cataloging-in-Publication Data

A companion to African-American philosophy / edited by Tommy L. Lott and John P. Pittman.
    p. cm. – (Blackwell companions to philosophy; 25)
   Includes bibliographical references and index.
   ISBN 1-55786-839-5 (alk. paper)
   1. African American philosophy.   I. Lott, Tommy Lee, 1946–   II. Pittman, John P.
   III. Series.

   B944.A37 C66 2002
   191'.089'96073 – dc21

                                                                                                2002066640

ISBN-13: 978-1-55786-839-8 (alk. paper)
ISBN-13: 978-1-4051-4568-8 (paperback)
ISBN-10: 1-4051-4568-4 (paperback)

A catalogue record for this title is available from the British Library.

Set in 10 on 12.5 pt Photina
by SNP Best-set Typesetter Ltd, Hong Kong

For further information on
Blackwell Publishing, visit our website:
www.blackwellpublishing.com

Contents

Part VI   Aesthetic and Cultural Values

Notes on Contributors

Anita L. Allen is Professor of Law at the University of Pennsylvania School of Law, where she teaches Privacy Law, Legal Philosophy, Bioethics, and Torts. Her numerous articles are published in philosophy and law journals. She is author of *Uneasy Access: Privacy for Women in A Free Society*. Allen received her Ph.D. in Philosophy from the University of Michigan and her law degree from Harvard University.

Bernard R. Boxill is Professor of Philosophy at the University of North Carolina, Chapel Hill. His articles are widely published in journals and anthologies. He is author of *Blacks and Social Justice* and editor of *Race and Racism*.

Patricia Hill Collins is Charles Phelps Taft Professor of Sociology in the Department of African American Studies at the University of Cincinnati. She is author of *Fighting Words: Black Women and the Search for Justice* and *Black Feminist Thought: Knowledge, Consciousness, and the Politics of Empowerment*.

Angela Y. Davis is Professor of Philosophy in the History of Consciousness Program at the University of California, Santa Cruz and has an appointment to a University of California Presidential Chair in African American and Feminist Studies. She is author of *Angela Davis: An Autobiography*; *Women Race and Class*; *Women, Culture and Politics*; and *Blues Legacies and Black Feminism*.

Annette Dula co-edited with Sara Goering *"It Just Ain't Fair": The Ethics of Health Care for African Americans*. She has published articles on race and health care policy for the Hastings Center.

Gerald Early is Director of the International Writers Center and Professor of English at Washington University in St. Louis. He is currently a research fellow at the National Humanities Center in North Carolina. He is author of *Tuxedo Junction* and *The Culture of Bruising: Essays on Prizefighting*. He is editor of *Speech and Power* and *Lure and Loathing*.

David Theo Goldberg is Director of the Humanities Research Institute, University of California and Professor of African American Studies and Criminology, Law and Society at University of California, Irvine. He is author of *The Racial State*; *Racist Culture:*

Philosophy and the Politics of Meaning; *Racial Subjects: Writings on Race in America*. He is editor of several anthologies including *Ethical Theory and Social Issues, Anatomy of Racism, Multiculturalism: A Critical Reader,* and co-editor of *Jewish Identity, Race Critical Theories, Relocating Postcolonialism, Blackwell Companion on Racial and Ethnic Studies,* and *Between Law and Culture*. He is the founding co-editor of *Social Identites: Journal for the Study of Race, Nation, and Culture*.

Lewis R. Gordon is Chair of Africana Studies and Professor of Africana Studies and Modern Culture and Media at Brown University. He is author of numerous articles and books, including: *Bad Faith and Anti-Black Racism*; *Fanon and the Crisis of European Man: An Essay on Philosophy and the Human Sciences*; *Her Majesty's Other Children: Philosophical Sketches of Racism from a Neocolonial Age* and *Existentia Africana: Understanding Africana Existential Thought*. He is editor of *Existence in Black: An Anthology of Black Existential Philosophy* and coeditor of *Fanon: A Critical Reader*.

Leonard Harris is Professor of Philosophy at Purdue University. He is editor of *Children in Chaos: A Philosophy for Children Experience*; *The Philosophy of Alain Locke: Harlem Renaissance and Beyond*; *Philosophy Born of Struggle: Afro-American Philosophy from 1917*; *Racism*, and *The Critical Pragmatism of Alain Locke* and co-editor of *American Philosophies; Exploitation and Exclusion: Race and Class*. He is founder of the Alain Locke Society and the Philosophy Born of Struggle Association.

Luke C. Harris is Chair of the Political Science Department at Vassar College. He has published and teaches about questions of equality. He is a co-founder of the African American Policy Forum, a black feminist think tank.

Trudier Harris-Lopez is J. Carlyle Sitterson Professor of English at the University of North Carolina at Chapel Hill. She is author, editor and co-editor of twenty volumes, including *The Literature of the American South: A Norton Anthology*, *Exorcising Blackness: Historical and Literary Lynching and Burning Rituals, Selected Works of Ida B. Wells-Barnett*, and her most recent book, *Saints, Sinners, Saviors: Strong Black Women in African American Literature*.

Paget Henry is Associate Professor of Sociology and Afro-American Studies at Brown University. He is author of *Peripheral Capitalism and Underdevelopment in Antigua* and *Caliban's Reason* and co-editor of *C. L. R. James's Caribbean*. He is also editor of *The C. L. R. James Journal*.

Joy A. James is Professor of Africana Studies at Brown University. She is author of *Resisting State Violence: Radicalism, Gender and Race in U.S. Culture, Transcending the Talented Tenth: Black Leaders and American Intellectuals*, and *Shadowboxing: Representations of Black Feminist Politics*. She is editor of several anthologies including *States of Confinement: Policing, Detentions and Prisons* and co-editor of *The Black Feminist Reader*. Her most recent book is *Imprisoned Intellectuals: U.S. Political Prisoners and Social Justice*.

Ronald A. T. Judy is Professor of English at the University of Pittsburgh, where he teaches courses related to the fields of American literature and culture, African litera-ture, Arab literature, contemporary Islamic thought, global English studies and literature. He has been a Fulbright Fellow at the Institut Bourguiba des Langues Vivantes, Universite de Tunis I. He is author of *(Dis)forming the American Canon: The Vernacular of African Arabic American Slave Narrative*. He is editor of a special edition of *boundary 2* on *Sociology Hesitant: W. E. B. Du Bois's Dynamic Thinking*. He is currently completing a book project tentatively titled, *The Last Negro or the Destruction of Categorical Thought: An Experiment in Hyperbolic Thinking*.

Frank M. Kirkland is Associate Professor of Philosophy at Hunter College and the Graduate Center, both at the City University of New York. He is editor of the volume *Phenomenology: East and West*. He co-edited with Bill E. Lawson *Frederick Douglass: A Critical Reader*. He is currently writing a book provisionally titled *Hegel and Husserl: Idealist Meditations*.

Bill E. Lawson is Professor of Philosophy at Michigan State University where he teaches courses on social and political philosophy. He is co-author of *Between Slavery and Freedom: Philosophy and American Slavery*, editor of *The Underclass Question*, and co-editor of *Frederick Douglass: A Critical Reader*.

Tommy L. Lott is Professor of Philosophy at San Jose State University. He is author of *The Invention of Race: Black Culture and the Politics of Representation* and *Like Rum in the Punch: Alain Locke and the Theory of African-American Culture*. He is editor of *Subjugation and Bondage: Critical Essays on Slavery and Social Philosophy* and *African-American Philosophy: Selected Readings*. He is co-editor of *The Idea of Race* and *Philosophers on Race: A Critical Reader*.

Howard McGary is Professor of Philosophy at Rutgers, The State University of New Jersey in New Brunswick where he teaches courses on African-American philosophy and social and political philosophy. He has published numerous articles and is author of *Race and Social Justice* and co-author of *Between Slavery and Freedom: Philosophy and American Slavery*.

Charles W. Mills is Professor of Philosophy at the University of Illinois at Chicago and a University Scholar at UIC. He is the author of numerous articles, as well as two books, *The Racial Contract* and *Blackness Visible: Essays on Philosophy and Race*. He is working on a third book, tentatively titled *Red Shift: From Critical Class Theory to Critical Race Theory*.

Michele Moody-Adams is Hutchinson Professor of Ethics and Public Life and Professor of Philosophy at Cornell University. She has published numerous articles in journals and anthologies. She is author of *Fieldwork in Familiar Places: Morality, Culture, and Philosophy*.

Albert G. Mosley is Professor of Philosophy at Smith College. He is editor of *African Philosophy: Selected Readings*. He is co-author of *Affirmative Action: Social Justice or Unfair Preference?* and *An Introduction to Logic: From Everyday Life to Formal Systems*.

Lucius T. Outlaw, Jr. formerly T. Wistar Brown Professor of Philosophy at Haverford College, is Professor of Philosophy and Director of the African-American Studies Program at Vanderbilt University where he teaches and engages in research devoted to

African Philosophy, African-American Philosophy, Marx, Critical Social Theory, Social and Political Philosophy, and the history of Western Philosophy. He is author of *On Race and Philosophy*. His forthcoming book is entitled *In Search of Critical Social Theory in the Interest of Black Folk*.

John P. Pittman teaches philosophy at John Jay College of Criminal Justice at the City University of New York. He is editor of *African-American Perspectives and Philosophical Traditions*. He is Associate Editor of *Philosophia Africana*, a journal devoted to the analysis of philosophy and issues in Africa and the black diaspora.

Thaddeus Pope formerly served as a Judicial Law Clerk to the Honorable John L. Coffey in the United States Court of Appeals for the 7th Circuit. His publications include articles on the Miranda rule, airline passenger security, smoker's choice, and the death sentence. He practices law in Beverly Hills, California.

T. Denean Sharpley-Whiting is Professor of Africana Studies and Romance Languages and Chair of Africana Studies at Hamilton College. She has been awarded fellowships from the Camargo Foundation in Cassis, France, the Rockefeller Foundation in Bellagio, Italy and the George A. and Eliza Howard Foundation. She is author of *Sexualized Savages, Primal Fears, and Primitive Narratives in French* and *Frantz Fanon: Conflicts and Feminisms* and co-editor of *The Black Feminist Reader, Spoils of War: Women of Color, Cultures, and Revolutions* and *Fanon: A Critical Reader*. Her most recent book is *Negritude Women: Race Women, Race Consciousness, Race Literature*.

Richard Shusterman is Chair of Philosophy at Temple University. Editor of *Analytic Aesthetics* and *Bourdieu: A Critical Reader*, he is also author of *The Object of Literary Criticism, T. S. Eliot and the Philosophy of Criticism, Pragmatist Aesthetics, Practicing Philosophy, Performing Live*, and *Surface and Depth*. He has held senior NEH and Fulbright Fellowships.

Lorenzo C. Simpson is Professor of Philosophy at the State University of New York at Stony Brook. He has published articles on hermeneutics, critical theory, philosophy of science, and African-American philosophy in journals and anthologies. He is author of *The Unfinished Project: Towards a Postmetaphysical Humanism* and *Technology, Time and the Conversations of Modernity*. He is also an aspiring jazz saxophonist.

Hortense J. Spillers is the Frederick J. Whiton Professor of English at Cornell University where she teaches courses in African-American and American literature. Recently, she was a visiting professor in cultural studies at the John F. Kennedy Institute, the Free University, Berlin. She is editor of *Comparative American Identities: Race, Sex, and Nationality in the Modern Text* and co-edited with Marjorie Pryse *Conjuring: Black Women, Fiction, and Literary Tradition. Black, White and in Color: Essays on Literature and Color*, a collection of her essays will be published in 2003 by the University of Chicago Press.

Clyde R. Taylor is Professor of Interdisciplinary Studies at the Gallatin School and in Africana Studies at New York University. His numerous articles on black cinema and culture are widely published in journals and anthologies. He is author of *The Mask of*

Art: Breaking the Aesthetic Contract and editor of *Vietnam and Black America*. He wrote the script for *Midnight Ramble*, a documentary about early independent black cinema.

Laurence M. Thomas is Professor in the Departments of Philosophy and Political Science, and a member of the Judaic Studies Program at Syracuse University. His numerous essays on moral and social issues have been widely published in journals and anthologies. He is author of *Living Morally* and *Vessels of Evil: American Slavery and the Holocaust* and co-author of *Sexual Orientation and Human Rights*.

Rudolph V. Vanterpool is Professor of Philosophy and Chair of the department at California State University – Dominquez Hills, where he teaches a variety of courses on moral and legal philosophy. His publications include articles on aesthetics, political philosophy, and African-American philosophy.

Cornel West is the Alphonse Fletcher, Jr. University Professor at Harvard University teaching in Afro-American Studies and Philosophy of Religion. He has numerous articles and books, including: *Race Matters, Keeping Faith: Philosophy and Race in America, Prophesy Deliverance! An Afro-American Revolutionary Christianity, The Ethical Dimensions of Marxist Thought*, and *The American Evasion of Philosophy: A Genealogy of Pragmatism*.

Naomi Zack is Professor of Philosophy at the University of Oregon. She is author of *Bachelors of Science: Seventeenth-Century Identity, Thinking about Race*, and *Race and Mixed Race*. She is editor of *American Mixed Race, Race/Sex, Women of Color in Philosophy* and co-editor of *Race, Class, Gender, and Sexuality*. Her most recent book is *Philosophy of Science and Race*.

Preface

African-American philosophy has only recently been established in the institutions of the philosophical world. The American Philosophical Association's Committee on the Status of Blacks in the Profession was created during the 1970s to deal with issues arising from the new, and growing, population of black philosophers. There are many who still proclaim that "Philosophy is philosophy, whether done by women, blacks, or white men." But it is also widely – and justly – acknowledged that this bare identity is in need of supplementation. Philosophical inquiry must confront the social realities of race and fruitfully develop the insights latent in the collective experience of black folk. Contemporary African-American philosophy emerged at a specific political moment in the 1960s to vie for recognition in the discipline, and is now an academic specialization that constitutes an evolving socio-historical reality.

It was the social movements of black people themselves – from Garveyism and the Harlem Renaissance to the Civil Rights movement and its more radical progeny – that compelled social change and forced the larger American society's grudging acknowledgment of the deep historical racial injustices. Out of the tumult of the 1960s African-American philosophers began to focus on some of the ideas expressed in this volume. Indeed, the advent of Black Studies in the academy is concurrent with the development of African-American philosophy as a field of inquiry. Without the 1960s political movements, however, Black Studies would not have been established. Hence, political activism gave Black Studies, and African-American philosophy, its initial momentum and reason for being, its ideological coloring, practical aims, and its first recruits.

Given the social reality that motivates the African-American orientation to philosophy, many of the anti-historical illusions of mainstream philosophy are less salient. As the articles in this volume attest, African-American philosophy is thoroughly interdisciplinary with a large, but not exclusive, focus on social, political, moral, and cultural issues. While the full sweep of African-American philosophic thought, including that which is devoted to standard topics in metaphysics and epistemology, cannot be represented in a single volume, we have attempted to make this volume representative of the major areas of current research, without attempting to be exhaustive. There are many African-American philosophers working in philosophy of language, the history of philosophy, or logic, for instance, who we have elected not to represent. At this moment, there remains a distinct set of concerns occupying the thought of some African-American philosophers. We envision an eventual merging of interests such that future generations of American philosophers of all racial and ethnic backgrounds working in this area will have come to recognize the importance of this initial contribution to the discipline.

Acknowledgments

The editor and publisher gratefully acknowledge the permission granted to reproduce the following copyright material in this book:

Chapter 1
Cornel West, "Philosophy and the Afro-American Experience," from *Philosophical Forum*, 1977–8 (Winter issue). Reproduced with permission of Blackwell Publishing.

Chapter 10
Tommy L. Lott, "African Retentions," *Social Identities* 1.1 (1995), pp. 200–20.

Chapter 12
Patricia Hill Collins, "Some Group Matters: Intersectionality, Situated Standpoints, and Black Feminist Thought," pp. 201–28 from *Fighting Words: Black Women and The Search for Justice* (University of Minnesota Press, 1998). Copyright © University of Minnesota Press. Also reproduced with the permission of the author Patricia Hill Collins.

Chapter 13
Joy A. James, "Radicalizing Feminisms from 'The Movement Era,'" pp. 73–92 from *Shadowboxing: Representations of Black Feminist Politics*. New York: St. Martin's Press, 1999. Copyright © by Joy A. James. Reprinted with permission of Palgrave Macmillan.

Chapter 14
Naomi Zack, "Philosophy and Racial Paradigms," *Journal of Value Inquiry* 33 (1999), pp. 299–317. © Kluwer Academic Publishers 1999. Reproduced with kind permission of Kluwer Academic Publishers and the author Naomi Zack.

Chapter 15
David T. Goldberg, "Racial Classification and Public Policy," pp. 27–58 from *Racial Subjects: Writing on Race in America*. New York: Routledge, 1999.

Every effort has been made to trace copyright holders and to obtain their permission for the use of copyright material. The publisher apologizes for any errors or omissions in the above list and would be grateful if notified of any corrections that should be incorporated in future reprints or editions of this book.

Part I

PHILOSOPHIC TRADITIONS

Introduction to Part I

Often the question "What is African-American philosophy?" is understood to demand evidence of a tradition of philosophic black thought in America. Many classic literary, social, and political texts representing the history of African-American thought are concerned with questions regarding rights, equality, and justice. It is no surprise to find that a lot of these writings have been greatly influenced by European-American philosophy. Some of the authors in Part I address questions regarding the limitations inherent in applying European ideas to the situation of African Americans, while others critically assess the major schools of thought within the African-American tradition so constituted. Whether it is fruitful for African-American thought to appropriate ideas from European-American philosophy appears as a theme in the chapters by Cornel West, Lewis Gordon, and Paget Henry, who critically examine the views of historical and contemporary black thinkers on various issues related to group progress. Frank Kirkland and Hortense Spillers focus on important positions taken by major figures within various schools of African-American thought. African-American philosophy is largely represented by a body of social and political thought related to the advancement of African Americans as a group.

Cornel West takes up the question of whether European and European-American philosophy can contribute to our understanding of the African-American experience. He combines the orientations of Martin Heidegger, Ludwig Wittgenstein, and John Dewey to offer a definition of African-American philosophy as "the interpretation of Afro-American history, highlighting the cultural heritage and political struggles, which provides desirable norms that should regulate responses to particular challenges presently confronting African Americans." His critical examination of four distinct historical traditions of black thought – vitalist, existentialist, rationalist, and humanist – all of which he finds problematic, leads him to endorse the humanist view because of its emphasis on the "universal human content of African-American cultural forms."

According to West, ideal types represent distinct conceptions of black people as either passive objects of history, or as active subjects; the former implying a pervasive denigration of African Americans and the latter suggesting their striving for self-respect. There are strong and weak versions of the doctrine associated with each

3

tradition. Vitalists laud the uniqueness of African-American culture, making – in the stronger case ontological, in the weaker one sociological – claims for African-American superiority. The rationalists view African-American culture as pathological, while the third tradition, existentialist thought, is a derivitive of these two, viewing African-American culture as restrictive, constraining, and confining. West rejects the existentialist emphasis on eccentricity and nonconformity in favor of the fourth, humanist, tradition, which affirms the humanity, while emphasizing the distinctiveness, of African-American culture.

West's focus on a narrow strand of African-American existentialist thought is in stark contrast with Lewis Gordon's claim that existential questions permeate the whole range of black thought. Gordon distinguishes between existentialism as a fundamentally European historical phenomenon and the questions concerning freedom, anguish, responsibility, and embodied existence as "the lived-context of concern." He cites Du Bois's interrogation of the meaning of black suffering and compares Toni Morrison's exploration of tragedy and ethical paradox with Kierkegaard's call for keeping faith. Because the question of race is "a source of anxiety pervading the New World," Gordon believes the appeal of Christian, Marxist, Feminist, and Pragmatic thought derives from what each contributes to "theorizing the existential realities of blackness."

One topic close to the core of existentialism is suicide. With regard to black people, Jean Paul Sartre and Simone de Beauvoir raised the question, "Why do they go on?" alluding to the existential enigma with which Camus was preoccupied. Fanon reflects on black suicide in *Black Skin, White Masks*. Black existentialist thought confronts the idea that the world would be better off without black people. With Fanon's notion of "the lived experience of the black" at hand, Gordon surveys the work of a variety of black thinkers to illustrate the multifarious ways in which black existentialist thought has been articulated to establish a tradition in African-American philosophy.

The insight, as well as the limitations, of West's and Gordon's accounts of African-American philosophy are discussed by Paget Henry. Henry wants to combine the existential–phenomenological orientation of Gordon with Lucius Outlaw's focus on discursive practice to identify a common unifying content of African-American philosophy. He endorses Gordon's use of the ontology of black and white egos to get at the origin and perpetuation of antiblack racism. But he insists on expanding Gordon's analysis in two ways: he calls for an analysis of the traditional African ego and an analysis of how this is linked with the discursive formations to which Outlaw refers. He wants to shift away from a European to an Africana perspective.

Henry maintains that Africana philosophy is constituted by an African-oriented phenomenology. The Africana project is grounded on the Pan-African task of reconstituting a racialized self to deal more effectively with what Gordon refers to as "the imperial ontology of white ego-genesis." Henry endorses Gordon's call for a reconstruction of the notion of a black self in the wake of the "phenomenological disappearance" of its African heritage. With regard to phenomenological similarities and differences, this is a move to accommodate many comparable aspects of contemporary philosophy practiced by African Americans, Caribbeans, and Africans. Henry recognizes that, although Africana philosophy draws upon European thought, it has a different set of concerns. He agrees with West and Gordon that cognitive activities are not the point of departure for Africana philosophy. Rather, it has an existential orientation which is primarily

4

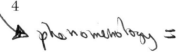 phenomenology =

social, not ontological. Henry favors Gordon's shift in focus from Jürgen Habermas's "angst over technology" to the black anguish caused by racism and colonialism. He wants to expand Gordon's analysis to include the mythic and religious discourses that inform the construction of a notion of the "traditional African ego."

Henry supports Anthony Appiah's cautious endorsement of so-called "ethnophilosophy." He believes the inclusion of a shared discourse and set of symbols that applies to all African peoples helps "to define, sustain, and legitimate the African ego." In place of timeless essences, Africana philosophy affirms the operation of "African cultural registers." Henry's appeal to the uniqueness of African symbols and discourses as an Africana foundation for African-American philosophy parallels similar reconstructions by African and Afro-Caribbean philosophers. While this does not exclude a role for the European-American heritage, Henry insists that, because the "pattern of exit" from the traditional world of myth and religion into the modern period was different for black people than for Europeans, African modernity must be seen as different from European modernity.

The question of the relation between modernity and the African diaspora is discussed by Frank M. Kirkland. He considers the coherence and relevance of the concept of modernity for people who have been enslaved and colonized by critically examining views held by Orlando Patterson and Toni Morrison regarding the claim that blacks are the first and most truly modern people. In his discussion of their opposing views, Kirkland distinguishes between "functionalist" and "cultural" modernism. On the functionalist conception, modernity is a culturally neutral development of reason (e.g., science) characterized by the secular point of view and value-naturalism, while the culturalist conception posits transformations essentially internal to the existence, or emergence, of a specific culture. Functionalism has been the prevailing conception of modernism, but Kirkland is concerned that it fails to accommodate the diversity of non-European cultures. Patterson's functionalism denies the significance of African cultural remnants. He maintains that "New World blacks lack all claim to a distinctive cultural heritage." Indeed, what is culturally distinctive, and makes them truly modern, is their lack of a cultural tradition. By contrast with this view of tradition as impediment, Morrison maintains the necessity of considering the culturally distinctive manner by which blacks have become modern. The present is bound to a sense of the past. According to Morrison, as blacks move from bondage to freedom they "reinhabit" the past. In this manner she believes black modernism recognizes slavery and racism as "the signature of a European-dominated modernity."

The role of aesthetics is an important point of contention between Patterson and Morrison. Morrison is concerned with free self-expression and artistic imagination – an aesthetic focus that Patterson rejects. Kirkland turns to the history of black thought to show that a black aesthetic modernism can be construed along functionalist lines. He cites Alexander Crummell's and Edward Blyden's discussions of the cultural unity of the African diaspora and the future of the race. Kirkland considers, as a precursor to Morrison's cultural modernism, Du Bois's notion of the color line to be a constitutive element of modernity in African diaspora societies.

Because black intellectuals have had to negotiate the color line, by definition, they embody what Hortense J. Spillers refers to as "the ongoing crisis of life-worlds in his-

5

torical confrontation with superior force." She critically examines the issues of assimilation versus separation and integration versus nationalism which have so dominated black thought. In doing so, she unearths several dimensions of "fantasy and blindness" that have attended the complex "masculinist" practices of black nationalism inherited from the nineteenth century. She cites Joy James's criticism of contemporary nationalists for adhering to the elitism that characterized the thinking by Crummell, Blyden, Du Bois and others. Noting the exclusion of women such as Ida B. Wells and Anna Julia Cooper from the Negro Academy founded by Crummell she claims that black male intellectuals were not "liberalized" by the urban experience, but became "less progressive."

Due to the central role of the black church in the history of activism, Spillers believes it was not until the consolidation of the social sciences at the turn of the century that a nonclerical black intellectual formation was possible. In *The New Negro*, Alain Locke spoke of a secular social formation of black thinkers who could redefine the past in accordance with what Spillers calls "a reformulated modernization project." She claims that the development of secular thought has led to a stigmatization of ideas as elitist and a tendency in black communities to link the efficacy of ideas with their pragmatic value.   sceptcsm?

Spillers discusses the scepticism of black thinkers toward the class reductionism of socialism. The attempt to subordinate the black problem to that of the working class has led to what she refers to as "a shrewd domestication of dissent." One prominent reason for Marxism's "checkered" career as a challenge to black nationalist thought is black activist practice itself, which militates against Marxism's race-neutral reading of the struggle. In her evaluation of the distinctive radical analysis developed in the Civil Rights movement – and the challenge posed to it by the Nation of Islam (Malcolm X) and the Black Panther Party – Spillers cites King's support of the black labor movement in Memphis and the Poor Peoples Campaign.

With the opposition between nationalist and socialist visions of black liberation in mind, Spillers cautions against a "suicidal" tendency of black intellectuals to behave as if post-modernist practices (and economies) do not have significant effects on the situation of African Americans. She notes the difference between pre- and post-1968 black intellectuals. According to Spillers, a rapid ascent of black intellectuals into the academy has granted them access, through publishing, to the "epistemic structures" crucial to the larger society's discursive formation.

do blacks need to " catch up" ?

1

Philosophy and
the Afro-American Experience

CORNEL WEST

How does philosophy relate to the Afro-American experience? This question arises primarily because of an antipathy to the ahistorical character of contemporary philosophy and the paucity of illuminating diachronic studies of the Afro-American experience.[1] I will try to show that certain philosophical techniques, derived from a particular conception of philosophy, can contribute to our understanding of the Afro-American experience. For lack of a better name, I shall call the application of these techniques to this experience, Afro-American philosophy. I will examine historical sources of these techniques and explore the way in which they underscore the feasibility of an Afro-American philosophy. Finally, I will attempt to show what results such a philosophy should yield.

The philosophical techniques requisite for an Afro-American philosophy must be derived from a lucid and credible conception of philosophy. The search for such a conception requires us to engage in a metaphilosophical discourse, in philosophical reflections on philosophy. The most impressive metaphilosophical formulations of our age which express displeasure with the ahistorical character of modern philosophy are those of Martin Heidegger, the later Wittgenstein and John Dewey.[2] Although the interests and reflections of these thinkers widely diverge they point to one idea essential for an Afro-American philosophy: a critical attitude toward the Cartesian philosophical world-view. The Cartesian Weltanschauung is the foundation of modern philosophy.

Briefly, the Cartesian perspective categorically distinguishes homo sapiens from the rest of the animal kingdom; posits the process of knowing as qualitatively different from all other human activities; claims mental entities, such as beliefs, desires and intentions, are separate from yet related to physical actions; and conceives language and thoughts as systems of representations which somehow "correspond" to the world.[3] This Cartesian picture – the first modern philosophical portrait – presents the perennial conundrums of contemporary philosophy, namely, the metaphysical nature of man, necessary truth, freedom of the will, the mind–body schism and the relation between ideas and objects, words and things. Despite gallant attempts to dissolve these problems into psychology (Hume), history (Marx) and culture (Nietzsche), the Cartesian tradition persists into the twentieth century.

Cartesians postulate the absolute autonomy of philosophy. They presuppose that there is a distinct set of philosophical problems independent of culture, society and history. For them, philosophy stands outside the various conventions on which people base their social practices and transcends the cultural heritages and political struggles of people. If the Cartesian viewpoint is the only valid philosophical stance, then the idea of an Afro-American philosophy would be ludicrous.[4]

Martin Heidegger launched the first major attack on Cartesian thought within the Continental tradition in his monumental work, *Being and Time* (1927). The task of philosophy, Heidegger suggests, is not to ascertain indubitable claims about the self and world, but rather to provide an interpretation of what it means for human beings to be.[5] He reconstructs Husserl's phenomenological method – a tool for conceptual description and interpretation – and applies it to the *Dasein* (Being) of the existing, thinking self.

For Heidegger, the preeminence of the Cartesian perspective, the predominance of epistemology in modern philosophy, is but a stage, an unfortunate one, in humankind's attitude toward *Dasein*.[6] This stage begins with Descartes, culminates in Kant and ends with Nietzsche; it originates with Cartesian gaiety about philosophical methodology and terminates in the grotesque, yet often alluring, Nietzschean vision. Heidegger claims the Cartesian viewpoint ultimately produces a scientific positivism that views any systematic analysis of *Dasein* meaningless and fanciful.

Besides criticizing the positivist doctrine that results from Cartesianism, Heidegger also rejects Cartesian viewpoints within the hermeneutic tradition of philosophy. Manifest in the works of Friedrich Schleiermacher and Wilhelm Dilthey, the Cartesian hermeneutic tradition claims that the understanding (subtilitas intelligendi) of a text, history or *Dasein* is distinct from its interpretation (subtilitas explicandi). Understanding refers to real meaning; interpretation to mere interpreted meaning. The Cartesian viewpoint in hermeneutics posits an unchanging meaning of a text, history or *Dasein* that is sharable owing to its reproducibility; this sharing consists of an interpreted meaning correctly corresponding to the real meaning. Correct correspondence assures the objectivity and validity of interpretation.[7]

Heidegger refuses to accept the traditional distinction between understanding and interpretation in Cartesian hermeneutics. He believes this quest for certainty is misguided; it attempts to overcome the historical and personal limitations of human interpretation. These limitations take the form of the inherent and inevitable circularity of interpretation.

Any interpretation which is to contribute understanding, must already have understood what is to be interpreted.[8]

For example, when interpreting a text, history or *Dasein*, we can only appeal to other interpretations we presently understand as the basis for our own interpretation. This circularity is not a vicious one because it continually provides new meaning and novel insights, while acknowledging the limits of who and what we are.

Heidegger claims that philosophical interpretation is an activity of understanding which makes explicit what implicitly people are. A successful interpretation gives meaning to what is originally present in an obscure, confused form. Every interpretation is grounded in a fore-having (Vorhabe), a fore-sight (Vorsicht) and a fore-conception (Vorgriff). It is always grounded in something we have, see and grasp prior to the act of interpretation; it is never free of presuppositions. In other words, all interpretative activity is rooted in historical situations and formulated in terms of a particular tradition, perspective and prejudice, owing to each individual's engagement in the world and attempt to project possibilities for the future.[9] Heidegger's metaphilosophical insight is: *Philosophy is the hermeneutic analysis that interprets what it means to be for personal selves who remember a past, anticipate a future and decide in the present.*

Afro-American philosophy appropriates from Heidegger the notion of philosophy as interpretation of what it means to be for people who, as a result of active engagement in the world, reconstruct their past, make choices in the present and envision possibilities for the future. Yet Heidegger's conception of philosophy is inadequate. His understanding of the "historicality" (Geschichtlichkeit) of *Dasein*, or the way in which historical circumstances influence individuals' choices in the present, is unsatisfactory. His constitutive categories of "historicality", namely, fate, destiny and heritage, fail to incorporate the current perceptions of the historical forces which constrain human activity.[10]

For Heidegger, fate is the crucial category of the "historicality" of *Dasein*. It is an awareness of each individual's limited possibilities, of their own finitude. Destiny is an extension of fate to the level of groups, nations and humankind. Heritage is the awareness of tradition as the central determining factor in the concept of self. Yet, as the young Marcuse noted, these categories ignore crucial historical forces e.g. social position within the mode of production, racist and sexist constraints, that significantly shape and mold the kind of choices available to people.[11]

Heidegger overlooks these vital historical forces because he views history in personal terms, as mere "stretchedness" (Erstrecktheit) extending through time. This conception of history neglects the social and political relations between people; it ignores their communal life, past and present. Calvin Schrag perceptively observes,

> Heidegger neglects, as do most existentialist thinkers, the community of selves with their common social memory which is the very stuff out of which history is made. To be sure, for Heidegger, being-in-the-world is always being-with-others, but it is the radically isolated *Dasein* who determines the significance of this communal world for his personal existence. The context of historical meaning arises not from the interdependent experiences and reflections of a community of selves, but from the individual projects of a solitary *Dasein* who is concerned for his authentic existence.[12]

Afro-American philosophy rejects Heidegger's personalistic conception of history.

The later Wittgenstein goes beyond Heidegger by investigating, in detail, various linguistic practices and illustrating how they are linked to, or constitute the basis of, particular forms of life (Lebensformen) or cultures. His philosophy becomes the description of the multi-faceted dimensions of language within distinct cultures.

Wittgenstein believes this descriptive activity is dispensable; philosophy is mere therapy for those still captured by the Cartesian picture of the world ("Philosophy is a disease of which it itself is the cure"). The endless insoluble philosophical problems that bewilder philosophers cannot be solved within the Cartesian framework and they dissolve when this framework is discarded. Any attempt to replace it with a new philo-

9

sophical perspective is symptomatic of the need to keep philosophy autonomous, to keep it pure.

According to Wittgenstein, philosophy has been inextricably linked to a notion of necessity. Philosophers have searched for the immutable, invariable and unquestionable. They have claimed that necessity derives from the essence of things (e.g. Plato, Aristotle), the structure of our minds (e.g. Kant, Hegel), the structure of history (e.g. Spencer, Marx) and language (some linguistic philosophers and structuralist thinkers). The later Wittgenstein tries to show that the very notion of necessity is anthropocentric: necessity rests upon the contingencies of social practice. His linguistic naturalism (or conventionalism) claims that the meaning of words in our language (or norms in culture, values in society) are linked not to abstract essences or inscrutable mental phenomena, but rather to the use we give them in particular language-games we create, modify and accept. David Pears, in his notable book on Wittgenstein, succinctly states,

> It is Wittgenstein's later doctrine that outside human thought and speech there are no independent, objective points of support, and meaning and necessity are preserved only in the linguistic practices which embody them. They are safe only because the practices gain a certain stability from rules. But even the rules do not provide a fixed point of reference, because they always allow divergent interpretations. What really gives the practices their stability is that we agree in our interpretations of the rules.[13]

Wittgenstein suggests that since necessity derives from human agreement on such rules and their interpretations, autonomous philosophy vanishes.[14] He equates this end of Cartesian philosophy with the end of philosophy *per se*. His own philosophical works, he claims, undermine the Cartesian picture of the world. Wittgenstein's metaphilosophical insight is: *Philosophy is the detailed description of linguistic [social] practices within distinct cultural ways of life.*

Despite obvious differences, Wittgenstein and Heidegger are kindred spirits. Both view philosophy as a move from the obscure to the obvious, rather than from doubt to certainty. Both attempt to discover the human conventions concealed by the Cartesian perspective, to decipher the Cartesian hieroglyphics that promote philosophical deceptions. For both thinkers, philosophy is an interpretative activity which renders the complex simple, the opaque clear and the strange familiar yet, paradoxically, each believes only the courageous will be able to accept the relatively simple truths revealed by their interpretations. To them, all philosophizing requires resolute fearlessness, fortitude and ultimately a change in living and perceiving. Afro-American philosophy subscribes to this approach.

Afro-American philosophy embodies Wittgenstein's stress on the cultural and social practices of people; it is concerned not only with the life-meaning of individuals but also the way such meaning is shaped by the cultural and social practices of a particular community. Yet Wittgenstein's conception of philosophy is incomplete. It lacks a normative component. His suspicion of any justification for norms allows him to "stop doing philosophy" more easily than most of us. It is no accident that his moral thought offers common yet unoriginal ideas derived from Schopenhauer, Kierkegaard and Tolstoy, e.g. the good life is one patterned after the historical examples of religious figures.[15] As to why this life is better than others, he remains silent.

10

John Dewey's metaphilosophical views serve, for our purposes, as a form of synthesis and corrective for those of Heidegger and Wittgenstein.[16] He recognizes that the Cartesian picture of the world rests upon specific historical circumstances e.g. the rise of science, the need for methodological purity in philosophy, the advent of capitalist production, which fall within a certain epoch of humankind's development. He acknowledges that an anthropocentric critique of Cartesian thought breaks down traditional distinctions between philosophy and science, art and science, morality and science. Philosophy is inextricably bound to culture, society and history.

For Dewey, the idea of an autonomous philosophy is culturally outmoded. It must submit to the fate of its first cousin, theology. Theology was once an autonomous discipline with its own distinct set of problems, now most of these problems lie at the mercy of psychology, sociology, history and anthropology. This is the path Cartesian philosophy (and its modern variants) must follow.

But the normative function of philosophy remains. Philosophy becomes the critical expression of a culture, the critical thought of a society, the critical component of a discipline. It no longer contains delusions of autonomy nor illusions of disappearance. The historical hermeneutics of Heidegger and the cultural descriptions in Wittgenstein are combined with Dewey's pragmatic orientation. Dewey's metaphilosophical insight is: *Philosophy is the interpretation of a people's past for the purpose of solving specific problems presently confronting the cultural way of life from which the people come.* For Dewey, philosophy is critical in that it constantly questions tacit assumptions and unarticulated presuppositions of previous interpretations of the past; it scrutinizes the norms these interpretations endorse, the solutions they offer and the self-images they foster.

From the metaphilosophical insights of Heidegger, Wittgenstein and Dewey, I shall define Afro-American philosophy in this way: *Afro-American philosophy is the interpretation of Afro-American history, highlighting the cultural heritage and political struggles, which provides desirable norms that should regulate responses to particular challenges presently confronting Afro-Americans.*[17] Afro-American philosophy is the application of the philosophical techniques of interpretation and justification to the Afro-American experience. The particular historical phenomena interpreted and justified by Afro-American philosophy consist of religious doctrines, political ideologies, artistic expressions and unconscious modes of behavior; such phenomena serve as raw ingredients to be utilized by Afro-American philosophy in order to interpret the Afro-American past and defend particular norms within this past.

The two basic challenges presently confronting Afro-Americans are those of self-image and self-determination. The former is the perennial human attempt to define who and what one is, the sempiternal issue of self-identity; the latter is the political struggle to gain significant control over the major institutions that regulate people's lives. These challenges are abstractly distinguishable, yet concretely inseparable. In other words, culture and politics must always be viewed in close relation to each other.[18]

The major function of Afro-American philosophy is to reshape the contours of Afro-American history and provide a new self-understanding of the Afro-American experience which suggests desirable guidelines for action in the present.[19] Afro-American philosophy attempts to make theoretically explicit what is implicit in Afro-American history to describe and demystify the cultural and social practices in this history and offer certain solutions to urgent problems besetting Afro-Americans.

11

Modernity is a central notion in my interpretation of the Afro-American past. I shall define it in this way: *Modernity is the descriptive notion that connotes the historical state of affairs characterized by an abundance of wealth resulting from the industrial and technologi-cal revolution and the ensuing cultural isolation and fragmentation due to a disintegration of closely-knit communities and the decline of religious systems.* Afro-American history chronicles the prolongation of the Afro-American entrance into the corridors of modernity; the long overdue reaping of the harvest they helped cultivate, the seizing of opportunities previously closed, and the bruising encounter with the emptiness, sterility and hypocrisy of contemporary life.

When Afro-Americans are viewed as passive objects of history, Afro-American history is a record of the exclusion of a distinct racial group from the economic ben-efits and cultural dilemmas of modernity. Politically, this exclusion has meant white ownership of Afro-American persons, possessions and progeny; severe discrimination reinforced by naked violence within a nascent industrial capitalist order; and urban enclaves of unskilled unemployables and semi-skilled workers within a liberal corpo-rate capitalist regime. Culturally, this has meant continual Afro-American degradation and ceaseless attempts to undermine Afro-American self-esteem.

When Afro-Americans are viewed as active subjects of history, Afro-American history becomes the story of gallantly persistent struggle, of a disparate racial group fighting to enter modernity on its own terms. Politically, this struggle consists of pru-dential acquiescence plus courageous revolt against white paternalism; institution-building and violent rebellion within the segregated social relations of industrial capitalism; and cautious reformist strategies within the integrated social relations of "post-industrial" capitalism. Culturally, this has meant the maintenance of self-respect in the face of pervasive denigration.

I will attempt to order and organize some significant aspects of the Afro-American past by delineating four ideal-types which embody distinct Afro-American historical traditions of thought and behavior. These categories incorporate abstract elements of Afro-American historical reality; they are, however, derived from an empirical exami-nation of this reality. Needless to say, they rarely appear empirically in their pure, con-ceptual form, but may serve as heuristic tools to confer intelligibility on Afro-American history and provide an understanding of this history by revealing its internal rationality.

The four theoretical constructs to be considered are the vitalist, rationalist, existen-tialist and humanist traditions in Afro-American history.[20] I shall try to stipulate clear definitions of these traditions so they will not be automatically associated with their previously established meanings within traditional historiography.

The Afro-American vitalist tradition lauds the uniqueness of Afro-American culture and personality. It claims a *sui generis* status for Afro-American life in regard to form and content. It stresses what qualitatively distinguishes Afro-Americans from the rest of humanity, especially what sets them apart from white Americans. This tradition con-tains two types: strong vitalism and weak vitalism. Strong vitalism makes ontological claims about Afro-American superiority; Afro-Americans stand above other racial groups because of their genetic makeup, divine chosenness or innate endowments. Weak vitalism makes sociological claims about Afro-American superiority; Afro-Americans stand above other racial groups because of certain values, modes of behav-

12

ior or gifts acquired from their endurance of political oppression, social degradation and economic exploitation.

The Afro-American rationalist tradition considers Afro-American culture and personality to be pathological. It rejects any idea of an independent, self-supportive Afro-American culture. It stresses the inability of Afro-Americans to create adequate coping devices to alleviate the enormous pressures caused by their dire condition. This tradition also contains two types: strong rationalism and weak rationalism. Strong rationalism makes ontological claims about Afro-American inferiority; Afro-Americans stand below other racial groups because of their genetic makeup, divine rejection or innate deficiency. Weak rationalism makes sociological claims about Afro-American inferiority; Afro-Americans stand below other racial groups because of certain values, modes of behavior or defects acquired from their endurance of political oppression, social degradation and economic exploitation.

The Afro-American existentialist tradition posits Afro-American culture to be restrictive, constraining and confining. It emphasizes the suppression of individuality, eccentricity and nonconformity within Afro-American culture. This tradition is parasitic in that it rests upon either the rationalistic or humanist traditions.

The Afro-American humanist tradition extolls the distinctiveness of Afro-American culture and personality. It accents the universal human content of Afro-American cultural forms. It makes no ontological or sociological claims about Afro-American superiority or inferiority. Rather it focuses on the ways in which creative Afro-American cultural modes of expression embody themes and motifs analogous to the vigorous cultural forms of other racial, ethnic or national groups. This tradition affirms Afro-American membership in the human race, not above or below it.

My conception of these four traditions in Afro-American thought and behavior assumes that culture is more fundamental than politics in regard to Afro-American self-understanding. It presupposes that Afro-American cultural perceptions provide a broader and richer framework for understanding the Afro-American experience than political perceptions. As noted earlier, culture and politics are inseparable, but as I believe Antonio Gramsci has shown, any political consciousness of an oppressed group is shaped and molded by the group's cultural resources and resiliency as perceived by individuals therein.[21] So the extent to which the resources and resiliency are romanticized, rejected or accepted will deeply influence the kind of political consciousness individuals possess.

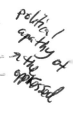

These four traditions of thought and behavior in Afro-American history can serve as guides for understanding Afro-American culture and politics. They shall represent distinct Afro-American responses to the challenges of self-image and self-determination; they will also be the alternatives from which we choose a desirable response to these challenges.

Vitalist Tradition

The self-image of Afro-Americans in the vitalist tradition (both types) is one of pride, self-congratulation and often heroism. Afro-Americans are considered to be more humane, meek, kind, creative, spontaneous or nonviolent than members of other racial groups; less malicious, mendacious, belligerent, bellicose or avaricious. This tradition posits Afro-American superiority, not over all others, but specifically over white Americans.

The strong vitalist tradition in Afro-American history does not appear until the rise of a secular Afro-American intelligentsia. The early religious Afro-American intellectuals, though vehemently opposed to black oppression and the doctrine of white supremacy, did not subscribe to any form of strong vitalism. Despite the fierce fight continually waged for Afro-American enhancement they refused to make any ontological claims about Afro-American superiority, primarily because of inhibitory, deep, Christian roots.

The first major formulation of strong vitalism in Afro-American thought appears in the "germ" theory of New England-born, Harvard-trained W. E. B. Du Bois. Ironically, he borrowed this theory from his teacher at Harvard, Albert Bushnell Hart, who used it to support Teutonic (Anglo-Saxon) superiority. This theory maintains that each race possesses its own "race idea and race spirit" embodying its unique gift to humanity. Du Bois writes,

> At the same time the spiritual and physical differences of race groups which constituted the nations became deep and decisive. The English nation stood for constitutional liberty and commercial freedom; the German nation for science and philosophy; the romance nations stood for literature and art, and the other race groups are striving, each in its own way, to develop for civilization its particular message, its particular ideal . . . Manifestly some of the great races today – particularly the Negro race – have not as yet given to civilization which they are capable of giving.[22]

And what is this message? In *The Souls of Black Folk* (1903) and *The Gift of Black Folk* (1924), he suggests it is essentially that of meekness, joviality and humility manifest in the Afro-American gift of spirit. His essay, "Of Our Spiritual Strivings", found in the earlier work, rhetorically asks,

> Will America be poorer if she replace her brutal dyspeptic blundering with light-hearted but determined Negro humility? or her coarse and cruel wit with loving jovial good-humor? or her vulgar music with the soul of the Sorrow Songs?[23]

He ends the latter work casting "the sense of meekness and humility" of Afro-Americans against the white man's "contempt, lawlessness and lynching" for domination of the emerging American spirit. The uniqueness of Afro-Americans is even more explicitly endorsed when he writes,

> Negroes differ from whites in their inherent genius and stages of development.[24]

Under the influence of Franz Boas and Marxism, Du Bois abandons the "germ" theory, yet he planted and nurtured its seed long enough for the strong vitalist tradition to establish a continued presence in Afro-American thought and behavior.

James Weldon Johnson gives the strong vitalist tradition new life with his notion of the unique creativity of Afro-Americans. In the famous preface to his well-known anthology of Afro-American poetry, he claims that the true greatness of a civilization should be measured by its creative powers in the arts. He then adds,

> the Negro has already proved the possession of these powers by being the creator of the only things artistic that have sprung from American soil and have been universally acknowledged as distinctive American products.[25]

He attributes these creative powers to the "racial genius" of Afro-Americans,

> us who are warmed by the poetic blood of Africa – old, mysterious Africa, mother of races, rhythmic-beating heart of the world . . .[26]

And what does this "racial genius" consist of? Like that of Du Bois, it is a god-given (or Nature-given) spirit revealed in the pietistic, primitive Christianity of rural Afro-Americans.

The majority of literary works during the Harlem Remaissance mark a shift in the strong vitalist tradition. The urban setting and close interaction with alienated white literary figures groping for the vitality of "noble savages" adds new content to Afro-American uniqueness: the primitivism of Afro-Americans manifest in their uninhibited and spontaneous behavior.

In the past decade, the strong vitalist tradition has flourished in the religious doctrine of the Black Muslims under the leadership of the late Honorable Elijah Muhammad, the black theology of Joseph Washington and Albert Cleage, and the Black Arts Movement promoted by Imamu Baraka, Hoyt Fuller, Addison Gayle and others. These groups provided ontological justifications for the inhumanity of white Americans, hence Afro-American superiority over these whites. The evidence usually adduced was American history; the conclusion was to deny American (white) values, defy American (white) society and preserve the small dose of humanity left in America.

The weak vitalist tradition began with the African Methodist Episcopal intelligentsia. The humanity of white people is not denied, but they are relegated to a lower moral status than Afro-Americans. For example, R. R. Wright, a leading intellectual of the A. M. E. Church at the turn of the century writes,

> The white man is selfish and the American white man is the most grasping breed of humanity ever made.[27]

Wright concludes that whites, due to their materialist greed and moral self-centeredness, have never understood the Christian message. Only the peaceful loving and forgiving Afro-Americans can instill the spirit of Christianity in the violent, vicious white race.

> African Methodism will carry the Christian message of brotherhood to the white man.[28]

The weak vitalist tradition continued with the Garvey Movement of the nineteen twenties. Garvey heralded Afro-American pride, beauty and strength without claiming innate white inferiority. His program of racial purity, black religion (including a black

Christ, Mary and God) and Back-to-Africa doctrine was juxtaposed with, for example, the following judgment on white people,

> We are not preaching a propaganda of hate against anybody. We love the white man; we love all humanity, because we feel that we cannot live without the other.[29]

Yet Garvey believed white people behaved in a demonic fashion within the existing social order.

> I regard the Klan as a better friend of the race than all the groups of hypocritical whites put together. You may call me a Klansman if you will, but potentially, every white man is a Klansman, as far as the Negro in competition with whites socially, economically, and politically is concerned, and there is no use lying about it.[30]

The most recent instance of weak vitalism is Martin Luther King's doctrine of non-violence. This doctrine tends to assume tacitly that Afro-Americans have acquired, as a result of their historical experience, a peculiar capacity to love their enemies, to endure patiently suffering, pain and hardship and thereby "teach the white man how to love" or "cure the white man of his sickness". King seemed to believe that Afro-Americans possess a unique proclivity for nonviolence, more so than other racial groups, that they have a certain bent toward humility, meekness and forbearance, hence are quite naturally disposed toward nonviolent action. In King's broad overview, God is utilizing Afro-Americans – this community of *caritas* (other-directed love) – to bring about "the blessed community". He seemed confident his nonviolent movement of predominately Afro-Americans was part of a divine plan. He was the drum major of,

> this mighty army of love, and I am sure that the entire world now looks to the Negro in America for leadership in the whole task of building a world without want, without hate, and where all men live together in shared opportunity and brotherhood.[31]

The self-image fostered by the vitalist tradition (both types) is defensive in character and romantic in content. It is a reaction to the doctrine of white supremacy, an attempt to build Afro-American pride and self-worth upon quixotic myths about the past, exaggerated expectations of the present and chiliastic hopes for the future.

This self-image reveals the real roots of the Afro-American vitalist tradition: the rise of the Afro-American petit bourgeoisie. The vitalist claim of Afro-American superiority can be seen as a cloak for the repressed self-doubts, fears and anxieties of an emerging Afro-American middle class. It results from the inevitable questioning of personal identity and the belated quest for wealth, status and prestige among the Afro-American *parvenu* petit bourgeoisie caused by interacting with a hostile white (American) society.

In the cultural sphere, Afro-American vitalism was begun by talented Afro-Americans extolling the cultural achievements of the West, searching for Afro-American ones commensurate with those of the West, and ending by conjuring up mythologies that put Afro-American achievements on superior footing with the West. Personal identity becomes cushioned by racial myths of superiority; the search for this

16

identity is motivated primarily by the white opposition. Hence, it is extrinsic, containing no enduring sustenance, potency or authenticity.

In the political sphere, Afro-American vitalism started with ambitious Afro-Americans who pursued wealth, status and prestige in American society, ran up against racist barriers, then returned to the Afro-American world to continue this pursuit, with an acquired hostility toward the society in which they unsuccessfully sought entrance. They amassed wealth, status and prestige in this world ("big fish in a little pond") and concerned themselves with helping other ambitious socially mobile Afro-Americans, sometimes under the banner of anti-whitism, and often at the expense of the Afro-American masses.

The bourgeois roots of the vitalist tradition is most clearly seen in its aims and conceptions of political struggle. Its major form is Afro-American vocation ideology: a calling for Afro-Americans to acknowledge their uniqueness, utilize it to organize and mobilize themselves against the white world, and undermine the inhumanity and hypocrisy of this white world. A cursory examination of the Afro-American vitalist approach to political struggle substantiates a revised version of Lenin's famous quip: "scratch a vitalist and underneath is a budding bourgeois".

Du Bois's "germ" theory has its political analogue in his doctrine of the Talented Tenth. He promoted both simultaneously. While the Afro-American masses are busy giving the world its meekness, humility and joviality, the Talented Tenth is provided leadership and guidance for these spiritual masses, a leadership and guidance that presupposes the sustained wealth, status and prestige of the Talented Tenth. In other words, the Untalented Ninetieth possess the idealized gift of spirit, while the Talented Tenth acquire the essentials of power, namely education and skills.[32]

> The Negro race, like all races, is going to be saved by its exceptional men. The problem of education, then, among Negroes must first of all deal with the Talented Tenth; it is the problem of developing the Best of this race that they may guide the Mass away from the contamination and death of the Worst, in their own and other races.[33]

James Weldon Johnson's important role in the NAACP (its first black executive secretary) embodies the same relationship, with an integrationist twist: a middle-class approach while idealizing the religious "primitivism" of the Afro American masses.

The literary artists of the Harlem Renaissance, as well as the Black Arts Movement in the sixties, represent petit bourgeois fascination with the spontaneity of Afro-American proletarian (and lumpenproletarian) life; the first movement remained much less political than the later one. The Harlem Renaissance writers basically portrayed stereotypical lifestyles with which they were scarcely acquainted; the Black Arts figures promoted so-called "black" values that rest completely outside the cultural framework of most Afro-Americans. Both movements produced mediocre art, romanticized the Afro-American lower class and launched lucrative careers for a few middle-class artists previously excluded from the white (American) world of art.

R. R. Wright's weak vitalist approach culminated in an energetic attempt to organize an Afro-American interest group, an Afro-American political party and an Afro-American voting bloc: early middle-class attempts to utilize Afro-American cohesion to gain entrance to the political mainstream.

The Garvey Movement, after great popular support, resulted in an aborted trip to Africa. The thousands of dollars it acquired from Afro-Americans (mainly from small entrepreneurs) who purchased stocks in Garvey's business concerns, was squandered, through ineptitude and graft. The Black Muslims (under the late Honorabic Elijah Muhammad) opted for entrepreneurship in urban centers – a gallant yet hapless attempt to secure a notch within a declining entrepreneurial capitalism and an ever-expanding corporate-dominated economy. The same holds for the "black capitalism" promoted in the past decade by some Black Power advocates.[34]

King's political viewpoint was more candid than the others: it literally proclaimed American middle-class status its goal. After harsh political struggle, the federal government was persuaded to legitimize this pursuit. Federal legislation removed certain racist barriers e.g. disenfranchisement, segregated housing, which increased possibilities for skilled and educated Afro-Americans to acquire some degree of wealth, status and prestige in American society. Results for the Afro-American poor have been minimal.[35]

The vitalist response to the challenges of self-image and self-determination is this: a romanticization of Afro-American culture that conceals the social mobility of an emerging opportunistic Afro-American petit bourgeoisie. Afro-American vitalism offers symbols and rituals to the Afro-American masses which are useful for enhancing the social mobility of Afro-American professional and business groups.[36] It generates cathartic and amorphous feelings of Afro-American pride, self-congratulation and heroism that contain little substance.

The hypocrisy of Afro-American vitalism is revealed usually *ex post facto*: when bourgeois nationalists, after acquiring some status, prestige and wealth, begin to "outgrow their childish past", namely begin to interact, commune and even marry the previously "inferior enemy"; and when bourgeois integrationists, after gaining a desired place in American society, remain complacently inert and satisfied in their Promised Land, the coveted suburbs. So the Afro-American vitalist tradition (both types) is a stream of thought and behavior in Afro-American history which serves principally as a covert strategy for Afro-American entree into the mainstream of American society.

Afro-American philosophy deems the vitalist response undesirable. The romanticization of Afro-American culture is an escape from reality. It fosters cultural stagnation and leaves Afro-Americans vulnerable to insidious manipulation by charismatic figures or socially mobile groups. In other words, it does not enhance the cultural life or ameliorate the socioeconomic conditions of the majority of Afro-Americans.

Rationalist Tradition

The self-image of Afro-Americans in the rationalist tradition (strong and weak types) is one of self-hatred, shame and fear. Afro-Americans are viewed as morbid subhuman monsters. This tradition posits Afro-American inferiority, not against everyone, but specifically to white Americans.

Like the vitalist tradition, this stream of thought and behavior in Afro-American history did not appear until the rise of a secular Afro-American intelligentsia. Aside from occasional remarks by Alexander Crummell and Edward Blyden regarding missionary emigrationism, the early religious Afro-American intelligentsia refused to engage in any talk about Afro-American inferiority, primarily because they headed the institutions (Churches) around which Afro-American culture evolved.

The unchallenged theoretician of the weak rationalist tradition in Afro-American history is E. Franklin Frazier.[37] The Chicago school of sociology serves as the context in which his brand of weak rationalism flourished. Borrowing from the social theory of W. I. Thomas (especially his work on Polish peasants) and Robert Parks (notably his work on urban class and status conflict), Frazier views the history of Afro-American culture as a series of devastating social shocks – the initial act of enslavement from Africa, the cruel voyage across the Atlantic Ocean, the "peculiar institution" of slavery, the vicious post-emancipation life and the disintegration of folk culture in the cities.

ok!

In his well-known book, *The Negro Family in Chicago* (1932), Frazier suggests that the Afro-American culture basically amounts to superstition, ignorance, self-hatred and fear. It emanates from political despair and produces a wholly negative self-image. He hopes it will soon disappear.[38]

The weak rationalist tradition under the aegis of Frazier provided the theoretical framework for legal and political argumentation of civil rights during the past two decades. The message was clear: Afro-Americans have been environmentally created less equal and normal than whites, so only assimilation with whites can break the circle of political oppression and pathological behavior.

Powerpoint "do you think this is true"

This message contains the chief aim of political struggle in the Afro-American weak rationalist tradition, an ideology of Afro-American uplift: The only hope for Afro-American enhancement is increased interaction with whites because only assimilation can civilize, refine and modernize Afro-Americans. Frazier makes this point crystal clear,

what about Blk scholars & blk success?

> If the Negro had undertaken to shut himself off from the white culture about him and had sought light from within his experience, he would have remained on the level of barbarism.[39]

Later in life, Frazier began to recognize the belated consequences of his viewpoint. In his scathing critique of the Afro-American middle-class, *Black Bourgeoisie* (1962), he castigates their aping of white bourgeois society, their fanciful world of status, wealth and prestige, and their inability to take each other seriously as professionals. In a later essay, he advises Afro-American intellectuals to provide positive self-images for black people and don't confuse assimilation with self-effacement.[40] Yet, despite these late attempts that acknowledge the limitations of the weak rationalist tradition, Frazier almost singlehandedly set in motion a stream of Afro-American thought and behavior which remains highly influential today.

Like the vitalist tradition, the rationalist one is a petit bourgeois affair; it promotes a self-image which inheres primarily among an insecure, socially mobile Afro-American middle class (and adopted as true by some misguided white social scientists) and posits this largely negative self-image as the only one for all Afro-Americans. Yet, unlike the vitalist tradition, it does not romanticize Afro-American culture; instead, it deprecates this culture.

The rationalist response to the challenges of self-image and self-determination is this: a rejection of Afro-American culture and total assimilation into American society. It assumes that the universal must wipe clean all particulars, that cosmopolitan society erases all provincialities.

Afro-American philosophy holds the rationalist response to be unacceptable. The wholesale renunciation of Afro-American culture only denigrates Afro-Americans. It deprives them of the autonomous elements of their way of life, the genuine creations of their cultural heritage. The rationalist tradition, like the vitalist one, is a rash reaction against a hostile white society rather than a responsible response to particular challenges. Both traditions represent the peculiar predicament of the Afro-American middle class. Just as the vitalist tradition looks at Afro-American culture and sees no evil, so the rationalist tradition looks and sees no good. The major shortcoming of the latter is that it overlooks the possibility of cultural vitality and poverty-ridden living conditions existing simultaneously in Afro-American life.

Existentialist Tradition

The Afro-American existentialist tradition promotes a self-image of both confinement and creativity, restriction and revolt. It encompasses a highly individualistic rebellion of Afro-Americans who are marginal to, or exist on the edges of, Afro-American culture and see little use in assimilating into the American mainstream. It expresses a critical disposition toward Afro-American culture and American society.

The early manifestations of Afro-American existentialist thought and behavior were found in the critical attitudes of religious leaders toward their own church members and American society. But the result was rarely personal rebellion against both, owing to the need for conformity and community under severe oppression.

The existentialist tradition appears more fully in the works of Sutton Griggs and Charles Chesnutt. For both, the problematic status of the mulatto – the physically marginal person between Afro-American culture and American society – is central. The authors and their characters maintain a distance and express a denial of Afro-American culture which leaves them uprooted. Their rejection and distrust of American society makes them vindictive.

Griggs and Chesnutt are the first archetypes of Afro-American existentialists: individualistic, alienated, searching for a home. Their talent and imagination lift them above what they conceive to be the uncouth, vulgar and unrefined Afro-American folk culture, yet this same talent and imagination is denied recognition by whites, hence turned against the white world. In the end, both sought escape from this predicament – Griggs to Africa, Chesnutt ("passing") into the white world he had earlier assailed.

The existentialist tradition blossoms in the works, and lives, of Nella Larsen and Rudolph Fisher. Both were plagued by the inability to accept themselves and could not find comfort anywhere. Larsen's Helga Crane, the protagonist of *Quicksand* (1928), is an attractive well-bred mulatto who seeks to overcome her self-hatred and find herself in a provincial southern Negro college, the urban life of Chicago and Harlem, the cosmopolitan world of Copenhagen and finally the pietistic Christianity of Afro-American rural life. She – Helga (and Larsen) – is an incessant rebel, unable to come to terms with herself in either world, black or white.

Rudolph Fisher, the talented physician-writer, fostered early in life a deep hatred of the white world. He also found it hard to appreciate anything in Afro-American urban life. He praised the spirituals, but refused to acknowledge similar artistic richness in the blues and jazz. The latter are considered secular vulgarizations evolved from the former; the cruel urban environment destroys the pure, religious pathos of Afro-American rural life. Fisher was unable to feel at home in the city. This detachment allowed Fisher to portray Afro-American urban life more honestly than his literary contemporaries during the Harlem Renaissance. He was more conscious than they of the divisions within black city life because they affected him more acutely.[41]

The personal revolt of Wallace Thurman may serve as a turning point in the existentialist tradition. It marks the refusal to escape from self-hatred and shame. Prior to Thurman, Afro-American existentialists imagine heroic self-absorbing events, long for idyllic lifestyles of the rural past, or succumb to resignation. Thurman candidly confronts his negative view of self, and attempts to see something in it that can help him overcome it. Unfortunately, he discovers little to aid him.

This theme is presented, in embryonic form, in his first novel, *The Blacker the Berry* (1929). The jet-black complexion of Emma Lou, his protagonist, forces her to come to terms with who she is. Only a sincere acceptance of her dark skin color, in contrast to the attitudes of both her own culture and white society, leads to personal salvation. In his second novel, *The Infants of the Spring* (1932), Thurman portrays his own predicament and his efforts to get out of it. He parodies the Harlem Renaissance, its phoniness, self-deception and barrenness. He depicts how its praise of primitivism conceals self-effacement; how white patrons encourage literary compromise; how Afro-American pretentiousness hides inferiority complexes. For Thurman, only a Nietzschean *Ubermensch* or a Dostoevskian Underground Man can avoid these traps. Salvation lies in self-definition through art created out of no illusions about the self. Yet his self-acceptance precludes any usage of the positive aspects of Afro-American culture as ingredients for art. He creates from a cultural vacuum, from solely personal despair and self-hatred, resulting in an unusually truncated view of life, an extremely limited vision of human experience.

The Afro-American existentialist tradition reaches its zenith in the works and life of Richard Wright. The chief motif that pervades his writings is personal rebellion, against who he is, the culture that nurtures him, the society which rejects him and the cosmos which seems indifferent to his plight. Uprooted from the rural life of Mississippi, disgusted with the black bourgeoisie and predominately Jewish Communists in Chicago and New York, alienated within the cosmopolitan world of Paris and distrustful of emerging African countries, Wright is the marginal man *par excellence*.

Wright tried to create an Afro-American self-image that rests solely upon personal revolt, be it couched in the naturalism of Dreiser or crudely guided by the philosophical existentialism of Sartre or Camus. His revolt was intense, but it never crystallized into any serious talk of concerted action partly because such talk presupposes a community, a set of common values and goals, at which a marginal man like Wright can only sneer.

Wright's attitude toward Afro-American culture was twofold: A conscious embodiment and rejection of it.[42] In his major novel, *Native Son* (1940), Wright linked himself to the Afro-American community by presenting Bigger Thomas, his main character, as a symbol of this community, of its plight and hopes. Bigger gave visibility and recognition to Afro-Americans. Wright's sometimes subtle, and often overt, derogatory remarks about Afro-American culture were integral elements in the exposure of this culture, Wright's own fear, shame and self-hatred, he believed, made him intuitively close to the culture he rejected and rebellious against the society partially responsible for his negative self-image. Wright seemed to think he would always be a part of the culture from which he sought to escape, and the deeper his repudiation of it, the more tightly he remained tied to it. Why? Because his own negative self-image, he seemed to believe, only mirrored the self-image found in Afro-American culture. Artistic imagination allowed him (only him!) to overcome the deep scars of oppression. These livid scars became, for Wright (who had escaped from the inferno), the chief sources of his art. Hence, the assertions of being in his fiction take the form of violent acts against his culture, society and world.

The first major critique of Wright's perspective was written by the young James Baldwin. In his influential *Partisan Review* essays, (reprinted in *Notes of a Native Son*), he claims Wright succumbed to the cold, lifeless, abstract categories of social scientists; in short, Wright endorsed the Afro-American self-image found in the rationalist tradition. For Baldwin, such a view overlooks the richness and beauty in Afro-American life. Wright adopts a self-image that distorts Afro-American culture, denies Afro-American humanity. Baldwin concluded his remarks stating,

> our humanity is our burden, our life; we need not battle for it; we need only to do what is infinitely more difficult – that is, accept it.[43]

The greatness of Baldwin as a person and the significance of his work as a writer is his candid portrayal of this burdensome acceptance. In his first, and best, work of fiction, *Go Tell It On The Mountain* (1953), Baldwin discovered that the positive side of Afro-American life is much easier for him to talk about in essays than depict in fiction. When he looked closely into his own life, he saw almost precisely what Wright saw – terror, fear and self-hatred.[44] These qualities evolved from a rigid, fundamentalist Christian home in the heart of urban America – Harlem.

Baldwin's protagonist, John Grimes, has an immense fear of God, his father (Gabriel) and white society. He is plagued by a cosmic terror. He feels trapped. If he revolts against his Superegos, he fears perdition; if he submits, he suffers frustration. The only way out is through a rebellious act of imagination.

Unlike Wright, Baldwin's rebellion is not for deeper marginality or further isolation. Instead, his is a search for community, a community of love and tolerance denied him by Afro-American culture. Baldwin does not abhor this culture; he simply cannot overlook the stifling effects it has on nonconformists. He wants desperately to identify with Afro-American culture, but takes seriously the Christian, humanist values it espouses and the artistic imagination (the nonverbal or literate expressions) it suppresses. As with Wright, Baldwin is intuitively close to Afro-American culture and simultaneously on the edge of it. But, in contrast to Wright, this marginality is an interim condition, not a permanent state. Baldwin can envisage an escape from the inferno which leads to salvation, whereas Wright's vision lands him in a perennial limbo.

The most recent exponents in the Afro-American existentialist tradition are Gayl Jones and Toni Morrison. They illustrate the restrictive boundaries which confine and stifle Afro-American women. Jones' novels, *Corregidora* (1975) and *Eva's Man* (1976), are essentially indictments of the Afro-American male's sexual exploitation of Afro-American females. Both novels are literally monologues or dialogues about deranged sexual relations within a repressive culture, a culture shaped by white racism and further reinforced by black machismo. Toni Morrison's first two works of fiction, *The Bluest Eye* (1970) and *Sula* (1973), are lucid portraits of what it is like to be a talented Afro-American woman growing up in a strangling culture which punishes creativity and fears nonconformity. Behavioral patterns for women are rigidly set; violation invariably results in marginality. And marginality for imaginative Afro-American women in a *machismo* culture and hostile white world often leads to personal rebellion and sometimes self-destruction. Morrison captures this progression in a passage from her second novel,

> In a way, her strangeness, her naivete, her craving for the other half of her equation was the consequence of an idle imagination. Had she paints, or clay, or knew the discipline of dance, or strings; had she anything to engage her tremendous curiosity and her gift for metaphor, she might have exchanged the restlessness and preoccupation with whim for an activity that provided her with all she yearned for. And like any artist with no art form, she became dangerous.[45]

It is difficult to discern the conception of political struggle in the existentialist tradition. Given the artistic preoccupation of its members, political matters are secondary. If this tradition contains any conception of political struggle at all, it is a highly moralistic one. For example, the frequently cited last chapter of Wright's *Native Son* which contains Max's speech more closely resembles a sermon than a Marxist analysis of society.

Baldwin's masterful essays are grounded in moralism, often echoing the rhythm, syncopation and appeal of an effective sermon. The salient values are love, mercy, grace and inner freedom. In his famous work, *The Fire Next Time* (1964), he views the racial problem as stemming from truncated personal relations, from the refusal of black and white Americans to confront each other as human beings. He sees whites as afraid of being judged by blacks, scared of being seen as they really are; blacks as viewing themselves through white eyes, so they know little of who they really are. Even Baldwin's more vitriolic writings about social change have a deep moral fiber which speaks to the heart of individuals rather than to a community planning to undertake concerted political action.

The existentialist response to the challenge of self-image and self-determination is this: a candid acceptance of personal marginality to both Afro-American culture and American society plus moral sermonizing to all Americans. The basic concern of this tradition is to loosen the constraints on individuality in Afro-American life. Thus, it does not provide acute observations on political struggle. The Afro-American existentialist tradition is parasitic in that its numbers accept the self-image found in the rationalist or humanist camps.

Despite this dependence on other traditions, the existentialist response is important because it grapples with a personal torment endemic to modernity. This torment is an inevitable alienation and sense of revolt from one's racial group, society and world, if felt only for a few moments. This tradition endorses a marginality which serves as an impetus to creativity.

Humanist Tradition

The humanist self-image of Afro-Americans is one neither of heroic superhumans untouched by the experience of oppression nor of pathetic subhumans devoid of a supportive culture. Rather Afro-Americans are viewed as both meek and belligerent, kind and cruel, creative and dull – in short, as human beings. This tradition does not romanticize or reject Afro-American culture; instead it accepts this culture for what it is, the expression of an oppressed human community imposing its distinctive form of order on an existential chaos, explaining its political predicament, preserving its self-respect, and projecting its own special hopes for the future.

The best example of the Afro-American humanist tradition is its music. The rich pathos of sorrow and joy simultaneously present in spirituals, the exuberant and lyrical tragicomedy of the blues, and the improvisational character of jazz, affirm Afro-American humanity. These distinct artforms, which stem from the deeply entrenched oral and musical tradition of African culture and evolve out of Afro-American experience, express what it is like to be human under black skin in America. Afro-American musicians are Afro-American humanists *par excellence*. They relish their musical heritage and search for ways to develop it. This search proceeds without their having to prove to others that this heritage is worth considering, or that it is superior to any other. Rather the Afro-American musical heritage develops and flourishes by using both its fertile roots and elements from other musical traditions – from the first religious hymns and work songs through Scott Joplin, Bessie Smith, Louie Armstrong, Mahalia Jackson, Ella Fitzgerald, Duke Ellington, Coleman Hawkins, Lester Young, Billie Holiday, Charlie Parker, Dizzy Gillespie, Miles Davis, Ornette Coleman and John Coltrane. The heritage remains vibrant, with innovation and originality ensuring continual growth. Indeed, it has become one of the definitive elements in American culture.

The chief literary figures of the Afro-American humanist tradition – the young Jean Toomer, Langston Hughes, Zora Neale Hurston, Sterling Brown and Ralph Ellison – turn to the culture of the Afro-American masses, to blues, jazz and folklore, as the ingredients of their art. They feel no need to be either superior to whites or marginal to Afro-American culture. They seem to consider themselves relatively secure with their heritage, as well as those of other groups or nations.

The first major literary expression of Afro-American humanism is found in Jean Toomer's still insufficiently studied *Cane* (1923). This work is a search for Afro-American humanity in the alluring, beautiful and burdensome black culture of the South. This unconventional collage of poignant stories and poems is a gem, a relatively untapped treasure that yields deep insights into Afro-American culture.

Toomer describes the myriad of constraining effects resulting from the attitudes and beliefs of Afro-Americans in rural settings. He portrays lives of spirituality and degradation. Women are objects, sex is sterile, human relations are exploitative and painful. The innocent Karintha is treated as a commodity; Becky is caught in a web of miscegenation, hypocrisy and sympathy; Fern's other-worldly life melts into nothingness, dissolves into anomie.

When Toomer shifts to the urban setting, despair persists, but possible liberation looms. This liberation lies in the artistic shaping of the past, the discovery of self by understanding the spiritual riches of this past. The central characters, Dan and Kabnis, are archetypes of the Afro-American artist. Dan, whose roots stem from the rural South, comes to the urban North with a messianic mission: to remind the "New Negroes" of their roots. He pursues the socially pretentious and haughty Muriel, who avoids him and ignores his message. Nevertheless, he emerges from the confining Afro-American urban world of self-hatred and shame, aware of the grand challenge of creating an ordered view of life from a fading folk past.

This theme of candid confrontation with the past is further illustrated in "Kabnis", the last and longest story in *Cane*. Kabnis is self-effacing and uncomfortable with Southern culture, a culture he knows little of. He confronts his roots in the person of Father John, a former slave. Kabnis, a mulatto, has denied any links with slavery by disavowing any black ancestors. When Father John utters his long-awaited words of wisdom (Christian quips about the sinfulness and mendaciousness of whites), Kabnis is disappointed and angry. He had expected more than mere small talk about an oppressive past, a past, he believes, filled with black docility fueled by a slave religion. Kabnis is ashamed of this past and looks into the future with perplexed eyes.

Toomer's insight is that any acceptable Afro-American self-image begins with unflinching introspection. For an oppressed people, a mere superficial glance will result in self-gratifying celebration of heroic resistance, or self-pitying lament over the great damage done. Toomer opts for neither alternative. Instead, he looks into the Afro-American past and sees the small yet cumulative struggles of human beings against overwhelming odds, the creation of both supportive values and stifling mores.

His profound message to Afro-Americans is that in modernity, where alienation is commonplace, it is important to be aware of roots, but even this provides no assurance of ability to achieve a positive self-image in the ever-changing present. The search for personal identity is never a pleasant one if only because the very need for it connotes a misplacement, dislocation and homelessness of the self. The act of self-definition forever remains open-ended, with no guarantee of triumph. Indeed, the process takes precedent over the result, since any static self-identity soon disintegrates the self.

Only a person highly knowledgeable of, and sensitive to the Afro-American past, moved by its many struggles, though not blind to its shortcomings, could give such a sympathetic and credibly convincing portrait of an old, God-fearing, Christian, black woman as did Langston Hughes with Aunt Hagar in his only novel, *Not Without Laughter* (1930). Although Hughes unequivocally objects to her orthodox religious beliefs, bourgeois values and white standards, he admires the perseverance and fortitude of Aunt Hagar. Despite adverse circumstances, she endures, with a joy derived from her Christian faith, and its Dionysian rituals. Aunt Hagar triumphs over overwhelming odds in her own dynamic and flexible way, without self-hatred, self-pity or self-deception. She overcomes by pure, unabated struggle.

25

This simple, but profound message of personal and communal struggle voices the wisdom of Afro-American folklore, blues and jazz. It guides the con life of Sterling Brown's Slim Greer in *Southern Road* (1932) and the tenuous and ultimately tragic plight of Zora Neale Hurston's Janie in *Their Eyes Were Watching God* (1937).

The Afro-American humanist tradition reaches its literary apex in the writings of Ralph Ellison. He stands out among Afro-American humanists, and all Afro-American artists of the other traditions, not only because of the superb mastery of his craft and the acuteness of his mind, but also because he takes the Afro-American art-forms of the past with more intellectual seriousness than other Afro-American artists. He understands the spirituals, blues, jazz and folklore of the Afro-American masses to be, not artifacts for self-congratulation or objects of catharsis, but rather aesthetic modes of expression that represent distinctive perceptions of reality. They serve as media of social communication which express the values for the joint communal existence of Afro-Americans. For Ellison, the task of the Afro-American artist is to locate, articulate and delineate the universal human core of these Afro-American art-forms and transform this discovery into a work of art that portrays the complexity and ambiguity of human existence.

The major aim of political struggle in the Afro-American humanist tradition is found in the works of the young A. Phillip Randolph and Chandler Owen of the *Messenger*, William Jones of the Baltimore *Afro-American* (all three during the 1920's), the later Du Bois, Paul Robeson, post-Mecca Malcolm X, Huey Newton, Angela Davis, the later Imamu Baraka and to a certain extent the theology of James Cone.[46] These thinkers share a certain common value: the necessity for the democratic control over institutions in the productive and political processes. The basic assumption of this Afro-American humanist political viewpoint is that the present economic system and social arrangements cannot adequately alleviate the deplorable socioeconomic conditions of the Afro-American masses. This assumption is linked to a corollary claim, namely that the circumstances of the black poor and those of the black working class (including both blue and white collar workers) are qualitatively similar and only quantitatively different. In other words, the Afro-American middle class merely (yet significantly, in human terms) have higher-paying jobs than the Afro-American lower-class; but neither have any meaningful participation in the decision-making process as to who gets hired or fired nor any control over the production of goods and services.

The ostensible oppressive circumstances of the Afro-American poor and the less visible ones of the Afro-American working class are both linked to the relative powerlessness of Afro-Americans, not only in the political process, *but, more importantly, in the productive process.* This lack of significant control in the work situation also holds for the white poor and working class. Historically, the white poor and working class have served as formidable obstacles for Afro-American enhancement. Racism has been a source of intra-class conflict. But the future looks different. Expansion of interracial unionization in the South, the radicalization of integrated unions in blue and white collar occupations and the concerted push for federalized policy concerning national problems of unemployment and health care, may provide the framework for a new era, an era in which the black and white poor and working classes unite against corporate domination of the economy and government. The Afro-American humanist political viewpoint eagerly endorses and energetically encourages action to make this era a reality.

26

The humanist political perspective acknowledges the complex interplay between pragmatism and ideology, electoral politics and structural social change. It discourages ideological programs which have no reasonable chance of succeeding and pragmatic ones that preclude the possibility of fundamentally transforming the present economic system and social arrangements. This perspective supports the continued participation of Afro-Americans in electoral politics, reformist strategies in the political and pro-ductive processes and reasonable radical agitation on persistent issues of common concern.[47]

The humanist response to the challenges of self-image and self-determination is this: a promotion of an unconstrained individuality strengthened by an honest encounter with the Afro-American past and the expansion of democratic control over the major institutions that regulate lives in America and abroad. This response contrasts sharply with the vitalist and rationalist ones. It neither romanticizes nor rejects Afro-American culture; it also avoids the self-serving pursuit of status, wealth and prestige. Instead, the humanist response provides a cultural springboard useful in facing the ever-present issue of self-identity for Afro-Americans and joins their political struggle to other progressive elements in American society.

Afro-American philosophy deems the norms of the humanist tradition desirable. These norms of unconstrained individuality and democratic control of the political and productive processes are acceptable because they promote personal development, cultural growth and human freedom. They foster the fulfillment of the potentialities and capacities of all individuals, encourage innovation and originality in Afro-American culture, and expand people's control over those institutions that deeply affect their lives.[48]

So Afro-American philosophy diachronically reconstructs the Afro-American past and critically evaluates Afro-American responses to crucial challenges in the present. It attempts to understand the Afro-American experience in order to enhance and enrich the lives of Afro-Americans; it demands personal integrity and political action.

Notes

1 I understand a diachronic study to be one that attempts to deal with a phenomenon as it changes over time; it contains a schema that sheds light on human thought and behavior over various historical periods. In contrast, a synchronic study is concerned with the complex of events within a specific time period. The most exciting Afro-American histori-ography being done focuses on the period of slavery. Stanley Elkins, Eugene Genovese, Herbert Gutman, John Blassingame and others have provided thought-provoking syn-chronic studies of this period, but few historians have tried to go beyond this era-bound approach and thereby broaden our understanding of the Afro-American experience.

2 In the following exposition of metaphilosophy, I follow closely the brilliant work of Prof. Richard Rorty of Princeton University. Most of this work remains unpublished. I am confi-dent his writings on metaphilosophical issues will be of paramount importance for thinkers in the future. A small taste of his views can be acquired from his article, "Keeping Philosophy Pure," *The Yale Review* (Spring, 1976), Vol. LXV, No. 3, pp. 336–56.

3 The idea that Descartes held a correspondence theory of truth recently has come under attack by Harry Frankfurt in his fascinating work, *Demons, Dreamers and Madmen* (New

York, 1970). This book indeed has infused new blood into Cartesian studies, but it is, I believe, wrong. For a convincing defense of the traditional view of Descartes, see Anthony Kenny, *Descartes: A Study of His Philosophy* (New York, 1968), esp. chapters five and eight.

4   By inadvertently presupposing the Cartesian viewpoint, some Afro-American philosophers, searching for something distinctly black and philosophical, engage in discussions about pseudo-issues, such as black epistemology, black ontology or black conceptions of time and space. This approach merely adopts the Cartesian categories and tries to fill them with "black" content. I believe it is confused, misguided, and will prove to be unproductive.

5   For Heidegger's contrast between the Cartesian perspective and his own, see *Being and Time* (New York, 1962), trans. Macquarrie and Robinson, the section entitled, "A Contrast Between Our Analysis of Worldhood and Descartes' Interpretation of the World," pp. 122–34.

6   In his famous essay, "The Overcoming of Metaphysics," Heidegger states, "the modern form of ontology is transcendental philosophy, which itself changes into theory of knowledge" found in *The End of Philosophy* (New York, 1973), p. 88. His comments echo the words of Nietzsche, who is for Heidegger the last Western metaphysician, "philosophy reduced to theory of knowledge . . . is philosophy at its last gasp, an end, an agony, something that arouses pity." Quoted R. J. Hollingdale, *Nietzsche* (London, 1973), p. 166.

7   The Schleiermacher-Dilthey view is merely a hermeneutic version of the Cartesian correspondence theory of truth. It is most clearly presented in the recent work of Eric Hirsch. This theory can be characterized as persons trapped in a veil of ideas; they get in touch with reality only by mental representations (analogous to interpreted meanings) correctly corresponding to external objects (real meanings, such as authorial intentions). Such a theory of truth is obsessed with objectivity because it is forever harassed by skepticism; that is, we can always question the correctness of the correspondence. This skepticism reaches its zenith in the writings of Bishop Berkeley and David Hume. Kant tries to undercut it by granting agnosticism of reality, yet positing an inescapable synthetic machinery that manufactures the raw manifold of intuitions into concepts which impose rational order on the phenomenal world. He sacrifices our knowledge of reality in order to preserve objectivity. Cartesian thinkers, like their Master, want both.

8   Heidegger, *Being and Time*, p. 194.

9   Hans-Georg Gadamer, one of Heidegger's students, has developed this viewpoint much further in his monumental work, *Truth and Method* (New York, 1975), translation edited by Garrett Barden and John Cumming from the second edition. For his discussion of Heidegger's insights, the Cartesian and Enlightenment attacks on prejudice and tradition, and his own notion of the "fusing of horizons" (Horizontsverschmelzung), see pp. 235–74.

10   For Heidegger's much too brief discussion of these notions, see *Being and Time*, section 74, pp. 434–9.

11   The young Marcuse's critique of Heidegger is found in his first published article, "Contributions to a Phenomenology of Historical Materialism" which appeared in the German periodical, *Philosophishe Hefte* I, 1 (1928). Martin Jay summarizes this article in his book, *The Dialectical Imagination* (Boston. 1973), pp. 71–3.

12   Calvin O. Schrag, "Phenomenology, Ontology and History in the Philosophy of Heidegger" in *Phenomenologv*, ed. Joseph J. Kocelmans (Garden City, 1967), p. 293.

13   David Pears, *Ludwig Wittgenstein* (New York, 1969), p. 179. Pears' book is a mini-classic on this enigmatic philosopher.

14   It is important to note that trenchant critiques of the notion of necessity within the philosophical tradition of the West leave philosophers with little subject-matter. For example, Hume's rejection of necessary causal inferences elevates the role of imagination in thought and custom and habit in behavior: it results in a psychological naturalism and an embry-

onic sociology of knowledge. W. V. O. Quine's repudiation of necessary true statements yields a behavioristic criterion (of assent or dissent to similar stimuli) for a grounding of epistemological validity and requires a holism that hints at a dynamic historicism (a la Kuhn and Feyerabend). For Hume's arguments, see his magnificent work, *A Treatise of Human Nature* (Oxford, 1968), ed. L. A. Selby-Bigge, Part III, Section XIV, entitled "Of the Idea of Necessary Connexion", pp. 155–72. For Quine's criticisms of analyticity, see his widely influential essay, "Two Dogmas of Empiricism," in his *From a Logical Point of View* (New York, 1961), pp. 20–46.

15   Wittgenstein's ethical views are clearly presented and elaborately discussed by Allan Janik and Stephen Toulmin in their provocative book, *Wittgenstein's Vienna* (New York, 1973), Chapter 6.

16   I have in mind his formulations in *Reconstruction in Philosophy* (Boston, 1948).

17   A brief methodological note. This philosophical inquiry into history should be distinguished from the history of ideas, history of philosophy and intellectual history. The history of ideas is concerned exclusively with concepts explicitly articulated by recognized thinkers; the objects of this discipline are formal ideas. The history of philosophy is the study of concepts or conceptual systems demonstratively presented by thinkers in response to distinctly philosophical problems as defined by present philosophical traditions. Intellectual history includes the history of ideas, history of philosophy plus the unformulated opinions, silent assumptions and inarticulated beliefs of people; the objects of this discipline are the relations between various sets of notions and the cultural way of life from which they emerge. A philosophical inquiry into history utilizes various aspects of historical phenomena in order to unearth, reject and endorse norms of existential and political dilemmas currently besetting a cultural way of life. For useful discussions of these distinctions, see Leonard Krieger, "The Autonomy of Intellectual History," *The Journal of the History of Ideas*, (Oct.–Dec., 1973), Vol. XXXIV, No. 4 and Maurice Mandelbaum, "The History of Ideas, Intellectual History and History of Philosophy," *History and Theory*, 5 (1965).

18   A particular conception of the Afro-American self-image deeply affects the political strategy of Afro-American self-determinism. Yet we must not assume a priori that certain correlations necessarily hold, such as that a positive self-image will always accompany the acquisition of power, or a negative self-image the absence of power. Afro-American philosophy must preserve the delicate symbiotic relation between culture and politics without resorting to a simplistic and all too often incorrect reductionism.

19   Based on my conception of Afro-American philosophy, there have been few conscious instances of it. Of course, there have been Afro-American philosophers, but, like most Afro-American intellectuals, they have exerted their energies either trying to convince the black middle class that the world of ideas should be taken seriously, serving as an ideologue for a particular political or cultural movement, or attempting to gain acceptance in the predominately white Academy. All three activities are essential for a potent intelligentsia, but leave little time for reflecting upon the basic assumptions of the theoretical frameworks wherein thinkers speculate. Effective propagandists and insecure academicians rarely question basic frameworks or ask fundamental questions with seriousness.

20   These four ideal-types represent the basic responses of any group, community or nation entering modernity. In the American context, they are found among emerging Irish, Italian, Polish, Jewish, et al. communities beginning to interact with the dominant WASP culture and society. In the European context, these traditions are salient in early 19th Century Germany, late 19th Century Russia, early 20th Century Spain, etc. They are presently forming in Third World countries. The best recent studies on this problematic of groups entering modernity are those of John Cuddihy on Jewish intellectuals, Rockwell Gray on Spanish thinkers (esp. Ortega y Gasset) and Elaine Showalter on British women novelists.

For samples of their work, see Cuddihy, *The Ordeal of Civility: Freud, Marx, Levi-Straus, and the Jewish Struggle with Modernity* (New York, 1974). Rockwell Gray, "Ortega y Gasset and Modern Culture", *Salmagundi* (Fall, 1976), No. 35, pp. 6–41. Elaine Showalter, *A Literature of Their Own: British Women Novelists from Bronte to Lessing* (Princeton, 1977).

21 Gramsci defends this viewpoint in his important essay, "Problems of Marxism" in his *Prison Notebooks*, ed. Quintin Hoare and Geoffrey Nowell Smith, (London, 1971).

22 W. E. B. Du Bois, "The Conservation of Races", *The Seventh Son: The Thought and Writings of W. E. B. Du Bois* (New York, 1971), Vol. One, ed. Julius Lester, p. 180.

23 W. E. B. Du Bois, *The Souls of Black Folk* (Greenwich, 1961), intro. Saunders Redding, p. 22.

24 This remark is quoted from S. P. Fullinwider's seminal work, *The Mind and Mood of Black America* (Homewood, 1969), p. 60.

25 *The Book of American Negro Poetry*, ed. James Weldon Johnson (New York, 1922), pp. 9–10.

26 Manuscript of speech delivered to Washington D.C. branch of the NAACP, 1924, Johnson papers, James Weldon Johnson Collection Yale University Library. Quoted from Fullinwider, *The Mind and Mood of Black America*, p. 89.

27 R. R. Wright, Jr. "African Methodism and the Second Century," *Christian Recorder*, Vol. 64 (April 13, 1916), p. 4.

28 Ibid.

29 Amy Jacques-Garvey, *Garvey and Garveyism* (Kingston, 1963), p. 98.

30 *Black Nationalism in America* (New York, 1970), ed. Bracey, Meier and Rudwick, p. 193.

31 Martin Luther King, Jr., "A Mighty Army of Love," *SCLC Newsletter*, Vol. 2, (Oct.–Nov., 1964), p. 7.

32 This interpretation puts the famous Du Bois–Washington debate in a slightly different light. Du Bois indeed favors struggling for political rights and a liberal education for the Talented Tenth, while Washington pushes for the acquisition of marketable skills and accumulation of property among Afro-Americans. But, in regard to Afro-American leadership, Washington preserves an important place for skilled workers and entrepreneurs, who have close contact with ordinary black people. For Du Bois, at this stage in his long career, only the educated elite could provide leadership, an elite that easily falls prey to idealization of the Afro-American masses.

33 W. E. B. Du Bois, "The Talented Tenth", *The Seventh Son: The Thought and Writings of W. E. B. Du Bois*, p. 385.

34 An important note should not be overlooked regarding Afro-American nationalist movements in the vitalist tradition, namely their invariable authoritarian and sexist character. These movements e.g. Garvey, Black Muslims, Congress of African People, delegate power from top to bottom within a highly rigid hierarchical structure wherein women are relegated to the lowest runs, the most powerless positions. As Christopher Lasch has suggested, these movements may contain elements of a machismo complex and express assertions of masculinity heretofore ignored. Lasch's insightful essay, "Black Power: Cultural Nationalism as Politics" is in his work, *The Agony of the American Left* (New York, 1969), pp. 117–68.

35 Despite ostensible gains during the past decade by the black white collar and stable blue collar working class, the black poor has increased, in numbers and percentage. In the last Government Census (in 1972), the poor and near-poor represented a staggering 42% of all Afro-Americans. See Sar Levitan, William Johnston and Robert Taggart, *Still A Dream* (Cambridge, 1975), Chapter 2, esp. p. 33.

36 Martin Kilson makes this acute observation in his article, "Black Power: Anatomy of a Paradox," *The Harvard Journal of Negro Affairs*, Vol. 2, No. 1, 1968, pp. 30–4. He writes, "Some professionals are adopting a Black Power ideological format not with the intent of preparing themselves for service to self-governing urban black communities but to make

themselves more visible to the white establishment, which is not at all adverse to offering such persons good jobs as alternatives to Black Power. The more viable Negro businessmen are also simulating the Black Power phenomenon in this way ... The Black Power advocates have virtually no control over this use of their political style by the professional and business black bourgeoisie, which means the Black Power advocates will eventually lose the payoff potential of nationalist politics. If so ... the Negro lower classes, whose riots legitimize Black Power, will be joined by the Black Power advocates in holding the bag – with nothing in it, save a lot of therapeutic miscellany . . ." (p. 34).

37 Fortunately, there are no Afro-American strong rationalists, though there are still a few white ones around e.g. Shockley, Jensen.

38 This viewpoint has been extremely influential in American sociological studies on Afro-Americans. For example, Gunnar Myrdal's renowned *An American Dilemma* (1944) states "American Negro culture . . . is a distorted development, or an unhealthy condition of American culture" (p. 928). Glazer and Moynihan's first edition of *The Melting Pot* (1963) reads "the Negro is only an American, and nothing else. He has no values and culture to guard and protect" (p. 53). And the list goes on and on e.g. Stanley Elkin's Sambo thesis about slave personality in *Slavery* (1959), the Moynihan report on the Afro-American family (1965), Kenneth Clarke's *Dark Ghetto* (1965), et al.

39 E. Franklin Frazier, "Racial Self-Expression", *Ebony and Topaz, a Collectionana* (New York, 1927), ed. Charles S. Johnson, p. 120.

40 In later life, like most active minds, Frazier makes claims inconsistent with his earlier views and engages in a fruitful exercise of self-criticism. Based on his earlier perspective, it is not surprising the black middle class dangles in a world of make-believe since white society excludes them and they abhor their own culture; Afro-American intellectuals also would be hard put to project positive self-images if Afro-American culture is what the early Frazier suggests it is. For Frazier's later essay on Afro-American intellectuals, see "The Failure of the Negro Intellectual," *Negro Digest*, February 1962.

41 Nathan Huggins concurs with this observation in his book, *Harlem Renaissance* (New York, 1971), p. 119, where, in discussing Fisher's novel, *The Walls of Jericho* (1928), he writes, "Joshua 'Shine' Jones, Rudolph Fisher's proletarian hero, has several walls to bring down. There is the barrier of race, of course, which remarkably is the least of his concerns. His resentment is directed primarily against class distinctions and the pretensions of high-toned Negroes. Thus, Fisher wrote the only novel of the decade that exposed class antagonisms among Harlem blacks." See also Robert Bone's perceptive comments on Fisher's attempt to bridge the gap between other cleavages e.g. rural vs. urban, artist vs. middle class, West Indian vs. Southern black, in his short stories. Robert Bone, *Down Home: A History of Afro-American Short Fiction from Its Beginning to the End of the Harlem Renaissance* (New York, 1975), pp. 150–9.

42 My reading of Wright is influenced by Martin Kilson's unpublished paper "Nationalism and Marginality in Black Writers: The Case of Richard Wright."

43 James Baldwin, "Everybody's Protest Novel," *Notes of a Native Son* (New York, 1955), p. 17.

44 My reading of Baldwin is influenced by Stanley Macehuh's *James Baldwin: A Critical Study* (Third World Press, 1973).

45 Toni Morrison, *Sula* (New York, 1973), p. 105.

46 The other important stream of thought and behavior in the Afro-American humanist tradition is "reformist". It extends from Frederick Douglass through Booker T. Washington to Benjamin Hooks. This stream is represented by those people who satisfy the cultural criteria of Afro-American humanism and advocate certain reforms in the capitalist system. They fail to promote structural change in society. The stream of thought and behavior mentioned above (in the essay) represent those people who satisfy the same cultural criteria, but

support the replacement of the capitalist system with one that extends democracy into the institutions of production so that the government and economy is truly "of the people, by the people, and for the people." This replacement constitutes a structural change in society, especially a redistribution of its wealth.

47 Acceptable reformist programs must meet two criteria: improve the deplorable living conditions of the poor and open up new possibilities for people gaining some control over the major institutions that deeply affect their lives.

48 Needless to say, this endorsement of the humanist tradition and its norms is not a justification of them. The latter indeed is necessary if people are to be convinced to accept them. Unfortunately, space does not permit such an endeavor in this essay.

2

African-American Existential Philosophy

LEWIS R. GORDON

African-American existential philosophy is a branch of Africana and black philosophies of existence. By Africana philosophy is meant the philosophical currents that emerged out of the experience of diasporic Africa. By black philosophy is meant the philosophical currents that emerged from the question of blackness. Black philosophy relates to a terrain that is broader than Africana communities because not all black people are of African descent. Indigenous Australians, whose lived reality is that of being a black people, are an example. Similarly, problems of blackness are but a part of Africana philosophy. The divide is not only philosophical – where black philosophy's normative and descriptive concerns may be narrower than Africana philosophy's – but also cultural: Although there are Africana cultures, it is not clear what "black culture" is. There are black communities whose cultural formations show convergence of many cultural formations – from Africa, Europe, Asia, and the Americas – but there, the focus may be Africana or something more than race. That being so, the turn to African America carries a similar divide. In African-American philosophy, there is focus on the unique features of African-American cultural experiences on the one hand, and the reality that African Americans are a black people and, hence, are impacted by the significance of race and racism. The same cultural and political concerns apply to African-American existential philosophy.

What is African-American existential philosophy? Perhaps its features will best be understood through an anecdote on my putting together a project in the area of black existential philosophy some years ago. In 1994, I issued a call for papers on black existential philosophy. Responses ranged from discussions of the African roots of black existential philosophy to the liberating struggles of blacks in a racially hostile world. There were, however, a few mysterious abstracts. There is no black existential philosophy, these argued, since existentialism is a European phenomenon addressing European experience. Look for thought from Søren Kierkegaard to Simone de Beauvoir, and one would find more bourgeois *Angst* than material conditions of black misery. To this criticism, I wrote letters with the following response: The body of literature that constitutes European existentialism is but one continent's response to a set of problems that date from the moment human beings faced problems of anguish and despair. That conflicts over responsibility and anxiety, over life affirmation and suicidal nihilism, preceded Kierkegaardian formulations of fear and trembling raised questions beyond Eurocentric attachment to a narrow body of literature. Existential philosophy addresses problems of freedom, anguish, dread, responsibility, embodied agency, sociality, and liberation. It addresses these problems through a focus on the human condition.

At the heart of existential thought are two questions: "What are we?" and "What shall we do?" These questions can be translated into questions of identity and normative action. They are questions, further, of ontological and teleological significance, for the former addresses being and the latter addresses what to become – in a word, "purpose." Such questions can be further radicalized through reflection on their preconditions: How are such questions, in a word, possible?

In my replies to the skeptics, I asked them if slaves did not wonder about freedom, suffer anguish, paradoxes of responsibility, concerns of agency, tremors of broken sociality, and a burning desire for liberation. Do we not find struggles with these matters in traditional West African proverbs and folktales that these slaves had brought with them to the New World? And more, even if we do not turn to the historical experiences of slaves of African descent and the body of cultural resources indigenous to the African continent, there are also the various dialogical encounters between twentieth-century African-American theorists and European and Euro-American theorists.

Problems of existence emerge wherever there are people confronting their freedom and degradation. In the nineteenth century, these concerns took similar and different forms on both sides of the Atlantic. In Europe, there were anxiety over the future to come and boredom over passions that were dying. In North America, there were other concerns. For white Americans there was a present and a future to conquer. There wasn't much room for boredom, and since they were self-assured, there seemed little room for anxiety. To find anxiety and dread, one needed to look beyond white America. And since North America was not populated solely by white people, finding these sources of concern isn't difficult. As W. E. B. Du Bois, Frantz Fanon, Ralph Ellison, and Toni Morrison have shown us, anxiety, dread, and despair was in the modern world's underside, in the blackness that it often sought to hide in its theoretical and aesthetic moments of self-representation. Few topics brought on particularly New World anxiety more than these questions of color. Such questions continue to forge the divide in modern loyalties. Who knows how many interracial friendships have fallen prey to those moments of candor?

So, racial problems serve a dominating role. In African-American existential philosophy, this reality has meant detailed explorations of this factor in the lived experience of African Americans. It has meant an exploration of their lived experience of blackness.

The racial problematic for African Americans is twofold. On the one hand, it is the question of exclusion in the face of an ethos of assimilation. On the other hand, there is the complex confrontation with the fact of such exclusion in a world that portends commitment to rational resolutions of evil. With regard to this latter concern, we could paraphrase Du Bois from *The Souls of Black Folk* and *Darkwater*: What does it mean to be a problem? and What is to be understood by black suffering?

These questions of problematized existence and suffering animate the theoretical dimensions of black intellectual existential productions. It is what signals the question

of liberation on one level and the critique of traditional, read "European," ontological claims on another. Together they inaugurate African-American liberation thought and African-American critical race theory. The former finds its fountainhead most poignantly in Frederick Douglass. His answer in 1857 was straightforward:

> The whole history of the progress of human liberty shows that all concessions yet made to her august claims, have been born of earnest struggle. This struggle may be a moral one, or it may be a physical one, and it may be both moral and physical, but it must be a struggle. Power concedes nothing without demand. It never did and it never will.

The latter ontological question was examined by many philosophers and social critics of African descent in the nineteenth century, including such well-known and diverse figures as Martin Delany, Maria Stewart, Anna Julia Cooper, and (the early) Du Bois. It was not until the 1940s, however, that a self-avowed existential examination of these issues emerged, and they emerged ironically through a European philosopher – namely, Jean-Paul Sartre.

Sartre stands as an unusual catalyst in the history of African-American existential philosophy, for he serves as a link between Richard Wright and Frantz Fanon (undoubtedly the two most influential "men of letters" among African-American existentialists of the twentieth century) on the one hand, and the historical forces that came into play for the ascendence of European Philosophy of Existence in the American academy on the other hand – forces that provided a context for the academic work of African-American philosophers such as William R. Jones (who wrote his Brown University dissertation on Sartre's critical methodology), Angela Y. Davis (who majored in French existential thought at Brandeis University while studying with Herbert Marcuse), and Anthony Bogues (whose path from theology to existential Marxism emerged from engagements with the writings of Sartre). Other black academic philosophers who have been influenced by Sartre's work, by way of either Sartre himself or by philosophers like Frantz Fanon or Merleau-Ponty, also include Robert Birt (whose dissertation was on Sartre's *Critique of Dialectical Reason*), Thomas S. Slaughter (whose phenomenology is of the existential variety and who wrote his dissertation on Frantz Fanon), Naomi Zack (who utilizes Sartre's ideas in her *Race and Mixed Race*), and the present author (who wrote his dissertation on Sartre's conception of bad faith).

It will, however, be an error to construct African-American academic existential philosophy as a fundamentally Sartrian or European-based phenomenon. For although there are African-American philosophers who have been influenced by both Sartre and European thought, it will nevertheless be fallacious to assume that that influence functions as the "cause" instead of the opportunity. African-American philosophers already have a reason to raise existential questions of liberation and questions of identity, as we've already suggested, by virtue of the historical fact of racial oppression – oppression manifested most vividly in the Atlantic Slave Trade. What that event brought about was not only a period of intense suffering for black peoples, but also the hegemonic symbolic order of Western civilization(s) itself, a symbolic order whose "place" for "the black," if we will, has been fundamentally negative as far back as the Middle Ages and antiquity. There is much debate on this issue, especially in light of postmodern scholarship that locates such phenomena in the modern era. The problem is that there are texts in the Middle Ages and antiquity that refer not only to the black, but also to the black in very negative terms, as argued by Eulalio Baltazar in his *Dark Center*. African-American philosophers' choice of European thinkers through whom to consider these questions is, therefore, already existentially situated. To place European thinkers as "cause" would be to place the proverbial cart before the horse.

There is, however, a distinction that can here be borne in mind. We can regard *existentialism* – the popularly named ideological movement – as a fundamentally European historical phenomenon. It is, in effect, the history of European literature that bears that name. On the other hand, we can regard *philosophies of existence* – the specialized term for what are sometimes called *existential philosophies* – as philosophical questions premised upon concerns of freedom, anguish, responsibility, embodied agency, sociality, and liberation. Unlike fashionable standpoint epistemology of the 1980s and early 1990s, philosophies of existence are marked by a centering of what is often known as the "situation" of questioning or inquiry itself. Another term for situation is the lived-context of concern. Implicit in the existential demand for recognizing the situation or lived-context of African-American people's being-in-the-world is the question of value raised by people who live that situation. A slave's situation can only be understood, for instance, through recognizing the fact that a slave experiences it. It is to regard the slave as a perspective in the world.

Given our conception of philosophy of existence, it is clear that the history of African-American philosophy – at least from David Walker's *Appeal to All Colored Citizens of the World* to Cornel West's Kierkegaardian call for keeping *faith* and Toni Morrison's tragic questions of identity and ethical paradox in the Present Age (in both her *Playing in the Dark* and *Beloved*) – has its own unique set of existential questions. We find a constant posing of the teleological question of black liberation, the ontological question of agency, and the question of black identity in the midst of an antiblack world. The irony is that, as Fanon has shown in *Black Skin, White Masks*, one cannot in critical good faith raise the question of the black without raising these accompanying existential questions.

What this is to say is not that African-American philosophy is existential in the sense of reducing it to philosophy of existence. It is to say that the impetus of African-American philosophy, when the question of the black or the situation of black people is raised, has an existential impetus. That African-American philosophy cannot, and should not, be reduced to existential philosophy is paradoxical because of a central dimension of philosophy of existence itself: The question of existence, in itself, is empty. Philosophy of existence is therefore always a conjunctive affair. It must, in other words, be situated. This is because, for complex reasons that will become evident to the reader of the essays in this volume, the sine qua non of an existential philosophical anthropology is the paradoxical incompleteness of existential questions. Consider the famous existential credo of existence preceding essence. If essence is read also as conceptualization, then the theoretical or conceptual domain is always situated on what can be called the reflective level. The reflective dimension of situated life always brings in an element of concrete embodiment of relevance. What this means, then, is that theory, any theory, gains its sustenance from that which it offers *for* the lived-reality of those who are expected to formulate it. African-American philosophy's history of Christian,

36

Marxist, Feminist, Pragmatic, Analytical, and Phenomenological thought, then, has been a matter of what specific dimensions each had to offer the existential realities of theorizing blackness. For Marxism, for instance, it was not so much its notion of "science" over all other forms of socialist theory, nor its promise of a world to win, that may have struck a resonating chord in the hearts of African-American Marxists. It was, instead, Marx and Engels' famous encomium of the proletarians having nothing to lose but their chains. Such a call has obvious affinity for a people who have been so strongly identified with chattel slavery.

Academic African-American existential philosophy has oscillated from time to time on the liberation question. In the contemporary academy, for instance, one will find priority placed on the identity question. The concern has taken many euphemisms, particularly in terms of questions of culture and ethnicity, but in the end, it usually amounts to the ever infamous "race question." This consequence is a function of an historical fact: race has emerged, throughout its history, as the question fundamentally of "the blacks" as it has for no other group. It is not that other groups have not been "racialized." It is that their racialization, if we will, has been conditioned in terms of a chain of being from the European human being to the subhuman on a symbolic scale from the light to the dark. As we have already noted, it is not that African-American philosophy has been the only situated reality of blackness, but instead that it has been a situated reality that is fundamentally conditioned by the question of blackness. The link between African-American philosophy of existence and the question of race is pronounced on the critical race theoretical problem of human designation. What African-American critical race theory has shown is that the situation of blacks cannot be resolved by any philosophical anthropology that places the human being as a consequence of essential properties of valuative determination. Race issues are not issues, in other words, of chromosomal make-up nor simply morphological appearance. Race issues, as Alain Locke has shown through several essays on values and identity, are issues by virtue of the values placed upon what has been interpreted as "given." Thus, in spite of biophysical evidence, all of world history, beyond black struggles for significance, questions the humanity of black peoples. As Fanon has so provocatively put it in his 1956 resignation letter from Blida-Joinville Hospital in Algiers, included in *Toward the African Revolution*, colored defiance to black dehumanization has been historically constituted as *madness* or social deviance. Blackness and, in specific form, *the black* thus function as the breakdown of reason, which situates black existence, ultimately, in a seemingly nonrational category of faith. It is the plight of, in other words, *the damned of the earth*. In the face of unreason, nihilism gnaws at black existence. The black stands as an existential enigma. Eyed with suspicion, the subtext is best exemplified in the question: "Why do they go on?"

One can readily see why such European existentialists as Jean-Paul Sartre and Simone de Beauvoir were particularly interested in the existential situation of African Americans in such works as Sartre's *Nausea*, *Notebook for an Ethics*, "Return from the United States," and many more instances, as well as De Beauvoir's reflections on Richard Wright and Frantz Fanon in her autobiographies. Their philosophies of existence, premised upon a critical encounter with bad faith and reconciliation with responsibility, requires an understanding not only of bourgeois or ruling-class self-delusions of *Angst*, but also the force of *their* circumstances (as de Beauvoir might put it) as social realities of those upon whose labor their society drew its luxuries.

"Why do they go on?," placed in the context of the black, is easily reformulated, simply, as, "Why go on?"

It is, as Albert Camus has so well noted in "Absurdity and Suicide," in *"The Myth of Sisyphus" and Other Essays, the* question. If there are readers who may be suspicious of this peculiar invocation of the question of suicide on questions of race, they need only consider that the question of whether blacks commit suicide was treated with such seriousness by psychiatrists in the first half of the century that Fanon had to address the question in *Black Skin, White Masks* in the midst of a *philosophical* argument. Blacks, it was believed, were incapable of committing suicide because, supposedly like the "rest" of the animal kingdom, there wasn't enough apperception or intelligence to understand the ramifications of their situation. This reasoning was based on the supposition of what a "true" human being *would* do if treated as blacks are treated.

This question of continuing to live on is connected to a controversial theme of all existential thought. It goes like this: there is a sense in which none of us has ever chosen to be born into this world and possibly any possible world. Yet, in our decision to live on, we live a choice which requires our having been born – in a word, our *existence*. In the context of blacks, the implication is obvious. No one chooses to have been born under racial designations, but the choice to go on living, and especially choices that involve recognizing one's racial situation, have implications on the meaning of one's birth. Applied to groups, it is the question of whether certain groups "should" have existed. The racist sentiment on this issue is summarized well by Henry Ward Beecher, as quoted by Anna Julia Cooper in her *Voice from the South*, when he remarks that

> Were the Africans to sink to-morrow, how much poorer would the world be? A little less gold and ivory, a little less coffee, a considerable ripple, perhaps, where the Atlantic and Indian Oceans would come together – that is all; not a poem, not an invention, not a piece of art would be missed from the world. (p. 228)

Antiblack racism espouses a world that will ultimately be better off without blacks. Blacks, from such a standpoint, "must" provide justification for their continued presence.

"Why go on?"

Well, the first thing to bear in mind is the illegitimacy of such demands for existential justification. What could *blacks* offer when it is their blackness that is called into question? The demand is loaded; failure emerges from the project of providing a suitable response. Asymmetry abounds in the performance of the question, since the *questioner's* existence is treated as pre-justified. If the questioner's existence alone is sufficient, why not the questioned's?

"Why go on?"

There is, however, another dimension to this question. One, in the end, goes on because one wants to, and in so doing seeks grounds for having *ought to* go on. The wanting, however, signifies an intentional framework that has already militated against nihilism, for self-value also emerges from valuing one's desire to bring meaning to one's existence.

38

See p. 54

In the course of any effort to describe a philosophical position there will always be people who, in the tradition of old, demand names. Who, in other words, are Africana existential philosophers? The problem is made particularly acute by virtue of there being both African-American existential philosophy and African-American philosophers of existence, the first category of which is broader than the second. Although there are many philosophers who have contributed to African-American existential philosophy, not all are African American nor *black* existential philosophers, as is clear not only by virtue of Sartre's and de Beauvoir's contributions to this area of thought, but also other nonblack philosophers such as David Theo Goldberg, Linda Bell, Joseph Catalano, Stuart Charmé, Patricia Huntington, and Martin Matuštík, all of whom have written on antiblack racism, problems of agency in black contexts, black invisibility, African Americans, and intersections of race and feminism, and, among African-American thinkers, not all who have contributed to African-American existential thought are, or ever were, existentialists, as can be seen by the work of Roy Morrison, II, Frank Kirkland, Charles Mills, Katie Canon, Josiah Young, III, Dwight Young, Jacquelyn Grant, Maulana Karenga, and Molefe Asante.

Further, the problem of identifying African-American existentialists and contributors to African-American existential thought is exacerbated by our point made earlier about the conjunctive dimension of existential philosophy, which makes suspect any unequivocal assertion of individuals' being black existentialists. There are, for example, black existential Christians, black existential Marxists, black existential nationalists. Thus, Cedric Robinson's characterization, in chapter 11 of *Black Marxism*, of Richard Wright living a journey from Communism to Existentialism to Black Nationalism is inaccurate, for example, because of Black Nationalism's being a concrete instantiation of a form of existential positioning – approaching the world through the situation of black people. Black Power demands, among its values, first and foremost the recognition and valuing of black people as sources of value. That being said, we can consider black existential thinkers in two ways.

First, there are theorists whose positions have an existential dimension, *among other dimensions*, and who may not have formally defined themselves as existentialists. These individuals fall under the designation of philosophers *of* existence. These individuals are existentialists in the way that Europeans like Søren Kierkegaard, Fyodor Dostoevsky, Martin Heidegger, Franz Kafka, and Martin Buber are studied in existentialism courses in spite of their never having *claimed* to be existentialists and, in some cases, for instance, Heidegger's "Letter on Humanism," have even outright declared that they are *not* existentialists. Given our considerations of what is involved in raising both the question of black suffering and the classical encounter with nihilism – that is, the struggle involved in deciding to go on – black existential thinkers of this type include such diverse figures as Frederick Douglass, Sojourner Truth, Anna Julia Cooper, W. E. B. Du Bois, Zora Neal Hurston, Alain Locke, Aimé Césaire, Angela Y. Davis, Toni Morrison, Cornel West, bell hooks/Gloria Watkins, Joy Ann James, and many of the central figures in black liberation and black womanist theology (by virtue of their point of focus in Biblical interpretation being similar to many black Marxists' point of focus in Marxian interpretation).

We find examples of existential dimensions in Douglass's thought throughout his published work but especially in his conception of struggle and his interpretation and various efforts to develop a theory behind the significance of his fight with the slave-breaker Edward Covey. Truth's provocative purported demand on the identity question – "Ain't I a Woman?" – is rooted in the concrete embodiment of both "what" she is (*black woman*) and "who" she is. It is both a generalized *I* and an individually emphasized *I*, since after all, one can also imagine, through her powerful words, her extending her strong, overworked arms in her ostensible challenge. For Cooper, an excellent example is her provocative essay, "What Are We Worth?," which can also be interpreted as her articulation of the conditions of responding to, "Why go on?" in her classic volume, *A Voice from the South*. There she addresses head-on the implications of demanding a race of people to justify their right to exist – in a word, their "worth."

The Du Boisian story is a complex one that is articulated through the course of many volumes and essays, but see especially his articulation of "the race problem" in *The Souls of Black Folk*, in his last autobiography, his *Soliloquy on Viewing My Life From the Last Decade of Its First Century* where he presents a portrait of the turning point of his political consciousness. His famous essay, "Conservation of the Races," has received much discussion since Anthony Appiah in his essay "The Illusion of Race" and his book *In My Father's House*, accused him of being racist. My take on Du Bois's essay, besides being concerned by its rather confused conceptions of race, is that Du Bois was dealing there, at the end of the nineteenth century, with an important anxiety and justified fear of North American black folk: That it was not only the case that if white America had it their way, they would eliminate black folks from the face of the earth, but that there were very powerful white individuals, from Jefferson through to Lincoln and onward, devising such a plan. This plan was certainly the case for indigenous Americans, who, according to Russell Thornton, in *American Indian Holocaust and Survival*, were reduced to 4 percent by 1900. Du Bois needed an argument to justify why black people, among all people, should not be condemned to the fate of the dodo. That is why his first and second concluding recommendations are most significant: "(1) We believe that the Negro people, as a race, have a contribution to make to civilization and humanity, which no other race can make; (2) We believe it the duty of the Americans of Negro descent, as a body, to maintain their race identity until this mission of the Negro people is accomplished, and the ideal of human brotherhood has become a practical possibility." Du Bois's remark, "which no other race can make," had to be made because he knew that if other races could make such contributions, the national response would have been, "Why, then, should we continue to tolerate the presence of Negroes?" Du Bois, I contend, knew that, without a Judaic notion of election, there was no "Negro mission," so his call for Negro identity until the achievement of such a mission was, in effect, a call for Negroes not to be exterminated. The essay was, in other words, in spite of its provocative explorations of consciousness and Herderian appeals to linguistic and cultural genius, a *policy* essay with existential significance. As Du Bois queried in that work, "Is this right? Is it rational? Is it good *policy*? Have we in America a distinct mission as a race – a distinct sphere of action and an opportunity for race development, or *is self-obliteration the highest end* to which Negro blood dare aspire?" (emphasis added). Nine decades later, Audre Lorde echoed Du Bois's concerns when she declared in *Sister Outsider*: "to survive in the mouth of this dragon we call America, we have had to learn this first and most vital lesson – that we were never meant to survive."

40

Zora Neale Hurston, too, will require discussion that is well beyond the scope of this chapter. But for a sample, see her discussion of religion in her *Dusk Tracks on a Road*. For Alain Locke, see especially his essay, "Values and Imperatives," in *The Philosophy of Alain Locke*, where Locke defends, among several theses, the view of values as "lived" – that is, *valuing*. Aimé Césaire is well known for his posing questions of black existence through the lens of what he coined *négritude*. I have already mentioned Angela Y. Davis. The reader could consult a developed representation and discussions of her work in the *Angela Davis Reader*, edited by Joy Ann James. Similarly, I have already mentioned both Morrison and West. Morrison's work probes not only problems of black consciousness and the constructions of blacks in American society, but also the complexity of asserting agency in oppressive environments. Her first novel, *Bluest Eye*, is a masterpiece of black existential analysis. It could easily be read along with Richard Wright's *Outsider* and Frantz Fanon's *Black Skin, White Masks* (which, by the way, offers many of the themes in Morrison's *Playing in the Dark*). Cornel West has engaged Kierkegaard's writings and the thought of black humanists like Ralph Ellison and James Baldwin as early as his *Prophesy, Deliverance!* but most obviously so in his essay "Black Nihilism" in *Race Matters* (and his Afterword in Yancy, 2001).

bell hooks/Gloria Watkin's existential positions are most influenced by the work of Paulo Freire, as she attests in many of her works, especially *Black Looks* and *Teaching to Transgress*, but one can argue that her centering of the liberation and identity questions are already rooted in black existential philosophy. Her affinity with Freire's work is, in other words, animated by the same concerns as black liberation theologians in certain sections of the Bible and black Marxists in certain sections of Marx's opus. Every one of hooks's books substantiates this claim. In addition, that Freire's *Pedagogy of the Oppressed* is clearly rooted in Sartre's and Fanon's philosophies of liberation instantiates the existential legacy here.

For Joy James, see her books *Transcending the Talented Tenth* and *Resisting State Violence*, as well as her award-winning edited volume, *Spirit, Space, and Survival*. These works challenge reductive readings of black feminism and defend models of agency and resistance in a world marked by what she describes, in her essay "Black Feminism," as "existence in gray."

Second, we can also consider black existential philosophers and social critics among those who have taken an openly admitted existential identity as philosophers of existence, those who were and those who are, in other words, "out of the closet." Those include Richard Wright, Frantz Fanon, Ralph Ellison, James Baldwin, William R. Jones, Lucius T. Outlaw, Naomi Zack, and this author. Wright's importance is Promethean. His investigations of existential paradoxes through such novels as *Native Son* and *The Outsider*, and his classic essays against simple-minded, reductive readings of African Americans' existential condition still call for careful existential analyses. His insight, at the end of *The Outsider*, that even African Americans who commit crimes suffer from a gnawing feeling of innocence raises the question of black existence beyond problems of inclusion: How can one have agency in a world of meaningless guilt? Fanon has provided perhaps the strongest *theoretical* statements in African-American existential thought. We can credit him with articulating the "epidermal schema," where blacks are historicized as pure externality; phobogenesis, where negrophobia collapses into a material value; sociogenesis, where the constructivity of racialization and the relation between meaning and life-formations are revealed; racist normativity, where the rationality of racism is unmasked; and many more observations. Ellison's existential thought is well known, particularly in terms of his classic *Invisible Man* and his collection of essays on literature, politics, and culture, *Shadow and Act*. There are numerous instances in Baldwin's writings, but a primary example is *The Fire Next Time*.

For William R. Jones's philosophy, there is his classic critique of Black Theology, *Is God a White Racist?* There, Jones defends a humanistic conception of agency in the project of black liberation. Lucius T. Outlaw has defended the place in American academic philosophy for not only African-American and Africana philosophy and critical theory, but also existential phenomenology. Through several important articles, he has issued what is ultimately an *existential* critique of the social-constructivist critical race theorists and Appiah's accusation of Du Boisian race theory as racist – that they fail to articulate the most relevant dimensions of the *lived*-realities of race and racism. In *On Race and Philosophy*, he, like Du Bois, urges us to take seriously the meaning of a future without black people. And Naomi Zack's positions can be found in her influential book *Race and Mixed Race*, which raises questions regarding the existential reality of mixed-race people, her anthology *American Mixed Race*, and her most explicitly existential essay, "Race, Life, Death, Identity, Tragedy and Good Faith," where her response to the Du Boisian question of black suffering and identity is, in stream with Appiah, for blacks to give up race and black identity.

This list is not, I should stress, an exhaustive list, and it is not necessarily the case that each of these thinkers converge on the same set of values. For instance, although all ultimately "humanist," Wright's (middle-period), Baldwin's, and Zack's works take a more individualistic turn, whereas (early and later) Wright's, Fanon's, Jones's, and my own work – represented, for example, by my *Bad Faith and Antiblack Racism; Fanon and the Crisis of European Man; Her Majesty's Other Children;* and *Existentia Africana* – are situated in what may be called black existential revolutionary thought.

I should like to conclude by stressing that not all contributors to African-American existential philosophy are existentialists in any sense. Some of the individuals who have something to say of value on that subject may also be those who are most critical of it, or at least suspicious of an existential philosophy premised upon what Fanon calls *l'expérience vécue du Noir* – "the lived-experience of the black." In that regard, the irony of African-American existential philosophy is that its best challengers are among its best contributors. Such is the way of existential paradoxes.

Bibliography

Adell, Sandra. 1994. *Double Consciousness/Double Bind*. Urbana and Chicago: Illinois University Press.

Allen, Earnest. 1997. "On the Reading of Riddles: Rethinking Du Boisian 'Double Consciousness.'" In *Existence in Black*, ed. by Lewis R. Gordon.

Allen, Norman (ed.). 1991. *African-American Humanism: An Anthology*. Buffalo, NY: Prometheus Books.

Appiah, K. Anthony. 1998. "The Illusions of Race." In *African Philosophy*, ed. by Emmanuel Chukwudi Eze.

Asante, M. K. 1988. *Afrocentricity.* Trenton, NJ: Africa World.

———. 1993. "Racing to Leave Race: Black Postmodernists Off-Track," *The Black Scholar: The Multicultural Debate* 23, nos. 3–4.

Baldwin, James. 1955. *Notes of a Native Son.* Boston: Beacon.

———. 1963. *The Fire Next Time.* New York: Dell Publishing Company.

Baltazar, Eulalio. 1973. *The Dark Center: A Process Theology of Blackness.* New York: Paulist.

Batstone, David, Eduardo Mendieta, Lois Ann Lorentzen, and Dwight N. Hopkins (eds.). 1997. *Liberation theologies, Postmodernity, and the Americas.* New York and London: Routledge.

Beauvoir, Simone de. 1947. *Pour une morale de l'ambiguïté.* Paris: Gallimard.

———. 1949. *Le deuxième sexe.* Paris: Gallimard.

Bell, Linda. 1993. *Rethinking Ethics in the Midst of Violence: A Feminist Approach to Freedom.* Lanham: Rowman and Littlefield.

Bogues, Anthony. 1997. *Caliban's Freedom: The Early Political Thought of C. L. R. James.* London and Chicago: Pluto Press.

———. 1998. "C. L. R. James, Black Radicalism, and Critical Theory: A Response." *Small Axe* 3 (March).

Boxill, Bernard. 1997. "The Fight with Covey." In *Existence in Black*, ed. by Lewis R. Gordon.

Buber, Martin. 1965. *Between Man and Man.* Trans. Ronald Gregor Smith, with an intro. by Maurice Friedman. New York: Collier Books.

Butler, Broadus. 1983. "Frederick Douglass: The Black Philosopher in the United States: A Commentary." In *Philosophy Born of Struggle*, ed. by Leonard Harris.

Camus, Albert. 1955. *"The Myth of Sysyphus" and Other Essays.* New York: Vintage Books.

———. 1956. *The Rebel: An Essay on Man in Revolt.* Trans. Anthony Bower, with a Foreword by Sir Herbert Read. New York: Vintage.

———. 1960. *Resistance, Rebellion, and Death.* Trans. with an intro. by Justin O'Brien. New York: Vintage Books.

Catalano, Joseph. 1980. *A Commentary on Jean-Paul Sartre's "Being and Nothingness."* Chicago: University of Chicago Press.

———. 1986. *A Commentary on Jean-Paul Sartre's "Critique of Dialectical Reason," Volume 1, "Theory of practical Ensembles."* Chicago: University of Chicago Press.

Charmé, Stuart. 1991. *Vulgarity and Authenticity. Dimensions of Otherness in the World of Jean-Paul Sartre.* Amherst, MA: University of Massachusetts Press.

Cone, James. 1969. *Black Theology and Black Power.* New York: Seabury.

———. 1970. *A Black Theology of Liberation.* Philadelphia: J. B. Lippencott.

———. 1975. *God of the Oppressed.* New York: Seabury.

———. 1989. "Black Theology as Liberation Theology." In *African American Religious Studies*, ed. by Gayraud Wilmore.

Cooper, Anna Julia. 1998. *A Voice from the South*, foreword by Henry Louis Gates, Jr., and intro. by M. H. Washington. New York and Oxford: Oxford University Press.

Davis, Angela Y. 1983. "Unfinished Lecture on Liberation – II." In *Philosophy Born of Struggle*, ed. by Leonard Harris.

———. 1988. *Angela Davis: An Autobiography.* New York: International Publishers.

———. 1998. *Angela Davis: A Primary Reader*, ed. with an intro. by Joy Ann James. Oxford: Blackwell Publishers.

Douglas, Jock D. 1970. *Freedom and Tyranny: Social problems in a Technological Society.* New York: Alfred Knopf.

Douglass, Frederick. 1950. *The Life and Writings of Frederick Douglass*, vols. 1–5, ed. by P. Foner. New York: International Publishers.

——. 1962. *The Life and Times of Frederick Douglass: The Complete Autobiography*, with an intro. by R. W. Logan. New York: Crowell-Collier.

——. 1968. *Narrative of the Life of Frederick Douglass, an American Slave, Written by Himself.* New York: New American Library.

——. 1987. *My Bondage, My Freedom*, ed. with an intro. by William L. Andrews. Urbana and Chicago: University of Illinois Press.

Du Bois, W. E. B. 1899. *The Philadelphia Negro: A Social Study.* Philadelphia: The University of Pennsylvania Press.

——. 1920. *Darkwater: Voices from within the Veil.* New York: Harcourt, Brace, and Howe.

——. 1968a. *Dusk of Dawn: An Essay Towards an Autobiography of a Race Concept.* New York: Schocken.

——. 1968b. *The Autobiography of W. E. B. Du Bois: A Soliloquy on Viewing My Life from the Last Decade of Its First Century*, ed. by Herbert Aptheker. New York: International Publishers.

——. 1969. *The Souls of Black Folk*, with intros. by Nathan Hare and Alvin Poussaint. New York: Signet Classics.

——. 1998. "On the Conservation of the Races." In *African Philosophy: An Anthology*, ed. by Emmanuel Chukwudi Eze.

Dussel, Enrique. 1996. *The Underside of Modernity: Apel, Ricoeur; Rorty, Taylor; and the Philosophy of Liberation*, trans. Eduardo Mendieta. Atlantic Highlands, NJ: Humanities Press.

Ellison, Ralph. 1990. *Invisible Man.* New York: Vintage.

——. 1992. *Shadow and Act.* New York: Vintage.

Eze, Emmanuel Chukwudi (ed.). 1998. *African Philosophy: An Anthology.* Oxford: Oxford University Press.

Fanon, Frantz. 1952. *Peau noire, masques blancs.* Paris: Editions de Seuil.

——. 1961. *Les Damnés de la Terre.* Préface de Jean-Paul Sartre, présentation de Gérard Chaliand. Paris: François Maspero éditeur S.A.R.L.; Paris: Éditions Gallimard, 1991.

——. 1963. *The Wretched of the Earth.* Preface by Jean-Paul Sartre, trans. Constance Farrington. New York: Grove Press.

——. 1967. *Black Skin, White Masks.* Trans. Charles Lam Markmann. New York: Grove Press.

Filonowicz, Joseph. 1998. "Black American Philosophy as American Philosophy: Transcendentalism, Pragmatism, and Black Existentialism: An Experimental Course and Syllabus," *APA Newsletter on Philosophy and the Black Experience* 97, no. 2 (Spring).

Freire, Paulo. 1990. *Pedagogy of the Oppressed.* New York: Continuum.

Friedman, Maurice (ed.). 1991. *The Worlds of Existentialism: A Critical Reader*, ed. with intro. and a conclusion by Maurice Friedman. Atlantic Highlands, NJ: Humanities Press.

Fulop, Timothy E. and Albert J. Raboteau (eds.). 1997. *African-American Religion: Interpretive Essays in History and Culture.* New York and London: Routledge.

Gilroy, Paul. 1993. *The Black Atlantic: Modernity and Double Consciousness.* Cambridge, MA: Harvard University Press.

Goldberg, David Theo (ed.). 1990. *Anatomy of Racism.* Minneapolis: University of Minnesota Press.

——. 1993. *Racist Culture: Philosophy and the Politics of Meaning.* Oxford: Blackwell.

——. 1997. *Racial Subjects.* New York and London: Routledge.

Gooding-Williams, Robert. 1993. *Reading Rodney King, Reading Urban Uprising.* New York and London: Routledge.

Gordon, Lewis R. 1995a. *Bad Faith and Antiblack Racism.* Atlantic Highlands, New Jersey: Humanities Press.

——. 1995b. *Fanon and the Crisis of European Man: An Essay on Philosophy and the Human Sciences.* New York and London: Routledge.

——. (ed.). 1997a. *Existence in Black: An Anthology of Black Existential Philosophy.* New York and London: Routledge.

——. 1997b. *Her Majesty's Other Children: Sketches of Racism from a Neocolonial Age.* Lanham, New York, Boulder, and Oxford: Rowman & Littlefield.

——. 1998. "Meta-ethical and Liberatory Dimensions of Tragedy: A Schutzean Portrait." In *Alfred Schutz's "Sociological Aspect of Liberature,"* ed. with an intro. by Lester Embree. Dordrecht: Kluwer Academic Publishers.

——. 1999. *Existentia Africana.* Ithaca and London: Cornell University Press.

——, with James L. Marsh. 1998. "Faith and Existence." In *The Encyclopedia of Continental Philosophy*, vol. 2, ed. by Simone Glendenning. Edinburgh: Edinburgh University Press.

——, with T. Denean Sharpley-Whiting and Renée T. White (eds.). 1996. *Fanon: A Critical Reader.* Oxford: Blackwell Publishers.

Guttman, Herbert. 1976. *The Black Family in Slavery and freedom: 1750–1925.* New York: Vintage.

Grant, Jacquelyn. 1989. *White Women's Christ and Black Women's Jesus.* Atlanta: Scholars Press.

Harris, Leonard (ed.). 1983. *Philosophy Born of Struggle: Anthology of Afro-American Philosophy from 1917.* Dubuque, Iowa: Kendall/Hunt.

——. 1993. "Postmodernism and Utopia: An Unholy Alliance." In *Racism, the City, and the State*, ed. by M. Cross and M. Keith. New York: Routledge.

Hayes, III, Floyd. 1996. "Fanon, African-Americans, and Resentment." In *Frantz Fanon: A Critical Reader*, ed. by Lewis R. Gordon et al.

Heidegger, Martin. 1977. "Letter on Humanism." In *Martin Heidegger: Basic Writings from "Being and Time" (1928) to "The Task of Thinking" (1964)*, ed. with an intro. by David F. Krell. San Francisco: HarperSanFrancisco.

Henry, Paget. 1993. "C. L. R. James, African and Afro-Caribbean Philosophy," *The C. L. R. James Journal* 4, no. 1.

——. 1997. "African and Afro-Caribbean Existential Philosophies." In *Existence in Black*, ed. by Lewis R. Gordon.

hooks, bell. 1981. *Ain't I a Woman?: Black Women and Feminism.* Boston: South End Press.

——. 1984. *Feminist Theory from Margins to Center.* Boston: South End.

——. 1990. *Yearning: Race, Gender, and Cultural Politics.* Boston: South End.

——. 1992. *Black Looks: Race and Representation.* Boston: South End Press.

——. 1994. *Teaching to Transgress: Education as the Practice of Freedom.* New York and London: Routledge.

——. 1997. "Rastafarianism and the Reality of Dread." In *Existence in Black*, ed. by Lewis R. Gordon.

Huntington, Patricia. 1997. "Fragmentation, Race, and Gender: Building Solidarity in the Postmodern Era." In *Existence in Black*, ed. by Lewis R. Gordon.

James, C. L. R. 1989. *The Black Jacobins: Toussaint L'Ouverture and the San Domingo Revolution*, 2nd Edition Revised. New York: Vintage.

——. 1992. *The C. L. R. James Reader*, ed. by Anna Grimshaw. Oxford: Blackwell Publishers.

James, Joy Ann and Ruth Farmer (eds.). 1993. *Spirt Space and Survival: Black Women in (White) Academe.* New York and London: Routledge.

James, Joy Ann. 1996. *Resisting State Violence*, with a foreword by Angela Y. Davis. Minneapolis and London: University of Minnesota Press.

——. 1997a. *Transcending the Talented Tenth*, with a foreword by Lewis R. Gordon. New York and London: Routledge.

——. 1997b. "Black Feminism: Liberation Limbos and Existence in Gray." In *Existence in Black*, ed. by Lewis R. Gordon.

Jones, William R. 1967. "Sartre's Critical Methodology." Providence: Brown University Dissertation in Religious Studies.

——. 1997. *Is God a White Racist?: A Preamble to Black Theology.* Boston: Beacon Press.

Kant, Immanuel. 1959. *Critique of Pure Reason (Unabridged Edition).* Trans. Norman Kemp Smith. New York: St. Martin's Press.

Kierkegaard, Søren. 1959a. *Either/Or,* volume 1, trans. David F. Swenson and Lillian Marvin Swenson, with revisions and a foreword by Howard A. Johnson. Princeton, NJ: Princeton University Press.

——. 1959b. *Either/Or,* volume 2, trans. Walter Lowrie, with revisions and a foreword by Howard A. Johnson. Princeton, NJ: Princeton University Press.

——. 1980a. *Kierkegaard's Writings,* VIII, *The Concept of Anxiety: A Simply Psychologically Orienting Deliberation on the Dogmatic Issue of Hereditary Sin.* Trans. and ed. with intro. and notes by Reidar Thompte in collaboration with Albert Anderson. Princeton: Princeton University Press.

——. 1980b. *Kierkegaard's Writings,* XIX, *The Sickness unto Death: A Christian psychological Exposition for Upbuilding and Awakening,* ed. and trans. by Howard V. Hong and Edna H. Hong with intro. and notes. Princeton: Princeton University Press.

——. 1983. *Kierkegaard's Writings,* VIII, *"Fear and Trembling" and "Repetition."* Trans. and ed. with intro. and notes by Howard and Edna Hong. Princeton: Princeton University Press.

Kirkland, Frank and Bill Lawson (eds.). 1998. *Frederick Douglass: A Critical Reader.* Oxford: Blackwell Publishers.

Locke, Alain. 1989. *The Philosophy of Alain Locke: Harlem Renaissance and Beyond,* ed. with an intro. and afterword by Leonard Harris. Philadelphia: Temple University Press.

Lorde, Audre. 1984. *Sister Outsider.* Trumansburgh, NY: Crossing Press.

Marcuse, Herbert. 1972. *From Luther to Popper,* trans. J. de Bres. London: Verso.

Matuštík, Martin. 1993. *Postnational Identity: Critical Theory and Existential Philosophy in Habermas, Kierkegaard, and Havel.* New York and London: The Guilford Press.

——. 1998. *Specters of Liberation.* Albany: State University of New York Press.

McGary, Howard. 1998. *Racism and Social Justice.* Oxford: Blackwell Publishers.

Mills, Charles W. 1998a. *The Racial Contract.* Ithaca and London: Cornell University Press.

——. 1998b. *Blackness Visible: Essays on Philosophy and Race.* Ithaca and London: Cornell University Press.

Morrison, II, Roy. 1994. *Science, Theology and the Transcendental Horizon: Einstein, Kant, and Tillich.* Atlanta, GA: Scholars Press.

Morrison, Toni. 1970. *The Blues Eye.* New York: Holt, Reinholt, and Winston.

——. 1987. *Beloved.* New York: Knopf.

——. 1992. *Playing in the Dark.* Cambridge, MA: Harvard University Press.

Moses, Greg. 1997. *Revolution of Conscience: Martin Luther King, Jr., and the Philosophy of Nonviolence,* with a foreword by Leonard Harris. New York and London: Guilford Press.

Natanson, Maurice. 1970. *The Journeying Self: A Study in Philosophy and Social Role.* Reading, Mass: Addison-Wesley Publishing Company, 1970.

——. 1986. *Anonymity: A Study in the Philosophy of Alfred Schutz.* Bloomington: Indiana University Press.

Outlaw, Lucius T. 1990. "Toward a Critical Theory of 'Race.'" In *Anatomy of Racism,* ed. by David Theo Goldberg.

——. 1996. *On Race and Philosophy.* New York and London: Routledge.

Patterson, Orlando. 1972. "Toward a Future that Has No Past: Reflections on the Fate of Blacks in the Americas," *Public Interest,* no. 27.

Preston, William. 1997. "Nietzsche on Blacks." In *Existence in Black,* ed. by Lewis R. Gordon.

Robinson, Cedric. 1983. *Black Marxism: The Making of the Black Radical Tradition*. London: Zed Press.

Sartre, Jean-Paul. 1943. *L'être et le néant: essai d'ontologie phénoménologique*. Paris: Gallimard.

———. 1956. *Being and Nothingness: A Phenomenological Essay on Ontology*. Trans. with an intro. by Hazel Barnes. New York: Washington Square Press.

———. 1991. *Critique of Dialectical Reason*, Volume I, *Theory of Practical Ensembles*. Trans. Alan Sheridan-Smith; ed. by Jonathan Rée. London and New York: Verso.

———. 1992. *Notebooks for an Ethics*, trans. David Pellauer. Chicago: University of Chicago Press.

———. 1997. "Return from the United States: What I Learned about the Black Problem," trans. with comparative notes by T. Denean Sharpley-Whiting. In *Existence in Black*, ed. by Lewis R. Gordon.

Slaughter, Jr. Thomas. 1983. "Epidermalizing the World: A Basic Mode of Being Black." in *Philosophy Born of Struggle*.

Walker, David. *Appeal to All Colored Citizens of the World*.

West, Cornel. 1982. *Prophesy, Deliverance!: An Afro-American Revolutionary Christianity*. Philadelphia: Westminster Press.

———. 1993a. *Keeping Faith: Philosophy and Race in America*. New York: Routledge.

———. 1993b. *Race Matters*. Boston: Beacon.

Willett, Cynthia. 1995. *Maternal Ethics and Other Slave Moralities*. New York and London: Routledge.

Wilmore, Gayraud S. (ed.) 1989. *African American Religious Studies*. Durham, NC: Duke University Press.

Wright, Richard. 1953. *The Outsider*. New York: Harper and Row.

———. 1972. "Blueprint for Negro Writing." In *The Black Aesthetic*, ed. by Addison Gayle. Garden City, NJ: Anchor/Doubleday.

———. 1977. *American Hunger*. New York: Harper and Row.

Yancy, George (ed.) 2001. *Cornel West: A Critical Reader*. Oxford: Blackwell Publishers.

Young, III, Josiah. 1992. *A Pan-African Theology: Providence and the Legacies of the Ancestors*. Trenton, NJ: Africa World Press.

Zack, Naomi. 1993. *Race and Mixed Race*. Philadelphia: Temple University Press.

———. 1994. *American Mixed Race*. Lanham: Rowman & Littlefield.

———. 1997. "Race, Life, Death, Identity, Tragedy, and Good Faith." In *Existence in Black*, ed. by Lewis R. Gordon.

3

African-American Philosophy:
A Caribbean Perspective

PAGET HENRY

For most of its history, African-American philosophy has existed outside of the mainstream academic institutions of America. It has existed as a parallel discourse that only touched the dominant Euro-American philosophical tradition at certain crucial points. Given its recent recognition by the academic guardians of the latter tradition, it is not surprising that several attempts have been made to specify the nature of African-American philosophy, and the path it should take within the academy. Like African-Caribbean philosophy, African-American philosophy is a hybrid discourse in which European, African, and American philosophical traditions are locked in what Rex Nettleford has called "a battle for space." Thus, it should come as no surprise that there are several competing positions on how we should approach the identity and substantive themes of this philosophy.

In this literature, two positions in particular have gained significance. The first is an approach that suggests an American reading of African-American philosophy, while the second suggests an Africana reading. The American readings have stressed the connections between African-American philosophy and the American pragmatist tradition. On the other hand, the Africana readings have stressed the connections of African-American philosophy to traditional African philosophy and to the discourses of the global struggles of African peoples for liberation from colonialism and racial domination.

In this paper, I will focus on the Africana readings of African-American philosophy. In particular I will review the attempts of Lucius Outlaw and Lewis Gordon to thematize this notion of an Africana philosophy. Building on their work, I will outline in detail my own view of this very important notion. My approach will be one that brings together phenomenological and discursive strategies, as well as insights drawn from the Caribbean philosophical experience. I will begin with a brief look at the American readings of African-American philosophy through the work of Cornel West. Next, I will examine the Africana readings and then present my own. I conclude the paper with the significance of such an Africana project for the future of African-American philosophy.

48

American Pragmatism

Two excellent examples of American readings of African-American philosophy can be found in the works of Johnny Washington and Cornel West (Washington, 1986). In spite of important differences, both develop the identity of African-American philosophy with detailed references to Euro-American pragmatism, and little or no references to traditional African philosophy. However, for reasons of space, we will here examine only the case of West.

For West, "African-American philosophy is an expression of the particular variation of European modernity that African-Americans helped to shape" (West, 1980). It is primarily an American philosophy that is rooted in the life-worlds created by American modernity: "the life-worlds of Africans in the United States are conceptually and existentially neither solely African, European nor American, but more the latter than any of the former" (ibid., 24). This American identity of African-American philosophy leads West to a very clear rejection of an African model of African-American philosophy: "while it might be possible to articulate a competing African-American philosophy based on African norms and notions, it is likely that the results would be theoretically thin" (ibid.).

As with Washington, West sees an important convergence between the African-American and pragmatist conceptions of philosophy as forms of engaged cultural criticism. These views West opposes to the more "epistemology-centered" conceptions of philosophy that have come out of Europe. Consequently, African-American philosophy is seen as "a textuality, a mode of discourse that interprets, describes, and evaluates Afro-American life in order comprehensively to understand and effectively to transform it" (ibid., 15). African-American philosophy is not concerned with foundations and transcendental grounds, but with being "a material force for African-American freedom" (ibid.).

It is within such a pragmatist conception of African-American philosophy that West identifies its primary tasks. These include two important dialogical engagements. One between African-American Christianity and Marxism, and the other between African-American Christianity and Euro-American pragmatism. The primary convergence that West sees between African-American Christianity and pragmatism is a shared commitment to social changes that enhance personal agency and increase democratic practices. In both, the commitment to change is ethically motivated. For West, one of pragmatism's important achievements is that it "dethroned epistemology as the highest priority of modern thought in favor of ethics" (ibid., 21). This position on ethics points to an important polarization in West's thought: that between epistemological and ontological concerns on the one hand and ethically motivated activism on the other. West associates the former with "the subjectivist turn" in modern European philosophy, which in his view, attempts to locate the grounds for truth in the transcendental activity of the thinking subject, and "outside of politics and power" (West, 1983: 52). Hence this turn is associated with a possible weakening of the activist thrust. Both African-American Christianity and pragmatism avoid this threat to their activism by the priority they give to ethically motivated action.

In addition to the case of African-American Christianity, West also argues that the work of W. E. B. Du Bois is another important instance of the convergence between

49

African-American philosophy and pragmatism: "Du Bois seems to have been attracted to pragmatism owing to its Emersonian evasion of epistemology-centered philosophy, and his sense of pragmatism's relevance to the Afro-American predicament" (West, 1989: 139). Even Du Bois's poeticism is seen in terms of its Emersonian resonances: "Like Emerson, Du Bois always viewed himself as a poet in the broad nineteenth century sense, that is one who creates new visions and vocabularies for the moral enhancement of humanity" (ibid., 142).

However, West is clear that this pragmatist reading of African-American philosophy does not imply a perfect fit. Thus he notes pragmatism's neglect of the self, its veneration of science, and its refusal to take seriously racial and class struggles. These are important divergences, the full implications of which are not developed by West. In spite of these limitations, pragmatism provides an American context for African-American thought, a context that imparts to it both a shape and a heritage of philosophical legitimacy. In this pragmatist setting, West sees no need for any special dialogical engagements with traditional or modern African philosophy.

Africana Thought

In contrast to West and Washington, Lucius Outlaw and Lewis Gordon are strong exponents of Africana readings of African-American philosophy. Here the dialogical engagements with pragmatism are replaced by exchanges with traditional African thought and the discourses of the global struggle for African liberation. For Outlaw, the core of African-American philosophy is to be found in the socially transformative discourses that African-Americans have produced. Thus the accommodationist position of Booker T. Washington, the assimilationist position of Frederick Douglass, the integrationist positions of Du Bois and King, the nationalism of Malcolm X are all vital expressions of an African-American philosophical tradition.

However, Outlaw does not link this activist orientation to American pragmatism. In his work, it is thematized in relation to European traditions of hermeneutic, critical and poststructuralist theory, but primarily in relation to an Africana tradition of resistance to European imperialism and racism. One of Outlaw's most pressing concerns about contemporary African-American philosophy is that it "is conducted with little or no knowledge of, or attention to, the history of philosophical activity on the African continent, or elsewhere in the African Diaspora" (Outlaw, 1992–3: 71).

In developing this Africana reading, the major problem Outlaw takes up is the specifying of common or unifying contents and the professional norms that would justify his claims for a field of Africana philosophy. At the most general level, Outlaw resolves the first of these two problems by seeking unity and commonality in "third order organizing, classificatory strategies" directed at the lived experiences and second order classification of continental and diasporic Africans (ibid., 74). However, the concrete implementing of this general solution turns out to be quite problematic as Outlaw's examination of Molefi Asante's Afro-centric strategy makes clear. Outlaw remains skeptical about the existence of a set of underlying principles or common contents that could unify the diverse practices of peoples of African descent. Consequently, the identity problem remains unresolved, but is indirectly addressed as a part of Outlaw's solution to the second problem regarding professional norms.

Given this absence of any clear third order unifying principle, Outlaw suggests that unity and Africana identity can only come from the discursive practices of African-American philosophers: "the presentation of commonality is a function of my discursive agenda. But not mine alone" (ibid.). Thus the Africana identity of African-American or African-Caribbean philosophy would not be rooted in a set of shared symbols, but in the agendas, norms, and practices that these and other philosophers have set for their fields.

This solution to the problem of a common Africana identity reflects Outlaw's view of philosophy as an activity that is grounded "in socially shared practices" (ibid., 73). This collectively oriented philosophy is mediated by rules of discourse in the Foucaultian sense of the term. Like West, Outlaw rejects the subjectivist turn of modern European philosophy: "there is no timeless essence shared by any and all forms of thought called 'philosophy' . . . There are no transcendental rules a priori that are the essential, thus defining features of 'philosophy' " (ibid.).

Although very important, Outlaw pushes these discursive factors too far. For example, this extreme discursivist solution to the problem of commonality does not allow Outlaw to answer his very important problem of "Africans-becoming-Americans as instances of philosophy" (ibid., 63). It does not, because this solution entails a radical displacing of the subject or ego, that puts the problem of identity beyond adequate reach. To keep identity within reach, a more interpenetrating, dialectical relationship between self formation and discursive formation is required. This greater visibility of the self is one of the distinctive marks of Gordon's approach.

Existential-Phenomenology

In the work of Lewis Gordon, we find an existential-phenomenological approach to the problems of an Africana philosophy that is quite different from the discursivist approach of Outlaw. Gordon embraces the subjectivist turn in modern European philosophy, and does not see it as a threat to black activism the way West does. On the contrary, like Fanon, he uses the ontological spaces it opens up to ground an activist philosophical position. Gordon uses the subjectivist turn to thematize more explicitly than West or Outlaw the problems of black self-formation, and in particular its racialization in the white societies. Consequently, he grounds the Africana project in the Pan-African task of reconstituting this racialized self in the wake of the "phenomenological disappearance" of its humanity and its African heritage (Gordon, 1995b: 40).

In his explicit foregrounding of the self, Gordon's focus is the ontology (not the psychology) of everyday black and white egos, the interactive dynamics between these ontologies, and their relations to the origins and maintenance of antiblack racism. The interactive dynamics between these ontologies have trapped black and white ego formation in classic imperial battles for ontological space. By ontological space, I mean space to be, to posit oneself and realize that self-positing. The imperial nature of this battle derives from the fact that Europeans and Euro-Americans have defined the ontological space of white ego genesis in a way that requires the evading of the human-ity of Africans. This evasion is effected through the racial redefining of Africans as blacks, negroes or more pejoratively as "niggers." The result is an imperial ontology that restricts the space of black ego genesis and appropriates its ego formative resources in the interest of white self formation.

To come to terms with this battle for ontological space, Gordon focuses even more closely on the source of these predatory and extractive relations that exist between white and black egos. These relations are motivated by the easy solutions they provide to the blockages, contradictions, polar divisions and unacceptable tendencies that are integral parts of white ego genesis. Their predatory transformation, Gordon theorizes with the aid of the Sartrean notion of bad faith (Gordon, 1995a: 94–103). In bad faith, human beings in all cultures deal inauthentically and evasively with the specific blockages and obstacles that stand between self-positing and self realization. These impediments may be political, racial or economic. But for both Gordon and Sartre, they are also ineliminably ontological. The ego that executes the project of being always falls short of making the self conform to the projected ideal. How we deal with the less than perfect selves we inherit from the structural limitations of the ego, will determine the extent to which we live in bad faith.

In bad faith, we feign or assert greater degrees of self integration and completion than our ego has in fact achieved. The full extent of the failure of the ego to create a well integrated, autonomous self that goes into its ideal without remainders, must be concealed through some type of compensatory, evasive or accumulative activity. For Gordon, white racism with its diminutive stereotyping of blacks is one such accumu-lative activity. It is a set of discriminatory attitudes and practices towards blacks that provide whites with counterfeit solutions to the problems and anxieties of incomplete self-formation. The black self thus becomes a zone of ontological struggle as colonized states become zones of political conflict. Racism is thus linked directly to the ontology of white egos, as it becomes a form of existential exploitation that leads to the accumulating of counterfeit solutions to ontological problems.

This practice of existential exploitation entails a "projective non-seeing" that enacts "the phenomenological disappearance" of black humanity (Gordon, 1995b: 24). Invisibility, absence, displacement, anonymity, physicality become the constitutive acts through which white ego consciousness reconstructs the meaning of Black existence. Although routinized institutionally, this invisibility is clearly not a stark social or physic fact. It is also fundamentally phenomenological, that is an absence that is constituted as a meaning in the white consciousness. This spell of phenomenological invisibility is an important contribution of the European and Euro-American philosophical consciousness to the larger encompassing cloud of non-seeing conjured by European imperialism to veil the humanity of Africans. Consequently, as long as blacks and whites continue to share social and ontological spaces the removal of this invisibility must include a calling to task of the white philosophical consciousness for this particular expression of bad faith.

This philosophical task of visible restoration would require an Africana oriented phenomenology that is capable of dissolving the defensive formations and layers of meaning that have enacted black invisibility in the consciousness of both blacks and whites. Among whites it would have to identify the blockages in self-formation, disrupt the defense of projective non-seeing, thus helping to restore sight. Among Blacks, it would have to uproot white images of blacks that the latter have internalized, thus restoring visibility, presence and ontological space to African elements of black identity. These once more visible African elements will of course not be the original ones. Noticeable or not, these symbols and discourses have been undergoing significant changes in response to European imperialism and racism. Yet, it is precisely in this shared task of reconstituting the racialized black self in the wake of the phenomeno-logical disappearance of its African heritage that Gordon roots the Africana identity of African-American philosophy. In doing so, he has established phenomenological reflection on the existential dynamics of the black self as a philosophical practice that is indispensable for an Africana philosophy.

I would like to build on this phenomenological solution to the identity and core of an Africana philosophy. I think it will be extremely helpful in the philosophical exami-nation of Outlaw's problem of Africans-becoming-Americans, Africans-becoming-Caribbeans, or modern Africans. I will argue that it is the phenomenologically significant similarities and differences between these processes of becoming that are capable of establishing the common core of an Africana philosophy. However, to do this, we need to expand Gordon's analysis in two important ways.

First, we need to expand the analysis so that it includes more systematic phe-nomenological analyses of the traditional African ego. Second, these expanded phenomenological analyses need to be dialectically linked to many of the discursive formations, emphasized by Outlaw, that have shaped the development of African-American philosophy. In other words, although extremely important, the dynamics of black self-formation cannot by themselves establish the identity of African-American philosophy as an on-going discourse. These dynamics must be supplemented by the specific processes of publishing, writing, argumentation, debate, institutional reco-gnition or non-recognition that have shaped the formation of African-American philosophy. In the next section, I will make use of such a dialectical synthesis in outlining my view of an Africana philosophy.

Phenomenological Foundations

Although my approach to an Africana philosophy is indeed a synthetic one, for pur-poses of presentation I will separate the phenomenological and discursive components that make up the dialectal synthesis. Space does not permit the elaborating of a case study that would clearly illustrate the ways in which they work in concert.

The phenomenological aspects of my Africana project are rooted in self-reflective practices that Gordon has established. In general terms, we can define phenomenology as self-reflective activity in which a conscious agent comes to a greater awareness of the constitutive determinants of the self-formative process that makes its everyday life possible. Because we are usually unaware of many of these determinants, phenome-nological self-reflection often results in a transcending of everyday levels of awareness that can change the conduct of an individual life. However, strategies of self-reflection vary widely, leading to different types of phenomenologies. Hence we need to specify some of the particulars of an Africana phenomenology.

In Descartes and Kant, European self-reflection was directed at the knowing activities of the conscious agent. Shaped by these concerns, self-reflection came to know itself as epistemology rather than phenomenology. The phenomenological self-determination came with Hegel, where the growth in consciousness produced by self-reflection was linked to a larger theodicy and philosophy of identity between spirit and nature. Although focused on spirit's loss and subsequent recovery of identity, the epistemological issue is still very present in Hegel's concern with absolute knowledge. The stronger "epistemology-centered" orientation of Descartes and Kant returns in Husserl, whose phenomenology included the search for an absolute ground for the practice of self-reflection.

In Heidegger and Sartre, there is a clear break with this type of transcendental or epistemology-centered phenomenology. Self-reflection is linked to the ontology of everyday egos, thus establishing the European tradition of existential phenomenology. In Habermas, European self-reflection regains somewhat its earlier epistemological focus. It takes the form of self-reflection on the methodologies of sciences and on Habermas's angst over the technocratic impact of these sciences on modern democratic life. The result is a socio-epistemic phenomenology in which Habermas articulates a theory of knowledge that is at the same time a theory of society.

The Africana phenomenology emerging from the work of Gordon does not fit neatly into any of the above phenomenologies. It shares with them the centrality of self-reflection, but links it to a different set of concerns. As West clearly suggests, African-American self-reflection has not made cognitive activities its point of departure. The same is true of African-Caribbean philosophy. The major exception here is the work of Sylvia Wynter. However, both philosophies have given high priority to the "existential deviations" that colonialism and racism have inserted into the self-formative processes of African-Caribbeans and African-Americans (Fanon, 1967: 16). This direct link between self-reflection and black ego genesis has given Africana phenomenology its existential orientation.

However, this existential orientation is defined by sources of ego negation that are primarily social and not ontological in nature, although the latter are extremely important for Gordon. Consequently, as in the case of Habermas's phenomenology, the second site of self-reflection in Africana phenomenology is also social in nature. However, the contents of these two social points of departure are quite different. In the place of Habermas's angst over technocratic colonization, Africana phenomenology reflects on black anguish over and in resistance to racial colonization. The discursive elaborations that have arisen from these existential and social sites of Africana self-reflection, meet and engage each other in a philosophical space that can be labeled a theory of the racialized self as a theory of society. Consequently, in contrast to Habermas's socio-epistemic phenomenology, Africana phenomenology can be described as socio-existential. Thus rather than attempting to fit Gordon's phenomenological analysis into any of the above European models, I think it will be better if we place it alongside them as the expression of a distinct type of self-reflection.

The first modification of Gordon's analysis that we must undertake is the suggested expansion of its phenomenological analyses to include the traditional African ego. In particular, the mythic and religious discourses that have been integral to its formation and stability over time. Phenomenological reflections on these ego-genetic cultural constructs, will enable us to examine the different ways in which they were made to "disappear," as the African self was racialized on the continent and in the diaspora. They will also permit us to focus more effectively on the different ways in which these traditional constructs are being incorporated by continental and diasporic Africans, into post-colonial and post-racial identities that now occupy less cramped ontological spaces. In other words, to address the problem of Africans-becoming-Americans or -Caribbeans as instances of philosophy, we will require a comprehensive phenomenological history of Africana subjectivity.

This question of a phenomenological history, and in particular its extension to the traditional African ego, raises some difficult methodological problems. Specifically, it poses the problem of the phenomenological study of the ego activities of predecessors. The work of Alfred Schutz demonstrates that this difficulty is not an insurmountable one. He shows that from the perspective of the meaning constituting activities of the ego, it is possible to divide the social universe into three domains: (1) the world of consociates with whom we are in immediate face-to-face relation; (2) the world of contemporaries with whom we are in mediated, non-face-to-face relations; and (3) the world of predecessors with whom we are in similarly mediated relations, but whose lived-experiences do not overlap in time with ours (Shutz, 1967: 142–3). Shutz demonstrates that phenomenological analyses of all three sub-universes are possible, although the last is clearly the most difficult.

The latter is possible because we can reach the world of predecessors through records, monuments, artifacts and expressions of their subjectivity that they have left behind. We can also approach this world through a living person who may have known a predecessor. These are all indirect relations that lack the reciprocity of face-to-face relations. However, Schutz points to one possible reciprocal relation to predecessors. That is, a relation in which the behavior of an individual is oriented toward an act of a predecessor. This one reciprocal relation for Schutz was the bequeathing of property (ibid., 28). It is certainly a relationship through which predecessors continue to influence our behavior. If we take the notion of property to include cultural heritages, then such bequests can constitute another set of important phenomenological links to the worlds of predecessors.

The nature of the links to the worlds of consociates, contemporaries, and predecessors will determine the methods that our phenomenological history will employ. Because of the predominantly oral nature of the traditional African heritage, the data on our traditional African predecessors will clearly be ethnographic in nature. The ethnophilosophical data from these analyses will be qualitatively different from the historical, conversational and self-reflective data that we will gather on more recent predecessors, contemporaries, consociates and from our individual lived-experiences. Thus, in spite of the controversy that has raged over the practice of ethnophilosophy, I think it is a necessary component of not only African philosophy, but all Africana oriented philosophies. Although with great caution, Anthony Appiah has argued for the viability of such an ethnophilosophical component for African-American philosophy (Appiah, 1992–3: 23). Elsewhere, I've suggested a similar component for African-Caribbean philosophy (Henry, 1993). Thus the approach in this phase of our phenomenological history will be ethnophilosophical.

55

Given this possibility of phenomenologically analyzing the world of our traditional African predecessors, we need to specify more precisely why their cultural symbols and discourses are so important for our project of an Africana philosophy. How will these cultural constructs help to define the identity of this philosophy? How will they help to establish its core? I will discuss two reasons why the traditional African heritage is extremely important for both of these concerns.

First, for many African, African-American and African-Caribbean philosophers, these cultural constructs are invaluable properties that our traditional African predecessors have bequeathed to us. This Shutzian property relation helps to constitute the complex, phenomenologically significant ties that bind us to this African heritage. Because of the meanings associated with this reciprocal relation, expectations (particularly of continuity), obligations and constraints are imposed on us. This legacy is our responsibility in ways that cannot be for non-African groups. The reciprocal nature of our relation to these African symbols and discourses links us more directly to the wishes and expectations of the predecessors who created and nurtured them. In short, unique ties of kinship and inheritance have given Africana philosophers a special responsibility for a shared set of symbols and discourses. To fulfill the obligations of this responsibility, Africana philosophers must preserve and develop this heritage by examining it ethnophilosophically, by reflecting on it in their own lived experiences, or collectively with contemporaries and consociates.

Second, African, African-Caribbean, and African-American philosophers are not only in unique proprietary relations with the symbols and discourses of traditional Africa, they are also in unique ego-genetic relations with them. These relations establish certain common cultural or mythopoetic elements in the formation of African, African-American, and African-Caribbean egos. The formative or ego-genetic role of these cultural elements will establish them as common elements in the self reflections of Africana philosophers on their own ego-genetic processes. This will also be the case when these reflections are ethnophilosophical in nature, or more conversational with contemporaries and consociates. In other words, because of the critical importance of tradition African symbols and discourses to the ego formation of African philosophers – continental and diasporic – they are crucial for the identity of an Africana philosophy. Let's develop this claim more fully.

By the nature of its formative process, the human ego is reproductively tied to a culturally specific set of symbols, or to a number of them. These cultural constructs help to define, sustain, and legitimate the ego. More than any other factor, it is the self-reflection of philosophers on the symbols and discourses of their own ego formation that gives a philosophy its cultural identity. Thus the similarities and differences that emerge from the self-reflections of African, African-American, and African-Caribbean philosophers will be extremely important for their cultural identities.

In spite of its universalistic and transcultural claims, philosophy shares the above cultural birthmarks with literature, music, dance, and other discourses that affirm a national, collective identity. The rational orientation of philosophy does not in any way negate this moment of cultural rootedness, or the filial ties with the arts. This cultural moment is indispensable for examining the Africana dimensions of African-American philosophy, as it forces us to confront the cultural identity of this rationally oriented discourse. This identity is the necessary moment of prior cultural definition and mythopoetic instituting that the philosophical cogito must inherit. It is the latter's necessary encounter with time-bound symbols and discourses. The philosophical cogito can ignore this cultural identity or affirm it through a phenomenological reconstruction of its self-formative process. In other words, the philosophical cogito must make its pre-philosophical or inherited identities and their changing discursive registers the objects of a self-reflective philosophical analysis.

Ultimately, the possibilities for an Africana philosophy rests upon our ability to affirm the operating of African cultural registers in the ego genesis of African, African-American, and African-Caribbean philosophers. Without claiming the status of timeless essences, such affirmations would allow us to identify specific philosophic cogitos whose unique features are in part determined by the formative influences of African symbols and discourses. These formative experiences are ones that philosophers of African descent do not share with other philosophers. They are responsible in part for our uniqueness and our original voice. Again, these symbols and discourses are not timeless essences. On the contrary, they change. But like so many other sets of ego forming symbols, they have a very long half-life.

To the extent that these identity legitimating constructs shape or influence the work of African, African-American and African-Caribbean philosophers in comparable ways, to that extent do these African symbols and discourses constitute important foundations for the Africana identity of African-American philosophy. If, for example, we are able to reconstruct their influence on the African-American philosophical consciousness over time and compare it with similar reconstructions in the African and African-Caribbean cases, then the Africana project will be on solid foundations. On the other hand, if we are not able to recognize the common influences in the ego genesis and work of philosophers of African descent, then the basis for an Africana philosophy will be severely weakened. This I do not think is the case.

This phenomenological history of Africana subjectivity is not the kind of project that one person can complete. Rather, it is an open-ended collective project to which many must contribute chapters. It should encompass comparative phenomenological analyses of ego formation, deformation (racialization) and transformation among continental and diasporic Africans. The works of Du Bois, Fanon, Richard Wright, James Baldwin, and Gordon are important founding chapters in this project. They have all focused on the deformation (double consciousness) that accompanied the racialization of African identities and their subjugation to the ontological needs of white ego genesis. This phenomenological history will of course be more existential than transcendental, descriptive rather than scientific, social as well as individual, its claims falsifiable rather than absolutely certain. The special value of our phenomenological history is that it will add a unique philosophical perspective to the study of African symbols and to the identities they continue to reproduce.

Discursive Foundations

Important as these phenomenological foundations are, we've already accepted the importance of Outlaw's suggestion that we take into account the discursive processes that have been vital to the formation of African-American, African-Caribbean and

African philosophies. In this section I will argue that in addition to similar intentional acts of bad faith, "the phenomenological disappearance" of the African heritage in Africa, the Caribbean and the United States was enacted by Europeans with the aid of similar arguments, debates, and practices of institutional exclusion. The arguments against the existence of African philosophy, and the exclusion of African religions from the table of religious dialogue are cases that reveal these discursive similarities.

Equally important to the arguments of this section is the fact that the resistance of African, African-American, and African-Caribbean philosophers to this discursive invisibility was also carried out with the aid of internally similar counter-discourses and struggles for institutional recognition. This is important for the project of an Africana philosophy. The similarities in these counter-discourses were not accidental, but the result of historical contacts and textual exchanges. Thus the level of invisibility that surrounded the African heritage at a given point in historical time and social space was in part the result of the nature of the discursive compromise produced by these contentious exchanges. The greater visibility of African philosophy today is in part the result of important reverses in the terms of these exchanges that have produced a new discursive compromise. The changing degrees of invisibility that accompanied these compromises, and the struggles to emerge from beneath their veils, are shared experiences of crucial importance for an Africana approach to African-American philosophy. These experiences point to at least three discursive facts that strongly support these broader Pan-African dimensions to the identity of African-American philosophy: (1) similarities in patterns of development with African and African-Caribbean philosophy; (2) the large number of scholars shared by the three traditions; and (3) their current emergence from more restrictive discursive compromises. I will briefly examine each of these with an emphasis on African-American and African-Caribbean philosophies.

African-American philosophy did not develop in an intellectual vacuum. On the contrary, it developed as an integral part of a larger intellectual tradition. Like its Caribbean counterpart, the African-American intellectual tradition has its roots in the discursive responses of Africans to the existential, political, economic and other challenges of the new world environment. These challenges came via the institution of slavery that framed the life of Africans in the Caribbean and the US. The discursive responses that founded these two intellectual traditions were critiques and rejections of the racist and imperialist arguments used by Europeans to justify the practice of slavery. In short, both traditions can be viewed as being rooted in two distinct series of contentious, delegitimating dialogues with European slaveowners, and white supremacists.

The initial set of counter-challenges must have been formulated primarily in the discourse of traditional African religions, and ably supported by responses in the more auxiliary discourses of African magic, ritual, song, and philosophy. These were the discourses that sustained African ego formation and hence the ones that Africans were able to reproduce in America and the Caribbean. However, surviving instances of this type of religiously coded resistance by Africans are much harder to find in the US than in the Caribbean.

Drawing on Caribbean religions such as Shango, Santeria and Voodoo, we can suggest two basic responses. First is a politicizing of religious cosmologies that gave greater visibility and power to the gods of war and strength as is clear in the case of

Voodoo and Shango. Here the appeal was to gods like Shango and Ogun for the strength to fight enslavers and colonizers. Self-reflection recognized itself as angry, anguished, and religious. In the second response, resistance was less direct. The experience of slavery was placed in the category of divine punishment and thus a form of redemptive or expiatory suffering. Self-reflection comprehended itself as religious fate. However, those who were the immediate cause of this suffering would in time also get their taste of divine punishment. In other words, liberation from slavery and colonialism would be by the hands of the gods. Responses of both types were a part of the first discursive compromises African-Caribbean and African-American thinkers were able to achieve *vis-à-vis* their European counterparts. In these compromises, the role of philosophy was clearly to supplement religious and ideological responses to slavery.

Over time, these primarily religious responses changed their discursive registers and became predominantly Christian rather than traditional African. Although rooted in the great Protestant revivals of the 1700s the processes of Christianization in the Caribbean and African-America were quite different. In the main, Caribbean Christianity was the product of classic colonial churches that did not become independent until the 1960s (Bisnauth, 1989). By contrast African-American Christianity emerged from black churches that were autonomous by the start of the American civil war (Lincoln and Mamiya, 1990). In the Caribbean, we have the two extremes produced by these processes of African-Christian syncreticism: the survival of predominantly African religions such as Shango and Voodoo on the one hand, and highly Europeanized churches on the other. The latter are products of centuries of colonial control during which pastors were predominantly European. In African-America, there has been a more uniform and intermediate pattern of syncretism that has produced a distinct African-American Christianity. This Christianity is more African in tone than the classic colonial churches of the Caribbean.

The discursive impact of these processes of Christianization is evident in the earliest published writing of African-Americans and African-Caribbeans. Richard Allen, Lemuel Haynes, Jupiter Hammond, Phyllis Wheatly, and David Walker are African-Americans whose works clearly reflect this change of religious registers. In the Caribbean, similar changes are evident in the workds of Ann Hart (1804), Jean-Baptiste Phillipe (1824), Mary Prince (1831), and Michel Maxwell Phillip (1854). This shift introduced important changes in the *dramatis personae* of African-American and African-Caribbean writing. Satan, Jehovah, Mary, Jesus Christ, his disciples and the saints replaced Legba, Obatala, Shango, Erzulie, Oshun, Damballah, and other African deities.

But in spite of these and other significant discontinuities, there were also important continuities. Slavery and colonial domination were still understood in terms of two basic categories: situations to be resisted with the aid of divine power, or cases of divine punishment from which they would be relieved after a necessary period of expiatory suffering. The insurrectionary activities of Denmark Vessey in African America, and Paul Bogle in Jamaica are instances of the first. Evidence of the second, can be seen in the work Hammond and Walker. Walker explicitly links the experience of enslavement to punishment for the disobedience of our African forefathers (Walker, 1995: 21). This belief can still be found among the Rastafarians of Jamaica (Owens, 1976: 192–3). In short, the basic religious characteristic of self-reflection as fate survived the change of registers.

The fact that these older arguments were now being made in Christian rather than African religious terms significantly altered the role of philosophy in this set of discursive compromises made by African-American and African-Caribbean thinkers. Instead of legitimating the African religious frameworks of these arguments, African-American and African-Caribbean philosophies were now legitimating their newly adopted Christian frameworks.

However, this change in religious registers was a particularly difficult one for these two philosophies. Blinded like other European discourses by its hegemonic concerns, the new Christian register was already deeply involved in the discursive production of African invisibility demanded by European imperialism and slavery. Binary oppositions were being specially marked and discursively mobilized on behalf of this effort. The new register made its contributions by using these binaries to maximize the differences between African and European religions. The former was labeled and evaluated through categories such as primitive, pagan, black, evil, and polytheistic, while modern, Christian, white, good and monotheistic were the categories used to evaluate the latter. A greater inequality between religions would be difficult to construct. This chasm became the basis for excluding African religions from the American and Caribbean communities of religious discourse. In spite of the difference in patterns of religious creolization, both African-Caribbean and African-American Christianity inherited this radical disenfranchising of traditional African religions. A similar deployment of binaries, led to European/Christian denials of the existence of an African philosophy.

These anti-African biases entered the philosophical and religious thought of African-Caribbeans and African-Americans with this shift in religious registers. It was the shift that raised the veil on African philosophy in both traditions. In this state of self-alienation, the African-American and African-Caribbean philosophical cogitos were overtaken by cases of Du Boisian double consciousness. This lack of public recognition should not be equated with the non-existence of traditional African philosophy, but rather with a discursive illegitimacy that made it disappear. With this submerging of their African heritage, African-American and African-Caribbean philosophies entered a long contradictory period in which they were marked by under-identifications with traditional African thought and over-identifications with modern European thought. In other words, philosophical versions of Fanon's black skins wearing white masks. These patterns of over and under identification are evident in Wheatly, Walker, Blyden, Garvey, James, and even Du Bois and Fanon, who have provided us with these powerful images of our alienation and self-alienation. In this state, African-Caribbean and African-American philosophies were forced to legitimate Christian critiques of slavery at the cost of contributing to the invisibility of traditional Africa. Only with the shift to the currently emerging compromise has this contradictory dynamic shown real signs of reversal. The full recovery of traditional African philosophy from a life beneath veils and masks must be a central concern of an Africana philosophy.

From this predominantly Christian phase, the African-American and African-Caribbean intellectual traditions moved into more secular and ideological phases in the second half of the nineteenth century. In the former case, this shift was marked by the rise of figures such as Frederick Douglass, Booker T. Washington, Alain Locke, Zora

Neale Hurston, W. E. B. Du Bois, and others. In the latter case, it was inaugurated by writers such as J. J. Thomas, Robert Love, Marcus Garvey, C. L. R. James, George Padmore, Aime Cesaire, Frantz Fanon, and others. However, in many of the transitional figures such as Douglass and Blyden, the impact of the earlier Christian phase is still very evident. In this more ideological phase, slavery and racism were seen primarily in terms of the motivations and historical practices of Europeans. Receding into the background were the religious explanations, particularly that of divine punishment. This shift in perspective is clearly captured in Du Bois's reflections on the period: "A way back in the days of bondage they thought to see in one divine event the end of all doubt and disappointment; few men ever worshipped Freedom with half such unquestioning faith as did the American Negro for two centuries" (Du Bois, 1990: 10).

These shifts in the dominant patterns of argument in their larger intellectual traditions had important consequences for both African-Caribbean and African-American philosophies. In both traditions, it led to dramatic increases in the importance of historicism and poeticism. However, with these philosophical shifts, Africana self-reflection did not recognize itself as phenomenological but primarily as poeticist. It came close in Du Bois and James, but really only assumed a phenomenological identity in Fanon. Consequently, the philosophical positions of historicism and poeticism assumed much greater prominence than positions of empiricism, scientism or transcendentalism. Poeticism became the philosophical discourse for analyzing the motives and mythopoetics of white and black subjectivities. Historicism became the philosophical discourse for analyzing institutions of racial domination and the conditions for their transformation. In some case, both of these philosophical positions were embodied in the same person in a complementary or oppositional fashion. Thus, Du Bois, Jean Toomer, Zora Neale Hurston, Cesaire, James and Fanon were all important individuals who embodied strong historicist and poeticist tendencies. Indeed, as a short characterization of the philosophies that emerged from the more secular discursive compromises of the late nineteenth and early twentieth centuries, I would suggest a label between poeticism and historicism.

It is in these third compromises that the politico-ideological orientation of the African-American and African-Caribbean philosophical traditions really becomes explicit. Also more visible is the auxiliary role of philosophy within the discursive formations of the larger intellectual traditions. Even a cursory examination of the role of philosophy in the works of Locke, Du Bois, Garvey or James should make this clear. It is particularly evident in the case of Locke. Although formally trained in philosophy, it very often functioned as the minor text in his culturally oriented writings. Locke's philosophy often took the form of a subtextual poeticism, which was used to discursively mobilize the rising power of African-American aesthetics in the fight against racial stereotypes that created and sustained double consciousness (Locke, 1968).

Finally in this brief account of the similarities in patterns of development, it is important to note that the philosophies associated with these compromises were also marked by high levels of invisibility with regard to traditional African thought. This was a characteristic they inherited from their larger intellectual traditions. As we have seen, this was an inheritance of the Christianizing of these traditions that the first secular philosophical formations were not able to effectively reject.

61

Closely related to these parallels and similarities in the historical development of these two philosophies is the second discursive factor that is crucial for the broader Africana identities of African, African-Caribbean, and African-American philosophies. This factor is the large number of important philosophical and other writers that these three traditions share. From African-America, the three traditions share the figures of Douglass, Du Bois, Washington, Hurston, King, Malcolm X, West and many others. From Africa, we share the heritage of traditional African religions, as well as figures like Kwame Nkrumah, Leopold Senghor, Julius Nyerere, Amilcar Cabral, Samir Amin, Paulin Hountondji, Anthony Appiah, Kwame Gyekye and many others. From the Caribbean, we have the figures of Edward Blyden, Marcus Garvey, C. L. R. James, Frantz Fanon, Aime Cesaire, Edouard Glissant, Wilson Harris, Derek Walcott, Sylvia Wynter, Stokely Carmichael, Jamaica Kincaid, Lewis Gordon and many more.

These historical and intertextual connections are important as they point to common problems, and shared solutions between these three intellectual traditions. In particular, these connections must have influenced the nature and pattern of development of philosophy in all three cases. Consequently African-American philosophy has not developed in complete isolation from either African or African-Caribbean philosophy. These connections, which are embedded in its larger intellectual tradition, constitute important foundations for its Africana identity.

The third and final discursive factor that is important for my Africana project is the current move toward a fourth compromise in both African-American and African-Caribbean philosophy. In both of these traditions, philosophy has been shaped by the discursive demands of religion, literature, history, music, and sociology. Work in these fields generated demands for philosophical arguments and transformative visions that would inform and support their creative productions. Given the politically charged nature of the issues that occupied scholars in the above fields, the philosophical demands they generated were largely ideological in nature. This ideological orientation was clearly visible in our earlier review of the works of West, Outlaw, and Gordon.

However, as I've argued in the case of African-Caribbean philosophy, this ideological orientation has its limitations (Henry, 1996: 226–30). In this position, philosophy remains a very subordinate discourse in intellectual traditions that have been dominated by religion, literature, history etc. In both traditions, philosophy has ably supported the work done in these fields, but really has not had an agenda of its own. Its existence has been a subtextual one, providing infrastructural support for more dominant texts. This comparatively weak presence may be what Deotis Roberts had in mind when he described African-Americans as "reluctant philosophers" (Roberts, 1989). From these specific ideological/subtextual positions, it has been quite difficult to establish substantive connections with traditional African philosophy. These weaknesses are reflections of the cramped spaces in which African-American and African-Caribbean philosophies developed.

In the less cramped spaces of the contemporary period, both philosophies have been moving out of the subtextual roles they have occupied in their respective divisions of intellectual labor. They have also been moving away from their near exclusive politico-ideological focus and have begun engaging a broader range of issues. This is evident in the growing relations with traditional and modern African philosophy, the contacts with Euro-American pragmatism and various branches of European philosophy. These new engagements together with the changing realities that constitute the lived experiences of African-Americans and African-Caribbeans, should dramatically widen the scope of these philosophies, and increase their presence in the emerging discursive orders. The above forces have already moved these philosophies from their earlier states of delicate suspensions between historicism and poeticism. The dominance of these positions will continue to decline as they are forced to establish new balances with a wider variety of philosophical positions.

The engagements with traditional African philosophy should make more explicit the largely implicit ethnophilosophical components in both African-Caribbean and African-American philosophies. Because of the greater retentions of African religions, this ethnophilosophical component may be stronger in the African-Caribbean case. In short, the increased contact with both traditional and contemporary African philosophy should bring these two diasporic traditions closer in form and spirit to continental philosophy.

The engagements with European, Euro-American or other traditions of philosophy we should expect to vary more widely. These variations will reflect difference in the lived experiences of African-Caribbeans and African-Americans. For example, the national experiences of the two groups, the ways in which these experiences have colored problems of class, race, gender, and economic development have already and will continue to make for differences in patterns of engagement. I suspect that differences in the struggle for economic development account for the greater visibility of economic thinking in African-Caribbean philosophy, and its less enthusiastic response to the post-structuralist turn in European thought.

Finally, as it shares societal space with a large Indo-Caribbean population, African-Caribbean philosophy will have to engage in more systematic dialogues with Indian and Indo-Caribbean philosophies. To a lesser degree, the latter have also been victims of the phenomenological and discursive invisibility mobilized by European racism and imperialism. Yet both groups have inherited a lot of this blindness, and have not been able to see each other's philosophies. Hence the urgent need for dialogue.

In spite of these important differences, current trends indicate that African-Caribbean and African-American philosophies are both moving from similar points toward new discursive formations. The latter are likely to be similar in their African components but dissimilar in their non-African components. If realized, these are changes that will take the philosophies out of their earlier ideological and subtextual roles. These similarities and continuities, which are clearly integral parts of this new phase, constitute important bases for the broader Africana identity of both African-American and African-Caribbean philosophies.

Africana Philosophy and Diasporic African Philosophies

My case for an Africana philosophy that embraces African, African-American, African-Caribbean and other diasporic African philosophies, rests on the above three discursive pillars. It rests as well on the prospects for a comparative phenomenological history of ego formation, colonization and decolonization among continental and diasporic Africans. The former would establish the important interchanges, parallels and similarities necessary for a shared discursive field. The latter would establish the common ego-genetic symbols that are necessary for this field to share an Africana identity and a distinct Africana tradition of philosophical self-reflection. To the extent that our comparative phenomenology reveals the continuing ego-genetic relevance of African symbols, and our discursive analyses reveal continuing patterns of textual exchange and shared patterns of discursive development, to that degree will we have a firm basis for an Africana philosophy.

As the above account of the contemporary phase suggests, the pursuit of such an Africana approach to African-American philosophy does not exclude engagements with its European or Euro-American heritages. The Africana approach is an extremely important possibility within the emerging discursive conjuncture of African-American philosophy. As noted earlier it is quite possible for philosophers to ignore the cultural identity of their discourse and completely immerse themselves in its technical problems and its universalistic or transcultural claims. I am sure there will be African-American and African-Caribbean philosophers who will adopt such positions.

However, in spite of being a possibility that philosophers can ignore, our Africana project remains extremely important for the futures of African, African-American, and African-Caribbean philosophies. I will conclude with three reasons why this is the case.

The first concerns the retaining of traditions of activism. If these philosophies are to retain their traditions of activism in the new conjuncture, then an Africana project that takes seriously the cultural identities of these philosophies becomes extremely important. In their respective societies, devalued ego-genetic African symbols have been re-producing devalued or illegitimate black existences. An intellectually honest re-valorizing of these symbols is thus an urgent task, as the self-worth of many African peoples depend upon it. As our Africana project takes this challenge seriously, it would commit these philosophies to contributing to this critical task of revalorization through their own independent revaluing of the cultural symbols of their inherited identity. In doing so, these philosophies will be contributing to increases in the value of the lives that depend on these symbols. This is an important form of personal empowerment that enhances the courage to resist invisibility, discrimination, sexual abuse and other forms of domination.

The second reason our Africana project will be important for the futures of African, African-American, and African-Caribbean philosophies is related to the place and status of African mythic discourses in these systems of thought. It is very likely that our comparative phenomenology will reveal patterns of exit from the traditional worlds of African myth and religion into the modern period that are very different from European patterns of exit. Indeed, an important dimension of a distinct modern identity is the extent to which members of the group have been able to symbolically represent the uniqueness of their path to modernity. Can contemporary appropriations of Oedipus, Electra, Prometheus and other members of the Greek pantheon adequately represent the African paths to modernity, or will we require modern appropriations of Ogun, Erzulie, Shango, and other members of the African pantheon? The paths of Africans, both continental and diasporic, have been marked by the survivals of strong mythic elements into the modern period. They have also been shaped by territorially limited enclaves or patrimonial of feudal social organization, and colonization by an imperial Europe that was transitioning from feudal to capitalist forms of social organization. The specific discursive shifts and changes in registers that mark the paths by which Africans have become modern Americans or Caribbeans are important prerequisites for any accurate account of the uniqueness of the modern African-American or African-Caribbean identity. To the task of assessing this uniqueness our comparative phenomenology can make a valuable contribution. With the results, African-Caribbean and African-American philosophies will be able to gauge more carefully the future of their current practices.

Third and finally is the significance of our unique paths out of the world of myth for the broader problem of human modernity. Are there distinct perspectives or special philosophical lessons indigenous to our paths that might throw new light on the crises threatening this global project? Next to the problem of the color line, the biggest challenge with which modernity has confronted African philosophies is the problem of science and technology, their marriage to commodity production, and the imperial scientism that has been their offspring. Because of the priority given to historicism and poeticism, neither African-American nor African-Caribbean philosophy has dealt adequately with the challenges of science or scientism. As we have seen, these philosophies have been practice- and not epistemology-oriented. Self-reflection on knowledge production has not been for them a primary point of departure. To meet this modern challenge, these philosophies will have to engage in new modes of self-reflection, and bring original and indigenous symbolic resources with which to reframe and recode scientistic problems.

For example, scientism requires the "phenomenological disappearance" of myth, religion and other non-scientific discourses. European phenomenology has been unable to stop the march of this science-driven invisibility that has overtaken many of these discourses. Can an Africana phenomenology be of help here? We certainly need to find out. By bringing different attitudes toward myth and science, by establishing interesting parallels between Black invisibility and mythic invisibility, African-American and African-Caribbean philosophies could make important contributions to empowering the critical impulses against scientism. Consequently, it is important that African-American philosophy express not only European modernity as West suggests, but also African modernity. Through the latter, African-American philosophy will be able to bring unique symbolic resources that are not only important for its future as a modern discourse, but also for the project of modernity itself.

References

Appiah, Anthony. "African American Philosophy?" *The Philosophial Forum*, vol. XXIV, No. 1–3, Fall–Spring (1992-3).

Bisnauth, Dale. *History of Religions in the Caribbean*, Kingston, Kingston Publishers (1989).

Descartes, Rene. *Meditations on First Philosophy*, Indianapolis, Bobbs-Merrill (1960).

Du Bois, W. E. B. *The Souls of Black Folk*, New York, Vintage Books (1990).

Fanon, Frantz. *Black Skin, White Masks*, New York, Grove Press (1967).

Ferguson, Moira (ed.). *History of Mary Prince*, London, Pandora (1987).

——. *The Hart Sisters*, Lincoln, University of Nebraska Press (1993).

Gordon, Lewis. *Bad Faith and Antiblack Racism*, New Jersey, Humanities Press (1995a).

——. *Fanon and the Crisis of European Man*, New York, Routledge (1995b).

Habermas, Jürgen. *Knowledge and Human Interest*. Boston, Beacon Press (1971).

Hegel G. W. F. *The Phenomenology of Mind*, New York, Harper Torchbooks (1967).

Heidegger, Martin. *Being and Time*, New York, Harper & Row (1962).

Henry, Paget. "African and Afro-Caribbean Existential Philosophies" in Lewis Gordon (ed.) *Existence in Black*, New York, Routledge (1997a).

——. "Sylvia Wynter: Post-structuralism and Post-colonial Thought" in L. Gordon and R. White (eds.) *Black Texts and Black Textuality*, Lanham, Rowman and Littlefield (1997b).

——. "Fanon African and Afro-Caribbean Philosophy" in L. Gordon, T. Sharpley-Whiting, and R. White (eds.) *Fanon: A Critical Reader*, Oxford, Blackwell Publishers (1996).

——. "CLR James, African and Afro-Caribbean Philosophy," *The CLR James Journal*, vol. 4, no. 1 (1993).

Husserl, Edmund. *Phenomenology and the Crisis of Philosophy*, New York, Harper Torchbooks (1965a).

Kant, Immanuel. *Critique of Pure Reason*, New York, St. Martins Press (1965b).

Lincoln, C. Eric and Lawrence Mamiya, *The Black Church in the African American Experience*, Durham, Duke University Press (1990).

Locke, Alain. "The Legacy of the Ancestral Arts" in Alain Locke (ed.) *The New Negro*, New York, Antheneum (1968).

Outlaw, Lucius "African, African American, African Philosophy," *The Philosophical Forum*, vol. XXIV, nos. 1–3, Fall–Spring (1992–3).

Owens, Joseph. *Dread*, Kingston, Sangster (1976).

Phillip, Michel Maxwell. *Emmanuel Appadocca*, Amherst, University of Massachusetts Press (1997).

Phillipe, Jean-Baptiste. *Free Mulatto*, Wellesly, Calalous Publications (1996).

Roberts, Deites. "Religio-Ethical Reflections Upon the Experimental Components of a Philosophy of Black Liberation," in Gayraud Wilmore (ed.) *African American Religious Studies*, Durham, Duke University Press (1989).

Sarte, Jean Paul. *Being and Nothingness*, New York, Philosophical Library (1956).

Schutz, Alfred. *The Phenomenology of the Social World*, Chicago, Northwestern University Press (1967).

Walker, David. *David Walker's Appeal*, New York, Hill and Wang (1995).

Washington, Johnny. *Alain Locke and Philosophy*, N. T. Greenwood Press (1986).

West, Cornell *The American Evasion of Philosophy*, Madison, University of Wisconsin Press (1989).

——. "Philosophy, Politics and Power: An Afro-American Perspective," in Leonard Harris (ed.) *Philosophy Born of Struggle*, Dubuque, Kendal/Hunt (1983).

——. *Prophesy Deliverance!*, Philadelphia, Westminster Press (1980).

4

Modernisms in Black

FRANK M. KIRKLAND

Any [Negro writer] destitute of a theory about the meaning, structure and direction of modern society is a lost victim in a world he cannot understand or control.

Richard Wright (1937)

I   Introduction

What is usually meant when the relation between modernity and the African diaspora is brought to account? Is the issue (1) simply a matter of giving an explanation of how those of the African diaspora are modern or go about their business in the modern world *despite* the history of racial enslavement, colonialism, and imperialism? Or is the issue (2) of giving an explanation of how they are modern, since they would normally be regarded, "Eurocentrically" or "Afrocentrically," (with different theoretical implications and political consequences of course) as *outside* the modern world *because* of the history of racial subordination, enslavement, and colonialism? Or is the issue (3) a matter of giving an explanation of how they are modern *due* to the questions racial enslavement and colonization in the "New World" pose for the coherency and relevance of the conception of modernity? As we shall see, all three are meant. And each sets the horizons by which three distinctive theories of modernity or modernisms in black have been framed. Let us call that which is set by (1), *functionalist*, by (2), *nationalist*, and by (3), *cultural* modernisms in black.

In what follows, I shall sketch the functionalist, nationalist, and cultural kinds of modernisms in black by profiling the thoughts of a number of noted intellectuals such as Edward Blyden, Alexander Crummell, Cheik Anta Diop, W. E. B. Du Bois, Ralph Ellison, C. L. R. James, Alain Locke, Toni Morrison, Theophile Obenga, and Orlando Patterson on the relation between modernity and the African diaspora. I shall examine these modernisms' respective strengths, weaknesses, and paradoxes, explore how and why they are at variance with one another, and scrutinize why none of them may sufficiently be intellectually and politically satisfying to redeem the relation between modernity and the African diaspora.

67

II   What is Modernity?

Modernity refers to the emergence and formation of a new awareness of temporality whereby one's own present is construed as constantly oriented toward the future (James 1977), as constantly representing a transition to things and events novel and innovative, and as constantly breaking with a sense of the past or tradition, since (a) one's own present cannot rely for its orientation on the past and (b) the past no longer carries any exemplary status by which the present can model itself (Koselleck 1985). In effect, modern experience stands in opposition or in no relation to tradition.

Furthermore, in that light, modernity entails the interdependence of two seemingly contrary elements, viz. historical experience and utopian-laden convictions. History no longer serves to countermand utopian expectations; utopian expectations are no longer considered to lie outside of historical experience. Rather modernity enables history to serve as the medium for continually displaying alternative and innovative existential possibilities, without constraint of tradition or past, which would be understood as intrinsic to history itself. In short, historical process necessarily reflects historical progress (Koselleck 1985). And, on the social front, modernity represents the clearing of the way for legitimate structures of human interaction to be informed by a conception of the person whose social significance is no longer defined by natural determinations (e.g., biological notions of race and sex), but by a person's reciprocally recognized self-determinations.

Besides modernity, the social-scientific thesis of "modernization" also plays a strong role. That thesis purports to show, both descriptively and prescriptively, that the achievements and innovations of the industrial democracies of the West (capital formation, resource mobilization, enhancement of labor productivity and forces of production, centralization of political power, establishment of national identities, expansion of rights of political participation, and secularization of values) are the *culturally neutral* conditions of modern social development in general. It speaks to the expansion and broadening of these modern achievements through globalization. Such achievements, so states the thesis, make the previously industrial and now post-industrial democracies of the West the standard bearers to measure the development or, say, "progress" of non-Western polities, economies, and cultures in becoming "modern," i.e., in following suit and "modernizing." In some circles, "modernization" becomes synonymous with "Westernization."

Since modernity and modernization generally signal breaks with the past or liquidations of traditional constraints, any modernism in black, endorsing these conceptualizations, would have to ignore in its account (1) the history of racial enslavement and stratification as well as the history of being subject to the colonizing enterprise and (2) the social persistence and variety of human devaluation by means of race and the history of its effects. Entering the modern world or adapting to modernization would come with discounting the importance and relevance of both the history of racial subordination and the social persistence of racial devaluation. Disregarding their relevance and importance would be necessary for cultures of the African diaspora to share in the modern proclivity toward innovations, be they aesthetic, cognitive, moral, political, or socioeconomic. As we shall see, functionalist modernisms in black and, in part, nationalist ones accept this view.

Cultural modernisms in black, on the other hand, generally reflect disenchantment with the manner in which modernity has been conceptualized. Clearly this disenchantment with modernity is distinct from the process of "disenchantment" identified by Max Weber to be the defining element of modernity in the European cultural world. For Weber, the "disenchantment" process moves irreversibly to the modern Occident. It refers to the religiously motivated and historically shaped tendency of those of the West to be increasingly aware that their cognitive, ethical, and value commitments do not rest on metaphysical or religious structures and are not anchored in traditions themselves shielded from any consideration of alternatives or innovations (Weber 1993).

The disenchantment pertinent to cultural modernisms in black with modernity's conceptualization reflects a dissatisfaction with the manner in which the African diaspora has not been given its due weight in the philosophical, literary, and political discourse of modernity. This dissatisfaction is motivated by what is taken to be the audacious equivalence of "modernization" and "Westernization," that strongly resonates in the "modernization thesis" despite its supposed cultural neutrality. Yet it is also stimulated by the recognition that modernity's achievements and innovations could not be had without the complicity of the now post-industrial democracies of the West historically involved in the racial enslavement, subordination, and colonialism of Africa and its diaspora. So cultural modernisms in black neither turn a blind eye to the significance of the histories of racial enslavement and subordination nor disregard the variegated ways in which the devaluation of individuals and cultures by means of race persists. Both tasks are essential to their account of modernity and consequently to their account of modernity's relation to the African diaspora. This seems to suggest that, for cultural modernisms in black, historical experience does not automatically mesh with utopian expectations. Historical experience, it appears, would be constantly entwined with dystopian convictions.

But such a conclusion would be premature. Indeed cultural modernisms in black do not underwrite a conception of modernity that would involve engaging ever rationally, with utopian convictions, life's incessant novelties without constraint. Yet neither do they validate a conception of modernity that would involve repeating unimaginatively and unwittingly, through the social coercion of racial subordination, life's incessant banalities. Usually by emphasizing aesthetic innovations, their accounts rather address the need to rescue the significance of those histories from falling into oblivion as a consequence of endorsing a conception of modernity that radically breaks with the past (Du Bois 1997a; Gilroy 1993a; Kirkland 1992; Morrison 1992). In so doing, they reveal how the African and African-diasporic presence, historically connected to the legacy of racial enslavement, contributes to what counts as modern.

Furthermore, usually by underscoring socio-political innovations, their accounts try to envision and justify the development of institutions that expand structures of recognition. These structures, they claim, would eliminate socially denigrating enterprises and enhance the way issues of justice are resolved ever more equitably in the equal interest of all. They would also form the social trust necessary for people of color to ever more strengthen their expectations and hopes in a global environment without reservation and commensurate with the aforementioned egalitarian and equitable way issues of justice are resolved (Du Bois 1947, 1945; Locke 1989). In this regard, cultural modernisms in black lay down an alternative in which the historical experience of African and African-diasporic people can mesh with utopian convictions without dismissing their sense of the past. In effect, it speaks to deepening the sense of modernity and modern achievements by reflexively widening arenas of social recognition in ways that are not adverse to discursively defending the sense of the past.

The epigraph at the beginning of this essay taken from Richard Wright's well-known 1937 article "Blueprint for Negro Writing" expresses his belief in the importance of black intellectuals to put forward a modernism or a theory of modernity. Indeed I share that belief because of the tendency to view African and African-diasporic people as being in, but not of, modernity, as being impervious or resistant to modernization. This tendency denies the possibility of entertaining racial enslavement and subordination as a prism, so to speak, through which the conceptualization of modernity has always passed. Consequently such a denial fails to grasp the manifold and complexity of configurations that modernity would have to undergo, configurations accounting for how the cultures of the African diaspora are of the modern world, neither just in it nor outside it.

Yet Wright never recognizes the intellectual development of different types of modernisms in black – functionalist, nationalist, and cultural – and the different conclusions each yields for understanding modernity and its relation to people of color. The issue, then, would not be whether black intellectuals are "destitute" of a modernism. It would be whether they are aware of the dissonance amongst the kinds of modernisms in black, aware of the discordant meanings and accounts they generate for understanding the relation between modernity and the African diaspora. To this point this essay now turns.

III   Functionalist Modernism in Black

In an essay entitled "Toward A Future That Has No Past: Reflections on the Fate of Blacks in the Americas," Orlando Patterson initiates what I have called a functionalist modernism in black. Blacks throughout the "New World" diaspora, he claims, "can be the *first* group in the history of mankind who transcend the confines and grip of a cultural heritage. In so doing, they can become the *most truly modern of all peoples* – a people who feel no need for a nation, a past, or a particularistic culture, but whose style of life will be a rational and continually changing adaptation to the exigencies of survival at the highest possible level of existence" (Patterson 1972). What is it about this remark to indicate that it is part of a modernism in black functionalist in kind, especially given the rich and subtle detail in that essay showing the cultural differences amongst African-diasporic peoples in the United States from those in the Caribbean and in South America? Since the answer is not immediately evident, a brief setting of the scene is necessary.

Functionalist modernisms are accounts that conceive of modernity as the development of reason, designated in a variety of ways as, for example, the development of the scientific enterprise or the development and expansion of a secular point of view or the escalation of instrumental rationality or the enhancement of an even more transparent distinction between fact-finding and value-judging. They also conceive of modernity in the light of social changes such as industrialization, socio-economic and geographical mobility, rise of nationalism, extension of political rights, and expansion of administrative bureaucracy.

In all these instances, functionalist modernisms construe modernity as rational and social innovations as well as an expansion of options without constraint that any and every culture can take up and accept, and that all will be obliged to take up and accept. These innovations and their development are described as operations, to which any culture, generally and fundamentally, could be suitable as "input," and which any culture would abide as inevitable. For example, any culture could tolerate the impact of expanding scientific practice; any culture could undergo secularization; any set of ultimate ends could be challenged by a growth of instrumental reasoning; any metaphysics could be displaced by the split between fact and value. Functionalist modernisms, then, are accounts of the modernization thesis. They delineate social innovations and achievements as culturally neutral operations, as a bundle of cumulative and interdependent processes that supposedly can take any specific culture as "input." In effect, those innovations are detached from the specificity and historical impulses of a particular cultural group.

However, modernisms of the functionalist type have been mostly of European provenance and the type most prevalent. This type carries an evaluative force and perspective in which an observer does not see her own culture as one among others. It is not surprising, then, that those cultures, which do not undergo the operations, are regarded as deficient or debased in some fashion or other. Since functionalist modernisms have almost exclusively relied on the "input" of Europe, it is not difficult to see how the synonymy between "modernization" and "Westernization" is established. Moreover, given this near exclusive reliance, it is quite easy for functionalist modernisms to fashion the "input" of Europe as a template, such that innovations peculiar to the modernity of European culture alone reflect a universal function. As a consequence, functionalist modernisms tend to prescribe a falsely invariable pattern on the range of alternative cultures throughout different parts of the world that could be in other ways modern in existence or in formation. As we know, this tendency has had devastating political and intellectual effects on the self-understanding of non-European cultures, especially African ones.

So in what way can Patterson's modernism in black be of the functionalist kind, since functionalist modernisms apparently have the paradoxical character of being regarded as "culturally neutral" *yet* exclusively relying on the "input" of Europe, not Africa or its diaspora, as the template for what counts as modern? In the light of this question, Patterson makes a very ingenious move. He makes his critique of ethnic and racial nationalism the basis for establishing his modernism in black. He is critical of a certain feature arising in the modern world, viz., the rise of ethnic nationalism and the chauvinism normally associated with it. This feature is usually not made very prominent in functionalist modernisms. Nonetheless, it is a specifically modern form of the group identity of a supposedly homogeneous population, an identity drawn from a heritage, tradition, or sense of the past independent of church and religion. This form of identity is posed as congruent with language, history, literature, the group's self-aggrandizement and the self-assertion of its nativism through a power politics set against all other groups. As Patterson knows, ethnic nationalism has been the breeding ground of a destructive chauvinism and imperialist terror allegedly supported by a historical knowledge in the service of ethnic/nationalist solidarity, political proselytization, and economic expansion (Patterson 1977; Taussig 1986).

However, in contrast, blacks of the African-diaspora, Patterson argues, do not have a tradition, a sense of the past that contributes anything of significance to their future-oriented present (Patterson 1972). The sense of the past, to which Patterson refers, is the legacy of slavery and cultural remnants from the African continent. As he formulates it, "the slave experience has little relevance for the present either as a collectively shared memory binding all the black people of the Americas or as a socio-historical continuity shared by them all." African cultural remnants, he further asserts, are only a miniscule part of any black community in the Americas and, by and large, have faded away as a consequence of the advancement of modern society. Thus blacks of the African diaspora "lack all claim to a distinctive cultural heritage," "have a past that has no meaning for the present," and lack the basis for a historical knowledge beneficial to their ethnic/nationalist solidarity and possible concomitant chauvinism. For Patterson, then, they should "feel no need for a nation, a past, or a particularistic cultural unity." They should be indifferent to their own aspirations toward ethnic nationalism or black/Pan-African cultural patriotism (Patterson 1972).

When this indifference to ethnically nationalist aspirations (through a repudiation of the legacy of slavery) is coupled with rational conduct, both enabling supposedly successful adaptation to social innovations and the expansion of options in the economic and political spheres, blacks become, for Patterson, first amongst all others "the most truly modern of peoples." With the emphasis placed on this indifference, Patterson is able to claim for blacks of the African diaspora a separation of the rise of ethnic nationalism from two other features of modernization, viz., the expansion of rights of political participation and socio-economic and geographical mobility. Notably he does not take this indifference on the part of blacks to represent anything culturally distinctive about them. Rather this indifference represents an exercise of an option that blacks supposedly have unavoidably taken, accustomed themselves, and accepted (as their "fate") prior to any other cultural group and that other groups will ineluctably accept as well.

If there were anything culturally distinctive of blacks' indifference to aspirations of ethnic nationalism, it would simply be the *manner* in which the indifference occurs, viz., the repudiation of slavery's legacy. But this point would always be ancillary, if not irrelevant, to Patterson's modernism in black. For Patterson's key issue is what makes them "truly modern" in the functionalist sense of serving as (1) the "input" for seemingly perennial social operations (the indifference to nationalist aspirations and the assumption of rational conduct), which all others must eventually undergo, and (2) the possible template according to which all others must inevitably conduct themselves.

Blacks of the African-diaspora become "truly modern," according to Patterson's account, not by placing emphasis on their knowledge of their historical legacy and tradition which serve their self-assertion of cultural patriotism and identity. They rather become "truly modern" (or are open to modernization fully) by adapting and acquiescing to social innovations in the political and economic spheres, greatly facilitated, if not wholly enabled, by foregoing any concern for nationalist self-assertion, especially since the historical legacy of both slavery and African cultural remnants carry no currency for them.

Indeed there is nothing explicit in Patterson's functionalist modernism claiming a synonymy between "modernization" and, say, counterfactually, "African-diasporization" in contrast to "Westernization." However, in his functionalist modernism, any commitment to nationalist aspirations is construed as an impediment to modernization, an impediment to rational adaptation to future novelty, an impediment to any group progressing "toward a future that has no past." Blacks of the African diaspora, then, can serve as the template for other groups in Patterson's scheme, because they are in the position to surrender ambitions of cultural patriotism for the sake of being truly "integrated" into the modern world by means of culturally neutral social innovations and expanding options continually emerging in the economic and political spheres. So if they are to sustain a way of life adequate to modernity, they must relinquish, as essential to their adaptations to modernization, the use of all matters concerning their heritage.

IV   Nationalist Modernism in Black

As we have seen, Patterson's functionalist modernism in black provides an account *detaching* the importance of tradition, specifically the legacy of slavery or of African cultural remnants, from the relation between modernity and those of the African diaspora in the Americas. In contrast, nationalist modernisms in black give an account *attaching* the importance of tradition to that relation. Yet, in so doing, their accounts of the relation between modernity and blacks of the African diaspora have been conceptually confused at best. They fail to give a sense of what must count as tradition and what sense of tradition can be attached to that relation in order to make its connection to modernity feasible, especially since modernity is normally understood in terms of the liquidation or nullification of traditional commitments, conventions, routines, and rituals.

Nationalist modernisms in general neither deny nor decry the proclivity toward aesthetic cognitive, ethical, economic, and political innovations and the adaptation to them. But rather than understand that proclivity and those innovations and adaptation as a "functional fit" that any and all cultural groups inevitably undergo, they declare that the proclivity to both is peculiar or exclusive only to a particular cultural group. This would entail that a group's cultural tradition is construed in a way not to be inimical to that proclivity.

Furthermore they assert that the penchant to both is exclusive to a particular cultural group, precluding all others, by virtue of that group's identity. The innovations and their adaptation are identified as belonging exclusively to a particular cultural group, because that group *wittingly* appropriates its history, legacy, tradition in such a way as to mark it as the only group, against all others, that could produce, adapt to, and appreciate such innovations as its own. Tradition serves as (a) the motive for the particular group to engage in those innovations, (b) the feature for identifying it as the

73

group whose innovations they are, and (c) the proscription against other groups sharing in those innovations because of their different cultural identities and legacies. In short, a cultural group's tradition and the group's allegiance to it carry, say, the resources for that group alone to regard the modern world as its own.

A nationalist modernism in general shows that it is incumbent on a cultural group to employ the scholarly disciplines such as the humanities or "human sciences" to assist in the promotion of that group's cultural or national identity with modern achievements. As I alluded earlier, in the eighteenth and nineteenth centuries, European intellectuals used the humanities to serve as the vehicle in which the cultural heritage of a modern European nation could emphatically represent and promote its ethnic/national identity, especially amongst its educated social strata, within its national boundaries. As a consequence, the scholarly character of the humanities and the exoteric processes of cultural transmission and nation-building were strongly combined to enable a cultural group to make its identity-forming tradition consistent with modern innovations.

The European humanities took a totally different tenor, as we know, when the focus turned toward Africa and the African diaspora. They were fashioned to discover nothing of intellectual and human significance in the numerous societies and heritages of those comprising the African continent and the African-diasporic populations, given the prevailing traditionalism of their many pre-modern cultures and the legacy of enslavement. The humanities were used, then, to promulgate the view that those heritages and societies could *never* bear the resources for black Africans and blacks of the African diaspora to put their identity-forming traditions in unison with modern innovations. Historically, in response to this scenario, African-diasporic and African intellectuals have provided two different theoretical strategies to formulate a nationalist modernism in black. But, in each case, for different reasons, never cogently, never successfully. For the purpose of this paper, let us call them the "Eurocentric" and the "Afrocentric" strategy.

The "Eurocentric" strategy of a nationalist modernism in black accepts the aforementioned view about African and African-diasporic cultures. In employing this strategy, Alexander Crummell (1995) and Edward Blyden (1990) believe nothing that could form cultural patriotism or identity emerges from the *traditions* of societies on the African continent and throughout the African diaspora. But that strategy also includes the belief that the variety of then contemporaneous African and African-diasporic societies could be rendered culturally unified through race. Crummell and Blyden use that strategy to forge two points. The first calls for the cultural unity of then contemporaneous African and African-diasporic societies in terms of the notion of race. The second calls for treating the relation between modernity and those of the African continent and its diaspora along the same lines as the relation between modernity and race.

Both points are extremely problematic. The first makes race a proxy for culture. This practice is not unusual, especially for the emphatic nationalist modernisms of European cultures in the nineteenth and early twentieth centuries. Yet it is conceptually awkward for a nationalist modernism in black following a Eurocentric strategy, because Crummell and Blyden already concede that blacks have no identity-forming traditions which could be made consistent with modernity. Although, in theory, the racial designation of any group cannot stand as a proxy for culture, it has been employed as so standing for European people, because their "humanities-induced" identity-forming

74

traditions have been allegedly suitable for being placed in unison with modern innovations. In contrast, it has been for the most part *not* employed as so standing for African and African-diasporic groups, because their traditions supposedly lack such suitability.

So Crummell and Blyden place the racial designation of African and African-diasporic groups *directly* in accord with modernity, a designation unable to serve in any way as a proxy for the identity-forming cultural tradition of those groups. In so doing, the second problematic point emerges, because race or any other natural determination cannot inform any aspect of modernity, especially modern structures of inter-action. Yet Crummell and Blyden regard the persistence and integrity of African traditions as well as the customs, habits, and unwritten ways of thought and action of traditional African societies to be respectively an inadequate milieu and a deficient source from which the modern formation and reception of an African cultural/national identity could be enacted. Modern Pan-African cultural patriotism, in their eyes, could never be dependent on anything culturally "African" and/or "African-diasporic."

Hence they use race, in an unwittingly specious manner, to claim a full, immediate, affective, and unimpaired bond between African and African-diasporic people. Moreover, they turn to the cultural codes and language of modern British society (Crummell 1995; Blyden 1990) as the identity-forming tradition a racially bonded African and African-diasporic people would inevitably emulate to be in unison with modernity. A racially bonded African and African-diasporic people, their accounts imply, would be ("providentially") adaptable to the "input" of English culture and language ineluctably and unproblematically in order to be in accord, as a group or people, with modernity. Yet this would seem to be more in line with a functionalist rather than with a nationalist modernism in black.

Again let us be reminded that nationalist modernisms in general assert that the penchant to modern innovations and to their adaptation is peculiar to a particular group, at one with and certifiable by that group's humanities-induced identity-forming tradition. Given their "Eurocentric" strategy, Crummell's and Blyden's nationalist modernisms in black, as we can see, do not converge with that characterization. Indeed it would not be implausible to discard the idea that theirs is a nationalist modernism at all. It would even not be far-fetched to dismiss theirs as some kind of functionalist modernism, since their accounts are not designed to endorse cultural neutrality.

Is the "Afrocentric" strategy of a nationalist modernism in black more cogent and successful? Adopted by scholars such as Cheikh Anta Diop and Theophile Obenga, the "Afrocentric" strategy rejects the view there is nothing of intellectual and cultural significance in African and African-diasporic traditions. In texts such as *Civilization or Barbarism* (Diop 1991) and "African Philosophy in Pharaonic Times" (Obenga 1989) they respectively stress this point and claim the tradition of ancient African societies to be vastly continuous with the project suited for modern Pan-African cultural patriotism. "A look towards the Egypt of antiquity is the best way to conceive and build our [Pan-African] cultural future" (Diop 1991). The traditions of ancient African societies are not devalued in their accounts. Like Crummell and Blyden, they discern nothing culturally worthy for black people in the legacy of enslavement and racial stratification. Unlike Crummell and Blyden, however, they utilize the humanities to claim that the proclivity to modern innovations and to their adaptation can be reflective of Pan-African cultural patriotism, *if* it is put in line with the artistic, religious, and

75

scientific accomplishments of Egyptian or Ethiopian antiquity as the resources of an identity-forming tradition of those of the African continent and its diaspora.

This point raises a subtle yet important difference between, on the one hand, Diop's and Obenga's accounts and, on the other, nationalist modernisms in general, including, hypothetically, cogent and successful ones in black. In general, nationalist modernisms would employ the humanities to assert that the resources or accomplishments of a group's tradition can be reflective of that group's modern cultural identity, *if* they are put in line with the orientation to modern innovations and to their adaptation. The success of pressing the scholarly disciplines into the service of cultural identity would be conditional on making the accomplishments of a group's culture, wherein tradition is operative, coincide with the proclivity to modern innovations and forms of life. The humanities would revamp, through scholarly interpretation, a group's cultural tradition to show how that group's accomplishments would be open to and used for modern ends. As a result, cultural identity, usually ensconced in the integrity and persistence of tradition and ritual, would be rationalized to sustain the belief that a group's proclivity to modernity bears the mark of that group's cultural tradition, but without its tradition becoming inimical in any way to its orientation. Such a view has led to the contention that, under the auspice of nationalist modernisms, cultural identities become factitious, cultural solidarities "imagined" (Anderson 1991), and cultural traditions "invented" (Hobsbawm and Ranger 1983).

Yet, for Diop and Obenga, the success of pressing the scholarly disciplines into the service of Pan-African cultural patriotism would be conditional on making the proclivity to modern innovations and forms of life coincide with the accomplishments of those ancient African societies wherein tradition is regarded as a monolithic source of cognitive, ethical, and aesthetic authority. The "African humanities" (Diop 1991) would be called upon, through scholarly interpretation, *not* to revamp the tradition of ancient African societies, but to discover and, ultimately, rely on that tradition as a single monolithic source of authority to bolster Pan-African cultural patriotism. As a result, this patriotism would be rationalized to sustain the belief that even the proclivity of African and African-diasporic people to modernity would be wholly subject to the cognitive, ethical, and aesthetic authority vested in the integrity and persistence of their ancient African tradition. "From Ancient Egypt's impact on the culture of the rest of the African continent to the unity of all African languages, African history is one continuous, unbroken narrative of a people with a shared consciousness" (Obenga 1989). Claims such as this have lead to the contention that, under the auspice of the "Afrocentric" strategy, Pan-African cultural patriotism becomes "ahistorical' (Marable 1995), Pan-African cultural solidarity "unanimist" (Appiah 1992; Hountondji 1983; Wiredu 1992), and Pan-African cultural tradition "seamless."

But if that orientation is totally subject to the integrity and persistence of the tradition or African antiquity, then it is difficult to fathom how Diop's and Obenga's accounts are modernist at all. The "African humanities" they employ remain bound in their interpretations to that which gives authority to ancient African tradition, viz., its integrity and persistence. Hence they could never conflict with it. Modern innovations and forms of life would be regarded, then, as bearing the mark of a tradition that would be wholly inimical to them as modern, because the tradition of African antiquity would possess an exemplary status which those innovations and forms of life would have to exemplify.

76

Given its orientation toward the future, no African or African-diasporic innovation calling itself "modern" could be shaped by a sense of the past that carries the overwhelming influence Diop and Obenga purport.

It is indeed quite commonplace to think that the "Afrocentric" strategy "invents" the ancient African tradition, leads one to "imagine" Pan-African cultural patriotism in similar manner to nationalist modernisms in general. This view emerges only in the context of that strategy's critique of the "Eurocentric" one utilized in the interpretation of the African continent and its diaspora as cultural geographies with no significant tradition or history. But its critique of the "Eurocentric" strategy is not the issue here, so matters like the long-standing and raging polemic over whether the antiquity of Athens or the antiquity of the cultural reticulation of the Nile Valley has primacy in the inauguration of so-called "Western" civilization are here not at stake. What is of significance here is whether the "Afrocentric" strategy and its *robust* attachment to the tradition of ancient Africa leave any room for a modernism in black? And to this query, the answer must be in the negative.

What stands out for the African humanities in Diop's and Obenga's accounts is not an ancient African tradition revamped (invented) to establish a way in which modern innovations can be culturally identified as black or Pan-African. Rather it is an ancient African tradition discovered to show that its integrity and persistence (a) are resistant to the "buffeting" of modern innovations and (b) align and bind the proclivity to modern innovation repeatedly to ancient African tradition. There is nothing modern about an innovation that is aligned and bound repeatedly to the integrity and persistence of tradition. Seen in this light, Diop's and Obenga's accounts not only disconfirm the "Eurocentric" devaluation of the tradition and history of African and African-diasporic cultures, but also provide grounds for us to dub them non- or anti-modernisms. So if a nationalist modernism in black is exhausted by the "Eurocentric" and "Afrocentric" strategies, then there is no avenue on which to drive it cogently or successfully as a modernism at all.

V   Cultural Modernism in Black

Let us summarize to this point. A functionalist modernism in black argues that African and/or African-diasporic people become "truly modern" by adapting and acquiescing to modern innovations in the political and economic spheres while foregoing or becoming indifferent to any nationalist aspirations their identity-forming tradition(s) would yield. This entails, however, a modernism that both explains and justifies their proclivity and adaptation to modern innovations as a culturally neutral operation that any group inevitably assumes and undergoes, and not as something historically shaping or identity-bearing about them. There would not, then, be conceptually *and* culturally conspicuous ways, through which blacks become "truly modern," in the relation between modernity and those of the African continent and its diaspora and, hence, nothing characteristic of this kind of account to distinguish it from other functionalist modernisms.

A nationalist modernism in black claims that African and/or African-diasporic people become "truly modern" by showing that their identity-forming traditions are reflectively attached to their orientation and adaptation to modern innovations. This entails the promotion and representation of their cultural identity with modern achievements. Yet a nationalist modernism in black must adopt either a "Eurocentric" strategy, which quashes for black people an identity-forming tradition of their own and gives this modernist account a functionalist cast, or an "Afrocentric" strategy, which wholly binds their orientation to modern innovations ever recurrently to the integrity of their Pan-African cultural patriotism and, thus, renders this account non- or anti-modernist. In effect, such a modernism can be neither designed nor articulated coherently.

Can there be a modernism in black that accounts for conceptually coherent yet culturally shaped manners, through which blacks become "truly modern," in the relation between modernity and the African diaspora without succumbing to the aforementioned pitfalls of nationalist modernisms in black? This question can be answered affirmatively. Unlike nationalist modernisms in black, cultural modernisms in black give an account critically attaching the importance of a distinctive legacy to that relation. But what "distinctive legacy" is being granted importance in a critically discriminating way by a cultural, not a nationalist, modernism in black? The "distinctive legacy" is that of racial enslavement (colonialism, imperialism), which can be employed in a way that precludes the account of nationalist modernisms in black.

Let us examine this point and, in so doing, ask the following question. Why should the legacy of racial enslavement (or colonialism or imperialism) have any more distinctiveness and importance to the relation of modernity and the African-diaspora than the legacy of, say, African antiquity? On the surface, it appears that we have merely the sheer emphasis given to a set of historical facts comprising one legacy over another set of historical facts comprising the other. Yet if that were the case, each modernism in black, cultural and nationalist, would involve historical narratives making positivistic appeals to different sets of historical phenomena, each treating its own set as facts. As a consequence, nothing would then distinguish a cultural from a nationalist modernism in black, since each would be engaged in a barren assertion of historical facts. They would be distinguished only by the facts each takes to be relevant in explaining the relation of modernity and the African-diaspora. Yet the jejune assertions of each would underdetermine any intellectual, let alone philosophical, weight each modernism in black would claim to have.

Nevertheless the legacy of racial enslavement (or colonialism or imperialism) has a distinctiveness and significance to the aforementioned relation, because a cultural modernism always presents that legacy and the critical attachment of those of the African-diaspora to it as a historical condition of modern experience. It serves as a historically authoritative presupposition of modern experience and is not simply an indicator of historical phenomena within it. In contrast, nationalist modernisms in black, especially those following the "Afrocentric" strategy, do not present the legacy of ancient African societies as such a condition, but as a discovered resource for the identity-formation or cultural patriotism of a group as "African" regardless of whether the experience is premodern, modern or, if plausible, post-modern. The historical phenomena disclosed to comprise that legacy are themselves phenomena of African antiquity. Yet knowledge of them is alleged to satisfy sufficiently self-knowledge and cultural patriotism, i.e., alleged to satisfy sufficiently the need for the positive realization of who or what African and

African-diasporic people "truly" are regardless of the historical experience in which such people are situated. So, according to the historical narrative of a nationalist modernism in black, the legacy of African antiquity establishes the identity of African and African-diasporic people. In contrast, according to the historical narrative of a cultural modernism in black, the legacy of racial enslavement (colonialism and imperialism) sets the way in which the identity of African and African-diasporic people is to be interpreted. Clearly the legacy that constitutes, say, my identity, constitutes who I am, cannot simultaneously be the legacy that makes possible the manners in which my identity, the manners in which who I am, is to be understood historically.

If the legacy of racial enslavement is a historical presupposition of modernity, a cultural modernism in black provides an account in which modern experience is enabled by it. To better illuminate these matters and their consequences, let me take, as an example, and briefly examine a remark by, perhaps, the first and foremost proponent of a cultural modernism in black, W. E. B. Du Bois in his *The Souls of Black Folk* (*SBF*). As we know, Du Bois concisely framed his near century-long panoramic life in terms of that poignant, pithy, and understated remark – "The problem of the 20th century is the problem of the color line" (Du Bois 1997a). In many circles, that remark is interpreted as Du Bois' empirical description or generalization of the twentieth century. The color line is understood as (1) the practice of racial stratification, (2) the legacy of racial enslavement, (3) the unfolding of colonialism and imperialism globally (which, at the time of *SBF*, is reaching its moment of consolidation in Africa and Asia), and (4) the history and currency of European intellectual discourse on the "real" differences between people based on the way they "appear." It is usually taken as an empirical description of how all these items matter in the lives and events, which come to characterize and will come to characterize specifically the twentieth century. The problem of the color line would be then *just* the problem of the twentieth century alone. But such an interpretation lends itself to pronouncements that, in the face of not only new empirical circumstances, but also innovative possibilities of experience, Du Bois' remark is bound to historicism and, hence, subject to skeptical rejoinder (Njeri 1993).

Yet if we take Du Bois' remark as an empirical generalization, then we fail to understand the authoritative character of the "problem of the color line" for him. As Du Bois explicitly infers on more than one occasion and across several decades, his remark takes us to the root of that which he considers characteristic of *modernity*. The problem, to which he refers, appears to exceed or extend beyond any specific historical and geographical boundary in which we might seek to situate it. So, for example, Du Bois claims that "it was a *phase* of this problem that *caused* the Civil War" (Du Bois 1997a). If Du Bois' remark were an empirical description, if the problem were only a phenomenon within the twentieth century, then how is it possible that a twentieth-century problem or a "phase" of it could be the *cause* of a nineteenth-century event that was inarguably America's severest crucible?

Rather than an empirical description, Du Bois' remark reflects an interpretation addressing a historical condition of modern experience in terms of the "problem of the color line" and its consequences. As he puts it, *"three centuries' thought has been the raising and unveiling of that bowed human heart, and now behold a century new for the duty and the deed.* The problem of the 20th century is the problem of the color line"

(Du Bois 1997a; my emphasis). The twentieth century newly acquires custody of the "color-line problem" from three prior centuries at least. That acquisition does not shape the twentieth century to be the one in which that "problem" originates and terminates. Rather it shapes that century to be a part of an ongoing historical narrative of how and why that "problem" can be construed as a presupposition of modern experience. Taken in this way, the problem of modernity is the problem of the color line (Kirkland 1992).

As a historical condition, the "problem of the color line" neither trumps other aforementioned conditions of modernity nor resolves difficulties of modern experience. Rather it establishes that any "objective characterization" of modern innovations detailing, say, socioeconomic and geographic mobility or the extension of political rights or the development of reason or the unleashing of aesthetic sensibility, all under the auspices of the constant severance from a devalued sense of the past in the name of freedom or autonomy, already inherits or presupposes the "color-line problem." And, for Du Bois, that compels one to rethink what counts as modern within a more encompassing and complex whole such that the innovations just mentioned and the proclivity toward them are already entwined with the practice of racial stratification, the legacy of racial enslavement, the global unfolding of colonialism and imperialism, and the spurious intellectual and political legitimation of "white" racial supremacy. This entwinement reflects the problem the color line brings to modernity.

It is usually acknowledged that Hegel is the first to understand modernity itself to be a problem (Habermas 1987). The problem, as Hegel viewed it, was the paradox of modernity's break with the sense of the past or tradition as something modern experience constantly inaugurates without any rational motivation for the severance. To undo that problem, Hegel proposed that modernity's break with tradition was something modern experience is rationally and unavoidably provoked to do. In Hegel's eyes, modernity's break with tradition relies on a connection with tradition that is reconstructed in a historical narrative to construe rationally that connection as modernity's legacy and as still "*reconcilable*" with the proclivity to future innovation, as still reconcilable with utopian expectations. Indeed this is the philosophical view behind nationalist modernisms of Europe.

In contrast, it is usually acknowledged that Nietzsche is the first to understand modernity as a problem by virtue of its legacy. That legacy, for Nietzsche, not only was "*irreconcilable*" with future innovation, but also signaled at the outset, in its own "Christian" and "Platonist" origins, a *perennial nihilism* of the very proclivity to future innovation. Nietzsche's historical narrative, then, reveals modernity to be a problem, because modernity's legacy is worthless, unsatisfying, and can never be in line with utopian expectations.

To some degree, Du Bois is like Hegel in recognizing that modernity is attached to a legacy all its own. To some extent, he is like Nietzsche in regarding modernity as a problem because of its legacy. But the entwinement of modernity with the "color line" does not mark Du Bois as the first to link modernity and race. More importantly, it marks him (prior to Horkheimer and Adorno in their *Dialectic of Enlightenment*) as the first to understand that modernity has a *divided legacy*, a "problem" generated by its entwinement with the "color-line." On the one hand, modernity's legacy affirms modern experience's continuous severance from the sense of the past in that experience. On the other hand, modernity's legacy affirms modern experience's connection with the sense of the past not to foreclose any *novel* role it could defensibly have in that experience (Du Bois 1997b).

Du Bois is of the mind that this divided legacy reflects the attitude and behavior not of slaveholders and slaves, but of certain legatees. The former is reflective of the attitude and behavior of future heirs apparent or legatees of those who enslaved and their allied bystanders, and the latter is reflective of that of future heirs apparent or legatees of those enslaved and their allies. None of this initiates or confirms who is praiseworthy or blameworthy between the different sets of legatees. But this difference is reflective of the divided legacy and reveals different historical burdens. So although legatees may be neither responsible for what transpired in the past nor bound to the authority of a tradition inimical to modern experience, they are responsible for the way they continue or interpret modernity's legacy.

One way is to render racial slavery and its legacy *banal* for a culture's support of the proclivity to future innovation insofar as both are inessential to and severed from the incessant novelty of modern experience. In effect, the legacy of racial enslavement cannot serve as modernity's legacy because, like all other legacies, it falls into oblivion. Another way is to render them significant for a culture's support of the proclivity to future innovation insofar as both can be discursively or aesthetically redeemed to play novel roles in modern experience. In effect, the legacy of racial enslavement can serve as modernity's legacy, because it is, unlike others, open to improvisation. Du Bois sees the legatees of those enslaved, those of the African-diaspora, for the most part, pursuing the latter way, while simultaneously finding themselves "unreconciled" and "warring" with the pursuit of the former (Du Bois 1997a). For a cultural modernism in black, here we have, in effect, the historical condition of modernity and its "doubles" (Gilroy 1993a; Kirkland 1992), i.e., "double consciousness" (Du Bois 1997a), "double vision" (Wright 1965), and "dual personality" (Johnson 1989). Although interpreters tend to treat these "doubles" in socio-psychological terms, these "doubles" are better construed in socio-historical ones (Kirkland 1992).

Modernity's divided legacy contributes to the disenchantment a cultural modernism in black has with modern experience, since a cultural modernism in black is ever contesting a conception of modernity in which the legacy of racial enslavement as a historical condition is dismissed and thereby thrown into oblivion. Following in Du Bois' footsteps on this point, Toni Morrison believes blacks can be "truly modern" only if the slave experience represents the distinctive vehicle or legacy for an African-diasporic culture to incorporate facets of modern experience. She argues that in her novel *Beloved* she aimed to place slavery in the center of African-diasporic literary and political culture. "Slavery," she states, "wasn't in the literature at all. Part of that . . . is because, on moving from bondage to freedom which has been our goal, we got away from slavery and also the slaves, . . . we have to re-inhabit those people" (Gilroy 1993b). Furthermore, her emphasis on the slave experience is done less, if at all, for the sake of cultural patriotism than for the sake of a self-conscious *disenchantment* with a culture "where the past is always erased and America is the innocent future . . . [where] the past is absent or romanticized. [American] culture doesn't encourage dwelling on, let alone coming to terms with, the truth about the past. That memory is much more in danger now than it was thirty years ago" (Gilroy 1993b; my addition).

81

That the legacy of racial enslavement is not a matter for primarily raising cultural patriotism requires explanation. As I have argued, nationalist modernisms in black do not believe that legacy to have the capacity to contribute to some kind of Pan-African cultural patriotism, because nothing venerable emerges from that legacy. But even if we were to accept the idea nothing venerable comes from that legacy, that idea would not have any bearing on that legacy serving as a historical condition of modern experience. The issue is not about the legacy of African antiquity being more venerable than others. It is rather about that legacy serving as a contributing factor of modern experience. Serving in this fashion is not dependent on the legacy's venerability or lack thereof, let alone the factual accuracy of the historical phenomena that comprise it.

Moreover, the legacy of racial enslavement permits those of the African-diaspora to engage in a prophylactic skepticism toward a modern form of historical knowledge and social discourse that discounts their experience or allows their experience to fall into oblivion. It also ripens a moral sensibility that guides the repair of their integrity and dignity, guides their inauguration of qualitatively new social relations and needs (with the deliverance of their experience from oblivion in mind), to become their idea of what modern people should be. This sensibility would re-establish the utopian potential of modern experience through respect and appreciation for the uniqueness and inalienable "difference" of others. So that the repair of their integrity and dignity and their inauguration of new social relations would not be taken solely as a rational culmination of the modern extension of inalienable rights previously interrupted by racial stratification and enslavement. In addition, that moral sensibility, a few cultural modernisms in black have proffered, requires a political arrangement, usually designated, albeit confusedly or problematically, as socialism, to flourish (Du Bois 1947).

Although the issue of modernity's divided legacy is important for cultural modernisms in black, it is not as ubiquitous in their accounts as one may think. Indeed they all work with the legacy of racial enslavement as a historical condition of modernity. But there are some whose authors contest the idea that modernity's legacy is divided and is a problem of modern experience. Representatives of this view are Alain Locke, Ralph Ellison, and C. L. R. James. The legacy of racial enslavement still remains a historical presupposition of modern experience for them, but it does not issue into a divided legacy, so that modernity's "doubles" are not given weight in their cultural modernisms in black.

Locke, for example, frames the issue around "modern imperialism," which consists of the political, economic, and social practices of a dominating group to substitute totally its culture for that of subjected groups (Locke 1992). He is of the mind that modern imperialism engenders the "problem of the color line." But, for Locke, the entwinement of modern experience with the color line engenders a *modus vivendi* learning process to overcome modern imperialism, i.e., the color-line problem, the existence of "theoretical and practical group supremacies" (Locke 1989). A learning process is a group's adaptation to modern innovations on the basis of the *exchange* of cultural novelties with other groups. The learning process is modus vivendi, because even a subjected group's proclivity and adaptation to modern innovation can be undertaken or acquired without hint or awareness of isolating its own or challenging others' historical achievements and burdens in the exchange, an isolation or challenge which could thwart social integration.

For Locke and Ellison, racial enslavement or imperialism still did not prevent the "creative tensions arising from the cross-purposes of whites and blacks." Their "social and economic injustices failed to keep Negroes clear of the cultural mainstream" (Ellison 1986). So the legacy of racial enslavement or imperialism, i.e., modernity's legacy, still reflects the pragmatic contribution to social integration, even in the face of the racial division yielded by imperialism's color-line problem, through the exchange of cultural groups' innovations, a legacy that is learned in modus vivendi. The entwinement of modernity with the color line, then, bears an undivided legacy pragmatically adjusted to be reconcilable with the proclivity to future innovation of both groups.

Locke as well as Ellison would see the legatees of both those enslaved and those who enslaved as rendering racial slavery and its legacy significant for, not banal to, a culture's support of the proclivity to future innovation. Neither would see the importance of the undivided legacy as irreconcilable and conflicting with the legatees of those who enslaved, unless those legatees regarded that legacy as banal. Yet, for Ellison at least, to regard that legacy as banal is to deny owning up to it, and such a denial would render a person not a legatee with another legacy all his own, but a "rootless American type" (Ellison 1999). Locke and Ellison would see that legacy as a matter to which and with which both sets of legatees respectively can "adjust" and can themselves be "reconciled" in modus vivendi by virtue of the continuous exchange of cultural innovations between them. "The progress of the modern world demands what may be styled 'free-trade in culture . . .' Culture-goods, once evolved, are no longer the exclusive property of the race or people that originated them. They belong to all who can use them; and belong most to those who can use them best. But for all the limitless exchange and transplanting of culture, it cannot be artificially manufactured; it grows" (Locke 1989).

The color-line problem for them does not trump the free exchange of cultural innovations or invoke anything that ought to thwart the socially integrative or "antiphonal" consequences of that exchange between legatees. Otherwise two things occur. First, the legatees of those who enslaved become modern and "rootless" more open to illusion than to pragmatic adjustment. Second, the legatees of those enslaved become modern and "black" on the basis of a "problem" more open to cognitive and moral conflict rather than on the basis of a style of life more open to socially integrative ways with others.

Such a "lifestyle" pragmatically contributes to a "civilization type" called "American" whose flourishing within its borders and beyond will rely on the political vehicle of democracy (Locke 1992; Ellison 1986 and 1999). Moreover disenchantment with modernity as a whole would not issue from Locke's or Ellison's cultural modernism in black. Nonetheless a critique of cultural groups engaged in "modern imperialism" would emerge from it as well as a critique of cultural groups whose innovations remain insular ("ghetto-mindedness") and unreconciled with socially integrative ways cultural exchanges enact and cultural groups adjust to and amplify over time (Locke 1989).

Finally, but all too briefly, a key feature that would distinguish C. L. R. James's modernism from Locke's and Ellison's would be James's replacement of a modus vivendi learning process for one that is reflexive. Modernity's undivided legacy, for Locke and Ellison, guides cultural innovations toward the future potential of social integration in the current "civilization type" through the "lifestyle" of the legatees of those enslaved who enlarge and bend to that potential over time. This is why Locke's and Ellison's modernisms tend to have the flavor of a "black petit bourgeois apologetics" to some. On the other hand, for James, modernity's undivided legacy connects the future potential of social integration to cultural innovations transforming, in this instance, the colonial "civilization type" through action which coordinates the "lifestyle" of the legatees of those enslaved/colonized who are cognizant of both that potential and their own innovations being at odds with that civilization type (James 1984).

VI   Concluding Remarks

In an earlier work, I argued that a modernism in black defended and promoted the conviction that a future-oriented present could be the fortunate occasion in which African-diasporic culturally distinctive innovations would be historically redemptive of the legacy of racial enslavement in novel ways and could couple that group's emancipation with happiness, rather than with meaninglessness (Kirkland 1992). Given the discussion presented here, these tasks appear to be best satisfied by cultural rather than functionalist and nationalist modernisms in black. However, further work is necessary to explore and evaluate more fully the two different kinds of cultural modernisms in black. To date this has not yet been done. Despite the insights of Paul Gilroy, for example, it is clear that his attention is focused on cultural modernisms in black that address the relation of modern experience to those of the African diaspora in terms of modernity's divided, rather than undivided, legacy of racial enslavement (Gilroy 1993a).

Moreover, questions need to be raised about whether cultural modernisms in black, supportive of the conception of modernity's divided legacy, foreclose the potential of social integration, as my piece seems to imply. A good deal more needs to be said about the two different learning processes (*modus vivendi* and reflexive) operative in those cultural modernisms endorsing the undivided legacy. Are they not operative in those endorsing the divided legacy? Further inquiry is needed into the difference between Du Bois' and James's socialism in the light of their distinctive modernist accounts. Are there elements of a functionalist modernism residing in Locke's and Ellison's accounts? Do cultural modernisms in black back an African-diasporic identity, which is rigid culturally or, if I may coin a phrase, modally extended culturally? If all cultural modernisms in black rule out the possibility of "blackness" being a "rigid designator," does that mean "blackness" becomes under their auspice an "open signifier" or rather something that can be discursively amplified? How do cultural modernisms in black stand up to Gilroy's conception of a "populist modernism" (Gilroy 1993b), or to post-modernism, or to what has recently been called "reflexive modernization" (Beck 1992)? Hopefully this contribution has prepared the way for an in-depth treatment of these questions and issues, since it has not only "greased the skillet," but has also "lit the fire" for the cookin' to commence.

References

Anderson, Benedict (1991) *Imagined Communities* (New York: Verso).
Appiah, Kwame Anthony (1992) *In My Father's House* (New York: Oxford University Press).

Beck, Ulrich (1992) *Risk Society: Towards a New Modernity* (London: Sage Publications, originally published in German in 1987).

Blyden, Edward W. (1990) *Christianity, Islam and the Negro Race* (Chesapeake: ECA Associates, originally published in 1887).

Crummell, Alexander (1995) *Civilization and Black Progress: Selected Writings* (Charlottesville: University Press of Virginia).

Diop, Cheikh Anta (1991) *Civilization or Barbarism: An Authentic Anthropology* (Brooklyn: L. Hill).

Du Bois, W. E. B. (1997a) *The Souls of Black Folk* (Boston: Bedford Books).

——(1997b) "The Development of a People" in *The Souls of Black Folk* (Boston: Bedford Books).

——(1947) *The World and Africa* (New York: International Publishers).

——(1945) *Color and Democracy* (New York: Harcourt Brace).

Ellison, Ralph (1999) "Notes" to *Juneteenth* in *Juneteenth* (New York: Random House).

——(1986) *Going to the Territory* (New York: Random House).

Gilroy, Paul (1993a) *The Black Atlantic: Modernity & Double Consciousness* (Cambridge, MA: Harvard University Press).

——(1993b) *Small Acts* (London: Serpent's Tail).

Habermas, Jürgen (1987) *The Philosophical Discourse of Modernity* (Cambridge: MIT Press, originally published in German in 1985).

Hobsbawm, Eric and Ranger, Terence (1983) *The Invention of Tradition* (Cambridge: Cambridge University Press).

Hountondji, Paulin (1983) *African Philosophy: Myth and Reality* (Bloomington: Indiana University Press).

James, C. L. R. (1984) *At the Rendezvous of Victory* (London: Allison & Busby).

——(1980) *Notes on Dialectics* (Westport: L. Hill).

——(1977) *The Future in the Present* (Westport: L. Hill).

Johnson, James Weldon (1989) *The Autobiography of an Ex-Colored Man* (New York: Vintage Press).

Kirkland, Frank M. (1992/93) "Modernity & Intellectual Life in Black" in *The Philosophical Forum* XXIV, 1–3. (Reprinted in book form in 1997 as *African American Perspectives & Philosophical Traditions* by Routledge).

Koselleck, Reinhart (1985) *Futures Past: On the Semantics of Historical Time* (Cambridge, MA: MIT Press, originally published in German in 1979).

Locke, Alain LeRoy (1992) *Race Contacts and Interracial Relations* (Washington, D.C.: Howard University Press).

——(1989) *The Philosophy of Alain Locke*, ed. L. Harris (Philadelphia: Temple University Press).

Marable, Manning (1995) *Beyond Black and White: Transforming African-American Politics* (New York: Verso).

Morrison, Toni (1992) *Playing in the Dark: Whiteness and the Literary Imagination* (Cambridge: Harvard University Press).

Njeri, Itabari (1993) "Sushi and Grits: Ethnic Identity and Conflict in a Newly Multicultural America" in *Lure and Loathing: Essays on Race, Identity, and the Ambivalence of Assimilation*, ed. G. Early (New York: Penguin Press).

Obenga, Theophile (1989) "African Philosophy in Pharaonic Times" in *Egypt Revisited*, ed. I. Van Sertima (New Brunswick: Transaction Publishers, 2nd edition).

Patterson, Orlando (1977) *Ethnic Chauvinism: The Reactionary Impulse* (New York: Stein & Day).

——(1972) "Toward a Future That Has No Past" in *The Public Interest* (Spring 1972), 27.

Taussig, Michael (1986) *Shamanism, Colonialism, and the Wild Man: A Study in Terror and Healing* (Chicago: University of Chicago Press).

Weber, Max (1993) *The Sociology of Religion* (Boston: Beacon Press).

Wiredu, Kwasi (1992) "Formulating Modern Thought in African Languages: Some Theoretical Considerations" in *The Surreptitious Speech: Presence Africaine and the Politics of Otherness*, ed. V. Y. Mudimbe (Chicago: University of Chicago Press).

Wright, Richard (1980) "Blueprint for Negro Writing" in *Race and Class* XXI, 4. (Reprint of the 1937 article.)

——(1965) *The Outsider* (New York: Harper & Row).

5

The Crisis of the Black Intellectual

HORTENSE J. SPILLERS

To suggest that African-American intellectuals today persist in a state of crisis will not be news to students and observers of American culture more broadly speaking, nor to its African-American witnesses regarding the specific nature of the case. In a very real sense, the black intellectual, by definition, embodies the ongoing crisis of life-worlds in historical confrontation with superior force. But the confrontational model, ironically enough, has limited usefulness and explanatory range in sight of a new century, or can it be positively asserted that such is now the case? This moment of revision and transition, in which the intellectuals are located, so uncertain of feature, so undetermined in the demands that it makes on social agents, renders the current crisis both emphatically new and sufficiently comfortable to familiar circumstances, and the very fact that the intellectual can no longer easily appropriate a ready-made body of myths and social practices likely marks the point at which this discussion should begin. But in keeping with the need to *situate* the problem and to map only some of the continuities and ruptures that score it, we will have recourse to the time line.

When, during the mid-1920s, Alain Locke assembled the items that would make up the special number of *Survey Graphic*, he had at his back a powerful tradition of practices, including discursive ones, devoted to the aims of emancipation and race uplift. Less than a century removed from the peace of Richmond and the bloody military campaigns that had radically altered the social and political status of millions of African Americans, Locke's "New Negro," according to his creator, was in the process of reversing the gaze. This benefactor of abolition movement across the Western world was, by 1925, a "changeling" in the lap of the sociologist, the philanthropist, and the race-leader, but these "three norns who [had] traditionally presided over the Negro problem . . . [were] at a loss to account for him" (*The New Negro*, 3). Locke's special number of Paul Kellog's magazine, surfacing in March, 1925, would enjoy "extraordinary success," certainly enough of it to inspire Albert and Charles Boni to bring out a discrete publication of the volume during the fall of the same year. Featuring poetry by Countee Cullen, Claude McKay, Langston Hughes, and Gwendolyn Bennett, fiction by Rudolph Fisher, Zora Neale Hurston, and Eric Walrond, and occasional prose pieces, penned by Charles S. Johnson, W. E. B. Du Bois, Arthur A. Schomburg, and E. Franklin

Frazier, among others, the miscellany offered an hospitable climate to the tenets of the Harlem Renaissance and, in a very real sense, might be thought of as its debut. Even though the Negro renascence, which proffered its own version of modernism in the arts, is inconceivable detached from the context of larger demographic shifts from the countryside to the city, new industrial patterns of labor emergent in post-war technologies, and a veritable "reign of terror," post-reconstruction style and reenforced by oppressive regimes of work that rendered much of the South menacing for its black populations – even if "Mr. Wilson's war" had been supposed to make "the *world* safe for democracy" – little of this dramatic backdrop is refracted through the optics of Locke's introductory essay to the volume. All in one go, it seems, a "new" configuration of black humanity erupts on the landscape, even against Locke's rhetorical disclaimer that the "metamorphosis" had *not* been as sudden as all that. It was in Locke's interest to give the appearance of driving a wedge between himself and his generation and the immediate past in order to make way, in effect, for a *secular* social formation of black thinkers who could redefine the past according to the dictates of the new learning in the social sciences and to project into the present a black nationalist consciousness empowered to do battle against the systematic ruin that Euroamerican supremacy had visited on the non-white and non-male citizenries of the world. If we read Locke carefully, it emerges, eventually, that the idea he wants to drive home above everything else is black subject's *power to name*, although we would do well to suspect that this self-naming subject/project of Locke's conceptual narrative shows all the traces, despite itself, of an elision inscribed at the heart of modernist thinking about the "black problem" – Locke's subject here is not only a hypothetical male figure, but a young one at that (Wall [1995], 4; Hull [1987], 7–8ff). While the notion of *episteme* is not available to Locke's generation, it is rather remarkable (for that precise reason) that the broad outlines of an epistemic reconfiguration – or strategies of knowledge production – are inchoate in this essay.

This son of the black elite, who belonged to the upper reaches of the "Philadelphia Negro," had, like Du Bois, attended Harvard University, graduating *magna cum laude* in 1907 (*The New Negro*, 415; *The Norton Anthology*, 960–1.) The first black Rhodes fellow, Locke earned an Oxford degree in 1910 and, again like Du Bois, studied in Germany, spending a year as a student of philosophy at the University of Berlin, 1910–11; in 1918, Locke completed a Ph.D. at Harvard, having written a dissertation on problems in aesthetics.[1] If Locke's tone in "The New Negro" strikes one as rather arch, for all that, with more than a hint of the fervor of self-appointedness, then perhaps there is some justification for such posturing, after all, inasmuch as the miscellany itself is intended to represent a collective act of assertion on the part of black artists, who could, for the first time, declare the political efficacy of art without having to look over their shoulder.

It might be said, however, that every one of the exigencies that visited the intellectual formation of the "New Negro" has returned to the current scene with a vengeance, while some might claim that the categories of alignment converging on the Harlem Renaissance were never dissipated in the first place, that is to say, the extent to which "black community" is allowed the freedom of "mind life" at all. Still others would contend that the big picture of intellectual life in black unfolds against the entire sociopolitical backdrop of African diasporic life in the West and that until social justice is achieved for the whole, then nothing else really matters. These competing views, which date back to the nineteenth century and what Wilson Moses identifies as the "golden age of black nationalism," can quite rightly be thought of as the cost of membership that freed black subjects have had to pay for entry into the body politic as "one 'man,' one vote," and to the extent that black life looks inward and outward at the same time, the "problem" appears to be irresolvable. Another way to think about the issues involved here is to bring them to boil under the heat of two major foci – "assimilation/integration" and "separation/nationalism," which trend-lines, or some combination of thinking and practice hospitable to aspects of both, dominated black intellectual life until ca. 1973–4; the latter dates, as arbitrary as they may seem, mark decisive changes nevertheless on the landscape of black American life in the post-Civil Rights era that rendered the major currents of practice, until then, impotent to register certain subtle transformations wrought by not-so-subtle contingency: (1) the *mediatization* of American political life, beginning with the Kennedy–Nixon presidential campaign of 1960, running through the massive debacle of Vietnam and Watergate, with the resignation of Richard M. Nixon as one of its highlights, (2) the collapse of the contemporary movement in cultural black nationalism, accompanied by the more or less "successful" absorption of aspects of the Civil Rights movement by the mainstream American academy, and (3) new trends in the economies of migration (internal) and immigration (external), boosted by the powerful surge of corporate globalism and the revised cartographies of minority positionings. (Can any assessment of change within the last quarter century be *thought* without a glance at computers? It seems that for all its marvelous capacity, to the contrary notwithstanding, the computer has done more to hasten the redefinition of the "nation-state" and the national boundary than any other conceivable thing, including improvements in the work habits of millions of worldlings, e.g., college freshmen, for example, still need courses in writing taught by live human beings.) In any event, trying to analyze what must be done in the African-American community against deep broad cuts through the fabric of the American/global life world in general is precisely where we are located today. But what's new about that?

According to Wilson Moses, the period 1850–1920 staked out the classical postures of black nationalism, dominated by two major groups of actors: Martin Delany, E. W. Blyden, and Alexander Crummell formed one such cluster, which acceded authority to another, chiefly commandeered by W. E. B. Du Bois, Marcus Garvey, and the "ghost of Booker T. Washington" (Moses [1978], 267). But the Victorian concepts of gentility, *noblesse oblige*, Christianity, and civilization, which had shaped the thinking of the parent cohort, was jettisoned by the latter in the interest of a "new sociology" that tended to "emphasize social, as opposed to racial, reasons for the existence of prejudice" (*The Golden Age*, 256). Moses goes on to argue that for half a century (1925–75), cultural black nationalism was hostile to certain elements of the older synthesis, primarily its views of sub-Saharan Africa, widely held to be backward and benighted. The complexity of black nationalist thought, however, consists in the levels of contradiction and inconsistency that it has sustained over the last 150 years, as the period of our current location has not witnessed the end of black nationalist sentiment so much as introduced a number of modifications and nuances to it, sometimes inadvertently, as varied in texture and intensity as the Afrocentric synthesis, the black feminist/womanist project, and the Black Studies movement of two or three distinct metamorphoses. We will have occasion to revisit this descriptive apparatus.

One realizes that the black nationalist perspective, as Wilson Moses, Harold Cruse, and others have described it, is neither inevitable nor static, but that it is, rather, exactly proportionate to the level of danger and menace that African-American communities experience at any given moment; in other words, black nationalist practices are not God-given – whatever features of narrative emplotment its various practitioners may adopt from time to time – are not an instance of spirit drooping down in the midst of things – whatever appeals to the apocalyptic and the transcendent that they may evoke – and, finally, do not demarcate a purity of motives, either moral or political. We should also point out that these practices, of whatever shade and complexity, are remarkably consistent along a single line of emphasis, and that is, their insistent *masculinism*. We hope to suggest, along the way, that this feature of practice is not only backward and anachronistic by now, but actually dangerous to the common good in its unexamined dimensions of fantasy and blindness. This ensemble of material practices, as well as its grammars of feeling, arises concretely out of the human and historical world. If that is so (and how could it be otherwise?), then this complex must borrow its ways and means of conduct from the real concrete specific circumstances of its locations: it is not at all a stretch to imagine, as Moses narrates, that black nationalist impulses drew their first breath of oxygen from the marronage phenomenon, which revolutions in Jamaica, Haiti, and Surinam, during the seventeenth and eighteenth centuries, gained impetus with the rebellions of Denmark Vesey and Nat Turner in the United States during the early- and mid-nineteenth century, respectively (*The Golden Age*, 17–18). It also stands to reason that black nationalism/Pan-Africanism movements are diasporic occurrences, inasmuch as African enslavement in the New World had effected a synonymity of motive between *skin color* and the status of slavery *across African ethnic groups*, as the entire enterprise of slaving illustrated the impressive staying power of the plantation labor regime. To that extent, black nationalism has been a nationalism "only in the sense that it seeks to unite the entire black racial family, assuming that the entire race has a collective destiny and message for humanity comparable to that of a nation. For this reason, it is impossible to speak of black nationalism without simultaneously speaking of Pan-Africanism" (*The Golden Age*, 17).

We might think of the latter practice as the *internationalist* dimension of black nationalism, as the Pan-African idea was fomented by the convocation of some six conferences over the first half of the new century, the initial one organized by Trinidadian barrister, Henry Sylvester Williams in 1900. Prior to the "golden age," black nationalism is said to have been expressed as a "proto Pan-Africanism" (1787–1817), with representative instances figured forth in the writings of Olaudah Equiano and Ottobah Cugoano (*The Golden Age*, 19; 25–6). Even though it is admittedly difficult to think of Equiano's *Narrative*, with its unabashed embrace of mercantilism, in the same moment of recall with David Walker's *Appeal*, in its powerful comminatory outrage against slavery, these writers did share black nationalism's most common denominator of thought, and that is the impassioned belief in black redemption. If Pan-Africanism persists in our time, it apparently replicates certain features of belief in common with the view that proposes a "movement of all African peoples throughout the world, who believe that all black people have interests in common. Its adherents accept as axioms the idea that no black person is free until all are free, and that the liberation and unification of Africa is (sic) essential to the dignity of African people everywhere" (*The Golden Age*, 19).

Because black nationalism is so sweeping and historic in its embrace of black populations across the spatio-temporal continuum, it might be regarded as *multiformal* and acquires its shape according to local conditions: perhaps the most vivid witness of this catholicity of meanings is nowhere more evident than in black ritual celebrations – for example, broadcast by Cable-Satellite Public Affairs Network (C-Span) on Easter Sunday, 1998, a program honoring Stokely Carmichael/Kwame Touré was held at the Marriott Hotel in Washington, D.C., Wednesday, April 8; sharing the podium with the handsome, now venerable gray-haired, black activist were representatives of an ideological *callaloo*, from Louis Farrakhan of the Nation of Islam, to [former] Washington, D.C. mayor Marion Barry, to Georgia Congressman, John Lewis. In the midst of this spectacle of quite elaborate African/Moslem dress and Islamic sacred reference and renaming, the casual evocation of "affirmative action" and Ward Connelly, in a fleeting moment of the proceedings, was almost funny, certainly surprising, and, in drawing out the semiotic richness and "confusion" of the event, helped to demonstrate just the sort of symbolic, pragmatic, policy intersection that gives black nationalism its ironically-scarred countenance. (One of the few dignitaries on the platform, by the way, to be dressed in Western garb was the *Tanzanian* ambassador to the United States.) While these features of ritual are usually bracketed in our discussions of the most crucial elements of black nationalist practice, they are nonetheless worthy of note as a key to understanding how black nationalism/Pan-Africanism *imagines* and *narrates* itself as public address and *performance*. Combining the purposes of fundraising and commemoration, the D.C. program was fertile in signifying content, no less crucial for what it *implied*, indeed actually "spoke," about the authoritarian face of the presentation. Wilson Moses in fact names the idea of *organic collectivism under authority* as one of the leading symptoms of black nationalist practice and belief, suggesting, after E. Franklin Frazier, that the collectivist ideal, accompanied by an "authoritarian political tradition," may be attributed to "the peculiar role served by the black church" (*The Golden Age*, 22). To my mind, both the most powerful and persistently unconscious impulse that has so far guided black struggle, the elitist principle, borne out of authoritarianism, has yielded a mixed harvest. To it, we may assign our most solid gains since emancipation (and likely even before), as well as our profoundest moments of blindness and error. But for a movement so enormous in scope and purpose, it is hardly surprising that its still-unfolding outcome describes a riddle at the center.

If Joy James is right, then black intellectuals today have travelled quite far in time from the assumptions that shaped the protocols of Alexander Crummell, E. W. Blyden, and W. E. B. Du Bois, among many others, but essentially have not let go the elitism that characterized their thinking (James 1997). Moses suggests that Crummell's program, for example, was based on the notion of the uplift of black people, which activity was dependent, in turn, on "character building and the elevation of moral life" (*The Golden Age*, 73). But the aim of regeneration constituted the moral and political work of an "educated elite." The genesis of the idea behind the American Negro Academy and the philosophy of the "talented tenth," the notion of an educated elite throws into sharp focus a sense of history, indeed of historiography and research, that is teleological, hagiographical, and can probably be shown to privilege, as a result, the figures of metaphor. (The student of literature might bear in mind that what I mean here concerning the behavior of metaphoricity might be captured in the contrast between Homer Barbee's sermonic discourse in Ralph Ellison's *Invisible Man* and the discursive currents released in the novel's Prologue/Epilogue.) In short, the elitist contribution – which today's intellectuals tend to replicate – pursues the "great man/woman" theory of history, which displaces the "lives of the saints," but just barely, onto secular ground. In any case, the elitist strain of thinking appears to be the rule of black nationalism, rather than – and this outcome marks a genuine surprise, to my mind – the *exception*, as Moses draws a contrast between Frederick Douglass on this point and the likes of Crummell and Blyden: "hostile throughout his life to the mystical, pseudo-Christian radical rhetoric of the [latter]," Douglass also did not support emigrationist schemes either and is thought to have been a lot closer in spirit to the "egalitarian radicals of the abolitionist school" than to the gentlemen of the American Negro Academy (*The Golden Age*, 90). Founded by Alexander Crummell on March 5, 1897, five years after the publication of Anna Julia Cooper's *Voice from the South*, the American Negro Academy – let's call it the "dream team" of its day – produced a series of "occasional papers" on topics of intense interest to African Americans, indeed, to students of American culture, invigilating the impact of the study and the reproduction of the social sciences on it. The occasional papers of the Academy, managed rather like annual reports, run through the 1920s. William Loren Katz's *American Negro: His History and Literature* (1969) reprints the 22 annual papers from this series, starting with Kelly Miller's "Review of Hoffman's *Race Traits and Tendencies of the American Negro*." The second paper in the series is Du Bois's much-invoked "Conservation of the Races," as the series concludes some years later, with Archibald Grimke's "Shame of America" and John W. Cromwell's "Challenge of the Disfranchised," no. 22.

Not *one* of these occasional pieces appears to have been submitted by a woman writer (although, as we have implied, there are some capable ones around and even though we're looking at significant overlap here between the time of this black gentlemen's club, really, and the time of the woman's era – the black women's club movement, e.g., the National Federation of Afro-American Women, the National Association of Colored Women, etc.). Looking at the content of *Occasional Papers No. 21*, Grimke's "Shame of America, or the Negro's Case Against the Republic," we observe the following: (1) as "object," five stipulated goals –

The Promotion of Literature, Science, and Art
The Culture of a Form of Intellectual Taste
The Fostering of Higher Education
The Publication of Scholarly Works
The Defense of the Negro Against Vicious Assault

(We should point out here what is likely not a little bit ironic to the observer, and that is to say that one of the most devoted activists, defending the "Negro Against Vicious Assault" during crucial years of the Academy's tenure, was Ida Wells Barnett, whose name does not appear among this visionary company.); (2) the roster of officers:

President: Arthur A. Schomburg
Vice Presidents: J. R. Clifford, Charles D. Martin, L. Z. Johnson, Joseph J. France
Recording Secretary: Thomas M. Dent
Librarian: T. Montgomery Gregory
Treasurer: Lafayette M. Hershaw
Executive Committee: John W. Cromwell, Kelly Miller, Alain Leroy Locke, F. H. M. Murray, John E. Bruce
Corresponding Secretary: Robert A. Pelham;

(3) facts of publication:

Washington, D.C., published by the Academy (153 Tea Street, N.W.)

This nicely printed broadside sold on the streets for fifteen cents over the years and was increased by a nickel about 1920. With members scattered across the United States (in the East, the Mid-West, and the South), the membership itself seemed closely circumscribed, with a single African correspondent, one Orishatukeh Faduma, whom Wilson Moses describes as a "West African patriot with affinities to the American Negro Academy" (*The Golden Age*, 203). In any event, the rosters of the membership and the officers would suggest that the Academy offered an intellectual "home" to some of the most important black voices of the era, but in doing so, it excluded some others. "Tradition," however, seems to work in precisely that way, as the solidity of practice that it wishes to invoke of necessity describes boundary around a putative circumference, perhaps even a fantastical one. That the Academy excluded women as a rule of play seems to me to take the romance of "tradition" to an extreme, even though we would do well to regard it as a shabby imitation of certain cultural practices inherent in patriarchal ideology; that African-American males, even some of those whose biographies we admire, were engaging in such practices does not make them any less odious, or one iota less destructive, both in terms of examples of democratic praxis that this generation passed on to their successors and in the disparagement and truncating of talent that the African-American community can always use. That men of learning so close to the ravages of slavery could not adopt a progressive political stance on this score is not only disappointing, but it is also instructive: educated black males in their guise as intellectuals in/of the metropolis locate a special instance of gender and sexual bias. In fact, in this specific configuration – of a socioeconomic order directly dependent on economies of excess – we lay hold of virtually pure laboratory conditions for examining male political behavior. In other words, the *city*, both in its specific topographical punctuality and in the symbolic and semiotic density of its diverse fruit, appears *not* to have been a liberalizing influence on the educated bourgeois black male elite: the farther away he moved from the countryside, either actually or figuratively, the less progressive he became in certain respects, probably in all ways, except for matters of race. I am certainly not suggesting that the inverse of this proposition is true, nor that my claim works every time – at least Alice Walker's *Color Purple* provides sufficient caveat, indirectly, against such stupefying romanticism – but I do mean that the eliminating of *need*, which often requires men and women to cooperate in stanching the ruin of scarcity, encourages a more finely calibrated articulation of role, of status

93

and the exclusionary. Once that happens, the male "graduates" to *manness* and the telos of heroic destiny. Therein lies no small clue in this bit of allegory, I believe, to sexual politics in black in our own time, especially in the mainstream academy.

Even though it would not be entirely accurate to read certain observations concerning male political behavior in an ahistorical, or a retroactive, way, we can guess, with at least a degree of justification, that some things do not quickly or unambiguously change. About women writers of the Harlem Renaissance generation, Gloria Hull notes:

> Yet, despite what appears to be full participation of women in the Harlem Renaissance, one can discern broad social factors and patterns of exclusion. One of the most basic is how male attitudes toward women impinged upon them, how men's so-called personal biases were translated into something larger that had deleterious effects. (*Color, Sex, and Poetry*, 7)

Hull goes on to say that such effects were especially invidious "when such men were in influential and critical positions. They then made blatant antifemale prejudice inherent in the whole of society" (*Color, Sex, and Poetry*, 7). Alain Locke, for instance, was reputed to have been a "certified misogynist," who, according to Zora Neale Hurston – apparently favored by Locke at some point – could be "a malicious, spiteful little snot," dispensing patronage in exactly the same way that we imagine it is always doled out, that is, by virtue of some quite arbitrary measure, which is then rationalized as "objective" and self-evident." "God help you," Hurston wrote to a correspondent, "if you [got] on without letting him represent you" (*Color, Sex, and Poetry*, 8).

Locke and Company, many of them young males, "functioned within a homosexual coterie of friendship and patronage that suggests that literary events were, in more than a few instances, tied to 'bedroom politics' and 'sexual croneyism'" (*Color, Sex, and Poetry*, 8). The kind of titillating fare on which gossip and tabloid journalism batten, the sexual orientation and performance of public persons, or persons of some modicum of celebrity, is only interesting to the extent that it influences public policy, or as Hull meticulously notes, to the degree that it determines how the resources available to minority social formations, conventionally limited and begrudged, at best, are dispensed; if the Harlem Renaissance circle of patronage concealed an "epistemology of the closet," whose maskings I suspect we have greater access to today than we realize, then we might well wonder how retrospectively the idea might be read against the formation of the American Negro Academy that preceded it, for example, or even, fast forward, in reference to degrees of influence wielded by black intellectual formations on the current scene, for another. In any event, our grasp of African-American intellectual development in its various eras and stages must leave room for contradictory evidence, which would suggest a grammar of motives scored by complex and duplicitous relations between the sexes. As Joy James observes of Du Bois' relationships with Anna Julia Cooper and Ida Wells Barnett, we might say about others among their contemporaries: "Just as it is disingenuous to minimize Du Bois' significant contributions toward women's equality, it would also be deceptive to ignore his problematic representations of and political relationships with independent, influential African-American women activists" (*Transcending the Talented Tenth*, 42).

Although we tend to focus on certain impression points in describing black intellectual movement, it is likely that diasporic communities were, from the very beginning of
their cultural apprenticeship in the New World, never without dreamers and doers
who defined themselves against their oppressors. For that reason, black intellectual life
has inclined toward the confrontational and defensive postures that soon expressed
themselves along the thematics and contours of race consciousness. Historians often
attribute the first organizational motive among new-world Africans to the religious
impulse, beginning with the "church invisible" of the countryside – perhaps a blend of
certain African retentions and Christian rituals – that finally works its way into the
denominational structures of differentiated Christian practice, notably the African-
Methodist Episcopal Church of the late eighteenth century, spearheaded by
Philadelphia's Mother Bethel. Relatedly, traditions of homilectics – both scriptive and
oral – define one clear and unbroken strand of black intellectual/imaginative work, that
is to say, black sermonic forms, from Jupiter Hammon's "Winter's Piece" (mid-
eighteenth century), through Martin Luther King's sermons and speeches in the middle
of the twentieth century. As Wilson Moses implies, the separation of clerical from
secular work in black thought is no simple task, just as what counts as "intellectual"
in black community is fraught with a certain hesitation of naming, on the one hand,
and a kind of classificatory impurity on the other. In other words, it is not until the
twentieth century and the consolidation of the perspectives and projects of the social
sciences that we can witness a black intellectual formation veering significantly
away from clerical centrality, and not until even later in this survey can we speak of
such formations *not* defined according to traditional notions of "activism" and public-
policy-geared ambition. But there is every reason to believe that the current circumstance of black intellectuals, centered in the mainstream academy, in large measure,
requires, not that it would simply be a commendable thing to happen, a profound
rethinking of what it means to be an "activist": in short, the current period – and by
that I mean the world from ca. 1968, on – will take us far toward deciding the *status of
ideas* as a *political object*, or should we say, more precisely, toward the removal of the
stigma of ideas as the "elitist" marque of irrelevance? While the signs of such a transition taking place are not always evident or positive, we should allow ourselves some
measure of hope for its fulfillment.

All along, it seems, the efficacy of ideas has been decidedly linked in black community to their *practical* import and application. For instance, the American Negro
Academy was founded with the aim of "undertaking 'the civilization of the Negro race
in the United States, by the scientific processes of literature, art, and philosophy'" (*The
Golden Age*, 73). This "ideology of elitist reform," however, was recurrent along several
lines of stress, not the least of which was the club movement among African-American
women. Between 1893 and 1895, the Colored Women's League of Washington, D.C.
and the Woman's Era Club of Boston solicited black American women's support in the
formation of a national network. The first national convention to that effect was held
at Berkeley Hall, Boston, July 29–31, 1895 (*The Golden Age*, 105–6). Arguing that the
women's club movement was closer in spirit to the radical egalitarianism of Frederick
Douglass than to the "committed mystical" nationalism of Alexander Crummell, Moses
points out that the women "accepted the idea that blacks as a group should be concerned about the problems of race recognition, self-help, and 'Civilization'" (*The Golden

95

Age, 103). In the post-reconstruction era, as a repressive regime once again clamped down on black movement, the National Association of Colored Women – the heir of the National Federation of Afro-American Women – identified two key problems: (1) the sexual exploitation of black women, one of slavery's fundamental legacies, and (2) the installation of bourgeois values in black family life – "They were concerned with trying to introduce standards of genteel Victorian domesticity into the cabins of Georgia and Alabama peasant women" (*The Golden Age*, 104). While it is fair to say that the black women's movement was solidly middle-class in origins, with many of its leaders – Ida Wells Barnett, Mary Church Terrell, Josephine St. Pierre Ruffin, among others – ensconced in male-headed households, it would be incorrect to read its class allegiances in a negative light. I am suggesting, consequently, that "elitism" and its bourgeois placement are not necessarily or automatically questionable and dubious, even though we are compelled, with a good deal of justification, to try to discern *motive* and keep it in mind.

In early chapters of Dorothy Sterling's *We Are Your Sisters* (1984), the organizational forms of mutual aid societies, founded by free black women in the northern United States, decades before the Civil War, are thoroughly explored. Attached in many cases to black churches, like New York's St. Philip's and Philadelphia's Mother Bethel, these early nineteenth-century protocols of self-help and mutual benefit offer a paradigmatic instance of the sorts of programs that would blossom on freedom's horizon. They also signal the extent of independent critical judgment that African-American women have often exercised in their own and their community's behalf. The iconography that congeals around the late twentieth century's "Welfare Queen," when viewed against the long perspective of the historic background, is adjudged, quite rightly, to belong to the repertoire of disparagement and dehumanization that is systematically pressed into service against African-American women.

An observer encounters various asymmetrical arrangements in the approach to historiographies on black intellectual work, and one of the forms that such asymmetries assume (which this writing has not altogether avoided) cuts along the gender divide: When the contributions of black women are considered at all, the emplotment takes the shape of the account of a collective action. In rather stark contrast, the conceptual narratives that track black men's creative enterprise pursue the fortunes of a normative biographical discourse, an "official" account that relies on what we called earlier the "great man" theory of history. Variously named, the "great man" theory positions itself at the top of a supposed hierarchical order that, in the words of certain black preachers, "sits high and looks low." It is almost as if female gender by definition here belongs to the "masses" that is itself as much a narrative or literary device and analytical tool as the "great man." This observation is not meant to say that there is in fact no social and economic differentiation among African Americans, but it seems to me that we can systematically address it only as the relatedness of class interests, rather than the reified agencies of an inherent distinctiveness, or its absence. Consequently, historical materialist analyses of African-American/Diasporic cultures have attracted, for all their prestige, only sporadic articulation, especially with regard to United States minority cultures. There are certainly notable exceptions, among them, the work of Angela Davis, Walter Rodney, Manning Marable, Adolph Reed, and the veteran thinkers of these formations, including W. E. B. Du Bois, C. L. R. James, and Eric Williams. More surprisingly, even when such analyses are attempted, *as praxes*, i.e., the sixties initiatives of the National Black Panther Party and its breakfast programs, they sometimes persist in uneasy juxtaposition with authoritarian, even para-military, display, and as a result, perpetuate masculinist dispositions, *tout court*. One looks long for a sustained social and political analysis of black culture that does not hanker after *essence* of one kind or another, so that even the collective narratives on black women's work are subtended by the presumption that collectivism "belongs" to African-American women, or ought to, as a metaphysical property. Consequently, one of the major tasks for culture workers now and to come will be a thorough rehauling of black intellectual/historiographical configurations with a couple of goals in mind. One of them is expressed in a formulation which I borrow from Theodor Adorno's *Dialectic of Enlightenment*: The cognizing subject is not merely concerned with a determination of "the abstract spatiotemporal relations of the facts which allow them just to be grasped, but on the contrary to conceive them as the *superficies, as mediated conceptual moments* which come to fulfillment only in the development of their social, historical, and human significance" (26–7; emphasis mine).

It is fair to say that black nationalist thought not only inscribes a sequence of "conceptual moments" and actions that we can trace, more or less successfully, from the marronnage movements of the seventeenth century, through the period of the Civil Rights movement and its Black Power stages in the latter half of the twentieth, but that it also demarcates amorphous layers of feeling about "blackness" that elude systematic categorization. From that angle, black nationalist sentiment might be inserted into any number of analytical and artistic determinations as a kind of pretextual motive. The latter is roughly analogous to Robert Stepto's concept of the "pre-generic myth of literacy" as the elusive moment of origination regarding black writing in the African Diaspora. Against strictures on the word, black personality asserted its will to knowledge/power at great peril to his/her physical being, as Frederick Douglass attested in his 1845 *Narrative*. But these instances of what might be thought of as the "always-already-there" of black culture are not mystical forces, but are, rather, located in the historical particularity of concrete material practices, borne out of the "juridical non-existence" of the enslaved, which, according to Louis Sala-Molins, constituted "their one and only legal definition" (*Le Code Noir ou le calvaire de Canaan* [*The Black Code or the Cross of Canaan*], 24). Black writing might be said, then, to be haunted by that "other" text, which does not always "announce" itself, whatever the provenance and destination of the project.

Marxist analysis, or historical materialist discourse, more generally speaking, has sustained a checkered career in African-American cultural work for quite complicated reasons, not the least among them, black nationalist practice and sentiment itself, serving as a brake on apparently race-neutral readings. That the American scene, under the impetus of Cold War politics, has been virtually bereft of any radical critique whatsoever throws its weight in the balance. The ravages of the McCarthy years and its frightening and widespread communist paranoia, while focused in the late forties and fifties, have exerted an enormous influence on national life. What it means, quite simply, is that any radical thought, native or otherwise, is assimilated, with stunning ease, to patterns of interpretation nearly as time-worn as the century itself. Even

97

though the US Civil Rights crusade might be regarded as the second emancipatory movement on behalf of African Americans (and other disenfranchised groups, as a result), the phenomenon itself, sweeping and inclusive in its focus and dynamics, from public accommodations, to voting rights, was, above all else, a high moral assault on the vast hypocrisies of American democratic institutions. The benefits flowing from it were decisive, but chief among them, the opening up of political discourse to an entirely new repertory of persuasions: in other words, it was a matter of utmost irony that the United States Constitution, virtually meaningless with regard to black rights, was redis-covered in a powerful surge of creative energies that melded Ghandian teachings (the "satyagraha," or the "truth-love force"), civil disobedience, American style, as defined by Henry David Thoreau, Protestant Christianity and its focus on the Gospels, with the affecting rhetorical arts of black preaching and witness; in short, the entire period, stretching, roughly, from the Potsdam Conference of 1945 and the end of World War II, to the withdrawal of US military forces from Vietnam, nearly three decades later, was one of the century's most vital lessons in a living democracy. From that angle, it is as though McCarthyism had not happened at all, or that its ill-effects were annulled by a Left movement that had renewed the efficacies of a progressive agenda. For our time, then, Civil Rights, naming an entire national era, was the profoundly radical analysis that owed little to European intellectual traditions of dialectical thought.

However, beneath its stunning successes, helped along by the electronics medium of television and the institution of the thirty-minute "Evening News" format, which brought into American living rooms unforgettable images of renegade American sher-iffs, siccing police dogs on American citizens, the Civil Rights Movement poised black middle and working classes to take greatest advantage of its initiatives. There is every reason to believe now that its rapid-fire united front, going, apparently, from campaign to campaign, was *theoretically* incoherent, or, at best, incomplete, in its reliance on charismatic leaders, as its rear flanks were exposed by the Nation of Islam, during the career of Malcolm El-Hajj Malik El Shabazz, on the one hand, and the National Black Panther Party, on the other, with various Africanist-inspired movements that accom-modated to neither in between. Martin Luther King himself sounded, perhaps, the most eloquent critique of the movement that he had led when he took up the cause of the black garbage workers in Memphis and vowed to return to the nation's capital for the Poor People's March of August 1968. Had this turn toward political economy and its implications for labor by the nation's finest preacher finally made him, by the spring of 1968, insuperable to his enemies? In any case, many observers regard the Poor People's Campaign as a new King phase that shifted his sights toward foreign policy and those elements of the black population lowest down: in effect, the heart of the transforma-tion had been rudely revealed – those men and women *not* bound for the university, or the four-star restaurants of the nation's leading cities, or even as King himself had observed, those who now had the right to vote unharrassed, but had nothing to vote for. From here, the next step would not be difficult to take, if one dared, to wit, the cross-racial, cross-cultural ramifications of *homo economicus*, and *that* would require a rather different analysis.

But what reading of political economy would be apposite to an intractable American scene? And would it have to be invented? The Civil Rights Movement had demonstrated what a homegrown radicalism could accomplish, but its work was incomplete, and, as

98

turn-of-the-century politics are revealing in fabulous differentials of wealth and access, remains unfinished. The impression, however, that post-Civil Rights questions of the most fundamental inquiry for Left intellectuals are unique to this moment is an erroneous one. American radicalism has struggled for a place on the American scene for the last century and more, as Philip Foner attends the problematics in *American socialism and Black Americans* (1977). Foner points out that communitarian movements in US society were fairly numerous as early as the pre-Jacksonian era by way of Owenite and Fourieristic utopian formations, many of them located in the then-western territories; between 1820 and 1850, the countryside "was liberally dotted" with land reform movements, bent on the revision of notions of private property (4–5ff). These secular and religious communities more often than not failed, as a large number of German immigrants, "exiles from the Revolutions of 1830 and 1848," entered the country with their own ideas about land reform and "cooperative handicraft enterprises." Marxist thought in its American provenance commenced with the entry of a young Prussian lieutenant, Joseph Weydemeyer, who met Karl Marx on a visit to Brussels, joined the Communist League, and with the decline of revolutionary fervor, left Germany in 1850. By way of Switzerland, Weydemeyer settled in New York in November 1851.

Foner's narrative suggests, contrary to what traditional scholarship on American socialism usually tells us, that socialists did take decisions on political issues concerning African Americans and could hardly have avoided it, given the deepening crisis of slavery, from the ban on the trade, down to the eve of war – approximately half a century. The cause of abolition for the utopian socialists, though, was ever the problem of labor that found expression in binaristic form – *wage slavery vs. chattel slavery*: if the former were the central concern for the working class, then was it not true that the latter was simply a "distraction" from the larger aim? (10). In fact, Frederick Douglass is said to have grown quite irritated with one John A. Collins, general agent of the Massachusetts Anti-Slavery Society, who wanted to exploit abolitionist sentiments to the advantage of the utopian socialists: crowds, for instance, who had come to hear Douglass speak (at the 1843 Anti-Slavery Convention in Syracuse, for example) were put upon, Douglass felt, to listen to Collins argue that the cause of slavery was "a mere dabbling with effects"! (12). The logic went something like this: the anti-slavery movement ought to be concerned "not to free Negro slaves alone, but to remove the cause which makes us all slaves" (11).

It does not take rocket science to understand how pressed a recently-emancipated black progressive (or even one, longer emancipated, as in *now*) might have felt in seeing himself caught between two related truths, simultaneously urgent. But this recorded instance would not be the last time by any stretch of the imagination that the black progressive/intellectual would be compromised in a pseudo-contradictory closure that would compel him to *choose* between his right eye and the left, between one of his limbs and an eyeball. (Today's gender politics in black community seem exactly analogous to this chapter from the long freedom struggle.) The dilemma was that Douglass and his abolitionist colleagues, among them, Charles Lenox Remond, supported the "utopian socialists' right – and even duty – to advocate their principles," but resented their insistence that "the abolition of wage slavery should take priority. . . ." (12). Certainly Douglass knew, on the pulse of the nerve, that the struggle against chattel slavery was hardly "meaningless," as Marx himself would write in the *Vienna Presse* of November 7, 1861: "Events themselves drive to the promulgation of the decisive slogan – the emancipation of the slaves" (32).

It appears, then, that positions in socialist thought have always been drawn up against race matters on the American scene and that the skepticism that black intellectuals have experienced regarding its efficacy is concentrated in this knotty complication. Foner's work traces this trajectory in considerable detail, from the career of Peter H. Clark, who, in March, 1877, would become "the first black American to identify himself publicly with socialism" (45), to the black labor movement on the eve of World War II and the role of A. Philip Randolph in the initiatives taken by the Negro Work Subcommittee of the socialist party (363ff). Revised cartographies of the American intellectual project will have to perform more of the sort of work that Foner accomplished in *American Socialism and Black Americans*, and that is to say, a comparative reading between the flows and distributions of stress and strain among variously positioned social subjects as culture workers. The peak points in radical praxis will have to be reexamined as well, with their center of gravity now running through the Russian Revolution of 1917 and "ten days that shook the world," through the subsequent "red scares" of the 1920s and leftist responses to the Great Depression, through the currencies of Civil Rights, the Vietnam War protest, and a revitalized women's movement, and the dormancy into which the American Left has supposedly fallen since the eighties and the diverse sociopolitical persuasions of Reaganism. While we usually attribute modernist innovations to the stage of the twenties, for example, and radicalism to the next decade, as if it were a revolt against a revolt, there is a good deal of evidence to suggest that twentieth-century American radicalism actually carries over from the period of the Civil War and post-Reconstruction, as it sustains a varied countenance: Foner's companion volume on black socialist preachers of the opening decade of the new century highlights the writings of this formation; for them – including the Reverends James Theodore Holly, George Washington Woodbey, and George W. Slater – the Socialist party had nothing to offer the Negro that it was not prepared to win for whites: "in the main, the plight of blacks under capitalism, like that of whites, would be solved automatically under socialism" (*Black Socialist Preacher*, 1–2). While the preachers did not criticize the party for not addressing disenfranchisement, segregation, lynching, and southern peonage, they did maintain that blacks would benefit from a "socialist victory" because, among the working class, they were the worst off, regarding wages, job protection, education, and the vitals of food, shelter, and clothing (*Black Socialist Preacher*, 2). Reverend Woodbey's "Plan to Reach the Negro," published in the *Ohio Socialist Bulletin*, February, 1909, advanced the notion that as members of the working class, blacks must be taught class consciousness, and inasmuch as the church was centrally installed in community life, then the socialists ought to go to the Negroes in their churches. Frequently jailed for his activism between 1902 and 1908, Woodbey joined the Populist party in 1900 and stood for office in both the Democratic and Populist parties, later on, effecting common cause with Eugene Debs and the Industrial Workers of the World.

As we have seen, the assimilation of the "black problem" to that of labor and the working class was not a new position for the socialists and, oddly enough, appears recycled in our time as the middling and eviscerated dogma of political centrism, having turned up as Bill Clinton's "answer" to American minorities, especially African Americans, during the 1992 presidential campaign as "job growth." It might be stated as a general rule that under the press of consumer marketing and advertising, the American waves of radicalism wash out, eventually, as pablum. This shrewd "domestication of dissent," which transforms the entire range of political speech into market equivalences, works hand-in-glove with the always-present-tense of television and now the internet to induce the profoundest historical oblivion. From that angle, the nation "forgets" its political and discursive past and how much of it is the unfolding of a twin fetish – that of race and capitalist exchange. An analysis that pursues only one element of this nested semiosis will be only partially articulate, as the conceptual narrative we continue to try to invent will expose such interrelatedness once again; but what appears as the brand new element of conceptualization perhaps overwhelms any other single factor, and that is the media combine in its threat to the cultures of literacy. For black intellectuals to behave as if post-modernist practices and economies (because they reject the idea) do not bear down with considerable force on the life worlds that they address marks a form of suicide. In brief, the modern and postmodern syntheses of material, discursive, epistemic, symbolic, and political practices constitute the full range of human activity that black intellectuals are called upon to penetrate – no less.

It is probably inaccurate to speak of changes in America's predominantly white institutions, as of fall 1968 and the subsequent period, as "revolutionary." But if we think of this outcome in relative terms – against what had been the case until that time – then the opening semester of that academic year did indeed play host to radical transformation in the constituent elements of higher learning in the United States. At the level of student personnel, young African Americans in larger numbers – many of them "veterans" from the Black Power revolt and its parent movement – enrolled in such institutions across the country. The installation of Black Studies programs complemented these initiatives that had been enabled by the 1965 Civil Rights Act and Lyndon Johnson's Executive Order #11246, forbidding race-based discrimination on the part of any interlocutor in contractural relations with the federal government. But there had been, at heart, nothing sudden about 1968, even though it strikes the memory, in the cold unblinking certitude of a handful of irrevocable facts – the assassinations of Martin Luther King and Robert F. Kennedy nearly eight weeks apart, to the day, and the massacre of youth in the streets of Chicago during the month of August – as the year that exceeded its calendrical allotment. Despite that, the court-ordered desegregation of the nation's public school systems had not only prepared the ground for '68, but had also established the southern tier – ironically enough – as the weather front of change; state universities throughout the region, under fire from black plaintiffs, had fallen like dominoes between 1959 and 1964, confirming the NAACP's legal defense team as a formidable opponent in the cause of social justice. From the vantage of *Brown V. (Topeka) Board*, 1954, and what its successes had permitted, fall '68 strikes the imagination as the next predictable step. In crucial ways, it became the theatre of action from which the current phase of black intellectual activity was launched.

We can do nothing more than sketch here, in the briefest of terms, what 1968 has entailed for black creative thought: with a velocity that its beneficiaries could not have anticipated with the least degree of accuracy, '68 marks the relocation of black creative thinkers; previously situated in the community, or its extension by way of what comprises membership in the United Negro College Fund, black intellectuals were largely responsible for training thousands of black youth for the professional markets; statistics here would be instructive, but it is safe to guess, in their absence, that the cadres of doctors, lawyers, teachers, preachers, engineers, homemakers, and the entire range of the skilled work force in black community were the principal charge of proud institutions from Xavier University, Louisiana, and Bethune-Cookman, Florida, to Fisk University, Nashville, and Lincoln University, Pennsylvania, and Howard University, Washington, D.C., from the close of the Civil War, to the period of Civil Rights – the better part of the inaugural (and difficult) century of freedom. Too many of these figures are anonymous, as their work achieved "publication" in the hearts of the sons and the daughters of the black working class. (Ralph Ellison recalls what must be a paradigmatic instance in the case of music teacher, Hazel Harrison, at Tuskegee, in the brilliant formulations that make up "The Little Man at Chehaw Station.") But "something within," to echo the words of Ma Rainey's piano man, Thomas Dorsey, must have been conveyed in these classrooms that sped the baccalaureate back to those venues from which he and she had come, although it would be dishonest to claim that the iron laws of segregation were not a critical factor in the outcome. The independent culture worker in this synthesis lived in the neighborhood, as poet Gwendolyn Brooks, when he was not the self-induced subject of exile, as Richard Wright and James Baldwin, as well as Chester Himes and others. In short, prior to 1968, the black intellectual might be thought of as something of a *mole* in the system – hidden, subterranean, and quite effective in the production of competence in subjects who were neither expected, nor encouraged, to be fine by the society at large. In short, the black teacher, preacher, coach, and principal taught their people to read, to speak, to claim the dignity and the responsibility of person as a God-given right. In the most radical sense of the word, these culture workers were "educators."

To suggest that institutions in the United Negro College Fund experienced sudden collapse as of 1968 would overdraw the picture, but a trend line was established that started to propel talent away from the traditional structures. Athletic recruiters from the Big Ten and the Big Eight Conferences occasionally offered scholarships to gifted athletes as early as the mid-fifties, as even more rarely, black prodigies in mathematics and the sciences were spotted by the Massachusetts Institute of Technology, Carnegie-Mellon, and Harvard, among other organizations, in the era of Sputnik. For the most part, however, the community's most talented young scholars were trained in black institutions by black personnel; at the level of the professoriat, the recruitment of black teachers by predominantly white schools was so unheard of that when it did occur, after 1960, it was genuine news and *one at a time*. Against this background of occasional, even exotic, penetration, then, 1968 marks a watershed.

When the definitive narratives concerning the subsequent thirty-year synthesis are finally drafted, the observers will want to investigate the following:

1   While we cannot assert, even remotely, that there was no intellectual social formation among African Americans, prior to the late sixties, we can say quite justifiably that a black intellectual class was granted access to the nation's discursive/epistemic structures in relatively dramatic ways; we mean primarily its participation in the "culture industry" by way of publishing apparatuses. Once open almost exclusively to black creative writers and a handful of iconic figures, who broke through the nation's

intellectual apartheid, the publishing industry created a market share (or *found* one) devoted to "Black Studies." This trend has not slowed down, as it has been encouraged by the proliferation of journals and periodicals in the fields of the Humanities, especially those related to literary/textual criticism, women's studies, and cultural studies.

2   Intellectual life in black community is now conducted, almost exclusively, in mainstream institutions, i.e., the premier state universities, the Big Ten, the Ivy League, the Seven Sisters, the Little Ivies, etc. For that reason, the intellectuals must now rethink the meaning of "community" itself and how their various repositionings have redrawn the boundaries of belonging and affiliation.

3   Because Black Studies/Africana is historically positioned the way it is, the intellectuals cannot abandon the *critical project*, now threatened by gestures too complex to articulate on the run, but among them, the appropriation of African-American scholarship and writing by self-interested commodification and "ownership," as well as an unexamined gender politics that bears all the earmarks of a retrogressive lapse. It would be unfortunate if this vital and historic movement bogged down now in mediocre practice, failed development, and conservative political trends, and the latter all seem as much a possibility as any other outcome. If the black intellectual remains in crisis today, it is precisely because she/he must shatter a *status quo* that has brought that very subject – ironically enough – a degree of visibility unprecedented in the life of the nation.

Note

1   Excerpts from Alain Locke's dissertation were published some years ago in a special number of the *Harvard Advocate*, "Odyssey: A Search for Home," vol. CVIII, no. 4 (Spring, 1974).

Works Cited

Adorno, Theodor and Max Horkheimer. *Dialectic of Enlightenment*. Trans. John Cumming. New York: Continuum, 1998.

Black Socialist Preacher: The Teachings of Reverend George Washington Woodbey and His Disciple, Rev. G. W. Slater, Jr. ed. with intro. Philip S. Foner. Foreword by Congressman Ronald V. Dellums. San Francisco: Synthesis Publications, 1983.

Foner, Philip. *American Socialism and Black Americans: From the Age of Jackson to World War II*. Contributions in Afro-American and African Studies, number 33. Westport, Connecticut: Greenwood Press, 1977.

Hull, Gloria. *Color, Sex, and Poetry: Three Women Writers of the Harlem Renaissance*. Bloomington: Indiana University Press, 1987.

James, Joy. *Transcending the Talented Tenth: Black Leaders and American Intellectuals*. New York: Routledge, 1997.

Katz, William Loren, ed. *The American Negro: His History and Literature*. New York: Arno Press, 1969.

Moses, Wilson. *The Golden Age of Black Nationalism, 1850–1925*. New York: Oxford University Press, 1978.

The New Negro, ed. Alain Locke, with a preface by Robert Hayden. New York: Atheneum, 1977.

The Norton Anthology of African-American Literature, ed. Henry Louis Gates, Jr. and Nellie Y. McKay. New York: W. W. Norton, 1996.

Sala-Molins, Louis. *Le Code Noir ou le calvaire de Canaan*. Pratiques Théoriques. Collection dirigée par Étienne Balibar et Dominique LeCourt. Paris: Presses Universitaires de France, 1987.

Stepto, Robert. *The Reconstruction of Instruction*. New York: Publications of the Modern Language Association, 1977.

Sterling, Dorothy, ed. *We Are Your Sister: Black Women in the Nineteenth Century*. New York: W. W. Norton, 1984.

Wall, Cheryl. *Women Writers of the Harlem Renaissance*. Bloomington: Indiana University Press, 1995.

Part II

THE MORAL AND POLITICAL
LEGACY OF SLAVERY

Introduction to Part II

The justification of slave revolts grounded the early appeal of black nationalism for unity and emancipation. To advocate violence as a means of liberation presupposes that such intentional social action can be carried out by slaves – a recognition of their agency and their ability to engage in reflective thought regarding their plight. Lewis Gordon's contention that the history of black thought in America has been shaped by these existential circumstances must be well-taken. In the white mind of nineteenth-century America the alternative to slavery was extermination. As in the historic case of Native Americans, the rationale for this policy was that blacks are not full-fledged humans. Under conditions of enslavement the entire social apparatus was constructed to maintain this view of African Americans, setting the stage for a protracted struggle for social change that continues into the present. There were many scientific and legal views adduced to support the conception of blacks as inferior that prevailed in the nineteenth century. Ronald A. T. Judy reflects on the status of blacks in nineteenth-century ethnology. Anita L. Allen and Thaddeus Pope discuss the appeal to social contract theory in several important nineteenth-century court cases regarding the legal status of African slaves. While subsequent legal change that resulted in a ban on slavery is to be applauded, some African-American philosophers maintain that the wrongness of slavery demands more than a moral correction of false reasoning in science and law. Bernard R. Boxill defends the claim that social justice requires a restoration of the moral order by compensating the injured.

A key ingredient in the reconceptualization of blacks as humans has been the scientific account of their ability to use language, especially with regard to its symbolic function. Ronald Judy discusses the rise of philology and ethnology as a science that aimed to provide an understanding of the meaningfulness of representations of the world in language by the fixing of linguistic expression in typography. This science operated on the assumption that there is a correspondence of language, experience and thought. Uncertainty about whether a transcription captures the meaning of a representational utterance stems from the ethnographer's lack of knowledge as to whether the representation has conveyed the utterer's experience. Such uncertainty raises the question of whether there is an objective basis for transcribing spoken language. This is not only a problem of translation, but also a problem of how knowledge is related to experience.

Judy discusses an 1839 letter written by a southern plantation owner, who also was a philologist, regarding the use of language by one of his slaves. He tells us that this letter, sent to another philologist, is concerned with the question of whether "Negro speech" involves a continuum of sound and expression, but no reference to "mental affectations." In his remarks regarding his slave's ability to speak Foulah, the plantation owner suggests that the slave has a conscious knowledge of his experience. This prompted a question regarding the adequacy of his transcription. Judy points out that the plantation owner was faced with a question of "cognitive indeterminacy," a problem that derives from the relationship between language use and cultural identity. The plantation owner's attempt to transcribe his slave's speech involves an understanding of how signs relate to other signs, that is, the relation of people, things, and thought. Judy notes that, in this case, "there is no adjudicating referential instance that can determine the proper correspondence between sign and referent."

Judy employs a Kantian view of the relationship between perception and thought to explicate certain problems of linguistic reference and "phenomenal intentionality." On his reading of Kant's *Inaugural Dissertation* the ability of reason to supersede the "phenomenal materiality of nature" is a basis for cognition. Kant's distinction between terror and fear is used to illustrate the superiority of thought over phenomenal events. Judy explains that terror involves a real threat of bodily harm, but fear results from thinking, and is not determined by phenomenal events. This bears on the question of representation with regard to the use of symbols as indirect representation in the case of a concept which only reason can think. Judy asks, "What happens when the symbol presents materiality and gives meaning as a lie?" The plantation owner's lack of understanding of his slave's "utterance" was due to his not having any universal concept that would make sense of his slave's experience. To the extent that his slave thinks symbolically, he appears exceptional for the plantation owner. In this case symbolic representation mediates between theoretical understanding and reflective experience. Through the slave's "disappearing expression" the plantation owner encounters "an active intellect that is unknowable."

The scientific view of African slaves as less than human held by the plantation owner and other nineteenth-century philologists was sustained by the legal system. Anita Allen and Thaddeus Pope argue that the courts sometimes relied on the social contract theory made popular by the Founding Fathers to justify excluding blacks from constitutional protection of their basic human rights. In the famous *Dred Scott* case the Supreme Court upheld the argument that because Scott was of African descent, he could not be understood to have the citizenship status necessary to sue in federal court. The upshot of this decision was that the framers of the Constitution never intended blacks to be included as equals with full citizenship rights.

Another way social contract theory was used by judges to support slavery was by positing a hypothetical contract under which blacks are understood to have exercised rational choice to subordinate themselves to whites. According to the logic of the Hobbesian account, blacks have consented to such an arrangement to escape the anarchy of the state of nature. Given their inferior position they have no choice but to agree to the disadvantageous terms offered by superior whites. This "best deal" argument appeals to an implied rational consent. The courts also relied on arguments based on consent and just war theory to support slavery. Conquered blacks assent to their own enslavement as the preferred alternative to death. In *Mitchell v. Wells* Justice Taney appealed to conquest as a justification of slavery, noting that blacks as a group are a "subjugated" race because "the victor might enslave the vanquished."

What the cases discussed by Allen and Pope show is that, although slavery is condemned by the liberal ideals of contemporary social contract theory, nineteenth-century judges also employed various tenets of that view to lend support to slavery. The injustice of slavery is not simply a legal issue that, through a constitutional amendment, has now been resolved. The lingering ethical question of whether those who were enslaved are due compensation is critically examined by Bernard Boxill. He prefers the narrower term "reparations" because it applies only to the repairing of losses and deficiencies that result from injustice. Along with slavery, the particular injustice includes Jim Crow policies and laws that discriminated against the ancestors of African Americans. As a sequel to his classic essay, "The Morality of Reparations," Boxill focuses here exclusively on a backward-looking argument he derives from John Locke's account in the *Second Treatise*. He interprets Locke to hold that when someone transgresses causing injury, a right of reparations is held against the particular transgressor who caused the damage, allowing the injured to seek as much reparation as will make "satisfaction" for the damage suffered. Rather than a sanction of vengeance, Locke understood reparations to be an attempt to bring the injured to the condition they were in before they were damaged.

Boxill takes Locke's remarks regarding the just conqueror's right of reparation to imply that the injured can lay claim to the goods the children inherit in order to repair the damages. He insists that this applies to the injury sustained as a result of slavery or discrimination. This suggests that children of unjust parents are not immune to claims for reparation from those their parents injured. To what extent, however, does this suggestion apply to inherited property? Following Locke, Boxill maintains that when the right of reparation conflicts with the right of inheritance, the right of reparation gets precedence over inheritance to the extent that the children will not be harmed by this, with the only stipulation being that there can be no claim against property the children did not inherit.

When applying Locke's doctrine to the case for black reparations Boxill points out that slaves had titles for reparation against their slavemasters and that Locke allows descendents to renew the appeal for reparation, with the understanding that African Americans inherit titles from their slave ancestors and the master's children have inherited estates. Boxill considers the question of whether whites who innocently benefit from discrimination against blacks owe reparations. He then challenges the assumption that most whites innocently benefit from injuries to blacks, charging that European immigrants came to America to take advantage of their white privilege. He denies that a person who receives benefits he does not consent to receive incurs no obligations. According to Boxill, if white immigrants would not have consented to receiving the benefits had they been fully informed, then preferential treatment provides an opportunity to reject the unfair advantage the benefits give them.

6

Kant and Knowledge of
Disappearing Expression

RONALD A. T. JUDY

Early on in philology's career in the US, in 1839 to be precise, just as historicism was becoming ensconced at Harvard as the doctrine of Americanization – expressed at the time in terms of "Manifest Destiny" – there circulated a document, a letter, that posed a problematic whose scope entailed the demise of the still young science. From our current perspective in space and time, we are very much aware that this early demise of the science of philology in the US did not take place. More than aspects of its methodology were subsequently in evidence in the academic fields of history and sociology, where Romantic historicism appropriated Darwin, producing the inanities of social Darwinism. To appreciate why the letter in question failed to bring about philology's demise, we need to recall some things about the uniqueness of philology in that country at that time.

Like its contemporary, Romance philology in Germany, philology in the US was committed to the idea of historical development manifest in the individual *Volksgeist*.[1] Unlike German Romance philology, however, the scholarship of US philology was not on the corpus of Latin and Latin derivative vernacular literatures, but on a disparate mass of expressions and practices, the study of which was known at the time as "ethnology." Ethnological philology, or as one of its earliest practitioners, William Hodgson, called it, "comparative philology," aimed at a rigorous scientific understanding of those *Volk* (here understood in the problematical sense of race) in whose expression historical development was not manifested. In the first instance, the scholarship of ethnological philology was concerned with those populations who had no literary record, and whose social forms were deemed to be so agrammatic that they could only be categorized by the indications of language, to paraphrase Hodgson, who invokes Herder's designation of language as *das ewige Band der Menschen* [the eternal binder of men] in order to relate the uncertain science of ethnological philology to its historicist roots (60).

What this meant, of course, was that the scholarship of ethnological philology aimed at generating a historic record of the intelligence – the way thought was manifested – of those peoples who were destined to extinction according to the laws of historical development. This was not the study of primitives who function as the thesis in the dialectic of historical human development, such that their intelligence forms the *almost like how do "we" talk to "them"? What is their voice of intelligence?*

basis for a common human experience or expression. On the contrary, for the scholars of ethnological philology, the peoples under investigation not only differed greatly among themselves, and from the people of Europe, whose intelligence the North American colonist and his descendants were heir to, but there was no common substrate of classical thought or culture which related them to Europe or colonial America.

This is an extremely problematic issue. For what is perhaps most unique about the situation of ethnological philology in the US is that it did not seek to delineate the unity of thought that characterizes historical development as manifested in the unfolding of human intelligence in material culture from the classical east towards the west. The principal difference between Romance philology in Germany and ethnological philology in the US was their respective object fields. Ethnological philology no less than Romance philology was conceptually firmly rooted in the absolute universality of historicism. That is, it remained committed to the dialectical conception of humanity as a function of historical development, manifested in the material cultural expressions of individual *Volksgeist*, whose relation to each other is determined by a law of dialectic so that what at first appears particular is ultimately revealed to be a moment in the movement of a unified thought. Their common conceptual foundations notwithstanding, ethnological philology in the US presumed to study almost exclusively those populations that supposedly could not be included in that development.

In other words, ethnological philology presumed a world outside of the history of thought, peopled by creatures whose expressions were not easily accessible to reason. The extent to which they could even be deemed to be human was determined by the extent to which it could be demonstrated that their material cultural expressions manifested recognizable thought. This, of course, ought to be the question: What is thought? But that was not at all in question for ethnology. The history of thought at all of concern was most clearly manifested in methodology – i.e., the history of ideas – and less clearly manifested in the variegated material expressions of culture. No, thought, per se, was not in question for ethnological philology in the US. What was in question was whether or not thought was manifested in the expressions of all those creatures who appear to be humans. The task of ethnological philology, then, was to establish a scientific basis for understanding and relating to those "peoples" engaged in thoughtless expression. *? such* In this sense, its chief object of study was language or all that is linguistic. More specifically, its scholarship was concerned with the classification of tribes and nations in terms of their formal linguistic similarities. Such classification on the basis of linguistic evidence became the chief preoccupation of the American Ethnological Society, which later became the American Anthropological Society, and which under the stewardship of Boas established the field of ethnolinguistics.

So we see that from its infancy ethnological philology was concerned with a scientific understanding of the relationship between thought and linguistic expression. This concern would long outlast its early presumptions of social Darwinism, and continue into its subsequent articulations as ethnolinguistics, sociolinguistics, cultural anthropology, and in particularly aberrant modes in composition theory and cultural studies. It is important to bear in mind that in its foundational moment US ethnological philology presumed the people under investigation belonged to a world other than that of thought, a world of impressionistic experience. And so the task for the pioneer ethnologists was to devise a rigorous conception and methodology for mapping the meaningful practices of signification in that world to those of thoughtful expression, to translate experience into thought.

Translation, therefore, was as crucial an element of the early scholarship, as was classification. Indeed, the stability of the latter depended on the veracity of the former. Such translation always began with the first order representation of experience in verbal speech, and the graphic representation of the verbal. The transcription of verbal expression was the first order of business. Because the field was still unstable, in nearly every early case this meant devising a theory and method of transcription suitable to the immediate circumstance. A good deal of the business of the American Ethnological Society in the first 30 years of its existence was dedicated to the reporting on and comparative analysis of these theories and methods, in a befuddled effort to develop a standard methodology. This proved to be very difficult demanding work. Yet, for all of that, there persisted the conviction in a relationship of correspondence between experience and thought mediated by linguistic expression, and that this relationship was most accurately analyzed through typographic record. The tenets of this conviction are straightforward enough. Assuming that so called agrammatic illiterate peoples are in their expressions representing and organizing into some meaningful patterns impressions of the world, and that the meaningfulness of these representations is a function of some order, access to understanding that meaningfulness is through a scientific understanding of their language. Because of the inherently dynamic nature of language, such scientific understanding was facilitated by the fixing of linguistic expression in typography.

That this would, according to the presumed correspondence of experience, language, and thought, amount to the arresting of experience is readily apparent. The yield would be a specimen, subject to rules of confirmation and analysis. The genius of ethnological philology was in its understanding that such specimens could not be identified with dynamic experience, but only with its representations in language. Through the systematic collection and analysis of those representations and the discerning of their patterns or order of meaningfulness, the ethnologist could, in theory, reconstruct the fading world of experience. Fade as it may, the presumed endurance of typography as a stable regularized material record of the sought after experience, and the identification of such typography with historic authenticity, assured that even immanently extinct experience would become subject to thought. That is, it would become amenable as an object to the methodological practice of ethnology. As such, it would contribute to the perpetuation of the field.

Admittedly, there were moments of instability in the field, in which there was a high degree of uncertainty as to whether or not the transcription had caught the representational utterance, or, for the matter, whether the representation had indeed conveyed experience. These are well known problems of methodology, concerning issues of memory, perspective, and even the presumed materiality of thought itself. All of which cast dubious light on the assumption of historical development, or more to the point, the idea that thought progressing in time towards ever increasing perfection manifests its progress in discrete material forms. That, however, is not our concern just at this moment. Nor was it for the emerging science of ethnological philology, the fundamental hypothesis of which was that there is a quadripartite relationship of correspondence between experience, speaking, hearing, and thinking, whose function is, let us say, the

112

sign. Without this hypothesis there could be no science of ethnological philology, at least not one that could claim the objective classification and analysis of thoughtless experience manifested in verbal utterance.

But what does all of this have to do with the letter that circulated in 1839? It is precisely the hypothesis of quadripartite correspondence that the letter problematized. Having given the context in which it circulated, perhaps it is time to present the letter. It was written by James Hamilton Couper, Esq., the relatively well known owner of Hopeton Plantation on Saint Simons Island, Georgia, to his friend and fellow planta-tion owner, William B. Hodgson. I have written at some length elsewhere about this letter, and the two correspondents.[2] It suffices for purposes here to point out that both Couper and Hodgson were members of the American Ethnological Society, and that Hodgson was a founding member of the Society. He was also one of America's first orientalists and founder of the American Oriental Society. Having spent a number of years as a United States diplomat in North Africa, he became a strong proponent for ethnological, or as he termed it, comparative philology, achieving a status as expert in ethnological and linguistic matters of Africa. It was because of that acknowledged expertise that his friend Couper sent him the following letter:

> There are about a dozen or so negroes on this plantation who speak the Foulah lan-guage; but with one exception, they appear not to have been native born Foulahs; and to have acquired the language by having been for sometime in servitude among that nation. The exception I mention is a remarkable man for his opportunities; and as his history, country, and the information he possesses are interesting, I will give you, in detail, the results of the conversations I have had with him; feeling that everything coming from a person to whom Timbucto, Jenne, and Sego are familiar as household words cannot fail to be gratifying to one who has made Soudan a subject of research. . . . His native town is Kianah, in the district of Temourah, and in the kingdom of Massina.
>
> Tom, whose African name was Sali-bul-Ali, was purchased about the year 1800 by my father from the Bahamas islands, to which he had been brought from Anamaboo. . . . He has quickness of apprehension, strong powers of combination and calculation, a sound judgment, a singularly tenacious memory, and what is more rare in a slave, the faculty of forethought. He possesses great veracity and honesty. He is a strict Mohametan [sic]; abstains from spirituous liquors, and keeps the various fasts, particularly Rhamadan.[3]
>
> In his personal appearance, Tom is tall, thin, but well made. His features are small, forehead well developed, mouth well formed, with lips less protruding than is usual with the negro race, the nose flat, but not thick . . . The portrait of a *native of Haoussa*, in Pritchard's Natural History of Man, gives the general character of his head and face, and approaches more nearly to it than that of any other given of the African tribes (*NNASS* 74; see note 3).
>
> I will now give you his African reminiscences; and in doing so I will put down all names as nearly in accordance with his pronunciation, as the difficulty of seizing upon, and expressing the peculiarities of a foreign language, will admit of. You will perceive, that the proper names differ slightly from the received spelling; and that the vocabulary varies somewhat from those given by you, in the *Encyclopedia Americana*, and Pritchard in his *Physical Researches* (*NNASS* 69).
>
> You will, however, readily identify the words as belonging to the Foulah and Fellatah language. You will notice that in the numerals, a part are Foulah and a part Fellatah; and some common to both. A few such as *child*, differ from both (69).

Our concern here is exclusively with how the letter entails a compelling problematic that somehow contradicts the hypothesis of the quadripartite relationship of correspondence between experience, speaking, hearing, and thinking. As a consequence, I will forego any consideration of the problems of ethnographic classification so clearly expressed in the letter.[4] We need only note here that for both Couper and Hodgson the Negro was an instance of those people who inhabited the world outside of history. Hence, it was presumed that, in accordance with their nature, the natural speech of the Negro was composed purely of *signa naturalia* (natural signs), formally characterized by monosyllabic interjections, diphthongs and song, expressing ideas by the nature of the things of experience, as in their material properties. Such language is almost totally void of any *signa data* (poetic signs), and so gives evidence of how natural life and unmediated experience imprisons the Negro through their idiom. The Negro *signa naturalia* involves a continuum of sound and expression, but no indicative referentiality to mental affections. It is wholly commemorative, such that there is always something expressed about experience in the Negro's utterance, but nothing about self-reflective thought. That is, it recalls past phenomenal experiences almost to the point of being onomatopoetic. Thus, this cannot be a language that symbolizes thought.

By this view, in the Negro's natural language, the emotive opacity of the utterance should cause the idiom to draw attention to itself, to its instance of formation. The idiom becomes rhythmic and repetitious, a message that is somehow identical with its articulation. The question is, why is this not the case with Tom? What is it that enables him to express the peculiarities of a foreign (not natural) language? What, after all, is so exceptional about a nineteenth-century West African from the Senegambia speaking the Foulah language?

What made Tom such an exceptional Negro for Couper, and subsequently for Hodgson, was his capacity for presenting informational material for penetrating the emotive opacity of the utterance. In speaking Foulah, Tom caused the idiom to become somehow more transparent, drawing attention away from itself and its instance of formation towards the experiencing of self-reflective thought, which cast him in another light, that of reason. Couper's insistence that Tom has some sort of proprietary claim to the Foulah language serves to reiterate his capacity for the production of meaningful expression (he can represent knowledge of experience in the world), taking him toward the propriety of humanity. Tom ceases to be and, in point of fact never was, a Negro as a beast, becoming instead a Negro as a man. "The exception I mention [Tom], is a remarkable man for his opportunities." And Tom's opportunities are those of becoming human because he displays the effect of reflective investment of language, in addition to conscious knowledge of his experience. Tom's properties of language include memory and the capacity to present the narrative representation of his story, he has history – all of which is idiomatic. In this way, he is exceptional among Negroes because he manifests thought, and so falls into the world of history.

Thinking the historical formulation of thought, then, is the exigency that compels Couper to write his letter. The experience of Tom is both thought provoking and given to thinking in its being articulated in the *signa data* of Foulah. And it is this thinking and provoking of thought through the representation of datum that draws the focus of attention to Tom as an agent of thought, that is, as a self-conscious subject. Tom's subjectivity, and so humanity, is manifest in the representational function of his utter-

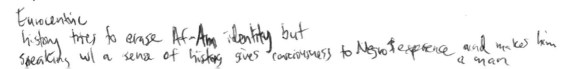
Eurocentric history tries to erase Af-Am identity but speaking w/ a sense of history gives consciousness to Negro experence and makes him a man

ances. Put differently, what he says to Couper in Foulah, and what he says about what he says in Foulah are symbolic representations of what he has experienced in the past. They are a type of signification that exhibit or display a systematic correlation of experience, thought, and expression. It is that system which attracts Couper's attention as the only material effects of Tom's experience available to him for analysis, and subsequently expert knowledge.

Initially, Couper's analysis amounts to no more than his gathering of Tom's thought in the Foulah language, which he presents to Hodgson so that the latter can elucidate the language with his expert knowledge. This gathering of thought, however, immediately encounters a problem of translation. As Couper puts it, regarding Tom's "African reminiscences": "I will put down all names as nearly in accordance with his pronunciation, as the difficulty of seizing upon, and expressing the peculiarities of a foreign language, will admit of" (*NNASS* 69). This signals a profound difficulty with apprehending the significance of Tom's speech; and apprehension is difficult because nothing can be seized upon in Tom's utterance, rather what can be "grasped" and transcribed by the letter is the ubiquitous process of difficulty in understanding everything expressed in the utterance of the idiom about the nature of the things of experience – i.e., their materiality. That materiality cannot be comprehend in the letter, and so there is a residual emotive opacity of the utterance that causes the idiom to still draw some attention to itself as the limitation of knowledge.

So the problem of translating Tom's *signa data* into a language of expertise proves to be a fundamental problem of how knowledge is related to experience. Let us tarry a while with this fundamental problem, for in so doing we will discover in it the threat that the letter poses for ethnological philology, as well as its subsequent derivative fields.

What Couper sends to Hodgson in the letter is as accurate a written reporting of what Tom said to him as he is capable of sending. In that report Couper uses paraphrase to portray in written words what the illiterate Tom has given him orally, presumably in English as well as Foulah, of his African experiences. In effect, Couper graphically describes the verbal representation of another's reminiscences. Contained in the letter is Couper's attempt to transcribe Tom's utterances, to graphically represent his experiencing of Tom's oral history. But, it turns out that as a transcription the letter is an absolute failure.

Simply put, Couper spells his idioms irregularly. In one instance he spells the name of one of the African cities of Tom's reminiscence as "Jenne"; elsewhere throughout the letter the same city is referred to as "Jennay." In reference to the fabled African city that so preoccupied the nineteenth-century European imagination, Couper first writes "Timbucto," and then five times "*Tumbootu*" (his italics).[5] Only the city of "Sego" appears throughout Couper's letter in a regular or consistent spelling. Nor is Couper alone in his irregular spellings. Hodgson spells the names of these cities with such irregularity in his *Notes on Northern Africa, the Sahara, and Soudan*, that confusion of reference is almost unavoidable. For example he spells Couper's "Timbucto" twice as "Timbuctoo," then once as "Tombutum," and "Tenbokto," and "Tombuctu" (the last three occurring all on the same page, 80). However, when citing from Leo Africanus he spells "Tombutu" (*NNASS* 61-2). Couper's "Jenne/Jennay" occurs once in Hodgson's book as "Jenneh," and then as "Yenni" (*NNASS* 80).[6] Regarding our concerns here, what is noteworthy about these instances of irregular spelling – or more accurately heterography – is how they indicate a persistent if not chronic problem that is not at all limited to the field of ethnological philology. This is the problem of determining an objective basis for transcribing spoken language.

In the instance of Couper's experience of Tom, the latter expresses more than disjuncted disembodied noise, he expresses a complexity of noises which as linguistic signs operate in a particular economy of conventional codes to signify something.[7] At the point where the effect of these codes and those of English meet, which, from our perspective, is in Couper's experiencing of this noise, there occurs an overlapping of signification processes, resulting in Couper's uncertain transcription. In Couper's employment of it, transcription is never meant to ground the scientific veracity of ethnology in the immediate representation of phenomenal experience (for Couper this would be the sounds of Tom's utterances). The objective validity of the transcriptions does not entail the correspondence of grapheme to phoneme (of graphic sign to sound), rather it entails the subsuming of the phenomenal impression (sound) under the schemata of understanding, in accordance with the language of ethnologists. What Couper's transcriptions signify are these schemata, and not Tom's phonemic significations.

The problem of Couper's heterography, therefore, threatens the very purpose for which Hodgson published his letter – i.e., the validation of ethnological philology's capacity to decipher experiential enigmas. This heterography is particularly troublesome because it indicates the failure of ethnology to establish a stable domain of reference. The uncertainty of Couper's spelling is not a trace of some residual material trait of Sali-bul-Ali's idiom (i.e., the material of its phonic qualities, its *continuum*) that resists the requisite comprehending expertise of the philologist. That poses no problem for Couper, having been displaced, along with Sali-bul-Ali, by Tom and his reminiscences. What is most significant about Couper's botched transcription is that it signals a fundamental conceptual crisis in the theory of signification on which his ethnology was predicated.

Recall that Couper was engaged in the project of achieving a scientific analysis and classification of diverse practices of articulating and organizing human experience into ordered systems of expression. While the first order concern of ethnological philology was linguistic expression in the specific sense of oral and graphic symbolizations of experience, the overall field of analysis was the ordering of symbols into systems of codes and meanings. Hodgson was clear in his understanding that these systems constitute the basis of the collective practices and customs of the African populations under study. Such an aggregation of practices according to a systematic code of meaning is what he understood as "culture." So, the scientific analysis of linguistic systems as symbolization of experience facilitated the analysis and categorization of human cultures in accordance with the then emerging "human sciences," or *Geisteswissenschaften*. Such a linguistic oriented *Kulturwissenschafte* ("cultural science"), whose principal premise was that there is a relationship of correspondence between language use and cultural identity, presumed a specific notion of the sign and its study.

In accordance with Hodgson's comparative philology (what we have been referencing as ethnological philology), studying the aggregation of diverse signifying practices specific to a people enables discerning the pattern and process of signification that defines the cultural horizon of that people, that is, the field in which their signs and

116

codes function as meaningful references to the world. The paramount interest with language, then, is in the relation of people, things and thought, which includes how signs
relate to other signs. It is not at all a far stretch, therefore, to infer that Hodgson's
working definition of the sign was, "something which stands to somebody for something in some respect or capacity."

A corollary to the premise that a sign is something that stands for something else
for somebody in some respect or capacity – a proof of which is provided in Tom's
articulation of the utterances – is that all signs as such are identical in this relationship of referentiality. Accordingly, the work of translation between signs – which is
what Couper is engaged in when transcribing Tom's utterances – is understood to be
that of transferring one instance of referentiality to another.

The question of referential value, or meaning, is at issue only insofar as the determination of the referential instance, the experience of reference, is concerned: the
exchange of signs results from the identification of different referential instances.
Establishing the sameness of what seems different is a matter of privileged perspective,
or expertise. There must, then, be an adjudicating referential instance, a transcendent
process of signification that establishes the totality of the domain of all referentiality,
which is to say, that can determine the proper correspondence between sign and referent. This, in turn, presupposes a theory or understanding of experience, or rather how
it is that signs refer to something. In other words, Hodgson asserting for ethnological
philology the status of scientific objectivity, rests upon specific epistemological claims
about the relationship between thought, expression, and experience.

In the face of such claims, the persistent illegibility of Tom's utterance for Couper
and Hodgson poses a significant problem of method. Which is why I have expressed the
problem of Tom's disappearing expression in an admittedly clumsy and involved formulation that seemingly inappropriately juxtaposes the problems of linguistic referentiality and phenomenal intentionality. That juxtaposition makes more obvious the
extent to which this problem necessarily entails an underlying challenge both to the
ideology of the history of philosophy which makes problematics of expression subordinate to the content of the idea, the issue of *cogito* (whether verifiable or axiomatic),
and the equally ideological conception of the history of semiotics which recognizes the
epistemological problematics of modern philosophy as problems of signifying by signs,
of conceptual relations.

With Couper's insistence on the translatability of that which remains unintelligible
we revisit a fundamental problematic of referentiality: the question of cognitive indeterminacy. By what means is the determination and reflection of a disparate object of
empirical experience, or intuition, possible when that intuited object cannot be adequately characterized by any determinate concept of reason? Given the significance of
this question for the fields of epistemology and anthropology as they have been construed since Kant, this problem posed through Tom's utterance warrants examination.

The way that the Tom problem poses the question of cognitive indeterminacy is by challenging somewhat anathematically ethnology's claims of there being a "cultural" experience. In order to apprehend, however fleetingly, what this means, a sighting must be
gained of the epistemological stakes entailed in the seemingly all too practical assertion
that one ought to know what one is talking about.

There is, after all, a tension between polyvariant relative knowledge and a reductive universality of reason that is implied in Couper's assertion that he has transcribed Tom's expressions. This tension describes the field wherein operates the major frame of reference for both the phenomenological project of transcribing and translating the appearance of phenomenal materiality into experience, and the anthropological project of transcribing and translating the material content of that experience into a reasonable textual form of developmental history. In short, it describes the field of philological based ethnology that Hodgson sought to validate with Couper's transcription of Tom's utterances, which is carefully articulated as a propositional statement that signals an economy whose specificity is a function of the statement's simply being uttered. Yet that transcription places the field in jeopardy by drawing attention to its specificity – what Couper calls its familiarity – by raising the fundamental question: What is ethnology? When asked in terms of Kant's architectonic, the question of ethnology is recognizably that of the theoretical understanding of man, anthropology; and as such it is a specific articulation of the question of the configuration of knowledge: What is *Wissenschaften*? Read in this manner, as a problematic of determinate reason, the problem of experience that subtends the Tom problem proves to be somewhat complex and involved.

If the problem of discovering a classificatory scheme capable of mapping the correlation between events in incommensurate systems of ordering is connected with Kant's conception of the mathematical sublime, it then becomes a problem of apprehension, comprehension. In support of this last point, we would do well to recall Kant's dictate: "Anschauung *ohne Gedanken ist 'leer.' Gedanken ohne Anschauungen sind blind* [Perception without thought is empty, thought without perception is blind]." A dictate whose critical affect is made more accessible by careful analysis of the passage between sections 27 and 28 of the *Critique of Judgment*, where Kant shifts consideration from the problem of apprehension engendered by the "Analytic of the Mathematical sublime" to terms of resistance entailed in the dynamic sublime.

How is it that Couper's inadequate transcription of Tom's utterances brings us to this Kantian problematic? Answering this question requires that the question of ethnology be more precisely formulated so as to give a clearer view of the stakes involved in its asking: How does Tom enable Couper to transcribe all that he says so that it becomes knowledge? How does he translate his experience into a suitable form for cognitive appropriation by Couper? Simply put: What problems does exhibiting pose for the *sensus communis* of the faculties of cognition, for Kant's architectonic in its attempt to determine the genesis of synthetic a priori judgments?

This is a paramount question of Kant's *Critique of Judgment*. The focus of this discussion, however, is on the manner in which Kant tries to address it in part 1 of the *Critique of Judgment*, "Critique of Aesthetic Judgment." The particular field of the "Critique of Aesthetic Judgment" to which our attention is drawn is book 2, "Analytic of the Sublime," which divides into two analytics: "On the Mathematically Sublime," and "On the Dynamically Sublime in Nature." The center of attention is the movement of Kant's passing from "On the Mathematically Sublime," to "On the Dynamically Sublime in Nature." This passage occurs between section 27 of the "Analytic of the Sublime," which is entitled "On the Quality of Liking in our Judging of the Sublime"; and section 28, entitled "On Nature as Might." In the passage from 27 to 28 Kant abruptly shifts consideration from the problem of apprehension encountered in "On the Mathematical Sublime" to terms of dynamic resistance.

Section 27 addresses how the feeling of the sublime in nature is the feeling of respect (*Achtung*) for the vocation of humanity. The inability of the imagination to comprehend its own apprehensions (of things in appearance) in a totality of intuition, in accordance with the law of reason that enjoins it to do so (i.e., the idea of the absolute whole), means that the imagination cannot exhibit the idea of reason through example: it cannot give the idea objective validity. While this inadequacy of the imagination engenders displeasure (*Unlust*) and fear (*Furch*) because the idea cannot be exhibited, it also is emancipating, because what it does exhibit is that the imagination's vocation is not at all determined by objects in nature, by phenomena, but, rather, its vocation is to strive to obey the laws of reason.

This respect for the idea of humanity (the realization within ourselves as subjects in accordance with the vocation to obey the laws of reason) is substituted for a respect for the object of intuition that engenders imagination's displeasure. This is achieved through what Kant calls *subreption*. In this *Inaugural Dissertation* Kant defines subreption as "the intellect's trick of slipping in a concept of sense as if it were the concept of an intellectual characteristics."[8] Subreption is how the sublime can be presented by the mind as being in nature, as though the object of nature makes intuitable the superiority of the rational vocation of our cognitive powers over the greatest of sensibility – i.e., the imagination in its greatest expansion.[9]

Hence, the feeling of the sublime in nature is respect for the fact that the inadequacy of the greatest power of sensibility is itself in harmony with rational ideas, insofar as the imagination inevitably strives to realize the rational idea of absolute totality. The agitation which the mind feels in presenting the sublime in nature is thus a rapid alteration of repulsion from the object of inadequacy and attraction to it, because of how it exhibits the conflict between the faculties of reason and imagination, and in that exhibition demonstrates that the dynamics of human cognition are emancipated from any basis in the determinate concept of the object of nature. This conflict gives rise to a subjective purposiveness of the mental faculties (*Vermögen*). Furthermore, the exhibition of vocation is all the more liberating in its exhibiting the feeling of the sublime to consist in its being a feeling, accompanying an object of displeasure but not determined by it.

This same exhibition centers on a particular confusion of sign production and sign function, of representation and reference; a confusion that is perhaps unavoidable and, from a certain perspective of meaningfulness (desire) in Kant's architectonics, is necessary. The resistance to a recognition of this confusion as a negative principle of meaningful productivity – it subtends the architectonics – derives from the first order confusion of representation and reference. This is made more readily available to the understanding in the "Analytic of the Sublime," where the relation of transcription to experience is thought in terms of force. Here Kant uses the term *Macht* instead of the word *Kraft*, which he employed with relative regularity in the *Critique of Pure Reason*, and consistently in *Metaphysical Foundations of Natural Science*.

This difference in terms is not without its theoretical consequences. *Kraft*, as it occurs in *Metaphysical Foundations of Natural Science* and *Critique of Pure Reason*, is a phenomenal experience which in its two aspects, repulsive and attractive, configures

119

RONALD A. T. JUDY

matter in space. Wanting to distance himself from both Leibniz's monadology and Newton's material atomism, Kant formulated a dynamic theory of physics according to which matter is a continuum of motive force (*Kraft*). Force's categorical status is as a predicative of the a priori category of causality, a category of the understanding which is a condition stipulated or postulated in reason, and which presents itself on the order of the possibility of any given experience and appearance; it is the relation between the two. *Kraft* is the fundamental property (*Eigenshaft*) of material change; the basis of its activity is exertion or endeavor (what Kant calls *Bestrebung*), which is constant and quantifiably measurable in terms of repulsion and attraction *energeia*. In this very Aristotelian sense, *Kraft*, is the phenomenal process of becoming actualized.

Macht, on the other hand, is a capacity or faculty (*Vermögen*) of the understanding to overcome (*Überlegen*) great resistance (*großen Hindernissen*). For Kant it is synonymous with will or possibility. As such it is more akin to Aristotle's concept of *dynamis*, a potential power to effect change, and the Scholastics notion of *potentia* as the capacity of being (which presupposes a corresponding potency). *Macht*, then, is that which has the potential to *cause* change, as opposed to *Kraft*, which *is* phenomenal change.

Section 28, by commencing with the term *Macht*, underscores that the issue at stake is the dominion of reason's potency as a force that operates in opposition to the mechanics of nature, of *Kraft*. When applied to the phenomenal materiality that correlates with the movements of sublimity (i.e., pain → pleasure → superiority of reason, or consciousness) as in §24–28 of *Critique of Judgment*, *Macht* signals the dynamic potential inherent in reason for overcoming, and to a certain degree forgetting, the phenomenal materiality of nature as the basis for cognition.

This overcoming is done for the sake of the productive subjection of imagination to reason, and the radical differentiation in the architectonics between reason and nature. That subjection occurs, because exhibition cannot be determined as it is without disrupting the a priori intuition of space and time – which is what is at stake in the disjunction between apprehension and comprehension, engendered by the experience of the sublime. Where time is seen as being contained by space, the disjunction forces the realization that there is not enough space for time. Implied in all of this is a mapping of space, a proper geography, which presents time as the articulating juxtaposition of discrete particulars.

Macht is the *arché* of the architectonic; it is the a priori basis for the equality of potential between the faculties of cognition, and to that extent it reveals that the grounding of cognition, of our representation of nature in all its possibility of totality, is purely in reason. In *Macht* Kant attempts to overcome the impossibility of reason realizing itself in nature (and hence in history as a process of worldly development) by introducing imagination's frustration at feeling a limit as being grounded in the logical (mathematical) conception of the boundlessness of the imagination's faculty for apprehension. The idea of totality, which is an idea of reason, and so is a priori and independent of material experience (nature), is the idea of the comprehensiveness of time. That is to say that the boundlessness of imagination's faculty of apprehension reveals the infinity of time from the smallest nanosecond to the hyper millennium. At the same moment, in *Macht* Kant discovers the most persistent antinomy inherent to the architectonic: the antinomy of translation. When time comprehends space, the resistance of phenomenal materiality is trivialized against the measure of rational speculation: "It

120

expands the soul." Thus the obscurity of the passage from Section 27 to Section 28 of the "Analytic of the Sublime" is unavoidable for Kant, because in the formulation of *Macht* he discovers as the result of all his labor, and it might be added, in spite of all his labor, exactly what he sought to dispel: an ontology grounded in the primacy of substance, of materiality.

This discovery is what prompts a lengthy digression on Kant's part, where he seeks to distinguish between terror and being afraid. Terror is empirical in its determination; it is predicated on purposiveness in the cognition of a real threat of material bodily harm. Fear, on the other hand, results from *thinking* and so is purely subjective and discursive: it is in no way determined by phenomenal materiality. The force by which the experience of the sublime overcomes Terror is realized in the recognition of thought's superiority over phenomenal events.

Thinking conquers death, and that is the consciousness of reason's superiority which the experience of the sublime gives us. In that experience imagination subjects itself to reason, in order to be free from the materiality of death. This is the resistance, the obstacle that must be forcefully dominated. But, it is not the death of matter that one is afraid of, it is the matter of death, the dissolution of the supersensible as the focal point of consciousness of being. It is the hierarchy of thought and being, thinking and writing, in which thought derives being, and thinking engenders writing, that is threatened by the phenomenal materiality of experience.

The architectonics employs fear to legitimate this hierarchy of thought and being; the fear of the experience of the sublime gives our consciousness of ourselves as transcending nature, as the autonomous being of reason. All of which is achieved through the dynamics of thought's transcribing the terror of materiality into the idea of fear as infinite emancipation. And thinking is in language, so this transcription is profoundly prosaic. The presentation of time as the articulation of discrete particulars that can potentially extend beyond the field of apprehension is in the end *parataxis*. The genesis of Kant's architectonics is in the subsumption of matter in narrative formulation, in the capacity to generate an effective fable. And if this subsumption is that which grounds the transcendence of reason, it is no more than the displacement of materiality through transcription.

As to the confusion of representation and reference, the production of the symbol as indirect representation is the process of its function. Kant calls this type of representation *hypotyposis*, and defines it as *subjectio ad adspectum* (subjection to inspection), consisting in making a sensible concept (*verinnlich*); and it is either schematic or symbolic. In schematic hypotyposis there is a concept that understanding has formed, and the intuition corresponding to it is given a priori. In symbolic hypotyposis there is a concept which only reason can think and to which no sensible intuition can be adequate, and this concept is supplied with an intuition that judgment treats in a way merely analogous to the procedure it follows in schematizing; in different terms, the concept is treated according to the same rule of procedure governing the treatment of empirical concepts that have determinate objects of intuition.[10]

What occurs, however, when the symbol, rather than displacing phenomenal materiality, and forgetting that displacement, presents it, when the symbol represents and is self-referential, giving meaning as a lie? Would there be a scandal that reason could not ameliorate? As a consequence of maintaining that the givenness of aesthetic

121

experience is inaccessible to either reason or understanding, but is only the pure work of imagination's articulating the conditions of experience (time and space) through its syntheses, Kant implies that natural force (material being) is other than reasonable. A larger implication is the law of reason's radical disassociation from the law of nature. Consequently, tracing the status of the "material body" as such, within reason, cannot but help to reveal that the very preconditions of the cognitive act are wholly dependent on imagination.

What Tom provides for Couper, then, is symbolic hypotyposis and not phenomenal perception. It is this hypotyposis that enables the transcribing of the particular event (or particular multiplicity of events) of Tom's "utterance" for which Couper's understanding could not provide any universal concept that would make sense of it as an experience. And he transcribes it into a (symbolic) code which mediates between the particular event and the understanding, so that the latter can attain a meaningful experiencing of the former. Even though this code is not schematic, which is to say that the event cannot be represented in its specificity as determined by understanding's having an a priori concept of the possibility of the experience, that does not mean any sort of representation is precluded. Not represented immediately in terms of the determinate concepts of understanding, there is an indirect, or negative representation of the event in a symbol. The symbol, while not enabling objective knowledge, does enable knowledge of how conceptual relations are established, which is knowledge of thinking as judgment itself. Since this knowledge of relation is a knowledge of knowledge, the symbolic representation will also be a reflection on the very establishing of the symbol, a symbol of symbolic thinking.

To think a symbolic relation is to represent both the particular and the universal in terms of the act of thinking that makes representation possible. To think symbolically is to trace in the given the contour of the event of knowledge's finiteness in relation to the supersensible, the "I think," as the focal point of cognitive experience. This is how Tom appears as exceptional for Couper. Thinking presents for cognitive appropriation an event of indirect representation (the symbol) that connects the event and experience in terms of the limitation of knowledge in the face of experience. This knowledge of limitation, the symbol's rigorous negativity, evokes a feeling of both pleasure and pain in the self-reflective awareness of the conceptual possibility of experience, and the denial of that possibility in the limited knowledge which presents it.

What we may now recognize as Tom's thinking is eventful. It is most definitely so for Couper. And as an event, it is somewhat sublime. In the manner of his persistence in transcribing Tom's eventful thinking, Couper presumes reflective judgment's capacity to arrive at a liberating synthesis of the faculties of knowledge, the *sensus communis aesthetica*. We need only recall here that for Kant the experience of the sublime may initially evoke a feeling of terror or pain, brought about by the experience of Imagination's impotence in comparison to an idea of reason. But such a discord between imagination and reason will eventually engender an accord, in which imagination acquires the feeling of being unbounded, of being presented with the infinite. The result is the thought of the supersensible, the "I think," as the site of connectedness. That is to say, Tom's intellectual agency is, for Couper, a function of the effective mapping of the spatial dimensions of the event in time so as to achieve a determination of difference between the possible object of knowledge (the very possibility of

122

an objective knowledge) and that which remains to be thought (*gedanken*) but not known (*erkennen*). Mediating between thinking and knowing, between the negativity of knowledge and knowledge of that negativity, the symbol becomes a negative representation that maps the limits of cognition's possibilities. Intellect emerges as a discursive figuration of eventfulness where something happens which can only be thought to happen.

Symbolic representation, then, is the dynamics of thought in language that charts the close connectedness between the particular given and its universal, and, thus, relates thinking to being. In accordance with the purely formal reflection of the transcendental aesthetic judgment, symbolic representation mediates between theoretical understanding and reflective experience, making critical thinking about what is and what is not a symbol possible. At stake in this determination is the transcribing of the thinking of the supersensible as the precondition of the connectedness of experience and event.

Insofar as the intellect of Tom's utterance effects an intervention into the objective economy of ethnological philology by displacing givenness with historical function, it is an event encountered but not known. Couper's transcription as symbolic hypotyposis [re]presents the giving of the conditions of experience (time and space). As such it is a function of productive imagination's figurative synthesis in schemata. The intellect of Tom's utterance, however, must remain unknowable, because the experience of experientiality in the negativity of symbolic representation presents the subject of knowledge to itself by resting on the event as that which resists the cognitive and so gives the subject as that of experience, as that which exhibits agency (force and motion). Couper's problem with transcribing Tom's thinking teaches the fallacy of presuming this agency to be an attribute of the subject of knowledge. Yet, it is just as fallacious to conceive of this agency as an attribute of the subject of experience, because that which provides the very possibility of the event's being given to cognition as resistance, imagination's schemata, is in itself indeterminate, thus placing a restriction on the definitive determination of subjectivity.

When thinking about this agency in his essay "*Bildung*," Kant argues that humanity is achieved through discipline (*Zucht*) and culture (*Bildung*). The combination of *Zucht* and *Bildung* achieves what we call education, which Kant also calls *Bildung* (hence the essay is translated into English as "Education"). According to Kant, discipline turns the animal *homo sapien* into the human. The problem with imagination is that its process cannot be comprehended in culture. That is, it cannot be a product of education, or discipline articulated as culture; this is because imagination as the pure process of intellect (as the schemata that enable perception, *Erfahrung*, and cognition, *Erkenntnis*) is necessarily incomprehensible, and groundless (Kant, is quite explicit about the impossibility of knowing the grounds of Imagination, these are "lost in the soul"). Such unbridled imagination, such agency of intellect, precludes culture – the *sensus communis* is thus a postulate. What is at stake here is not merely the unity of cognition but the possibility of thinking unity.

The "knowledge" that Couper claims for Hodgson of Tom's expressions, then, is a knowledge of disappearance, not a knowledge of that which is disappearing or has already disappeared. Thus knowledge of disappearing expression gives way to an active intellect that is encountered but unknowable.

Notes

This chapter is a revised version of a paper given at Villanova University in the first week of March 1996, on the occasion of a conference entitled "The Academy and Race: Toward a Philosophy of Political Action," that was organized by Kevin Thomas Miles in the Department of Philosophy.

1   Cf. Erich Auerbach, *Literary Language and its Public in Late Latin Antiquity and in the Middle Ages*, trans. Ralph Manheim (Princeton: Princeton University Press, 1993), 5.

2   See Ronald Judy, *(Dis)forming the American Canon: African Arabic Slave Narrative and The Vernacular* (University of Minnesota Press, 1993).

3   William B. Hodgson, *Notes on Northern Africa, The Sahara, and Soudan* (New York: Wiley and Putnam, 1844), 68.

4   For those interested in a somewhat involved consideration of the instability of the classifications of the Negro in Couper's correspondence with Hodgson see Judy, *(Dis)forming the American Canon*.

5   When Ivor Wilks reproduces a portion of Couper's letter in Curtin's *Africa Remembered* he regulates the spellings according to current conventions of English transliteration and orthography, producing: *Timbuktu, Jenne*, and *Segu*; see Ivor Wilks, "Ṣāliḥ Bilalī of Massina," *Africa Remembered: Narratives by West Africans from the Era of the Slave Trade*, ed. Philip Curtin (Madison: University of Wisconsin Press, 1967), 147–51, passim.

6   There are numerous other examples of the same problem, names such as *Zāgha, Dia, Jagha*, and their cognates, *Zāhawī Diahinké*, and *Jahinke*. All of these refer to the same metropolis and the same societal grouping.

7   As a point of information, in the case of the Foulah that he knew, there was an orthography as well. However, it was not Latin but Arabic.

8   Immanuel Kant, *De Mundi sensibilis atque intelligibilis forma et principiis, Kants gesammelte Schriften*, Königlich Preußische Akademie der Wissenschaften (Berlin: Walter Gruyter & Co. and Predecessors, 1902) 2: 412.

9   Immanuel Kant, *The Critique of Judgement*. Trans. James C. Meredith (Oxford: Clarendon Press, 1964), p. 114.

10 Ibid., 226.

7

Social Contract Theory, Slavery, and the Antebellum Courts

ANITA L. ALLEN AND THADDEUS POPE

Introduction

Social contract theory holds that political order "is legitimate if and only if it is (or could be) the outcome of a collective agreement of free, equal, and rational individuals" (Anderson, 1990: 1794). American law has a special relationship to social contractarian theory. According to some scholars, American colonists relied upon liberal, Lockean notions of a social contract to justify revolution against British rule (Henkin, 1989: 1029; McLaughlin, 1900: 467; Sutherland, 1965: 6; Tate, 1965: 376). Historians maintain that social contractarian theories of political order significantly influenced the people who wrote and defended the Declaration of Independence, the original Constitution, and the Bill of Rights (Bailyn, 1967: 59; Wood, 1969: 282–91).

Although much has been written about the contractarian foundations of the Declaration of Independence and the Constitution, little has been written about the role contractarian thought played in subsequent jurisprudence. One scholar has even concluded that "the idea of the social contract implicit in America's rights ideology served the new nation well at the beginning, but had no further use" (Henkin, 1989: 1033). Yet, social contract theory has had noteworthy further uses.

The idea of the social contract as a source of legitimate authority has surfaced in important constitutional, statutory, and common law cases in this century and the last. For example, in *Pavesich v. New England Life Insurance Co.*, 122 Ga. 190, 50 S.E. 68 (1905), the Supreme Court of Georgia became the first American court expressly to recognize a right to privacy. The Georgia court argued that, although the right to privacy was not yet a part of the positive law, the social contract implied by natural law required common law judges to recognize privacy rights protecting interests in personal identity. To take another example, one of the leading constitutional decisions establishing the right of government to restrict individual liberty in the interest of public health, *Jacobson v. Massachusetts*, 197 U.S. 11, 27 (1905), relied on contractarian reasoning. There the United States Supreme Court argued that one of the purposes for which persons embrace civil society is to reap the benefits of government police powers

125

exercised in the interest of public health. *Pavesich* and *Jacobson* are nearly a century old. But contractarian rationales like theirs are no mere historical artifacts found only in older precedents. Judges continue to offer contractarian rationales for everything from criminal punishment to civil forfeiture.

Of central concern here is a particular use judges made of contractarian thought in the nineteenth century. A number of state and federal judges explicitly used social contractarian rationales in their written opinions defending slavery. The defense of slavery is perhaps the most troubling use of social contract theory in the history of American law. Today social contract theorists disdain human chattel slavery. John Rawls rejects hereditary forms of involuntary servitude outright (Rawls, 1971: 248). Some nineteenth-century contractarian sympathizers similarly rejected slavery (Miller, 1977; Morrow, 1985–6). Yet, respected judges in the Antebellum period appealed to contractarian ideas in opinions supporting the inequality of people of African ancestry.

Nineteenth-century jurists employed an arsenal of arguments in defense of slavery, only some which owed a debt to social contractarian philosophy. A popular class of non-contractarian pro-slavery arguments relied on Biblical texts and non-textual under-standings of divine teleology. Another familiar class of arguments relied on the paternalistic premise that, as a practical matter, blacks were incapable of caring for themselves and would perish or degenerate without the protection of white owners. Other popular classes of arguments justified slavery as the consequence of fair commercial exchanges and conquests. Judges combined these several categories of argument with distinctly contractarian arguments to shape a powerful, pro-slavery jurisprudence. According to Edmund S. Morgan, "the central paradox of American history [is that] the rise of liberty and equality was accompanied by the rise of slavery" (1972: 5–6). Social contract theory was an intellectual tool nineteenth-century lawyers and judges manipulated to avoid a sense of paradox. They reconciled the enslavement of blacks with white freedom and equality by depicting slavery as the product of rational choices.

This article identifies distinctly contractarian "justifications" for black slavery found in antebellum court opinions. We elaborate three lines of contractarian argument. The first justifies permitting slavery on the ground that the US Constitution is a white-only social contract under which blacks are not free and equal. The second justifies permitting slavery on the ground that slavery is blacks' best deal for escaping the state of nature, given (putative) black inferiority. The third justifies slavery on the ground that death to the vanquished is a just consequence of war; and that slavery is a rationally preferable fate to death. We limit our attention here to social contractarian arguments. Judges also embraced commercial contract-based arguments for slavery, according to which the slave holder's "power over his slaves is derived from bargaining and purchase, explicitly equating slaves with other chattels" (Drescher, 1988: 502). The judges who routinely enforced agreements to buy, sell, and hold blacks were typically silent about what legitimated the free market in involuntary servants. Judges may sometimes have assumed that persons of African descent were properly bought, sold, and held as property by reasons of social contract.

In a provocative study, African-American philosopher Charles Mills posits the exis-tence of what he terms "the Racial Contract," a centuries old global agreement among white men to restrict the possession of freedom and equality to their own kind (Mills, 1997: 20). Mills would doubtless greet our evidence of pro-slavery jurisprudential contractarianism without surprise, having already concluded in his book that "legal decisions" reflect the historical reality of the Racial Contract (*id.*). Mills does not go into detail about the jurisdiction and era of the legal decisions he has in mind. We offer no opinion about the overall plausibility of Mills' case for the existence of a global Racial Contract; we merely present objective evidence that some white jurists put contractarian thought to use in the interest of black subjugation. The small, striking selection of judicial opinions cited here expressly exclude blacks from the privileges of liberal society on contractarian grounds.

The Constitution as a White-Only Social Contract

St. George Tucker wrote of the Founding that "the American Revolution has formed a new epoch in the history of civil institutions, by reducing to practice what, before, had been supposed to exist only in the visionary speculations of theoretical writers" (1803: 4). The American Constitution is "an instrument of democratic sovereignty, created and sustained by the sovereign people to provide for conditions enabling them effectively to exercise these basic rights" (Freeman, 1992: 28). Yet, the Founders did not construe slaves as among those sovereign people. In support of this observation scholars cite three specific provisions of the original Constitution that clearly presuppose the perpetuation of slavery as a legal institution. The Fugitive Slave Clause, Article IV §2, permitted the forcible return of runaway slaves to their owners. The so-called "3/5ths Compromise," Article I §3, counted slaves as only partial persons for purposes of allocating Congressional representation to the states. The Slave Trade Clause, Article I §9 prohibited a national ban on the slave trade before the year 1808.

Notwithstanding the document's unequal treatment of persons based on race, courts have long construed the original United States Constitution as a social contract. In *Calder v. Bull*, 3 U.S. 386, 388, 397 (1798), Supreme Court Justice Samuel Chase tied the erection of the United States Constitution to the formation of a "social compact" whose "nature and term" depends upon the "purposes for which men enter society." One of those purposes was the protection of slavery as a social and economic institution. Justice Roger B. Taney, author of the Supreme Court's opinion in the notorious *Dred Scott* case of 1856, observed that "[f]ree states had obligated themselves to respect the institution of slavery because they had bound themselves by the social compact of the Constitution to uphold it" (Baade, 1991: 1055). Taney vindicated the opinion of Supreme Court Justice Joseph Story in *Prigg v. Pennsylvania*, 41 U.S. 539, 660 (1842), who defended slave-holding as a "cherished right, included in the social compact, and sacredly guarded by law."

Judges supported chattel slavery on the ground that blacks were not parties to the social contract embodied in the U.S. Constitution. Judges opined that blacks were not entitled to any of the federal protections afforded by the Bill of Rights because they were not parties to the federal social contract forged by and among whites. The usual form of argument excluding blacks from the U.S. social contract was an argument about positive law and its history. The argument did not go so far as to exclude slaves as parties to the political moralists' social contract proper, sometimes termed *pactum societatis*. It only excluded them as parties to the *pactum subjectionis*, the pact that established the formal, legal government in the Antebellum United States. It was not uncommon in the nineteenth century for judges to embrace natural law as a constraint on positive law. Judges failed, however, to write opinions condemning slavery on the natural law ground that slaves ought ideally to have been included in the United States' *pactum subjectionis*.

The question of whether free blacks were parties to the *pactum subjectionis*, remained unsettled in American law until the Supreme Court handed down its decision in *Dred Scott v. Sanford*, 60 U.S. (19 How.) 393 (1856). Dred Scott was a slave of African ancestry owned by Dr. John Emerson. Emerson was employed as an army surgeon and traveled from the slave holding state of Missouri to Illinois and Wisconsin territory (areas prohibiting slavery) as a part of his duties. Emerson brough Scott with him to serve as his slave. Three years after Emerson's death Scott sued Emerson's widow, Irene Emerson, for formal declaration of his freedom. Scott argued he was free because he had resided in areas that prohibited slavery. A state court in Missouri declared Scott free, relying on the state's long standing legal principle "once free, always free." John F. A. Sanford took over the interests of the Emerson estate and sought to reestablish ownership of Scott. Scott then instituted a suit in federal court against Sanford. Sanford argued that because Scott was of African descent, he could never attain the citizenship status necessary to sue in federal court. The Supreme Court agreed.

The stunning holding of *Dred Scott* was that neither free blacks nor slaves were citizens of the United States entitled to the protection of the federal courts. Earlier cases, of which *Ely v. Thompson*, 3 A.K. Marshall 73 (1820) is an example, had held that free blacks, at least, were parties to the social contract with some Constitutional rights. Chief Justice Taney offered a contractarian justification both for upholding slavery and for denying federal citizenship to free blacks. Taney argued that the Founders intended to extend no rights under the Constitution to black people, free or enslaved. Blacks were: "[n]ot included, and were not intended to be included under the word 'citizens' in the Constitution, and can therefore claim none of the rights and privileges which that instrument provides for and secures to citizens of the United States" (Dred Scott: 404–5). Taney contended that, in the eyes of the Founding Fathers, blacks were: "[b]eings of an inferior order, and altogether unfit to associate with the white race either in social or political relations; and so far inferior, that they had no rights which the white man was bound to respect" (Dred Scott: 417). Taney's support for this bold claim included the false observation that slavery then existed in all the civilized nations of Earth (Fehrenbacher, 1978: 359).

Nevertheless, Taney was right about the intentions of the men who established the United States (Finkelman, 1996). Principal author of the Declaration of Independence, Thomas Jefferson considered the black race inferior to the white race in both body and mind. Moreover, examination of the debates in the Constitutional convention and in state ratification conventions reveals clearly that the Founders were fully aware of achieving constitutional agreement by adopting a document that reserved a place of inequality for persons of black African descent. The Supreme Court's decision in Dred Scott's case vindicated lower court judges' perceptions of black exclusion from the United States' social contract.

128

Slavery as the Best Deal

A second way in which judges used social contract theory to support slavery was by positing a hypothetical "contract" under whose terms rational blacks agreed to subordinate themselves to whites. Judges argued, in effect, that if blacks were parties to a social compact with whites to escape the anarchy of the state of nature, blacks would assent to their own enslavement. Why? In light of blacks' (imagined) limited natural endowments, reason would compel voluntary submission to the authority and protection of (presumably) better endowed whites. Out of practical necessity, persons of African ancestry would strike a deal less favorable than the deal that white European males strike while seeking to escape the perils of the state of nature.

This version of the justification of slavery embraced by members of the judiciary was a twist on basic Hobbesian political theory (Allen and Morales, 1992). According to Hobbes, the natural condition of humankind is a condition of war. Virtually equal in body, mind and hope, human beings in a state of nature will employ violence to gain and defend power, possessions, and reputation. So conceived, the natural predicament of humanity is the "warre of every man against every man" (Hobbes, 1991: 90). Two dispositions incline rational, self-interested human individuals to seek peace. First, they fear death. Second, they desire necessities, comforts, and the fruits of personal industry. To escape the perils of violent competition among equals over resources and social standing, individuals seek the protection of a common power or sovereign "to keep them all in awe" (*id.* at 88). To escape a life that is "solitary, poore, nasty, brutish, and short," rational persons will compact to form a commonwealth in which they are all subject to a single sovereign with absolute political authority and the ability to maintain peace (*id.* at 89).

The main point here is that the power of the sovereign is not imposed on the individual, but rather, is *chosen* by the individual. Human beings are by nature free. Individuals exercise their autonomy by rationally choosing to cede some power to a Leviathan in order to escape the perils of violent competition. It is sometimes viewed as a corollary of this principle that those who are especially vulnerable in the real world (e.g., children, women, and blacks) might have to make bigger sacrifices to enter into the social contract. Since "[a]ll contract law is mutual translation or exchange of right," if one party is in an inferior position, then he has no choice but to agree to the disadvantageous terms offered by the superior party (Hobbes, 1991: xiv).

The premise that blacks would be in an inferior position in a state of nature supports the argument that blacks have rationally compelling grounds for consenting to subordination. Or so concluded Justice James S. Nevius of the New Jersey Supreme court in *State v. Post*, 20 NJL 368 (1845). The issue in *State v. Post* was the status of slavery in New Jersey after the adoption of a new state Constitution. Prior to the enactment of the then new New Jersey constitution, the New Jersey legislature enacted the "Act for the Gradual Abolition of Slavery" which accounted for the freeing of slaves born after July 4, 1804. Unaccounted for by the aforementioned law were slaves born prior to the year 1804. William and Flora were both owned by John A. Post. The abolitionist law left their status as slaves unaltered because the dates of their births preceeded 1804. On its face, the state constitution enacted in 1844 seemed to promise freedom to them as well as those similarly situated in bondage, as the document declared *all* persons free and equal. The Abolitionists argued that slavery in New Jersey ended completely with the ratification of the new constitution and that the law calling for gradual manumission was therefore invalid.

The Supreme Court of New Jersey argued that slavery was consistent with the egalitarian language of the state constitution, much as slavery was consistent with similar language in the Declaration of Independence and the US Constitution. Furthermore: "[a]uthority and subordination are essential under every form of civil society, and one of its leading principles is that the citizen yields a portion of his natural rights for the better protection of the remainder" (*id.* at 374). But slaves must give up more than others, the judge implied.

The logic of bargain and consent seemed to dictate that blacks accepted slavery as their "best deal." The defense of slavery on these grounds rests ultimately on bias. Specifically it rests upon ethnological prejudice. The "best deal" argument assumes that the Negro is inferior and that he belongs to an inferior race (Frederickson, 1987). In the last century, experts expended much effort trying to demonstrate black inferiority empirically. They used tainted historical data to show that blacks had always occupied a position of inferiority. They tried to show that by virtue of anatomical and physiological differences blacks are inferior to whites (Wilson, 1949: 242–3).

The "best deal" argument is distinguishable from a non-contractarian paternalistic argument for slavery mentioned earlier. The "best deal" argument tries to explain why an arrangement which seems unfair is really quite fair, by maintaining that Negroes are so inherently inferior that they would be willing to strike whatever deal they could for white protection. The paternalistic argument, on the other hand, characterizes slavery as a fair and beneficial institution to help persons of an inferior race.

Paternalists did not use the inferiority assumption to justify implied rational consent to the best available deal; they used it to justify interference with liberty. After the ratification of the Constitution, it became increasingly obvious that "in order to explain the contradiction of slavery in liberal society, nineteenth century Southerners developed the . . . paternalist myth as a necessary corollary" (Cottrol, 1987: 364–5). The paternalists depicted slavery as the caring option (McGary and Lawson, 1992: 24–9). Paternalists sometimes argued that slaves were better off than free wage laborers whom employers could simply fire when they were no longer of use (Fitzhugh, 1857: 205). Thus, "[m]asters enjoy the labor and obedience of their slaves, but provide them in return food, housing, moral and religious guidance, and care in their infancy and old age" (Fischer, 1993: 1065). In *State v. Mann*, 13 N.C. 263 (1829) the court concluded that slavery on balance "has a beneficial influence . . . rendering both [races] better and happier than either would be without the other."

Conquest

A third kind of argument for slavery found in nineteenth-century jurisprudence relied on notions of assent, but had less clear ties to social contract philosophy than the "best deal" or "white-only Constitution" arguments. This is the argument from conquest, according to which slavery is justified on the ground that blacks were enslaved as a consequence of just wars. Conquered blacks assent to their own enslavement as the preferred alternative to death.

The argument from conquest constructs the slave as a rational person who chooses slavery over death: "[a]rchetypically, slavery was a substitute for death in war, . . . a conditional commutation. The execution was suspended only as long as the slave acquiesced in his powerlessness" (Patterson, 1982: 5). Thomas R. Dew, relying on Grotius and Pufendorf, defended slavery on these grounds in his *An Essay On Slavery* (Wilson, 1949: 2). John Locke justified slavery on these grounds in the course of advising Governor Nicholson of Virginia in 1698. Locke argued that "Negro slaves were justifiably enslaved, having been taken captives in a 'just war' thus forfeiting their liberty" (Morrow, 1985–6: 237).

Locke indeed held that slavery is just if the slaves were "captives taken in just war" (Locke, 1948: 42). A just war is one waged against unjust aggressors by an innocent people defending its rights and its property. Thus, slavery is nothing else but the state of war continued. The slave, by violating the rights of the innocents, "forfeited his own life, by some act that deserves death; he, to whom he has forfeited it, may (when he has him in his power) delay to take it, and make use of him to his own service, and he does no injury by it" (Locke, 1948: 13–14).

The jurisprude Blackstone perceptively questioned this justification as "built on false foundations" (Jones, 1973: 115). He attributed Locke's defense of slavery arising from *jure gentium*, from a state of captivity in war, where slaves are called *macipia quasi manu capti*, as one of the three origins of slavery assigned by Justinian. Yet, Blackstone argued that "war is itself justified only on principles of self-preservation, and therefore it gives no other right over prisoners but merely to disable them from doing harm to us. . . ." Furthermore "[s]ince the right of making slaves by captivity depends on a supposed right of slaughter, [and] that foundation fails, the consequence drawn from it must fail likewise" (*id.* at 115).

The conquest justification for slavery took on a strongly consensual character in Hobbesian philosophy. In Hobbes' theory, conquest counts as a form of consent. "If one male individual manages to conquer another in the state of nature the conqueror will have obtained a servant. Hobbes assumed that no one would willingly give up his life; so, with the conqueror's sword at his breast, the defeated man will make a [valid] contract to obey his victor" (Pateman, 1988: 47). Of course, neither Hobbes nor Locke adequately explains why the children and grandchildren of conquered persons should become slaves from birth.

Justice Taney relied upon the conquest justification of slavery in addition to his more formalistic white-only Constitution arguments. Explaining that blacks were not citizens, he wrote, "[o]n the contrary, they were at that time considered as a subordinate and inferior class of beings, who had been subjugated by the dominant race, and, whether emancipated or not, yet remained subject to their authority, and had no rights or privileges but such as those who held the power and the Government might choose to grant them." In *Mitchell v. Wells*, 37 Miss 235, 263 (1859), Judge Harris also insisted that slavery presumed that Africans were a "subjugated" race. The Supreme Court itself noted that "war confers rights in which all have acquiesced," one of them "that the victor might enslave the vanquished," *Antelope*, 23 U.S. 66, 120–1 (1825).

131

Conclusion

Slavery is antithetical to contemporary ideals of liberal social contract theory. Nevertheless, nineteenth-century judges were able to deploy the apparatus of social contract theory to lend support to slavery in the United States. Social contract thought and rhetoric remain popular in American culture and jurisprudence despite their ignoble applications on behalf of slavery before the Civil War. Resurrecting that past and remaining mindful of it makes repetition unlikely. Judges today may be less able to prevail with social contractarian argument to the extent that the public is familiar with repressive uses of the rhetoric of rational agreement.

References

Allen, A. L. and Morales, M. H.: "Hobbes, formalism, and corrective justice," *Iowa Law Review*, 77 (1992), 717.

Alpert, J.: "The origin of slavery in the United States – the Maryland precedent," *American Journal of Legal History*, 14 (1970), 187.

Anderson, E. S.: "Women and contracts: no new deal," *Michigan Law Review*, 88 (1990), 1794.

Baade, Hans W.: "Original Intent in Historical Perspective: Some Critical Glosses," *Texas Law Review*, 69 (1991), 1001, 1054–5.

Bailyn, B.: *The Ideological Origins of the American Revolution* (Cambridge, Mass.: Belknap Press, 1967), 59.

Barker, A. J.: *The African Link: British Attitudes to the Negro in the Era of the Atlantic Slave Trade, 1550–1807* (London: F. Cass, 1978), 51, 78–9.

Cottrol, R. J.: "Liberalism and paternalism: ideology, economic interests, and the business of slavery," *American Journal of Legal History*, 31 (1987), 364–5.

Davis, D. B.: *The Problem of Slavery in Western Culture* (Ithaca, NY: Cornell University Press, 1960).

Drescher, S.: "On James Farr's 'so vile and miserable an estate'," *Political Theory*, 16 (1988), 502.

Elliot, E. N.: *Cotton is King, and Proslavery Arguments* (Augusta, Ga.: 1860); (New York: Johnson Reprint Corp., 1968), 44.

Fehrenbacher, D. E.: *The Dred Scott Case: Its Significance in American Law and Politics* (New York: Oxford University Press, 1978), 349, 359.

Finkelman, P.: *Slavery and the Founders: Race and Liberty in the Age of Jefferson* (Armonk, NY: M.E. Sharpe, 1996).

Fischer, W. W.: "Ideology and imagery in the law of slavery," *Chicago-Kent Law Review*, 68 (1993), 1064.

Fitzhugh, G. 1960: *Cannibals All! or, Slaves without Masters* (Richmond, Va.: 1857); (Cambridge, Mass.: Belknap Press, 1960), 205.

——: *Sociology for the South; or the Failure of Free Society* (1857) (New York: B. Franklin Press, 1960), 82–83, 105–107.

Frederickson, G. M.: *The Black Image in the White Mind: the Debate on Afro-American Character and Destiny, 1817–1914* (Middletown, Conn.: Wesleyan University Press, 1987), 71–96.

Freeman, S.: "Original meaning, democratic interpretation, and the constitution," *Philosophy and Public Affairs*, 21 (1992), 28.

Henkin, L.: "Revolutions and constitutions," *Louisiana Law Review*, 49 (1989), 1029.

Hobbes, T.: *Leviathan* (1651), ed. R. Tuck (Cambridge: Cambridge University Press, 1991), 88–90.

Jones, G.: *Blackstone's Commentaries on the Laws of England*, Vol. 1 (Toronto: University of Toronto Press, 1973), 115.

Locke, J.: *Two Treatises of Government* (1690), ed. P. Laslett (Cambridge: Cambridge University Press, 1960).

——: *The Second Treatise of Civil Government* (1690), ed. J. W. Gough (Oxford: Basil Blackwell, 1948).

Loesch, M. C.: "Motive testimony and a civil disobedience justification," *Notre Dame Journal of Law, Ethics and Public Policy*, 5 (1991), 1074.

Maier, P.: *From Resistance to Revolution: Colonial Radicals and the Development of American Opposition to Britain, 1765–76* (London: Routledge & K. Paul, 1973), 27.

McGary, H. and Lawson, W. E.: *Between Slavery and Freedom: Philosophy and American Slavery* (Bloomington: Indiana University Press, 1992), 24–9, 55–70.

McLaughlin, A. C.: "Social compact and constitutional construction," *The American Historical Review*, 5 (1900), 467.

Miller, J. C.: *The World by the Ears* (New York: Macmillan Press, 1977), 4.

Mills, C. W.: *The Racial Contract* (Ithaca, NY: Cornell University Press, 1997).

Morgan, E. S.: "Slavery and freedom: the American paradox," *Journal of American History*, 59 (1972), 5–6.

Moore, W. E.: "Slave law and the social structure," *American Journal of Negro History*, 26 (1941).

Morrow, N. V.: "The problem of slavery in the polemic literature of the American enlightenment," *Early American Literature*, 20 (1985–6), 236.

Pateman, C.: *The Sexual Contract* (Cambridge: Polity Press, 1988), 68.

Patterson, O.: *Slavery and Social Death: A Comparative Study* (Cambridge, Mass.: Harvard University Press, 1982), 5.

Phillips, W.: *The Constitution: A Proslavery Compact or Extracts From the Madison Papers, Etc.* (New York: American Anti-Slavery Society, 1857), 6–7.

Rawls, J.: *A Theory of Justice* (Cambridge, Mass.: Belknap Press, 1971), 248.

Robinson, D.: *Slavery in the Structure of American Politics, 1765–1820* (New York: Harcourt, Brace, Jovanovich, 1971).

Sutherland, A. E.: *Constitutionalism in America: Origin and Evolution of its Fundamental Ideas* (New York: Blaisdell Publishing Comp., 1965), 6.

Tate, T. W.: "The social contract in America, 1774–1787: revolutionary theory as a conservative instrument," *William and Mary Quarterly*, 22 (1965), 376.

Tucker, N. B.: "An essay on the moral and political effect of the relation between the caucasian master and the African slave," *Southern Literary Messenger*, 10 (1844), 330.

Tucker, S. G.: *Blackstone's Commentaries: with Notes of Reference to the Constitution and Laws of the Federal Government and of the Commonwealth of Virginia*, 5 vols. Appendix H (Philadelphia: 1803); (Buffalo, NY: Dennis & Co., 1965), 4.

Wayland, F.: *The Elements of Moral Science* (1835) (Cambridge, Mass.: Belknap Press, 1963).

Wilson, F. G.: *The American Political Mind: A Textbook in Political Theory* (New York: McGraw-Hill Book Corp., 1949).

Wood, G.: *The Creation of the American Republic, 1776–1787* (Chapel Hill: University of North Carolina Press, 1969), 282–91, 541.

8

The Morality of Reparations II

BERNARD R. BOXILL

The debate over affirmative action began when preferential policies were first implemented around 1970, and it has continued to this day. Many of the early contestants
have retired from the fray, but their places have been filled, and the exchange is as lively
as it was thirty years ago. There has, however, been a change of emphasis. Although
the arguments in dispute can still be classified as roughly "backward looking" or
"forward looking," the former justifying preferential treatment as compensation, and
the latter justifying it in terms of its results, the defenders of preferential treatment seem
to be relying more and more on forward looking arguments. Practical considerations
go a long way in explaining this. It was natural to think of preferential treatment as
compensation when African Americans were its main beneficiaries; but now that preferential treatment is being extended to groups and individuals that do not seem to have
the strong claims for compensation against American society that African Americans
have, its defenders naturally have to emphasize other arguments; further, the Supreme
Court seems to have adopted Justice Powell's opinion in Bakke, that although the state's
interest in remedying the generalized effects of society's racial discrimination cannot
justify its treating blacks preferentially, a university's interest in attaining a "diverse"
student body may justify its using racial and ethnic criteria in its admission policies.
But I suspect that many defenders of preferential treatment emphasize forward looking
arguments because they worry that backward looking arguments are afflicted with
insuperable philosophical problems. In this essay I try to put this worry to rest: backward looking arguments for preferentially treating African Americans do raise difficult
philosophical problems, but these problems can be resolved; further, the US has special
compensatory obligations to its black citizens that take precedence over its aim to create
a more diverse society.

First some terminological details: "compensation" is a broad term that covers
making up for, or trying to make up for, losses and deficiencies in general; "reparation"
is a much narrower term that covers repairing losses and deficiences that result from
injustice. Consequently, although the case for black compensation may include arguments to make up for black losses where no one is at fault, the case for black reparations includes only arguments for repairing black losses caused by injustice. I focus here

on the argument for black reparations, in particular the argument that present generations of black people deserve reparation for the injustices practiced against their ancestors, especially the injustices of slavery and Jim Crow policies and laws. If it is sound,
the further argument that they also deserve reparation for the injustices they themselves suffer from will be sound too. Throughout I will be guided by the theory of reparation adumbrated by John Locke in the *Second Treatise on Civil Government*. I hope that
this approach will appeal to the critics of preferential treatment because many of them
claim to be Lockeans, and Locke's moral and political philosophy is still the source of
much American theorizing on social issues.

According to Locke, when one person violates the law of nature, and another person
"receives damages by his transgression," the latter has a "particular right to seek reparation from him that hath done" the damage, and others may assist him in "recover-
ing from the Offender, so much as may make satisfaction for the harm he hath suffered"
(Second Treatise, section 10). Locke's language suggests that he had intentional violations of the law of nature especially in mind, but there is no reason to believe he would
deny that damages caused by unintentional, though negligent or reckless, violations of
right could also deserve reparation. Supposing this to be the case, Locke seems to be
making at least four claims about the right of reparation:

1   It is an acquired right.
2   One acquires the right when someone transgresses on one's rights, and one is
    damaged, injured or harmed as a result.
3   The right is held against the particular individual who transgressed on one's rights
    and caused one damage.
4   The reparation one may seek is as much as will make "satisfaction" for the damage
    one has suffered.

The first of these claims means simply that the right to reparation is not a right one has
simply because one is a person, like the right to liberty, but a right one comes by because
someone does something to bring it into existence. The second says what someone has
to do to bring a right to reparation into existence; he has to transgress on another's
rights, and cause him damage, harm or injury as a result. When this happens the one
whose rights he has transgressed against and injured as a result, acquires a right to
reparation. Locke's comment, that "Besides the crime which consists in violating the
laws," there is "commonly injury done," implies that he thought that transgression was
not the same thing as damage, harm or injury, and that though it did "commonly"
cause damage, harm or injury it did not necessarily or always do so (*Second Treatise*,
section 10). He probably had something like the following in mind: if Mary walks across
a farmer's field without his permission, she transgresses against his property rights, and
perhaps should be punished for this, but if she did not damage his crops she cannot owe
him reparation for such damage. It does not follow that she owes him no reparation.
Transgression does not necessarily cause harm, but it may cause a variety of harms.
For example, even if Mary's transgression did not damage the farmer's crops, it could
have damaged his reputation as a person whose rights had better be respected, and
if it did, she may owe him reparation for that harm. Even in that case, however, the
distinction between transgression and damage or harm remains: her transgression

135

may, but need not damage his reputation as a person whose rights had better be respected.

Locke did not mention a second point, although it is implied in his view that transgression and harm are different things, and that both are necessary, the transgression and the harm, to give rise to a right to reparation: my actions may harm, damage, or injure someone else without also transgressing on his rights, and in that case he has no right to seek reparation from me. For example, my winning a competition may harm the other competitors, but if I did not transgress on their rights in winning, if for example, I win fairly, they have no right to seek reparation from me. But here again we should be careful not to overstate this conclusion. Locke does not mean that the losers in a competition can have no right to assistance to remedy the harm caused by their loss. If the harm it causes is "extream want," Locke's views suggest that they may have a right to others' "Plenty," although that right is a right of charity rather that a right of reparation.

Let us turn to the fourth point, that reparation must be "so much as may make satisfaction" for the "harm suffered." What did Locke mean by satisfaction? We can set aside vengeance; the right of reparation is a right sanctioned by natural law, and natural law does not sanction vengeance. We can also set aside the satisfaction the transgressors' victims feel in seeing their transgressors punished. Locke never says that the point of punishment is to give them satisfaction; its point, he says, is to deter transgressors and others from repeating the crime (*Second Treatise*, section 8). However, much later in the book, when he is discussing the rights of the lawful conqueror, Locke implies that the point of reparation is to "repair" the damages caused by transgression (*Second Treatise*, section 182). Since to repair something that has been damaged is to bring it to the condition it was in before it was damaged, this suggests that the "satisfaction" the victim of harmful transgression may seek is to be brought to the condition he was in before he was harmed.

But this proposal is unsatisfactory. It may be what we mean when we speak of repairing damages to machines, but the idea of damage to a person, which is the damage reparation is intended to repair, depends on a conception or ideal of human nature. Suppose, for example, that Dick steals Tom's bicycle. Then the proposal in question implies that the reparation Tom may seek from Dick is that Dick return his bicycle to him. But this is unsatisfactory, even in the simple cases when the transgression was theft and the harm is loss of property. Suppose that Dick destroys or loses Tom's bicycle after he steals it; surely it would be absurd to argue that since Dick cannot return to Tom the very bicycle he stole from him that therefore Tom cannot seek reparation from him. Neither does it seem quite enough to say that the reparation Tom can seek from Dick is the money to buy another bicycle comparable to one Dick stole from him. Suppose that Tom had planned to use his bicycle to deliver flowers and would have earned $100 doing that job but for Dick's theft. Returning his bicycle, or giving him enough money to buy another one, may put him in the condition he was in before Dick stole it, supposing he can still use it or its replacement to earn $100, but he is likely to feel that this is not quite enough, for if Dick had not stolen his bicycle, he would not only be in a position to earn $100, he would already have earned $100. Very likely he will feel that the reparation he can seek from Dick is his bicycle plus the $100 he would have earned had Dick not stolen it.

136

It may be objected that Tom is confusing what he has a right to with what he would have had a right to had something not happened that did in fact happen. If Dick had not stolen Tom's bicycle Tom would have earned the $100 and would have had a right to it. But in fact Dick did steal Tom's bicycle, and as a result Tom did not earn the $100, did not have a right to that sum, and consequently cannot claim it as compensation. This objection underestimates Tom's rights, at least as Locke would have understood them. Such rights depend on a conception or ideal of human nature, and on Locke's account that ideal was of man as an industrious, progressive, and rational planner. On this account, human beings are harmed when they are prevented from being industrious, progressive, rational planners, and they have rights to the kind of society that would enable them to be such persons. According to Locke, the "Freedom of men under Government," is among other things, "not to be subject to the inconstant, uncertain, unknown, Arbitrary Will of another Man." I think he was remembering Hobbes's warning that the insecurity of the state of nature is the main reason for the poverty and misery of its denizens. People who are subject to the inconstant, uncertain, unknown and arbitrary will of others are likely to be poor, miserable, and ignorant because they are likely not to invest much in long scale plans and projects – what would be the point? – and such investments are necessary for material and intellectual progress. In Locke's view, such progress is a desideratum, indeed without it people cannot be free; consequently government, which people create to protect their freedom must provide them with the stable environments in which they feel secure enough to invest in long scale plans and projects. Locke did not mean, of course, that government can give people complete assurance that no one will prevent them from bringing their plans to fruition; he thought that people should be free to act within their rights, and people acting within their rights can prevent others from bringing their rights to fruition. He meant that government should give people reasonable assurance that others would not frustrate their plans by violating their rights. Further, since he believed that the object of government is to protect peoples' rights, he meant that people have a right to such assurance.

If this is correct, government must punish rights' violators, because if it does not, most people would have no assurance that others would not violate their rights and probably wreck their plans, human nature being what it is. But a policy of merely punishing rights' violators would not be sufficient to give individuals the assurance they have a right to. Even if such a policy deterred many potential rights violators, it would probably not deter all of them; those it did not deter may make a shambles of others' plans; and people would know this. Of course, people could still feel somewhat secure about investing in their plans if the policy discouraged most potential rights violators, but they would feel more secure if government also compelled rights violators to pay their victims what their plans would have earned them, had their rights not been violated. Such a policy would be unacceptable if it violated the rights of the rights violators, for example by compelling them to pay more reparation than they owed. But Locke would not have thought that it did. On his account, transgressors must repair the damage their transgressions cause; that is the reparation they owe their victims. But given Locke's conception of human nature, that persons are ideally rational, industrious and forward looking, that is, rational planners, the damage transgressors cause and which they are obliged to repair, must include the damage they may do to that ideal.

Suppose, for example that after long research and study Harry determined that a certain batch of cigars is likely to increase tremendously in value after the cigars are aged, and that he bought them planning to age them and to make a profit. If the government punishes thieves, Harry will feel more secure about his plan than if the government did not punish thieves, assuming he believes that punishing theft deters theft. But he is not likely to feel as secure as he has a right to feel because he knows that if someone is undeterred by the government's policy and steals his cigars, he will not get back the time and effort he put into his investment. Nothing in life is certain, and our best laid plans can always be undone by accident or transgression, but to give Harry the assurance he has a right to, government must compel the thief to pay him the appreciated value of the cigars. Most will agree with this if the cigars are stolen after they are aged, and after they have appreciated in value. But given Locke's conception of human beings as ideally rational planners, and consequently as having a right to a society that enables them to be rational planners, as long as securing that society does not violate people's rights, it also seems true if the cigars are stolen before they have aged, and before they have appreciated in value.

Since it is wrongful damage to a person's plans that requires repair, generally, Harry has a right to be compensated only for the frustration of plans he actually made, not for the "frustration" of plans he might have made, but did not. Suppose Harry bought his cigars to smoke them the next day, but forgot about them in the basement; if Dick smokes the cigars he owes Harry only a smoke, even if they would have been worth a million dollars had they remained undisturbed for twenty years. But this may only be true for violations of the right to property. It is certainly not true for violations of the right to liberty. If I imprison you for an hour, and you had planned to and would have earned $1000 in that hour, you have a right to seek reparation from me for $1000. But suppose I imprison you for thirty years. In that case your losses will include all the financial, cultural and educational gains you would have made had you been free, plus less measurable but perhaps more important losses like the diminution of experience, self-knowledge, self-confidence and self-esteem that may have resulted from the restriction of your liberty. Even if you did make plans, without these losses you would have made better, more informed, and more reasonable plans. If you have a right to a society that would enable you to be a rational planner, I may owe you reparation for frustrating the plans you would reasonably have made if you had been free. And, of course, the point applies with even greater force if I enslaved, or unjustly imprisoned you or discriminated against you from the time you were born.

Let us now consider the third claim implied in Locke's comment on the right of reparation, namely that this right is held against the particular individual who transgressed against one's rights and thereby caused one harm, injury or damage. This claim, if it were true, would deliver the deathblow to preferential treatment considered as reparation for injuries blacks suffer that stem from the transgressions of slavery. As the critics of preferential treatment point out, since slaveholders are long since dead, and the right to seek reparation for harm can only be pressed against those whose transgression caused the harm, then clearly no one now exists who can legitimately be made to pay for the harms slavery caused. This difficulty cannot be met by arguing that the slaveholders' descendants probably did something to transmit the harms their fathers' caused to the present generation of blacks. This may well be true, but it does not follow that they owe the present generation of blacks any reparation unless what they did transgressed on that generations' rights. It is therefore important to notice that Locke allowed that the right for reparation can sometimes be pressed against people who did not commit the transgressions that caused the damages for which reparation is sought. This is clear in his comments about the just conqueror's rights to reparation, although at first Locke seems to be making the opposite point; he claims that although the unjust man who opposes the just conqueror, may "forfeit" his life by his "miscarriages and violence," these "are no faults of the children, who may be rational and peaceable," and his goods "which Nature . . . hath made to belong to the children to keep them from perishing, do still belong to his children." But although this says that the innocent children of unjust parents inherit their parents' goods, Locke immediately adds that their rights to these goods may be qualified by the just conqueror's rights to reparation. The just conqueror, he says, "may have some right" to the goods the children inherit in order "to repair the damages he has sustained by the war, and the defence of his own right."

There are two ways to intepret Locke's argument for this conclusion. The first takes inheritance to depend on the father's consent. On this account, when Locke says that a man has a "right before other men, to inherit, with his brethren, his father's goods," he means that in the absence of a father's express consent or dissent we can assume that he tacitly consents to his property passing to his children on his death. The second takes inheritance to be independent of the father's consent, relying on the view defended by James Tully that, for Locke a "family man's property is not his property at all; it is the common property of the whole family." On this account, when Locke claims that a man has a "right before other men, to inherit, with his brethren, his father's goods," he does not mean that, in the absence of a father's express consent or dissent, we can assume that he tacitly consents to passing on his property to his children on his death; he means that children are, with their father, the joint owners of his property, so that when he dies they automatically and independently of his consent – or dissent – become its exclusive owners. But whichever interpretation we adopt, Locke's comment makes it clear that the right to reparation can sometimes be pressed against people who are not guilty of wrongfully causing the harm for which reparation is sought, and in particular, that the bare fact that the children of unjust parents are not implicated in their parents' crimes, and are totally innocent of these crimes, does not make them automatically immune to claims for reparation from those their parents wronged and injured. If they inherit goods from their parents, they may have to give up some of these goods to repair the damages their parents inflicted on those they wrongfully harmed.

It is true that Locke qualifies the rights of the just conqueror to the goods inherited by his opponents' children. But he does so in a way that emphasizes the weight he gives to the right of reparation, even when this right is pressed against the totally innocent. The just conqueror has a right to reparation against the estates of his opponents, and his opponents' children have rights to subsistence against those same estates, or as Locke puts it, "The conqueror has a title to reparation for damages received, and the children have a title to their father's estate for their subsistence." But when "there be not enough fully to satisfy both – viz., for the conqueror's losses and the children's main-tenance," then according to Locke, "he that hath and to spare must remit something

139

of his full satisfaction, and give way to the pressing and preferable title of those who are in danger to perish without it." In other words, the just conqueror's right to seek reparation against the estates of his opponents takes precedence over all the rights of his opponents' children to those estates short of their right to subsistence; he can legitimately take all that he needs to repair the damages he wrongfully sustained, as long as he does not endanger the lives of the children in doing so.

This is a strong conclusion, but we should be careful not to inflate it. It does not say or imply that the lawful conqueror's right to reparation takes precedence over the rights in general of his opponents' children; it says that his right to reparation takes precedence over their rights to their fathers' estates. Thus it would be wrong for the lawful conqueror to press his right for reparation against any of their rights other that their rights to their fathers' estates, for example by taking property from them that they did not inherit from their fathers. Of particular importance is the children's right to liberty. The just conqueror's right to reparation does not take precedence over these rights, and it would be wrong for him to compel them to work off their fathers' debt. It is only the liberty of the innocents that is thus sacrosanct. The lawful conqueror may not legitimately press his right to reparation against the right to liberty of his enemies' children, but he may legitimately press his right to reparation against his enemies' liberty. That is, Locke would have no difficulty with the idea that the lawful conqueror may legitimately compel such people to work off their debts to him. Normally we think of compulsion, imprisonment, for example, as punishment. But if, as Locke believed, serious criminals forfeit their rights to liberty, and indeed may be justly enslaved, compelling them to work to repair the damages they wrongfully inflict on others would involve no violation of right. The principle I am suggesting here can never be used to justify violating anyone's rights, even a criminal's; a thief, who forfeits his right to liberty, may perhaps be justly compelled to work off his debt to those he wrongfully injured, but he cannot justly be killed and his organs harvested for the same end, supposing that he has not forfeited his right to life. But it does apply broadly. If the children of unjust parents inherit their parents' goods and then knowingly try to prevent those their parents wrongfully injured from pressing their claims for reparation against these goods, they lose their innocence, and may forfeit their right to liberty.

Let us now consider the case for black reparations. I assume that it is no longer controversial that the slave masters wronged and harmed the slaves, and that the slaves therefore had titles for reparation against their masters. Further, Locke's answer to the question what his "Remedy" is against a "Robber" who broke into his house: "Appeal to the law for justice. But perhaps justice is denied, or I am crippled and cannot stir, robbed and have no means to do it. If God has taken away all means of seeking remedy, there is nothing left but patience. But my son, when able, may seek the relief of the Law, which I am denied: He or his son may renew their appeal, till he recover his Right," clearly implies that titles to reparation can be inherited, and that, in particular, the present generation of African Americans have probably inherited titles for reparation from their slave ancestors. If we can also assume that the present white population of the US have inherited "estates" from the slave masters, the case for black reparations would follow directly from Locke's claim or implication that the lawful conqueror or his beneficiaries can press claims for reparation against estates inherited by his enemies' children.

140

But critics have been outraged by the idea that the present white population in general is the beneficiary of the slave masters. The complaint, usually stated vehemently and in tones of violated innocence, is that most white people in the US, usually including the complainer, are descended from European immigrants who arrived in the country after slavery had been abolished. Justice Antonin Scalia has been fit to burden us with his version of this objection: "My father," Justice Scalia writes, "came to this country when he was a teenager. Not only had he never profited from the sweat of any Black man's brow, I don't think he had ever seen a Black man. There are, of course, many White ethnic groups that came to this country in great numbers relatively late in its history – Italians, Jews, Poles – who not only took no part in, and derived no profit from, the major historic suppression of the currently acknowledged minority groups, but were in fact, themselves the object of discrimination by the dominant Anglo-Saxon majority. To be sure, in relatively recent years some or all of these groups have been the beneficiaries of discrimination against Blacks, or have themselves practiced discrimination, but to compare their racial debt . . . with those who plied the slave trade, and who maintained a formal caste system for many years thereafter, is to confuse a mountain with a molehill."

Justice Scalia is on sound ground when he implies that what makes a person a beneficiary of slave masters is not that she is descended from them, but that she receives benefits from them. But his claim, that white ethnic groups "derived no profit from, the major historic suppression of the currently acknowledged minority groups," is at least controversial; Eric Williams has argued famously that slavery and the slave trade financed the industrial revolution and enhanced Europe's prosperity. More particularly, if Anglo-Saxons started the practice of racial discrimination in the US the white ethnics certainly profited from it because it prevented black people from competing for opportunities that were kept wide open for them to take advantage of. It does not matter if they were not the ones preventing blacks from competing for the opportunities; what matters is that they benefited from blacks' exclusion from a chance to compete. In his excellent discussion of Justice Scalia's passage Albert Mosley allows that Italians were discriminated against in the US, adding that many emigrated to Argentina and Brazil instead to avoid that discrimination. To his reasonable argument that this does not justify them holding on to the advantages they gained because of racial discrimination practiced against blacks, I would add that the fact that so many of them decided to emigrate to the US instead of to Brazil and Argentina – despite the prospect of being discriminated against in the US – only underlines how attractive the opportunities must have been in the US, opportunities possible in part because blacks were excluded from competing for them.

Professor Ellen Paul raises different objections. According to Paul arguments for black reparations run into the problem that claims for compensation became "stale with the passage of time," and that this is "perfectly sensible" because if a person does not "act to claim his lost possessions within a reasonable amount of time, he and his heirs are forever barred from complaining." Further, on her account, "Intervening events, and the reliance of innocent third parties on legitimate transactions involving the stolen property, make it likely that others' rights will be violated if we attempt to repair damages that are of ancient lineage." There seem to be two arguments here. The first of these arguments seems to be that if a person does not speak up to claim his lost possessions then he tacitly transfers his right to those possessions to the one who now holds them. The folly in this kind of argument should be well known by now. It has long been exposed in the disputes about tacit consent in the history of political philosophy. Failure to speak up to claim one's rights cannot mean that one tacitly transfers them or gives them up because one may be prevented from speaking up, or may face harsh penalties for speaking up. Indeed, a person retains his right to his lost possessions if he fails to speak up because he has good grounds for believing that his complaints will be ignored or dismissed. And it does not matter if potential complainants are silenced for generations. Locke's comment cited earlier, that his son or even his grandson can inherit his right to reparation indicates that he saw this point clearly.

Paul's second argument that time makes claims for compensation stale is that "Intervening events and the reliance of innocent third parties on legitimate transactions involving the stolen property make it likely that others' rights will be violated if we attempt to repair damages that are of ancient lineage." I admit, of course, that the passage of time can make it difficult to prove that there is a claim for compensation and even more difficult to prove who should pay it; witnesses die, move away, or forget. For example, if property is stolen, often, perhaps usually, the passage of time, and the number of transactions the stolen property is involved in make it difficult or impossible to know who has it, and how to get it from him without violating his rights. In such cases the victim of the robbery must simply accept the fact that he cannot collect on his claim for compensation. But this is not necessarily, or always, the case. Sometimes, despite the passage of time, and despite the large number of transactions the stolen property is involved in, we do know who benefited from it. The claim for black reparations is a case in point. We know that whites in general were allowed to compete for advantages blacks were not allowed to compete for.

A more philosophically interesting objection starts with the reminder that Locke said only that the lawful conqueror can press his right for reparation against the estates his enemies' children inherit from them; he did not say that the lawful conqueror can press that right against their rights to anything else, as, for example their rights to their liberty and earnings. This suggests the following objection: perhaps black claims for reparation can be pressed against concrete physical items some white people inherit directly from slaveholders, like plantations and mansions; this follows directly from Locke's claim that the lawful conqueror can press claims for reparation against the "estates" his enemies' children inherit from them. But relatively few white people have inherited concrete physical items directly from slaveholding ancestors. Perhaps most of them enjoyed enhanced opportunities because of the enslavement of blacks, but many, especially perhaps the newly arrived white ethnics, may have done so innocently, not realizing the unjust source of the opportunities they enjoyed; further the benefits they received from these opportunities took the form of better education, greater human capital, and higher earnings, rather than the inheritance of "estates" from slaveholders. But in that case, Locke's view of reparation may not justify preferential treatment. By giving blacks an edge in the competition for jobs and university places, preferential treatment restricts the liberty of white people who might have innocently benefited from the injuries done to blacks; but it seems that on Locke's view of reparation, blacks may not justifiably seek reparation for their injuries by restricting the liberty of innocent people, even if these people innocently benefited from their injuries.

142

The following example seems to suggest how to resolve this difficulty. Suppose I find an unconscious man, near death (call him George) and I use up some of my resources to save his life. Although George owes me a sincere, "thank you, very much," it may seem inappropriate and wrong for me to insist that he compensate me for saving his life. Why? One plausible answer is that my saving his life is an act of charity, but it is not the answer Locke would give. The first difficulty with it is that it trades on an ambiguity about the resources I used to save George's life. Suppose that George was dying of cold and I used a warm and expensive suit to save his life. Even if my act was an act of charity, it need not be inappropriate for me to ask George to return my suit when he recovers, for my act of charity – my gift to George – might have been only to allow him to use the suit to recover; it need not have been to give him the suit. But a deeper difficulty with the answer is its assumption that the beneficiary of charity incurs no obligations that can be exacted from him. This assumption is false. It follows from the further assumption that charity is a gift, but although charity is often or even usually a gift, it is not always a gift. We think that charity is a gift when we think of it as a "duty of imperfect obligation." A duty of imperfect obligation is one which is not correlated with any right; the person with such an obligation is obliged to act in a certain way, but no definite person has a right against her that she act in this way. If charity is a duty of imperfect obligation – and John Stuart Mill picked it out specifically as an example of such a duty – then the beneficiary cannot exact it from his benefactor. This suggests that when charity is given it must have been given freely, and consequently must have been a gift. The tendency to think of charity as something that the rich do for the poor furthers this view, for we naturally assume that the rich can afford to part with what they give in charity to the poor, and consequently that they must have parted with it freely.

Sometimes, however, we think of charity not as something freely given, and consequently not as a gift. This is when we think of it as a duty of perfect obligation, that is, a duty we are obligated to perform and which some others are entitled to exact from us. Locke sometimes thought of charity in this way: "Charity gives every Man a Title to so much out of another's Plenty, as will keep him from extream want, where he has no means to subsist otherwise." But if someone has a "title" to my "plenty," then it seems that even if I part with it, and "give" it to him in charity, I cannot make a gift of it to him, since making a gift involves transferring a title, and he already has the title.

But if something transferred to another in charity is not a gift, the presumption that he incurs no obligation to return it or its equivalent becomes difficult to defend. This may sound preposterous. If charity is sometimes a duty of perfect obligation it is sometimes a duty of justice because duties of perfect obligation are duties of justice; Mill made the latter point explicitly, and Locke at least drew a parallel between the duty of charity when it implies a correlative right and the duty of justice. But if justice demands that I turn something over to someone else, then how can it be that he must return it to me? We can put this another way: if what a person receives in charity is not a gift because, as Locke puts it, he has a "title" to it, why should he be obligated to return what he has a title to?

This question may seem unanswerable because of an ambiguity about what the person in question has a title to. Locke derives his claim that the needy have a title to help from others from his "Fundamental Law of Nature" which says that "all as much as may be, should be preserved." But satisfying this law does not imply that the needy do not have to pay for the help they get. Locke did not make this point clear probably because when he spoke of the "needy" having a "Right to the Surplusage" of others, he was thinking of the needy as poor, and their beneficiaries as rich. But not every needy person is necessarily poor, and not everyone who has a "surplusage" to help the needy is necessarily rich. Consider the case of George again, and suppose that George is very rich and I am very poor. George in his unconscious and helpless state is certainly needy, and if I have more than I need at the moment to save my own life, the Fundamental Law of Nature requires me to use my surplusage to preserve his life; he has, if you like, a "title" to my surplusage. But he need not have a title to it in the sense that he does not have to pay me for it when he recovers; certainly the Fundamental Law of Nature would be satisfied even if he had to pay me, for his paying me would not mean that I failed to preserve him. Indeed the Fundamental Law of Nature may fail to be satisfied if George did not pay me for my surplusage, since I may be in "extream want" because I used my surplusage to save his life. Suppose that George was not unconscious, but was lost in the wilderness and dying from hunger, when he came across my cabin well stocked with food. George would do no wrong if he ate my food; in this sense the Fundamental Law of Nature would give him a title to it; but it would not give him a title to it in the sense that he would not have to pay for it.

These considerations suggest that for Locke at least the decisive reason why I cannot insist that George pay me for saving his life is not that my saving his life was an act of charity; for Locke, the decisive reason is that George can incur enforcible obligations to me for benefits he receives from me only if he consents to receiving these benefits, knowing that in doing so he may incur enforcible obligations to me, and George being unconscious when I saved his life could not possibly have consented to any such thing. Thus on Lockean grounds there are two reasons why a person's liberty may be justifiably restricted – he commits a crime by which he forfeits his liberty, or he consents directly or indirectly to the restriction of his liberty. Now although whites who innocently benefit from injuries to blacks necessarily commit no crime, it seems that they may, nevertheless consent to receive these benefits knowing that in doing so they incur enforcible restrictions on their liberty. But in that case blacks may be justified in seeking reparation from them by restricting their liberty; that is, preferential treatment may be justified.

But this argument defeats itself. If whites innocently benefit from injuries to blacks, they cannot have understood the tainted source of these benefits, and consequently they cannot have consented to receiving them knowing that in doing so they incur enforcible restrictions on their liberty. Consequently, if there are only two ways to justify restrictions on individuals' liberty – guilt and informed consent – Locke's sketch of a theory of reparation seems opposed to all restrictions on the liberty of innocents as a way to enforce the claims of reparation.

It is possible to challenge this objection to preferential treatment by challenging its assumption that most whites innocently benefit from injuries to blacks. White ethnics were not racial innocents before they arrived from Europe, even if most of them had never seen black people. They knew that America was the land of opportunity for white people and they came fully prepared to take advantage of that fact. How else can we explain the fact that they took to racism as ducks take to water? As historians of the period tell us, one of the first words the immigrants learned when they set foot on land was "Nigger." But it is more interesting philosophically to see that it can be rebutted even if we give it that assumption. We must reconsider the claim that a person who receives benefits he does not consent to receive incurs no obligations that can be exacted from him. I argue that this claim is false. It seems to be obviously true because it gets illicit support from the tendency to rely on the examples of unconscious people being saved from death. This tendency is understandable because we want examples where it is clear that the one receiving benefits did not consent to receive them either expressly or tacitly, for tacit consent may generate obligations as surely as express consent. But although the idea of tacit consent is clear enough, it is often unclear and controversial whether or not it is given. Locke's claim that a person gives tacit consent to the authority of the state by residing within its borders is a case in point. Most philosophers believe that Locke's claim was mistaken, but other examples are more genuinely controversial. Suppose, for example, that I am walking along a street and someone thrusts a book into my hands; assuming that I can easily tell the book thruster "No thanks," I believe that I tacitly consent to receive the book, but many will disagree. Examples of unconscious people being saved avoids these tangential disputes because such people cannot possibly consent to receiving benefits either expressly or tacitly. The problem is that they insinuate that those receiving assistance without their consent receive charity – who can deny that an unconscious and presumably helpless man deserves charity – and since most people believe, though mistakenly as I have argued, that charity generates no obligations that can be exacted from them, they create a prejudice in favor of the conclusion that those who receive assistance without their consent incur no obligations they can be compelled to satisfy.

Let us therefore work with an altogether different kind of example. Suppose that I am a poor man, though I have a rich neighbor, and suppose that she is away. El Niño is bringing torrential rain, the roof of her house unexpectedly springs a leak, and her expensive furniture will be ruined unless I act quickly; and suppose I do act quickly, and pay a roofer a considerable sum to fix her roof, thereby saving her a lot of money. This example is a special case of Locke's general principle of charity that the "needy' have a "title" to the "surplusage" of others; as I indicated, even the rich are needy when, despite their wealth, they require the assistance of others if they are to avoid serious loss, and even the very poor have a surplusage when, despite their poverty, they can part temporarily with some of their income without causing themselves harm. If this is correct, and if my neighbor would have hired a roofer and paid a similar sum to save her furniture if she had been present, then although she did not consent, either expressly or tacitly, to my hiring and paying the roofer, it would not violate her rights to require her to reimburse me.

This argument depends on two crucial conditions: My assistance must not have been a gift and it must be true that if she had been present she too would have hired and paid a roofer to save her furniture. In the case under consideration we can be reasonably certain that the first condition obtains. But this may not always be true. Certainly we cannot assume that every transference of property from one person to another is a gift; if I offer you a book, saying, "This is a gift," the book belongs to you, and you are entitled to think that it does, assuming that I know what I am saying, and was not coerced or duped into saying it; it does not matter that I did not really intend that you have the book. But if the transferor does not say that it is a gift, the context must make it clear that he intends to be taken as making a gift, and sometimes the context makes it clear that he does not intend to be taken as making a gift. Often, however, there can be considerable confusion and misunderstanding whether the transference of property is a gift. It is probably even more difficult to establish whether the second condition obtains. We can presume that it does in matters of life and death; if we come upon an unconscious dying person we can assume that he would be willing to pay to save his life. Often, however, the matter is far from clear.

Because it is often controversial whether the two conditions obtain, assisting others without their consent and expecting to be paid for one's assistance is a risky business. For example, the second implies that if those you assist without their consent would not have done what you did to help them had they been able, that is, if they would have rejected your assistance had they been able to do so, then they may not be obligated to pay you for your assistance. The problem is not only that you can be mistaken about whether they would have consented to your help if they had been able to; people being what they are, many of those you assist without their consent will claim – falsely – that they would not have consented to your help had they been able to do so, and refuse to compensate you on that ground. This is one reason, I believe, that assistance given without consent is so often taken to be charity or a gift. Since the risk of not being reimbursed is so high, it is natural to assume that no one would take that risk expecting to be reimbursed; and this suggests that the assistance must have been given without any expectation of reimbursement, and consequently must have been an act of charity or a gift.

But these complications do not affect the argument that people who receive benefits without their fully informed consent may incur obligations that can be legitimately exacted from them if they would have consented to receiving the benefits had they been fully informed, and if the benefits were not gifts. Both conditions are satisfied even if whites innocently receive benefits from injuries to blacks. These benefits cannot be gifts, since one can only make a gift of what one has a right to, and the benefits are forfeited to blacks. And it seems that whites would rationally have consented to receiving the benefits had they been fully informed for they are better off with the benefits than without them, even with preferential treatment. It may be objected that they would not have consented to receiving the benefits had they been fully informed because they would have rejected the unfair advantages these benefits give them. But in that case preferential treatment gives them an opportunity to reject the unfair advantages the benefits give them; the case for it is that unless blacks are given some preference, the competition for available places and positions will be unfair because whites have advantages in human capital gained as a result of injustices to blacks.

Bibliography

Boxill, Bernard R. "The Morality of Reparation," in *Social Theory and Practice* 2.1 (Spring 1972).

Darity, William. "A Model of 'Original Sin': Rise of the West and Lag of the Rest." *American Economic Review*, Vol. 82 No. 2 (May 1992): 162–7.

Fullinwider, Robert, "Preferential Hiring and Compensation," *Social Theory and Practice*, 3 (Spring 1975).

146

Locke, John. *Two Treatises of Government*, ed. Peter Laslett. (Cambridge: Cambridge University Press, 1988).

McGary, Howard, Jr. "Justice and Reparations," *Philosophical Forum*, 5 (Fall–Winter 1977–8): 250–63.

Mill, John Stuart. "Utilitarianism," in *Utilitarianism, Liberty and Representative Government*, edited by H. B. Acton (New York: Dutton, 1951).

Mosley, Albert "Affirmative Action: Pro" in *Affirmative Action, Social Justice or Unfair Preference* (Lanham: Roman and Littlefield, 1996), 1–63.

Nozick, Robert. *Anarchy, State and Utopia* (New York: Basic Books, 1974), 93.

Paul, Ellen Frankel "Set-Asides, Reparations and Compensatory Justice," in *Compensatory Justice, Nomos XXXIII*, edited by John W. Chapman (New York: New York University Press, 1991).

Scalia, Antonin. "Commentary – The Disease as Cure," 1979 *Washington University Law Quarterly*.

Williams, Eric. *Capitalism and Slavery* (Chapel Hill: University of North Carolina Press, 1944, 1994).

Part III

AFRICA AND DIASPORA THOUGHT

Introduction to Part III

The idea of Africana philosophy is closely associated with fairly recent developments in the discipline, most notably the arrival of a critical mass of African, Caribbean, and African-American philosophers. The relevance of a distinctive "African" world-view to Africana philosophy is a matter of controversy. Molefi Asante's concept of Afrocentricity, along with some of the prevailing views regarding Africanisms in African-American thought are critically examined in the chapters by Lucius Outlaw and Tommy Lott. Albert Mosley stakes out a middle position in the debate regarding the place of traditional African philosophy, or ethnophilosophy, in contemporary African thought. A fundamental issue informing the development of Africana philosophy is the question of whether the African heritage has a significant role to play.

Outlaw's critical examination of Afrocentric doctrine takes for granted the episte-mological view that "species-specific" knowledge is needed to insure survival and prosperity for every group. What is at issue is whether this implies that the needed knowledge is universal, or whether knowledge-needs vary with the lived experience of particular cultural groups. Outlaw maintains that notions of validity and truth must be included among the criteria governing the production of all knowledge, even if there is cultural variation. But this raises the worry that knowledge production conditioned by partisan social or political commitments cannot satisfy these criteria. One source of this worry, as Outlaw points out, is that, since the Renaissance, the prevailing conceptions of rationality and universalism have been entrenched in the pursuit of global capitalism. Consequently, a particular ideology that excludes Africans and their descendants from the human category has developed to legitimate the inequalities that result from this pursuit. Outlaw maintains that the situation of African-descended people under this kind of white supremacy, by existential necessity, demands a radical critique of Eurocentric knowledge-production "to play a crucial role in the struggle for emancipation."

In Asante's so-called "Africalogical" inquiry, language, myth, dance, music, art and ancestral memory provide the sources of knowledge and canons of proof, along with science. Outlaw is dissatisfied with Asante's failure to spell this out. He criticizes Asante's discussion of cosmological, epistemological, axiological, and aesthetic issues as not much more than promissory, and, in some respects, seriously inadequate. Especially problematic is Asante's rejection of the regulative ideal of objectivity as appropriate for "Africalogy." Asante claims that what often passes for objectivity is some kind of collective European subjectivity and proposes, as an alternative, what is ultimately verifiable in the experience of all humans, with procedures that are fair and open, as the final empirical authority. Outlaw claims that Asante wrongly attributes the norm of objectivity to Europeans and reveals the inconsistency of Asante's reliance on the rejected idea of objectivity in his claims about fair interpretation. Despite this rather serious limitation, Outlaw thinks Afrocentricity can still provide a "guiding concept" for knowledge-production in the interests of African-descended people.

Outlaw supports the conceptual unity Asante has brought to Africana Studies with the emphasis on the African origins of civilization. But there has been a bevy of criticism of this aspect of the Afrocentric view. In *The Black Atlantic*, Paul Gilroy questions Asante's claim to an African culture anterior to slavery as having a role to play in the emancipatory struggles of the African diaspora. He proposes a notion of surviving Africanisms that has been articulated in the work of Toni Morrison and Amiri Baraka.

Tommy Lott critically examines Gilroy's account of African retentions in African-American culture. He notes that the suggestion that there is an African element in African-American culture always stands in need of scientific verification. The debate between Melvin Herskovits and E. Franklin Frazier reflects the ambivalence in African-American thought towards the question of African retentions. Lott maintains that, despite this history of debate there is sufficient evidence to support the claim that many African-American cultural practices are grounded at least partly on principles and ideas that derive from an African cultural heritage. He argues that Gilroy's attempt to specify criteria on the basis of which we are entitled to speak of African-American cultural practices in terms of their African roots is grounded on a confused notion of cultural hybridity. According to Lott, this confusion hinders full appreciation of the African ingredient in African-American culture.

Lott begins with a consideration of Frederick Douglass's orientation to Africa. The main features of Douglass's view, reflected in the two issues he invoked to argue against emigration, indicate a political dimension of the debate about retentions. First, he questioned whether the interest of the black race is best served by African-Americans returning to Africa, or by their remaining in America to uplift the race. Secondly, he asserted that African-Americans are a mixed race and hence are American, not African. As Gilroy points out, even emigrationists such as Martin Delany and Edward Blyden shared Douglass's low esteem for African culture and were in agreement on the need for the modernization of Africa.

Gilroy asks, "what elements of invariant tradition heroically survive slavery?" but does not treat this as a straightforward empirical question. Rejecting Molefi's view of slavery as the source of a "dangerously negative image" of African-Americans (as disconnected from their African origin), Gilroy maintains that "the most enduring Africanism of all" exhibits a priority of form over content. He uses the Percy Mayfield song, "By the River's Edge" to illustrate how vernacular expressions of African retentions have been transformed by the experience of enslavement. The slave's music is premodern, modern, and antimodern all at once. Many twentieth-century love and loss songs, such as Mayfield's, are transcoded expressions of slavery's "unspeakable horror."

152

Because music need not have survived relatively unaltered to count as retentions, it best fits Gilroy's model of tradition as the enduring "changing same."

Taking issue with several overstatements by Gilroy regarding the preslave past, Lott sees the idea of reclaiming an anterior culture as less problematic in certain isolated cases such as the case of the Saramakas in Surinam and other maroon cultures that have survived in other parts of the New World. Although he believes Gilroy rightfully insists that there is no anteriority for African-American culture that can override the profound influence of slavery, he supports Alain Locke's view of a role for retentions in the development of a unique cultural contribution by African-American artists. Gilroy is critical of Locke's notion of authentic folk culture, but Lott defends Locke's idea that, as a criterion of its authenticity, African-American music expresses the experiences of African Americans. On Lott's view, the latent function of transformed retentions is to facilitate the adaptation of African-descended people to the alienation engendered by a modern world.

The question of the significance of ethnophilosophy in African thought is no less controversial than the question of African retentions in African-American culture. Underlying the debate about the definition of African philosophy is the question of whether philosophy requires a tradition of written communication that is foreign to Africa. Albert Mosley considers three senses of the notion of African philosophy to indicate the manner in which certain versions of ethnophilosophy have been opposed by African philosophers aligned with universalist and hermeneutical schools of thought.

Ethnophilosophy takes the set of values, categories, and assumptions implicit in the language, practices, and beliefs of African cultures as fundamental. Negritude philosophers, for instance, argue that Africans have a distinctive orientation to reality that is based on emotion rather than logic, encourages participation rather than analysis, and is manifested in the arts rather than in the sciences. This contention has been opposed by some African philosophers. Cheikh Anta Diop, John Mbiti, and Julius Nyerere have stressed the unique nature of African cultures, but disagree with Leopold Senghor's claim that Africans are more oriented towards the arts than to science and technology. Diop cites the achievements of the Egyptians in science, math, architecture, and philosophy and their influence on the Greeks. Critics of ethnophilosophy argue that a focus on the past detracts from a critical posture that evaluates all practices in terms of what they contribute to the liberation of Africa. Mosley cites Paulin Hountondji's and Anthony Appiah's criticism that ethnophilosophy benefits European colonizers and placates Africans, for African philosophy need not express a particular outlook of Africans.

Arguing from a universalist perspective, Kwasi Wiredu supports Hountondji's view that African philosophy need not be unique to African languages and cultures. According to Hountoundji, philosophy is a critical literature produced by Africans for Africans. Hountoundji's claim that written discourse (critical literature) is a necessary condition is opposed by Odera Oruka. Oruka cites active engagement in critical reflection on the assumptions of one's culture as the only requirement for philosophy – independent of a written discourse. Wiredu observes that the development of philosophy in Africa parallels the development of philosophy in Europe – that traditional thought in either case is not paradigmatic. He argues that African philosophers have a pivotal responsibility to "domesticate" topics in logic, epistemology, metaphysics and philosophy of mind into materials usable by Africans. He cautions that indigenous sources may

153

yield insights that are valuable to Africans and nonAfricans, but must also be critically viewed.

Wiredu argues for "conceptual decolonization" to avoid an uncritical assimilation of Western ideas by African people. The imposition on Africa of foreign conceptual schemes through language, religion and politics has fostered the acceptance of concepts, categories, and relationships that are often of little use, and sometimes even detrimental. Mosley objects to this suggestion by pointing out that there are many African languages in Africa, even within a single modern nation state. He cites this as a limitation of Wiredu's position by questioning the extent to which the peculiarities of one language e.g., Zulu, Hausa, or Ga reflects the linguistic peculiarities of another, e.g., Xhosa, Yoruba, or Akan.

According to the hermeneutical school, African philosophy operates in concert with the struggle against cultural and economic imperialism. Tsenay Serequeberhan borrows from Hans-Georg Gadamer and Martin Heidegger to frame the central dilemma of the postcolonial situation. On one horn is the continuining hegemony of Europe under neocolonialism and, on the other is the continuing influence of precolonial traditions on the rural masses. Mosley points out that Serequeberhan's theme of a return to the source has shortcomings similar to the inadequacy of Wiredu's account of conceptual decolonization. Both fail to note that many features of modern life have no analogues in traditional practices and cannot be validated by reference to them. Mosley believes Kwame Gyekye's proposal to fuse traditional and modern features of society to meet African needs, by forging a synthesis whereby Africans appropriate imported tools and expertise to readapt traditional technologies, also fails for a similar reason.

Mosley criticizes the universalists and hermeneuticists with regard to their embrace of western sources as a basis for African philosophy and their failure to appreciate the extent to which modern technological orientations may be incompatible with traditional technologies. They have faltered in a manner similar to the ethnophilosophers they criticize. For Mosley, ethnophilosophy is problematic because of a tendency of its adherents to identify some essential difference between Africans and non-Africans – an endeavor that quickly succumbs to racialism. He invokes postmodern philosophy to point out that there need be no essences for there to be kinds of things. This need not imply that there is no internal coherence to the notion of African philosophy, only that there need be no one factor. He insists that a cluster of factors combine to characterize this category. The solution to racism is not to deny the existence of racial differences, but to reject the manner in which those differences are used to disadvantage Africans relative to Europeans. Mosley's recommendation is twofold. Mainstream American society first must recognize the positive value of attributes traditionally associated with Africans, without suggesting that such attributes are unique to Africans and, secondly, insist that modern institutions be transformed to reflect the value of those attributes. According to Mosley, Africa might benefit more from learning to use its music to teach mathematics, instead of adopting mathematics as the principal means of teaching its music.

154

9

"Afrocentricity": Critical Considerations

LUCIUS T. OUTLAW, JR.

The production, validation and justification, legitimation, refinement and maintenance, distribution and mediation, and utilization of various forms of certified "knowledge" are endeavors (hereafter referred to collectively as "knowledge production") that
must be undertaken, more or less successfully, by authorized persons of every generation in every society that wishes to survive, reproduce, and live well across successive generations. For members of the human species do not enter the world already
equipped with programs of beliefs, understandings, and action-guiding strategies –
forms of knowledge – that will insure survival and well-being. Consequently, such "programs" must be produced; and those effective in enhancing the prospects of survival
and well-being must be sorted out from those less effective. These imperatives, then, give
rise to the need for "knowledge programs" for sorting programs of knowledge: that is,
for epistemologies or accounts of and criteria for knowledge production. Furthermore,
to whatever extent tens of thousands of years of evolution, of successful survival and
flourishing (more or less) through adaptation, have affected the genetic make-up of
humans, the genetic programs of each individual, and those of the pools of genes
of the population groups from which an individual's genes are derived, while directly
determining most of physical make-up and development, provide only the important
boundary-conditions for the acquisition, retention, reformulation, and utilization of
the action-guiding knowledges acquired by way of learning-experiences. Genes condition – but do not strictly and completely determine – the development, acquisition, and
utilization of knowledge-programs except for the ways in which the production and
utilization of such programs are species-specific (for example: the use of a human language and of symbol systems for developing, communicating, and mediating programs,
programming, and learning; the use of particular brain-capacities and the nervous
system for imagining, perceiving, conceptualizing, and communicating). What assur-
ances are to be had that knowledge production is conducive to survival and well-being
must be achieved, ultimately, through experiments in thinking, believing, valuing, and
acting in various situations of living, experiments that prove successful in all contexts
important to surviving and living well.

155

Figuring out the whats, hows and whys of success, and anticipating what will or ought to be needed for successful living, are fundamental aspects of knowledge production. So, too, the certification of what has been figured out as validated and justified "knowledge" to be legitimated, distributed, and mediated authoritatively to appropriate recipients. But the production of knowledge, as well as experiments of living, are inextricably and thoroughly social endeavors: they require coordinated, deliberate cooperation sanctioned and guided by shared norms. So it is for all human collectivities organized and maintained for the longevity, durability, and prosperity of individuals (who can only endure and prosper through the coordinated efforts of others) and through them the prosperity, durability, and longevity of the collectivity. For it is the condition of the collectivity and its resources, repertoires of knowledge included, not of individuals alone, that is utterly decisive for human endurance and well-being.

The need of species-specific knowledge of various kinds to insure survival and prosperity is *recurrent*, for *all* human collectivities. Does this mean, then, that the kinds of knowledge needed are thereby invariant across encultured times and spaces and can thus be produced, certified, legitimated, distributed, and mediated in accord with success-securing norms that are likewise "universal" (that is, throughout the earth . . .) and invariant? Or, do knowledge-needs vary with evolutionary development and the lived-experiences of particular self-reproducing human population groups in particular geographical and socio-cultural "ecological niches"? Consequently, that the kinds of knowledge needed, as well as the criteria to govern the production of knowledge, vary according to populations and environments and according to the life-agendas of biocultural reproductive social groups in their particular environments?

A review of the long histories of concern with these (and similar) questions will reveal that elaborate "yes" answers have been given to each, but that no one answer has been able to prevail over all others, certainly not across all fields and kinds of knowledge. Even in the most secure of the systematic and formal sciences there remain ineradicable indeterminacies and conditions that affect the production of these forms of knowledge and thus affect their range and forms of validity. Nonetheless, notions of "validity" and "truthfulness" – if not timeless, universal Truth – continue to serve as regulative ideals for the production of knowledge in virtually all fields. And in the formal and systematic natural sciences at least, appeals to these ideals, as well as claims that the conditions for meeting them have been met in various instances, can be made without seemingly self-serving regard for who will be helped by the justified knowledge – that is, without violating appropriate canons of objectivity and impartiality in the pursuit of conditional (if not absolute) truth. By many accounts, that is the way knowledge-production at its best is *supposed* to work in all fields of inquiry. And much effort has been expended over several thousand years by thinkers concerned with these matters to certify and perfect the production of such truthful and valid knowledge.

Still, "impartially"? "Objectivity"? "Truth"? Appropriate and viable specifications for each of these notions is dependent on what forms of what passes for knowledge are the focus of discussion and on the agenda for knowledge production. Nonetheless, today there is fairly widespread consensus that in almost no fields of inquiry with certified understanding is the knowledge "absolute" in terms of being wholly unconditioned by contingent particularities of historical time or socio-cultural place (though for formal

156

systems such as mathematics and logic, for example, neither truth nor validity is much conditioned by these factors). There is substantially less agreement, however, about whether knowledge-production more generally can be conditioned by partisan social or political commitments and still satisfy appropriate criteria for truthfulness or validity. For many persons, meeting these criteria requires rather strict impartiality and objectivity: the production of knowledge proper cannot be achieved if affected by partisan commitments other than commitments to truthfulness, validity, and impartiality, the norms for which do not depend for their viability on the partisan social, political, or other preferences of the knowledge producers, but rather (should) transcend all such preferences while being viable and valid for all persons – producers and consumers – who commit to them.

There is widespread belief that the ordering of individual and social life on the basis of knowledge produced and certified by rigorous adherence to just such norms has been the driving force in the achievement of distinctively progressive, enlightened, modern communities of free, autonomous individuals: that is, mature, self-actualizing persons who are bound only by duty to the dictates of reason alone, thus are (or should be) unencumbered by uncritical adherence to tradition, dogma, and parochial prejudices including those of natal tribal collectivities. Liberal and social democratic, more or less capitalist, social formations are thought to be the highest achievement and best nurturing context for these free individuals to flourish.

But with full acknowledgment of the substantial progress in many areas of life achieved through the formation of modern nation-states and other organizations and communities, in significant part due to commitments of various kinds and degrees to reason-grounded norms for truth and validity to govern the production of knowledge by which to meet recurring and new challenges of living in the ordering of personal and social life, there is much more to the story of "modern" developments. These same historic, indeed revolutionary, developments have also been explicitly, thoroughly, even brutally partisan: the projects of forming modern, "free" nation-states were initiated and carried out by, and in the interests of, various nations or peoples of Europe who, in establishing state sovereignty for themselves (as Anglo-Saxons, Germans, Frenchmen, Americans, etc.), extended that sovereignty over other non-Anglo-Saxon, German, or French peoples, lands, and resources in establishing white racial supremacy, the modern grounds of sovereignty in conflictual encounters of European peoples with peoples of other lands. Retrospectively, these projects, taken together, constituted what has come to called "Eurocentrism"[1]: a cultural complex of attitudes, sentiments, customs, habits, ideas, ideals, norms, and practices that motivated, informed, and legitimated the social and cultural, economic, and political orderings of life, of peoples. Two key aspects of this Eurocentric complex have been the notions of racialized hierarchies of peoples ordered by notions of white racial supremacy, and a capitalist political economy with universalist aspirations: that is, a desire to dominate the globe – even the solar system, perhaps – economically, civilizationally, and racially by peoples from Europe.

The "Eurocentric project" became a global political and economic project, because, in the view of Samir Amin (and quite a few others), it was (and is) informed and fueled by a particular theory of world history complemented, I must add, by a particular philosophical anthropology: namely, that the "progressive" modernization of the world was the historic mission of the "race" of European "white" peoples. This self-constructed orientation emerged during the Renaissance as a decisive "qualitative break" in human history: "Europeans become conscious of the idea that the conquest of the world by their civilization is henceforth a possible objective. They therefore develop a sense of absolute superiority, even if the actual submission of other peoples to Europe has not yet taken place." To these convictions a second key element was joined: the crystallization of capitalist society in Europe into the fundamental rules and practices of a capitalist economic system and the increasingly rationalized character of decision-making in social organization and state policies. Thus, the two definitive motivations of Eurocentrism: aspirations for rationality and universalism both to be realized through the political-economic and cultural systems of capitalism through which Europe progressively imposes itself and its values on a worldwide scale.[2]

From the Renaissance, through the Enlightenment, and on into the nineteenth century, a particular ideology was developed, institutionalized, legitimated, and deployed to legitimate the expansive, imperialist Eurocentric project and to legitimate, as well, the inequalities that accompany and result from its realization, an ideology constructed of four key enabling mythical elements (that is, narrative stories peoples fabricate and tell themselves that are designed to provide relief from and reassurance in the face of existential anxieties with regard to the meanings of the most crucial things in the ordering and continuation of individual, family, tribal, and social life generally, stories the salience and viability of which are not – cannot be – secured via empirical confirmation no matter how "scientific"):

- the myth of "Western History" narrated as the story of an "eternal West" with Greek ancestry through which there was the establishment of the idea that this Greek heritage – in truth, a reconstructed heritage that was removed from the milieu of the Orient and annexed to Europe – predisposed Europe to rationality which predisposition "supposedly accounts for capitalism's [and the theoretical and practical sciences'] emergence in Europe first . . .";
- racialism as the fundamental basis for the attempted construction of the presumptive cultural unity of Europe, which serves, in turn, as the basis for invidious characterizations and distinguishing of other peoples as less than fully human "Orientals," "Negroes/Africans," "Indians";
- the "Christianophile" myth: the appropriation of Christianity from its milieu of origination and its annexation to Europe through reinterpretations that make of it a principal factor in the maintenance of Europe's presumptive cultural unity, particularly after notions of white racial supremacy are increasingly discredited;
- use of this refashioned and reinterpreted religion against the religions of Semitic peoples, against Islam, Hinduism, and other non-Christian, non-European white – thus, not fully human – peoples of the Near East, the distant Orient, Africa, the New Worlds.[3]

Consequently, a great deal of the knowledge produced to fuel, guide, and legitimate the centuries-long expansive projects of continental and diasporic European peoples served also to rationalize and justify their racist imperialism and other modes of exploitation. Western modernity's reasonable life and justice were not the order of the day except for those who met the racial and/or ethnic, gender, religious, socio-economic class criteria for being a proper human being blessed and chosen by a Christian God and ready, because of His annointment, to exercise and benefit from the proper exercise of Reason.

With great and determined effort, expended across centuries and thousands of miles and aided by several authoritative forms of knowledge, Africans and their descendants were defined as not meeting the criteria. Consequently, millions were killed, millions more maimed and their lives distorted, still millions more herded worse than cattle and transported thousands of miles from their homes and families to live and die – never to flourish – in New Worlds being fashioned for the free living of white male citizens and their charges and the supremacy – *vis-à-vis* any and all black folk and other peoples of color – of any and all white folk.

The struggles of African and African-descended peoples to be free of and to recover from the holocaust of this racist exploitation and the oppressions of white racial supremacy have required, then, radical critiques of knowledge production by peoples of European descent (and by African and African-descended peoples substantially influenced by them, as well), particularly in those instances in which such knowledge was produced and utilized to rationalize and justify oppression and exploitation. The production of various forms of knowledge by black folk in these historic circumstances has thus had to be decidedly partisan *by existential necessity*: that is, to aid emancipatory struggles for creative freedom in and through which to engage in the reconstruction of lives while being guided by devotion to the humane well-being and flourishing of African and African-descended peoples, first and foremost. There has been, and continues to be, a compelling need for decidedly *partisan* knowledges centered on and devoted to the interests of African and African-descended peoples. Hence, the call for an *Afrocentric* orientation to and vision of knowledge production: for decidedly partisan knowledge production by virtue of explicit commitment to and guidance by the interests of African and African-descended peoples.[4]

While this call, formulated in such terms, is especially associated with the very influential writings and other prominent efforts of Molefi Kete Asante and Maulana Karenga in particular, recognition of the need for, and engaging in the production of, knowledge (historical, social scientific, literary, philosophical, aesthetic, religious and theological ...) in service to the emancipatory interests of African and African-descended peoples have been imperatives pursued by engaged black intellectuals for centuries. Contemporary Black, African American, some instances of African, and Africana Studies ventures are clusterings of efforts in colleges and universities of knowledge production and mediation devoted to Afrocentric agendas, many of which such efforts grew out of situations of struggle of the Civil Rights and Black Power Movements from the 1950s through the 1970s and '80s. Yet the self-consciously partisan production of knowledge in the interest of Negroes and other colored peoples in the Americas, Africa and elsewhere predates by many decades these more contemporary efforts, and was taken up by dedicated persons many of whom did not hold positions in academic institutions – or, even when they did, because they were persons of African descent their productive labors were generally denied recognition, validation, and legitimation as providing settled knowledge. All the more compelling, then, the need for the institutions and organizations, agendas and strategies, and African and African-descended knowledge-workers to produce partisan knowledge in the interest of African peoples, knowledge unencumbered by the constraints of the Eurocentric project of white racial supremacy.[5]

But a call to what, precisely? What does it mean, how is one, to be properly "Afrocentric"? Many persons have responded to the call and committed themselves to being "Afrocentric," a majority of them, I suspect, in their cultural life primarily since they are not involved professionally in the production of knowledge. Yet this was, indeed, what was intended, in part, by Molefi Asante when, in an initial effort to work out his idea, he offered a conception of "Afrocentricity" (the state or modality of *being* Afrocentric, we might say . . .) as a matter or process of being "centered" in and on the values and interests, and these on the historical experience, of African people.[6] For all living and knowing, Asante argues, occur in and from some "place" or "position" in history, culture, and locale in which the living and knowing person is situated or "centered," which he or she shares experientially with others similarly positioned, and which affects their living and knowing. Caught up in the Eurocentric project, to involve oneself in *becoming* Afrocentric is to adopt a critical posture as a life-orientation, one that begins with "the primary measure! Does it place Africans in the center?" One *has become* Afrocentric "when the person becomes totally changed to a conscious level of involvement in the struggle for his or her own mind liberation."[7]

With what implications and explicit guidance for the production of knowledge, however? These issues have been a focal preoccupation of Asante's (and of a significant number of other thinkers and scholars) over the years due, in large part, to the responsibilities of his position as founding chairperson of the Department of African American Studies at Temple University (Philadelphia, Pennsylvania) which provided the first, and until recently the only, Ph.D.-granting program in African American Studies in the United States of America. In his *Kemet, Afrocentricity and Knowledge* ("Part I: Interiors," pp. 3–40), Asante attempted to provide a more developed response to this question and to challenges to his (and others') previous conceptualizations of "Afrocentric." As set forth in this work, his goal is still "freedom from the constraints of Eurocentricists in connection with critical theory . . ."; and "place" is still the focal and grounding metaphor (no pun intended) and heuristic notion for working out his conception of Afrocentricity:

> Our place is the constantly presenting and re-presenting context, the evolving presentation context, the perspective – that is, history to us.
> The Afrocentrist sees knowledge of this "place" perspective as a fundamental rule of intellectual inquiry because its content is a self-conscious obliteration of the subject/object duality and the enthronement of an African wholism [*sic*]. A rigorous discipline is necessary to advance the intellectual movement toward a meaningful concept of place. In saying this I am challenging the Afrocentrist to maintain inquiry rooted in a strict interpretation of place in order to betray all naïve racial theories and establish Afrocentricity as a legitimate response to the human conditions. All knowledge results from an occasion of encounter in place. But the place remains a rightly shaped perspective that allows the Afrocentrist to put African ideals and values at the center of inquiry . . . The Afrocentrist seeks to uncover and use codes, paradigms, symbols, motifs, myths, and circles of discussion that reinforce the centrality of African ideals and values as a valid frame of reference for acquiring and examining data.[8]

160

This metaphor of being oriented in a determinate space, of being "centered" in an appropriate "place," is a way of getting at the all important matters of the situated *interests* that set the *orientation* and *agenda* that structure the production of knowledge. Since all knowledge, Asante is convinced, "relates ultimately to some human interest . . . ," in struggling against Eurocentrism and for African peoples there is thus a compelling need for African and African-descended producers of knowledge to take pains to insure that the ends and means of their knowledge-producing efforts serve appropriate values, ideals, and interests of African people – namely, those that, first and foremost, preserve and enhance our cultural lives and prospects (but that also contribute to the well-being of others).[9]

If this is the Afrocentric agenda, what is required for such knowledge production? For Asante, "Africalogical" inquiry (his preferred term for Afrocentric knowledge production) is a quest for *meaning*, defined first and foremost by "place" and "framed by cosmological, epistemological, axiological, and aesthetic issues."[10] In terms of cosmological issues, "The fundamental assumptions of Africalogical inquiry are based on the African orientation to the cosmos" within which orientation, he suggests, there are several concerns to be considered as fundamental matters of inquiry (race as a social factor; culture; gender; and class) though he does not provide much at all in the way of explications of these concerns, nor spell out fully and clearly how they should properly be addressed in knowledge production.[11]

Epistemological issues, the context in which these concerns should be discussed, are thus at the very heart of endeavoring to forge an Afrocentric approach to knowledge production, to developing Africalogy as a multi- and interdisciplinary venture. Yet, just where the most important and demanding work is called for, especially with regard to rehabilitating the notion of *truth* in the production of knowledge about and for African peoples, and for others, Asante has astonishingly little to offer: "What constitutes the quest for truth in the Afrocentric enterprise? In Africalogy, language, myth, ancestral memory, dance–music–art, and science provide the sources of knowledge, the canons of proof and the structures of truth."[12] And what *are*, precisely, the crucial "canons of proof" and "structures of truth" in these endeavors? Asante doesn't recover or spell these out for our consideration supported by his persuasive argument in their behalf. Rather, we get, at most, the likes of the following regarding language as one of the sources of Afrocentric knowledge production: "In the United States Ebonics serves as the archetype of African-American language."[13] Two more short paragraphs follow, each one devoted to a discussion of "*Myth*" and "*Dance–Music–Art*," and the explicit discussion of "Epistemological Issues" is completed, the whole discussion taking up less than a full page of the book. There is no more to be had from his discussion of "Axiological Issues" (a discussion of "good" that concludes with "Doing good is equivalent to being beautiful," and two sentences on "right conduct" that conclude "The Afrocentric method isolates conduct rather than physical attributes of a person in literary or social analysis"[14]) and "Aesthetic Issues." The latter discussion draws on the work of Kariamu Welsh-Asante in offering seven "aesthetic senses" (polyrhythm, polycentrism, dimensional, repetition, curvilinear, epic memory, and wholism [*sic*]) as "the leading elements of the African's response to art, plastic or performing."[15]

What Asante provides in the way of discussion of cosmological, epistemological, axiological, and aesthetic issues is not much more than promissory and seriously inade-

161

quate for what is needed to underwrite Africalogy as a determinedly partisan venture in knowledge production. Not only is this disappointing, the absence of a much needed fuller account leaves his conception of the enterprise seriously underdeveloped and vulnerable to critique and to the challenges to be met in the politics of knowledge that are the normal life of institutions of research and education. Still, much to his credit, as Maulana Karenga has pointed out, Asante has made major contributions to Africana Studies through his continuing efforts to bring conceptual unity to African-centered approaches in the form of his elaborations of the notion of *Afrocentricity*.[16] In this regard there is real value in the rest of his conceptualization of Africalogy in the first part of *Kemet, Afrocentricity and Knowledge*, particularly in his discussions of the "shape of the discipline"; its subject fields (social, communication, historical, cultural, political, economic, psychological); arguing the case for "The uses of African origins of civilization and the Kemetic high culture as a classical starting point . . ." as "the practical manifestations of the ways the scholar secures centrism when studying Africa"; mapping out the geographical scope of the African world, of the field(s) of study of Africalogy ("includes Africa, the Americas, the Caribbean, various regions of Asia and the Pacific. Wherever people declare themselves as African, despite the distance from the continent or the recentness of their out-migration . . ."); and touching on appropriate data-sources for inquiry ("oral, written and artifactal records").[17]

Nonetheless, there are many pertinent issues to be addressed and resolved having to do with appropriate norms and strategies for identifying and querying the various data-sources, important tasks that are hindered significantly, were we left to rely on Asante's programmatic articulations alone, by the absence in these articulations of a more fully developed and vetted epistemology. This problem becomes especially poignant when Asante takes up the matter of methodology ("The Problems of Method," pp. 23–40), which, it turns out, is really his most sustained discussion of epistemological matters in *Kemet, Afrocentricity and Knowledge* (though apparently he does not view them as such). It is, however, a troubled discussion. Of particular note, having earlier expressed concern for "canons of proof" and "structures of truth" in Africalogy (p. 10), Asante takes care to reject the regulative ideal and normativity of "objectivity" as appropriate for Africalogy:

> The Afrocentrist does not accept the European concept of objectivity because it is invalid operationally . . . what often passes for objectivity is a sort of collective European subjectivity. Therefore it may not serve any useful purpose to speak of objectivity and subjectivity as this division is artificial in and of itself. The Afrocentricist speaks of research that is ultimately verifiable in the experiences of human beings, the final empirical authority. Of course, the methods of proof are founded upon the principles of fairness and openness. Both concepts are based in the idea of doing something that can be shown to be fair in its procedure and open in its application.[18]

There are several quite troubling aspects to this line of argument. First, there is the conflation of the notion of objectivity with raciality/ethnicity given his characterizing the concept/norm as a "European concept" which thus renders it inappropriate for an Afrocentric knowledge producer even though Africalogy is to have methods of proof governed by principles of fairness and openness. Moreover, within the space of two pages after the quoted passage, Asante asserts that "The Afrocentric method insists that the researcher examines [sic] herself or himself in the process of examining any subject . . . The reason . . . is to ascertain what obstacles exist to an Afrocentric method in the researcher's own mind. Retrospection is the process of questioning one's self after the project has been completed to ascertain if any personal obstacles exist to a fair interpretation."[19] So, there can be "personal" obstacles in "the researcher's own mind" that prevent "fair interpretations" as required by principles of fairness and openness? What distinction is operative here if not the rejected one of objectivity (fair interpretation) versus subjectivity (personal obstacles – obstacles in the researcher's own mind – that prevent them from producing a "fair" interpretation)?

This self-contradictory approach is made worse by Asante's attempt to appeal to a supposedly distinguishing aspect of African cosmological life that is supposed to be normative for the epistemological structuring of Africalogy: namely, the commitment to "wholism" [sic] ("The Afrocentricist finds the wholistic [sic] impulse naturally from the cultural environment . . . Afrocentric method suggests cultural and social immersion as opposed to 'scientific distance' as the best approach to understand African phenomena") rather than to what he regards as the "artificial" Eurocentric separations of subject/object, speaker/audience, dancer/spectators or investigator/subject.[20] What he does not provide, however, is an adequate, fleshed-out account of this "wholism" that makes the case, as well, for its absence as a commitment among peoples of Europe, a case I do not think Asante can make. For there have been many instances of European thinkers attempting to develop integrative, sometimes self-described "holistic" explanatory and ontological schemes as counter to what they took to be atomistic, too individualistic, reductive, linear accounts which they regarded as based on and contributing to serious misunderstandings of realities, with equally serious consequences. The rich promissory note of a methodological commitment to "wholism" is yet to be fully and properly cashed out by Asante.

Much of the difficulty plaguing Asante's methodological efforts is due to his over-reliance on "Eurocentric" as a tool for making certain critical distinctions. This notion is much too blunt, and much too loaded with complicated and complicating semantic weightings of notions of raciality and ethnicity, to do the fine-grained work called for without especially deft handling when attending to epistemological and methodological matters. By way of his training, and his own continuing self-education notwithstanding (note his discussion of Husserlian phenomenology on pages 26ff), Asante has not yet cultivated sufficient deftness of understanding and articulation with regard to epistemological matters. Moreover, too often his distinguishing matters as either being European or African is simplistic; and frequently he bequeaths to the possession of Europeans what cannot rightly be claimed to be the property of or patented by any particular people, such as the important norm of "objectivity" in knowledge production. Ironically, in this way Asante participates in the very Eurocentric project of hegemonic appropriation against which he continues to struggle so valiantly.

Epistemology and methodological considerations, vital to efforts to articulate a contestatory venture in knowledge production, as is very much the case with Afrocentric Africana Studies or Africalogy, are by no means Asante's strong suits though, again, there is much of value in his handicapped discussion of methodology, such as his concern that those studying realities having to do with African and African-descended

163

peoples immerse themselves in the cultural lives of those they study before producing and pronouncing findings; setting a heuristic vision of a methodology in Africalogical knowledge production as "wholistic [sic] and integrative" and "devoid of obvious prejudices"; requiring that the epistemology be "participatory and committed."[21] Further, he argues that "The fundamental theoretical bases for Africalogy are derived from the Afrocentric perspective. Since the Africalogists must select from a vast galaxy of facts for a study; it is the theoretical principle which assists the Africalogist in determining the questions to ask and the methods to use in acquiring data which will answer the questions."[22] However, to my mind his own efforts, while promising, have yet to provide an adequate set of theoretical principles or account of their application to do this work effectively. Even in *Kemet, Afrocentricity and Knowledge* the discussion of methodology continues to rely too much on contestatory rhetoric and inadequately developed heuristic metaphors and insights, however promising.

What to conclude regarding the viability of "Afrocentricity" as the defining and guiding concept and motif for knowledge production in the interests of African and African-descended peoples? First, that Asante's creative, valiant, and generous efforts notwithstanding, no one conception of the notion is sufficiently intellectually persuasive to provide coherence and uniformity to efforts in Africana Studies or Africalogy. To a large extent because the notion can really only function heuristically – that is, as an orienting commitment in terms of which knowledge workers in Africana Studies are called upon to make the experiences, needs, accomplishments and failures, unfinished projects and desires of African and African-descended peoples, their life-worlds and historicities, their "fundamental point of departure and intellectual concerns."[23] In this way "Afrocentric" can (and for many scholars does) serve well as a vehicle for the committed *envisioning* of an ongoing project (to paraphrase Karenga), an important *agenda-setting orientation* that helps to guide "the delineation of a conceptual framework for a self-conscious, unified, and effective way of understanding, appreciating, and utilizing the rich and varied complexity of African life and culture."[24] The call for Afrocentricity in knowledge production is thus a call to commitment to a partisan vision and agenda *for* knowledge production, and a reminder of who those are who are the subject–object foci of, and are to be well served by, the knowledge produced even in serving others neither African nor African-descended.

However, the notion "Afrocentricity" itself is not, cannot be, the embodiment of that fulfilled agenda for knowledge production, cannot provide much of what will be needed to complete that agenda. Africana Studies has been unduly burdened in many instances over the years by being straight-jacketed by well-intended but misguided and simplistic demands, and by efforts to meet these demands, that the knowledge produced be "Afrocentric" and not "Eurocentric" when neither notion can provide fully adequate critical or guiding concepts or strategies for producing or evaluating intellectual work – for working out, for example, canons of warrantability, objectivity, or truthfulness. After an orientation to knowledge production has been set and commitments and interests clarified accordingly, then a great deal of the work to be done will not be much helped by a notion of "Afrocentricity" except as an aid in checking to make sure the work is "on course," as it were, in some larger sense though even then there will be the need to satisfy the relevant criteria for appropriate knowledge production in whatever the field of endeavor.

And in Africana Studies there will be several fields since the studies will make use of pertinent tools and strategies of inquiry in virtually all fields of knowledge production given that the agenda is to produce viable and truthful knowledge about African and African-descended peoples in the totality of their lives. Which is why it is not appropriate to require a single methodology for Africalogical inquiry. Africana Studies must always be comprised of a cluster of disciplinary and interdisciplinary ventures in knowledge production. We would do well to be especially cautious in invoking demands or nourishing desires to pursue inappropriately conceived, ultimately unattainable "unity" and "coherence" in Africana Studies both methodologically and in terms of the results of knowledge producing efforts. The regulative ideal of "holism" has its own promise but may impose much more than the subject matter – African and African-descended peoples whenever and wherever they have been and are, in all aspects and dimensions of their lives – can possibly support. Here, I think, it is much more appropriate and fruitful for knowledge production to have full and critical accounts of similarities and commonalities, as well as of differences, among African and African-descended peoples rather than of a presumptive "unity" of African and African-descended peoples. After appropriate particular and comparative studies, it would be best to determine which studies might best be *integrated* into complete pictures-of-understanding of any particular African or African-descended people or person, or grouping of several of the same. To my mind, Africalogical knowledge production would benefit from serious, open-minded, critical (and self-critical) examination of usages and commitments to notions of "unity" in thinking about African and African-descended peoples and the consequent implications for the propriety of regarding notions of "holism" as ontological and epistemological regulative principles.

These very important issues require the kind of sustained, expansive treatment devoted to them by several scholars, one of the more prominent efforts being, of course, Maulana Karenga's *Introduction to Black Studies*, particularly his discussion of "Challenges and Possibilities."[25] Given the focus of the present essay, it is especially worth noting that this discussion by Karenga is decidedly unburdened by a constant need to insure – and reassure the reader – that his articulations are Afrocentric though he has made clear throughout the book that such, in fact, is his committed orientation. Rather, in addressing the concept early in the book ("The Concept of Afrocentricity," pp. 34–8), he offers that "it is important to note that there is no single conception of Afrocentricity, only a general conceptual agreement that Afrocentric means essentially viewing social and human reality from an African perspective or standpoint."[26] Karenga goes on to devote nearly five hundred pages to working out his ideas, aided by the acknowledged ideas of others, for knowledge of the history, religious life, sociology, politics, economics, creative productions (art, music, literature), and the psychology of African and African-descended peoples, in the United States of America in particular (though the account, by historical necessity, begins with classical civilizations on the continent of Africa) because these areas, in his judgment (and the judgment of many scholars), constitute the core disciplinary foci of Africana Studies. It is particularly noteworthy that Karenga takes great care to stress (as does Asante, it should be said) that the fullest measure of the viability of knowledge produced by workers in Africana Studies must be judged, ultimately, by its contributions to the enhancement of human understanding and living well beyond communities of African and African-descended

peoples: the particularity of the partisan commitments of Afrocentric knowledge production must be reconciled with more general commitments to service to the well-being
and flourishing of other humans. It must be knowledge that finds its fullest productive
and ethical measures, in Karenga's words, "in the service of humankind."[27]

Does an Afrocentric orientation provide a new paradigm for knowledge-production and
validation, as some proponents proclaim, that adequately satisfies this requirement?
Yes, and no. Better put: in some important ways, yes; in other, but equally important,
ways, no. Yes, for providing a crucial set of orienting commitments to producing, validating, legitimating, distributing and mediating knowledge of African and African-
descended peoples that affirms and validates them as fully human, history-making
beings of significance and accomplishment certainly provides paradigmatic alternatives of enormous significance compared to the ways in which they were characterized in, and treated as a consequence of, the philosophical anthropology of white
supremacy–black subordination fashioned and institutionalized to facilitate imperialism and enslavement as part of the Eurocentric project. No – at least not quite yet – to
the extent that all of the efforts of producing, validating, legitimating, distributing, and
mediating "Afrocentric" knowledge satisfy appropriate criteria for warrantability, justification, truthfulness, validity, etc., such that in serving the interests of African and
African-descended peoples, the better interests of others who are not of African descent
are also well served. That is, Africalogical knowledge production satisfies appropriate
criteria for justified belief that, in some cases, have long been advocated by guardians
of knowledge of European descent, philosophers especially, but which they failed mis-
erably to satisfy.

   In important, even ironic respects, then, the emergence and pursuit of Afrocentric
orientations in knowledge-production are but chickens of truth-seeking coming home to
roost: that is, a reclaiming of the crucial norm of truthful knowledge from the distorting
corruption of the Eurocentric Project in order to have knowledge production be much,
much more fully of service, on the very best of terms, to African and African-descended
peoples and for the humane service and just well-being of all the world's peoples.

   The shortcomings in the efforts to work out appropriate "canons of proof" and
"structures of truth" in Afrocentric inquiry as well as the unfinished work of addressing these and other methodological issues in whichever field understanding is to be had
that enhances our knowledge of African and African-descended peoples are opportunities – responsibilities, even, for those of us who would have them be such – for African
and African-descended philosophers to join in the efforts and to lend a helping hand.
Doing so would be good for us – challenging us in our ongoing existential projects of
taking stock of and constituting who we take ourselves to be – and further enable and
empower us in our efforts to contribute to the transformation and rehabilitation of professional Philosophy wherein very substantial work remains to be done in the form of
critiques of and correctives to the philosophical core – the rationalizations and justifications – of the Eurocentric project. Then we, too, as philosophers, would share in one
of the ongoing contributions to knowledge production that was and continues to be an
intended focal contribution of what has come to be called "Afrocentric" Africalogical
or Africana Studies: critique and corrective as a joint project in the educational enterprise that is to be of service to *all* who would partake of them.

166

Notes

1   See Samir Amin, *Eurocentrism* (New York: Monthly Review Press, 1984).

2   Ibid., pp. 72–3.

3   Ibid., pp. 72–96.

4   See, for example, Molefi Kete Asante, *Afrocentricity: The Theory of Social Change* (Buffalo, New York: Amulefi Publishing Co., 1980); *The Afrocentric Idea* (Philadelphia: Temple University Press, 1987); and *Kemet, Afrocentricity and Knowledge* (Trenton, New Jersey: Africa World Press, 1990).

5   For an especially informed, comprehensive, and conversant discussion of the long and complex history of such knowledge production, see St. Clair Drake, *Black Folk, Then and Now*, 2 Vols. (Los Angeles, CA: Center for Afro-American Studies, University of California, 1987).

6   Asante, *Afrocentricity: The Theory of Social Change*, p. 26.

7   Ibid., pp. 52–6.

8   Asante, *Kemet, Afrocentricity and Knowledge*, pp. 5–6.

9   Ibid., p. 6.

10 Ibid., p. 8.

11 Ibid., p. 9.

12 Ibid., p. 10.

13 Ibid., p. 10.

14 Ibid., p. 11.

15 Ibid., p. 11.

16 Maulana Karenga, "Afrocentricity and Multicultural Education: Concept, Challenges, and Contribution," in Benjamin P. Bowser, Terry Jones and Gale Auletta Young, eds., *Toward the Multicultural University* (Westport, CT: Praeger, 1995, pp. 41–61), p. 43.

17 Asante, *Kemet, Afrocentricity and Knowledge*, pp. 12–23.

18 Ibid., pp. 24–5.

19 Ibid., p. 27.

20 Ibid., p. 27.

21 Ibid., p. 28, 30.

22 Ibid., p. 30.

23 Karenga, "Afrocentricity and Multicultural Education: Concept, Challenges, and Contribution," pp. 43–4.

24 Ibid., p. 43.

25 Second edition (Los Angeles, CA: The University of Sankore Press, 1993), pp. 475–505.

26 Karenga, *Introduction to Black Studies*, pp. 34–5.

27 Karenga, "Afrocentricity and Multicultural Education: Concept, Challenges, and Contribution," p. 46.

10

African Retentions

TOMMY L. LOTT

James Brown's music reconnected Bamako's youth to a pre-Atlantic-slavery energy that enabled them to master the language of independence and modernity and to express the return of Africanism to Africa through Black aesthetics. (Manthia Diawara 2001)

In 1925 Melville J. Herskovits published an article titled "The Negro's Americanism" in Alain Locke's anthology, *The New Negro*. Speaking from a scientific standpoint he explicitly rejected the idea of African-American cultural difference.

To what extent, if any, has the Negro genius developed a culture peculiar to it in America? I did not find it in the great teeming center of Negro life in Harlem, where, if anywhere, it should be found. May it not then be true that the Negro has become acculturated to the prevailing culture and has developed the patterns of culture typical of American life? (Locke, 1925b: 353–4)

These remarks revised his earlier statement in the special "Harlem" issue of *Survey Graphic*, also edited by Locke. Indeed, his earlier stance was a more strident counterpoint to the view Locke wanted to promote under the auspices of the new Negro movement. "Is the cultural genius of the Negro, which is supposed to have produced jazz and the spiritual, the West African wood-carving and Bantu legalism, non-existent in this country, after all?" (Locke, 1925a: 676). Herskovits's view, if true, had the potential to undermine any notion of African-American culture conceived in terms that would support Du Bois's pronouncements in "The Conservation of Races" regarding Negro genius and group loyalty – especially his argument for the obligation of African Americans to retain their racial identity in order make a unique cultural contribution.

Following Du Bois, Locke often portrayed the mission of the Negro Renaissance largely in these terms. In some of the correspondence between Herskovits and Locke there is evidence that pressure from Locke may have influenced Herskovits to reverse his view. Along with Arthur Schomburg's proposal to study black cuisine and Du Bois's early writings on black religion and family, Herskovits's *The Myth of the Negro Past* published in 1941, was a pioneering study of African retentions – and directly influenced Lorenzo Turner, a student of Herskovits, whose *Africanisms in the Gullah Dialect* is another classic published in 1949. There are two related concerns that have a bearing on how we should understand Herskovits's earlier failure to notice any retentions in African-American culture – as well as his subsequent tendency to rely mainly on evidence from the Caribbean and Latin America. First, he operated with an assimilationist, rather than a pluralist, paradigm to interpret the culture he observed in Harlem. Secondly, as Locke pointed out in the editorial section of *Survey Graphic*, Herskovits's interpretation failed to account for the "inner" aspects of Harlem culture – the "race-soul striving for social utterance" (Locke, 1925a: 676).

The well-known debate between Herskovits and E. Franklin Frazier reflects a general ambivalence in African-American thought regarding the affirmation and denial of African retentions. In common parlance, and mass media, cultural distinctions between black and white Americans are frequently drawn in a manner that parallels cultural distinctions between whites and Asian or Mexican Americans. Yet, the suggestion that there is an African element in African-American culture is always a matter of controversy – a claim standing in need of scientific verification. This latent contestation is especially evident when the concept of African-American culture is employed in the context of educational policy. The mass media's success at discrediting the Oakland School Board's recent proposal regarding Ebonics, a proposal well-grounded on scientific research, is a case that clearly indicates why the policy-oriented context for raising questions regarding African retentions in African-American culture cannot be ignored (Perry and Delpit, 1998).

Despite a history of debate, there is sufficient empirical evidence to support the claim that many African-American cultural practices are grounded partly on principles and ideas that derive from an African cultural heritage – principles and ideas that have evolved to accommodate the complexity of modern life in American society. For a new generation of scholars Herskovits's earlier question of whether any remnants of African culture survived slavery has been superseded by a different set of concerns. Recent research by folklorists, historians, cultural anthropologists, and sociolinguists indicates a shift towards the empirical study of transformations that retentions (or Africanisms) have undergone since slavery. If, however, all we can presently observe are various aspects of African culture in some later stage of transformation, how do we identify a given cultural practice as African?

In his recent book, *The Black Atlantic*, Paul Gilroy has attempted to meet this demand for a specification of criteria on the basis of which we are entitled to speak (explicitly or implicitly) of African-American cultural practices in terms of their African roots. Gilroy presents an account of black diaspora identity that addresses questions regarding the nature and function of transformed retentions in contemporary black cultures. My examination of Gilroy's account aims to shed light on a confusion in his discussion of cultural hybridity that hinders full appreciation of the African ingredient in African-American culture. After a brief consideration of nineteenth-century thought, I respond specifically to Gilroy's interpretation of Alain Locke's view. I propose an alternative reading of Locke's teachings regarding the nature and function of African retentions in African-American culture.

Douglass's Eurocentric Perspective

Gilroy cites Frederick Douglass's account of the magic root given to him by another slave, Sandy, as an indication of how certain aspects of a premodern African culture were employed by slaves to engage in resistance. Although Douglass was sceptical of the root's power, he acknowledged that it nonetheless gave him the confidence to resist being whipped by Covey. The root itself seems to stand between two different world-views. Gilroy notes that Douglass considered Sandy's belief system regarding the magical powers of the root as mere superstition, but does not consider Sandy's opinion of its metaphysical status. Douglass represents an assimilated house slave who relies on a cultural retention maintained by a less assimilated field slave. By juxtaposing the quite different cultural orientations of Douglass and Sandy to the root, the complexity of the relationship between slaves and their cultural retentions can be highlighted. Was Douglass unable to enter into Sandy's African worldview perhaps because he lacked the cultural sensibilities that were necessary to fully appreciate the field slave's African reli-gious practices? The predominantly Eurocentric worldview that governed Douglass's cultural sensibilities suggests an erasure of some sort that was not true of Sandy.

An important political dimension of the transformation of African retentions in the context of slavery can be gleaned from a consideration of Douglass's position on the relationship of African Americans to Africa. He insisted that the native land of African Americans is America. In his argument against colonization he maintained that the African American owed no more to blacks in Africa than he owed to blacks in America. He claimed that a blow struck for blacks in America was a blow struck for blacks in Africa, and cautioned that emigration to Africa would be detrimental to uplifting the race as a whole.

> If we cannot make Virginia, with all her enlightenment and Christianity, believe that there are better uses for her energies than employing them in breeding slaves for the market, we see not how we can expect to make Guinea, with its ignorance and savage selfishness, adopt our notions of political economy. (Douglass, 1859: 265)

His concern with the future development of African Americans prompted him to respond to the advocates of emigration to Africa as enemies to "moral progress" (ibid.). He raised the issue of racial hybridity as a ground for his stance against emigration.

> It is pertinent, therefore, to ask . . . where the people of this mixed race are to go, for their ancestors are white and black, and it will be difficult to find their native land anywhere outside of the United States. (Douglass, 1894: 330)

Douglass's appeal to a notion of racial hybridity to speak of the destiny of African Americans as a group led him to conclude that the African American "will be absorbed, assimilated, and will only appear finally, as the Phoenicians now appear on the shores of the Shannon, in the features of a blended race" (Douglass, 1886: 309). His refer-ence to the Phoenicians as a blended race echoes earlier remarks regarding the racial composition of the Egyptians that were presented in his public lecture, "The Claims of The Negro Ethnologically Considered." In his dispute with ethnologists Douglass saw no need to insist upon viewing Egypt as a part of black Africa, although, for the sake of counterpoint, he argued quite forcefully that it was. He instead asserted the enlightenment doctrine that "all mankind have the same wants, arising out of a common nature" (Douglass, 1854: 243). Under the banner of human rights Douglass proclaimed the equality of even the most "savage" African.

Nineteenth-Century Nationalism: Delany and Blyden

Douglass's unfavorable view of Africa as a homeland for African Americans displays a common assumption shared by many of his adversaries. Although his opposition to emigration was bitterly opposed, his low esteem for the role of traditional African culture in the modern world was widely shared. Douglass and many of his emigrationist detractors were in agreement regarding the need to modernize Africa. For this reason the political agendas of nineteenth-century nationalists such as Martin Delany and Edward Blyden displayed little concern with reclaiming an anterior African culture. Their political-economic concerns were focused on securing a modern nation state that would ensure the social elevation of black people. As Gilroy notes, they were quite sceptical of "Africa's capacity for civilization" (Gilroy, 1993a: 192). Blyden, for instance, saw colonization as a means to civilize Africa, whereas Delany considered Texas, Haiti, and Central America as alternative sites for emigration. Douglass's exchange with Garnet provides a very good illustration of how his disagreement with emigrationists reflected this concern. Garnet wrote to Douglass asking him to reply to the question, "What objection have you to colored men in this country engaging in agriculture, lawful trade, and commerce in the land of my forefathers?" (Douglass, 1859: 266) Garnet's question, as well as Douglass's reply, expressed a desire to modernize Africa, a desire that was prevalent among nineteenth-century black intellectuals.

Blyden cast his argument for the modernization of Africa in religious terms. He invoked the notion of God's providence to ground his claim that African Americans have a duty to return to their "fatherland" (Blyden, 1862: 115). He argued, by analogy with the ancient Hebrews, that slavery was God's way of preparing African Americans for their civilizing mission – a kind of "purifying by fire" (Blyden, 1890: 130). Gilroy points out that Blyden's black Zionism was based on a notion of racial purity. He spoke of African Americans as "exiled Africans" in an alien land. He even questioned whether mulatto spokespersons, such as Douglass, should be included in the black race. Underneath the political disagreement between Blyden and Douglass lay more fundamental issues concerning biology and racial identity. Blyden's advocacy of black racial purity as a criterion for racial classification reflects the influence of scientific racism on nineteenth-century black intellectuals.

Delany's class analysis of the plight of African Americans contrasted sharply with Blyden's religious-based argument for emigration. According to Delany, any such appeal to spirituality as a means of social elevation is fundamentally misguided, for religion cannot provide the means for achieving an economic goal. For this reason, he maintained only a tenuous commitment to Africa as the site of emigration. This was due in part to his belief that African Americans had been reduced by slavery to a class of servants based on racial heritage. Although he had great pride in his African heritage, unlike Blyden, the African origin of black people held little significance for his view of emigration and was not the basis for his argument. He argued that African Americans should emigrate to any country that would allow them to flourish.

Various notions of "progress" and "civilization" were central to the social elevation theories of nineteenth-century black nationalists. I have already indicated how the civilizing mission of their political agendas speaks to their recognition of the importance of modernization. In many cases their vision of the role of the Black Atlantic in the modern world generated a quest for a black nation-state that would be economically competitive with Europe. To a large extent then their view of modernization was based on the model of the European Enlightenment. The utopia sought was a black version of Western society. Given the resolve of many nineteenth-century black nationalists to stake a claim for African people in a global economy dominated by Europe, it seems that, rather than reject the political agenda of the Enlightenment, they aimed to carry it through in a manner that served the interests of black people.

Afrocentric Nationalism

Gilroy's observation that a preoccupation with the discourse of tradition is a crucial part of the Black Atlantic critique of modernity seems to be the basis for his somewhat rhetorical question, "what elements of invariant tradition heroically survive slavery" (Gilroy, 1993a: 189). He resists treating this as a straightforward empirical question, for one consequence of the Afrocentric emphasis on African antiquity is that the memory of slavery becomes something that inteferes with the discernment of the elements that survived. To show that this orientation to tradition is misguided Gilroy quotes Molefi Asante's claim that the slave experience only produced "made-in-America Negroes" (ibid.). Asante insists that the focus on slavery, an aberration, as the womb of African-American culture must be rejected as perpetuating a dangerously negative image of African Americans as disconnected from their African origin. Gilroy criticizes the Afrocentric doctrine for its commitment to a narrative of Western civilization that only couches a different set of political interests in the same terms. He takes to task the Afrocentric notion of tradition as a means of establishing a contiguous relationship between contemporary black life and its African past and criticizes advocates of Afrocerntricism who aim to "rescue and reconstruct" this African tradition.

Stories about death that are repeatedly told in black vernacular culture, with or without music, according to Gilroy, "constitute the Black Atlantic as a non-traditional tradition" (ibid., 186). This tradition can be defined as an "asymmetrical cultural ensemble" that cannot be understood in terms of the binary codes of "African authenticity–purity–origin versus New World hybridity–creolization–rootlessness"; it evades the contrast between a positive image of ancient Africa and a negative image of contemporary America. Tradition, in Gilroy's sense of the term, refers to "the living memory of the changing same" (ibid., 198).

Rather than place tradition in opposition to modernity Gilroy's revisionist notion instead establishes a two-way connection between them. Recognizing that Africa has also been transformed by cultural influences from the diaspora he argues for a "crossroads" view of the relationship between tradition and modernity that captures the suggestion of "intermixture and cross-fertilization" (ibid., 199). Surprisingly, rather than deny a role for African retentions in contemporary Black Atlantic cultures, Gilroy's reflections on black vernacular culture are grounded on his acknowledgment of what he calls "the most enduring Africanism of all" (ibid., 200).

Everyone knows that black music has an African origin. Gilroy points out, however, that "there is a direct relationship between the community of listeners constructed in the course of using that musical culture and the constitution of a tradition" (ibid., 198). He focuses on the active dynamic process of music making in Black Atlantic cultures to show the political significance of the deceptive content of the love stories. Recognizing the priority of form over content is a necessary move because it accords with the changing role of the storyteller in a modern world. Gilroy presents his conception of the history of Black Atlantic music as an illustration of Benjamin's dictum that, in modern society, the practice of remembrance is organized in novel ways due to the fact that "the gift for listening is lost and the community of listeners has disappeared" (ibid., 200).

This shift in the role of the storyteller is matched by another shift in content away from the nineteenth-century stories regarding the ordeal of slavery toward love and loss stories in the twentieth century. Gilroy tells us that this new genre indicates a group desire, tantamount to a "cultural decision," not to communicate about the experience of slavery openly in story and song. These love and loss stories, nonetheless, express displaced feelings of mourning and yearning caused by the "unspeakable terror" of slavery. Gilroy identifies an African retention in Percy Mayfield's song "The River's Invitation" (ibid., 1987: 35–6). The lyrics express a consciousness of African ecology and cosmology that illustrates the persistence of a theme of death as freedom from suffering. This example shows how vernacular expressions of African retentions in black popular culture have been transformed by the experience of enslavement. Tradition in this sense is a derivative of cultural activity that has been shaped by social memory.

Retentions as Reconstructions

Gilroy seems to allow that there is some sense in which the slave's music is pre-modern, modern, and anti-modern all at once. Indeed, for the artistic practices of the slaves to have been both "inside" and "outside" of modernity one would think that there had to be some residue of their anterior African culture (Gilroy, 1993b: 135). Music is Gilroy's paradigm of a transformed cultural retention: Love and loss songs in twentieth-century black music constitute a disguised expression of the suffering caused by slavery, a "transcoding" of its "unspeakable horror" (Gilroy, 1993a). He deliberately positions black music at par with other representational art forms in order to challenge Hegel's privileging of written language (cognitive, conceptual) as the highest expression of human consciousness. He selects music from the various cultural forms that survived slavery because it best fits his model of tradition as an enduring "changing same" (ibid., 198). For Gilroy, African musical practices need not have survived relatively unaltered to count as retentions.

Gilroy's emphasis on the survival of form rather than content is a key to understanding his account of music as a transformed retention. References to the premodern usually suggest vestiges of a traditional African culture. Similarly, the idea of modernity is usually associated with European cultural influences. Since, according to Gilroy, modern black cultural forms originated in the West as hybrid creations, African-American music is a "cultural mutation" produced by the "creolization" of premodern African and modern European elements. The status of African-American music as a transformed retention involves the inescapable "doubleness" that derives from its hybrid form, a feature that accounts for its being both "inside" and "outside" of modernity's aesthetic conventions.

Gilroy is committed to saying that the critique of modernity embedded in black music practices articulates a memory of a preslave past, as well as a memory of slavery itself. To the extent that the critical stance in black music opposes the rationality of modernity it is a premodern variety of antimodernity. This is suggested, for instance, by Gilroy's claim that utopia enters the consciousness of the Black Atlantic as a form of "jubilee" (ibid., 212). Gilroy uses the concept of jubilee to mark a break with the Western concept of time. He tells us that it is "a liberatory, aesthetic moment which is emphatically anti- or even prediscursive," a moment that "has the upper hand over the pursuit of utopia by rational means" (ibid., 68 and 71). There is no static African tradition frozen in time because remembrance of a preslave past is *actively practiced* in black music as recurring acts of identity operating through the call and response mechanisms produced in the interaction of performer and audience.

The memory of slavery itself provides the basis for what Gilroy refers to as "rescuing" or "redemptive" critiques. Toni Morrison's *Beloved* is a retelling of the Margaret Garner story that involves the construction of a social memory. Gilroy's endorsement of Morrison's reconstruction of the memory of slavery seems inconsistent with his criticism of the Afrocentric reconstruction of the memory of a preslave past. He rightfully criticizes the Afrocentric focus on the preslave past, for in the history of African Americans that memory of the past has been occluded by the memory of slavery. As I have already noted in the case of Douglass and Sandy, this is not entirely true with regard to all of the Black Atlantic.

Gilroy does not consider that New World slaves had a *right* to resist in the manner carried out by slaves in Surinam. This right entails overthrowing their masters, burning the plantations, and returning to a traditional village life. In the light of this implication the criticism that Herskovits relied too heavily on his research in Surinam and the Caribbean to make the case for African retentions in the New World tends to ignore the role culture has played as a mode of resistance. The case of the Saramakas is troublesome, in different ways, for views held by Asante and Gilroy. In the documentary film "I Shall Moulder Before I Be Taken" we are shown the rituals by means of which a reconstruction of the preslave past was carried out in Surinam *during slavery*. The film depicts contemporary cultural practices that are the end-result of a process Sterling Stuckey has deemed an early form of Pan-African cultural synthesis (Stuckey, 1987: 35–6). We can now observe in Surinam the manifestation of African retentions in the form of cultural practices that express a social memory that incorporates the experiences of a group of former African slaves. In this case the transformed African retention involves much more than Gilroy's idea of "jubilee." Rather, it is constituted by a reconstruction of a premodern village life that has endured well into the twentieth century.

174

Gilroy's account of the transformation of African retentions does not adequately accommodate Black Atlantic cultures in other parts of the New World where slavery was less disruptive and where there was less contact with European culture. The cultural transformations experienced by slaves in the United States cannot serve as a paradigm of the retention of African religious practices in Brazil, Cuba, and other places in Latin America where erasure was far less than in the United States. The rescuing and redemptive critiques Gilroy approves are reconstructions that ritualize the practice of remembrance. The idea of reclaiming an anterior culture appears less problematic when consideration is given, in this isolated fashion, to the influence of transformed retentions in New World African religious music. But this appearance is misleading, for, as Gilroy rightfully insists, with very few exceptions there is no anterior African-American culture that can override the profound influence of slavery. It would be an error, however, to suppose that this insight, even if true in the case of African-American culture, uniformly applies throughout the Black Atlantic. Perhaps most of the Black Atlantic is closer to Douglass's modern orientation to the magical root. Nevertheless, there has to be some allowance made for Sandy's premodern orientation as well.

Alain Locke on Transformed Retentions

In many of his writings, beginning in 1911, Alain Locke championed the idea of a unique cultural contribution by African-American artists and intellectuals. The historical schema he employed in his theory of culture to represent the various stages of African-American cultural development indicated progress in each phase by reference to whether folk forms have entered a process of transformation into high art. He explained the uneven development of music and art in African-American culture in terms of African retentions. Noting that advancement had occurred in those areas of cultural expression in which there had been an early start in well-developed folk art forms, Locke concluded that faster progress had been made where African retentions were strongest. In *Negro Art: Past and Present* he remarked that "there was some memory of beauty . . . toward the only channels of expression left open – those of song, graceful movement and poetic speech," a list he expanded to include retentions in pantomime and folklore (Locke, 1936b: 3). By contrast with these forms, he believed that no such retentions existed in sculpture or the decorative arts. He appealed to environmental influences to explain both what was retained, as well as what was lost of the African cultural heritage.

This view of retentions was a basis for Locke's advocacy of a Negro racial idiom in art that aimed to restore a lost African tradition in sculpture and the decorative arts which had been literally erased by the toils of slavery. The crudeness of slave labor caused physical damage to the hands of the slave, consequently, there was an eventual loss of the manual dexterity required for sculpturing, carving, and similar physical skills. By comparison with music, dance and poetry, slavery reduced African Americans to a "cultural zero" in visual art (ibid., 2). The uneven development of various art forms was used by Locke to support his claim that, with regard to artistic temperament, there is no kinship between African and African-American cultures. The ordeal of slavery had caused African-Americans to emphasize the "emotional" forms of cultural expression. This lopsided development and neglect of the plastic and pictorial forms has resulted in a reversal of the African artistic temperament. Beneath the African-American's acquired artistic temperament, however, "slumbers" an original, more basic, one waiting to be reawakened. According to Locke, since the African spirit is at its best in abstract decorative forms, it is this "slumbering gift" that needs "reachievement and reexpression" (Locke, 1925b: 267).

Locke's appeal to a Negro artistic temperament to account for the unique element in Negro art and music sometimes has been interpreted to imply that the kinship between African and African-American cultures is rooted in genetics. None of his remarks need be construed in this fashion, given that he only assumed an emotional bond between peoples of African origin. For example, his remark that, "we must believe that there still slumbers in the blood something which once stirred will react with peculiar emotional intensity toward African art" has been taken to mean that, due to a blood tie, the emotional bond between African-American and African artists is genetically determined (Washington, 1986: 196). Here, as in several other places, Locke's use of the term "blood" is misleading since he only meant this bond to be understood in terms of a reconstructed social memory peculiar to those whose cultural roots trace back to Africa. The rapid progress of African-American self-expression in art following the Negro Renaissance emboldened Locke to predict in 1933 that sculpture would be the great forte of African-American artists. "It is rather the feeling that there is some connection between unusual plastic sense and skill and the naive emotional approach to life (Locke, 1933: 320–1)." He seems to deny any role for retentions in this case. Instead he draws a parallel with African-American artistic achievement in music. "The instinctive spontaneous harmony of the Negro in music ought to be expected to have some counterpart in the other arts, and here, I think, it is" (ibid.). When specifically discussing the work of African-American artists, Locke shifts his paradigm of the underlying African aesthetic endowment to music, whereas in his article on Negro art in *Encyclopedia Britannica* (1951) he maintains that the reason the African-American artistic temperament found expression in music was because it was unable to express itself in the characteristic African forms of sculpture, smithing, and weaving. Taken altogether these remarks suggest that the "transplanted" African-American aesthetic endowment has not been a static African retention, rather it too has undergone transformation along with the African-American artistic temperament.

In the *Negro Art: Past and Present* Locke acknowledged that the African-American artist had not yet completely "recaptured his ancestral gifts or recovered his ancient skills." He believed this recovery of a lost African tradition in the plastic arts would occur "not as a carry-over of instinct," but instead as "a formal revival of historical memory" based on "the proud inspiration of the reconstructed past" (Locke, 1936b: 5). It was important that African-American artists gain inspiration from exposure to their lost African heritage – both to creatively express racial themes in their art, as well as to acquire the advanced skill and technique of their ancestors. The rediscovery of an African tradition in art by African-American artists would be second remove, through the work of European masters such as, Picasso, Barlach, Lipchitz, and Modigliani. Consequently, the race tradition instituted by African-American artists will draw upon both European and African masters to produce uniquely African-American art.

Locke's reference to a Negro temperament "transplanted" to the soil of the New World can be understood in terms of his belief that, although the strength of African retentions may vary in the three Americas, there remains a common cultural denominator. He held that, even when the interpenetration of European and African cultures has rendered the African element difficult to specify, this element is not difficult to recognize, for it dominates "like rum in the punch" (Locke, 1939: 452). He appealed to the retention of an African aesthetic endowment to explain the diverse ways European music and art have been reconfigured by African descendants throughout the New World. He proposed to understand both the lack of affinity, as well as the close affinity, of African and New World black cultures in terms of a relationship between environmental influences and the retention of a basic aesthetic endowment responsible for the African artistic temperament "creeping back" into the "overtones" of creative expression (Locke, 1928: 439).

Gilroy's Concept of Cultural Hybridity

Gilroy maintains that New World black cultures have drawn upon "one of their adoptive, parent cultures: the intellectual heritage of the West since the Enlightenment" as well as upon "premodern images and symbols that gain an extra power in proportion to the brute facts of modern slavery" (Gilroy, 1993a: 2, 56). These modern and premodern elements are combined through a process of "cultural mutation." On the face of it the suggestion that African-American culture is a mutation from its parent cultures seems quite plausible, but underneath lies a troublesome question regarding the nature of this mutation. What does it mean to speak of a given black culture as a "mutation?" There seems to be an inherent tension in Gilroy's use of the terms "hybridity" and "mutation" to characterize Black Atlantic cultures, for both terms can refer either to *stages* of a process, or to the *end result* of that process. A hybrid culture that is the end result of a process of mutation sometimes may have a different social status than a hybrid culture that is still in formation, for in some cases, once this process has reached a certain level of maturity, the former ceases to be thought of as a hybrid.

The inclination to think of a group's cultural hybridity as a by-product of the biological hybridity of its members is irresistible, although in many cases the biological hybridity of a group does not always yield a corresponding hybrid culture. In many parts of Brazil there is a noticeable African element that is manifested in both a biological hybridity and a hybrid culture, whereas in Mexico, perhaps due to a much smaller number of slaves imported, the contribution of Africans to Mexico's biologically hybrid population is less apparent, and, while not totally absent, there are even fewer traces of any African elements in Mexico's hybrid culture. Although in both cases there is a biological hybridization of Native Americans, Africans and Europeans, to use Du Bois's expression, Brazil's dominant culture has been "Africanised" to a far greater extent than Mexico's. For this reason a lot of "Brazilian" music is typically included among the cultural products of the Black Atlantic, whereas "Mexican" music typically is not included.

The interplay of race and culture can be shown to be quite complex in certain instances of cultural contact and exchange. Consider, for example, a group of biologically mixed Africans and Native Americans who have a Native American cultural identity as compared with a group of Africans who are not biologically mixed with Native Americans, but have acquired a Native-American identity by adopting the language and cultural practices of a particular Native-American group. These two cases represent different types of cultural hybridity, yet we continue to refer to the two groups categorically as either Native Americans or African American, depending on the weight attached to race or culture. Given the history of legal segregation "Zamboes" as a separate racial category has never been fully established in the United States, any more than "mulattoes," or "creoles."

Race, Culture, and Diaspora Identity

Gilroy points to a basis for a "new metacultural identity" for New World black people in the common history of slavery and the intercultural connection established by the transnational structure of the slave trade itself. His readiness to combat what he considers "the easy claims of African-American exceptionalism," downplays the troublesome nature of the metacultural identity he endorses. He proposes to replace "the lure of ethnic particularism and nationalism" with "a global, coalition politics in which anti-imperialism and antiracism might be seen to interact if not fuse" (ibid., 4). But if anti-imperialism and anti-racism are the basis for the group identity of the Black Atlantic, the cultural links that establish race solidarity seem to have been replaced entirely with a multiracial political coalition against economic and racial oppression. This global struggle encompasses much more than the Black Atlantic and, hence, cannot provide a basis for understanding the particularity of black diaspora race identity.

This worry has not entirely escaped Gilroy's attention for he highlights a similar feature of Du Bois's view by connecting Du Bois's notion of double consciousness with the internationalist outlook of his famous remark that "The problem of the Twentieth Century is the problem of the color-line" (Du Bois, 1903: 33). Double consciousness involves not only a tension between African-American and black diaspora identity, but also between a diaspora identity grounded on race and a Third World identity based on the struggle against global imperialism. If the black diaspora identity sought by Du Bois (or Gilroy's metacultural identity) is grounded on resistance to European global domination, it cannot be employed to designate a specific racial or cultural group since it refers to all people of color who are engaged in this resistance. Although the point of this criticism must be well-taken I want briefly to consider an alternative available to Du Bois and Gilroy which seems to mitigate some of its force.

What if we were to view the relationship between the various ethnic groups comprising the Black Atlantic as having a metacultural link with each other on the model of the culturally diverse Jewish diaspora, or similar to the relationship between the culturally diverse Islamic groups throughout the world? Just as there are many different races and cultures that are Jewish or Islamic "bound and welded together" by a common religion, similarly, the various black ethnic groups have some commonly held cultural feature that provides the basis for a bond and by virtue of which these diverse groups are referred to as "Negro" (or black). Unfortunately, specifying this commonly held cultural feature is not as easy as Du Bois and Gilroy would have it. Du Bois understood the cultural link to derive primarily from having a common African heritage, while Gilroy insists upon including the history of New World slavery as equally important. But, in addition to Britain's Asian-descended population, there is another "UK Blak" group in Australia that has no history of slavery and is not of African descent. In the case of black Australians, these criteria are neither necessary nor sufficient. The appeal to cultural continuity loses plausibility given that their identity as a distinct black ethnic group is a political construction based largely on their own rich cultural heritage and the biologically-based racism they face. Although there are "cultural links" with other diaspora black people, it seems more plausible to consider similarity of race, in some biologic sense, rather than similarity of culture per se as what connects black Australians with the Black Atlantic.

The notion of cultural hybridity Gilroy employs applies to quite different phenomena. New World black cultures "are configured by their compound and multiple origins in the mix of African and other cultural forms" (ibid., 75). With regard to this "mix" of different cultural forms he has in mind the contacts and exchanges between African and European cultures. But he is equally concerned with contacts and exchanges between various black cultures such as those that have occurred between Brazilians, West Indians, and African Americans. Where the former leads to double consciousness, the latter establishes the cultural links within the Black Atlantic. One quite significant aspect of the difference between a European–African cultural hybrid and cultural hybridity between black diaspora groups is that the latter, but not the former, does not seem to disturb the group's identity. This issue ties in with Du Bois's observation regarding the cultural hegemony of imperialism, which grants European cultural influences a greater impact than others.

The Spiritual as a Transformed Retention

When Gilroy speaks of black vernacular culture as a link between the Black Atlantic he has in mind primarily music. His reflections on the social and political significance of black music practices are skillfully employed to show the connection between Black Atlantic cultures as well as to specify their premodern, modern, and antimodern elements. He attributes to Du Bois the insight that music can be a primary mode of expressing a nontextual popular black critique of racial subjection. Supplementing this thesis with his own contention that music was the central medium through which black identities were constructed and linked throughout the diaspora, he argues that the commonly shared "rituals of performance" provide the chief mechanism, for in these rituals "the closeness to the ineffable terror of slavery was kept alive" (ibid., 73).

Despite the importance of the role of music in establishing the self-identity of a group, Gilroy maintains that it is problematic to hold that a given form of music is "expressive of the absolute essence of the group that produced it" (ibid.). He protests some of the ways music has been used to prove racial authenticity. When authenticity is based on origins there is a problem of dislocation created by the global dissemination of black music. The value placed on its origins is contested by the occurrence of "opposing mutations" (ibid.). He cites Alain Locke's reference to the double value of the spirituals as both nationally as well as racially characteristic to indicate the mishandling by African American intellectuals of issues pertaining to cultural mutation. It is far from clear, however, how Locke's remarks are supposed to confront the intellectual tradition that relies on "an image of the 'authentic folk' as an essentially invariant, anti-historical notion of black particularity" (ibid., 100). Although Locke did not hold this essentialist view his general critique of African-American cultural practices was influenced strongly by a non-essentialist demand for more "authentic" representations of African-American folk culture.

Locke's conception of "authentic" folk representation emanated from his account of African-American cultural growth and development. His various remarks regarding the doubleness of the spirituals are grounded on his view of cultural mutation as the outcome of an historical process. Even while bemoaning the passing of a dying black folk culture he spoke favorably of contemporary versions of the spirituals. He held the general view that "truly Negro music must reflect the folk spirit and eventually epitomize the race experience" (Locke 1934: 115). His theory of African-American music schematically represented the various stages of its development from the "primitive" African survivals, to classic folk expressions, to sophisticated hybrid folk art forms. The amount of interest in African-American music shown by classical composers led Locke to declare that "the masters of Negro musical idiom so far are not Negro" (ibid., 110). The pioneers, in Locke's opinion, were white composers such as Dvorak, Aaron Copeland, Alden Carpenter, George Gershwin, Paul Whiteman, and Sesana. Moreover, Locke criticized black composers for giving treatments of the spirituals that he claimed resulted in the most "sophisticated and diluted arrangements" (Locke, 1934: 111). Gilroy's citing of Locke's view of the doubleness of the spirituals omits the nuanced criteria Locke used to gauge their authenticity.

Gilroy instead chooses Hurston and Wright to represent a tradition of African-American intellectuals who have appealed to a notion of the "authentic folk." Hurston, for example, accused the Fisk singers of performing inauthentic versions of the spirituals. It is interesting that Gilroy points to this criticism to show that her appeal to cultural authenticity was self-serving. Gilroy fully understands the political significance of her question regarding the representation of the spirituals by the Fisk Singers. Given his own endorsement of rap artist Rakim's cultural malpractice charge against the rap group 2-Live Crew it seems inconsistent for him to dismiss Hurston's similar charge against the Fisk Singers. Needless to say Hurston was not alone in expressing this worry. Locke, for instance, thought the Fisk singers were far better than any of the other theater groups because they maintained the "real simplicity and dignity" of the spirituals, yet he concurred with Hurston's criticism and quotes it in his analysis of the historical development of the spirituals (Locke, 1936a: 20).

The Question of Authenticity

In keeping with his general aesthetic theory, Locke believed that "much classical music is folk music at second or third remove from the original source." According to his historical account of the development of African-American music there were seven stages between slavery and the present (1936a). The age of the sorrow songs (1830–50) was the classic folk period of the great spirituals. This folk tradition was disrupted between 1850 and 1895 by the predominance of the minstrel tradition, but in the twentieth century it has steadily evolved towards the age of classical jazz. Locke noted that "Spirituals are still being created, but no one doubts that the real age of the sorrow songs has passed" (Locke, 1936a: 11).

Locke's view that the spirituals, and the Negro folk idiom in general, are in some sense both "racial" and "national" is an important feature of his account of race and culture. He did not conceive of race in biological terms. He maintained that we call racial what is "only an intensified variety of the same elements that we called national." With regard to the European elements in black music Locke maintained that, "To say that one of these strands is more Negro than the other is entirely out of place. . . ." He denies any genetic basis for the musical abilities of black people by citing the peasant stocks of the Irish, Italian, German and Russian nations as "the well-springs of folk music" in European societies. "It has simply been the lot of the Negro in America to be the peasant class, and thus to furnish the musical subsoil of our national music." There is a twofold reason for this historical development. First, African Americans had a peculiar need for emotional expression, given their experience under slavery. Secondly, the Anglo-Saxon white population that is "the dominant force in American civilization" is relatively less musically endowed (ibid., 13–14).

Locke shared Hurston's concern regarding the authenticity of the spirituals because he worried that under the influence of minstrelsy and the concert stage "pseudo-Negro characterization led to misrepresentative music" (Locke, 1936a: 54). By this he did not mean that truly representative music would be "invariant" folk forms. Instead, Locke claimed,

> Negro folk melodies and their harmonic style have been regarded by most musicians as the purest and most valuable musical ore in America; the raw materials of a native American music. Eventually on another level, they will come back to their original power and purity. We should always remember that they are not sentimental nor theatrical, but epic and full of simple dignity" (ibid., 21).

For Locke, "purity" does not mean "unmixed" for he acknowledged the hybridity of the spirituals in his historical account. Locke's concern with authenticity then was focused on the *nature* of the fusion and hybridization of African-American folk music. He often criticized both black and white musicians for creating "terrible" hybrid forms that were "artificial," "unstable and anaemic" (ibid., 152). We must keep in mind that Locke's point here was not that hybridity itself is artificial, or anaemic, and therefore inauthentic, but that some hybrid forms are artificial, or anaemic, and less authentic in this sense than others.

Locke cited the music of George Gershwin as a case in which "the effort to lift jazz to the level and form of the classics has devitalized it" (ibid., 112). He endorsed Olin Downes' critical advice to the Negro University Chorus to do more singing in "the true Negro idiom and less imitation of other types of choral singing" (ibid., 24). This advice reflected Locke's opinion that even African-American composers had been too much influenced by formal European idioms and mannerisms in the quest to transform the spirituals from a folk-form to an artform. What Locke's demand for authenticity sought was a "true union and healthy vigourous fusion of jazz and classical tradition." He insisted upon "a style more fused and closer to the original Negro musical idioms." Rather than "artificial hybrids" he wanted "genuine developments of the intimate native idioms of jazz itself." He emphasized that this demand does not stipulate any one style of rendering spirituals, rather it requires only that "the folk quality and atmosphere should be preserved as much as possible" (Locke 1936a: 113–14).

Locke's aesthetic concern with the authenticity of the spirituals, and African-American folk culture in general, sometimes manifested a sharp political focus. For example, he protested the popularity of Stephen Foster's music. He believed that because of it, the plantation legend that glorified slavery "wormed its way into the heart of America" (ibid., 48). Locke applied a similar criticism to later forms of minstrelsy.

> Superficially they reflected some of the characteristic traits of the Negro, but instead of his real peasant humor, his real folk farce, his amazing ribaldry, the minstrels made a decoction of their own of slap-stick, caricature and asininity. (Ibid., 53)

Locke's relatively strong position on the question of whether minstrelsy is always to be condemned as inauthentic is vulnerable to the objection that sometimes the answer is a matter of whether the alleged minstrelsy aims to perpetuate oppression, or whether it has emancipatory aims. For example, the subversive elements in minstrelsy account for the ironic interplay between "authentic" jubilee singing and minstrel versions. Locke claimed that the Fisk singers saved a by-gone folk form from extinction. Toll has pointed out, however, that jubilee music in minstrelsy was a "more authentic" religious music than that sung by the Fisk singers (Toll, 1974). Whatever we may think of these various claims regarding the authenticity of the spirituals sung by the Fisk singers, as Jon Cruz has pointed out, the political dimension of this debate over the representation of the spirituals derives from their hybridization under the influence of a thoroughly racist mainstream popular culture (Cruz, 1999).

Black Music and Black Identity

Gilroy refers to "our enduring traditions – the African ones and the ones forged from the slave experience" as a basis for the creation of modern black traditions (Gilroy, 1993a: 101). Although he frequently acknowledges that African retentions are an important component of black Atlantic cultures, he places a great deal more emphasis on the vernacular forms that derive from the slave experience because they constitute rituals of active remembrance in contemporary practices.

For Gilroy there is no retention of a static African tradition because remembrance of a preslave past is actively practiced in black music as recurring acts of identity that operate through the antiphony of performers and listeners. As a paradigm of a transformed retention, twentieth-century black music constitutes a transcoded expression of slavery's unspeakable horror. This disguised expression of the memory of slavery does not erase the anterior culture, for "The irrepressible rhythms of the once forbidden drum are often still audible" (Gilroy, 1993a: 76).

Gilroy's recognition that black identity is often experienced as "natural and sponta-neous" and "is lived as a coherent (if not always stable) experiential sense of self" is what inclines him to reject anti-essentialist claims regarding cultural continuity (ibid., 102). He quotes Foucault to lend force to his assertion that music can produce "the imaginary effect of an internal racial core or essence" (ibid.). He adds that, by this, Foucault did not mean that the soul is only an illusion. It has a reality, but "as the product of the social practices that supposedly derive from it" (ibid.). Once the notion of a black essence is understood in this manner, music can be shown to represent the endurance of the past in the form of a "changing same" (ibid.). Gilroy insists that this "changing same" can be explicated only in terms of a "dramaturgy," and not in terms of "textuality and narrative." Black diaspora music practices developed within the surviving oral structures, along with gesture and dance, to create the "pre- and anti-discursive constituents of black metacommunication" (ibid.). These performative aspects of black music comprise the foundational element in the continuity of post-slave cultural forms. The significance of what Gilroy calls anti-anti-essentialism lies in his criticisms of both "a squeamish, nationalist essentialism and a sceptical, saturna-lian pluralism" (ibid., 102). He charges that both sides of this debate have ignored the dramaturgy and performative aspects of music. Racialized subjectivity is the outcome of practical activity such as "language, gesture, bodily significations, desires" (ibid.). Black identity is produced in relation to a body through the process of musical perfor-mance involving the production and reception of black music.

Gilroy's position here seems much too strong. Why not allow identities to be recon-stituted *and* expressed (or represented) through music? He admits that music does not have a monopoly on the construction of racial identity, but nonetheless employs it to present his notion of a "changing same" to satisfy the demand for an internalized racial essence. He proposes to understand identity construction in terms of a fluid ongoing process of hybridization, rather than the preservation of certain static elements that are supposed to represent a racial core. By virtue of the performative aspects of black music, black identity is constantly reconstituted. According to Gilroy, "Its characteris-tic syncopations still animate the basic desires – to be free and to be oneself – that are revealed in this counterculture's unique conjunction of body and music" (ibid., 76). This point seems to be less emphasized at various crucial places in his account of cul-tural identity. His discussion of the impact of hybrid influences often leaves out the fact that music can represent the experiences of a group by expressing certain very particu-lar thoughts and emotions that are exclusive to people who have been victimized on the basis of their color.

He invokes Locke's view of the spirituals as a hybrid cultural form without giving due consideration to Locke's concern that not all mutations are equally expressive of the black experience. Locke distinguished those hybrid elements that "mixed in" from others he thought were only "artificially fused" or "grafted." As I have noted above, he rejected ethnic absolutism by refusing to define African-American music in terms of African-American authorship. Yet he was known to be critical at times of the black music performed by white musicians, or written by white composers. He referred, for instance, to the "white spirituals" as "sterile" and "stereotyped." The distinction he made between black and white versions of the spirituals invokes ethnic particularity as a ground for his criticism, for his various comments regarding the racial element can be taken to mean that white versions sometimes fail to represent the African-American experience. It was for this reason that he proclaimed that black composers such as Duke Ellington would most likely "create the classical jazz towards which so many are striving" (Locke, 1936a: 99).

It is not clear whether on Gilroy's account of the hybridity of black music Locke's criticism of white renderings of African-American music can be sustained. Gilroy views black music as constitutive of black identity and contends that black identities can be produced in other races by their participation in black music practices. But if black identities can be acquired by whites in this manner then Locke's distinction between black and white versions of the spirituals is misguided. Here Gilroy's critique of ethnic absolutism seems to rely too heavily on the black British paradigm. If the meaning of the term "black" as a racial designation differs in England and the United States, some of Gilroy's claims may apply in England, but not in the United States. Unlike African Americans, the black British were, until the 1985 riots in London, a newly combined multiracial group that included Asians from India and Pakistan. Gilroy's point is that, though constituted primarily by a fragile political alliance, they nonetheless have a commonly shared black vernacular culture. Given the racial apartheid of the music industry in the United States, however, it makes no sense to speak of a black vernacular culture in the United States that is commonly shared with whites. Instead, there is a black vernacular culture produced by African Americans primarily for a black audience that, in turn, is selectively mass-marketed by the culture industries to white audiences.

Perhaps what Gilroy discerns in Locke's view of the doubleness of the spirituals is the suggestion that because they are simultaneously racial and national they can both retain and lose their racial distinctiveness. White composers who work in a black musical idiom are tapping into a national treasure of American folk culture. How do their appropriations differ from the music composed by blacks? In *Small Acts*, Gilroy speaks of the symbolic invocation of the premodern in black music and refers to Locke's "celebratory enthusiasm for the primitive" as one notable instance of this (Gilroy, 1993b: 162). He claims that in *The New Negro* Locke appeals to the premodern as part of the black artist's critique of the modern. He does not, however, attempt to square this interpretation with some of the social implications of Locke's concept of the "New Negro." This concept represents the historical stage in a process of African-American cultural hybridization at which the synthesis of diverse cultural forms yield syncretized forms. Rather than view black music as only a symbolic invocation of premodernity, Locke thought instead that it would *express* this premodernity in modern terms.

Gilroy and Locke maintain similar views regarding the dynamic history of black cultural traditions. Nonetheless, their focus on aesthetic production to represent African retentions in African-American culture tends to foster a modern-versus-traditional conception of cultural expression. Two important considerations regarding the African element in African-American culture caution against this tendency.

Although John Coltrane's rendition of the Rogers and Hammerstein song, "My Favorite Things," is influenced in obvious ways by the traditional music of South Indian, it is sometimes taken to be like many other jazz versions of a popular tune from a Broadway musical. Perhaps it would be better compared with appropriations of jazz by classical composers such as Stravinsky. In accordance with Locke's paradigm of a transformed folk idiom Coltrane's music incorporates highly evolved principles of pre-modern and modern music making that have been synthesized and transmitted within a black cultural tradition by successive generations of African-American musicians. If we recall Locke's proposal that "Negro" folk forms provide the raw materials for both black and white composers to fuse with European classical forms to create genuine American hybrids, the history of African-American music provides many illustrations of how a different version of this proposal has occurred in accord with many of Locke's principles of cultural exchange. We can readily notice on Coltrane's different recordings of "My Favorite Things" that he treats the highly commercial music of Rogers and Hammerstein as the "ore" for his musical explorations within an African-American tradition that is continuous with its African origins. In his article on "Spirituals" Locke remarked that the frequency of references to Jordan in the Spirituals was a "primitive carry over of water symbolism of West African religions." Gilroy's analysis of Percy Mayfield's treatment of "The River's Edge" is an extension of Locke's thought. In keeping with these examples I propose to understand Coltrane, similarly, to have transformed a commercial show tune into a spiritually inspired, almost sacred, piece, by relying on principles of music-making derived partly from an African heritage that has undergone continual change since slavery.

This application of Locke's and Gilroy's view of transformed retentions to the music of John Coltrane, or to sixties avant garde jazz in general, reiterates a concept of cultural practice that focuses on art, literature, music, and dance. But their view can also be applied to cultural practices that are less concerned with aesthetic production. Arthur Schomburg proposed to study black cuisine "to uncover if possible such traces of Africanisms which still persist in American dishes" (Schomburg, n.d.). Schomburg noted that the slave's adaptation of European recipes parallels their adaptation of the Christian hymns that constitute the spirituals. Moreover, as John Brown Childs has argued, by converting the cheapest food available to an oppressed group into a "culinary synthesis" that had no rival in the south, the slaves subverted the dominant culture with a cuisine that became the basis for *all* southern cooking. This display of "Negro genius" represents a different paradigm of black cultural expression requiring an even broader analysis of the manner in which transformed African retentions continue to function in American and African-American culture.

References

Adams, Edward Clarkson Leverett. 1876–1946. *Congaree Sketches*. Chapel Hill: University of North Carolina Press.
Abrahams, Roger D. and John F. Szwed. 1983. *After Africa: Extracts from British Travel Accounts and Journals of the Seventeenth, Eighteenth, and Nineteenth Centuries Concerning the Slaves, Their Manners, and Customs in the British West Indies*. New Haven: Yale University Press.
Aptheker, Herbert. 1943/93. *American Negro Slave Revolts*. New York: International Publishers.
——. 1951. *A Documentary History of the Negro People in the United States*. New York: Citadel.
Asante, Molefi K. 1987. *The Afrocentric Idea*. Philadelphia: Temple University Press.
——. 1988. *Afrocentricity*. Trenton, NJ: Africa World Press.
Bascom, William. 1972. *Shango in the New World*. Austin: African and Afro-American Institute, University of Texas.

——. 1992. *African Folktales in the New World*. Bloomington: Indiana University Press.

Blyden, Edward Wilmot. 1862. "The Call of Providence to The Descendants of Africa in America." In Brotz, ed., *Negro Social and Political Thought*.

——. 1887. *Christianity, Islam and the Negro Race*. Black Classic Press, 1993, rpt.

——. 1908. *African Life and Customs*. Liberia: *The Sierra Leone Weekly News*/Baltimore: Black Classic Press, 1994, rpt.

——. 1890. "The African Problem and the Method of its Solution." In Brotz, ed. 1966. *Negro Social and Political Thought*.

Brandon, George. 1993. *Santeria from Africa to the New World: The Dead Sell Memories*. Bloomington: Indiana University Press.

Brotz, Howard, ed. 1966. *Negro Social and Political Thought: 1850–1920*. New York: Basic Books, 1995 rpt. *African-American Social and Political Thought 1850–1920*. New Brunswick: Transaction Publishers.

Childs, John Brown. 1984. "Afro-American Intellectuals and the People's Culture." *Theory and Society* 13: 69–90.

Crane, T. F. 1880–1. "Plantation Folk-Lore." *Popular Science Monthly* 18: 824–33.

Crowley, Daniel J. 1962. "Negro Folklore: An Africanist's View." *Texas Quarterly* 5: 65–71.

——. 1977. *African Folklore in the New World*. Austin: University of Texas Press.

Cruz, Jon. 1999. *Culture on the Margins: The Black Spiritual and the Rise of American Cultural Interpretation*. Princeton: Princeton University Press.

Delany, Martin R. 1852. *The Condition, Elevation, Emigration and Destiny of the Colored People of the United States*. Baltimore: Black Classic Press, rpt. 1993.

——. 1859–62. *Blake*. Boston: Beacon Press; collected serial from *Anglo-African Magazine*, rpt. 1970.

——. 1879. *Principia of Ethnology: The Origin of Races and Color*. Philadelphia: Harper & Brother, Publishers/Black Classic Press, rpt. 1991.

Diawara, Manthia. 2001. "The 1960s in Bamako: Malick Sidibe and James Brown." *The Andy Warhol Foundation for the Visual Arts: Paper Series on the Arts, Culture and Society*. Paper Number 11.

Dorson, Richard M. 1975. "African and Afro-American Folklore: A Reply to Bascom and Other Misguided Critics." *Journal of American Folklore* 88: 151–64.

——. 1977. "The African Connection: Comments on 'African Folklore in the New World.'" *Research in African Literatures* 8: 260–5.

Douglass, Frederick. 1854. "The Claims of the Negro Ethnologically Considered." In Howard Brotz, ed. 1966. *Negro Social and Political Thought*.

——. 1859. "African Civilization Society." In Brotz, ed., *Negro Social and Political Thought*.

——. 1886. "The Future of The Colored Race." In Brotz, ed., *Negro Social and Political Thought*.

——. 1894. "The Folly of Colonization." In Brotz, ed. 1966. *Negro Social and Political Thought*.

Du Bois, W. E. B. 1897. "The Conservation of Races." In Brotz, ed. 1966. *Negro Social and Political Thought*.

——. 1903. *The Souls of Black Folk*. Henry L. Gates and Terri H. Oliver, eds. 1999 rpt. New York: Norton.

——, ed. 1907. *Economic Co-operation among Negro Americans*. Atlanta: Atlanta University Press. 1969 rpt. *The Atlanta University Publications Nos. 3, 4, 6, 7, 10, 12, 20*. New York: Arno Press.

——. 1908. *The Negro American Family*. Westport, CT: Negro Universities Press.

Dundes, Alan. 1965. "African Tales among the North American Indians." *Southern Folklore Quarterly* 29: 207–19.

——. 1976. "African and Afro-American Tales." *Research in African Literatures* 7: 181–99.

Ellis, A. B. 1895–6. Evolution in Folklore: Some West African Prototypes of the Uncle Remus Stories. *Popular Science Monthly* 48: 93–104.

186

Esser, Janet Brody, ed. 1988. *Behind the Mask in Mexico*. Santa Fe: Museum of New Mexico Press.

Ewers, Traute. 1996. *The Origin of American Black English:* Be-*Forms in the Hoodoo Texts*. Berlin: Mouton de Gruyter.

Fabre, Genevieve and Robert O'Meally, eds. *History and Memory in African-American Culture*. New York: Oxford University Press.

Foner, Philip S., ed. 1950/75. *The Life and Writings of Frederick Douglass*. 5 vols. New York: International Publishers.

Gates, Henry Louis, Jr. 1988. *The Signifying Monkey: A Theory of African-American Literary Criticism*. Oxford: Oxford University Press.

——and Nellie McKay, eds. 1997. *The Norton Anthology of African American Literature*. New York: Norton.

Geiss, Imanuel. 1968. *The Pan-African Movement: A History of Pan-Africanism in America, Europe and Africa*. New York: Holmes & Meier Publishers.

Gerber, A. 1893. "Uncle Remus Traced to the Old World." *Journal of American Folklore* 6: 245–57.

Gilroy, Paul. 1993a. *The Black Atlantic: Modernity and Double Consciousness*. Cambridge, MA: Harvard University Press.

——. 1993b. *Small Acts*. London: Serpent's Tail.

Harris, Leonard, ed. 1999. *The Critical Pragmatism of Alain Locke*. Lanham: Rowman & Littlefield.

Henry, Paget. 2000. *Caliban's Reason: Introducing Afro-Caribbean Philosophy*. New York: Routledge.

Herskovits, Melville J. 1925. "The Dilemma of Social Pattern." *Survey Graphic*, 6.6. (March): 676–8.

——. 1941/58. *The Myth of the Negro Past*. Boston: Beacon Press.

Herskovits, Melville J. 1966. *The New World Negro*. Edited by Frances S. Herskovits. Bloomington: Minerva Press.

Hill, Patricia Liggins, ed. 1998. *Call and Response: The Riverside Anthology of the African American Literary Tradition*. Boston: Houghton Mifflin.

Hill, Robert A., ed. 1987. *Marcus Garvey: Life and Lessons*. Berkeley: University of California Press.

Holloway, Joseph E., ed. 1990. *Africanisms in American Culture*. Bloomington: Indiana University Press.

Holloway, Joseph E. and Winifred K. Vass. 1993. *The African Heritage of American English*. Bloomington: Indiana University Press.

Hurston, Zora Neale. 1938a. *Tell My Horse*. Berkeley, CA: Turtle Island.

——. 1938b. *The Sanctified Church*. Berkeley, CA: Turtle Island.

James, Joy. 1995. "Politicizing the Spirit: American Africanisms and African Ancestors in the Essays of Toni Morrison." *Cultural Studies* 9.2.

——. 1997. *Transcending the Talented Tenth: Black Leaders and American Intellectuals*. New York: Routledge.

Jacques-Garvey, Amy, ed. 1971. *Philosophy and Opinions of Marcus Garvey*, 2 vols. New York: Atheneum.

Kochman, Thomas, ed. 1972. *Rappin' and Stylin' Out: Communication in Urban America*. Urbana: University of Illinois Press.

——. 1981. *Black and White Styles in Conflict*. Chicago: University of Chicago Press.

Labov. 1972/84. *Language in the Inner City: Studies in the Black English Vernacular*. Philadelphia: University of Pennsylvania Press.

Legum, Colin. 1962. *Pan-Africanism: A Short Political Guide*. New York: Praeger Publishers.

Locke, Alain LeRoy. 1915. *Race Contacts and Interracial Relations*. Edited by Jeffrey C. Stewart. 1992. Washington, DC: Howard University Press.

——. 1925a. "The Art of the Ancestors." *Survey Graphic*, 6.6. (March): 673.

——, ed. 1925b. *The New Negro: An Interpretation*. New York: Albert and Charles Boni.

——. 1927. "Our Little Renaissance." *Ebony and Topaz*. Ed. Charles S. Johnson. New York: National Urban League.

——. 1928. "The Negro's Contribution to American Art and Literature." In Stewart, ed., *The Critical Temper of Alain Locke*.

——. 1933. "The Negro's Contribution in Art to American Culture." *Proceedings of the National Conference of Social Work* (Chicago): 320–1.

——. 1934. "Toward a Critique of Negro Music." In Stewart, ed. *The Critical Temper of Alain Locke*.

——. 1936a. *The Negro and His Music*. Washington, DC: Associates in Negro Folk Education.

——. 1936b. *Negro Art: Past and Present*. Washington, DC: Associates in Negro Folk Education.

——. 1939. "The Negro's Contribution to American Culture." In Stewart, ed., *The Critical Temper of Alain Locke*.

Mintz, Sidney W. and Richard Price. 1976. *The Birth of African-American Culture: An Anthropological Perspective*. Boston: Beacon Press.

Morrison, Toni. 1992. *Playing in the Dark*. Cambridge, MA: Harvard University Press.

Moses, Wilson Jeremiah. 1998. *Afrotopia: The Roots of African American Popular History*. Cambridge: Cambridge University Press.

——. 1978. *The Golden Age of Black Nationalism, 1850–1925*. Oxford: Oxford University Press.

Mufwene, Salikoko S., ed. 1993. *Africanisms in Afro-American Language Varieties*. Athens, GA: University of Georgia Press.

Murray, Albert. 1996. *The Blue Devils of Nada*. New York: Vintage Books.

Neeley, Bobby Joe. 1988. *Contemporary Afro-American Voodooism (Black Religion): The Retention and Adaptation of the Ancient African-Egyptian Mystery System*. Doctoral Dissertation: University of California, Berkeley.

O'Meally, Robert. 1988. *The Jazz Cadence of American Culture*. New York: Columbia University Press.

Padmore, George. *Pan-Africanism or Communism*. 1972. Garden City, NY: Anchor Books.

Perry, Theresa and Lisa Delpit. 1998. *The Real Ebonics Debate*. Boston: Beacon Press.

Piersen, William D. 1971. "An African Background for American Negro Folktales." *Journal of American Folklore* 84: 204–14.

Raboteau, Albert J. 1978. *Slave Religion: The "Invisible Institution" in the Antebellum South*. Oxford: Oxford University Press.

Robeson, Paul. 1958. *Here I Stand*. Boston: Beacon Press.

Schomburg, Arthur. N.d. Proposal for Book on Black Cuisine. Schomburg Papers, Box 12. New York, Schomburg Center, New York Public Library.

Southern, Eileen, ed. 1971. *Readings in Black American Music*. New York: Norton.

Simpson, George Eaton. 1978. *Black Religions in the New World*. New York: Columbia University Press.

Segal, Ronald. 1995. *The Black Diaspora*. New York: Farrar, Straus and Giroux.

Spencer, Jon Michael. 1995. *The Rhythms of Black Folk: Race, Religion and Pan-Africanism*. Trenton, NJ: Africa World Press.

Stewart, Jeffrey C. 1983. *The Critical Temper of Alain Locke: A Selection of His Essays on Art and Culture*. New York: Garland Publishers.

Stuckey, Sterling. 1987. *Slave Culture: Nationalist Theory and the Foundations of Black America*. Oxford: Oxford University Press.

——. 1994. *Going Through the Storm: The Influence of African American Art in History*. Oxford: Oxford University Press.

Sykes, Roberta B. *Black Majority: An Analysis of 21 Years of Black Australian Experience as Emancipated Australian Citizens*. Victoria, Australia: Hudson Publishing.

Szwed, John F. and Roger D. Abrahams. 1978. *Afro-American Folk Culture: An Annotated Bibliography of Materials from North, Central and South America and the West Indies*. 2 vols. Philadelphia: Institute for the Study of Human Issues.

Taylor, Clyde. 1998. *The Mask of Art: Breaking the Aesthetic Contract – Film and Literature*. Bloomington: Indiana University Press.

Thompson, Robert Farris. 1979. "Siras Bowens of Sunbury, Georgia: A Tidewarter Artist in the Afro-American Tradition." In Michael Harper and Robert B. Stepto, eds. *Chant of Saints: A Gathering of Afro-American Literature, Art, and Scholarship*. Urbana: University of Illinois Press.

——. 1981. *Flash of the Spirit: African and Afro-American Art and Philosophy*. New York: Vintage Books.

——. 1993. "Divine Countenance: Art and Altars of the Black Atlantic World." In Phyllis Galembo, ed. *Divine Inspiration*. Albuquerque: University of New Mexico Press.

Thompson, Vincent Bakpetu. 1969. *Africa and Unity: The Evolution of Pan-Africanism*. Harlow: Longmans.

Toll, R. C. 1974. *Blacking Up: The Minstrel Show in Nineteenth-Century America*. Oxford: Oxford University Press.

Toop, David. 1991. *Rap Attack 2: African Rap to Global Hip Hop*. London: Serpent's Tail.

Washington, Johnny. 1986. *Alain Locke and Philosophy: A Quest for Cultural Pluralism*. Westport, CT: Greenwood Press.

Werner, Alice. 1899. "The Tar-Baby Story." *Folklore* 10: 282–93.

11

African Philosophy at the Turn of the Century

ALBERT G. MOSLEY

Because of a legacy of denigration that portrays Africans as incapable of abstract thought, the question "What is African philosophy?" is often the first that occurs to those outside the field. This legacy is reinforced by the assumption that philosophy requires a tradition of written communication that is foreign to Africa. In answer to the question "What is African philosophy?" it has become standard in the many anthologies and texts that have recently been published on the subject to delineate three senses of African philosophy: ethnological, universalist, and hermeneutical.

As a form of ethnology or "ethnophilosophy," African philosophy can be considered the set of values, categories, and assumptions that is implicit in the language, practices, and beliefs of African cultures. One of the major expressions of philosophy as ethnology is Negritude, the principal exponent of which was Leopold Senghor. Senghor argued that Africans have a distinctive approach to reality that is based on emotion rather than logic, an approach that encourages participation rather than analysis, and has its primary manifestation in the arts rather than in the sciences. Precursors of negritude can be found in the work of Alexander Crummel, Edward Blyden, W. E. B. Du Bois, and Alain Locke.

Another major expression of ethnophilosophy is Placide Tempels' *Bantu Philosophy*, published in 1959. Following the Sapir–Whorf thesis so popular during the first half of this century, Tempels argues that the linguistic categories of the Bantu people reflect the metaphysical categories that shape their view of reality. On this view, extended and refined by Father Alexis Kagame of Rwanda, every culture is organized around a set of philosophical principles that are implicit in its language, beliefs and practices, whether or not it is stated explicitly by any member of that culture.

Others who have been characterized as ethnophilosophers include Marcel Griaule, Cheikh Anta Diop, John Mbiti, and Julius Nyerere. As such an extensive list would suggest, what is called ethnophilosophy has taken many different forms, not all of which agree with one another. Thus, while Cheikh Anta Diop stresses the unique nature of African cultures, he disagrees with Senghor's claim that Africans are "naturally" more oriented towards the arts than to science and technology. On the contrary, Diop argues that Egypt was an African culture whose achievements in science, mathematics, architecture, and philosophy was the basis for the flowering of classical Greek civilization. John Mbiti also assumes a distinctiveness among African cultures, which accounts for similar beliefs about personhood, supernatural causality, and the nature of time. Marcel Griaule's conversations with the Dogon priest Ogotommeli and Odera Oruka's interviews with his father and other Luo elders portray them as African sages comparable to Thales and Socrates.

Advocates of ethnophilosophy have claimed that African philosophy should be concerned with articulating those factors that make African people unique and different, and provide them with a special contribution to make to the evolution of civilization. Thus, Diop contrasts the matriarchal nature of African civilizations with the patriachial nature of European civilizations, and argues that such differences should be reflected in the political organization of African states. On the other hand, Tempels considered the chief difference between African and Western philosophy to be the difference in the concept of a being, the African concept being one based on force, while the Western concept was that of a static object.

Critics of ethnophilosophy (of both universalist and hermeneutical persuasion) argue that a focus on the past as the source of authenticity detracts from a critical posture that evaluates all practices relative to their contribution to the liberation of Africa. Thus, Hountoundji claims that Tempels' analysis was made to placate Africans and aid European colonial administrators. Similarly, in response to the view that African philosophy should express the particular outlook of the African race, Appiah claims that the very notion of race was invented to benefit Europeans, not Africans. In fact, Appiah argues, there are no races and the very notion is one that African philosophers should reject.

The universalist school (advocates of which I would include Kwasi Wiredu, Paulin Hountoundji, the late Peter Bodunrin, and Kwame Gyekye) denies that African philosophy should be unique to African languages and cultures. In his famous article "How Not to Compare African Philosophy with Western Philosophy" Kwasi Wiredu argues that the development of philosophy in Africa parallels the development of philosophy in Europe, and traditional African thought should not be taken as paradigmatic of African philosophy any more than traditional European thought is considered paradigmatic of European philosophy. Similarly, Paulin Hountondji argues that philosophy is a critical literature and African philosophy is a critical literature produced by Africans for Africans. While Wiredu and Hountondji construe literacy as essential to the practice of African philosophy, Odera Oruka insists that active engagement in critical reflection on the assumptions of one's culture is the only requirement for philosophy, and this can take place independently of a written discourse. For Oruka, African sages that critically reflect on the assumptions of their culture are just as much philosophers as was Socrates. But for Hountondji, had there been no Plato, a thousand Socrates would not have produced philosophy.

Expanding on his earlier views, in *Conceptual Decolonization in African Philosophy: Four Essays* (1995) Wiredu argues that the fight against colonialism in Africa gave rise to activists like Nkrumah, Nyerere, Kaunda, Sekou Toure, and Senghor who used philosophy for political purposes. By contrast, postcolonial philosophy in Africa is the era of the professional philosopher, whose philosophical interests have been formatively shaped by training in the Western philosophical tradition.

ALBERT G. MOSLEY

Wiredu is aware that African professional philosophers who deal with esoteric topics in logic, epistemology, metaphysics, and the philosophy of mind are often accused of being sell-outs. But he rejects such a characterization, and argues that African philosophers have a pivotal responsibility to domesticate the products of western thought into materials usable by Africans both on the continent and in the Diaspora. He continues to maintain that just because something may have developed in the West is no argument against its proving useful for Africans.

But Wiredu is careful to stress that the professional African philosopher should be as concerned to utilize indigenous as foreign sources of wisdom. For indigenous sources may yield insights that are valuable to Africans as well as non-Africans. He insists nonetheless that in the construction of a postcolonial African philosophy, traditional sources be viewed with just as critical an eye as are modern sources.

For Wiredu, a critical function of postcolonial African philosophy is what he calls "conceptual decolonization," by which he means, avoiding or reversing the unexamined assimilation of western ideas by African people. The necessity of a decolonization of the African mind derives from the imposition on Africa of foreign languages and foreign conceptual schemes through the mediums of language, religion, and politics. Through the use of colonial languages, Africans have accepted concepts, categories, and relationships that are often of little use, and sometimes even detrimental. He enjoins each of us to carefully question whether we might not be carrying a substantial amount of "philosophical deadwood" concealed beneath the foreign terms and concepts we use to express our interests and concerns.

Wiredu's recipe for conceptual decolonization is that we try to translate conceptual projects and notions posed in western terms into indigenous African languages. If the project makes sense in the indigenous language, then it is worthy of further consideration. Investigating the problem using an indigenous African language holds open, for Wiredu, the possibility of revealing novel and useful perspectives that might be much less obvious (if present at all) in a modern European language. If, on the other hand, a problem posed in a Western language appears ridiculous or unintelligible when translated into an indigenous language, then this should alert us to the possibility that it is a pseudo-problem introduced by linguistic imperialism.

But Wiredu's prescription for decolonization is not without its problems. Given the multiplicity of languages in Africa, even within a single modern nation state, we may question to what extent the peculiarities of one language (e.g., Zulu, Hausa, or Ga) should be expected to reflect the linguistic peculiarities of another (e.g., Xhosa, Yoruba, or Akan)? And what of Africans in the diaspora, whose indigenous language is English or French or Portuguese? Finally, one wonders how different Wiredu's recipe for conceptual decolonization is from the recent recommendations of ordinary language philosophy, and whether it harbors similar weaknesses?

A third approach to African philosophy is hermeneutical, and includes Tsenay Serequeberhan, Okondo Okolo, Franz Fanon, Leonard Harris, Lucius Outlaw, and V. Y. Mudimbe among its exponents. In the hermeneutical approach, philosophy takes lived experience as its starting point, and the lived experience of most Africans revolves around a struggle to cope with the omnipresent effects of the cultural and economic imperialism of Europe. As such, the principle objective of African philosophy for hermeneuticists is how to achieve liberation from the injuries imposed by European

192

hegemony. Traditional beliefs and oral discourse are not valuable in themselves, but only relative to the contribution they make to this end.

In his book *The Hermeneutics of African Philosophy* Tsenay Serequeberhan makes use of the work of Hans Gadamer and Martin Heidegger to approach African philosophy from a point of view of what he considers to be the central dilemma of the postcolonial situation. This is the problem of resolving the tension between the continuing hegemony of Europe in the guise of its neocolonial puppets and the continuing influence of pre-colonial traditions especially on the rural masses. Serequeberhan's aim is to provide a means whereby Africans can reassert themselves as the subjects rather than as mere objects in the historical transformation of human kind.

For Serequeberhan, both ethnophilosophers and Western trained professional philosophers have imposed on Africa paradigms that have their primary origin in European social development. Both have reproduced European visions of Africa. He views ethnophilosophers such as Senghor and Tempels as merely appropriating the taxonomy of racial differences developed by Europe, and construing as positive the same characteristics derided by Europeans as evidence of African inferiority. On the other hand, professional philosophers such as Nkrumah and Hountondji would merely replace the capitalist yoke with a communist one. Each, Serequeberhan holds, is a form of "colonialism in the guise of theory."

As an antidote to this globalization of European civilization, Serequeberhan recommends the work of liberationists like Aime Cesaire, Franz Fanon and Emile Cabral, who argue that Europe's violent conquest of Africa is to be opposed by an equally violent expulsion. In the service of ousting the neocolonial remnants of European domination, westernized urban Africans must fuse their talents and concerns with the non-westernized masses of rural Africa. "In the fusion of these two fractured 'worlds'," Serequeberhan writes, "the possibility of African freedom is concretized. . . ."

It is in this "return to the source," where urbanized Africans put their knowledge to the service of the rural masses (rather than merely manipulating them for urban advantages), that Serequeberhan sees the key to true African liberation. In this fusion, both the ossified traditions of the past and the imposed traditions of the colonizer are transformed, and the modern African emerges as a new hybrid capable of acting rather than merely being acted upon. This "return to the source" is not the uncritical and romantic adoption of traditional beliefs and practices for their intrinsic value. Rather, both the weaknesses and strengths of traditional African cultures are exposed to critical review and the stunted potential of African cultural development is released. Clearly, Serequeberhan's theme of a "return to the source" and Wiredu's program of "conceptual decolonization" bear a strong family resemblance.

In a recent paper, "Technology and Culture in a Developing Country," Kwame Gyekye also directs his attention to the problem of how to fuse traditional and modern currents to meet contemporary African needs. Gyekye, far from giving blind respect to traditional African beliefs and practices, openly acknowledges their failure to encourage scientific and technological development. On the other hand, he is aware that the wholesale adoption of Western technology is equally as much a part of the problem. His solution is to forge a synthesis whereby the African appropriates imported tools and expertise to readapt traditional technologies.

Serequeberhan's concern with the fusion of traditional and modern Africa is thus mirrored in the concerns expressed by Wiredu and Gyekye. Yet each flounders in the details of how this fusion is to take place, raising our fear that their concerns may be more utopian than realistic. Wiredu fails to note that many features of modern life have no analogues in traditional practices, and hence cannot be validated by reference to them. And Gyekye fails to appreciate the extent to which modern technological orientations may be incompatible with traditional technologies. Following Fanon, Serequeberhan defends the necessity of violently expelling the African puppets of neocolonialism. But it is difficult to see how this advocacy of violence is any less an extension of a European initiative than Nkrumah and Hountondji's embrace of Marxist–Leninism, Senghor's embrace of racialism, or Tempels' embrace of an ontology of Being (*pace* Heidegger).

For universalists and hermeneuticists, having aspects of the Western canon as a principal source for intellectually modeling Africa's problems is not a flaw. They consider use of the Western idiom as a necessary rather than incidental aspect of the program of Africans trained in the Western tradition. But this is not seen as making them any less African. As Kwame Anthony Appiah is fond of saying, intellectuals are now as African as fetish priests.

Yet if this is a valid disclaimer for universalists and hermenueticists, I believe it is also a valid disclaimer for Blyden, Du Bois, and Senghor's appeal to racialism and an ontology of racial difference. With regard to sources, Wiredu, Hountondji, Serequeberhan, and Appiah have done no more or less than the ethnophilosophers they criticize.

This does not mean that there are no problems with racialism that we need beware of. Certainly there are. One especially that I wish to address here is that of essentialism. There is no denying the attempt of ethnophilosophers to identify a factor that marks an essential difference between Africans and non-Africans. Emotion, matriarchy, the concept of being, and the concept of time have all been cited as establishing an essential difference. Yet, one of the most prominent aspects of postmodern philosophy is its critique of essentialism. Recognizing intra-specific variation as natural rather than aberrant and the pervasiveness of family resemblance concepts has shown that there need be no essences in order for there to be kinds of things.

Ethnophilosophers need to integrate this insight into their treatment of African philosophy. But this need not imply that there is no internal coherence to the notion of African philosophy. Rather than one or the other of them defining its essence, epistemological, metaphysical, social, political, and historical factors may combine to give African philosophy a distinctive cast. Yet, there need be no "unamism," to use Hountoundji's term. That there is no one factor that distinguishes chairs from benches, or males from females, does not mean there are no chairs, benches, males, and females. Nonetheless there is a cluster of factors that do combine to characterize typical members of each of those categories.

Imbo warns that we must be wary of how we characterize differences, because "in the dominant frameworks of Western philosophy, 'different' means 'inferior'." But this is not just a problem for African philosophy. Given similar histories of struggling against domination, African, African-American, and feminist philosophical enterprises must satisfy the political imperative of deconstructing traditional philosophical methods and assumptions to expose hidden agendas of domination.

Feminists such as Sandra Harding have called attention to the similarity of African and feminist agendas. And just as Harding carefully distinguishes between being female, feminine, and a feminist, I believe we should as carefully distinguish between being an African, an Africanist, and an Afrocentrist. One can be feminine and a feminist without being female, and likewise, I would hold that one can be an Africanist and an Afrocentrist without being African. To be an Africanist implies being interested in African languages, cultures, and peoples. To be an Afrocentrist is the attempt to see events and situations from the point of view of the Africans affected. Not all Africanists and Afrocentrists need be Africans and not all Africans need be Africanists and Afrocentrists.

Difference oriented feminists such as Carol Gould have contrasted women as care givers with men as reciprocating rational agents, in much the same manner that ethnophilosophers such as Senghor have contrasted Africans as emotive and Europeans as intellectual. But in neither case need we insist that such differences be biologically based or without exception. The dilemma is how to affirm differences without perpetuating the exclusionary myths that have been historically associated with them. It is as false that men cannot be nurturing and women cannot be rational as it is that Africans cannot be scientists and Europeans have no rhythm.

Denying that there are races is much like insisting that each of us is androgynous. While androgyny is certainly a legitimate option for some, the solution to racism and sexism is not in denying the existence of racial and sexual differences, but in rejecting the manner in which those differences are used to disadvantage Africans relative to Europeans and women relative to men. Rather than deny the existence of differences, African philosophy in its neo-ethnological guise should insist that the dominant framework recognize the positive value of attributes traditionally associated with Africans, without suggesting that such attributes are unique to Africans. And it should insist that modern institutions be transformed to reflect the value of those attributes, instead of passively acquiescing to the demand that Africans and African-Americans be shaped and transformed to fit criteria already esteemed by those institutions.

D. A. Masolo perceptively notes that "At the beginning, African philosophy did little more than echo the premises which had been expressed by the Harlem Renaissance and negritude movements." I have argued that many of those premises need reassessment in light of developments in feminist and African-American philosophical critiques. Nonetheless, I believe that W. E. B. Du Bois, Alain Locke, Aime Cesaire, and Leopold Senghor were onto something important.

At the gates to Western philosophy Plato declared "Let no one enter who has not studied mathematics." At the gates to African philosophy we may imagine the ethnophilosopher to have declared "Let no one enter who has not communicated with ancestral spirits and internalized the rhythms of traditional music." While the neo-ethnophilosopher should resist the implicit essentialism that would exclude those who did not satisfy those requirements, it remains true that Africa might benefit from learning to use its music to teach mathematics instead of (*pace* Schoenberg) adopting mathematics as the principal means of teaching its music. For there is a difference, I believe, with regards to which, mathematics or music, one chooses as African philosophy's primary model.

195

References

Appiah, Kwame Anthony. 1992. *In My Father's House: Africa in the Philosophy of Culture*. New York: Oxford University Press.

Coetzee, P. H. and A. P. J. Roux (eds.). 1998. *The African Philosophy Reader*. New York: Routledge.

Diop, Cheikh Anta. 1987. *Precolonial Black Africa: A Comparative Study of the Political and Social Systems of Europe and Black Africa from Antiquity to the Formation of Modern States*. Trans. Harold Salemson. Trenton, NJ: Africa World Press Edition.

——. 1991. *Civilization or Barbarism: An Authentic Anthropology*. Trans. Yaa-Lengi Meema Ngemi. Brooklyn: Lawrence Hill Books.

English, Parker and Kibujjo Kalumba (eds.). 1996. *African Philosophy: A Classical Approach*. Upper Saddle River, NJ: Prentice Hall.

Eze, Emmanuel (ed.). 1997. *African Philosophy: An Anthology*. Cambridge, MA: Blackwell.

Griaule, Marcel. 1965. *Conversations with Ogotemmeli: An Introduction to Dogon Religious Ideas*. London: Oxford University Press.

Gyekye, Kwame. 1995. "Technology and Culture in a Developing Country." In *Philosophy and Technology*. 1995. Supplement 38 to *Philosophy*. London: Royal Institute of Philosophy. Reprinted as the lead essay in Emmanuel Eze, ed. 1997. *Postcolonial African Philosophy: A Critical Reader*. Cambridge, MA: Blackwell.

Harding, Sandra. 1991. *Whose Science? Whose Knowledge?* Ithaca, NY: Cornell University Press.

Hountondji, Paulin. 1983. *African Philosophy: Myth and Reality*. Bloomington: Indiana University Press.

Imbo, Samuel. 1998. *An Introduction to African Philosophy*. New York: Rowman & Littlefield.

Langer, Susanne. 1953. *Feeling and Form*. New York: Scribner.

——. 1957. *Philosophy in a New Key*. Cambridge: Harvard University Press.

Masolo, D. A. 1994. *African Philosophy in Search of Identity*. Bloomington, IN: Indiana University Press.

Mbiti, John. 1969. *African Religions and Philosophy*. New York: Praeger.

Mosley, Albert (ed.). 1995. *African Philosophy: Selected Readings*. Englewood Cliffs, NJ: Prentice Hall.

Mosley, Albert. 1997. "Are Racial Categories Racist." In *Research in African Literatures*, 28:4 (Winter).

Mosley, Albert. 2000. "Science, Technology and Tradition in Contemporary African Philosophy." *African Philosophy* 13.1 (March).

Mudimbe, V. Y. 1988. *The Invention of Africa*. Bloomington, IN: Indiana University Press.

Nietzsche, Frederich. 1967. *The Birth of Tragedy out of the Spirit of Music*. Trans. Walter Kaufmann. New York: Random House.

Nyerere, Julius. 1968. *Ujamaa – Essays on Socialism*. Dar-es-Salaam, Tanzania: Oxford University Press.

Oruka, Henry Odera. 1990. *Sage Philosophy*. Leiden: E. J. Brill.

Rhode, Deborah. 1996. "The Ideology and Biology of Gender Difference." *The Southern Journal of Philosophy* 35. Supplement, pp. 73–98.

Serequeberhan, Tsenay (ed.). 1991. *African Philosophy: The Essential Readings*. New York: Paragon House.

Serequeberhan, Tsenay. 1994. *The Hermeneutics of African Philsophy*. New York: Routledge.

Tempels, Placide. 1959. *Bantu Philosophy*. Trans. Rev. Colin King. Paris: Présence Africaine.

Wiredu, Kwasi. 1995. *Conceptual Decolonization in African Philosophy*. Selected and introduced by Olusegun Oladipo. Ibadan, Nigeria: Hope Publications.

Part IV

GENDER, RACE, AND RACISM

Introduction to Part IV

Questions regarding the structuring of gender and race in institutions and practices are a central concern in African-American philosophy. Black feminists have challenged the hegemony of ideas that support patriarchy. While maintaining a commitment to the theoretical thrust of black feminism, Patricia Hill Collins and Joy James question certain practices that fail to adequately accommodate the intersection, or hybrid manifestations, of race, class, and gender. The idea of racial categories also has been subjected to criticism from these different standpoints. Naomi Zack, David Theo Goldberg, and Charles Mills address a wide range of issues related to the social and political function of racial categorization.

Collins is concerned with the relation between standpoint epistemology and black feminist thought. She begins with the idea that the standpoint of African Americans and the knowledge that can influence their political action is situated in unjust power relations. The nationalist idea of racial solidarity that fueled the Civil Rights movement has been criticized for its commitment to an essentialist ideology of racial authenticity. The use of a standpoint theory that focuses on the lived experience of women has also been criticized by feminists. Collins acknowledges the importance of diverse elements among African-American women, but she believes there are problems stemming from hierarchies of power based on age, gender, economic class, region, and sexuality.

Collins is worried that even if a group's position in power relations, and the shared experiences that accompany this, were effective in past struggles, under new conditions, such as the politics of containment, group-based identities of this sort may no longer be effective. She asserts that group-based identities such as those advocated by standpoint theory may ultimately disempower African-American women because they unduly suppress differences and heterogeneity among black women. Restating the connection between black women's identities as individuals and their historically constituted group identity, she maintains that, because individuals cannot always choose to opt out of a group, race creates what amounts to "immutable" group identities. Gender marks the body in similar fashion – by assigning it a classification, and meaning. For this reason, she believes the notion of standpoint can be employed to refer to groups having shared histories based on their shared location in unjust power relations. The twin binaries of whites dominating blacks and men dominating women require a recognition of intersectionality to accommodate the interplay between race, class and gender, adding complexity to the view of how black women are positioned within unjust power relations.

Collins wants to deny a "new myth of equivalent oppressions." Individual and collective experiences of black women are not the same as white women, gay men, or working-class Latinos. The fact that they are connected obscures the differential effects of intersecting systems of power. Black and white women participate in the same system of institutionalized racism and sexism, but each group assigns a different salience to race and gender. African-American women are differently positioned in race–class groups and gender-organized groups. She cites, as the major shortcoming of intersectionality theory, the suggestion that all such intersections produce equivalent results for all oppressed groups.

Collins cautions that class connotes more than just economic status because groups are situated in a specific history of a society. She points out that Marx analyzed class relations in terms of historically concrete, lived experience. Collins proposes to generate class categories from actual lived experience to reveal the manner in which social hierarchies construct group or class relationships with visible economic dimensions. She considers the manner in which African Americans participate in race–class intersectionality in the US to show that structural features bring people into proximity who have common economic interests. She maintains that there are no "shared economic conditions" on the basis of which all women can organize. Women are sorted into clearly defined categories of race, economic class, ethnicity, and citizenship status.

Collins's view that class is a major factor inhibiting the social formation of women with a commonly shared group identity is supported by Joy James's critique of the lumping of all black feminists into a monolithic category. She proposes to follow Ella Baker's assessment of the contradictions of liberalism among black elites involved in the civil rights struggle. James distinguishes between the political agenda of becoming a part of the American scene and the more radical struggle to transform American society. At a time when leaders were positioned above the masses, Baker advocated the right of all people to participate in the decision-making that affected their lives. James is concerned that contemporary feminists who embrace "the bourgeois ideology of race uplift" display an antirevolutionary tendency, which facilitates their integration into, or suppression within, corporate-consumer culture. She praises Baker for advocating a more grass-roots form of leadership. James is dissatisfied with the fact that these leaders and organizers have gone largely unrecognized and undocumented in the history of radical feminism.

She aims to rectify this by drawing attention to the Combahee River Collective, a group of radical black feminists that took its name from the guerrilla foray led by Harriet Tubman in South Carolina's Port Royal region in 1863. She points out that, as feminists and lesbians, they claimed solidarity with black men around the issue of race, distinguishing themselves from white feminists. They were committed to radical change aimed at the destruction of capitalism, imperialism, and patriarchy. With this paradigm in mind, James proposes an integrative analysis to overcome the marginalization of black feminism and the antiradical tendencies within black feminism. She focuses on ideology to distinguish between liberal, radical, neoradical, and revolutionary politics among feminists. She believes the difficulty of articulating defining criteria for radical black feminism is due to the fact that feminist ideology and practice can only be understood as revolutionary within context.

According to James, the marginalization of all black feminism is often the basis for attributing a radical view to liberal and conservative feminists. But she believes this over essentializes black women and black feminisms. Just as conservative black feminists have benefited from the association and conflation with liberalism, radical black feminists have also benefited from association and conflation with liberal black feminists – a legitimation process that is dynamic and two-way. James uses a mat metaphor to assert that a mat over the political vision of black feminism establishes newer borders that frequently "blot out" revolutionary activists, and allow "professional radicals" to appear within this new frame as the only "insurgents."

Although all black feminists are marginalized, the revolutionary feminist remains on the margin more than any other. James believes the symbiotic relationship between subordinate black feminists and the "white" masculinist state precludes any presumption of a unified politics. Black feminisms function as shadows in their subordinate status, while their plurality is portrayed as monolithic. According to James it is the shadow boxer's dilemma to fight male domination while simultaneously battling internal conflict and contradictions among competing feminisms.

Many philosophers maintain that, along with gender, the category of race is socially constructed for political purposes. The argument that the concept of race functions as ideology is presented by Naomi Zack. She aims to promote a healthy scepticism regarding the continued use of this concept. According to Zack, empirical research shows that race does not exist; nonetheless, we still operate with related ideas and practices that rely on racial paradigms. Although American society seems to be moving away from the old oppressive and racist paradigm, involving issues of racial hierarchy, toward a new liberatory and nonracist one that aims to promote racial equality, Zack argues that both are problematic.

Beginning with the seventeenth century, she traces the history of the concept of race to set up her argument for the "demolition" of this construction. The influence of this history of the idea of race on current thought is evidenced by the fact that belief in the existence of race is a core issue of the "New Paradigm." This paradigm is employed with the understanding that people are divided into natural groups with common physical traits that can be studied in the biological sciences and that racial terms refer to them. Zack relies on John Searle's analysis in *The Construction of Social Reality* to support her critique of racial paradigms. On Searle's account, social facts about physical facts and other social facts are related through language. The process of constituting and regulating objects on different levels of social reality gives new meanings to constructions from less abstract levels. She maintains that Searle's formula: X counts as Y in C can be used to describe the American social realities of race, specifically the manner in which certain features of the "Old Paradigm" survive into the "New Paradigm." Searle's formula can be used to trace lines between facts about racial difference and social constructions based on the facts in any given context. Using a paradigm other than our own that she calls the "Last Paradigm," she criticizes both the "Old" and "New" paradigms.

Zack uses the example of a paperweight to illustrate her thesis. A stone can be a paperweight only in an observer-relative sense. Similarly, being black, white, or Asian is observer-relative and not something intrinsic about the person. She maintains that, unlike the case of money, where there is common agreement that everyone benefits from having a functional monetary system, we do not know if people would continue to do everything they now do with race in conjunction with widespread belief that there is nothing to back it up. According to Zack, it is an empirical question whether discrimination would decrease if people came to generally believe that there is no biological basis for race.

Zack views mixed-race identity as problematic for "Old" and "New" paradigms. She acknowledges that there are psychological and moral aspects of racism in the absence of the biological foundation that has generated a worry among some African Americans, who are concerned that a recognition of mixed-race status will dilute the gains of the Civil Rights movement. David Theo Goldberg does not view this concern as a matter of changing existing categories to create new categories that are more accurate. He argues that the role of racial classification in the practice of census-taking is "a mechanism of racial governance." With an eye to the institutional level at which racial distinctions operate on the basis of census data, he recommends self-identification as a means of changing social policy. Unlike Zack's proposal to use mixed-race categories to depoliticize race as a means of ending racism, Goldberg urges a strategic employment of race consciousness to subvert the practice of racial classification. Self-identification allows the victims of racial classification to intentionally render the collection of statistical data useless.

Given the ideological function of racial classification in the census, Goldberg believes, paradoxically, that it is necessary to count by race in order to undo counting by race. He views racial knowledge in terms of "using racial characteristics, making racial claims, asserting racial truths, and assessing racial value." By assuming a scientific cloak, the census lends racial knowledge legitimation, especially in popular media.

Interpreting charts from the two hundred years of census-taking, Goldberg traces its history to indicate the manner in which it has functioned politically. With an eye to Zack's recommendation regarding mixed-race, it is worth noting that Goldberg reports that enumerators were cautioned to take special care in reporting mulatto and mixed race because "important scientific results depend upon the correct determination of these." He goes on to point out, however, that in 1900 the distinctions between various mixtures, such as quadroon and octoroon, began to collapse with the single-drop rule. In the 1940 census Mexicans were listed as white in accordance with the trend to introduce ethnoracial categories while maintaining a majority white population.

Goldberg seems to agree with Zack regarding the political implications of racial classification. He points out that the reason we are concerned at all with counting by race, given the complexity of mixed race identities, is because of a legislative mandate to manage effective resource distribution and voting access. He cites the use of Hispanic, a term crafted in the 1970s as a nonracial, panethnic term to cut across racial designations, and notes that now in its generality it serves as a new ethnoracial category. Hispanic is at once racialized and deracialized. Because an Hispanic person can be white, black, or nonwhite, according to Goldberg, it is a racialized category that functions to garner political support, a move "to reorder the structure of whiteness."

Goldberg notes that the ideological functions of racial categories are often inconsistent. For example, colorblindness is an ideal espoused in the Constitution, Bill of Rights and Civil Rights Acts, yet these founding laws have been racialized in order to be instituted. The Dale Sandhu case against Lockheed for racial bias was dismissed because the law considered East Indians to be Caucasian, but Sandhu cited the 1980 census category of Asian Indian to win an appeal. Indeed, the Census Bureau recognizes that race is not the same in all the various census counts of the past. Goldberg's point is that a political interest is served. Race is to be counted only where it signals "class exploitation and exclusion."

The idea that the interest of whites is served by the census is consistent with the central claim of Critical Race Theory – that a state apparatus of this sort functions to maintain white privilege. The argument that white supremacy has not vanished, but only changed from *de jure* to *de facto* is presented by Charles Mills. White supremacy is a term usually restricted to formal juridico-political domination, as in the case of slavery in the US, or apartheid in South Africa. Mills wants to extend the concept of white supremacy beyond these overt racist practices, as well as beyond its common use to refer to the beliefs of radical white separatist groups such as the Ku Klux Klan (KKK) or Aryan Nation. He agrees with Zack and Goldberg regarding the ideological function of the prevailing paradigm of race as natural, or biological. He opposes this idea with a constructivist theory that maintains that race is not natural, but "an artifact of sociopolitical decision-making." In keeping with Goldberg's analysis of the history of census-taking, he maintains that where the boundaries are drawn is a function of political power.

Mills's account of white supremacy involves several features. Central to his view is the idea that the white race is an invention. He cites David Roediger's work as the source of a debate over the role of the state and the working class in making themselves white. Along with the change from a *de jure* to a *de facto* form of white supremacy there was also a change in the rules as to who is counted as white. Based on the analysis offered by Matthew Frye Jacobson, Mills identifies "three great epochs of US whiteness." He notes that Mediterraneans, Celts, Slavs, and Teutons who were once recognized as distinct races have now disappeared into an expanded white race.

Another important feature of Mill's view is the thesis that the global influence of European colonialism has rendered white supremacy transnational. The age of global white supremacy overlaps pre-World War II European colonialism, under which the world was in fact formally ruled by white nations. Mills wants the concept of white supremacy to have "an overarching holistic reconceptualization of social relations as a system of group domination" on par with the focus on power in Marxist and feminist political theory. White supremacy has a parallel conceptual function in political discourse regarding race. Mills presents his concept of white supremacy as a repudiation of the epiphenomenalist treatment of race in Marxist theory. Rather than reduce race to class, he insists upon treating it as "real" in the sense that it is materialized by white supremacy in social practices and by victims in "felt phenomenologies."

According to Mills, subjugation is no longer maintained primarily through legal mechanisms, rather it is a multidimensional system of domination that involves "a racialization of the social world that determines one's being and consciousness." He believes that the consciousness of both blacks and whites has been shaped by the negative effects of white supremacy. Whites are socialized into an ethical code that is itself structured by race. Mills refers to this as a "Herrenvolk ethics" in which whiteness itself becomes property. This involves a characteristic and pervasive pattern of "structured ignorance, self deception and moral rationalization" with which blacks, for their own survival, have to learn to become familiar. Mills cites a list of nineteenth-century African-American writers who addressed their racial concerns in global terms that fostered a diaspora consciousness. Given the work of black intellectuals on white supremacy, the project of Critical Race Theory and Critical White Studies amounts to a "belated catching up" with the insights of black thought.

Some Group Matters: Intersectionality, Situated Standpoints, and Black Feminist Thought

PATRICIA HILL COLLINS

In developing a Black feminist praxis, standpoint theory has provided one important source of analytical guidance and intellectual legitimation for African-American women.[1] Standpoint theory argues that group location in hierarchical power relations produces shared challenges for individuals in those groups. These common challenges can foster similar angles of vision leading to a group knowledge or standpoint that in turn can influence the group's political action. Stated differently, group standpoints are situated in unjust power relations, reflect those power relations, and help shape them.

I suspect that one reason that the ideas of standpoint theory (in contrast to the vocabulary deployed by standpoint theorists, including the term *standpoint theory* itself) resonate with African-American women's experiences lies in the resemblance of standpoint theory to the norm of racial solidarity. Created in response to institutionalized racism and associated with Black nationalist responses to such oppression (see, e.g., Franklin 1992; Van Deburg 1992), racial solidarity within Black civil society requires that African-Americans stick together at all costs. The civil rights and Black Power movements certainly demonstrated the effectiveness of Black politics grounded in racial solidarity. In the former, racial solidarity among African-Americans lay at the center of a multiracial civil rights effort. In the latter, racial solidarity was expressed primarily through all-Black organizations. Collectively, these movements delivered tangible political and economic gains for African-Americans as a group (but not for all members within the group). Differences could be expressed *within* the boundaries of Blackness but not *across* those same boundaries. In this sense, the notion of a Black women's standpoint gains meaning in the context of a shared Black consciousness dedicated to sustaining racial solidarity. Notions of racial solidarity and a shared Black women's standpoint both invoke explicitly political objectives. Just as adhering to racial solidarity was important for Black emancipation in the United States, so might a collective Black women's standpoint be seen as essential for Black feminist praxis. Since Black women, like African-Americans overall, are oppressed as a group, collective as compared to individualized strategies remain important.

Much has happened since the 1970s. Depending on their placement in hierarchies of age, gender, economic class, region of the country, and sexuality, African-American women encounter new challenges associated with the new politics of containment in the United States. These changes require fresh ideas that analyze the complexities of contemporary lived Black experience and suggest adequate political responses to them. The intellectual climate currently housing Black feminist thought has also changed. In academic contexts influenced by postmodern rubrics of decentering, deconstruction, and difference, the norm of racial solidarity itself has come under increasing attack. Within Black cultural studies in particular, critiques now stress how racial solidarity has far too often been constructed on the bedrock of racial authenticity and essentialism (see, e.g., Dyson 1993; West 1993; and Collins 1998c, 83), leading some to emphasize the pitfalls of unquestioned racial solidarity for African-American women (Grant 1982; Terrelonge 1984; Richie 1996). Academic feminism in North America takes aim at similar targets. Whereas Black academics question the utility of racial solidarity in addressing social issues of lived Black experience, feminist theorists increasingly criticize standpoint theory on theoretical grounds (Hekman 1997). Collectively, many Black and/or feminist academics question the assumptions that underlie solidarities of all sorts. This has great implication for Black feminist praxis generally, and a Black women's standpoint situated in unjust power relations in particular.

Given these shifting patterns, the situated standpoints that Black women collectively construct, and even the question of whether African-American women self-define as a group, become vitally important. In historical contexts in which racial segregation more visibly organized geographic, symbolic, and political space assigned to African-Americans, the links between a group's common positionality in power relations, the shared experiences that accompanied this commonality, the mechanisms for constructing group standpoints, and the significance of group standpoints for political activism were fairly straightforward. Under the changed conditions that accompany the new politics of containment, however, these links are neither clear nor assumed. Despite the historical significance of the ideas of standpoint theory to African-American women, questions remain concerning the efficacy of group-based identities of this sort for contemporary political struggles. In situations in which increasingly sophisticated practices, such as controlling populations through constant surveillance (Foucault 1979), as well as strategies of everyday racism (Essed 1991) and symbolic racism (Jhally and Lewis 1992), obscure the continued effects of institutionalized injustices of all sorts, political theories that seem to advocate pulling together and storming the factory gates can seem simplistic. Moreover, the decreasing effectiveness of an identity politics currently associated with standpoint theory raises questions of its continued relevance (see Collins 1998c, 44–76). Are group-based identities that emerge from standpoint theory and the politics they generate still empowering for African-American women? Do group-based identities such as those advocated by standpoint theory ultimately disempower African-American women because they unduly suppress differences and heterogeneity among Black women? Quite simply, in what ways, if any, does standpoint theory remain relevant for Black feminist thought?

Intersectionality and Social Groups

Since standpoint theory remains predicated on the notion of a group with shared experiences and interests, addressing these questions requires revisiting the connections between African-American women's identities as individuals and Black women's historically constituted group identity. Individuals can assemble associations by coming together as already formed persons. African-American women who join sororities come as individuals and participate as voluntary members. In contrast, a historically constituted group identity is neither fleeting nor chosen. As Iris Marion Young points out, "One *finds oneself* as a member of a group, which one experiences as always already having been" (1990, 46; emphasis in original). For example, for the vast majority of the population in the United States, race creates immutable group identities. Individuals cannot simply opt in or out of racial groups, because race is constructed by assigning bodies meaningful racial classifications. Gender marks the body in a similar fashion.[2] Within the framework provided by their historically constituted group identity, individuals take up and perform their classification in diverse ways. African-American women, for example, all encounter some variation of what is expected of them as "Black women." How individual Black women construct their identities within these externally defined boundaries varies tremendously. However, it also occurs in response to the shared challenges that all Black women encounter.

Within unjust power relations, groups remain unequal in the powers of self-definition and self-determination. Race, class, gender, and other markers of power intersect to produce social institutions that, in turn, construct groups that become defined by these characteristics. Since some groups define and rule others, groups are hierarchically related to one another. Within this overarching hierarchical structure, the ways in which individuals find themselves to be members of groups in group-based power relations matters. In some cases, individuals may be aware that their classification in a particular group matters, but they have little contact with other group members or believe that group membership is not important in everyday lived experience. Other groups have clearly defined histories, traditions, and patterned forms of behavior dedicated to ensuring that individual members "find themselves" as members of groups quite early in life.[3]

I stress this difference between the individual and the group as units of analysis because using these two constructs as if they were interchangeable clouds understanding of a host of topics, in this case, assessing the contributions of group-based experiences in constructing standpoints.[4] The type of reductionist thinking that uses individual experience to theorize group processes falters, because the treatment of the group in standpoint theory is not synonymous with a "family resemblance" of individual choice expanded to the level of voluntary group association. The notion of standpoint refers to groups having shared histories based on their shared location in unjust power relations – standpoints arise neither from crowds of individuals nor from groups analytically created by scholars or bureaucrats. Common location within power relations, not the result of collective decision making of individuals, creates African-American women as a group. What collective decision making does produce is a determination of the *kind* of group African-American women will be in a given social context.

Under race-only or gender-only conceptual frameworks, it is fairly easy to see how unjust power relations create social groups. Within binary thinking, men rule women and Whites dominate Blacks in schools, the labor market, government organization, and other social institutions. However, the emerging paradigm of intersectionality problematizes this entire process of group construction. As a heuristic device, intersectionality references the ability of social phenomena such as race, class, and gender to mutually construct one another. One can use the framework of intersectionality to think through social institutions, organizational structures, patterns of social interactions, and other social practices on all levels of social organization. Groups are constructed within these social practices, with each group encountering a distinctive constellation of experiences based on its placement in hierarchical power relations. African-American women, for example, can be seen both as a group that occupies a distinctive social location within power relations of intersectionality and as one wherein intersectional processes characterize Black women's collective self-definitions and actions. Whereas race-only or gender-only perspectives classify African-American women as a subgroup of either African-Americans or women, intersections of race, class, and gender, among others, create more fluid and malleable boundaries around the category "African-American women." Within this logic, Black women as a historically constituted group in the United States are no less real – how the group is theoretically defined, however, changes markedly.

Intersectionality thus highlights how African-American women and other social groups are positioned within unjust power relations, but it does so in a way that introduces added complexity to formerly race-, class-, and gender-only approaches to social phenomena. The fluidity that accompanies intersectionality does not mean that groups themselves disappear, to be replaced by an accumulation of decontextualized, unique individuals whose personal complexity makes group-based identities and politics that emerge from group constructions impossible. Instead, the fluidity of boundaries operates as a new lens that potentially deepens understanding of how the actual mechanisms of institutional power can change dramatically even while they reproduce long-standing group inequalities of race, class, and gender. As Kimberle Crenshaw points out, "Intersectionality captures the way in which the particular location of black women in dominant American social relations is unique and in some senses unassimilable into the discursive paradigms of gender and race domination" (1992, 404). In this sense, African-American women's group history and location can be seen as points of convergence within structural, hierarchical, and changing power relations.

Given the tendency of state power to manipulate groups that rely too heavily on narrowly defined identity politics, it is especially important to keep intersectional analyses of group construction in mind. In their assessment of how the government policy of positive action (affirmative action) in Great Britain effectively weakened racial and ethnic identity politics, Floya Anthias and Nira Yuval-Davis (1992) identify an important pitfall confronting groups that allow themselves to be constructed around essentialist definitions. When state distribution of social rewards in relation to group membership fosters a situation of group competition for scarce resources, policing the boundaries of group membership becomes much more important. Anthias and Yuval-Davis illustrate how initial efforts to express self-defined group standpoints can easily be co-opted by state powers that recognize and use identity politics for their own interests.

Retaining this focus on groups constructed within and through intersectionalities remains important for another reason. Intersectionality works better as a substantive theory (one aimed at developing principles that can be proved true or false) when applied to individual-level behavior than when documenting group experiences. The construct of intersectionality works well with issues of individual agency and human subjectivity and thus has surface validity in explaining everyday life. Individuals can more readily see intersections of race, gender, class, and sexuality in how they construct their identities as individuals than in how social institutions rely on these same ideas in reproducing group identities. On the level of the individual, using race, class, gender, sexuality, and national belonging as mutually constructing categories of experience that take on shifting meanings in different contexts makes sense. It is perfectly reasonable to compare, for example, an individual African-American woman to an individual White American woman and to ask how each constructs an identity informed by intersections of race, class, and gender across varying social contexts. On the level of the individual, these kinds of comparisons work, because the unit of comparison – the individual – is deemed equivalent, constant, and not in need of analysis.

Unfortunately, the compatibility of intersectionality with individual-level analyses can foster the consequence of elevating individualism above group analyses. This valorization of individualism to the point where group and structural analyses remain relegated to the background has close ties to American Liberalism. Despite the significance of racial, ethnic, economic, and other types of groups in U.S. society, individualism continues as a deep taproot in American law and social theory. David Goldberg describes the roots of liberalism:

> Liberalism is committed to *individualism* for it takes as basic the moral, political, and legal claims of the individual over and against those of the collective. It seeks *foundations* in *universal* principles applicable to all human beings or rational agents. . . . In this, liberalism seeks to transcend particular historical, social, and cultural differences: It is concerned with broad identities which it insists unite persons on moral grounds, rather than with those identities which divide. . . . Liberalism takes itself to be committed to equality. (1993, 5; emphasis in original)

Whether we are talking about the explicit individualism of bourgeois liberalism or the explicit individualism permeating postmodern renditions of difference, individualistic models define freedom as the absence of constraints, including those of mandatory group membership. Freedom occurs when individuals have rights of mobility into and out of groups – the right to join clubs and other voluntary associations or to construct their subjectivity as multiple and changing. Little mention is made of the collective struggles that preceded any group's gaining individual rights of this sort. Within this logic, race, class, gender, and the like become defined as personal attributes of individuals that they should be able to choose or reject. Thus, because it fails to challenge the assumptions of individualism, intersectionality when applied to the individual level can coexist quite nicely with both traditional liberalism and a seemingly apolitical postmodernism.

When discussing intersectionality and group organization, however, assumptions of individualism obscure hierarchical power relations of all sorts, from race- and gender-only perspectives through more complex frameworks such as intersectionality. Can one argue that African-American women and White American women as *groups* are so equivalent that one can take the reality of the social group itself as an assumption that does not need to be examined? Moreover, not only does intersectionality, when applied to the level of groups, become more difficult to conceptualize, but because groups do not operate as individuals do, intersectionality on the group level becomes difficult to study. When examining structural power relations, intersectionality functions better as a conceptual framework or heuristic device describing what kinds of things to consider than as one describing any actual patterns of social organization. The goal is not to prove intersectionality right or wrong, nor to gather empirical data to test the existence of intersectionality. Rather, intersectionality provides an interpretive framework for thinking through how intersections of race and class, or race and gender, or sexuality and class, for example, shape any group's experience across specific social contexts. The existence of multiple axes within intersectionality (race, class, gender, sexuality, nation, ethnicity, age) means neither that these factors are equally salient in all groups' experiences nor that they form uniform principles of social organization in defining groups. For example, institutionalized racism constitutes such a fundamental feature of lived Black experience that, in the minds of many African-American women, racism overshadows sexism and other forms of group-based oppression. In contrast, if the literature on the social construction of Whiteness is any indication (see, e.g., Frankenberg 1993), despite their comfort with identifying themselves as women, many White women in the United States have difficulty seeing themselves as already part of Whites as a group. Although African-American women and White American women participate in the same system of institutionalized racism and sexism, each group assigns a different salience to race and gender. Race and class and gender may *all* be present in *all* social settings in the United States, yet groups will experience and "see" them differently. Within this logic, examining historically constructed groups that exist not in theory but in everyday practice requires having an open mind about what types of groups will actually be uncovered.

Given the significance of both group membership and intersectionality, African-American women's group classification and its connection to intersectional analyses of Black women's common history become important. African-American women participate in two distinctive yet overlapping ways of organizing groups in the United States, one organized around a race–class axis and the other around the axis of gender. Because both operate as defining principles of American national identity – recall the race–gender categories of "free White men," "free White women," and "Slaves" – both constitute groups in which Black women find themselves members quite early in life. However, despite the significance of, on the one hand, race–class groupings and, on the other, gender groupings as core forms of social organization, race, class, and gender mutually construct one another in historically distinctive ways.

Although race, class, and gender may share equal billing under the paradigm of intersectionality as a heuristic device, most African-American women would identify race as a fundamental, if not the most important, feature shaping the experiences of Black women as a group. Race operates as such an overriding feature of African-American experience in the United States that it not only overshadows economic class relations for Blacks but obscures the significance of economic class within the United States in general. Even though race and economic class are intertwined, mutually constructing, and intersecting categories, race is often manipulated to divert attention from economic class concerns (Katz 1989; Quadagno 1994). At the same time, race and

210

economic class are such tightly bundled constructs in shaping actual economic outcomes in the United States that one construct loses meaning without referencing the other. Recall that in interpreting the intent of the framers of the Constitution, Chief Justice Roger Taney referred to African slaves as "a subordinate and inferior class of beings" (qtd. in Estell 1994, 130). In this remark, Taney uses a language of class to describe a racialized population and thus illustrates how race and class often stand as proxy for one another. For the sake of argument, I'll refer to this relationship as one of articulation between race and class or, for the context of the United States, race–class intersectionality.[5]

As women and men, African-Americans also encounter gender as a fundamental organizing principle of social structure. Race and economic class not only articulate with one another but also intersect with gender. Although race and gender both mark the body in similar (but not identical) ways, in the United States they are organized in social relations quite differently. Race–class intersections operate primarily through distancing strategies associated with racial and economic segregation. Groups remain separated from one another and do not see themselves as sharing common interests. Blacks and Whites, labor and management are defined in oppositional terms. Although race–class groups may be in close proximity – slavery certainly represented full employment for Blacks coupled with close proximity to Whites – they do not see themselves as sharing common interests. For African-Americans in particular, segregated spaces of all sorts – in particular, housing segregation with its concomitant effects on educational opportunities, employment prospects, and public facilities – accentuate these oppositional relationships. In contrast, gender is organized via inclusionary strategies where, via family, neighborhood, and religious groups, women live in close proximity to or belong to common social units with men. Women are encouraged to develop a commonality of interest with men, despite the gender hierarchy operating within this category of belonging.

Examining how race and class, on the one hand, and gender, on the other, have been historically organized in the Untied States suggests that they represent two divergent ways of constructing groups, each with different implications for the meaning of standpoint theory. African-American women's positionality within both race–class collectivities and gender collectivities as two overlapping yet distinct forms of group organization, provides a potentially important lens for evaluating standpoint theory overall. Specifically, standpoint theory seems useful in analyzing issues associated with a new politics of containment that places Black women in segregated housing, schools, and jobs designed to keep them on the economic "bottom." But standpoint theory seems less applicable to gender relations in the United States. Because women are separated from one another by race and class, they face different challenges both in conceptualizing themselves as a group at all and in seeing themselves as a group similar to race–class groups. This suggests that standpoint theory might be better suited for particular types of groups or, alternately, that groups formed via different mechanisms have varying relationships with standpoint theory.

I realize that in an intellectual climate in which viewing race, class, gender, sexuality, and nation as intersecting categories of analysis has now become more accepted, highlighting differences between race–class and gender as forms of organization may seem counterintuitive to some and intellectually conservative to others. However, despite my commitment to intersectionality as an important conceptual framework, continuing to leave intersectionality as an undertheorized construct contributes to old hierarchies (and some new ones) being reformed under what I see as a new myth of equivalent oppressions. In the United States, to be a Black woman is not the same as to be a White gay man or a working-class Latino. Similarly, Black women's collective experiences differ from those of White gay men and working-class Latinos. Although these experiences are all connected, they are not equivalent. Moreover, in a situation in which far too many privileged academics feel free to claim a bit of oppression for themselves – if all oppressions mutually construct one another, then we're all oppressed in some way by something – oppression talk obscures actual unjust power relations. Within these politics, some groups benefit more from an assumed equivalency of oppressions than others. Although this approach is valid as a heuristic device, treating race, class, and gender as if their intersection produces equivalent results for all oppressed groups obscures differences in how race, class, and gender are hierarchically organized, as well as the differential effects of intersecting systems of power on diverse groups of people.

Black women's social location in the United States provides one specific site for examining these cross-cutting relationships among race, class, and gender as categories of analysis. Its particularity may also shed light on how rethinking the connections between social group formation and intersectionality points to the potential relevance of standpoint theory for Black feminist praxis. In the next two sections of this chapter, I examine two groups in which African-American women "find themselves" – race–class groups in the United States, and gender-organized groups shaping women's experiences. My analysis is not meant to be exhaustive but instead sketches out some patterns for beginning to examine how intersectionality might relate to situated standpoints.

Race–Class Group Formation: Standpoint Theory Revisited

Reviewing the origins of standpoint theory in a more general theory of economic class relations associated with the critical social theory of Karl Marx sheds light on race–class intersectionality in the United States generally and standpoint theory in particular. Although current scholarly attention restricts its attention to standpoint theory, the idea of experiential bases of knowledge is much broader than Marxist social theory. Social theorists as diverse as American functionalist Robert Merton, German critical theorist Karl Mannheim, and French postmodernist Michel Foucault all explore the experiential base of knowledge to some degree. Marxist social thought, however, most clearly situates knowledge within unjust power relations.[6]

Although Marx may be better known for his analyses of capitalism and socialism, I find that revisiting Marx's historical work provides new directions for conceptualizing how race and economic class mutually construct one another in the United States.[7] Marx's 1852 essay *The Eighteenth Brumaire of Louis Bonaparte* provides a historical examination of how economic class relations both constrained and shaped human agency during a period of social uprising in France. The following passage from this work contains several interrelated ideas that collectively provide an interpretive context for understanding how economic class represents a specific type of group formation.

212

> In so far as millions of families live under economic conditions of existence that separate their mode of life, their interests and their culture from those of the other classes, and put them in hostile opposition to the latter, they form a class. In so far as there is merely a local interconnection among these small-holding peasants, and the identity of their interests begets no community, no national bond and no political organization among them, they do not form a class. They are consequently incapable of enforcing their class interest in their own name. (Marx 1963, 124)

Four features of economic class analysis are germane to conceptualizing how race–class intersectionality in the United States constitutes a particular type of group formation. First, although economic class remains rooted in economic analysis, dual meanings of economic class exist. On a specific level, economic class refers to the economic status of historically identifiable groups in capitalist political economies such as the United States. Concentrations of economic power (owning income-producing property), political power (running workplaces and the government), and ideological power (controlling the schools, media, and other forms of representation) distinguish economic classes from one another (Higginbotham and Weber 1992). Analyses that define the middle class as comprising managerial and professional workers, the working class as encompassing factory workers and clerical workers, and the underclass as populated by workers who move between secondary labor-market jobs, government transfer payments, and the informal economy represent one important dimension of economic class relationships. Relying on analyses of segmented labor markets, industrial sectors, or other indices of placement in political economy, these approaches attribute economic class outcomes to economic causes (Baran and Sweezy 1966; Edwards 1979; Wilson 1978, 1987).

Ways of conceptualizing class relations exist other than those accompanying the familiar labor market, industrial sector, and human capital variables. Understanding classes whose "economic conditions of existence" distinguish them from other groups requires situating those groups in the specific history of their society. This history might resemble the familiar bourgeoisie and proletariat of Marxist conflict theory constructed from studies of industrializing, racially homogeneous nineteenth-century European societies. However, in the post-colonial, desegregated contexts of advanced capitalism, Marxist class categories seemingly lose validity. The approach taken to constructing class, however, remains valuable. Rather than starting with a theory of how capitalist economies predetermine economic classes, analysis *begins* with how social groupings are actually organized within historically specific capitalist political economies. Class categories are constructed from the actual cultural material of historically specific societies. This is exactly the method that Marx used in constructing his class categories – the bourgeoisie and proletariat were not theoretically derived categories but emerged from historical analysis.[8]

Analyzing class relations via historically concrete, lived experience sheds light on race–class intersectionality in the United States. One might ask whether African-Americans "live under economic conditions of existence that separate their mode of life, their interests and their culture from those of other classes" or, alternately, whether African-Americans continue to bear the intergenerational costs associated with the denial of citizenship stemming from their being branded "a subordinate and inferior class of beings." For African-Americans, group positionality is determined less by theoretical categories constructed within assumptions of distinct discourses of class or race, and more by actual lived Black experience. Although economic outcomes remain fundamental to conceptualizing Black economic class relations, such relations may not be defined *solely* by labor markets, industrial sectors, and other economic criteria. A more complex analysis of class formation might encompass an intersectional analysis attentive to institutionalized racism, slavery as a mode of production, and other factors shaping the social location of African-Americans as a group. The forces constructing African-Americans as a group living under economic conditions that distinguish them from other groups in the United States are far more complex than simple economic determinism.

This leads to a second feature essential for exploring how race–class intersectionality in the United States might foster a specific type of group formation – the necessity of historic specificity in examining both economic class relations and any standpoints that might ensue. Nowhere is it written that only two or three classes exist. Yet this parsimonious number persists. It seems just as reasonable to argue that actual class relations are much more complex. Since Marxist class analysis is heavily influenced by its origins in racially homogeneous European societies as well as its construction of class categories from the individual's relationship to capital and labor, it underemphasizes the importance of race in conceptualizing class. However, given how institutionalized racism and capitalism have constructed one another in the United States (Marable 1983), restricting analysis to a few economic classes shorn of racial meaning oversimplifies a series of complex relationships. Rather than taking a class analysis developed for one specific historical context – for example, Marx's discussion of the bourgeoisie and proletariat developed for nineteenth-century France or industrializing England – and applying it uncritically to other social settings, one might assume that differently organized class differences will *always* characterize unjust power relations.

This shift in perspective that both views class relations in more than purely economic terms and generates class categories from actual lived experience creates space to examine how social hierarchies construct group or class relationships with visible economic dimensions. It also creates space to think about class in relation to race, nationality, and ethnicity (see, e.g., Anthias and Yuval-Davis 1992). Within the United States, race, ethnicity, and nationality have long been intertwined in historically complex ways in producing pronounced economic inequalities among groups (Takaki 1993). Moreover, the institutional mechanisms by which unjust power relations of class, race, nation, and ethnicity are organized are similar – namely, separation and exclusion. Issues of purity and separation, whether of geographical space or occupational and employment space, or in school curricula, the media, or other forms of symbolic space, appear central to maintaining unjust power relations of race, class, nation, and ethnicity in the United States. Despite a rhetoric of individualism associated with liberalism, Americans seem to be profoundly group-oriented. As sociologist Joseph Scott succinctly puts it, "Group rights are the American practice; individual rights are the American promise" (1984, 178).

If groups with historically identifiable histories and traditions become the focus of class analysis (class cannot operate in the abstract – it always works through actual lived experience), African-Americans participate in class relations in particular ways.

214

The complexity of class analysis is limited only by the degree of specificity used to delineate groups with shared "economic conditions of existence." Class relations can thus be drawn with broad brush strokes, as in the case of nineteenth-century industrializing England, or more finely crafted into intersectional categories such as race–class intersectionality in the late-twentieth-century United States. Within this logic, race–class groups are constructed less from theoretical models advanced by governmental officials and academics, and more from actual group histories.

A third feature of class analysis that is especially germane to both group formation and race–class intersectionality in the United States concerns the nature of class as a construct. Class does not describe a "thing" but rather a *relationship* among social groups unequal in power. Classes represent bounded categories of the population, groups set in a relation of opposition to one another. Within Marxist social theory, group relationships describe power relations such that one group's privilege is predicated upon another group's disadvantage. One group or class exploits the other, excludes the other from equitable social rewards, or somehow benefits from the other's disadvantage. The main insight here concerns the relationship between group structure, group membership, and unjust power relations. Groups become defined largely by their placement within historically specific power relations, not from choices exercised by individual group members concerning issues of identity and belonging.

From this perspective, it makes little sense to talk about the middle class as an entity or a thing unto itself, because such a class could not exist without other economic classes to which it is linked in relationships of, at best, mutuality and, at worst, exploitation. In a similar fashion, historically in the United States, the notion of Whiteness as a meaningful group category was formed in relation to Blackness as a separate and allegedly inferior way of constructing groups. Moreover, these group relationships within race–class intersectionality persist over time. Although patterns of race–class intersectionality may be distinctive for any given era, the basic oppositional relationships among groups constructed within and linked by these intersections remain constant. As long as the basic relationship of intergenerational disadvantage and privilege in which White and Black individuals "find themselves" persists, the relationship is one of class.

I stress the intergenerational nature of this process of mutually constructing privilege and disadvantage because, in the United States, such relationships remain organized through family units. With the important exception of feminist analyses of the family, the concept of family remains simultaneously underanalyzed and fundamental to how people conceptualize groups of all sorts. In his discussion of class, Marx identifies families as the unit of class analysis. Recall the passage quoted earlier: "In so far as millions of *families* live under economic conditions of existence that separate their mode of life, their interests and their culture from those of the other classes, and put them in hostile opposition to the latter, they form a class" (1963, 124; emphasis added). Consider how differently that passage would read if the term *individuals* were substituted for the term *families*. In this passage, classes are constructed not from the building blocks of *individuals* but from those of *families*, the same building blocks of nations, races, and ethnic groups. Thus, class, race, and nation all become linked in a common cognitive framework that relies on separation and exclusion to define family groups. This shift from the individual to the family as the basic unit of class analysis leads to

215

very different notions of how hierarchical power relations become reproduced over time. As the long-standing debate on Black family deviance indicates, most Americans seem comfortable with the idea of the intergenerational transfer of property from one generation to the next, as long as the property under consideration is *cultural* capital. Any resulting inequalities can then be attributed to the workings of good or bad parenting. However, analyzing how the intergenerational transfer of *wealth*, or actual capital, participates in shaping these same outcomes leads to different conclusions (Collins 1997). Here one encounters inherited patterns of opportunity or disadvantage, based on the class position of one's family. Moreover, if family is used to conceptualize other types of groups – race as family, nation as a large extended family, ethnicity as a large kinship group – then relations within the family and the treatment of family members and outsiders become significant to social relations of all sorts (Collins 1998b).

Rather than trying to determine the essential features that distinguish African-Americans from other social groups, a more fruitful approach might explore how African-Americans participate in race–class intersectionality in the United States at any given time, especially in oppositional relationships with other groups. This approach accommodates a dual emphasis on fixity and change. On the one hand, inter-generational patterns of family inequality in which Whites and Blacks largely replicate the economic status of their parents signal the fixed nature of race–class intersection-ality in the United States. On the other hand, because history is seen as changing, race–class formations also change, as the new politics of containment suggest, often in quite dramatic ways. Within such changes, opportunities for struggle continually are being remade. Historicizing race–class relations as specific power relations in this way not only highlights how race–class relations change over time but also reintroduces the question of human agency in bringing about such changes.

Exercising agency in response to and/or in behalf of a group requires *recognizing* groups by seeing how past circumstances have profound effects on the present. Thus, a final dimension of class approaches to group formation specifically related to race–class intersectionality in the United States concerns the centrality of group culture and consciousness in developing self-defined group standpoints. Shared disad-vantage and shared interests are not sufficient – *separate* modes of life that distinguish groups from one another remain important. Although structural features such as shared location in the economy can bring people into proximity who have common economic interests, they do not become classes without some sort of self-defined group knowledge. Individuals within the group must develop and proclaim a consciousness of their connections with one another, and the group itself must come to see its rela-tionships with other groups within this same system of power relations:[9] "In so far as there is merely a local interconnection among these small-holding peasants, and the identity of their interests begets no *community*, no national bond and no political or-ganization among them, they do not form a class" (Marx 1963, 124; emphasis added). In other words, a group consolidates its class interests through community infrastruc-tures that actively reproduce its particular group interests for its own membership.

Historically, African-Americans have recognized themselves as a group in this way, with shared interests constructed in opposition to those of more powerful Whites as a dominant group. The longevity of Black nationalism in Black civil society stems in part from its repeated denouncements of institutionalized racism, coupled with an insistence that Blacks center political action on lived Black experience. Recall that Black cultural nationalism encourages African-Americans to claim an independent Black culture. Aiming to develop a radical Black consciousness that recognizes how existing race–class relations are unjust, such a culture is designed to give voice to Black political struggle. In exploring these relations, African-American legal scholar Derrick Bell has the Curia, fictional Black women judges, point to the importance of situated standpoints for theories of Black liberation:

> Some of you . . . will leave here seeking theories of liberation from white legal philosophers, who are not oppressed, who do not perceive themselves as oppressors, and who thus must use their impressive intellectual talent to imagine what you experience daily. Black people, on the other hand, come to their task of liberation from the battleground of experience, not from the rarefied atmosphere of the imagination. (1987, 253)

Bell's fictional account in which the Curia chides Black people who fail to trust their own experiences with racism, who deny the perspectives that often emerge from these experiences, and who look to Whites for answers resonates with the type of independent thinking advocated by Black nationalist leader Malcolm X, who once advised a group of Black youth to think for themselves (Collins 1992). Within this framework, culture, consciousness, and political struggle become inextricably intertwined.

Overall, the ideas of standpoint theory seem more suited to groups structured via segregated spaces such as residential racial segregation, employment discrimination, and other exclusionary practices characterizing race–class intersectionality in the United States. Despite its insights into the workings of power through segregated spaces, this race–class approach to group construction routinely fails to address hierarchy *within* groups that are differentially positioned within unjust power relations. This failure to address internal hierarchy has great implications for constructing group standpoints. Even though a social group may occupy a distinctive structural location within hierarchical power relations, it can simultaneously remain quite uninformed about unjust power relations operating within its own boundaries. Thus, one fundamental challenge lies in ensuring that neither group practices nor any ensuing standpoints replicate other hierarchies, particularly those of gender and sexuality.

Gender and Group Formation

Because women in the United States are distributed *across* groups formed within race–class intersectionality, gender raises different issues. Long-standing exclusionary practices that separate women by race, economic condition, citizenship status, and ethnicity result in social groups that *include* women, organized via these categories. For example, Black women and White women do not live in class-stratified women's neighborhoods, separated from men and children by processes such as gender steering, bank redlining that results in refusal to lend money to women's neighborhoods, inferior schools in women's inner-city neighborhoods due to men moving to all-male suburban areas, and the like. Instead, for the most part, Black and White women live in racially

217

segregated, economically stratified neighborhoods (Massey and Denton 1993). The experiences they garner in such communities, especially via the powerful social institution of family, reflect the politics of race–class intersectionality in the United States. Stated differently, although women in the United States may share much as women, residential patterns, schools, and employment opportunities that routinely sort women into clearly defined categories of race, economic class, ethnicity, and citizenship status mean that few opportunities exist for having the type of intimate, face-to-face contact that would reveal women's "shared economic conditions," if they exist at all, let alone for organizing around those conditions.

At the same time, as a collectivity, women experience distinctive gendered mechanisms of control that remain specific to women's patterns of inclusion within race–class groups. Specifically, regardless of actual family composition, all women encounter the significance of American society's preoccupation with family. As a familiar and seemingly natural form of group organization, the idea of family serves as a particular foundation on which many types of groups are built (Collins 1998a). Members of all sorts of collectivities are often encouraged to treat one another as "family," a perspective illustrated by family references to, for example, the "brothers" in gangs, the "sisterhood" of feminist struggle, the Black "mothers" of the church, and the founding "fathers" of America. Recall that Marx himself falls back on the image of the family as the smallest social unit having a shared interest. By definition, families stick together against outsiders. Within idealized notions of family, family units protect and balance the interests of all of their members – the strong care for the weak, and members contribute to and benefit from family membership in proportion to their capacities. Though there may be differentiation within the family, family members share a common origin through blood and a commonality of interests.

By providing compelling arguments that family functions as a primary site for conceptualizing and organizing women's oppression, feminist scholarship challenges these assumptions. Analyses of bourgeois family structure or the traditional family ideal, in particular, unpack the relationship between particular ideas of family and gender oppression. Defined as a natural or biological arrangement based on heterosexual attraction, a normative and ideal family consists of a heterosexual couple who produce their own biological children. Formed through a combination of marital and blood ties, the traditional family ideal views this nuclear unit as having a specific authority structure, arranged in this order: a father-head earning an adequate family wage, a stay-at-home wife and mother, and children. Assuming a relatively fixed sexual division of labor, wherein women's roles are defined as primarily in the home and men's in the public world of work, the traditional family ideal assumes the separation of work and family. Viewing the family as a private haven from a public world, family is seen as held together through primary emotional bonds of love and caring (Andersen 1991; Thorne 1992).

Feminist scholarship reveals that despite a rhetoric of equality in this ideal, a good part of women's subordination is organized via family ties. In contrast to idealized versions of family, actual families remain organized around varying patterns of hierarchy. As Anne McClintock observes, "The family image came to figure *hierarchy within unity* as an organic element of historical progress, and thus became indispensable for legitimating exclusion and hierarchy within nonfamilial social forms such as nationalism, liberal individualism and imperialism" (1995, 45). Thus, because the family is per-ceived as a private sphere that is naturally and not socially constructed, relying on the traditional family ideal as a model for group organization replicates a naturalized hierarchy. For women, domination and love remain intimately linked. Through their contribution of socializing family members into an appropriate set of "family values," women participate in naturalizing the hierarchy within the assumed unity of interests symbolized by the family while laying the foundation for systems of hierarchy outside family boundaries. As people often learn their place within hierarchies of race, gender, ethnicity, sexuality, nationality, and class from their experiences within family units, they simultaneously learn to view such hierarchies as natural social arrangements, as compared to socially constructed ones. As feminist analyses of family suggest, women's families remain central to their subordination. Moreover, because women's shared eco-nomic conditions as women remain organized within families across race–class groups, women remain disadvantaged in seeing their connections with other similarly situated women.

Developing group culture and consciousness for all women as a collectivity involves extracting them from historically constituted groups within which family serves as part of the conceptual glue giving meaning to race, class, ethnicity, and nation. It also involves creating a new group identity based on gender affiliation. For women as a col-lectivity, building this type of group constitutes an intellectual and political project dis-tinctly different from that confronting groups organized via the segregated spaces of race, class, ethnicity, and nation. Moreover, differences in group construction and the challenges that face different types of groups have implications for any ensuing standpoints. Using standpoint theory both as a tool for analyzing gender relations in the United States and as a strategy for organizing women raises a different and complex set of issues. Because women are distributed across a range of race–class groups, all women confront the initial task of developing a shared understanding of their common interests as women. However, they must do so in close proximity to, and often in sexu-alized love relationships with, members of the group that allegedly oppresses them. Since women must first construct a self-definition as a member of a group, ideas may precede the building of actual group relations. Women certainly know other women within their own race, economic, ethnic, and/or citizenship groups, but most have dif-ficulty seeing their shared interests across the vast differences that characterize women as a collectivity. The process of constructing a group standpoint for women differs dramatically from that confronting groups with histories of group-based segregated spaces. Women come to know themselves as members of a political collectivity through ideas that construct them as such.

By invoking the rhetoric of family in constructing women's groups and any hoped-for standpoints that might follow, a feminist politics may inadvertently undermine the logic of its own organization. The longed-for group solidarity promised under the rubric of "sisterhood" posited by contemporary feminists seems designed to build a commu-nity among women that is grounded in shared conditions of existence. However, imag-ining multicultural, multiethnic, multiracial, multiclass women's groups predicated on family-based notions of sisterhood is much easier than building such communities across lived, institutionalized segregation. The path from women conceptualized as a numerically superior "minority group," through feminist organizing designed to generate a shared consciousness of women's oppression or standpoint under the banner of sisterhood, to building actual women's groups organized around sisterhood encountered considerable resistance, much of it from African-American women and other similarly situated women (Dill 1983).

White American feminist critiques of standpoint theory may emerge in part from discouragement with the seeming failure of feminist struggles for sisterhood. In part, the increasing attraction of postmodernism for many White American feminists may lie in its deconstructive move. By arguing that multiracial, multicultural women's collectivities are neither desirable nor possible, postmodernism seems to offer a way out. Turning attention away from challenging women's oppression to deconstructing the modern subject provides conceptual space to sidestep the theoretical failures of Western feminism. If women cannot be organized as a group, then groups themselves must go, and everything associated with them, including standpoints. Although this theoretical move seems highly plausible when directed toward the fragile solidarity of women, applying similar deconstructive moves to groups organized through segregated spaces of race and economic class remains far less convincing. Despite well-intentioned gestures (e.g., placing "race" in quotation marks to signal the socially constructed notion of race as a category of analysis), declaring a moratorium on using the word *race* does not make housing segregation, underfunded inner-city schools, and employment discrimination any less real.

Because groups respond to the actual social conditions that they confront, it stands to reason that groups constructed by different social realities will develop equally different analyses and political strategies. For example, White American feminist thinkers who theorize that feminist standpoints are untenable may be inadvertently expressing the standpoint of a group that has no need of such thinking. Moreover, despite the support and leadership of many women's studies professionals for intersectional analyses, such support may evaporate quickly if any real sharing of power appears on the horizon. Ironically, within unexamined assumptions of individualism, intersectionality can be reconfigured so that it makes things worse. Just as academic talk of centers and margins flattened and in some cases erased hierarchical power relations, the construct of intersectionality used to analyze differences among women can be similarly depoliticized. When extracted from hierarchical power relations, recognizing differences among women can become so watered down that power simply vanishes.

In a fundamental way, African-American women are caught in the crossfire of two different ways of organizing groups. Race, class, nation, and ethnicity all rely heavily on segregation and other exclusionary practices to maintain hierarchy. In contrast, because women often find themselves in close proximity to men, gender relies more heavily on surveillance and other inclusionary strategies of control targeted toward the proximate other. Because it reproduces the naturalized hierarchy that also informs the self-definitions of race–class groups, the idea of family permeates both types of group organization. On the one hand, due to its overreliance on a gender-blind racial solidarity constructed via family metaphors, Black civil society fosters a problematic paradigm of sacrifice for African-American women. On the other hand, because structural power attached to race–class intersectionality in the United States can be recast within apolitical frameworks of differences among women, White American feminist theories in particular maintain the illusion of gender solidarity while allowing hierarchy to be reformulated via actual practices. For African-American women, hierarchy flourishes in *both* approaches to constructing groups.

Situated Standpoints and Black Feminist Thought

How might these complexities introduced by intersectionalities and group organization shed light on the relationship between standpoint theory and Black feminist thought? A more intricate view both of African-American women as a group and of any accompanying Black women's standpoint might emerge by first agreeing that African-American women have a shared (though not uniform) location in hierarchical power relations in the United States. The existence of group interests means neither that all individuals within the group have the same experiences nor that they interpret them in the same way. Acknowledging a shared location means neither that African-American women's experiences become collapsed into stereotypes of welfare queens or Black Lady Overachievers, nor that images of "natural," "African," or "real" Black women that are conjured up in Black nationalist discourse constitute what is shared. A paradigm of intersectionality stressing how race, class, and gender mutually construct one another suggests that unitary standpoints of the type associated with traditional racial solidarity are neither possible nor desirable. However, if groups themselves need not be organized via essentialist principles, neither do group-derived standpoints. Group-based experiences, especially those shared by African-American women as a collectivity, create the conditions for a shared standpoint that in turn can stimulate collective political action. But they guarantee neither that such standpoints will follow nor that efforts to develop standpoints constitute the most effective way of empowering a group in a given context.

Shared group location is better characterized by viewing Black women's social location as one of a heterogeneous commonality embedded in social relations of intersectionality. Despite heterogeneity among African-American women that accompanies such intersections, differences in Black women's experiences generated by differences of age, sexual orientation, region of the country, urban or rural residence, color, hair texture, and the like theoretically can all be accommodated within the concept of a shared standpoint. When it comes to oppression, there are essentials. A passage in *The Eighteenth Brumaire* speaks to this critical element of what might actually be shared: "Men make their own history, but they do not make it just as they please; they do not make it under circumstances chosen by themselves, but under circumstances directly encountered, given and transmitted from the past" (Marx 1963, 15). "Shared" refers to the "circumstances directly encountered, given and transmitted from the past," not to uniform, essentialist responses to those conditions. Stated differently, a shared standpoint need not rest on a list of essential rules or Black feminist articles of faith to which Black women must subscribe in order to be considered a true sister. Rather, it rests on the recognition that when it comes to being African-American women in the United States, as Fannie Lou Hamer points out, "we're in this bag together" (qtd. in Lerner 1972, 613).

By primarily emphasizing only one historically specific dimension of hierarchical power relations, namely, economic classes in industrializing political economies, Marx posited that, however unarticulated and inchoate, oppressed groups possessed a particular standpoint concerning the "bag" they were in, that is, their own oppression. Contemporary analyses of social structure that stress the complexity created by intersections of race, economic class, gender, ethnicity, sexuality, and nationality ask how to invoke a comparable complexity in defining and studying groups. What we now have is increasing sophistication about how to discuss group location not in singular "fighting words" paradigms of economic class, race, or gender, but with a growing recognition of the significance of intersectionality. This suggests that the complexity characterizing African-American women's group identity under a new politics of containment will generate a comparably sophisticated Black women's standpoint.

As the preceding discussion of race–class and gender groups suggests, actually thinking through this complexity represents a daunting task. However, at a minimum, it points to the need to develop a more sophisticated language for discussing social groups that takes power relations into account. Traditional discussions of standpoint theory leave this notion of group unexamined, if they make mention of it at all, allowing unexamined family metaphors to fill the void.

Because actual family relations are rarely fair and just, using family as metaphor for constructing an understanding of group processes can duplicate inequalities that are embedded in the very definition of what constitutes a well-functioning group. This has profound implications for any group that understands its internal dynamics through the lens of "family." Since the 1970s, increasing numbers of African-American women have recognized how this notion of naturalized hierarchy within a family constitutes a problematic organizing principle for the organization of actual Black families. However, challenging conceptions of Black civil society that naturalize hierarchy among African-American men and women has proved more difficult. This recognition requires questioning long-standing norms that simultaneously have used family language to define African-Americans as a race and have often conceptualized Black political struggle via the rhetoric of family.

Protesting gender hierarchies internal to Black civil society certainly framed the feminism of African-American women participating in the civil rights and Black Power movements of the 1960s and 1970s. As Frances Beale succinctly observed in "Double Jeopardy: To Be Black and Female," her groundbreaking 1970 essay,

> Unfortunately, there seems to be some confusion in the movement today as to who has been oppressing whom. Since the advent of black power, the black male has exerted a more prominent leadership role in our struggle for justice in this country. He sees the system for what it really is for the most part, but where he rejects its values and mores on many issues, when it comes to women, he seems to take his guidelines from the pages of the *Ladies' Home Journal*. (Beale 1995, 147–8)

Beale's comments reveal how African-American women's placement in political struggles organized by both race and gender reveal two overlapping and important uses of family in constructing groups. On the one hand, a Black civil society in which race-as-family metaphors are used to construct group identity misses potentially problematic internal hierarchies such as those of gender and sexuality. On the other hand, African-American women who see themselves as part of a women's collectivity organized around women's subordination within families confront the ongoing difficulties of organizing across deeply entrenched patterns of segregated space.

In thinking through these relationships, it may prove useful to revisit standard sociological categories of macro-, meso-, and micro-levels of social organization yet to view them as organized within and through power relations. Hierarchical power relations operate on all three levels – no one level "rules" the others. Collectively, these levels of social structure frame what Black women as a group are, what they do, and what they might think. On the macro level, schools, labor markets, the media, government, and other social institutions reproduce a social position or category of "Black women" that is assigned to all individuals who fit criteria for membership. One does not choose to be a "Black woman." Rather, one "finds oneself" classified in this category, regardless of differences in how one got there. On the meso level, Black women as a group encounter accumulated wisdom learned from past interactions between what was expected of them as Black women and what they actually did. On this level, Black women develop strategies for how African-American women grapple with these socially assigned positions. On the micro level, specific contexts of everyday life provide each Black woman multiple opportunities to play the social role of "Black woman" as it has been scripted or to negotiate new patterns. In this sense, each Black woman constructs the type of Black woman she chooses to be in different situations. All of these levels work together recursively, shaping one another to create specific social outcomes.

In analyzing the question of situated group standpoints, the meso level provides considerable insight on how Black women's group organization mediates between categories that are socially assigned to Black women and options that individual African-American women perceive in constructing their unique ways of being Black women. Although all Black women remain defined by the social role of Black women, how individual African-American women act in specific situations depends on at least two factors. The distinctive patterns of their individual biographies constitute one important factor. In addition, their access to historically created and shared Black feminist wisdom, for want of a better term, matters. This is of immense importance for Black feminist thought, because it suggests that Black women's collective, lived experiences in negotiating the category "Black woman" can serve a purpose in grappling with the new politics of containment. Despite its importance, scholarship on this meso level that examines Black women's agency in accessing cultural knowledge to construct individual expressions of self within socially defined categories of "Black woman" remains modest. What does exist, however, is provocative. Signithia Fordham's study of "loud Black girls" in education (1993) reveals strategies deployed by Black women who routinely encounter institutional silencing. Jacqueline Bobo's study of Black women as cultural readers (1995) informs us that Black women do not sit passively by, watching movies and believing everything they see. Rather, they actively negotiate cultural meanings.

Developing Black feminist thought as critical social theory requires articulating a situated standpoint that emerges from rather than suppresses the complexity of African-American women's experiences as a group on this meso level. British sociologist Stuart Hall's notion of articulation works well here – the idea of "unity and difference," of "difference in complex unity, without becoming a hostage to the privileging of difference as such" (qtd. in Slack 1996, 122). Such a standpoint would identify the ways in which being situated in intersections of race, economic class, and gender, as well as those of age, sexuality, ethnicity, and region of the country, constructs relationships *among* African-American women as a group. At the same time, a situated standpoint would reflect how these intersections frame African-American women's distinctive history as a collectivity in the United States. This involves examining how intersectionality constructs relationships *between* African-American women and other groups. Thus, the challenge confronting African-American women lies in constructing notions of a Black female collectivity that remain sensitive to Black women's placement in distinctively American hierarchical power relations, while simultaneously resisting replication of these same relations within the group's own ranks.

The ability of Black feminist thought to make useful contributions to contemporary freedom struggles hinges on its ability to develop new forms of visionary pragmatism. Within the new politics of containment that confronts African-American women, visionary pragmatism in turn hinges on developing greater complexity within Black women's knowledge. In this regard, remaining situated is essential. Vision can be conjured up in the theoretical imagination, yet pragmatic actions require being responsive to the injustices of everyday life. Rather than abandoning situated standpoints, becoming situated in new understandings of social complexity is vital. Despite the importance of this project, changes in Black civil society, coupled with the growing importance of academia as a site where Black feminist thought is produced and circulated, raise real questions concerning the future of this type of functional knowledge. Whether Black feminist standpoints survive remains to be seen.

Notes

1 Standpoint theory alone cannot explain Black women's experiences. Instead, it constitutes one of many conceptual frameworks that I use in analyzing Black feminist thought. Despite the overtly claimed and clearly stated eclecticism of my own work, I remain amazed at repeated efforts to categorize my ideas in one theoretical framework or another, generally without full knowledge of the scope of my work. I interpret this pressure to classify works in this fashion as a shortcut way of analyzing social phenomena. Grounded in circular reasoning, one identifies what one perceives as the essence of one approach, classifies thinkers and/or their works in those categories, and then accepts or rejects their ideas based on one's initial classification. Intellectual work typically reflects much more complexity than this, and Black women's intellectual traditions in the United States certainly cannot be adequately addressed by any one approach (standpoint theory or any other).

2 Although bodies receive race and gender classifications, people routinely try to escape from, blur, or challenge the legitimacy of the boundaries between their assigned category and others. The history of racial and gender "passing" (when Blacks "pass" as White and women "pass" as men) speaks to one way of transgressing boundaries. The strength of these performances reveals how classifications are rooted not in nature but in power relations. Similarly, the current attention to racially mixed individuals (as evidenced by the ongoing debate to change the racial categories of the U.S. census) and to intersexed individuals (those whose sex cannot easily be assigned at birth) also speaks to the permeability of racial and sexual borders. Although these cases are transgressive, installing these specific acts as a new transgressive politics writ large seems shortsighted. It's like chipping away at the edges of a giant

mountain, claiming that each chip weakens the structure while failing to realize that the mountain of race and gender classification is far from crumbling.

3 Iris Marion Young contends that the New Left social movements of the 1960s and 1970s introduced new meanings of oppression by stressing group location in social institutions: "In its new usage, oppression designed the disadvantage and injustice some people suffer not because a tyrannical power coerces them, but because of the everyday practices of a well-intentioned liberal society" (1990, 41). Oppression became less associated with individual intentionality and more with the everyday workings of social structures that manufactured groups in hierarchies. In my brief analysis of intergenerational transfer of group privilege later in this chapter, I build on Young's notion of group-based oppression carried out by social institutions. As Young continues, "We cannot eliminate this structural oppression by getting rid of the rulers or making some new laws, because oppressions are systematically repro-duced" (41).

4 This slippage between the individual and the group as units of analysis also fosters a re-ductive and problematic reading of "voice" as symbolic of group consciousness. Individual "voice" is not the same as group "voice" or standpoint. Typically, this reduction operates by imagining how *individuals* negotiate self-definitions and then claiming that through a "family resemblance," *collectivities* undergo a similar process. Because collectivities certainly do construct stories in framing their identity, this approach appears plausible. However, can the individual stand as proxy for the group and the group for the individual? Moreover, can this particular version of the individual serve as the exemplar for collective group identity? If an individual reasons from his or her own personal experiences that "since *we* are all the same under the skin, therefore, what *I* experience must be the same as what *everybody else* experi-ences," a certain perception of group narrative structure emerges. If an individual believes that his or her personal experiences in coming to voice – especially the inner voices within his or her individual consciousness, which are hidden from hierarchal power relations – not only reflect a common human experience but, more to the point, serve as an exemplar for how *group* consciousness and decision making operate, then individual experience becomes the model for comprehending group processes. This approach minimizes the significance of conflict between groups in generating group narratives. In the model wherein individuals conduct inner dialogues among various parts of their "selves," the process of mediating conflicting identities occurs within each individual. The individual always holds complete power or agency over the consciousness that he or she constructs in his or her own mind and over the voice that she or he uses to express that consciousness.

5 For the moment, I am deliberately choosing to use the term *intersectionality* instead of its related term *articulation*, even though articulation approximates my understanding of inter-sectionality. In her essay "The Theory and Method of Articulation in Cultural Studies," Jennifer Daryl Slack examines the meaning of articulation in the work of British sociologist Stuart Hall. Recognizing the difficulty of developing a precise definition of articulation, Slack notes that articulation "isn't *exactly* anything" (1996, 117, emphasis in original). Although articulation is obviously a very powerful concept that closely parallels what I am calling inter-sectionality, there may be a difference between them. Slack describes the relationship between ideas and social structure that she sees emerging in cultural studies and that is captured by articulation: "The context is not something *out there, within which practices occur or which influence the development of practices*. Rather, *identities, practices, and effects generally, constitute the very context in which they are practices, identities or effects*" (125; emphasis in original). Although I value the effort to infuse a more dynamic dimension into analyses of social phe-nomena, this definition seems too much of a closed loop for me. I prefer, at least analytically, to retain the distinction between context and ideas that Slack collapses into one. Thus, the notion of intersectionality seems more closely wedded to notions of articulation that assume

225

an independent existence for social structure. For additional insight into Hall's use of the term *articulation*, see Grossberg (1996).

6 Many thinkers have worked within a sociology-of-knowledge framework. At first glance, the links between a sociology of knowledge associated with Robert Merton and a standpoint theory associated with Karl Marx may seem surprising. Merton is typically associated with a structural-functionalism that omits questions of power. Although Merton is known for his contributions to the sociology of science, he treats science as one knowledge among many. Merton has been central in bringing ideas of the sociology of knowledge, historically associated more with theoretical and historicist traditions of Europe than with empiricist traditions in American sociology, to American sociology. As Merton suggests in his important essay "Paradigm for the Sociology of Knowledge," originally published in 1945, "The perennial problem of the implications of existential influences upon knowledge for the epistemological status of knowledge has been hotly debated from the very outset" (Merton 1973, 13).

In contrast, Marx's entire focus seems to be hierarchy. The fundamental questions that link diverse thinkers in this field are flexible enough to accommodate a considerable variability on the connections between knowledge and social structure. Merton places far less emphasis than Marx on the hierarchical or power dimensions of social structure. In contrast, Marx focuses on the power dimensions of social structure; his ideas that are now known as standpoint theory are designed to explore the connections between hierarchical power relations and ensuing knowledges or standpoints. Moreover, thinking through the connections between knowledge and power is an especially sociological concern, because sociology examines social structure. French philosopher Michel Foucault (1977) points out that it is not a question of emancipating truth from systems of power. Rather, the issue lies in detaching the power of truth from its hegemonic institutional contexts. Foucault suggests that rather than being outside power or deprived of power, truth remains grounded in real-world politics. Each society has its own "regime of truth" or "general politics" of truth. These regimes consists of the types of discourses harbored by a particular society that it causes to function as true; epistemological criteria that distinguish truth from falsehoods; and legitimating mechanisms that determine the status of those charged with constructing truth (Foucault 1977). Using a more general definition of class as group leads one in a different direction. Like Robert Merton (1973), I see Karl Mannheim's work (1954) as extending the idea of class as a group with a connection to knowledge, to broader types of social groups. Thus, although the language of standpoint remains affiliated with Marxist social theory, the idea of knowledge emerging from groups differentially placed in social conditions transcends its origins in Marxism.

7 The literature on economic class is vast, and I make no attempt to review it here. Both Grimes (1991) and Vanneman and Cannon (1987) provide useful resources for summarizing and critiquing American scholarship on economic class. In brief, within American social science, economic class is routinely associated with either Karl Marx (social class) or Max Weber (status). The status-attainment perspective has garnered the most attention in American social science. Sacks (1989) takes the position that economic class should be conceptualized as group relationships and that efforts to assign a class category to individuals in order to examine economic class consciousness overlook the more significant features of economic class analysis. Thus, the approach that I use in developing a context for standpoint theory is already a minority position. For a discussion of the origins of feminist standpoint epistemology in a Marxist standpoint theory of labor, see Smith (1987), especially pp. 78–81.

8 Bourdieu makes a similar point about the difference between the ideas in Marxist social theory and the use to which those ideas are put: "Marxism, in the reality of its social use, ends up by being a mode of thought completely immune to historical criticism, which is a paradox, given the potentialities and indeed, the demands inherent in Marx's thought" (1990, 17).

226

9 Current debates that juxtapose class and culture as if these were two oppositional and distinct processes may create artificial boundaries where none exist. Economic class is typically theorized on the level of macrosociological structures – labor markets, industrial sectors, and the like. In contrast, historically, studies of group culture have emphasized ethnic and tribal cultures emerging from small-group interactions. This seeming division of the themes of economics, political science, and sociology as being best suited for one type of issue, namely, economic class, and the humanities of history, literary studies, English, and literature as dealing with another, reflects the problems inherent in relying too heavily on disciplinary approaches to each concept. Sociology claimed the concept of social class and, from its inception, has studied economic class as a structural phenomenon largely divorced from culture. In contrast, until the advent of British cultural studies and its subsequent impetus on communications studies generally to take on the theme of mass culture, culture remained largely the province of anthropologists who carried out studies of culture in other societies.

References

Andersen, Margaret, 1991. "Feminism and the American Family Ideal." *Journal of Comparative Family Studies* 22.2 (Summer): 235–46.

Anthias, Floya, and Nira Yuval-Davis. 1992. *Racialized Boundaries: Race, Nation, Gender, Colour, and Class in the Anti-racist Struggle.* New York: Routledge.

Baran, Paul, and Paul Sweezy. 1966. *Monopoly Capital.* New York: Monthly Review Press.

Beale, Frances. 1995 [1970]. "Double Jeopardy: To Be Black and Female." In Beverly Guy-Sheftall, ed. *Words of Fire: An Anthology of African American Feminist Thought.* New York: New Press.

Bell, Derrick. 1987. *And We Are Not Saved: The Elusive Quest for Racial Justice.* New York: Basic Books.

Bobo, Jacqueline. 1995. *Black Women as Cultural Readers.* New York: Columbia University Press.

Bourdieu, Pierre. 1990. *In Other Words: Essays Towards a Reflexive Sociology.* Stanford: Stanford University Press.

Collins, Patricia Hill. 1992. "Learning to Think for Ourselves: Malcolm X's Black Nationalism Reconsidered." In Joe Woods, ed. *Malcolm X: In Our Own Image.* New York: St Martin's.

——. 1997. "African-American Women and Economic Justice: A Preliminary Analysis of Wealth, Family, and Black Social Class." *University of Cincinnati Law Review* 65.3, pp. 825–52.

——. 1998a. "Intersections of Race, Class, Gender, and Nation: Some Implications for Black Family Studies." *Journal of Comparative Family Studies* 29.1, pp. 27–36.

——. 1998b. "It's All in the Family: Intersections of Gender, Race, Class, and Nation." *Hypatia.*

——. 1998c. *Fighting Words: Black Women and the Search for Justice.* Minneapolis: University of Minnesota Press.

Crenshaw, Kimberle Williams. 1992. "Whose Story Is It Anyway? Feminist and Antiracist Appropriations of Anita Hill." In Toni Morrison, ed. *Race-ing Justice, En-gendering Power.* New York: Pantheon, pp. 402–40.

Dill, Bonnie Thornton. 1983. "Race, Class, and Gender: Prospects for an All-Inclusive Sisterhood." *Feminist Studies* 9.1, pp. 131–50.

Dyson, Michael Eric. 1993. *Reflecting Black: African-American Cultural Criticism.* Minneapolis: University of Minnesota Press.

Edwards, Richard. 1979. *Contested Terrain: The Transformation of the Workplace in the Twentieth Century.* New York: Basic Books.

Essed, Philomena. 1991. *Understanding Everyday Racism: An Interdisciplinary Theory.* Newbury Park, CA: Sage.

227

Estell, Kenneth. 1994. *The African-American Almanac*, 6th edn. Detroit: Gale Research.

Fordham, Signithia. 1993. "'Those Loud Black Girls': (Black) Women, Silence, and Gender 'Passing' in the Academy." *Anthropology and Education Quarterly* 24.1, pp. 3–32.

Foucault, Michel. 1977. "The Political Functions of the Intellectual." *Radical Philosophy*. 17 (Summer): 12–14.

——. 1979. *Discipline and Punish: The Birth of the Prison*. Translated by Alan Sheridan. New York: Schocken.

Frankenberg, Ruth. 1993. *White Women, Race Matters: The Social Contruction of Whiteness*. Minneapolis: University of Minnesota Press.

Franklin, V. P. 1992. *Black Self-Determination: A Cultural History of African-American Resistance*. Chicago: Lawrence Hill.

Goldberg, David Theo. 1993. *Racist Culture: Philosophy and the Politics of Meaning*. Cambridge, Mass.: Blackwell Publishers.

Grant, Jacqueline. 1982. "Black Women and the Church." In Gloria T. Hull, Patricia Bell Scott, and Barbara Smith, eds. *All the Women Are White, All the Blacks Are Men, But Some of Us Are Brave: Black Women's Studies*. Old Westbury, Conn.: Feminist Press, pp. 141–52.

Grimes, Michael D. 1991. *Class in Twentieth-Century American Sociology*. New York: Praeger.

Grossberg, Lawrence. 1996. "On Postmodernism and Articulation: An Interview with Stuart Hall." In David Morley and Kuan-Hsing Chen, eds. *Stuart Hall: Critical Dialogues in Cultural Studies*. New York: Routledge, pp. 131–50.

Hekman, Susan. 1997. "Truth and Method: Feminist Standpoint Theory Revisited." *Signs* 22.2, pp. 341–65.

Higginbotham, Elizabeth, and Lynn Weber. 1992. "Moving Up with Kin and Community: Upward Social Mobility for Black and White Women." *Gender and Society* 6.3, pp. 416–40.

Jhally, Sut, and Justin Lewis. 1992. *Enlighten Racism*. Boulder: Westview.

Katz, Michael B. 1989. *The Undeserving Poor: From the War on Poverty to the War on Welfare*. New York: Pantheon.

Lerner, Gerda, ed. 1972. *Black Women in White America: A Documentary History*. New York: Vintage.

McClintock, Anne. 1995. *Imperial Leather: Race, Gender and Sexuality in the Colonial Conquest*. New York: Routledge.

Mannheim, Karl. 1954 [1936]. *Ideology and Utopia: An Introduction to the Sociology of Knowledge*. New York: Harcourt, Brace & World.

Marable, Manning. 1983. *How Capitalism Underdeveloped Black America*. Boston: South End.

Marx, Karl. 1963 [1852]. *The Eighteenth Brumaire of Louis Bonaparte*. New York: International Publishers.

Massey, Douglas S., and Nancy A. Denton. 1993. *American Apartheid: Segregation and the Making of the Underclass*. Cambridge, MA: Harvard University Press.

Merton, Robert K. 1973. *The Sociology of Science: Theoretical and Empirical Investigations*. Chicago: University of Chicago Press.

Quadagno, Jill. 1994. *The Color of Welfare: How Racism Undermined the War on Poverty*. New York: Oxford University Press.

Richie, Beth E. 1996. *Compelled to Crime: The Gender Entrapment of Battered Black Women*. New York: Routledge.

Sack, Karen Brodkin. 1989. "Toward a Unified Theory of Class, Race, and Gender." *American Ethnologist* 16.3, pp. 534–50.

Scott, Joseph W. 1984. "1984: The Public and Private Governance of Race Relations." *Sociological Focus* 17.3, pp. 175–87.

Slack, Jennifer Daryl. 1996. "The Theory and Method of Articulation in Cultural Studies."

228

In David Morley and Kuan-Hsing Chen, eds. *Stuart Hall: Critical Dialogues in Cultural Studies*. New York: Routledge, pp. 112–27.

Smith, Dorothy E. 1987. *The Everyday World as Problematic: A Feminist Sociology*. Boston: Northeastern University Press.

Takaki, Ronald. 1993. *A Different Mirror: A History of Multicultural America*. Boston: Little, Brown.

Terrelonge, Pauline. 1984. "Feminist Consciousness and Black Women." In Jo Freeman, ed. *Women: A Feminist Perspective*. 3d edn. Palo Alto: Mayfield, pp. 557–67.

Thorne, Barrie. 1992. "Feminism and the Family: Two Decades of Thought." In Barrie Thorne and Marilyn Yalom, eds. *Rethinking the Family: Some Feminist Questions*. Boston: Northeastern University Press.

Van Deburg, William L. 1992. *New Day in Babylon: The Black Power Movement and American Culture, 1965–1975*. Chicago: University of Chicago Press.

Vanneman, Reeve, and Lynn Weber Cannon. 1987. *The American Perception of Class*. Philadelphia: Temple University Press.

West, Cornel. 1993. *Race Matters*. Boston: Beacon.

Wilson, William Julius. 1978. *The Declining Significance of Race*. Chicago: University of Chicago Press.

——. 1987. *The Truly Disadvantaged: The Inner City, the Underclass, and Public Policy*. Chicago: University of Chicago Press.

Young, Iris Marion. 1990. *Justice and the Politics of Differences*. Princeton: Princeton University Press.

13

Radicalizing Feminisms from "The Movement Era"

JOY A. JAMES

In order for us as poor and oppressed people to become a part of a society that is meaningful, the system under which we now exist has to be radically changed. This means that we are going to have to learn to think in radical terms. I use the term radical in its original meaning getting down to and understanding the root cause. It means facing a system that does not lend itself to your needs and devising means by which you change that system. That is easier said than done. But one of the things that has to be faced is, in the process of wanting to change that system, how much have we got to do to find out who we are, where we have come from and where we are going.

Ella Baker, speech at the Institute for the Black World, Atlanta, GA, 1969

Ella Baker, "The Black Woman in the Civil Rights Struggle"

During the height of the black liberation and black power movements, veteran activist Ella Baker's cogent assessment of the political contradictions of liberalism among black elites advocating civil rights distinguished between attempts to become "a part of the American scene" and "the more radical struggle" to transform society. According to Baker, "In . . . struggling to be accepted, there were certain goals, concepts, and values such as the drive for the 'Talented Tenth.' That, of course, was the concept that proposed that through the process of education black people would be accepted in the American culture and they would be accorded their rights in proportion to the degree to which they qualified as being persons of learning and culture. . . ." For Baker, the common belief that "those who were trained were not trained to be part of the community, but to be leaders of the community" implied "another false assumption that being a leader meant that you were separate and apart from the masses, and to a large extent people were to look up to you, and that your responsibility to the people was to represent them." This precluded people from acquiring their own sense of values; but the 1960s, according to Baker, would usher in another view: "the concept of the right of the people to participate in the decisions that affected their lives."

Political agitation and movements have historically increased the scope of black leadership; however, African-American participation in political decisions has historically been translated through corporate, state, or philanthropic channels. A century ago, the vision and resources of the American Baptist Home Missionary Society (ABHMS) allowed wealthy, white Christian missionaries to support the black elite Talented Tenth as a shadow of themselves as influential, liberal leaders and to organize privileged black Americans to serve as a buffer zone between white America and a restive, disenfranchised black mass. During the Reconstruction era, funding elite black colleges such as Spelman and Morehouse (named after white philanthropists) to produce aspirants suitable for the American ideal, the ABHMS sought to encourage the development of race managers rather than revolutionaries. To the extent that it followed and follows the founders' mandate, the Talented Tenth was and remains antirevolutionary. Supported by white influential liberals, the Talented Tenth historically included women. It therefore liberalized or deradicalized the protofeminism of historical black female elites. Contemporary black feminist politics as pursued by elites imbued with the bourgeois ideology of "race uplift" evince the same antirevolutionary tendency as the early Talented Tenth. Vacillating between race management and revolutionary practices, black feminisms are alternately integrated into or suppressed within contemporary American corporate-consumer culture.

Yet as Baker noted, the 1960s ushered in a more democratic, grass-roots-driven form of leadership. The new "wave" of black feminisms originating from that time invariably connects with historical antiracist struggle in the United States. Black women created and continue to create feminisms out of militant national liberation or antiracist movements in which they often function as unrecognized organizers and leaders. Equally, their contributions to American feminisms are inadequately noted even among those who document the history of contemporary radical feminism. Emerging from black militant groups, African Americans shaped feminist politics. These sites of emergent antiracist feminism influenced the more radical dimensions of black feminisms despite their inherent contradictions. For instance, the Combahee River Collective traces its origins to political formations now generally perceived as uniformly sexist:

"Black feminist politics [has] an obvious connection to movements for black liberation, particularly those of the 1960s and 1970s. Many of us were active in those movements (Civil Rights, Black nationalism, the Black Panthers), and all of our lives were greatly affected and changed by their ideologies, their goals, and the tactics used to achieve their goals. It was our experience and disillusionment within these liberation movements, as well as experience on the periphery of the white male left, that led to the need to develop a politics that was antiracist, unlike those of white women, and anti-sexist, unlike those of Black and white men."

The Combahee River Collective took its name from the June 2, 1863, guerrilla foray led by the black revolutionary Harriet Tubman. This excursion in South Carolina's Port Royal region freed hundreds of enslaved people and became the first and only military campaign in the United States planned and executed by a woman. During the Civil War, Tubman, the first American woman to lead black and white troops in battle, headed the Intelligences Service in the Department of the South. Before making a name for herself as a military strategist and garnering the people's title of "General Tubman," the formerly enslaved African woman had proven herself to be "a compelling and stirring orator in the councils of the abolitionists and the anti-slavers." Tubman's distinct

231

archetype for a black female warrior belies conventional narratives that masculinize black history and resistance. Although males remain the icons for black rebellion embattled with white supremacy and enslavement, women also engaged in radical struggles, including the strategy of armed self-defense. As fugitives with bounties on their heads, they rebelled, survived, or became casualties of state and racial–sexual repression.

Despite being designated "outlaws" and made outcasts because of their militancy, historical or ancestral black women such as Tubman have managed to survive in political memory. A few have been gradually, marginally, accepted into an American society that claims their resistance by incorporating or "forgiving" their past revolutionary tactics for humanitarian goals. Tubman's antebellum criminalized resistance to slavery, like Ida B. Well's post-Reconstruction antilynching call to arms, typifies a rebellion that later became legitimized through American reclamation acts. The anomaly or contradiction is that the nation's racial progressivism seeks to reclaim black women who bore arms to defend themselves and other African Americans and females against racial–sexual violence in a culture that continues to condemn black physical resistance to political dominance and violence while it supports at the same time the use of weapons in the defence or expansion of the nation-state, individual and family, home, and private property.

Seeking explicitly to foster black female militancy in the 1970s, without the reservations of ambivalence that national culture exhibits toward black insurrectionists, Combahee black feminists selected an African-American military strategist and guerrilla fighter as their archetype. Their choice of Tubman over her better-known contemporary, Sojourner Truth, suggests an intent to radicalize feminism. Truth, not Tubman, is closely identified with feminism because of her work as a suffragette and collaboration with prominent white feminists of her day. Tubman is identified with black people – men, women, and children – and military insurrection against the US government. Her associations with white men are better known than those with white women; for instance, she allegedly planned to participate in John Brown's raid on Harper's Ferry despite the warnings of the prominent abolitionist and profeminist Frederick Douglass. With this African warrior and freedom fighter as their feminist model, the Combahee River Collective emerged in 1977 to contest the liberalism of the National Black Feminist Organization (NBFO) that preceded it.

In its manifesto, the collective expresses its "serious disagreements with NBFO's bourgeois-feminist stance and their lack of a clear political focus" and offers an activist alternative. The collective, which included Barbara Smith, Gloria Hull, and Margo Okazawa-Rey, would later organize against a series of murders targeting black girls and women in the Boston area. Combahee's black feminist manifesto emphasizes radical activism rather than liberal politics:

> Although we are feminists and Lesbians, we feel solidarity with progressive Black men. . . . Our situation as Black people necessitates that we have solidarity around the fact of race, which white women of course do not need to have with white men, unless it is their negative solidarity as racial oppressors. We struggle together with Black men against racism, while we also struggle with Black men about sexism.

Given the prevalence of antiradical bias in American society, and despite cultural critic bell hooks's definition of feminism that evokes the collective's ideology, one must continue to wade deeply into the mainstream to retrieve critiques such as the following issued by the Combahee River Collective:

> We realize that the liberation of all oppressed peoples necessitates the destruction of the political-economic systems of capitalism and imperialism as well as patriarchy. We are socialists because we believe that work must be organized for the collective benefit of those who do the work and create the products, and not for the profit of the bosses. Material resources must be equally distributed among those who create these resources. We are not convinced, however, that a socialist revolution that is not also a feminist and antiracist revolution will guarantee our liberation.

Ideology and Feminist Identity

Black feminists face the challenge of how to maintain Combahee's integrative analyses combining race, gender, sexuality and class with more than rhetoric, the challenge, that is, of how to express their critiques in viable political practice amid organizing in nonelite communities. Rhetoric nonwithstanding, all antiracist and antisexist politics are not equally ambitious or visionary in their confrontations with state dominance and in their demands and strategies for transforming society by rechanneling economic and political power. Conservative attempts to bring "closure" to or contain the black revolutionary struggles that fueled radical black feminism such as Combahee altered the transformative potential of black feminist ideology. "Closure" itself is likely an illusory pursuit, given the continuance of repressive conditions, impoverishment, abrogation of rights, and racial and sexual denigration that engendered revolutionary struggle.

Although the greatest opponent to antiracist and feminist revolutionary struggles has been the counterrevolutionary state (arguably, in the twentieth century, embodied by the United States), black feminist writings may pay insufficient attention to state repression and the conflictual ideologies and divergent practices (from liberal to revolutionary) found within black feminisms. This may be partly due to the considerable energy that some focus on the marginalization of black feminisms in European-American and African-American culture (as well as in African and Latin American cultures); and partly due to the often-obscured antiradical tendencies found within black feminisms.

Liberal, radical, and revolutionary black feminisms may be presented as ideologically unified and uniformly "progressive" while simultaneously being viewed as having little impact beyond black women. Sorting out progressive politics within black feminisms, we may distinguish between ideological trajectories that reveal the at times compliant, often ambiguous, and sometimes oppositional relationship of black feminisms to state hegemony. Delineating ideology works to place in context black feminist attitudes toward institutional and political power. In the blurred political spectrum of progressives that broadly includes "liberal," "radical," "neoradical," and "revolutionary" politics and their overlap, all of these camps change character or shape-shift to varying degrees with the political context and era. For instance, no metanarrative can map radical or "revolutionary" black feminism, although the analyses of activist-intellectuals such as Ella Baker serve as outlines. Some reject while others embrace the self-proclaimed "revolutionary" that manifests through rhetorical, literary, cultural or conference productions. "Revolutionary" denotes dynamic movement rather than fixed stasis within a political practice relevant to change material conditions and social consciousness. As the revolutionary has a fluid rather than fixed appearance, its emergence remains episodic. As conditions change, what it means to be "revolutionary" changes. "Revolutionaries" or "radicals" are not disembodied; rather they are understood (and so definable) only within context. (As a result, the articulation of a final destination for radical or revolutionary black feminisms remains more of a motivational ideal and the pronouncement of an arrival at the final destination is a depoliticizing mirage.)

Despite ideological fluidity and bordercrossings, some valid or useful generalizations can be made. Black feminisms that accept the political legitimacy of corporate-state institutional and police power but posit the need for humanistic reform are considered *liberal*. Black feminisms that view female and black oppression as stemming from capitalism, neocolonialism, and the corporate-state that enforces both are generally understood to be *radical*. Some black feminisms explicitly challenge state and corporate dominance and critique the privileged status of bourgeois elites among the "left"; those that do so by connecting political theory for radical transformation with political acts to abolish corporate-state and elite dominance are *revolutionary*.

Differentiating between liberalism and radicalism or even more so between "radical" and "revolutionary" to theorize about black feminist liberation politics is extremely difficult but essential for understanding some limitations of "left" politics and black feminisms. Part of the difficulty in delineating the "left" of black feminisms stems from the resurgence of the right and its modification of liberal and progressive thought.

New terminology that denotes the pervasive influence of conservatism as "neo" becomes a standard political prefix for the postcivil rights and postfeminist movements era. The efficacy of a rightist conservatism has led to the coupling of reactionary with conservative politics to construct the rightist hybrid "neoconservative"; the merger of the conservative with liberal politics to create the right-leaning "neoliberalism"; and the marriage of liberalism with radicalism to produce "neoradicalism" as a more statist or corporate form of radical politics. Alongside "neoconservatism" and "neoliberalism," one finds "neoradicalism." All denote a drift toward conservatism. This drift has led to deradicalizing trends that include the hegemony of bourgeois intellectuals within neoradicalism and the commodification of the "revolutionary" as performer who captures the attention and imagination of preradicalized masses while serving as storyteller for apolitical consumers. Responding to revolutionary struggles, the counterrevolutionary, antirevolutionary, and neoradical surface to confront and displace activism inspired and sustained by vibrant rebellions.

Neoradicalism, like liberalism, denounces draconian measures against women, poor, and racialized peoples; and, like liberalism, it also positions itself as "loyal" opposition to the state. Therefore what it denounces is not the state itself but its excesses, prison exploitation and torture, punitive measures toward the poor, environmental degradation, counterrevolutionary violence, and contra wars. Abolition movements, directed by neoradicals, rarely extend their rhetoric consistently to call for the abolition of capitalism and the corporate state. Movements led or advocated by those representing the disenfranchized are marked by the appearance of the symbolic radical.

All black feminists, including those that follow conventional ideology to some degree share an outsider status in a commercial culture. That marginalization is not indicative of, but often confused with, an intrinsic or inherent radicalism. Ideological differences among African Americans belie the construction of black women or, even more significantly, black feminists as a "class." Refusing to essentialize black women or feminism, writers such as bell hooks have noted the conflictual political ideologies found among black women. In 1991, hooks's "Must We Call All Women 'Sister'?" questioned feminist championing of Anita Hill that made little mention of the fact that the then Reagan Republican had promoted antifeminist, antigay/lesbian, anti-disabled, and anticivil rights policies at the Equal Employment Opportunity Commission (EEOC) under the supervision of Clarence Thomas. The gender solidarity that surrounded Hill obscured her support for ultra-conservative policies. Prior to her courageous testimony at the Senate Judiciary Committee hearings, hearings that eventually confirmed Thomas as a Supreme Court Justice, she had implemented reactionary attacks on the gains of the civil rights and women's movements; movements that had enabled non-activists such as Hill and her former supervisor to attend Yale Law School.

Legal theorist Kimberlé Crenshaw has noted the consequences of African Americans' failure to distinguish between and to discuss political ideologies among black public figures. Crenshaw criticizes a racial uniformity in black solidarity that includes reactionaries. At a C-SPAN gathering of black lawyers critical of the American Bar Association invitation to Thomas to keynote its annual meeting, Crenshaw gave a scintillating critique of black support for Thomas (televised, July 1998). She contended that because of his race, African Americans paid little attention to his right-wing politics and so failed to distinguish between "conservative" and "reactionary" ideologies. (The endorsement of neo-Nazi David Duke of Thomas's appointment to the Court underscores the affinity rightwing ideologues felt for the Republican replacement to the late Justice Thurgood Marshall.) According to Crenshaw, ideological distinctions eroded black opposition to former President George Bush's Supreme Court nominee, but if black Americans had maintained and sharpened the distinction between conservative and reactionary positions, more would have actively opposed Thomas's appointment.

Crenshaw's argument has merit. Conservatism has some respectability among black women and men immured in the "race uplift" of Booker T. Washington's black capitalism (even thought they are not fully compliant with his prohibitions against competing with whites). Reactionary politics, however, hold no respectable public place among African Americans. Historically viewed as an extension of white supremacy and racial dominance, reactionaries have been considered an anathema for black and female lives. Yet African Americans seem unwilling to publicly, critically discuss black reactionaries in service to the state and to distinguish their counterrevolutionary service from the antirevolutionary disavowals of black liberals and neoradicals. (In similar fashion, maintaining distinctions between revolutionaries and radicals appears to be equally problematic.)

Just as blurring the lines between black reactionaries and conservatives politically accommodates reactionaries by reclassifying them as respectable "conservatives," some black feminisms have erased distinctions between liberalism and the radicalism that incited dynamic, militant formations (like the Combahee River Collective). Given that liberalism has accrued the greatest material resources and social legitimacy among progressives, the coalition of liberals and radicals to foment neoradicalism means that respectability has been designated to dual beneficiaries. Liberal black feminism garners the image of being on the "cutting edge" by appending itself to symbols of radicalism and hence increases its popularity as "transformative." Radicals are able to maximize their visibility and the market for their rhetoric via legitimization through association with liberalism. The terms for merger may be weighted toward the more privileged liberalism and its offshoot neoliberalism than radicalism or neoradicalism. Liberalism also allows black feminisms to increase their compatibility with mainstream American politics and with mainstream African-American political culture.

From their strong fidelity to the Democratic Party (which under the Clinton administration increased police powers and punitive measures against the poor), it may be inferred that African Americans generally do not favor political "extremism." Shunning reactionary or revolutionary politics, most black Americans support a progressive liberalism (left of center) that has a greater social conscience, and therefore moral content, than that of the general society. Yet this and their sometimes outraged, and at times outrageous, condemnations of white supremacy, consequently places most African Americans outside narrowly-construed conventional politics and allows them to be portrayed as political "extremists."

With centrism the conventional political stance, some black feminisms have reconfigured radicalism to fit within liberal paradigms. Doing so enables a black feminist erasure of revolutionary politics and a rhetorical embrace of radicalism without material support for challenges to transform or abolish, rather than modify, state-corporate authority. An analogy for black feminist erasures can be made with the framing of a painting. The mat establishes the official borders for viewers. Often matting crops off the original borders of the picture. If incorrectly done, the mat encroaches upon the image itself and the signature of the image-maker. Framing black feminisms for public discourse and display, the extreme peripheries of the initial creation are often covered over. Placing a mat over the political vision of black feminisms establishes newer (visually coordinated) borders that frequently blot out the fringes – revolutionaries and radical activists – and allow professional or bourgeois intellectuals and radicals to appear within borders as the only "insurgents." With layered or overlapping mats that position rhetoric as representative of revolutionary struggle, the resulting portrait will even obscure radicals, leaving liberals or neoradicals in the position of gender and race "rebels." . . .

Conclusion

The legacies of black female radicals and revolutionaries contest arguments that state repression and resistance to it are not "black women's issues" or are too "politicized" for "feminism." Such legacies also contradict contentions that feminism is inherently "bourgeois" and therefore incapable of an organic revolutionary politics. Yet even the "revolutionary" is marked in a corporate culture (where commercials at one time proclaimed that the Revlon Corporation made "revolutionary cosmetics for revolutionary women"). Revolutionary black feminism transgresses corporate culture in its focus on female independence; community building/caretaking; and resistance to state dominance, corporate exploitation, racism, and sexism. Emphasizing economic and political power rather than social service programs for the disenfranchised, it challenges basic social tenets expressed in "law and order" campaigns, the respectability of political dissent channeled through lobbying and electoral politics, and acceptance of a corporate-state as a viable vehicle to redress disenfranchisement.

In the United States, the blurred lines between revolutionary, anti-revolutionary, and counterrevolutionary politics allow for the normative political and discursive "sisterhood" that embraces conservative and liberal women of various ethnicities yet rarely extends itself to radical or revolutionary women. Adherence to mainstream political ideology appears key in the normative appeal of antiracism, feminism, and antiracist feminism. Because political marginalization usually follows challenges to repressive state policies (and critiques of female or feminist complicity in those practices), the revolutionary remains on the margin, more so than any other form of (black) feminism.

The symbiotic relationship between subordinate black feminists and the "white" masculinist state contest any presumption of a unified politics. Seeking a viable community and society, antiracist feminisms can serve as either sedative or stimulant. Conflicting messages about the nature of political struggle and leadership can be found within black feminism, which function as "shadows" – both in the negative aspects attributed to them and in their subordinate status on the American scene. Ever present, often ignored but completely inescapable, their plurality is seen as monolithic and depicted as the antithesis of the "robust American" body. Fending their shadows as American alter political egos, black women paint varied portraits of the shadow boxer as radical: as lone warrior; successful corporate fund-raiser for and beneficiary of progressive issues; individual survivalist, and community worker receptive to the leadership of nonelites in opposing state-corporate dominance.

Progressive black feminisms face the predicament of struggling to maintain radical politics despite their inner conflicts. Yet this, after all, is the shadow boxer's dilemma: to fight the authoritative body casting the boxer off while simultaneously battling with internal contradictions.

Bibliography

Baker, Ella. "The Black Woman in the Civil Rights Struggle" in Joanne Grant, *Ella Baker* (New York: John Wiley & Sons, 1998).

Chomsky, Noam. *The Culture of Terrorism* (Boston: South End Press, 1988).

Collins, Patricia Hill. *Black Feminist Thought* (Cambridge, MA: Unwin Hyman, 1990/rpt., New York: Routledge, 1991).

Combahee River Collective. "The Combahee River Collective Statement," in Barbara Smith, ed., *Home Girls* (New York: Kitchen Table: Women of Color Press, 1983).

Conrad, Earl. "I Bring You General Tubman." *The Black Scholar*, Vol. 1, Nos. 3–4 (January–February 1970).

Du Bois, W. E. B. *The Souls of Black Folk*. (New York: A. C. McClurg & Co, 1903).

Gates, Henry Louis Jr. and Cornel West. *The Future of the Race*. New York: Knopf, 1996.

Higginbotham, Evelyn Brooks. *Righteous Discontent: The Women's Movement in the Black Baptist Church, 1880–1920*. Cambridge, MA: Harvard University Press, 1993.

hooks, bell. "Must We Call All Women 'Sister'?" *Z Magazine*. February 1992.

Hull, Gloria T., Patricia Bell Scott, and Barbara Smith, eds. *All the Women Are White, All the Blacks Are Men, But Some of US Are Brave* (New York: Feminist Press, 1982).

14

Philosophy and Racial Paradigms

NAOMI ZACK

Introduction

In a sufficiently comprehensive cultural context, such as contemporary American society, the ways in which people think and behave concerning race constitute a paradigm.[1] The ideational part of a paradigm of race generates social constructions that are part of social reality.[2] Viewing sets of related ideas and practices concerning race as paradigms makes it possible to consider the sets in their appropriate historical contexts without anachronism, and to criticize ideas and practices from paradigms other than our own, without semantic confusion.

Since the eighteenth century, there have been two paradigms of race, an Old Paradigm that was oppressive and racist, and a New Paradigm that is liberatory and nonracist. Outside of both paradigms, empirical research in the human biological sciences yields the insight that race does not exist. That insight might turn out to be the main component of The Last Paradigm of Race, or it might continue to be ignored.[3]

I will use "racial paradigm" to refer to a set of ranges of beliefs about issues. Everyone holding some belief on each issue shares a general core belief on that issue, although not everyone thinking within a paradigm has to have the same beliefs on any given issue. Also, it is not necessary that everyone thinking within the paradigm have a belief on every issue within the paradigm.

The issues in a racial paradigm are applied to human behavior, social situations, and events, so that the paradigm as a whole is a mechanism, and its ideational content a theory that provides explanations, predictions, and normative claims. The ability of a racial paradigm to generate normative statements results from the normative nature of some of the core beliefs and variable beliefs within the paradigm. The normative statements may be moral judgments or rules that are socially or legally enforced. In this normative dimension, a racial paradigm may function as an ideology.

Racial paradigms also function as critical theories. The explanations generated from critical theories may not be recognizable or acceptable to people, acting individually or as members of groups, to whom a critical theory is applied.[4] Similarly, explanations and normative statements generated from a racial paradigm may be unrecognizable or unacceptable to people to whom the paradigm is applied.

It will clarify matters to stipulate distinctions between paradigms, and conceptual schemes and theories. A conceptual scheme is made up of symbols that are related through their meanings. A theory is a conceptual scheme that is primarily used for explanation and prediction, although it may be of epistemic or aesthetic value as a description in its own right. The correct use and appreciation of theories tends to be restricted to specialists in professional fields of inquiry, even though many theories have been popularized for specialists in other fields, amateurs and the lay public. Both conceptual schemes and theories are linguistic-ideational entities.

However, a paradigm, in the sense at issue, includes not just linguistic-ideational entities but their applications to persons, things, and events that exist independently of language and ideas. When Thomas Kuhn included scientific practice and research programs in his definition of paradigms, he seems to have had something like this in mind. But, Kuhn's usage of "paradigm" was restricted to scientific communities, whereas racial paradigms operate in political discussion and everyday life, as well as science.[5] The political and daily scope of a racial paradigm means that it is an unplanned, dynamic system that may contain contradictory beliefs on some issues, even though there are shared core beliefs. Politicians and their public do not go out of their way to resolve contradictions, and neither are they perplexed that anything at all may be logically implied by a contradiction. Therefore, a paradigm that spans both science and common sense can be expected to be messy and with the mess comes instability and the probability of change.

The advantage of viewing an entire cultural system of beliefs and behavior pertaining to race as a paradigm is that it fits several different kinds of facts about race and allows for a wide variety of explanations. Also, philosophers and others in the humanities and sciences are already familiar with the ways in which paradigms operate, and cease to operate when they are supplanted by other paradigms. We also know how what Kuhn called the "incommensurablity" of paradigms may preclude rational, empirically-based argument between agents from competing paradigms.[6] What we do not know is what external and internal factors are required before one racial paradigm can be supplanted by another, to what extent the factors are psychological, intellectual, economic, or demographic, or what their critical masses are. We also do not know the extent to which liberatory laws can correct oppressive custom. Thus, in a representative democracy where public policy is largely determined by majority interests and corporate business interests, official commitments to universal human rights may at times be taken seriously and at other times reduced to mere ceremonial rhetoric.

Comparison of the Old and New Paradigms of Race

The core ideational components of the Old and New Paradigms of race can be summarized as follows. Each component is also an issue that has a range of more specific beliefs.

Old

1_o. There exist distinct human races, constituted by hereditary traits.

2_o. The white race is naturally culturally superior, its members aesthetically, intellectually and morally superior, to other races.

3_o. Racial mixture is biologically common but unnatural; it is and should be illegal.

4_o. Racial difference can be scientifically studied on an empirical, physical level. It may be part of the divine order of things.

5_o. Human racial difference has appropriate moral and political consequences. Laws and government action should support natural inequalities based on race, especially when they exist in society, based on custom.

6_o. All knowledge and policy concerning racial difference does and should come from whites.

New

1_n. There exist distinct human races, constituted by hereditary traits

2_n. The white race is economically and politically advantaged over all others based partly on a history of oppression of non-white races.

3_n. Racial mixture is biologically common but socially odd; it is and should be legal.

4_n. Cultural racial difference can be scientifically studied but it is the result of environmental differences, alone, especially in education and opportunity.

5_n. Human racial difference has appropriate moral and political consequences. Laws and government action should have a liberatory effect on non-whites. Inequality based on race is a social and legal problem.

6_n. Non-whites as well as whites can and should contribute to the construction of knowledge and policy based on racial difference.

The main differences between the two paradigms are the issues of racial hierarchy and racial equality as stated in issues 2_o and 2_n, and 5_o and 5_n. While these issues appear to be solely matters of evaluation that are *about* race, they are instead closely related to how race is objectively defined during the historical period of each paradigm. The definitions facilitate social constructions of race that are characteristic of their paradigm.

The ideational part of the Old Paradigm of Race was formulated in Europe during the late eighteenth century; it reigned in America from then until the Civil Rights legislation of the 1960s, after which the New Paradigm of Race supplanted it. These dates are of course imprecise because some members of society subscribed to elements of the New Paradigm in the eighteenth century and some still operate within the Old Paradigm today. For instance, Thomas Jefferson, although otherwise living and thinking within the Old Paradigm, thought that slavery was a major social problem, as did nineteenth-century abolitionists.[7] Also, not everyone before the 1960s thought that blacks were culturally inferior by heredity. At present, some racialist scientists continue to search for physical proof of hereditary white cultural superiority, and ideological white supremacists explicitly adhere to the components of the Old Paradigm.

What is still needed is more careful work within intellectual history to track the conceptual connections between eighteenth and nineteenth, and nineteenth and twentieth, century theories of racial difference.[8] Such tracking would lead from the intellectual content of the Old to the New Paradigm, and it might also yield clues about what is coming next. It is probably easier to track the intellectual construction of both racial paradigms than to chart their demolition. The evidence of intellectual construction lies in the published record, whereas demolition is largely the result of lack of interest to the point where certain ideas no longer find authoritative fora in speech or print. This is not to say that there is only one intellectual path that can be traced to the complete development of either paradigm, one mental story that can be told. I like a philosophical story but, as we shall see, this is far easier to come by for the construction of the Old, than New Paradigm.

Hume and Kant between them settled contemporary disagreements to the concluding effect that there existed human races with hereditary differences that were both cultural and physical. No eighteenth-century thinkers of comparable rank were recognized as having refuted them and Hume's opinion was widely cited by defenders of slavery, and accepted as a major obstacle by abolitionists.[9] All of the eighteenth-century writers on race considered so-called black skin color to be the determining racial difference between Europeans and Africans, but early on in the racial project, there was a speculation that dark skin color was the result of environment and therefore not permanently hereditary.[10] George Louis-Leclerc, Comte de Buffon, wrote in 1748: "Thus it appears that the existence of Negroes is confined to those parts of the earth where all the necessary circumstances concur in producing a constant and an excessive heat."[11] Buffon speculated that black skin color would be gradually lightened over eight to twelve generations in a cold climate.

Hume objected, in what was received as a refutation of Buffon, that while climate had a powerful influence on the natures of all plants and animals, human beings developed culturally through custom and imitation. He disclosed, in an infamous footnote, that he was "apt to suspect the negroes and in general all other species of men (for there are four or five different kinds) to be naturally inferior to the whites."[12] Hume went on to claim that the constant differences between whites and others would not exist, "if nature had not made an original distinction between these breeds of men."[13]

James Beattie challenged the sweep of Hume's generalization on several grounds: Europeans had been uncivilized two-thousand years earlier; the civilizations of all Negroes were unknown to Hume; there were many counter-examples to Hume's sweeping claims that non-whites were uniformly inferior in civilized achievement.[14] Hume's response was to change "There never was a civilized nation of any other complexion than white" to "There scarcely ever was a civilized nation of that [Negro] complexion."[15]

Hume does not seem to care whether he is talking about species or breeds, but it is safe to assume that he intends both terms to be synonymous with "race." He accepts skin color as a sign of racial difference, even though he acknowledges that skin color could be an effect of climate. He then associates cultural differences, which are much more important than skin color differences, with the different races of mankind. He also posits the cultural differences as the effect of an original racial distinction.

Hume's argument is incomplete. If skin color is the relatively superficial effect of climate, then it cannot be the basis of racial difference. If racial difference is responsible for cultural difference, then it cannot be the same thing as cultural difference.

242

What, then, is racial difference, or, what is race? Hume seems unaware that this question can be posed and that he has not answered it.

Kant, who cited Hume as an authority on the subject of race, does seem to address the question of what race is. He begins with a claim that all human beings must belong to the same genus in order to be comprehensible under a system of natural laws. He reasons that within the genus there are hereditary variations, in the form of resemblances and deviations from the "stem genus" of humanity, which cannot be restored.[16] Then, he seems to define race on an empirical basis:

> Among the deviations – i.e., the hereditary differences of animals belonging to a single stock – those which, when transplanted (displaced to other areas), maintain themselves over protracted generation, and which also generate hybrid young whenever they interbreed with other deviations of the same stock, are called *races*. . . . In this way Negroes and Whites are not different species of humans (for they belong presumably to one stock) but they are different *races* for each perpetuates itself in every area, and they generate between them children that are necessarily hybrid or blendlings (mulattoes).[17]

Kant's reasoning here appears to be that if there are races, then interbreeding will result in hybrids. There are hybrids. Therefore, there must be races. On the face of his reasoning, Kant has not made a case for the existence of races. First, logically, he affirms the consequent in claiming that if there are races, there are hybrids, and, there are hybrids, so therefore there are races. Second, and more important, his suggestion that hybridity is evidence for the existence of races is undermined by the fact that "hybridity" is itself defined as racial mixture, so its existence, and the perception of its existence, presupposes the prior existence of pure races, and our ability to identify them.

Kant may not have intended to use hybridity to confirm the existence of race, either logically or empirically, but to explicate a taxonomy of human species and races, of which hybridity is a part. If this is so, he still does not have an independent empirical foundation for the existence of races but merely applies a pre-existing taxonomy of species, races, and hybridity to what he identifies as instantiating instances.

Kant posited four races from which he claimed to be able to derive all observed human differences. But, after brief descriptions of the Hunnic and Hindu races, he asserts, "The reason for assuming the Negroes and Whites to be fundamental races is self-evident."[18]

Kant's assumption that races exist was consistent with his *a priori* answer to the question, What is race? He posited unseen formative causes of races, namely, "germs and dispositions."[19] He asserted that from these causes, together with geographical differences, "national characteristics," resulted, the differences among them depending on "the distinct feeling of the beautiful and sublime."[20] On the subject of this feeling, Kant made subtle distinctions among the French, Germans, and English. However, in his description of Africans, he merely took a short step back to Hume, saying:

> The Negroes of Africa have by nature no feeling that rises above the trifling. Mr Hume challenges anyone to cite a single example in which a Negro has shown talents, and asserts that among the hundreds of thousands of blacks who are transported elsewhere from their countries, although many of them have even been set free, still not a single one was ever found who presented anything great in art or science or any other praise-worthy quality,

even though among the whites some continually rise aloft from the lowest rabble, and through superior gifts earn respect in the world. So fundamental is the difference between these two races of man, and it appears to be as great in regard to mental capacities as in color.[21]

As stated, Hume and Kant between them settled the question of race, and racial difference, in the eighteenth century. By 1797, Georges Léopold Cuvier could definitively set out the entire human racial taxonomy based on the thought of Hume and Kant. This was Cuvier's classification in *Animal Kingdom*:

Although the promiscuous intercourse of the human species, which produces individuals capable of propagation, would seem to demonstrate its unity, certain hereditary peculiarities of conformation are observed which constitute what are termed *races*.

Three of them in particular appear very distinct: the *Caucasian* or white, the *Mongolian* or yellow, and *Ethiopian* or negro.

The Caucasian, to which we belong, is distinguished by the beauty of the oval formed by its head, varying in complexion and the colour of the hair. To this variety, the most highly civilized nations, and those which have generally held all others in subjection, are indebted for their origin.

The Mongolian is known by his high cheek bones, flat visage, narrow and oblique eyes, straight black hair, scanty beard and olive complexion. Great empires have been established by this race in China and Japan, and their conquests have been extended to this side of the Great Desert. In civilization, however, it has always remained stationary.

The Negro race is confined to the south of Mount Atlas; it is marked by a black complexion, crisped or woolly hair, compressed cranium, and a flat nose. The projection of the lower parts of the face, and the thick lips, evidently approximate it to the monkey tribe; the hordes of which it consists have always remained in the most complete state of utter barbarism.[22]

Except for Hegel's thesis that Africa stands outside of the civilizing and legalizing progress of human history, the Old Paradigm philosophical story about race ended with Kant.[23] The nineteenth-century development of the conceptual components of the Old Paradigm of Race consisted of attempts to provide an empirical basis for the hierarchical taxonomy: measurements of skull size, and limb proportion; speculations about different kinds of blood, because blood was believed to be the hereditary medium of race. Stephen Jay Gould and Nancy Leys Stepan have well chronicled the circular and metaphorical reasoning behind those attempts to develop an empirical foundation for race. Gould explains how the empirical data were reported inaccurately and sometimes even fraudulently; Stepan anlyzes how metaphors for black race were used to explain female gender inferiority and how female gender metaphors were used to explain black racial inferiority.[24] I will not retrace that ground here. Suffice it to say that by 1900, no racial essences had been discovered, and it was known within the sciences of human biology that differences in human blood do not correspond to racial differences.[25]

Despite widespread miscegenation among American Negroes, a mythology about the physical and mental debilities of mixed-race people and their inability to reproduce successfully, continued to define "hybridity" during the nineteenth and much of the twentieth century.[26] Interracial marriage was illegal in most American states after emancipation.[27] By the early 1900s the so-called one drop rule was used as a legal definition of whiteness: a white person was someone with no known black ancestors; a black person was someone with some known black ancestors.[28] As in the eighteenth century, the Old Paradigm of Race needed cases of mixed race to prove the value of racial purity or the existence of the white race. A stated ideal of Thomas Jefferson was thus fulfilled: slavery had been abolished but racial mixture was unacceptable.[29]

When the U.S. Supreme Court struck down the remaining anti-miscegenation laws in *Loving* v. *Virginia*, 1967, the appellee's arguments rested on the desirability of what they considered to be racial integrity. Chief Justice Warren based the Court's decision on the argument that because marriage is a basic social liberty, states are not entitled to prohibit and punish marriage on the invidious basis of racial difference alone. Warren argued that such regulation violated the equal protection clause of the four-teenth amendment and that it was designed to maintain "White Supremacy."[30]

By the 1930s, cross-cultural investigations in anthropology had been interpreted by Franz Boas and Claude Lévi-Strauss as proof that cultural traits were not biologically inherited.[31] It was assumed that Euro-American cultural attainments were universally desirable, and by the 1950s, educated emancipatory thinkers developed critical theo-ries and public policy toward the goal of achieving civic and social equality between blacks and whites.

The views of non-whites on their own identity and liberation, based on racial dif-ference, are recognized in the New Paradigm, 6_n. Non-white traditions of liberation have been in basic accord with goals and policies for racial equality that have been formulated by whites, except when non-white projects of identity affirmation have cultural content in conflict with white ideals. For instance, indigenous advocates in the United States, and throughout the world, have tried to retain land-based social values that are not recognized within the Western technological project.[32]

A core issue, 4_n, of the New Paradigm of Race is that human cultural traits and individual aptitudes are not variably inherited within distinct racial categories. As a result, there is a general presumption, based on the equal protection clause of the fourteenth amendment to the United States Constitution, that different treatment in non-racial legal and civic matters cannot be based on racial difference alone. This is evident in the Civil Rights Act of 1964, The Voter Registration Act of 1965, and the Immigration Act of 1965. Nonetheless, this legislation does not so much affirm equal-ity among racial groups as it prohibits discrimination against individuals, on the basis of race.[33]

Logically, the implementation of equal protection under the law depends on prior identification based on race. If people were not presumed to be racially different, there would be no basis on which to insist that they be treated equally, regardless of that racial difference. Different criteria for racial discrimination, as well as appropriate policies for correcting racial discrimination have been formulated in varied ways, within issue 5_n, of the New Paradigm. However, belief in the existence of race is a core issue of the New Paradigm of Race, as it was of the Old, 1_o and 1_n. Almost everyone in American society assumes that people are divided into natural groups with common physical traits that can be studied in the biological sciences, and that the groups are the referents of racial terms. The subject of serious difference within the New Paradigm is how members of the different racial groups have, do, and ought to relate to one another, based on racial difference, or in spite of it.

In both paradigms, racial difference is associated with cultural difference that includes varied kinds of human character, skills, and behavior, which are all subject to evaluation. In the Old Paradigm, race is defined as hereditary biology and hereditary culture. But, in the New Paradigm, race is defined as hereditary biology only, and assumptions or explicit statements that cultural differences associated with racial difference are inherited are defined as racist by educated thinkers holding beliefs in the range on issue 4_n. Within the Old Paradigm, charges of racism according to the New Paradigm either do not make sense or appear to be changing natural differences into political and moral ones.

Let us assume that adherents of both paradigms assume that justice consists in treating equals equally, and that they are willing to process empirical information about the connection between human biological racial difference and culture. On that assumption, some instances of racism within the New Paradigm may not have constituted injustice within the Old Paradigm, because relevant information was not available. Nonetheless, there is an important residue of psychological and moral illwill toward people of different races, which is not fully captured by this semantic, paradigmatic analysis of racism as based on available empirical information. Kwame Anthony Appiah and others, have tried to identify exactly where race-based ill will intersects with factual ignorance.[34] Without doubt, some of the ill will is moral and psychological in ways that overflow the ideational content of either paradigm. Even without such ill will, racial matters in society go far beyond ideation, into social reality.

The Social Construction of Race

John Searle's analysis in *The Construction of Social Reality* can be applied to racial paradigms to clarify the connection between the ideational and social aspects of race. Searle observes that human beings live in realities made of physical facts that can be studied in the natural sciences, and social facts that are about physical facts and other social facts. Broadly speaking, social facts are related to physical facts through language. Much of the language used in social reality contains words that are presumed ultimately to refer to physical facts. However, there are levels and meta-levels within social reality, so that on each level, constructions from less abstract levels can be given new meanings. The new meanings regulate objects on the new level of social reality and to some extent constitute them as social objects on that level. This process of regulating and constituting is the construction of social reality.[35]

Searle's primary example of a construction within social reality is money. Originally, money, as a store of value and medium of exchange meant, because it was, precious objects. That M, a general term, was instantiated by a precious object, was a physical fact. That the precious object was money was a social fact. In time, money came to be non-precious objects that represented precious objects, such as paper that was backed up by gold or silver held in vaults in central banks. Eventually, money came to be pieces of paper and notations that are not backed up by any object of value and have no significant value in themselves.[36]

Searle's general formula for social construction is *X counts as Y in C*, where the following conditions obtain. First, X is some object; Y is some object, reason for action, or

246

symbol; *C* is a social context. Second, the term "counts as" means that *X* is assigned a new status or function in *C*, which it could not fulfill before, outside of *C*, as just *X*. This assignment constitutes and regulates *Y* at the same time. Third, and as an important correlative of the second condition, although *X* and *Y* may refer to the same object outside of *C*, which may be either a physical object or a social construction in C_{1-n}, sentences containing *X* cannot be substituted for sentences containing *Y* with preservation of the same truth value. Sentences containing *X* and *Y* are intensional with respect to substitutability. For example, if an electronic blip, E, counts as B, a $100 bill, in C, then the truth of a sentence about E may not be preserved if "B," the name for B, is substituted for "E," the name for E, in that sentence.[37]

We can view a racial designation in the Old or New Paradigm as an instantiation of *X*, and view some treatment based on that *X* as an instantiation of *Y*, where *C* is American society. Searle's formula, *X counts as Y in C* can thus be used to describe the American social realities of race. The advantage of applying Searle's analysis in this way is that we may describe social practices relating to racial difference, without speaking as though the subjects of racial designation are the same as what they count for in society. We thus have a simple way in which to separate race from how people behave on the basis of race. For example, under the Old Paradigm, "black" counts as "being a slave," "being subject to Jim Crow regulations," or "being prohibited from marrying a white person." Under the New Paradigm, what is presently described as institutionalized racism, becomes instances in which "black" counts as "being poor," "being unlikely to be hired or promoted to top management," or "being likely to have grown up in an inner-city ghetto." If "white" is an instantiation of *X*, it may count as "being respectable," "being a likely candidate for President," or "being likely to have grown up in an affluent suburb." Everything that can be understood to be a social result of prior biological racial designation, including derogatory stereotypes and liberatory identities, is an instantiation of some *Y* in *C*.

To repeat, we now have neutral language for drawing lines between facts about racial difference, and social constructions based on the facts, in any given context. The paradigmatic assumption up to now has been that there is some factual *X* about race, on the basis of which *X* can count as something else, as *Y*. Often, *Y* has been whatever else those with power and authority to regulate and constitute *Y* have decided. In the Old Paradigm, *X* was presumed to be instantiated by hereditary biology and culture, in the New Paradigm, by hereditary biology only.

There are empirical grounds for arguing that in the next, Last Paradigm of Race, there will be no physical fact believed capable of instantiating *X*. The grounds are the kinds of evidence which rational, empirically-minded, people, who currently adhere to the New Paradigm of Race, are otherwise likely to consider: there are no physical racial essences; there are no general genes for black, white, Asian, or any other race; there is greater physical variation within any race than between any two races; the genes for traits that have been designated as racial in American society do not automatically get inherited together but, like other physical traits, are subject to dispersal and recombination at conception. Furthermore, there is no evidence that mixed-race individuals have any physical or mental debilities, including reproductive difficulties, or that they are even an anomaly over the history of humankind. There is a pretense in the media that racial identity can be detected by DNA testing but in fact DNA differences correlate with racial differences only if race has already been picked out according to social criteria that include family relation.[38]

Searle's distinction between intrinsic and observer-relative facts about objects is relevant to the distinction between the existence of race in the Old and New Paradigms, and its non-existence according to realist criteria that have been applied to other entities by many people who have believed in the existence of race. Consider Searle's example of a stone paperweight. That the object is a stone is an intrinsic fact about it, but its being a paperweight is an observer-relative fact.[39] Observer-relative facts depend on common intentions in cultural contexts, and on complex systems of rules, actions, functions, and conscious, as well as potentially-conscious, beliefs. They are the stuff of both subjective and objective social reality, just as intrinsic facts are the stuff of objective, physical reality.[40] Applying Searle's distinction, we can say that for a long time a person being black, white, or Asian was believed to be an intrinsic fact about that person and that it is now clear that being black, white or Asian is an observer-relative fact. As an observer-relative fact, racial identification exists as a result of collective intentions or beliefs that are held in large part because it is believed that others hold them. If the majority of educated Americans came to believe that there are no physical facts capable of instantiating any racial X in the formula X counts as Y in C, the first core issue of the Last Paradigm of Race would be:

1_1. There is no evidence that there are distinct human races constituted by hereditary traits of any kind.

There are objections to the kind of naive realism or belief in objective external reality that seems to motivate taking the trouble to articulate 1_1. Searle's presumption is that ultimately, all of the X's that can count as Y's in C's can be instantiated by physical facts that exist independently of social reality. However, his own example of money in the contemporary world, falsifies the presumption. Insofar as all money is fiat money, with nothing of value backing it up, all of the referents of money are dependent on social reality. The electronic and numerical notations, paper money, and coin are physical things, but they are not as such objects of value that form a factual base for money, in any of its socially constructed forms. All of the different forms of money are no more than symbols of the very social constructions that rest on them.

Given the ultimate symbolic nature of money, combined with its ability to drive and do so much in contemporary society, someone today could claim that physical race is really nothing more than dark skin hues. Dark skin hues already function as symbols that ground all of the other social constructions of race.[41] Therefore, someone today may ask, "Why should it matter if people suddenly realize that what they thought was a general biological difference is merely a particular symbolic difference, as long as they believe that the symbol continues to have the same meaning in society that it has had thus far?"

This question overlooks an important distinction. It is true that people already do everything they do with money in conjunction with the belief that there are no precious objects backing it up. However, this is mainly due to common agreement that everyone benefits from having a functional monetary system. We do not know if people would continue to do everything they now do with race in conjunction with widespread belief that there is nothing to back it up. There is no common agreement that everyone benefits from the existence of a socially-constructed racial taxonomy. Therefore, the fact that there is nothing to instantiate a biological racial X, does matter.

Related to the objection to the social-construction analysis of race is a more general idealist skepticism about physical reality that should be addressed. Consider, borrowing from Berkeley, that our idea of a physical reality that exists independently of our idea of it, is no different from our idea of such a reality as existing only because we believe it does. The lack of an independent biological substratum for our idea of race does not mean that there is anything wrong with Old and New Paradigm ideas of race as something physical. Since all we have are our ideas, it does not matter if some ideas that we thought were accompanied by something else, never were. That something else, in this case, a biological substratum, was nothing but another idea, anyway.

The answer to this objection, oddly enough, comes from Berkeley himself.[42] Our world is organized by the relations among our ideas. In the Old and New Paradigms, it has been assumed that X counts as varied Y's in C because the general nature of X justifies the general Y constructions and provides detailed justifications in specific instances. If X is not biological in the ways believed, then the Y constructions are arbitrary and where they are harmful to the people who were previously believed to instantiate X, they should be changed.

Implications for Philosophers

The paradigmatic and socially-constructed nature of race has ethical and philosophical implications for future philosophical work on the topic. The ethics include matters of professional ethics.

Race has never been a traditional topic in Western philosophy. The idea of races as general biological categories, abstract general ideas in Berkeley's sense, is a relatively new idea in the West.[43] It begins in the eighteenth century at the earliest, and philosophy is an ancient discipline. Furthermore, the social and moral issues raised by racial difference and racism are not sufficiently abstract and universal to interest most philosophers. Therefore, Hume's offhand footnote and Kant's publications in anthropology and geography do not weigh heavily in evaluations by philosophers of their work as philosophers. But, a number of professional philosophers are beginning to write about race at this time and that is why the ethical points are relevant. Race has become a philosophical topic.

If we give race a fraction of the kind of systematic thought reserved for traditional philosophical topics, and begin to sort out some of the current disagreements in the literature with the standing tools of the trade, it is obvious that race is not a burdensome subject. It is not difficult to get the empirical and semantic facts about race right. Even if the full and final theory is elusive, plausible abstract clarity can be brought to the issues. If individuals who are not philosophers find the ontology of race conceptually confusing and emotionally distressing, this does not mean that philosophers, who for the most part do earn a professional reputation of detachment, need be confused and upset.

Philosophers who are concerned about the social reality of race ought to use the tools of their trade on it. For instance, philosophers who otherwise operate in the mainstream of the discipline might set the record straight given everything that the non-philosophical sciences have yielded about race since Hume and Kant wrote. There is little diffidence in the profession in criticizing Hume and Kant, or anyone else in the history of philosophy, about their ideas on topics other than race. Once it is understood that Hume and Kant were addressing race within a paradigm different from the contemporary one, it should be possible to systematically revisit their ideas on this subject, without blame or embarrassment. The way in which nineteenth-century racial investigations were completely taken over by scientists might also be a topic of some historical interest to philosophers. What were the conceptions of philosophy and science that accompanied this shift? Of course, to suggest that a subject might be of interest to philosophers is not the same thing as saying that any particular philosopher is obligated to pursue it.

Given the history of ideas about race and the present knowledge that race does not have the biological foundation that the lay public continues to think it does, philosophers addressing race at this time would seem to have a professional obligation to think through the implications for related topics of the biological non-existence of race. For instance, what are the implications for the content of liberatory public policy? What can we say about the psychological and moral aspects of racism in the absence of the biological foundation?

This situation resembles the position of a philosopher who lacks religious faith and has realized, here, with thanks to Hume, that there is no rational or empirical proof for the existence of God. Does such a philosopher leap into a religious dispute on the side of practitioners who have been persecuted for their religion, taking up their theology and vocabulary in the process? Or, should the philosopher try to explain to all contending religious groups that there is no rational basis for any of their theological claims? It would not be intellectually honest were the philosopher, for political reasons, to downplay the failure of proofs for the existence of God. The philosopher could remain aloof, but is it right to do this if religious tensions cause great social and individual harm? Perhaps the philosopher ought to reformulate secular principles of morality and human identity that will be acceptable to all religious practitioners.

At any rate, philosophers need to consider whether it is possible to construct a professional code about illusion. There could be a parallel in the code of medical doctors regarding disease – they are against it. Philosophers who are against illusion generally, and in favor of social justice in particular, could think about the content of The Last Paradigm of Race. Four issues will have to be resolved, ideationally and socially, before the Last Paradigm of Race can fully develop.

One issue concerns racial historical criticism. Working within the New Paradigm of Race, it is not difficult to find grounds to excoriate the ideas and behavior of people who thought and lived within the Old Paradigm. It can be plausibly argued that, at the least, otherwise liberatory white thinkers in the Enlightenment tradition were guilty of grave omissions. Charles Mills makes this point in a way impossible to answer with moral conviction:

Where is Grotius's magisterial *On Natural Law and the Wrongness of the Conquest of the Indies*, Locke's stirring Letter *Concerning the Treatment of the Indians*, Kant's moving *On the Personhood of Negroes*, Mill's famous condemnatory *Implications of Utilitarianism for English Colonialism*, Karl Marx and Frederick Engels's outraged *Political Economy of Slavery*?[44]

However, before the Enlightenment, the biological concept of race as an hereditary tax-onomic system did not exist. As recently as the seventeenth century, distinctions among human groups that divided Europeans from Africans and American Indians, were drawn on the basis of non-hereditary cultural practices such as the use of money and religious behavior.[45] To interpret such differences as racial differences, because they were drawn to the disadvantage of those who would be designated non-white within the Old and New Paradigms of race, is anachronistic. Furthermore, given the lack of a confirmed biological substratum for race, there is no reliable epistemological basis on which specific racial groups can be identified as subjects of pre-racial oppressive social constructions.[46] For that matter, the lack of a confirmed biological substratum, in prin-ciple casts doubt on the accuracy with which racial groups can be picked out within the periods of the Old and New Paradigms of race. As Appiah has explained in the context of non-white racial identity, if we base racial identification on culture or history, the net is too wide because members of different races may share the same history.[47] If we rely on biological distinctions, the best we can do is refer to individuals who have been picked out based on the distinctions falsely drawn in specific cultural contexts. Of course, that is all we need in order to address historical oppressions based on race, as long as we realize that we are talking about historical oppressions based on what race was falsely thought to be.

Another issue concerns non-white identity commitments. Some parts of some non-white racial identities presuppose the truth of the Old and New Paradigm core beliefs that there are biological races. Given the lack of evidence for biological race and the racisms that have been perpetrated using biological race as an excuse, care should be taken with liberatory identities so that they do not continue to reproduce false deter-ministic taxonomies of biological race. One way in which this can be done is through a reconfiguration of race as ethnicity, because ethnicity is known to be cultural. Another way is to reconstruct race as family heredity only, because human families do transmit biological traits and much of the false taxonomy of race has supervened on existent human genealogy. Still, to the extent that non-white liberatory identities are forms of resistance and protest, they have a rhetorical dimension that is based on fictive oppressive attributions. Those attributions have been social constructions that are in themselves real in specific contexts.

Still another issue concerns affirmative action. Much of white American discrimi-nation against non-whites has been based on Old Paradigm core beliefs about the hered-ity of cultural traits. The Civil Rights legislation of the 1960s, which is based on New Paradigm beliefs that racial difference does not necessarily involve cultural difference, is intended to oppose that kind of racial discrimination. However, there is a residue of the effects of past discrimination, as well as continued aversion based on perceived racial difference, which laws against discrimination are widely believed not to correct.

Affirmative action policies were initially formulated as correctives of such discrimi-natory effects and aversions. Whether or not present aversion and effects of past discrimination would subside if it came to be generally believed that there were no biological bases for race, is an empirical question. We do not know if affirmative action would still be considered necessary were such facts broadly known. Amy Gutman, and others, who defend affirmative action with the knowledge that race lacks a biological foundation, ignore the contingent effects of broad education about the biological facts.[48] The status of affirmative action in a Last Paradigm of Race is presently undetermined.

One more issue concerns mixed-race identity. Mixed-race identification and self-created mixed-race identities are problematic for both the Old and New Paradigms of Race. On the one hand, what Kant called hybridity is necessary to confirm that there are races in the first place. On the other hand, the recognition of mixed-race identity destabilizes racial taxonomy because it interferes with the ability to sort everyone into one or another of a recognizable group of races.[49] In fact, mixed-race individuals do not fulfill Kantian notions of hybridity by being in some ways biologically defective, or even odd. Since there is no confirmation for the biological existence of race itself, mixed-race has no biological basis. Nevertheless, anyone who persisted in some belief in the existence of races, would have to say on that basis that the vast majority of people has always been racially mixed.

The most vexing present problems with mixed-race appear to be political. There is concern among some African-Americans that if mixed-race Americans, especially those who are black and white, are recognized as such, it will dilute recent legal gains and entitlements that have been race-based according to traditional racial taxonomy. In this sense, mixed-race seems to work against broad goals of liberation. But, the growing population of mixed-race Americans, most of whom are the result of the 1967 Supreme Court legalization of interracial marriage, is the result of at least partial realization of the same broad liberatory goals.

Notes

This paper was presented as my presidential address to the American Society for Value Inquiry on 29 December, 1998, at the American Philosophical Association, Eastern Division meeting in Washington, D.C.

1   For more on this use of "paradigm" see Thomas S. Kuhn, *The Structure of Scientific Revolutions* (Chicago: University of Chicago Press, 1970).
2   For more on this use of "social construction" see John Searle, *The Construction of Social Reality* (New York: The Free Press, 1995).
3   See Naomi Zack, *Thinking About Race* (Belmont, Calif.: Wadsworth, 1998), pp. 108–9.
4   Raymond Geuss, *The Idea of a Critical Theory* (Cambridge, England: Cambridge University Press, 1981), pp. 22–5.
5   Kuhn, "Postcript," in *The Structure of Scientific Revolutions*, pp. 176–7.
6   Ibid. pp. 144–59.
7   Thomas Jefferson, "Manners" from *Notes on the State of Virginia*, ed., W. Peden, University of North Carolina Press, 1955, in Emmanuel Chukwudi Eze, *Race and the Enlightenment: A Reader* (Cambridge, Mass.: Blackwell Publishers, 1997), p. 97.

8   See Eze, *Race and the Enlightenment*; Ivan Hannaford, *Race: The History of an Idea in the West* (Baltimore: The Johns Hopkins University Press, 1996).

9   Richard H. Popkin, "Hume's Racism," *Philosophical Forum*, vol. 9, No. 2–3.

10 Ibid., pp. 212–13, 223–4.

11 George-Louis Leclerc, Comte de Buffon, *A Natural History, General and Particular*, vol. 1, trans. W. Smellie, 1860, in Eze, *Race and the Enlightenment*, pp. 23–4.

12 David Hume, "Of National Characters," in *Essays Moral and Political*, rev. ed 1748, in Eze, *Race and the Enlightenment*, p. 33.

13 Ibid.

14 James Beattie, *An Essay on the Nature and Immutability of Truth, in Opposition to Sophistry and Skepticism* (Philadelphia: Solomon Wieatt, 1809), in Eze, *Race and the Enlightenment*, pp. 34–7. See also Popkin, "Hume's Racism," pp. 219–21.

15 Beattie, *An Essay*, p. 37.

16 Immanuel Kant, "On the Different Races of Man," in *This is Race*, ed., E. W. Count (New York: Henry Schuman, 1950), in Eze, *Race and the Enlightenment*, pp. 38–9.

17 Ibid. p. 40

18 Ibid. p. 42.

19 Ibid.

20 Kant, *Observations on the Feeling of the Beautiful and Sublime*, trans. J. T. Goldthwait (Berkeley, Calif. University of California Press, 1960), in Eze, *Race and the Enlightenment*, pp. 49–58.

21 Ibid. p. 55.

22 Georges Léopold Cuvier, "Varieties of the Human Species," in *Animal Kingdom*, trans. H. McMurtie, New York, 1831, in Eze, *Race and the Enlightenment*, pp. 104–5.

23 G. W. F. Hegel, *Lectures on the Philosophy of World History*, trans. H. B. Nisbet (Cambridge, England: Cambridge University Press, 1975) section, "Africa" in *Geographical Basis of World History*, in Eze, *Race and the Enlightenment*.

24 See Stephen Jay Gould, *The Mismeasure of Man* (New York: W. W. Norton, 1981); Nancy Leys Stepan, *The Idea of Race in Science: Great Britain, 1800–1950* and "Race and Gender: The Role of Analogy in Science," in David Theo Goldberg, ed., *Anatomy of Racism* (Minneapolis, Minn.: University of Minnesota Press, 1990).

25 N. P. Dubinin, "Race and Contemporary Genetics," in Leo Kuper, ed., *Race, Science and Society* (New York: Columbia University Press, 1965).

26 See Naomi Zack, *Race and Mixed Race* (Philadelphia: Temple University Press, 1993), pp. 112–26.

27 See *Loving v. Virginia* in *United States Reports*, vol. 388, Cases Adjudged in The Supreme Court at October Term, 1966 (Washington, D.C.: United States Government Printing Office, 1968).

28 See Naomi Zack, *Thinking About Race*, pp. 5–6.

29 Jefferson, *Notes* in Eze, *Race and the Enlightenment*, p. 103.

30 *Loving v. Virginia*, pp. 1–13.

31 Franz Boas, *Anthropology and Modern Life* (New York: Norton, 1928); Claude Lévi-Strauss, "Race and History," Leo Kuper, ed., *Race, Science and Society*.

32 Ward Churchill, ed., *Marxism and Native Americans* (Boston: South End Press, 1993); Naomi Zack, "Lockean Money, Indigenism and Globalism," *Canadian Journal of Philosophy*, 1999 supplementary volume 25, *Civilization and Oppression*, pp. 31–53.

33 See Nathan Glazer, "Individual Rights against Group Rights," in Will Kimlicka, ed., *The Rights of Minority Cultures* (Oxford: Oxford University Press, 1995); and Michael Walzer, "Pluralism: A Political Perspective," in Kimlicka, *The Rights of Minority Cultures*.

34 Kwame Anthony Appiah, "Racisms" in Goldberg, *Anatomy of Racism*.

35   Searle, *The Construction of Social Reality*.

36   Ibid., pp. 48–58, 79–112.

37   Ibid., pp. 18–19.

38   See K. Anthony Appiah, " 'But Would That Still Be Me?': Notes on Gender, 'Race,' Ethnicity, as Sources of 'Identity,' " in Naomi Zack, ed., *RACE/SEX: Their Sameness, Difference and Interplay* (New York: Routledge, 1997); "Race, Culture, Identity: Misunderstood Connections," in K. Anthony Appiah and Amy Gutman, eds., *Color Conscious: The Political Morality of Race* (Princeton, N.J.: Princeton University Press, 1996); Naomi Zack, "Race and Philosophic Meaning," in Zack, ed., *RACE/SEX*.

39   Searle, *The Construction of Social Reality*, pp. 11–13.

40   Ibid., pp. 177–9.

41   See Kevin Thomas Miles, "Body Badges: Race and Sex" in Zack, ed., *RACE/SEX*.

42   George Berkeley, *A Treatise Concerning the Principles of Human Knowledge*, ed., Kenneth P. Winkler (Indianapolis, Ind.: Hackett, 1982) para. 105, p. 68.

43   Ibid. para. 9–14, pp. 9–15.

44   Charles W. Mills, *The Racial Contract* (Ithaca, N.Y.: Cornell University Press, 1997), p. 94.

45   See: Naomi Zack, *Bachelors of Science: Seventeenth Century Identity, Then and Now* (Philadelphia: Temple University Press, 1996) chs. 12 and 14; Hannaford, *Race*, pp. 147–84.

46   Naomi Zack, "The Racial Contract According to Charles Mills," forthcoming in the *Radical Philosophical Review*.

47   Kwame Anthony Appiah, "The Uncompleted Argument: Du Bois and the Illusion of Race," reprinted in Naomi Zack, Laurie Shrage and Crispin Sartwell, eds., *Race, Class, Gender and Sexuality: The Big Questions* (Malden, Mass.: Blackwell Publishers, 1998), pp. 28–47.

48   Amy Gutman, "Responding to Racial Injustice," in Appiah and Gutman, eds., *Color Conscious*, pp. 106–37.

49   See Zack, *Thinking about Race*, ch. 3, "Mixed Black and White Race and Public Policy," in Zack, Shrage and Sartwell, *Race, Class, Gender and Sexuality*, pp. 73–84.

15

Racial Classification and Public Policy

DAVID THEO GOLDBERG

Introduction

Modern social subjects have become more or less unself-conscious in establishing, if not quite in using, racial characteristics. They have come to take for granted the recognition of racial difference: they make racial claims, assert racial truths, assess racial value – in short, create (fabricate) racial knowledge. So much is this the case that it seems paradoxically to characterize as much those promoting commitment to colorblindness as it does racists and racial nationalists. Racial knowledge accordingly has become integral to articulating the common sense of modernity's self-understanding.

In the (re-)production of social consent that underpins racial common sense in societies with long racially inflected histories, formal and informal racial categorizing acts as social cement. It sets the terms, not to mention the limits, of public policy formation, licensing and delimiting forms of socially sanctioned thought and action. Possibilities thus become conceived along racially inflected lines, and this not simply by grouping and so casting people off or against one another. Racially inflected policy making, whether explicit or subtle, intentional or consequential, serves to reify existing divides. Curiously, though, it also enables resistance and counterformation to be waged by fashioning commonalities and commitments that otherwise likely wouldn't exist or be recognized (or recognizable), often with a view to promoting policy change. Mapping the social terrain in racial terms accordingly may be a tool, as it is often a product, of modern governmentality, a mode of agenda setting and outcome shaping. Nevertheless, it might also – though (given its genealogy) perhaps not quite as readily – be an instrument shaped by and for social movements in the drive for popular justice.

Knowledge production, and this is especially true for social knowledge and its in*form*ing of social policy, does not take place independent of social circumstance. The production of knowledge is sustained and restricted by political economy and culture – by its own and that of the society more generally. Productive practices act upon the epistemological categories invoked, shaping the knowledge thus produced, imparting assumptions, values, and goals. These categories that frame knowing, in turn, order their users' terms of articulation, fashioning content of the known and constraining what and how members of the social order at hand think and what they think about. So while power obviously orders the terms of knowing, the grounds of knowledge also offer "foundations" or frames for the constitution of social power (Habermas 1988, 272).

What I am calling "racial knowledge" is defined initially by two principal features. First, such knowledge assumes as its own the modes and premises of the established scientific fields, especially anthropology, natural history and biology, but also of sociology, politics, and economics. This scientific cloak imparts to racial knowledge seemingly formal character and universality, authority and legitimation. Racial knowledge acquires its apparent authority by parasitically mapping its modes of expression according to the formal authority of the scientific discipline it mirrors. It can do this – and this is its second constitutive feature – because it has been historically integral to the emergence and elaboration of these authoritative scientific fields, for instance, physical anthropology and eugenics. Race accordingly has been a basic categorical object, in some cases a founding focus, of scientific analysis. More recently though, and in keeping with the crisis in epistemological legitimation that has gone under the name of the "postmodern," racial knowledge and representation have assumed license less directly from such authoritative sources so much as from popular media, from the repeated public circulation of sometimes old or reinvented racially assertive claims precisely with the view to affecting public policy formation. So Charles Murray and Richard Herrnstein (1994) did not have to produce any new data to make claims, and through clever media management to promote an enormous public debate with obvious policy implications, about the long dismissed standard deviation between intelligence of whites and blacks in the United States. Tired old racial science is reinvigorated by captivating a public imagination all too quick to the racial draw.

Epistemologically, power is exercised in naming and evaluating. In naming or refusing to name, existence is recognized or refused, meaning and value are assigned or ignored, people and things are elevated or rendered invisible. Once defined, symbolic order has to be maintained, serviced, extended, operationalized. In this sense, racial others are nominated into existence. As Said makes clear (1978, 31–49), the Other is constituted through the invention of projected knowledge. The practices of naming and knowledge construction tend to deny meaningful autonomy to those so named and imagined, extending over them power, control, authority, and domination.

The U.S. Census has served to weave racial categorization into the social fabric, blending scientific strands with public policy threads. After all, the census is an exercise in social naming, in nominating into existence. The wiser governing powers appear about those they nominated as subject races, the less will their administrative rule require raw force. Racial governmentality thus requires information about supposed racial natures: about demography and economy, housing and education. Information thus has two meanings: detailed facts about racial nature, and the forming of racial character. The census has been a formative governmental technology in the service of the state to fashion "racial" knowledge – to articulate the categories, to gather data, and to put them to work. Individuals and interest groups, in the United States and elsewhere, have lobbied the state regarding the promotion or dismissal of some or other racial category, thereby mediating or delimiting the hegemonic imposition and diffusion of state categories. Here, the state agency serves, as Stuart Hall and his collaborators (1978, 57–62) put it, as "primary definers"; individual or interest group intervention serve at best as "secondary." Secondariness in the case of the census is best illustrated by the fact that, in the lead up to the 1980 U.S. Census, oversight hearings were scheduled, somewhat cynically, months *after* Congress had signed off on the categories presented to them by the director of the U.S. Census Bureau.

The U.S. Census serves, and was initially designed to serve, state interests, functioning to furnish information crucial to state revenue collection, and to distributional and voting purposes. But the census has also always had an ideological mandate; namely, to articulate, if not to create, a national profile, a mapping and a mediation of the nation's demographic contours. I examine here the practical intersection of social science, state-directed social policy, and racialized discourse by focusing on the ways that U.S. Census counts throughout their history have helped to fashion and fix the racializing of the US body politic. The census has worked thus to draw racial lines around and within the society, reifying as it reflects prevailing racial common sense, channeling social policy in certain directions.

Taking the National Stock

A national census, by all accounts, is a stocktaking of the country's human assets, of the state's population capital. The census maps the geographical contours of population distribution, fashioning a social understanding strongly predicated on historical records. So, ironically, a census is always too late, tied as it gives new life to past reports of social division and diffusion, presupposing categories crafted from the material of past records (Cohn 1987, 231–2).

In the United States, the national census is as old as the republic itself, mandated decennially by the Constitution. Beyond its crucial administrative mandates with respect to tax collection and voting apportionment, the census has functioned also to secure recognition and material benefits for groups otherwise ignored. Ideologically, the census is a kind of "collective self-portrait" that serves to invent and renew – to reimagine – the national identity (Starr 1987, 19). The U.S. Census has always ordered this national image in racial terms, both in its imagined (pre-)formation and in its statistical (re-)creation, racial antinomies are produced and defined by the census, as it reflects and refines the racially patterned social formation.

Arjun Appadurai (1993, 799–800) suggests that census classification in a wide variety of modern societies, marching to their own technological requirements, has been influential in producing or reproducing fractured, fearful, and fixed social identities, which would be otherwise fluid and negotiable. The fabrication of panethnicities – Hispanic, Asian American, indeed, white and black – are cases in point. The snapshot of the national profile freezes momentarily into givens, thereby objectifying, the racializing categories it at once assumes and fashions. This body count, authorized by state mandate and its legal instrumentality, thus offers racial categories the mark of respectability. It thus enables these indices of otherness, apartness, and fracture to extend over, to seep silently into, the social concepts and categories of the nation which are not so straightforwardly racial, especially those of class, with more or less direct policy implication. A national census profiles the laboring classes, mapping their regional and locational availability, their racial un/suitability, providing a snapshot of capital's labor needs.

The administrative mandate of the U.S. Census was racially concerned (just as it was engendered) from its inception. In 1787, the Constitution required the census to distinguish between "free white males," "free white females," "all other free persons" (by sex and color), "untaxed Indians," and "slaves." "The slave," presumed silently to be black, was defined as three-fifths a person for the purposes of resource allocation. Given that the constitution opens by declaring all "men" equal, this implies, if it did not assume, that slaves – black slaves, to emphasize the point – were assumed not to be "men," that is, not fully human. Stephen Steinberg (1989) points out that by 1790, slaves still included some Indians and whites, but their numbers were overwhelmingly black. Indeed, it is hard to think how the three-fifths clause could have been entertained, let alone sustained, if not premised upon black dehumanization (Lively 1992, 1–39).

It may help to group the racial categories employed in the two hundred years of census taking in America into five periods. The first period runs from 1790 to 1840 during which the initial categories are baldly fashioned, framing the premises for all future conceptualization. The period offers no instructions as to the categories' definition or scope. The second period runs from 1850 to 1880, during which precise categories were streamlined as a reflection and in the expressed service of (racial) science. The third period spans from 1890 to 1920, during which categories covered for the first time all of settled America (Lee 1993, 76) and responded to the significant thrusts of (im)migration. The fourth period covers 1930 to 1970, during which racial distinction in the United States began to proliferate against (or in spite of) the assimilationist grain. The fifth period includes the U.S. Census counts of 1980 and 1990, significant for transforming the presumptive basis of category formation from "objectively" given constructs to "self-identifying" ones.

The accompanying charts offer an overview of the categories in order and sequence of appearance, employed throughout the history of the U.S. Census. (For 1800, 1810, and 1820, I rely largely on the categories formulated by Massachusetts, the state that seems to have been most coherent in its administration). In what follows I offer simply some interpretive reflections upon this history of classification (for a fuller account, see Goldberg 1997, 27–58).

Instructions to census takers were initiated in 1820, though instructions regarding race first appeared for the 1850 census. Lacking explicit definitions of the racial categories, the census relied in its first half century on establishing the racial body count upon the "*common* sense" judgments, the (pre-)supposed views, of its all-white enumerators. Persons were racially named, the body politic measured, and resources distributed based on prevailing racial presumptions and mandated fractional assessments. The society was literally marked in black and white.

By 1840, as more black people gained freedom and the operation of the census had begun to assume centralized and national proportions, the census was invoked ideologically to shore up the institution of enslavement. Thus, as William Petersen notes (1987, 230, n. 90), the 1840 U.S. Census "measured" insanity and idiocy, claiming to show the percentage of blacks suffering both conditions to be greater in the North than in the South. These "facts" were then used to license the argument that though blacks were at ease with slavery, they were clearly incapable of adjusting to freedom. The argument and the data supposedly supporting it were vigorously challenged by Edward Jarvis, a Massachusetts physician supported by the Massachusetts Medical Society and

258

Table 15.1 Census categories from 1790 to 1990 (compiled with the assistance of Barbara Lammi)

1790	1800	1810	1820	1830	1840	1850	1860	1870	1880	1890
Free White Males & Females	Free White Males & Females	Free White Males & Females	Free White Males & Females	Free White Persons	Free White Persons	White	White	White	White	White
All Others Free Persons, Except Indians Not Taxed	All Other Free Persons, Except Indians Not Taxed	All Other Free Persons, Except Indians Not Taxed	All Other Persons, Except Indians Not Taxed							
Slaves	Slaves	Slaves		Slaves	Slaves					
			Free Colored Persons	Free Colored Persons Gender Age	Free Colored Persons					
						Black (B) Mulatto (M)	Black Mulatto	Black Mulatto	Black Mulatto	Black/Negro Mulatto Quadroon Octoroon
								Chinese		Chinese Japanese
								Indian		Indian

1900	1910	1920	1930	1940	1950	1960	1970	1980	1990
White	White	White	White	White	White	White	White	White	White
Black (Negro or Negro Descent)	Black Mulatto	Black Mulatto	Negro	Negro	Negro	Negro	Negro or Black	Black (or Negro)	Black or Negro
Chinese Japanese	Chinese Japanese	Chinese Japanese	Mexican Chinese Japanese Filipino Hindu Korean	Chinese Japanese Filipino Hindu Korean	Chinese Japanese Filipino	Chinese Japanese Filipino	Chinese Japanese Filipino Korean	Chinese Japanese Filipino Korean Vietnamese Asian Indian Guamanian Samoan Hawaiian	Chinese Japanese Filipino Korean Vietnamese Asian Indian Guamanian Samoan Hawaiian
						Hawaiian Pan Hawaiian	Hawaiian		
Indian	Indian	Indian	Indian	Indian	American Indian	American Indian Aleut Eskimo	Indian (Amer.)	Indian (Amer.) Aleut Eskimo	Indian (Amer.) Aleut Eskimo
	Other	Other	Other Races	Other Races	Other Race	Etc. (Inc. Asian Indians)	Other (Specify Race)	Other	Other Race Other API (Asian Pacific Islander)

the American Statistical Association, who demanded that the many miscalculations be formally corrected. Instead, John Calhoun, then Secretary of State and so in charge of the census, censored the critique and persisted in invoking the figures in support of slavery. A separate study conducted by Dr. James McCune Smith for a convention of free black Northerners found that eight towns in Maine where thirty insane black people were claimed to be institutionalized had no black residents at all. Moreover, Aptheker (1974) reveals that where the census had reported 133 black patients in the mental institution of Worcester, Massachusetts, they were all white, consistent with the nineteenth-century tendency to identify idiocy and blackness.

From 1850 on, increasingly fine distinctions began to appear for those considered "nonwhite," and the growing complexity of these distinctions seemed to require issuance for enumerators of instruction schedules concerning the racial categories. Thus, in 1850, under the leadership of U.S. Census Superintendent, J. D. B. De Bow (for whom "the negro was created essentially to be a slave"), enumerators were asked to mark the color of "Free inhabitants." Slaves were to be counted separately, and their color indicated also.

These categories informed a significant Californian case, *People v. Hall*, in 1854. In 1850, the Californian legislature had passed (in an act regulating California criminal proceedings) a clause prohibiting the court testimony of a black, mulatto, or American Indian person directed against a white defendant. Hall, a white man, had been convicted of murder because of witness testimony by a Chinese man. Hall appealed his conviction on the basis that the Chinese belonged with American Indians to a common Mongoloid race, and so the testimony of the Chinese witness was inadmissible. Appealing to the Bering Straits theory of American Indian migration and invoking the most vituperative antiblack rhetoric, the California Supreme Court upheld Hall's appeal and vacated his conviction (Renoso 1992, 833). The heart (not to mention the mind) of whiteness, it seems, is naturally set apart from the heart and mind of an alien(ated) and singular "nonwhiteness."

In 1870, further distinctions were introduced into the census: "Chinese" (largely because of the importation of coolie labor in the West) and "Indian" (marking the policy shift to removing American Indians to reservations). The new instructions cautioned enumerators to take special care in reporting "Mulatto (including quadroons, octoroons, and all persons having any perceptible trace of African blood)." The reason? "Important scientific results depend upon the correct determination of this class." The instructions for the 1890 count reflected not only the rapid diversification of the US population, but the intensifying administrative concern (in the face of this expanding diversity) with racial distinction, hierarchy, and imposed division. Thus, while the categories for "white," "Chinese," and "Indian" remained unchanged, explicit and superficial distinctions were introduced between "black," "mulatto," "quadroon," and "octoroon." "Black" was to refer to any person with "three-fourths or more black blood"; "mulatto" referred to those having "from three-eighths to five-eighths black blood"; "quadroon" to those persons having "one-fourth black blood"; and "octoroon" to those "having one-eighth or any trace of black blood."

In 1990, these distinctions began to collapse in the wake of the widespread social belief that "black" was any person "with a single drop of black blood" (Davis 1991, 5). So "black" was indicated on the instructions as "a negro or of negro descent." The 1924

National Origins Act, strongly promoted by the eugenics movement in the United States and sponsored by Senator Albert Johnson, president at the time of the Eugenics Research Association at Cold Spring Harbor, Long Island, cut immigration from those countries already represented in the US to 2 percent of their numbers already residing in the US, as determined by the 1890 U.S. Census. Difficulties soon arose in determining the figures on national origins, so that by 1929 a flat cap of 150,000 immigrants per annum was introduced, 71 percent of whom were to be from Britain, Germany, and the rest of Europe generally. Japanese immigration was restricted completely (Gossett 1965, 406–7).

By 1930, the prevailing institutional mandates of racial segregation and immigration restriction had prompted seemingly precise specifications for reporting race. Enumerators were required to enter as "Negro" any person of "mixed white and Negro blood" irrespective of how small "the percentage of Negro blood." Moreover, a person "part Indian" and "part Negro" was to be listed as "Negro unless the Indian blood predominated and the person is generally accepted as Indian in the community." Similarly, someone of "mixed white and Indian blood" was to be counted as "Indian, except where the percentage of Indian blood" was deemed very small or the person was generally considered white in the community. In general, any "racially mixed person" with white parentage was to be designated according to the race of the parent who was not white; by contrast, "mixtures of colored races" were to be racially designated from the father's race, "except Negro-Indian." For the first time, also, "Mexican" was introduced as a separate *racial* category, and defined as "all persons born in Mexico, or having parents born in Mexico, and who are definitely not white, Negro, Indian, Chinese, or Japanese." In the next count, however, partly in response to objections by both the Mexican government and the U.S. State Department, "Mexicans" were to be listed as "white" unless they were "definitely Indian or some race other than white." While the concern by 1940 with racial purity may have been waning in the wake of Aryanism, the concern with the growing ethno-coloring of America, and not the least with policing access to the privileges of whiteness, seemed to demand a way of keeping whites separate and distinct.

This trend toward introducing ethnoracial categories while looking for ways to maintain a majority of whiteness continued unabated through the 1970 census. Accordingly, in 1950 the category of "Filipino" was introduced under the section on "Race," white American Indians were listed according to "degree of Indian blood: full blood; half to full; quarter to half; less than one quarter." This calculus was presumably tied to the New Deal undertaking to reestablish tribal administrative authority. Blood counts would provide the insidious technology for determining the range of bureaucratic control: the "purer" the "blood" the less assimilable and so the more they were to suffer governmental imposition. To illustrate just how far the concern with the racially conceived body count was carried, enumerators were warned, in an implicit nod to the intersection of race, class, and gender distinction, that "knowledge of the housewife's race tells nothing of the maid's race."

These transformations in race designation were carried forward into the 1980 U.S. Census in a way that altogether undermines any cross-census comparisons. Most important, the census introduced the standard of racial *self*-identification that had begun in the early 1970s to be assumed in almost all fifty states. For census purposes, however, the injunction to declare oneself racially as one chooses was circumscribed. Respondents were still required to choose from *given* designations, a mix of traditionally racial, ethnic, and national categories.

Whatever happened to the right of self-identification to *refuse* to identify oneself racially? The denial of such a right implies (if it does not presuppose) that race is a primary, indeed, a primal category of human classification, one so natural to the human condition that it can be ignored only on pain of self-denial. Underlying the imperative of racial self-identification is the presumption of naturalism: one is expected to identify oneself as what one "naturally" is (Goldberg 1993b). The democracy of self-naming is undermined by the authoritarianism of imposed identity and identification. Those resisting literally become the new "Others," identified in (and by) their self-subscribed lack of identities.

This apparent paradox of racial self-naming highlights the tensions faced by any nation committed to a racial numeration. The technology of counting can impose categories of identification or it can allow completely open self-identifying response. The former will furnish a set of consistent categories and a statistically manipulable data base. The latter won't. Nevertheless, at best, the former will seriously undercount; at worst, it will have little objective reference to the nuances of people's felt identities. For example, on the basis of national origin and native language reports in the 1930 census, there were an estimated 200,000 Spanish speakers in New Mexico (roughly half that state's population). But the census count in 1930 listed only 61,960 for the category "Mexican" (Petersen 1980, 223). For the overwhelming majority, the category did not apply. Unfortunately, unrestricted self-identifying response will be statistically useless, for there is unlikely to be any categorical uniformity. Social identities, in other words, belie simplicity, and bureaucratic-statistical requirements (elevated by managed multiculturalisms) simply serve to enforce the racializing imperative of the census.

These elastic racial, ethnic, and national characteristics mean, as the U.S. Bureau of Census (1990, 2) readily admits, that "Data on race and Hispanic origin . . . are not totally comparable between censuses." The bureau's publication (1990, 3, n. 2) attributes this difficulty in crosscensus comparisons not only to "changes in the census questionnaire and the way persons report race and ethnic origin," but also to "improvements in census procedures." Thus, we are faced by a strange paradox: as census procedures improve, the transhistorical comparisons – the very mandate of the census undertaking – become increasingly unreliable.

The shifting politics of (self-)identification prompted and reified by the history of the census raise deep difficulties for any social science relying unproblematically on cross-census population group comparisons from census reports on "Race and Hispanic Origin." The mix of legal and bureaucratic technologies reduces the nuance of experienced identity to the certitude of categorical identity. For instance, Teja Arboleda's maternal grandparents are European, his father's mother African-American, and his father's father Filipino/Chinese. He is listed as white on his birth certificate. In responding to the 1990 Census, he refused to complete the ethnic/racial section. On the basis of his name, skin, and hair color an enumerator marked him "Hispanic" (see *The New York Times*, July 8, 1994, A18). So much for the (pre)supposed correlation between race and IQ driving the agenda of *The Bell Curve*. The underlying question is why we are concerned at all with counting by race.

263

Counting by Race

This line of analysis demonstrates that one should be deeply wary of drawing any intra-census implications based on racial categories. The racial politics of numbers and the numerical politics of racial naming and placing must be comprehended in the context of their primary legislative mandate. The initial mission of the census in US history was to manage effective resource distribution and voting access. These economic and political mandates in the United States have always been racially conceived, and the apparent contemporary democratizing of census self-identification serves only to hide from view newly framed racial tensions that remain as managed with respect to initiating the reconceived missions as they always were. Thus the census now serves also to map the contours of ethnoracialized labor supply as well as to furnish corporate America with cost free market research. The censal managing of these matters is revealed, for instance, by the fact that "Hispanics" may catch up with "Blacks" in their percentage of the US population early in the twenty-first century and may pass them within the first decade of the next century. But this "fact" is as much a fabrication of racial designation as it is of demographic growth. "Hispanic" was crafted in the 1970s as a nonracial, panethnic term to cut across racial designations, yet in its generality it has served, and serves, as a new ethnoracial category.

Racially inflecting the body count in this way has (had) significant implications for voting rights. The voting rights of blacks are now guaranteed (in more or less complex ways) by the Fifteenth Amendment (1871), and by the 1965 Voting Rights Act and its 1982 amendment. One of the ways to dilute blacks' voting rights, perhaps one of the only permissible alternatives now, is to set them against "other" statistically dominant but discretely maintained "minorities," minorities whose racial configurations are precisely ambiguous. Blacks are marked hegemonically as politically and socially liberal (and in the 1980s liberal came to be case as literally un-American); whereas those configured as "Hispanic" (and perhaps also Asian American) are often cast as socially (and perhaps economically) conservative. Using exactly what I have questioned here, namely, racial categories, 78 percent of black voters support the Democratic Party compared to 54 percent of Hispanic voters, and only 34 percent of white voters. In the equally fabricated tensions between liberals and conservatives that characterize US politics, the drive to bring those referenced as "Hispanic" under the "right" wing is under way (just as the New Deal and Great Society Democrats sought to capture the black vote). A social statistics that purports to report the truth underpins the new racial dynamics. This new dynamic may be fueled, paradoxically, by the very instrument designed to democratize the social body count, namely, racial self-identification.

The parameters of formalized self-definition have never been open-ended in the US, for the state has always furnished the range of available, credible, and reliable – that is, of licensed and so permissible – censal categories in terms of which self-definition could occur. Simultaneously, in the 1970s, the overwhelmingly white-faced image of the United States was becoming dramatically shaded. There is a sense, then, in which the nominal politics of panethnicizing – "Hispanic," "Asian American" – is serving to soften, if not to undermine, this racial transformation. In census terms, "Hispanic" is only ambiguously a racial category, placed alongside, as an additive to, "Race." It is thus, at once, racialized and deracialized. "Hispanics" may now be white or black, where they once were certainly deemed "nonwhite" (George Bush, Sr., in a televized family profile before the 1988 election, referred to his grandson, whose mother is Mexican, as "the little brown one"). In the past, the boundaries of blood counts were quite rigidly policed, evaded by some through "passing," though only at considerable psychological cost. Now this restriction has given way to a licensed and encouraged passing via redefinition; that is, a restructured white identity at once referencing as it passes over racial distinction. This restructured racial identity reflects material interests. Examples include the intersection of race and class interests around "Mexicans" in the debate leading up to the Congressional vote on NAFTA, reading Mexican businessmen as white and the Mexican poor as not, and the ongoing debate concerning extension of health care to "illegal aliens." The census promotion of "Hispanic" while censoring categories like "Chicano" or "Latino" reorders the structure of whiteness as it strictures the boundaries of blackness.

We find in the example of the census, then, a technology which has racially ordered the social fabric and reflected the distinctions alive in the general culture. This bureaucratic document, distributed decennially throughout the population with a strong request for response, provides to the cultural categories it disseminates the imprimatur of official approval. Via the limits that census forms place upon self-identification and self-understanding (the categories are given, their order of appearance set – never alphabetical but with white always first, the categorical exclusions significant in their absence – Jews, for instance, are never counted) (see Yanow 1993; Lee 1993), the census serves also to endorse, reify, and normalize the categories available in the general culture. The census count, thus, naturalizes this national profile, authorizing the prevailing language of imposed identity and identification, licensing it in the name of the law and the state – from the constraints of which there is little or no escape.

Consider, for instance, a recent racial discrimination appeal to the Sixth District Court of Appeal. Dale Sandhu had been ruled ineligible by a Superior Court judge to bring a claim against Lockheed, his former employer, stating that his layoff had been prompted by racially discriminatory animus. Lockheed argued that, as someone of East Indian origin, Sandhu was considered "Caucasian" by the law, and so his argument failed to have standing under the California Fair Employment and Housing Act. But, appealing to the appearance in the 1980 census of the category "Asian Indian," the Appeals Court ruled that Sandhu was "subject to a discriminatory animus based on his membership in a group which is perceived as distinct" (see *American Lawyer Media, L.P., The Recorder*, July 7, 1994, p. 4, which ironically reported the case under the byline, "Court Allows *Caucasian's* Bias Suit" (my emphasis)). The appeal succeeded only in view of the censal endorsement – the classificatory standing – of the category "Asian Indian" in the 1980 census. This case reveals the possibility of turning categories against their history of formation, for "Asian Indian" in the 1980 census is a legacy of the more sinister because exclusionary inclusion of "Hindoo" as a separate racial category in the census counts of 1930 and 1940. Similarly, recent jury discrimination suits have turned on demonstrating a significant disparity between the racial composition of a jury pool, or jury and alternates, of jury foreperson, and the racial composition of the jurisdiction in which the jury trial is located as measured by the most recent census tract count (Hiroshi Fukurai, Edgar Butler, and Richard Krooth 1993), and yet the

265

crosscensal complexities, gaps and silences make for some awkward interpretations and decisions. So Fukurai, Butler, and Krooth, for example, commit the error of unproblematically reading the category "Hispanic" back into the pre-1970s historical record. Thus, they interpret *Hernandez v. Texas* (347 U.S. 475 1954) as the first recognition by the Supreme Court of the need for protection by Hispanics from jury discrimination. The *Hernandez* Court, in fact, recognized the claims of *Mexican*-Americans.

This, then, becomes the dilemma: We (the People) hold out the ideal of colorblindness in the Constitution, Bill of Rights and Amendments, and in the Civil Rights Acts. No sooner is this done than these founding laws are racially inflected. To institute the ideal racialized categories have to be invoked to rectify past injustice and present legacy. Two implications immediately follow. The ideal becomes racially conceived; that is, tied to its history, de-idealized, necessarily unrealized. Yet, at once, given the historicity of racial categories – given their own formative conditions – the terms of racial fabrication themselves change, marking social formation anew. The census, I have argued, plays a central role in this process. Political technologies like the census accordingly render "race" natural, making it appear that race naturally characterizes social formation. This naturalism freezes the prevailing terms of social relations into natural givens, seemingly inevitable and unchangeable.

To demonstrate, as I have, that racial terms are transformable does not alone undo the marking of social formation by race, for the new terms may serve simply to re-mark social relations, thereby recoding social exclusion and exploitation. As this recoding renews racially ordered social structure and relations, it ties present racial formation in a superficially apparent similitude to the past by hiding from view its transformed signification – its codes, meanings, and significance. Race today seems just like race last century, or last decade. The U.S. Census Bureau now recognizes that races are not the same, indeed, they warn us not to make crosscensus racial comparisons. Confusion may be the death knell of counting by race.

I want to suggest that insofar as the paradox of racial counting is of the imagined making of those in a society thus racially ordered, it is within the collective horizon of those in such a social formation also to undo or to reorder. To this end, I want with the view to public policy to identify some reasons why in the race to count we in the United States cannot (and should not) count by race.

First, race codes past *and* present discrimination, offering a rough and ready indication of opportunities that were (un)available at different moments in time. It serves as a "measure" therefore of the sorts of odds against or under which middle-class black persons, say, attained or retained their middle-class status; or of the degree to which poorer blacks have been denied socioeconomic mobility, or the degree to which just trials by jury are denied those in this country not white, male, or wealthy. Counting by class doesn't quite do, for in a social order so deeply marked by racist exclusion, not only does it undercount the racially marginalized, but it benefits the whitened marginalized at the expense of the black. In any case, if we want to determine whether there has been any improvement among those discriminated against because of racial membership, we need to count the poor by race (however problematically defined), and race by wealth. Second, it follows that if the society collectively is committed to some other form of compensatory justice, and of programs that facilitate compensation, reference groups are imperative. Given that much discriminatory exclusion has been effected in terms of racial definition, a racial count referenced to the sorts of groups racially excluded in the past becomes crucial. Third, it is necessary – again, paradoxically – to count by race in order to undo racial counting.

This latter suggestion prompts a twofold strategy. Looking back to relieve the past, racially defined injustices, and their consequent inequities, the injunction is to count by race – primarily, that is, in terms of "blacks" and "whites," but also in terms of "American Indians." Latter-day "Hispanics," "Asians," and "Pacific Islanders" whose racial experience in or at the hands of this country qualifies them for compensatory justice will count on this mandate as not-white; historically, that is, as "black." This suggestion is meant to apply only for administrative technologies of counting; I do not mean to undermine the importance of multicultural histories like those that have long been narrated though only recently publicly celebrated, or to flatten the various discriminatory experiences of different groups. In any case, this form of "racial lumping" (Winant 1994) – a different kind of panethnicizing – has the virtue of destigmatizing blackness through the promotion of coalitions. If race is a social construction, perhaps one form of resistance is creative reconstruction. Looking forward, by contrast, and enjoined by a rough motivational mix of color-blindness and democratic self-definition, the implication is to encourage open-ended (I am prompted to add open-faced) self-identification. The undertaking here is to undermine the social control of racial naturalism. Promoting open-ended self-identification takes us beyond the insistence on reified racial categories required by managed multiculturalism and the bureaucratization of diversity. From the point of view of bureaucratic manipulation and control, counting by properly open-ended self-identification is statistically useless. But that, precisely, is its virtue.

So race is to be counted only where it signals class exploitation and exclusion – past, present, and predictably future. Where race indicates a class that is socially, politically, and economically marginalized, there is a need – if justice is to be served – to identify members, not to ensure their social distance but to promote programs to facilitate their self-defined (that is, autonomous) self-development. In that sense, taking stock is not a matter simply of making a body count but of making the numbers count, defining where we have been, where we are coming from and now are, and where, dialogically conceived and policy wise, we see ourselves headed.

References

Acosta-Belen, Edna and Barbara R. Sjostrom, eds. (1988) *The Hispanic Experience in the United States: Contemporary Issues and Perspectives.* New York: Praeger.

Aptheker, Herbert (1974) *A Documentary History of the Negro People*, 3 vols. New York: Citadel Press.

Arjun Appadurai (1993) "The Heart of Whiteness," *Callaloo* 16, 4, 799–800.

Balibar, Etienne (1991) "*Es Gibt Keinen Staat in Europa*: Racism and Politics in Europe Today," *New Left Review* 187 (May–June) 5–19.

Chavez, Linda (1991) *Out of the Barrio.* New York: The Free Press.

Cohn S. Bernard (1987) *An Anthropologist among the Historians and Other Essays.* Oxford: Oxford University Press.

Conk, Margo A. (1987) "The 1980 Census in Historical Perspective." In William Alonso and Paul Starr (eds.), *The Politics of Numbers.* New York: Russell Sage Foundation.

Davis, Cary, Carl Haub, and JoAnne L. Willette (1988) "U.S. Hispanics: Changing the Face of America," in Acosta-Belen and Sjostrom (1988).

Davis, James (1991) *Who is Black? One Nation's Definition*. University Park, PA: Pennsylvania University Press.

D'Souza, Dinesh (1995) *The End of Racism*. New York: The Free Press.

Fukurai, Hiroshi, Edgar Butler, and Richard Krooth (1993) *Race and the Jury: Racial Disenfranchisement and the Search for Justice*. New York: Plenum.

Goldberg, David Theo (1993a) *Racist Culture: Philosophy and the Politics of Meaning*. Oxford: Basil Blackwell.

Goldberg, David Theo (1993b) "The Semantics of Race," *Ethnic and Racial Studies* 15, 4 (October) 543–69.

Goldberg, David Theo (1997) *Racial Subjects: Writing on Race in America*. New York: Routledge.

Gossett, Thomas (1965) *Race: The History of an Idea in America*. New York: Schocken Books.

Gotanda, Neil (1995) "A Critique of 'Our Constitution is Colorblind'," in K. Cosenshaw et al. (eds.) (1995) *Critical Race Theory: The Key Writings that Formed the Movement*. New York: The New Press, 257–75.

Habermas, Jürgen (1988) *Philosophical Discourse on Modernity*. Cambridge, MA: MIT Press.

Hacker, Andrew (1991) *Two Nations: Black and White, Separate, Hostile, and Unequal*. New York: Scribner's.

Hall, Stuart, Chas Critcher, Tony Jefferson, John Clarke, and Brian Roberts (1978) *Policing the Crisis: Mugging, the State, and Law and Order*. London: Holmes and Meier.

Hero, Rodney E. (1992) *Latinos and the U.S. Political System: Two-tiered Pluralism*. Philadelphia: Temple University Press.

Kilson, Martin (1993) "Anatomy of Black Conservatives," *Transition* (59) 4–19.

Lee, Sharon M. (1993) "Racial Classifications in the US Census: 1890–1990," *Ethnic and Racial Studies* 16, 1 (January) 75–94.

Lively, Donald (1992) *The Constitution and Race*. New York: Praeger.

Marin, Gerardo and Barbara VanOss Marin (1991) *Research with Hispanic Populations*. Newbury Park: Sage, 1991.

Murray, Charles and Richard Herrnstein (1994) *The Bell Curve*. New York: The Free Press.

Peterson, William (1980) "Politics and the Measurement of Ethnicity." In William Alonso and Paul Starr, eds., *The Politics of Numbers*. New York: Ressell Sage Foundation.

Renoso, Cruz (1992) "Ethnic Diversity: Its Historical and Constitutional Roots," *Villanova Law Review* 37.

Smith II, George P. (1988) *The New Biology: Law, Ethics, and Biotechnology*. New York: Plenum.

Said, Edward (1978) *Orientalism*. New York: Vintage Books.

Starr, Paul (1987) "The Sociology of Official Statistics." In W. Alonso and Paul Starr, *The Politics of Numbers* (1987). New York: Russell Sage, 7–58.

Steinberg, Stephen (1989) *The Ethnic Myth*. Boston: Beacon Press.

Stepan, Nancy Leys *"The Hour of Eugenics": Race, Gender, and Nation in Latin America*. Ithaca: Cornell University Press.

U.S. Bureau of the Census (1990) Census Profile #2 (1991).

U.S., Department of Commerce (1989) *200 Years of U.S. Census Taking: Population and Housing Question, 1790–1990* (November).

Wilson, William Julius *The Truly Disadvantaged* (1989) Chicago: University of Chicago Press.

Winant, Howard (1994) *Racial Conditions*. Minneapolis: University of Minnesota Press.

Yanow, Dvora (1993) "Administrative Implications of American Ethnogenesis." Paper presented to the Public Administration Section, American Political Science Association Annual Meeting, Washington DC. Sept 1–5. Paper on file with author.

16

White Supremacy

CHARLES W. MILLS

Conceptualization and Scope of White Supremacy

"White supremacy" is the term that has traditionally been used to denote the domination of whites over non-whites. In mainstream social theory, it is usually restricted to *formal* juridico-political domination, as paradigmatically exemplified by slavery, Jim Crow and black disenfranchisement in the United States, and by apartheid in South Africa (Fredrickson, 1981; Cell, 1982). Since official segregation and political exclusion of this sort no longer exist in the United States, the term has now disappeared from mainstream white American discourse, except to refer to the unhappy past or, in the purely ideological sense, to the beliefs of radical white separatist groups (e.g., the Ku Klux Klan, Aryan Nations).

However, the term has recently been revived by those theorists in critical race theory and critical white studies (Crenshaw et al., 1995; Delgado, 1995; Delgado and Stefancic, 1997) who would claim that American white supremacy has not vanished, but only changed from a *de jure* to *de facto* form. Typically, these writers argue that the merely formal rejection of white supremacist principles will not suffice to transform the United States into a genuinely racially egalitarian society, since the actual social values and enduring politico-economic structures will continue to reflect the history of white domination. Given this analysis, a conception of white supremacy that encompasses the non-juridical as well as the juridical is the more useful one. Frances Lee Ansley suggests the following: "a political, economic, and cultural system in which whites overwhelmingly control power and material resources, conscious and unconscious ideas of white superiority and entitlement are widespread, and relations of white dominance and non-white subordination are daily reenacted across a broad array of institutions and social settings" (Ansley, 1989). Though white–black racial domination has obviously been central to this system, a comprehensive perspective on American white supremacy would really require attention to, and a comparative analysis of, white relations with other peoples of color also: Native Americans, Mexican Americans, and Asian Americans (Takaki, 1990; Okihiro, 1994; Almaguer, 1994; Foley, 1997).

In this more latitudinarian supra-juridical sense, white supremacy could be said to characterize not merely the United States but the Americas as a whole. In contradiction to the promulgated myths of color-blind racial democracy, most Latin American nations have historically stigmatized and subordinated their Afro-Latin populations (Twine, 1998). *Mestizaje* (race mixture) as an ideal has in actuality been predicated on the differential valorization of the European component and the goal of *blanqueamiento*, whitening, and, to this socially meliorist end, many Latin American nations have had white immigration policies (Minority Rights Group, 1995).

Finally, insofar as the modern world has been profoundly shaped by European colonialism, there is a sense in which white supremacy could be seen as transnational, global, the historic domination of white Europe over nonwhite non-Europe and of white settlers over nonwhite slaves and indigenes, making Europeans "the lords of human kind" (Kiernan, 1981; Cocker, 1998). I have argued in my own work that this domination can enlighteningly be conceptualized through the idea of a global "racial contract" between whites, a set of agreements to regard themselves as morally equal while non-whites are treated as moral unequals who can legitimately be exploited for white benefit (Mills, 1997). Before World War II, most of the planet was in fact formally ruled by white nations. To the extent that this domination persists, albeit through different mechanisms (military, economic, cultural), into the postcolonial period, we could be said to be still living in an age of global white supremacy.

Origins and Evolution of White Supremacy

White supremacy as a system, or set of systems, clearly comes into existence through European expansionism, and the imposition of European rule through settlement and colonialism on aboriginal and imported slave populations – the original racial "big bang" that is the source of the present racialized world (Winant, 1994). But this domination need not itself have taken a "racial" form. The causes for the emergence of "race" as the salient marker of exclusion, and the corresponding growth and centrality in the West of racist ideologies, continue to be contested by scholars. What are sometimes called "idealist" accounts would focus on the role of culture, color-symbolism, and religious predispositions, for example the self-conceptions of "civilized" Europeans opposed to a savage and "wild" Other, the positive and negative associations of the colors white and black, and the assumption of a Christian prerogative to evangelize the world and stigmatize other religions as the devil-worship of heathens (Jordan, 1977; Jennings, 1976). On the other hand, so-called "materialist" accounts, primarily Marxist in inspiration, would see such factors as either irrelevant or subordinate to the causally more important politico-economic projects of obtaining a supply of cheap labor, expropriating land, and imposing particular super-exploitative modes of production, for which "race" then becomes the convenient superstructural rationale (Cox, 1948; Fields, 1990; Allen, 1994–7). Other explanations, not readily fitted into a materialist/idealist taxonomy, regard white racism as a systematized and sophisticated extrapolation of the primordial ethnocentrism of all humans, or as linked with particular psychosexual projections on to the dark body (Kovel, 1984).

Debates over origins also have implications for the conception of "race" itself, and the evolution of white supremacy. Race has paradigmatically been thought of as natural, biological, the carving of humanity at its actual ontological joints. By contrast, contemporary radical thought on race almost universally assumes what has come to be called a "constructionist" theory (Omi and Winant, 1986; Lopez, 1995). For this account, race is not natural but an artefact of socio-political decision-making, so that where the crucial boundaries are drawn is a function of political power. From this perspective, "whites" and "nonwhites" do not pre-exist white supremacy as natural kinds, but are categories and realities themselves brought into existence by the institutionalization of the system. The white race is in fact invented (Allen, 1994–7), though theorists will differ on the relative significance of the role of the state (from above) in making race and whiteness (Marx, 1998) as against the role of the Euro-working class (from below) in making themselves white (Roediger, 1991). Correspondingly, white supremacy evolves over time not merely in its transition from a *de jure* to a *de facto* form, but in the changing rules as to who is counted as white in the first place. Matthew Frye Jacobson, for example, has recently argued that US whiteness is not temporally monolithic but should be periodized into "three great epochs": from the 1790 law limiting naturalization to free white persons to the mass influx of Irish immigrants in the 1840s; from the 1840s to the restrictive immigration legislation of 1924; and from the 1920s to the present. In the process, groups once recognized as distinct races (Mediterraneans, Celts, Slavs, Teutons) have now disappeared into an expanded white race (Jacobson, 1998). Similarly, other authors have delineated how over time the Irish and the Jews *became* white in the United States (Ignatiev, 1995; Brodkin, 1998).

White Supremacy as Political

In radical oppositional political theory, such as that centered on class or gender, a crucial initial conceptual move is often the redrawing of the boundaries of the political itself, and the corresponding entry of new, hitherto unrecognized actors on to the theoretical stage. What is taken for granted by mainstream theory as natural, or at least apolitical, is reconceptualized as itself problematic and political. A case can be made that "white supremacy" should play the same role in oppositional racial theory that "capitalism"/"class society" and "patriarchy" respectively play in Marxist and feminist political theory: providing an overarching holistic reconceptualization of the polity as a system of group domination. In this way, a diverse array of phenomena can be illuminatingly conceptually integrated as constituting different aspects of what is in fact a global system.

In the Marxist model, capitalism is not seen, as in neo-classical economic theory, as a set of market transactions disconnected from societal structure. Rather it is viewed as a system dominated by a bourgeoisie whose differential economic power ramifies throughout society, making them a "ruling class," so that even with universal suffrage the polity is no more than a "bourgeois democracy." Thus the atomistic social ontology of liberal contractarianism is profoundly misleading. Similarly, the radical feminists of the 1970s, who devised the use of "patriarchy," argued that men as a group dominate women as a group, but that this is mystified by limiting the boundaries of the political to the so-called public sphere. The ubiquity of patriarchy as a political system is therefore obfuscated through the seemingly "natural" relegation of women to the apolitical domestic space of childrearing and care of the household. Male domination becomes conceptually invisible rather than being recognized as itself the oldest form of political rule (Jaggar, 1983; Pateman and Gross, 1987).

In both cases, then, the challenge of class and gender theory to mainstream thought involves a revision of what counts *as* political in the first place, and a focus on power relations and manifestations of domination not recognized and encompassed by the official/formal definition of the political (political parties, formal contests in the electoral arena, delegated representatives in parliamentary bodies, etc.). The deliberate employment of the term "white supremacy" (in contrast to the orthodox paradigm of "race relations") constitutes a parallel challenge. The idea is that it is politically illuminating to see whites in the United States as ruling as a group, thus constituting the "ruling race" of what was originally – and is in some ways still – a *Herrenvolk* democracy" (Van den Berghe, 1978), a "white republic" (Saxton, 1990), historically founded on a notion of racial, Anglo-Saxonist "manifest destiny" (Horsman, 1981).

It will be obvious that such a conceptualization is radically at variance with a mainstream white American political theory which generally ignores or marginalizes race (Smith, 1997). The hegemonic race relations paradigm largely confines discussions of race to sociology – race is not seen as *political*. Moreover, apart from this disciplinary confinement, the paradigm itself is fundamentally misguided insofar as it seeks to conflate the experience of assimilating off-white European immigrants (Irish, Jewish, Mediterranean) with the radically different experience of subordinated nonwhite non-European *races* (black, red, brown, yellow), the former within, the latter beneath, the melting pot. "It erases the crucial difference between the incorporation of the colonized minorities by force and violence – not only the intensity of their repression but its systematic nature – and that of the European immigrant groups" (San Juan, Jr., 1992). Where "racism" is dealt with in mainstream political theory, it is standardly seen as anomalous, marginal, and conceived of in ideational, attitudinal and individualist terms, a tragic "American dilemma" (Myrdal, 1944). As such, it is to be redressed through moral suasion and enlightenment, having no substantive conceptual implications for American political theory, which can take over without modification the (facially) raceless categories of European sociopolitical thought.

"White supremacy" as a concept thus registers a commitment to a radically *different* understanding of the political order, pointing us theoretically toward the centrality of racial domination and subordination. Within the discursive universe of white social theory on race, liberal or radical, it disrupts traditional framings, conceptualizations and disciplinary divisions, effecting what is no less than a fundamental paradigm shift (Blauner, 1972; Steinberg, 1995).

(1) To begin with, attention is displaced from the moralized realm of the ideational and attitudinal to the realm of structures and power which has been the traditional concern of political theory. Correspondingly, the facile and illusory symmetry of an individualized "prejudice" (Allport, 1979) equally to be condemned wherever it is encountered, which opens the conceptual door to the later notion of "reverse discrimination," and the Supreme Court's opting for the "color-blind" "perpetrator perspective," is revealed as a mystificatory digression from the clearly *a*symmetrical and enduring system of white power itself. "The perpetrator perspective presupposes a world composed of atomistic individuals whose actions are outside of and apart from the social fabric and without historical continuity" (Freeman, 1990). (2) Secondly, this

conception blocks mainstream theory's ghettoizing of work on race through rejecting its conceptual framing of the polity as a raceless liberal democracy. Instead, the polity is conceptualized as a white supremacist state, a system as real and important historically as any of those other systems formally acknowledged in the Western political canon (aristocracy, absolutism, democracy, fascism, socialism, etc.). (3) Thirdly, the notion of a global racial system with its own partial autonomy constitutes a repudiation of the too often epiphenomenalist treatment of race in the most important Western theory of group oppression, Marxism. Instead of treating race and racial dynamics as simply reducible to a class logic, this approach argues that through constructions of the self, proclaimed ideals of cultural and civic identity, decisions of the state, crystallizations of juridical standing and group interests, permitted violence, and the opening and blocking of economic opportunities, race becomes "real" and causally effective, institutionalized and materialized by white supremacy in social practices and felt phenomenologies.

Finally, it should be noted that this alternative paradigm – race as central, political, and primarily a system of oppression – is not at all new, but has in fact always been present in oppositional African-American thought. Thirty years ago, for example, Stokely Carmichael and Charles Hamilton argued in their classic *Black Power* that essentially white Americans "own the society," that the most important kind of racism is "institutional," and that blacks should be seen as an internal colony facing whites who on issues of race "react in a united group to protect interests they perceive to be theirs," dominating blacks politically, economically, and socially (Carmichael and Hamilton, 1967). From the struggles against slavery to the battles against Jim Crow, from David Walker's militant 1829 *Appeal* (Walker, 1993) to Malcolm X's matter-of-fact 1963 judgment that "America is a white country and all of the economy, the politics, the civic life of America is controlled by the white man" (Malcolm X, 1971), blacks have historically had little difficulty in grasping that the central political reality of the United States is, quite simply, that it is a "white man's country." But this "naive" perception has apparently been too sophisticated for mainstream white political theory to apprehend.

Moreover, as earlier noted, white domination has traditionally been seen as an *international* political system. Walker's *Appeal* is addressed not merely to black Americans but to the "coloured citizens of the world," a global racial perspective that anticipates the later anti-imperialism and anti-colonialism of Pan-Africanism: Du Bois's assertion of an international "color-line," Marcus Garvey's message to Africans "at home and abroad," Frantz Fanon's vision of a planetary "wretched of the earth," Malcolm X's prediction (somewhat premature) of "the end of white world-supremacy." Paul Gilroy points out that black radical political thought is "hemispheric if not global" in orientation and scope (Gilroy, 1993), and this is fictionally dramatized in such novels of international slave rebellion and anti-imperialism as Martin Delany's *Blake* (1859–62), Du Bois's *Dark Princess* (1928), and George Schuyler's pseudonymously authored science fiction serials *The Black Internationale* and *Black Empire* (1936–8), with their pulp fantasies of a black international dedicated "to destroying white world supremacy." Current work on white supremacy in critical race theory and critical white studies can thus be seen as a belated catching-up with the insights of black lay thought, simultaneously disadvantaged and advantaged by lacking the formal training of the white academy.

Dimensions of White Supremacy

White supremacy should therefore be seen as a multi-dimensional system of domination, encompassing not merely the "formally" political that is limited to the juridico-political realm of official governing bodies and laws, but, as argued above, extending to white domination in economic, cultural, cognitive-moral, somatic, and in a sense even "metaphysical" spheres. There is a pervasive racialization of the social world that means that one's race, in effect, puts one into a certain relationship with social reality, tendentially determining one's being and consciousness.

Juridico-political

For the alternative paradigm, the state and the legal system are not neutral entities standing above interracial relations but for the most part themselves agencies of racial oppression (Kairys, 1990). To Native Americans, the white man's law has constituted an essential part of "the discourses of conquest" (Williams, 1990). For blacks, the history has been similar. As Judge A. Leon Higginbotham has documented in detail, blacks have consistently been legally differentiated from, and subordinated to, the white population, not merely with the obvious case of the enslaved, but also in the lesser rights of the free black population (Higginbotham, 1978, 1996). The Philadelphia Convention notoriously enshrined slavery without mentioning it by name through the three-fifths clause, and in 1790 Congress made whiteness a prerequisite for naturalization. The 1857 Dred Scott decision codified black subordination through its judgment that blacks were an inferior race with "no rights which the white man was bound to respect." The promise of Emancipation and Reconstruction was betrayed by the Black Codes, the 1877 Hayes–Tilden Compromise, and the 1896 *Plessy v. Ferguson* decision that formally sanctioned "separate but equal." For the next sixty years, Jim Crow was the law of the land, with widespread black disenfranchisement, exploitation, and inferior treatment in all spheres of life (Litwack, 1998). Thus for most of US history, white supremacy has been *de jure*, and blacks have either been non- or second-class citizens unable to appeal to the Federal government to provide them equal protection (King, 1995).

While the victories of the 1950s and '60s over Jim Crow have led to the repeal of overtly racist legislation, and thus to real racial progress, substantive racial equality, as earlier noted, has yet to be achieved. The failure to allocate resources to implement anti-discrimination law vigorously, the placing of the burden of proof on the plaintiff, conservatively narrow interpretations of civil rights statutes, the backlash against affirmative action and desegregation, and the general shift since the 1960s from the "victim" to the "perpetrator" perspective (Freeman, 1990), in effect mean that the anti-discrimination provisions are increasingly formal. Moreover, since the United States, unlike apartheid South Africa, has a white majority, a democratic vote guided by white group interests will itself continue to reproduce white domination in the absence of opposition from a Supreme Court committed to "veiled majoritarianism" (Spann, 1995). Donald Kinder and Lynn Sanders' research shows that, in contradiction to the expectations of classic postwar pluralist theory, racial group interests are nationally the most important ones, cutting across and overriding all other identities, and that whites see black interests as antagonistic to their own (Kinder and Sanders, 1996). Whether through legalized inferiority, electoral disenfranchisement, or majoritarian group-interest-based domination, then, blacks have been systematically subjugated for nearly four hundred years in the white American polity.

Finally, in mapping the juridico-political, the role of official and unofficial white violence in perpetuating white rule also needs to be taken into account: the sanctioned tortures and informally connived-at killings of slave penal codes; the "demonstration effects" of lynchings in terrorizing the local black population; the freedom to operate given the Klan; the differential application of the death penalty; the race riots which, until well into the twentieth century, were basically white riots; and the part played by the repressive apparatus of the state (slave patrollers, federal militia, police, military, the prison system) in suppressing first slave uprisings and then later targeting legitimate black protest and activism to gain the rights enjoyed by white Americans (Berry, 1994; Garrow, 1981; Shapiro, 1988). In effect, for most of US history the state has functioned as a racial state protecting white supremacy.

Economic

Marx's theorization of the dynamics of capitalism famously rests on the claim that it is intrinsically an exploitative system, since even when the working class are being paid a "fair" wage, surplus value is being extracted from them. But with the discrediting of the labor theory of value, this claim is no longer taken seriously in mainstream neo-classical economics, though John Roemer has recently attempted to develop a general theory of exploitation in other terms (Roemer, 1982).

In the case of white supremacy as a system, however, there is a pervasive "exploitation" ongoing throughout society that is, or should be, quite obvious, and that is wrong by completely conventional *non*-Marxist liberal standards. What could be termed "racial exploitation" covers an extensive historical variety of institutionalized and informal practices much broader than proletarian wage-labor: slavery itself first and foremost, of course; but also the refusal to blacks of the opportunity to homestead the West; the debt peonage of sharecropping; the exclusion of blacks from certain jobs and trades, and the lower wages and diminished promotion chances within those employments permitted; the blocking of black entrepreneurs from access to white markets; the denial of start-up capital by white banks; the higher prices and rents for inferior merchandise and housing in the ghettoes; the restricted access of blacks to state and Federal services that whites enjoyed; the Federally-backed segregation and restrictive covenants that diminished the opportunities for most blacks to accumulate wealth through home ownership; the exploitative business contracts that took advantage of black ignorance, or, when recognized as such, had to be signed because of lack of an alternative to white monopoly control; and many others (Massey and Denton, 1993; Oliver and Shapiro, 1995; Lipsitz, 1998; Brown, 1999).

An adequate theorization of white supremacy would require a detailed taxonomy and analysis of these different varieties of racial exploitation that have jointly historically deprived blacks as a group of billions, or even (globally) trillions of dollars of wealth, and have correspondingly benefited whites, thus in effect constituting the "material base" of white supremacy, the "wages of whiteness" in Du Bois's classic phrase (Du Bois, 1992). (The wealth of the median black American household is less than one-eighth the wealth of the median white household.) And globally there is a longstanding black and Third World argument that slavery, colonialism, and the exploitation of the New World were crucial in enabling European development and producing African underdevelopment, so that racial exploitation really has to be seen as planetary in scope (Williams, 1966; Rodney, 1974; Blaut, 1993).

Cultural

Given recent debates about "multiculturalism," the cultural dimension of white supremacy at least is familiar: a Eurocentrism that denigrates non-European cultures as inferior, or even non-existent, and places Europe at the center of global history (Amin, 1989). What is not usually articulated is the role such denigration played in teleological theories of history that made Europeans the master race, destined either to annihilate or lead to civilization all others, generating a discourse that could be regarded as "fantasies of the master race" (Churchill, 1992; Said, 1993). Colonial peoples in general, of course, have suffered this denial of the worth of their cultures, but the centrality of African slavery to the project of the West required the most extreme stigmatization of blacks in particular. Thus sub-Saharan Africa was portrayed as the "Dark Continent," a vast jungle inhabited by savage "tribes" lost in a history-less and culture-less vacuum, to be redeemed only by a European presence (Mudimbe, 1988, 1994). The Tarzan novels and movies, the Phantom comic strip, the thousands of African "adventure" stories of pulp and ostensibly highbrow fiction of the last hundred years, are all part of this master-narrative of white cultural superiority (Pieterse, 1992). From north to south, from Ancient Egypt to Zembabwei, the achievements of the continent have generally been attributed to anybody other than the black population themselves. Blacks in the United States and the Americas generally were, of course, tainted by their association with such a barbarous origin (Fredrickson, 1987). African survivals were actively suppressed both as part of the project of Christianizing and civilizing the slaves, and, in some cases, for fear of their possibly subversive employment. Finally, apart from this well-known pattern of white cultural hegemony, there is also a phenomenon that deserves more theoretical attention of cultural *appropriation* without acknowledgment, so that civilization in general seems to have an exclusively white genealogy. "You took my blues/and now you're gone," complained Langston Hughes, a form of exploitation that is again uneasily fitted within the categories of the best-known mainstream theory of exploitation, Marxism. Cultural white supremacy manifests itself not merely in the differential valorization of Europe and European-derived culture, but in the denial of the extent to which this culture – "incontestably mulatto" in the phrase of Albert Murray (Murray, 1970) – has itself been dependent on the contributions of others, a "bleaching" of the multicolored roots of human civilization.

Cognitive-evaluative

More generally, white supremacy as a system will necessarily, though in different ways, have a negative effect on the consciousness of both whites and nonwhites, shaping both

276

their descriptive and evaluative conceptualizations of the world. Living in a situation of white privilege in a society based on racial oppression, whites will tend to develop theories that justify their position, both morally and in terms of alleged facts about reality. Thus Paul Gilroy suggests that we need to investigate "the complicity of racialised reason and white supremacist terror" (Gilroy, 1993). Being constructed as white means, inter alia, learning to understand the world in a certain way, developing particular patterns of perception, conceptualization and affect. The clearest manifestation of this will be in the development of racist ideology itself, in its numerous variants, theological and secular: polygenesis, craniometry, Social Darwinism, IQ theory (Gould, 1981). But racialized perceptions will continue to shape cognition in unconscious and subtle ways even in apparently non-racist contexts. Morally, whites will be socialized into an ethical code that is itself color-coded, structured by race, and predicated on differential white entitlement – a "*Herrenvolk* ethics" (Mills, 1998b) in which whiteness itself becomes "property" (Harris, 1993) – so that it will be difficult for them, even when acting in good faith, to break free of this (Lawrence, 1995). Thus there will be characteristic and pervasive patterns of structured ignorance, motivated inattention, self-deception, and moral rationalization, that blacks, for their own survival, have to learn to become familiar with. In Ralph Ellison's classic novel *Invisible Man*, the eponymous narrator describes the "peculiar disposition" of white eyes, a blindness arising not out of physiology but socialized psychology, "the construction of their *inner* eyes" (Ellison, 1972). For their part, blacks who have internalized a belief in their own mental inferiority will be cognitive cripples, deferring automatically to white epistemic authority, unable to develop theorizations and moral evaluations that challenge white supremacy, and as such accepting an "ethics of living Jim Crow" (Wright, 1991).

Somatic

White supremacy also has a pivotal somatic dimension, especially where the black population is concerned. Since this is a political system predicated on racial superiority and inferiority, on the demarcation and differential evaluation of different races, the "body" in the body politic naturally becomes crucial in a way it does not in the abstract polity of (official) Western theory. A white "somatic norm" assumes hegemonic standing, and serves as an important contributory measure of individual worth (Hoetink, 1962). The black body, on the other hand, being both the sign of slave status and the body physically most divergent from the white one, is derogated and stigmatized as inferior, grotesque, ugly, simian; it is mocked in blackface minstrelsy, cartoons, advertising, animated films, memorabilia (Turner, 1994; Pieterse, 1992). Blacks who have accepted this norm will then be alienated from their own bodies, in a sense estranged from their own physical being, be-ing, in the world (Russell et al., 1992). This alienation will manifest itself both in attempts to transform the body to more closely approximate the white somatic norm, and in a racialization of sexual relations in terms of the differential attractiveness of certain bodies (Fanon, 1967). Correspondingly, black resistance to oppressive corporeal whiteness has taken the form of a guerrilla insurgency on the terrain of the flesh itself (White and White, 1998). Recent philosophical work on the body has generally focused on gender rather than race (Welton, 1998), but some philosophers of color, for example Lewis Gordon and Linda Martin Alcoff, are beginning to explore racial embodiment from a phenomenological point of view (Gordon, 1995; Alcoff, 1999).

Metaphysical

Finally, there is what could be termed a central "metaphysical" pillar to white supremacy, though this is metaphysical in the sense of a *social* ontology. Mainstream Anglo-American analytic philosophy tends to separate metaphysical issues of being and consciousness, identity and the self, from the social; one thinks of the classic iconography of the isolated solipsistic Cartesian ego, of the atomic and pre-social individuals of contract theory. By contrast, in the Continental tradition in its numerous variants (Hegelian, Marxist, poststructuralist) there is a greater appreciation of the notion of the socially-constituted, or at least socially-formed, self. From this perspective, white supremacy could be seen as a bipolar system whose ontological underpinnings lift a white *Herrenvolk* above non-white, particularly black *Untermenschen*. Black intellectuals have always recognized that racial subordination is predicated on regarding blacks as less than human, as sub-persons rather than persons. Frederick Douglass writes: "My *crime* is that I have assumed to be a man." Sojourner Truth asks: "And ain't I a woman?" Du Bois ironically describes black Americans as this curious "*tertium quid*," this third thing "between men and cattle." Ralph Ellison recounts the fate of an "invisible man." James Baldwin complains that "nobody knows my name." And black civil rights demonstrators in the 1950s and 1960s carry placards that declare simply: "I *AM* A MAN."

The virtue of using white supremacy as an overarching theoretical concept is that it enables us to pull together different phenomena and integrate these different levels: socio-political, economic, cultural, somatic, metaphysical. Race is best thought of not primarily as ideational, not as in the head, but as embedded in institutions, networks of belief, and social practices that so shape the world with which we interact as to constitute an "objective" (deriving from intersubjectivity), though socially constructed, "reality." Seeing white supremacy as objective, systemic, multi-dimensional, constitutive of a certain world that evolves over time, thus provides us with the appropriate framework for understanding what, in an evocative phrase, Lewis Gordon terms "being black in an anti-black world" (Gordon, 1995).

References and Recommended Reading

Alcoff, Linda. 1999: "Towards a Phenomenology of Racial Embodiment." *Radical Philosophy* (special issue on race and ethnicity), 95.

Allen, Theodore, W. 1994–7: *The Invention of the White Race* (in two volumes). New York: Verso.

Allport, Gordon. 1954; rpt. 1979: *The Nature of Prejudice*. Reading, Mass.: Addison-Wesley.

Almaguer, Tomas. 1994: *Racial Fault Lines: The Historical Origins of White Supremacy in California*. Berkeley: University of California Press.

Amin, Samir. 1988; rpt. 1989: *Eurocentrism*, trans. Russell Moore. New York: Monthly Review Press.

Ansley, Frances Lee, 1989: "Stirring the Ashes: Race, Class and the Future of Civil Rights Scholarship." *Cornell Law Review* 74.

Berry, Mary Frances. 1971; rpt. 1994: *Black Resistance, White Law: A History of Constitutional Racism in America*. New York: Allen Lane.

Blauner, Robert. 1972: *Racial Oppression in America*. New York: Harper & Row.

Blaut, J. M. 1993: *The Colonizer's Model of the World: Geographical Diffusionism and Eurocentric History*. New York: The Guilford Press.

Brodkin, Karen. 1998: *How Jews Became White Folks and What That Says About Race in America*. New Brunswick, NJ: Rutgers University Press.

Brown, Michael K. 1999: *Race, Money, and the American Welfare State*. Ithaca: Cornell University Press.

Carmichael, Stokely and Hamilton, Charles V. 1967: *Black Power: The Politics of Liberation in America*. New York: Vintage Books.

Cell, John W. 1982: *The Highest Stage of White Supremacy: The Origins of Segregation in South Africa and the American South*. Cambridge: Cambridge University Press.

Churchill, Ward. 1992: *Fantasies of the Master Race: Literature, Cinema and the Colonization of American Indians*. Monroe, Maine: Common Courage Press.

Cocker, Mark. 1998: *Rivers of Blood, Rivers of Gold: Europe's Conflict with Tribal Peoples*. London: Jonathan Cape.

Cox, Oliver. 1948: *Caste, Class, and Race: A Study in Social Dynamics*. New York: Modern Reader.

Crenshaw, Kimberlé, Gotanda, Neil, Peller, Gary, and Thomas, Kendall (eds.). 1995: *Critical Race Theory: The Key Writings That Formed the Movement*. New York: The New Press.

Delgado, Richard (ed.). 1995: *Critical Race Theory: The Cutting Edge*. Philadelphia: Temple University Press.

Delgado, Richard and Stefancic, Jean (eds.). 1997: *Critical White Studies: Looking Behind the Mirror*. Philadelphia: Temple University Press.

Du Bois, W. E. B. 1935; rpt. 1992: *Black Reconstruction in America, 1860–1880*. New York: Atheneum.

Ellison, Ralph. 1952; rpt. 1972: *Invisible Man*. New York: Vintage Books.

Fanon, Frantz. 1952; rpt. 1967: *Black Skin, White Masks*, trans. Charles Lam Markmann. New York: Grove Weidenfeld.

Fields, Barbara. 1990: "Slavery, Race and Ideology in the United States of America." *New Left Review*, 181.

Foley, Neil. 1997: *White Scourge: Mexicans, Blacks, and Poor Whites in Texas Cotton Culture*. Berkeley: University of California Press.

Fredrickson, George. 1971; rpt. 1987: *The Black Image in the White Mind: The Debate on Afro-American Character and Destiny, 1817–1914*. Hanover, NH: Wesleyan University Press.

——. 1981: *White Supremacy: A Comparative Study in American and South African History*. New York: Oxford University Press.

Freeman, Alan David. 1990: "Legitimizing Racial Discrimination through Antidiscrimination Law: A Critical Review of Supreme Court Doctrine." Abridged in Crenshaw et al. (1995).

Garrow, David J. 1981: *The FBI and Martin Luther King, Jr.: From "Solo" to Memphis*. New York: W.W. Norton.

Gates, Henry Louis, Jr. (ed.). 1991: *Bearing Witness: Selections from African-American Autobiography in the Twentieth Century*. New York: Pantheon Books.

Gilroy, Paul. 1993: *The Black Atlantic: Modernity and Double Consciousness*. Cambridge, Mass.: Harvard University Press.

Gordon, Lewis R. 1995: *Bad Faith and Antiblack Racism*. Atlantic Highlands, NJ: Humanities Press.

Gould, Stephen Jay. 1981: *The Mismeasure of Man*. New York: W.W. Norton.

Harris, Cheryl I. 1993: "Whiteness as Property." *Harvard Law Review* 106.

Higginbotham, Jr., A. Leon. 1978: *In the Matter of Color: Race and the American Legal Process – The Colonial Period*. New York: Oxford University Press.

279

——. 1996: *Shades of Freedom: Racial Politics and Presumptions of the American Legal Process*. New York: Oxford University Press.

Hoetink, Harmannus. 1962: *Caribbean Race Relations: A Study of Two Variants*. London: Oxford University Press.

Horsman, Reginald. 1981: *Race and Manifest Destiny: The Origins of American Racial Anglo-Saxonism*. Cambridge, Mass.: Harvard University Press.

Ignatiev, Noel. 1995: *How the Irish Became White*. New York: Routledge.

Jacobson, Matthew Frye. 1998: *Whiteness of a Different Color: European Immigrants and the Alchemy of Race*. Cambridge, Mass.: Harvard University Press.

Jaggar, Alison. 1983: *Feminist Politics and Human Nature*. Totowa, NJ: Rowman & Allanheld.

Jennings, Francis. 1975; rpt. 1976: *The Invasion of America: Indians, Colonialism, and the Cant of Conquest*. New York: W.W. Norton.

Jordan, Winthrop. 1968; rpt. 1977: *White over Black: American Attitudes Toward the Negro, 1550–1812*. New York: W.W. Norton.

Kairys, David (ed.). 1982; rev. ed. 1990: *The Politics of Law: A Progressive Critique*. New York: Pantheon Books.

Kiernan, V. G. 1969; rpt. 1981: *The Lords of Human Kind: Black Man, Yellow Man, and White Man in an Age of Empire*. New York: Columbia University Press.

Kinder, Donald R. and Sanders, Lynn M. 1996: *Divided by Color: Racial Politics and Democratic Ideals*. Chicago: University of Chicago Press.

King, Desmond. 1995: *Separate and Unequal: Black Americans and the U.S. Federal Government*. Oxford: Clarendon Press.

Kovel, Joel. 1970; rpt. 1984: *White Racism: A Psychohistory*. New York: Columbia University Press.

Lawrence, III, Charles R. 1995: "The Id, the Ego, and Equal Protection: Reckoning With Unconscious Racism." Abridged in Crenshaw et al. (1995).

Lipsitz, George. 1998: *The Possessive Investment in Whiteness: How White People Profit from Identity Politics*. Philadelphia: Temple University Press.

Litwack, Leon F. 1998: *Trouble in Mind: Black Southerners in the Age of Jim Crow*. New York: Alfred A. Knopf.

Lopez, Ian Haney. 1995: "The Social Construction of Race." In Delgado (1995).

Malcolm X. 1971: *The End of White World Supremacy*. New York: Little, Brown.

Marx, Anthony W. 1998: *Making Race and Nation: A Comparison of the United States, South Africa, and Brazil*. New York: Cambridge University Press.

Massey, Douglas S., and Denton, Nancy A. 1993: *American Apartheid: Segregation and the Marking of the Underclass*. Cambridge, Mass.: Harvard University Press.

Mills, Charles. 1997: *The Racial Contract*. Ithaca: Cornell University Press.

——. 1998a: *Blackness Visible: Essays on Philosophy and Race*. Ithaca: Cornell University Press.

——. 1998b: "White Right: The Idea of a *Herrenvolk* Ethics." In Mills (1998a).

Minority Rights Group (ed.). 1995: *No Longer Invisible: Afro-Latin Americans Today*. London: Minority Rights Publications.

Mudimbe, V. Y. 1988: *The Invention of Africa*. Bloomington: Indiana University Press.

——. 1994: *The Idea of Africa*. Bloomington: Indiana University Press.

Murray, Albert. 1970: *The Omni-Americans: New Perspectives on Black Experience and American Culture*. New York: Outerbridge & Dienstfrey.

Myrdal, Gunnar. 1944: *An American Dilemma: The Negro Problem and Modern Democracy*. New York: Harper & Brothers.

Okihiro, Gary Y. 1994: *Margins and Mainstreams: Asians in American History and Culture*. Seattle: University of Washington Press.

Oliver, Melvin L. and Shapiro, Thomas M. 1995: *Black Wealth/White Wealth: A New Perspective on Racial Inequality*. New York: Routledge.

Omi, Michael and Winant, Howard. 1986: *Racial Formation in the United States: From the 1960s to the 1980s*. New York: Routledge & Kegan Paul.

Pateman, Carol and Gross, Elizabeth (eds.). 1987: *Feminist Challenges: Social and Political Theory*. Boston: Northeastern Press.

Pieterse, Jan Nederveen. 1990; rpt. 1992: *White on Black: Images of Africa and Blacks in Western Popular Culture*. New Haven: Yale University Press.

Rodney, Walter. 1972; rpt. 1974: *How Europe Underdeveloped Africa*. Washington, D.C.: Howard University Press.

Roediger, David R. 1991: *The Wages of Whiteness: Race and the Making of the American Working Class*. New York: Verso.

Roemer, John. 1982: *A General Theory of Exploitation and Class*. Cambridge, Mass.: Harvard University Press.

Russell, Kathy, Wilson, Midge, and Hall, Ronald. 1992: *The Color Complex: The Politics of Skin Color Among African Americans*. New York: Harcourt Brace Jovanovich.

Said, Edward. 1993: *Culture and Imperialism*. New York: Alfred A. Knopf.

San Juan, Jr., E. 1992: *Racial Formations/Critical Transformations: Articulations of Power in Ethnic and Racial Studies in the United States*. Atlantic Highlands NJ: Humanities Press.

Saxton, Alexander. 1990: *The Rise and Fall of the White Republic: Class Politics and Mass Culture in Nineteenth-Century America*. New York: Verso.

Shapiro, Herbert. 1988: *White Violence and Black Response: From Reconstruction to Montgomery*. Amherst: University of Massachusetts Press.

Smith, Rogers. 1997: *Civic Ideals: Conflicting Visions of Citizenship in U.S. History*. New Haven: Yale University Press.

Spann, Girardeau. 1995: "Pure Politics." In Delgado (1995).

Steinberg, Stephen. 1995: *Turning Back: The Retreat from Racial Justice in America*. Boston: Beacon Press.

Takaki, Ronald. 1979; rpt. 1990: *Iron Cages: Race and Culture in 19th-Century America*. New York: Oxford University Press.

Turner, Patricia A. 1994: *Ceramic Uncles and Celluloid Mammies: Black Images and Their Influence on Culture*. New York: Anchor Books.

Twine, France Winddance. 1998: *Racism in a Racial Democracy: The Maintenance of White Supremacy in Brazil*. New Brunswick, NJ: Rutgers University Press.

Van den Berghe, Pierre. 1978: *Race and Racism*. 2nd edn. New York: Wiley.

Walker, David. 1993: *Appeal*. Baltimore, MD: Black Classic Press.

Welton, Donn (ed.). 1998: *Body and Flesh: A Philosophical Reader*. Malden, Mass.: Blackwell Publishers.

White, Shane and White, Graham. 1998: *Stylin': African American Expressive Culture, from its Beginnings to the Zoot Suit*. Ithaca: Cornell University Press.

Williams, Eric. 1944; rpt. 1966: *Capitalism and Slavery*. New York: Capricorn.

Williams, Jr., Robert A. 1990: *The American Indian in Western Legal Thought: The Discourses of Conquest*. New York: Oxford University Press.

Winant, Howard. 1994: *Racial Conditions: Politics, Theory, Comparisons*. Minneapolis, Minn.: University of Minnesota Press.

Wright, Richard. 1991: "The Ethics of Living Jim Crow." In Gates (1991).

X, Malcolm. 1971: *The End of White World Supremacy*, ed. Imam Benjamin Karim. New York: Arcade Publishing.

Part V

LEGAL AND SOCIAL PHILOSOPHY

Introduction to Part V

The social implications of several landmark Supreme Court decisions has generated a great deal of disagreement regarding a wide variety of public policy issues. Many of these issues have been debated within African-American philosophy, as well as within mainstream American thought. With notions of self-respect and fairness at hand, Laurence Thomas subjects the general moral framework of American society to close scrutiny, whereas Michelle Moody-Adams, Howard McGary, Luke Harris and Rudolph Vanterpool focus on specific constitutional issues. Annette Dula and Angela Davis critically examine policies that are created by institutional practices sanctioned by the law. The essays in this section exhibit the manner in which the interplay of jurisprudence and social policy is a major theme in African-American moral and political thought.

In the opening selection, Laurence Thomas deals with an important ethical concern underlying social institutions and practices. Moral worth and self-respect are based on the idea that all humans are equal. Thomas considers why the obviousness of our humanity is no guarantee of self-respect. With the question of how widespread and systematic injustices influence the self-respect of victims, he focuses on African Americans to highlight the hostile conditions under which their self respect has to operate. With a scepticism much similar to Zack's and Goldberg's, Thomas raises the question of what makes a person a black person to contest the prevailing definitions in current use with a laundry list of examples and names of black people who do not fit the categories. He acknowledges, however, that, because of the *social* reality of racial categorization, it is more convenient to adopt the language of racial groups than not, even though the notion is "intellectually bankrupt."

Social views regarding the moral nature and the natural temperament of groups are "underwritten" by practices that incline many members of the racial group alleged to be inferior to hold negative views of themselves. Citing Du Bois's claim in *Dusk of Dawn* that there is no better remedy to end self-doubt about one's abilities than a record of success, Thomas points out that Du Bois was not concerned with the innate abilities of blacks, rather he was concerned with the circumstances under which blacks might have a secure sense of their own innate abilities. Thomas points to American society's

INTRODUCTION TO PART V

negative view of African-American language interference as an indication of a systematic denial of self-worth.

Thomas believes the daily injustice to which black people are subjected in American society is not conducive to their living morally. He compares the situation of blacks treating whites with respect after centuries of injustice to the situation of a woman who has been raped by a neighbor whose house is being burglarized. Thomas claims that because we believe that "when wronged by someone we generally want a moral leveling between us," a person cannot be expected to do what is right under these circumstances. He notes that, despite the racial injustice in America, black people "found the will to live morally." According to Thomas, the case of African Americans shows that persons whose lives are lacking self-respect may nonetheless exhibit morally proper behavior that counts as supererogatory.

In 1892 Homer Plessy refused to comply with a conductor's request that he take a seat in the Jim Crow car of a train in Louisiana. He was convicted in violation of the Railway Accommodations Act. He appealed to the Supreme court, but the badge of inferiority argument presented on his behalf was defeated by a majority opinion upholding racial segregation. Michele Moody-Adams reflects on this historic legal case. She points out that *Plessy* introduced the idea that a principle of color blindness is implicit in the equal protection clause of the Fourteenth Amendment, and that prior to this the equal protection clause offered no explicit protection against racial discrimination. Plessy's supporters advocated a color blind reading of the constitution – a reading that helped bring about much of the current protection of individual rights.

Moody-Adams cautions against giving full weight to the principle of color-blindness in shaping social policy. She is worried about the unwavering commitment to color blindness – apart from whatever facts of discrimination. Given the history of institutional racism in America, she believes more compelling considerations can sometimes outweighed colorblindness. With the passing of Jim Crow legislation well into the middle of the twentieth century, legal liberation from the constraints of the *Plessy* decision did not occur until the 1954 *Brown* decision. For this reason Moody-Adams believes that, in a social context of racial injustice, where color conscious remedies such as affirmative action are needed, color blindness is problematic. She claims that many whites now believe that lack of merit, not opportunity, accounts for any remaining social and economic disparities between black and white Americans. Against this idea she insists that it is implausible to think that either the internal perspective on segregation, or inequality of opportunity, would disappear with the demise of legally sanctioned and enforced segregation.

In keeping with Charles Mills's account of the nature of white supremacy, she endorses Critical Race Theory's claim that the law operates on the principle of property in whiteness and recommends color-conscious social policies as the only appropriate response. She confronts the reverse discrimination argument advanced by advocates of anti-affirmative action with the contention that there is no reason to think the reverse property interest in blackness would ever be established. For this to transpire, color-conscious policies would have to be based on principles of black superiority. She insists that "a principled demand to remedy oppression cannot be the functional equivalent of the property interest in whiteness." She is nonetheless aware that critics of color-conscious remedies believe affirmative action is morally unfair because it challenges the principle of merit. As Bernard Boxill points out, with changing patterns of immigrants, these concerns will be exacerbated. Moody-Adams is worried that looking at the contemporary problem solely through Plessy's "lens" of individual rights is "intrinsically unlikely to succeed."

Moody-Adams's hesitation regarding the color-blind principle is matched by Howard McGary's equally hesitant stance on the *Brown* decision. McGary notes that the position taken by the court in this landmark case has been praised and criticized. He believes that even though it eliminated *de jure* segregation in schools and paved the way for equal opportunity, it was "well-intentioned but legally unsound." McGary claims that specifically, the court was wrong to conclude that all black schools necessarily caused inferiority and low black self-esteem. He distinguishes *de jure* from *de facto* segregation in terms of the former, but not the latter, involving intentional segregation of races. With this distinction he joins the present debate about whether the courts can and should attempt to eliminate *de facto* segregation and whether the constitution gives the state authority to use its coercive power to achieve equity.

The *Brown* decision was twofold. Along with the declaration that *de jure* segregation in schools is unconstitutional, the Court also fashioned a remedy. McGary points out that the debate over this remedy revealed the ambiguous nature of what was declared unconstitutional. He analyzes four interpretations of *Brown*, each representing a different view of remediation. McGary is concerned that the Court's declaration that *de jure* segregation is unconstitutional implies that all single-race schools are unjust. The line of reasoning that *de jure* legal segregation of school children violates equal protection involves an empirical claim that required the Justices to appeal to a body of research on the damaging psychological effects of racial isolation and segregation. To show that the self-esteem of black children would still be harmed if they were in a racially segregated school with equal facilities, Kenneth Clark's doll studies were used. McGary objects to the stipulation established on this ground, because it entails a legal conception of black people as psychologically unhealthy.

McGary believes *Brown* leaves unclear whether the Court's remedy meant to address a question of racial isolation, or inadequate funding. He points out that the Court did not rule that the doctrine of separate but equal was logically or legally inconsistent, nor that all single race institutions were necessarily unconstitutional. Hence, the remedy for *de jure* segregation did not require the total dismantling of *Plessy* and was consistent with the rulings in other important legal cases involving race and educational opportunity. The burden in *Brown* shifted to making the case that racially segregated schools always cause serious harm and that separate educational facilities are inherently unequal. According to McGary, critics of the reasoning of *Brown* rightfully argue that appeal to research about black inferiority was not needed to justify a conclusion that legal segregation violates equal protection, for school children should have this protection even if denying it did not make them feel inferior.

McGary questions the Court's appeal to the "feelings of black inferiority rationale" because it applies no matter how good the all-black schools might be. He believes that, on this view, the Court unwittingly contributes to the idea of white supremacy. His objection does not deny the wrongness of legal segregation, rather it rests on the claim that racial isolation does not always entail feelings of inferiority. A dominate group can sometimes isolate a group it considers superior. Neither the isolating, nor the isolated group, need to view this group as inferior – although the group is perceived and referred to pejoratively. McGary argues that the '"feelings of black inferiority" rationale is a "myth." He maintains that the question is whether public institutions violate a right of African Americans to be treated equally by the state, not whether an institution is predominantly black or white.

McGary refers to the National Basketball Association to indicate why racial balance is not necessary for black self-esteem, but rather respect for rights is necessary. He believes that black institutions will be necessary to overcome the vestiges of slavery and segregation. To those who believe that racial isolation is bad altogether, and that it goes against the grain of the Civil Rights movement McGary points out that the offensiveness of racial isolation does not override an equally important question for liberal democratic society: Do such schools violate anyone's rights, or cause serious harm to innocent persons? McGary insists that if these schools do not violate anyone's rights, or cause serious harm to innocent persons, then, on principles of liberalism, it is not appropriate to deny public funds to a school because there is racial imbalance.

Along with policies that aim to foster the integration of schools to achieve racial balance, affirmation action has been a source of great controversy in American Society. The four people Luke Harris quotes at the beginning of his essay represent ideological diverse viewpoints in the black community, yet all seem to oppose race-based programs that offer preference to African-Americans. Harris examines the hostility and ambivalence informing this perspective with the aim of showing that the misgivings dominating public debate over affirmative action are generated by a series of misunderstandings. He attributes the negative response to affirmative action to certain distortions. He argues that, once affirmative action is accurately portrayed, it can be seen not to afford preferences to its beneficiaries, but offers instead a greater equality of opportunity.

Harris notes that critics raise the reverse discrimination objection, while proponents appeal to the compensation justification. Noting that legal scholars have already challenged a widespread belief that affirmative action departs from standards of merit, Harris attributes the persistence of the moral dilemmas cited in affirmative action debates to the use of the language of preference. He cites, for example, Shelby Steele's appeal to the idea of unjustified preference to raise the issue of self-doubt among recipients and resentment among nonbeneficiaries. He also cites Stephen Carter's view of affirmative action as patronizing and demeaning, noting that Carter, however, calls in question the legitimacy and value of affirmative action while supporting it. According to Carter, racism is receding for the black middle class, but getting worse for poor people. Carter's criticism dovetails with the concerns raised by Steele and championed by conservatives. His view that middle-class blacks are harmed by the circumvention of "legitimate academic and professional standards" resonates with Thomas Sowell's argument that affirmative action undermines black achievements – making them look like "gifts from government," and William Julius Wilson's claim that middle-class blacks are the main beneficiaries of affirmative action.

Harris considers the extent to which there is a general misconception about the scope of affirmative action – the widespread belief that these programs do nothing for truly disadvantaged blacks. To ward off this criticism Harris notes that there are autobiographical accounts of how affirmative action has helped many blacks at the bottom. He points out that Blauner attributes the growth of the black middle class to the Civil

Rights movement and affirmative action, and provides evidence of social mobility that included many blacks from the bottom. Harris takes to task the assumption that middle-class minorities do not need, or deserve affirmative action. Steele, for instance, thinks the black middle class should be treated exactly like their white counterparts. Harris points out that Steele assumes that middle-class blacks are similarly situated, when studies suggest that blacks are treated worse than equally qualified whites. He cites the black-to-white ratio of median income and white male dominance in senior management positions to argue that these structural inequities have not been ameliorated by color-blind policies.

Harris invokes Kimberlé Crenshaw's account of the intersection of race and gender to support his claim regarding the joint operation of intersecting discriminatory factors. He insists that, because affirmative action policies can target blue collar trades as well as elite universities and colleges, critics who assume that class is the only reason minorities need affirmative action are mistaken. Against Boxill's backward-looking argument for reparations, Harris maintains that the aim of affirmative action is not to compensate for past injuries, but rather to promote equality by eradicating the unfair exclusionary practices. He is dissatisfied with the compensatory and social utility rationales for affirmative action because they do not contest the idea that affirmative action is preferential treatment. According to Harris, there is no stigma because affirmative action addresses unfair practices that privilege whites. He wants to trade in talk of preference for talk of fairness and equal opportunity such that the costs are more accurately construed as a loss of privilege derived from using old criteria that works against minorities.

While there is disagreement over the question of whether affirmative action benefits disadvantaged blacks, the debate regarding welfare reform involves a matter of public policy that clearly affects the lives of African-American poor people. The passage of the *Personal Responsibility and Work Opportunity Reconciliation Act* (1996) poses new constitutional challenges. Rudolph Vanterpool reflects on the moral and legal controversy surrounding public assistance programs. He points out that law is influenced by politics and that public policy tends to shift in response to existing political and economic conditions. Although much current debate centers on a range of reform initiatives, Vanterpool is concerned primarily with legal decisions involving public assistance programs. By tracing certain similarities between legal and moral discourse, he wants to address the question of whether people have obligations to assist other persons in need.

With regard to legal theory, Vanterpool cites several important Supreme Court decisions in which welfare benefits were characterized as mere government gratuities, or charitable contributions, and welfare interests were not regarded as earned property entitlements but treated as privileges. In *Shapiro* the issue revolved around the constitutionality of statutory provisions in several states that denied welfare assistance to nonresidents. Justice Brennan cautioned that welfare aid to subsist could not be denied by the argument that public assistance benefits are a privilege rather than a right. In the *Goldberg* case the issue was whether the state of New York could terminate federal public assistance payments without affording the claimant an opportunity for an evidentiary hearing. Justice Brennan again invoked the rights-privilege distinction and held that welfare benefits constitute statutory entitlements and that due process requires an adequate hearing before termination of benefits. Justice Black presented the argument against the statutory entitlements rationale by characterizing public assistance programs as allowances, or gratuities. Vanterpool points out that this case raised the policy issue of whether taxes from the most affluent could be used to support the less fortunate.

With regard to the ideological function of these legal decisions, Vanterpool points out that the earlier Warren Court was committed to liberalism, whereas the later Burger Court was more closely aligned with libertarianism. Liberals advocate the use of government intervention to enable individuals to engage in fair open competition in the marketplace on equal terms. Vanterpool notes that proponents of the statutory entitlements doctrine found support in liberal ideology – specifically, the idea that everyone is entitled to access government authority to remedy inequalities of opportunity produced by the laissez-faire marketplace. He points out that Charles Reich's view of the changing nature of property, as reflected in subsidies to farmers, businesses and national defense contractors, was cited by Brennan in *Goldberg*. He believes that Rawls's theory of distributive justice would support the liberal ideology that influenced the earlier Court. The Difference Principle is designed to ameliorate economic inequalities. On this principle, welfare allocations are categorized as equitable shares in redistributed wealth. Liberals envision a democracy in which the rights of the needy require constitutionally guaranteed minimum protection.

Vanterpool considers the manner in which Peter Singer's utilitarian proposal aims to balance relevant interests by assimilating welfare programs to the case of giving aid to people in famine stricken nations. Singer maintains that, rather than appeal to charity, affluent people have a moral responsibility to prevent others from starving. He appeals to the principle of preventing bad things from happening rather than a principle of promoting good. Vanterpool points out that, importantly, this principle is not framed in terms of charity. Vanterpool's own Kantian proposal starts with fundamental moral obligations, instead of entitlements to aid. Although there is no uniformity in dealing with solutions to providing for subsistence needs there is a recognition of universal vulnerability. Vanterpool urges new solutions with viable alternatives to the limiting modes of welfare rights discourse. He thinks the entitlement era is a thing of the past and endorses the inclusion of education incentives and employment training requirements in the *Reconciliation Act*. He insists that either some form of the present welfare system be retained, or that a viable alternative for dealing with the needs of the poor is required to bring about the overall realization of the pursuit of happiness in America.

In sharp contrast with the racial overtones surrounding the question of welfare reform, the question of race has been absent from medical ethics discourse. Annette Dula argues that, unlike cloning, race is not just another issue because, when race is ignored, the ethical dilemmas are misrepresented. According to Dula, empirical evidence shows that the poor health of African Americans is a consequence of institutional racism in the health care system and that the gap in the health status of African Americans and whites is getting wider. She maintains that this is an ethical issue involving unequal and unfair treatment.

According to the prevailing view, claims that genetics contribute to the high death rate among blacks, that there are cultural influences on the attitudes of African Americans toward health care providers resulting in less mammograms and screening for prostate cancer, and that the abuse of cigarettes and alcohol is greater among blacks, have gained currency. Citing studies that show that blacks and other minorities do not get the same treatment as whites Dula questions whether racism in the delivery system is a more important factor, and whether differential treatment of minorities is related to racism. For example, whites receive more hip replacements, flu shots and twice as many cardiac procedures and mammograms, while blacks receive more amputations and more castrations for prostate cancer. Even government programs such as Medicaid practice differential, and substandard, treatment of African Americans.

Dula discusses the relationship between racism in medical research and the issue of informed consent. Although the Tuskegee Experiment is among the most egregious, blacks and other minorities continue to be overrepresented in unethical experimental research with the added irony that, along with women, minorities have been excluded from ethical research that might benefit them. These practices have detrimental consequences, for African Americans sometimes respond differently to the same treatment as whites with certain drugs such as lithium, a fact that makes access to new therapies imperative. Dula ties this issue of access to care to the issue of being enrolled in a research protocol. She is wary, however, that research involves a possibility of abuse of informed consent because regulations allow experimentation in emergency, or traumatic, situations without informed consent. This could have a disproportionate effect on minorities, given that a large number of trauma centers are located in public hospitals in, or near, inner cities. Many of these hospitals are affiliated with the teaching and research interests of universities.

The debate about solutions to some of these problems involves a universalist color-blind versus a multicultural-diversity moral viewpoint. Dula favors a multiculturalist orientation and criticizes universalist policy. She cites, as a limitation of the universalist view, the fact that the problem of access would continue, because, even when money is not the issue, access to procedures and services is not equally distributed. Add to this the fact that, due to their having poorer health, African Americans would require more. But any attempt to meet this need would amount to preferential treatment. A universalist policy also would mask the history of intentional and unintentional discrimination, fostering explanations in terms of genetic mishap, irresponsible lifestyle, and poor education. Denial of racism obscures the facts that created the need for the remedy in the first place. Advocates of diversity and multiculturalism insist on recognition of difference. Racism is not a phenomenon of the past. A color conscious approach insists that African Americans have been wronged by the health care system and compensation is in order. This requires programs and services that explicitly address the health of African Americans and eliminates disparities.

Dula argues that group survival provides a justification for preferential treatment in health care. Differential treatment has harmed African Americans by contributing to their poor health. Color-conscious programs aim toward greater equality in health status by eliminating the unjust distribution of health goods. She maintains that, in addition to universal needs, health care policy must address group-specific needs, because the history of racism has affected the health of minorities in such a manner that special needs have been created.

With the rapid growth of the black prison population in recent years the extent to which racism is a factor in the functioning of the criminal justice system is another policy issue presently of great concern to African Americans. Angela Davis reflects on Michel Foucault's *Discipline and Punish* as the most influential text in contemporary studies of prison, noting that the category of class plays a pivotal role in his analysis, but gender and race are virtually absent. She maintains that there is a need to move beyond a strictly Foucauldian genealogy in examining histories of punishment. She considers instead the influence of slavery on American systems of punishment to show the connections between confinement, punishment, and race.

Prior to Emancipation southern prisoners were primarily white, but afterwards the percentage of black convicts rose 90 percent higher. As prison populations became predominantly black, penitentiaries were either replaced by convict leasing, or restricted to white convicts. Davis cites the fact that there was widespread use of torture in connection with convict leasing to contest Foucoult's assumption that torture had become historically obsolete in industrial capitalist countries. She points out that slavery's philosophy of punishment insinuated itself into prison practices.

The tendency to treat racism as a contingent element of the criminal justice system results in part from its marginalization in histories and theories of punishment. The conjunction of crime and punishment is criticized by abolitionists who cite the fact that few people who break the law are called upon to answer for their crimes. Given that a large number of people who commit crime will not go to prison, but a large number of blacks will, being black is a factor influencing whether a person will go to jail. Davis is concerned that there is no sustained analysis of the part antiracism might play in abolitionist theory and practice and calls for a critique of race and punishment.

17

Self-Respect, Fairness, and Living Morally

LAURENCE M. THOMAS

The idea of self-respect is inextricably tied to the equality to all human beings. But if it is obvious that all human beings are created equal, it is considerably less obvious in what way this is so. In fact, it is only in recent decades that the idea that all human beings are created equal has gained a seemingly unshakable hold upon social thought, although it was the Enlightenment period just under 300 years ago that gave this notion its philosophical underpinnings. Approximately 1,500 years earlier, Aristotle thought it natural that there should be slaves, although he did not take skin color to mark the difference between slaves and non-slaves; and he thought it natural that women should be subordinate to men.

With the Enlightenment (two key figures of which are Jean-Jacques Rousseau and Immanuel Kant) came the recognition that there is a fundamental moral commonalty and equality among human beings notwithstanding the vast differences between them. The commonalty aspect is that every human being has more in common with human beings than with creatures of any other kind. Thus, for example, only human beings are susceptible to the full range of moral sentiments which includes not only anger – a sentiment which many non-human creatures can experience – but gratitude, resentment, and indignation. And only human beings are capable of language. The equality aspect is that every human being is capable of being guided by moral considerations; accordingly, only human beings admit of moral praise and blame. What is more, any creature that is capable of the full range of moral sentiments is also one who is capable of being guided by moral considerations, and conversely. Taken together, these two considerations are thought to bespeak a moral worth which all human beings have in virtue of being such. Moreover, on account of this moral worth, it is maintained that there is a proper moral way in which all human beings should be treated notwithstanding the differences among them in physical features, social standing, or natural talents and accomplishments.

The contemporary idea of self-respect is to be located in the notion of moral worth just explicated. Self-respect is the psychological attitude that consists in having the conviction that, as with any other person, one is fully worthy of the moral treatment that is proper for any and all persons. As a psychological notion, self-respect admits of

293

degrees of conviction. A person's conviction that she is deserving of proper moral treat-ment could be so strong – that nothing short of the very worst forms of wrongful moral treatment would cause her to doubt whether she is deserving of proper moral treat-ment. By contrast, a person's conviction in this regard could be sufficiently weak that even mild forms of wrongful moral treatment would incline her to wonder whether she really deserves proper moral treatment. The self-respect of the former person is very secure, but not so with the latter.

My first aim in this essay is to offer a general account of self-respect, explaining why the very obviousness of our humanity is no guarantee that persons will have self-respect. Next, I look at the ways in which widespread and systematic injustices impact upon the self-respect of persons who are the target of such practices. Although the racial treatment of blacks in the United States is the focus of this section, there is no shortage of examples in world history where one group has systematically oppressed another. What perhaps is unique about the American case is that so much inequality took place in a country whose self-confessed commitment to equality for all peoples has had no equal in the world. Finally, I raise a rather poignant question concerning this very matter. What shall we say about the moral character of persons who live morally in a society the social institutions of which do not just fail to underwrite their self-respect, but actively conspire to undermine it? I offer an example to show that there are instances in which it is plausible to suppose that doing what is morally right, in the sense of doing's one's duty, might be properly understood as supererogatory behavior. I want to make this very claim regarding blacks who lived morally in a society that was openly and sometimes viciously hostile toward them, regarding blacks who lived in a society that was on all accounts a systematic affront to their self-esteem.

I   Self-Respect, Personhood, and the Fragility of the Self

The basis for self-respect is so straightforwardly tied to being a person that, at first glance, it can be difficult to see how anyone could fail to have secure self-respect. Yet, we know that one of the profound effects of the institution of American Slavery, for instance, is that the self-respect of blacks was, in a great many instances, severely undermined. And, again, we know that sexist practices have been a most formidable obstacle to women having secure self-respect. But how can these things be? If people have never doubted whether they have limbs like others, how can people have ever doubted whether they are as deserving of proper moral treatment as others are?

The intuition behind this question, of course, is that from the moral point of view, there can be no doubt that personhood is an all-or-nothing matter. From this intuition, it follows that if one person is deserving of proper moral treatment simply in virtue of being a person, then all persons are. But this intuition is very much a contemporary one, which fails to appreciate the ingenuity of human beings to fix upon a difference and invest it with great moral significance. While the most indisputable difference among human beings is the divide between males and females, others have supposed that there are natural differences between groups of human beings. Looking at the divide between women and men will be instructive.

294

I remarked at the beginning of this essay that Aristotle held that women were morally inferior to men. As a master biologist, the issue for him was never whether women belonged to the same species as men. Rather, he took it to be obvious that as persons, women and men differ with respect to their "nature." For Aristotle, the "nature" of a woman elevated her above a slave, allowed that she should be able to exercise deliberative powers in the home, yet placed her below a man in that she did not have a place in the body-politic, nor could she participate in the highest form of friendship between equals. Why? Aristotle held that women are more temperamental and given to jealousy than men; hence, they were not as capable as men of the virtue of self-command. Thus, women could command (and, therefore, raise) children, but women commanding men was simply out the question. Women, Aristotle thought, are properly subordinate to men.

This view of the difference between women and men has to varying degrees been embraced down through the ages and across cultures. What is significant, for our purposes, though, is that without ever denying the personhood of women, it is had been held that women are not entitled to the same moral treatment as men, because women and men differ in their moral nature and the moral nature of the former is, in some fundamental respect, inferior to the moral nature of the latter.

We have, then, an answer to the question with which I began this section. Down through the ages, personhood has been regarded as compatible with a range of different moral natures, with some being inferior to the other. Accordingly, neither the moral nature of a group of people nor, therefore, what counts as the proper moral treatment of them has been regarded as entirely settled by the fact of their personhood.

Looking at this way of thinking through contemporary lenses, it is easy to dismiss it as just so much nonsense. But that would be a mistake. For one thing, if this line of thought is just so much nonsense, then surely we need to explain how some of the most talented thinkers in the history of ideas could have embraced various forms of it. As some contemporary philosophers have noted (Goldberg 1993), the formidable philosopher Immanual Kant took it to be obvious that Negroes, as he would say, were morally and intellectually inferior to white people; and he also thought that Jews were somewhat morally bereft, though he held them to be superior to Negroes. Yet, his writings, perhaps more than those of any other thinker, have inspired the idea of moral equality among all persons. Kant's idea that all persons, in virtue of being such, should regard themselves and one another as members of what he called the Kingdom of Ends has no equal in terms of moral inspiration. There are two considerations which shed some light on the discrepancy between what people have believed and the obvious truth that there is a moral point of view from which all persons are equal.

First of all, there is nothing about the logic of a false view which prevents it from being widely embraced; and a false view regarding people that is widely embraced makes for a social reality. A classic example here is that of racial differences (see Zack 1993; 1998). Biologists and social scientists have argued with great force that the very notion of a race, over and above the human race, is a bogus one. And common sense attests to this.

Does an abundance of melanin make someone a black person? Well, not if the individual is from the sub-continent of India. Does it suffice, then, that one has African ancestry? Well, not quite, since there are whites who satisfy that condition; for the Dutch populated the southern tip of Africa more than 400 year ago. On the other hand, having both African ancestry and an abundance of melanin will not do, since there are people who would regard themselves (and are regarded by others as) black who do not meet both of these criteria. Among others, the actress and singer Lena Horne, the writer Richard Wright, and the politician Adam Clayton Powell come readily to mind. None have possessed the physical features characteristically associated with being black, so much so that each could have passed for a non-black had he or she chosen to do so.

With regard to what makes a person a black person, things do not fare any better if the question is: What makes a person of African descent? A present day white person could have a lineage of 400 years in Africa. These considerations alone suggest that the notion of race is hardly about facts of the matter, at least not in any rigid way.

Still, no matter how untenable the notion might be from a scientific point of view, the social significance of the idea of race remains undeniably real; and phenotypical features used to make racial classifications are still treated by many as if these features represented deep biological differences. The notion of racial groups has such a social reality among the way people generally view one another that it is often more conveni- ent, as in this essay, to adopt the language of racial groups than not – more convenient, even though one is self-consciously aware that as a conceptual idea the notion is intel- lectually bankrupt.

A second, and perhaps more philosophical consideration, regarding the idea that people may differ in moral nature according to their biological group has its basis in the obvious truth that individuals belonging to the same biological group differ with respect to their talents and moral temperment. From this truth, it is a small slide to the view that each individual has a natural moral temperment; and this view is easily extended, although erroneously, to entire biological groups which are considered a product of nature and which are treated on the model of an individal. Thus, if per- sonhood is no barrier to persons of the same biological group differing with respect to their natural moral temperment, then personhood can hardly be a barrier to groups, which are supposedly based upon biological differences, differing with respect to their moral nature, where the idea of a moral nature is essentially a way of talking about natural temperment with respect to groups.

One very profound aspect of the fragility of the self is that prevailing and long- standing social views about a group are often embraced, albeit to varying degrees, by many members of the group itself, even if the views are false and portray the group in a quite negative fashion. This happens because social views are underwritten by a myriad of social practices which significantly shape the beliefs and feelings which people have about themselves. In *Dusk of Dawn*, Du Bois observed that nothing was a more successful threat to blacks having a positive view of themselves than the absence of a record of actual success. His point, which is readily generalizable to any group that has known little or no success, is that nothing better staves off self-doubt about one's abilities like a record of success. Accordingly, a society which does not allow an identi- fiable group of its citizens to pursue well-established avenues of success thereby ensures that many members of this group will be plagued with self-doubt about its abilities. Du Bois's point was not about the innate abilities of blacks, which he took to be equal to the innate abilities of others. Rather, he was addressing the circumstances under which blacks might have a very secure sense of their own innate abilities being equal to that of others.

If this is right, then the most eloquent rhetoric of equality cannot make up for the absence of success. This is because imagined successes, no matter how vivid, cannot bring about the feelings of affirmation that come with actual success. Nor can imagined successes silence those who would question one's abilities with the force that actual successes can. Perhaps nothing can force others to believe in one's successes. But this gets to the very heart of Du Bois's observation. When others refuse to believe in one's abilities, nothing staves off the self-doubt that would be caused by the disbelief of others than a history of actual successes.

Thus, it is important to distinguish a society's official political rhetoric from its prevailing social views – that is, the views actually embraced by most of the members of society. Arguably, The Declaration of Independence and The Constitution of the United States both contain some of the most eloquent political language of equality even written. Recall the powerful words of The Declaration: "We hold these Truths to be self-evident that all Men are created equal, that they are endowed by their Creator with certain inalienable Rights. . . ." The Preamble of The Constitution reads: "We the people of the United States in order to form a more perfect Union, establish Justice, . . . and secure the Blessings of Liberty . . . do hereby ordain and establish this Constitution of the United States of America." Yet, when the magisterial words of these two documents were penned, the prevailing social view was that blacks did not even count as full-fledged persons. Neither did women, although (harkening back to Aristotle) their social status was superior to slaves in some respects.

The fragility of self-respect, then, can be put as follows: Generally speaking, in order to have self-respect, persons need a social environment wherein they are, simply in virtue of one's humanity, treated as an individuals who are worthy of moral respect. The obvious truth that one is just as much a human being as any other person does not entail that one will have the conviction one is as much deserving of full moral treatment as any other person. Having this latter conviction is inextricably tied to the ways in which others actually treat one. This truth brings out the extent to which human beings are quintessentially social creatures. The moral uptake, if you will, of indisputable factual claims is tied to the ways in which persons are treated. Accordingly, self-respect is not something that persons can just will in or out of place, which is not to say that persons cannot do things which will have the effect of underwriting or, for that matter, undermining one's self-respect.

II   Self-Respect and Fairness

If, following John Rawls (1971), justice is properly regarded as the first virtue of social institutions, then fairness is surely the fundamental pillar of justice. It is conceptually impossible that a society could be just but not fair, and conversely. On the one hand, though, fairness hardly requires equality of outcome or distribution of goods in all cases. Presumably, some win–lose situations are surely fair. Not everyone can win the same lottery drawing or have the winning entry of the best painting. And even Marixist theory, which is diametrically opposed to capitalist theory, allows that need, which differs across persons, can be a fundamental basis for distribution of important social goods. On the other hand, it is clear that fairness and equality are very much interconnected. A fair society could not be one in which gross inequities prevailed. The issue, of course, is what counts as an (unacceptable) inequity. For Marxists, the vast inequities of wealth permitted in a capitalist society are unacceptable and, therefore, a capitalist society is an unjust society. Capitalists are simply not persuaded.

Fortunately, we need to settle this debate in order to arrive at an important insight regarding self-respect, fairness, and justice. While both Marxists and capitalists differ with regard to what counts as acceptable inequities, they are all humanity egalitarians. That is, they all agree that natural talent is randomly distributed across humanity and, therefore, no ethnic group, as such, is from the standpoint of biological endowment the bearer of greater natural talent than another. There are, to be sure, preferences and acumen owing to traditions, culture, and upbringing. However, the preferences and acumen of groups do not point to a deeper fact pertaining to the biological endowment of one group as opposed to another.

In the United States, for instance, it was often said in times past that blacks have "rhythm" and whites do not. This was said as as if the difference really had some biological basis. Contemporary times, however, makes it abundantly clear that the only basis this difference really had was early exposure on the part of whites to the music of blacks. According to humanity egalitarians, the alleged deep differences between blacks and whites in the United States has turned out to have just the sort of explanation it should have had. As an aside, the issue of rhythm is a paradigm example of a false view that is widely embraced by everyone. It is not just whites who have held that blacks, unlike whites, have rhythm, but blacks themselves. Yet, the issue of rhythm is just about perfectly analogous to accent. As a social phenomenon, it is true that persons who learn to speak a foreign language after their thirties will almost certainly speak that language with an accent that bespeaks their native language. And everyone supposes that the explanation for this is precisely what it is, namely that the foreign language was not learned until well-after a given speaking pattern had been informed. No one has ever claimed, or even been tempted to proffer, a biological difference between nations as an explanation for this phenomenon.

At any rate, if it is true that natural talent is randomly distributed across all of humanity, then in a just society, and so one which treats all of its citizens fairly, it should not turn out that one group (identifiable along ethnic or religious lines, for instance) languishes while all others flourish, whatever the economic structure of the society might be, unless that group has explicitly adopted a set of values whereby success and thriving are quite differently measured. Religious groups such as the Amish come readily to mind here. It is neither an accident of history nor the result of injustice that Amish homes do not have modern appliances in their homes (dishwashers, washers and dryers, microwave ovens, and so forth), that the horse and carriage remain their basic mode of transportation, and that they are not on university campuses as either faculty or students or that in general they are not a part of the American mainstream. The Amish do not, for instance, run for political office. As a people, the Amish have self-consciously and freely chosen this lifestyle in accordance with their conviction that their lifestyle pleases God. Needless to say, it would not occur to the Amish to think of themselves as languishing. And surely we should not either.

But with other ethnic and religious groups in America, things are quite different. The treatment of blacks in the United States stand as a paradigm example of a people being treated unfairly and, therefore, unjustly by American society. If blacks have languished in the United States this is not surprising. The ignominy of racism is that society takes a palpably irrelevant set of features of an identifiable group of persons in society and maintains as a societal truth that, on the basis of this set of features, these individuals are not worthy of being treated fully in accordance with the precepts of justice. And this American institutions did with an ingenuity that borders on incredulity.

From the one-drop rule according to which a person with one drop of black blood is black and so is to be consigned to the dustbin of society (whatever her physical features might in fact be) to the Jim Crow practices of the Old South, requiring among other things separate water fountains for blacks and whites, to treating blacks as second-class citizens in an army which, in the name of humanity, sought to liberate Jews from the Nazis: Political, social, and educational institutions across the country took a palpably insignificant, and sometimes elusive, set of features of a group of people and endowed those features with moral significance. A black could not count upon the very law which held him accountable for his misdeeds to protect him in the face of even blatant wrongdoing against him. Thus, in a country where political equality was regarded as the fundamental cornerstone, it was possible for a white person who was utterly lacking in either moral sensibilities or accomplishments to feel morally superior to any black, regardless of the moral virtues which that black might possess.

In a word, then, owing to systematic unfairness, the institutions of America were a brazen affront to the self-respect of all black citizens. That is, the lack of freedom and privileges accorded blacks and the concommitant indifference was tied to a normative conception of blacks which if they came to embrace would entail that they saw themselves as not worthy of being treated fully in accordance with the precepts of justice. What is more, and this gets to the very heart of the matter, if it is true that how people feel about themselves is profoundly shaped by the ways in which they are treated in the society in which they live, then there can be no doubt that the self-respect of many blacks was deeply undermined by the unjust practices that prevailed. In terms of modern psychology, the widespread unjust practices of the American society resulted in considerable cognitive dissonance on the part of many blacks regarding the belief that they are as worthy as anyone of proper moral treatment. For their belief in themselves as full moral beings was shorn of experiential anchoring, of the affirmation that springs from experience which not even the most vivid imagination can match.

To be sure, blacks could gather among themselves and affirm their moral worth (McGary 1999); and this must have had a salubrious effect in numerous instances. In this connection, the black church comes to mind as having been of considerable importance (Freedman 1993. All the same, affirmation such as this did not remove, and could not have removed, the daily reminders of inequality that existed throughout society. Likewise, such affirmation was not, and could not have been, a substitute for the experience of equality.

Now I have claimed that the vast inequality towards blacks was an affront to their self-respect. I also want to make another claim, namely that as a result of this systematic affrontery a great many blacks suffered from a lack of self-respect. But these two claims are logically distinct. A piece of behavior can certainly be an affront to a person's dignity or self-respect or character in general without diminishing that person's dignity or self-respect or character. Accordingly, systematic affrontery undoubtedly affects different people differently. This is true of all forms of egregious wrongful behavior. The will to survive and the wherewithal to believe in oneself is a function of a variety of factors, contingencies, and confluences. It is said that the refusal of Rosa Parks to give up her bus seat to a white person precipitated the Civil Rights Movement. But it is also true that she was sitting in the "colored section" located at the rear of the bus; and the bus then became crowded. Suppose that she had mistakenly sat in the "white section" of the bus, and she was then asked to take an available seat in the "colored section." It is not inconceivable that she would have complied with this request, although the very idea that tax-paying blacks should have had to sit in the back of buses paid for by tax dollars is an affront to the self-respect of blacks.

Did the widespread affront of social inequality have an adverse effect upon many blacks? I believe that it did. Many blacks were willing to accept their inferior position in society. In fact, some rationalized the acceptance of their inferior place in society by insisting that their just reward would be in heaven. This should come as no surprise. The best psychological evidence available suggests that systematic abuse, of which systematic and egregious unfairness is surely an instance, takes its toll. The issue here is not whether black families loved their children or whether blacks were in various ways supportive of one another. Surely these things were true. The point, rather, is that neither parental love or community support as such is likely to be a sufficient buffer against the constant tide of systematic injustice.

We know that Frederic Douglass and Harriet Jacobs, for instance, threw off the mantel of slavery with incredible majesty and ingenuity. There can be no doubt that these two individuals had self-respect. But there is little evidence that their lives were representative of the lives of slaves in general. Accordingly, when we consider the case of blacks between the Reconstruction and Civil Rights eras, there is good reason to believe that the self-respect of many blacks was adversely affected by the injustices that the American society relentlessly visited upon its black citizens.

III Self-Respect and Living Morally

A most interesting question arises regarding the moral character of blacks who, in some cases, suffered from a diminution of self-respect owing to the deep and systematic injustices of American society which, in any case, was unquestionably an affront to the self-respect of all blacks. Significantly, such a society was not conducive to blacks living morally. This is so, at any rate, if one supposes that our will to live morally is profoundly affected by the way in which we are treated by others. Surely a person who later acts with good will towards someone who has egregiously harmed her exhibits considerable strength of character. Typically, the supererogatory is understood as going sufficiently over and above the call of duty. But we might also suppose that a person acts supererogatory in doing what is morally right by those who have treated her in a most oppressive and inhumane way. If a woman has been raped by the man who is her neighbor, would she not be exhibiting extraordinary moral fortitude if, the next day, she should report to the police the scoundrels who were then attempting to set his house on fire? If, instead, she turned a blind eye, would this not be entirely comprehensible? Assuming that she could so without bring on any harm to herself, it would certainly be wrong of her not to turn them in. Yet, if she turned a blind eye who could blame her? Would it not be something akin to moral arrogance to take the moral high ground here and insist that her failing to turn in the scoundrels renders her morally blame-worthy?

Or, to take a very different example, suppose that Mary has beaten up Rachel day after day for the past 4 years while they were in middle school. They are now in differ-ent high schools; and in the meantime, Rachel has been going to the gym, learning karate, and so forth. Finally, not only is she in a position to defend herself against the likes of Mary, she is able to demolish Mary completely. Now, the fact that Mary had beaten Rachel up daily in middle school hardly constitutes a moral reason for Rachel to beat Mary up – and certainly not a moral reason to pick a fight with her. It is morally permissible to defend oneself – not to showcase one's fighting abilities by picking fights with others! Still, I suspect that we would all understand Rachel if, as we say, she just so happened to find herself walking past Mary's high school, not with the intention to pick a fight with Mary, but to well-defend herself should Mary take the initiative, as in middle school.

In both examples, we have an attitude that I shall refer to as the expressive symme-try of self-defense. When we have been wronged by another especially in an egregious manner, we typically want there to be a moral leveling between us and the person who has wronged us. And to this end, we will often refrain from behaving in certain ways on behalf of the other, expecting that as a result a measure of moral leveling will occur. This is the case with the first example. Or, as with the second example, we may position ourselves in the hopes that the person's behavior will require us to exercise certain powers against her or him. When a person has been egregiously wronged by another, but nonetheless fails to have an expressive symmetry of self-defense posture towards that person, then the person who has been wronged exhibits a considerable level of moral excellence. It is not always easy to do what is right. And when one does so under the most trying circumstances this deserves commendation.

It is one thing to tell the truth, and quite another to do so at the risk of losing one's life. There are numerous occasions when doing what is morally right understandably requires all the strength of will that one can muster. Indeed, for just this reason, there are occasions when it is far from obvious that one could expect a person to do what is right.

Viewing morality in this vein, then the notion of supererogation might be usefully extended. As I have said, the root idea behind the notion of supererogatory is a morally good act that is morally permissible, but not morally required; accordingly, the person is not morally blameworthy for failing to perform the act although it is one that she could have performed. I suggest that there are times when an act may be supereroga-tory even though it is morally required, precisely because the circumstances under which the act must be performed are such that it is far too understandable if a morally decent person should nonetheless lack the will to act as is required of her or him. It is far too understandable if a mother should lie if that is the only way in which she can save the life of her child. If a person has just been raped, it is far too understandable they will lack the wherewithal to call for an ambulance because the rapist, in the attempt to escape, was hit and seriously harmed by a hit-and-run driver. Yet, this would be the minimally decent thing to do. The Jew in Auschwitz who made an extraordinary effort, who put her very life on the line, to save the life of a dying Nazi would strike us as almost too moral for words. In my view these are all acts of supererogation.

This extended view of supererogation will not be as neat as the traditional view, simply because the latter is defined in terms of doing a significant good that is not required of one. On the other hand, the extended view is very much in keeping with the spirit of the traditional view. Typically, an act of supererogation is not the same thing as an act of generosity. For a person can be enormously kind without burdening herself, as when a multi-billionaire gives a multi-million dollar gift to a charitable foundation. On the traditional view, an act of supererogation typically involves helping another at the risk of one's life or, at any rate, enormous harm to oneself. And the idea is simply that it cannot be reasonably expected of a person to risk his life or physical well-being for another. The idea behind the extended view is that sometimes it cannot be reasonable, in just the same sense of the traditional view, not to expect persons to behave in certain ways, even if this is precisely what morality requires.

Let us apply the extended view of supererogation to blacks in the United States. The viciousness of slavery and post-slavery racism in America is too obvious for words. During slavery, a black man had little or no legal standing in the courts of the United States. And this was de facto the case after slavery's end. Depending upon the mood that whites were in, a black man could be lynched for merely looking at a white person, especially a woman, the wrong way. Whites were utterly indifferent to the devastation that this would have upon his family. During slavery, a black woman could be raped by a white man without any legal recourse. After slavery, it was only a legal fiction that she had any legal recourse. From slavery up until the Civil Rights Era, white American society barely acknowledged the humanity of blacks. Quite the contrary, social institutions brutally and systematically called into question the humanity of blacks.

Yet, for all of this brutality and utter indifference on the part of whites, for all the unabashed ill-will that blacks had to endure at the hands of whites, instances of blacks turning on whites were relatively rare until after the Civil Rights Era. Why was this?

One explanation, of course, is fear which is as powerful a motivating factor as there is. Were blacks to have started turning on whites, then blacks would have seen uncompromising wrath at the hands of whites. So on this view, prudence alone suffices to explain the absence of widespread hostility on the part of blacks towards whites between the Reconstruction and Civil Rights Eras. There can be little doubt that prudence, anchored in the fear of being harmed, is an explanation for why persons sometimes do what is morally right. But as any good Kantian would say, in this instance, we have the right behavior but the wrong motivation for executing it. Indeed, one hardly has to be committed to a Kantian conception of morality to think this.

By contrast, however, suppose that, between the Reconstruction and the Civil Rights Eras, the moral sensibilities of blacks were such that in general blacks were never much concerned with behaving in a morally hostile fashion towards whites. Suppose that, notwithstanding all the ill-treatment which they endured at the hands of whites, blacks never lost sight of the humanity of whites; and this perspective stayed the moral hand of blacks. In steadfastly refraining from engaging in such behavior, were not blacks exhibiting a level of moral goodness that perhaps could not have been reasonably expected of them?

Again, recall the story of rape given above. Surely, one would naturally expect the woman to be sufficiently angry at her neighbor for having raped her that she could hardly bring herself to turn in the scoundrels who attempted to burn down his house. If in spite of having endured this horror, she found the wherewithal to turn in those who have attempted to harm her rapist, then her behavior is most admirable morally. Some might argue that no woman could be in the throes of all the pain of rape and yet have any feelings of compassion for her rapist – certainly none that would lead her to act as I have described. While it is understandable that one hold such an event unlikely, there is no argument that would show that such behavior is conceptually ruled out of court. An explicit Christian commandment is that one should love one's enemy. No one has ever argued that living up to this commandment constitutes a conceptual impossibility. Nor has anyone ever denied its inspirational power.

Christianity played an abiding role in the lives of blacks during slavery and up until the Civil Rights Era. Thus, to an extent that has never been acknowledged, it is possible that blacks in America have masterfully exhibited the moral virtue of good will and forgiveness. In a society that referred to them as "niggers" and treated them as such, blacks found the will to live morally – to do what is right by whites. This blacks did all the while receiving little or no moral credit for doing so. This is an extraordinary testimony to the strength of their moral character.

I want to bring this section to a close by briefly drawing attention to non-invidios distinction between American Slavery and the Holocaust that I have made elsewhere (Thomas, 1993). The aim of the Holocaust was the extermination of the Jews, and not they should behave in a morally decent way towards others. And to this end, sheer force was the fundamental weapon of the Nazis against the Jews. The aim of American Slavery was that blacks should exhibit morally decent behavior towards whites even as whites systemmatically ignored the humanity of blacks. On my view, morally decent behavior on the part of blacks towards whites and Jews towards Nazis would count as supererogatory behavior. However, there was not the expectation of such behavior on the Nazis with respect to the Jews. Indeed, the Nazis systemmatically used force to insure compliance on the part of the Jews. On the other hand, whites did expect such behavior from blacks. And in the absence of force, it is precisely such behavior that blacks exhibited.

Self-Respect and Moral Character

The arguments of this essay leaves us with some very poignant considerations. Self-respect may be a very fundamental good. Yet, it would not seem necessary to live a moral life – at least not if the history of blacks in America is any indication. With unparalleled commitment and integrity, many blacks did what was right by their slavemaster with an undying commitment. In the name of theory, one could insist that such moral behavior on the part of blacks missed the moral mark, since as black slaves failed to take themselves seriously as individuals with full moral status – as members of the kingdom of ends. But theory, however, elegant must always bow to reality. If slaves could be loyal and faithful to their masters, as surely many were, then their moral behavior towards their masters could be as robust as the moral behavior of any fully self-respecting person. Accordingly, we have seen that persons whose lives are lacking self-respect may nonetheless exhibit not just morally proper behavior, but moral behavior that deserves to be regarded as supererogatory, given the pain of inequality.

The good of self-respect, it seems, consists not so much in marking off the ways in which we should treat others, but the ways in which we should expect others to treat us. The authors of the *Declaration of Independence* thought it obvious that no self-respecting persons would tolerate injustices against them, insisting that people have a right to revolt when a government comes up short in this regard. Alas, the case of American slavery may show that regarding the significance of having self-respect, the authors of the *Declaration of Independence* got it exactly right. As Socrates claimed, and Martin Luther King, Jr. echoed so very much later: Perhaps the problem with self-respect, if you will, is just that one is prepared to die for some things.

Acknowledgment

In writing this essay, I am deeply grateful to Claire Zeppelli for conversations, to John Pittman for detailed and astute comments, and to the Centre de Recherche en Épistemologie Appliqué (CRÉA) in Paris for its constant philosophical support. In writing section III, in particular, a special word of thanks goes to Nasri Abdel-Aziz.

References

Baier, Annette (1995), *Moral Prejudices* (Cambridge, MA: Harvard University Press).

Boxill, Bernard (1983), *Blacks and Social Justice* (Rowman and Littlefield).

Meillassoux, Claude (1998), *Anthropologie de l'esclavage* (Paris: Presses Universitaires de France).

Freedman, S. G. (1993), *Upon This Rock: The Miracles of a Black Church* (New York: Harper Perenial).

David, Theo Goldberg (1993), *Racist Culture: Philosophy and the Politics of Meaning* (Cambridge, MA: Blackwell).

McGary, Howard (1999), *Race and Social Injustice* (Cambridge, MA: Blackwell).

Moody-Adams, Michelle (1998), *Fieldword in Familiar Places* (Cambridge, MA: Harvard University Press).

Nagel, Thomas (1986), *The View from Nowhere* (New York: Oxford University Press).

Ogien, Ruwen (1993), *Portrait Logique et Moral de La Haine* (Presses Universitaires de France).

Nussbaum, Marth (1999), *Sex and Social Justice* (New York: Oxford University Press).

Rawls, John (1971), *A Theory of Justice* (Cambridge, MA: Harvard University Press).

Thomas, Laurence (1989), *Living Morally: A Psychology of Moral Character* (Philadelphia, PA: Temple University Press).

——(1993), *Vessels of Evil: American Slavery and the Holocaust* (Philadelphia, PA: Temple University Press).

Vargnières, Solange (1995), *Éthique et Politique Chez Aristotle* (Presses Universitaires de France, 1995).

Wolf, Susan (1982), "Moral Saints," *The Journal of Philosophy* 72.

Zack, Naomi (1993), *Race and Mixed Race* (Philadelphia: Temple University Press).

——(1998), *Thinking About Race* (Belmont, CA: Wadsworth Publishing Co., 1998).

18

The Legacy of *Plessy v. Ferguson*

MICHELE MOODY-ADAMS

In the summer of 1890, the state of Louisiana passed the *Railway Accommodations Act*, requiring "equal but separate accommodations for the white and colored races" on all passenger railways within Louisiana (Blaustein and Zangrando 1991). One year later, a small group of black Americans, drawn primarily from the New Orleans community of "Creoles of color," organized a Citizens Committee to test the constitutionality of the Act. Their plans came to fruition in 1892 with the hoped-for arrest of Homer Plessy, for his refusal to comply with a conductor's request that he take a seat in the Jim Crow car. Plessy was convicted. But he appealed that conviction to the Supreme Court of Louisiana, arguing that Louisiana's Railway Act violated the thirteenth and fourteenth amendments to the US Constitution. When that appeal was denied, Plessy appealed the case to the United States Supreme Court.

The US Supreme Court decision in Plessy's case would not come for four more years. But legal and social developments during those years – including the proliferation of Jim Crow laws, a marked increase in anti-black lynching, and the influence of Booker T. Washington's insistence upon the "folly" of "agitation of questions of social equality" – would have sent a powerful message about the national attitude toward racial segregation. Those black citizens of New Orleans who agitated for a constitutional test of segregation may not have been surprised, therefore, when the majority opinion in *Plessy v. Ferguson* enunciated what C. Vann Woodward has called the "national decision against equality" (Woodward 1964). Yet Homer Plessy and his fellows could hardly have anticipated the complex historical legacy of their protest. The unexpected triumphs, as well the frustrating limits, of *Plessy v. Ferguson* were revealed only gradually, as accompaniments to hard-won legal and social changes occurring over the next century – and to the moral and political debates to which those changes gave rise.

The immediate outcome in *Plessy* might have seemed to bear out Washington's conviction of the folly of protesting racial inequality; the majority opinion unequivocally declared that Louisiana's separate car law violated no thirteenth or fourteenth amendment rights. The Court not only maintained that segregation could not be unconstitutional so long as the segregated facilities were "equal," but also implied that racial segregation was in no way an obstacle to equal accommodations. Delivering the opinion of the Court, Justice Henry Billings Brown complained of the "underlying fallacy" of Plessy's claim that legally enforced segregation stamped black Americans with "a badge of inferiority." He allowed that this might sometimes be an effect of segregation. Yet "it is not because of anything in the law," he insisted, "but solely because the colored race chooses to put that construction upon it" (*Plessy* 1896). Several years later, assessing the judicial career of the lone dissenter in *Plessy*, Justice John Marshall Harlan, Brown finally acknowledged that the intent of the Louisiana law was in fact to exclude black passengers from white railway cars, and not the other way around (Brown 1912). But it is unlikely that critics of *Plessy* will find much consolation in Brown's belated concession of this fundamental premise of the "badge of inferiority" argument.

Yet there may be some consolation in the fact that, even in defeat, Plessy and his supporters accomplished something that neither the anti-discrimination interests in the 39th Congress, nor a thirty-year succession of plaintiffs in anti-segregation cases, could manage. Through Justice Harlan's now famous dissent in *Plessy*, the New Orleans Citizens Committee set in motion a chain of events which resulted in the first clear articulation in a constitutionally relevant forum of the idea that a principle of color-blindness is implicit in the "equal protection" clause of the Fourteenth Amendment. As early as 1864, opponents of slavery such as Wendell Phillips unsuccessfully sought the explicit inclusion of a doctrine of color-blindness in the Reconstruction Amendments (Kull). The failure of these efforts meant that central components of the Fourteenth Amendment – the "privileges and immunities" clause, the "due process" clause, and even the "equal protection" clause – could offer no explicit protection against racial discrimination. Moreover, for nearly three decades after the drafting of the Fourteenth Amendment, state and federal courts repeatedly denied that a principle of non-discrimination was even implicit in the Amendment (Kull 1992).

It is important that these results did not deter Plessy's legal counsel, Albion Tourgée, from charging that the Louisiana statute's rejection of color blindness was unconstitutional. But it is equally important that Tourgée had been sought out by the New Orleans Citizens Committee largely for the fit between his conception of social justice and their own, and that there is evidence of close and ongoing consultation between Tourgee and the members of the Committee throughout the *Plessy* case (Lofgren 1987; Oberst 1973). Taken together, these considerations lend compelling support to the claim made by some legal historians that Tourgée's understanding of the Consitutition clearly expressed the central arguments on which the black citizens of New Orleans based their legal case against racial segregation (Lofgren 1987; Oberst 1973). If the color-blind reading of the Constitution ever has the kind of influence its early supporters hoped it would have, the result will richly confirm Derrick Bell's claim that black Americans have helped to bring to the Constitution much of its current protection of individual rights (Bell 1995).

But what might it mean for the ideal of color-blindness to have the kind of influence which proponents such as Plessy, Tourgée, and Harlan, might have intended? To put the point a little differently, what would it be to give proper moral weight to the principle of color-blindness in shaping social policy in a liberal democratic society? A number of contemporary social critics and theorists insist that only an unwavering commitment to color-blindness – whatever that facts of discrimination might be – assigns proper moral weight to the principle. Yet others contend that in view of the lingering consequences of American apartheid, color-blindness can sometimes be outweighed by other, morally more compelling considerations (Boxill 1988; Gutmann 1996). On this view, then, the emergence of an ideal of color-blindness as a central component of American political morality at this point in history is, at best, a *Pyrrhic* victory.

This latter, more cautious commitment to color-blindness typically rests on several seemingly relevant historical considerations. To begin with, it will be argued, new Jim Crow legislation continued to appear well into the middle of the twentieth century. As late as 1944, for instance, the state of Virginia enacted legislation requiring racial segregation in airport waiting rooms and other public facilities (Oberst 1973). Critics who cite such facts must acknowledge that black Americans were legally liberated from the "Plessy prison" – in Roy Wilkins's apt phrase – with the 1954 US Supreme Court decision in *Brown v. Board of Education* (Wilkins 1963). But it can also be argued that America was still dismantling some of the legal structures of Jim Crow well into the late 1960s, and that deeply rooted resistance to *Brown v. Board of Education* could still be found in many parts of America for much of the final quarter of the twentieth century. The upshot of such claims is that American liberal democracy failed to genuinely dismantle segregation with "deliberate speed" during the post-*Brown* era, and that this failure exacerbated the social and economic consequences of American racial oppression and discrimination for much of the twentieth century (Bell 1992; 1995). The result, it may be argued, was the further exclusion of many black Americans from access to what John Rawls would call the social bases of self-respect (Moody-Adams 1992–3).

It must be noted that some who sought racial justice during the middle of the twentieth century nonetheless remained optimistic about the possibility that formal legal equality in America might eventually result in genuine equality of opportunity. This optimism overwhelmingly led them to welcome overt legal expressions of the color-blind ideal, for instance, in the *Civil Rights Act of 1964*, the *Voting Rights Act of 1965*, and the legal regulations governing the Equal Opportunity Employment Commission (Skrentny 1996). But the principle of color blindness has temporarily lost its luster for many who believe that the social and economic apartheid left in the wake of legal segregation requires color-conscious remedies such as affirmative action. According to these thinkers, in a political context still shaped by the existence of injustice (and its social and economic effects), color conscious social policies are a morally acceptable response to racial injustice and embody a morally defensible interpretation of the liberal democratic principle of fairness (Gutmann 1996). They accept that in a more nearly just political context – of the very the sort they seek to produce by a temporary reliance on color consciousness – the principle of color blindness would be the preferred interpretation of liberal democratic notion of fairness (Gutmann 1996). Yet, on this view, the color-blind interpretation of liberal democratic ideals cannot yet be separated from the history which produced that interpretation.

Some commentators have expressed profound pessimism about the fact that, in spite of their efforts, moral and political debates about racial justice so frequently sever the doctrine of color blindness from the history which produced it. Some of these pessimists even suggest, in response, that America may never attain genuine racial equality (Bell 1992). For many, the ease with which the doctrine of color blindness is so often separated from its history simply confirms the futility of the kind of protest carried out by the Citizens Committee of New Orleans. Legal scholars in the Critical Legal Studies movement have sometimes claimed that seeking racial equality from within a liberal democratic framework of individual legal rights can ultimately do no more than legitimate the racial inequality which, in their view, that framework of legal rights presupposes (Freeman 1978). Yet even sympathetic critics of this stance point out that the American civil rights movement did produce significant change – both in the "external" social worlds of many black Americans, and in the "internal" mindset of those black Americans who recognized the transformative potential inherent in some of the very legal structures that had been used to oppress and exclude them (Crenshaw 1988).

Equally important, even where civil rights protests have been unsuccessful in the short run, they have often forced public and critical scrutiny of the formerly untested assumptions underlying existing social arrangements that has proven fruitful in the long run. In this context, it makes to sense to suggest that the decision in *Brown* – ultimately rejecting the doctrine of "separate but equal" – was set in motion by the way in which segregation's opponents responded to their loss in *Plessy*. Justice Harlan's *Plessy* dissent (building on Tourgee's *Plessy* brief, and ultimately on the stance of the New Orleans Citizens Committee) entered into the legal record not only a particular reading of the Constitution, but an explicit statement of the central assumptions underlying the national decision against equality. To be sure, the socioeconomic implications of those assumptions would not be confronted in open national debate for six more decades. But the *Plessy* dissent – and its many antecedents in the abolitionist movement, and later legal challenges to segregation – helped to set the terms of that debate. Non-violent civil disobedience of the 1950s and 1960s proved to be a far more effective form of social protest than that carried out by Homer Plessy and his associates. Yet that is surely because the Civil Rights movement was able to build, at least in part, on the (initially unsuccessful) efforts of the New Orleans Citizens Committee.

The terms of the national debate about equality have changed dramatically in the decades since the Civil Rights movement. The changes can be traced, in part, to the emergence of color conscious social policies such as affirmative action, and to the increasingly vehement resistance to those policies. But changes in the way Americans talk about social equality can also be traced to the emergence, for many white Americans, of what might be called a moral fatigue about race. Some critics of this fatigue contend that it rests on a series of mistaken assumptions – including the belief that legal reforms accomplished by the civil rights movement created genuine equality of opportunity for all black Americans, and that any remaining social and economic disparities between black and white Americans simply reflect a lack of initiative or a lack of merit (or both) on the part of black Americans (Crenshaw 1988). But several increasingly vocal defenders of white American moral fatigue insist that it is justified, on the grounds that the emergence of the color-blind ideal has in fact been accompanied by the "end of racism" (D'Souza 1995; Sowell 1984). The end-of-racism theorist may admit the existence of racists beliefs, but is likely to argue that the vast majority of these are rational responses to allegedly supportable generalizations about the characteristics and behavior of African Americans, or to the presumed unfairness of color conscious social policies.

Yet there is resistance to these assertions about the end of racism. Implicit in much of this resistance is a notion, first defended by the philosopher of law H. L. A. Hart, that any legal system always includes a complex "internal perspective" on the law – a perspective from which agents subject to legal rules take demands for conformity to the rules, and take criticisms of breaches of the rules to be appropriate (Hart 1962). Those who accept Hart's conception of legal systems are likely to argue that the internal perspective on segregation and racial discrimination involved a complex set of beliefs about the racial inferiority of black Americans, and the racial entitlement of white Americans, that were transmitted from one generation to another throughout slavery and into the subsequent lengthy period of legally protected and enforced discrimination. On this view, it is simply implausible that the internal perspective on segregation – and the beliefs associated with it – would magically disappear with the end of legally sanctioned discrimination (Moody-Adams 1992–3).

This notion of an entrenched internal commitment to segregation helps explain Justice Brown's otherwise problematic assertion in *Plessy* that social prejudices could not be eliminated by legislation. We can assume that Brown was not simply expressing a personal commitment to the preservation of segregation, but articulating a reasonable inference based on segregation's structural consequences. In fact, Justice Brown's defense of segregation yields many insights relevant to contemporary debates about the controversial assertion of the "end" of racism. For Brown conceded that American social prejudices produced vast and deeply rooted inequality of opportunity. He did so by implicitly accepting Tourgee's claim (in the *Plessy* brief) that in a community where members of one race dominate another, being a member of the dominant race – or simply having the "reputation" of being a member – is the most valuable sort of property, being indeed "the master-key that unlocks the golden door of opportunity." But if it is implausible that the social prejudices which produce unequal opportunity could simply disappear with the end of legal segregation, it would seem to be equally implausible that inequality of opportunity would simply disappear with the demise of legally sanctioned and enforced segregation.

Many contemporary proponents of contemporary Critical Race Theory have argued this point quite forcefully, urging us to recognize the lingering social and economic importance of the notion (affirmed in the majority opinion in *Plessy*) that American legal and social institutions have long recognized a "property in whiteness" (Harris 1993; Bell 1995). According to many Critical Race Theorists, persistent social and economic racial inequality is the ongoing consequence of America's continued acceptance of a "property in whiteness," and color conscious social policies are the only appropriate response. They deny that, in the context of American history, color conscious policies could ever establish a "property interest in Blackness." In so doing, they deny what many critics of color conscious policies implicitly suggest. That is, they reject the notion that color conscious policies could possibly transform being a black American into a socially effective "master-key" to social and economic opportunity. To be capable of establishing a "property interest in blackness," they contend, color conscious policies would have to be based on principles of black superiority. Since they are rooted, instead, in a principled demand to remedy oppression and subordination, they therefore cannot be the "functional equivalent" of the longstanding property interest in whiteness (Harris 1993).

310

Even those who purport to acknowledge the persistence and consequences of unjust racial discrimination, however, may deny that color conscious policies can ever simply be modes of remedying oppression and subordination. For many of these critics, color conscious remedies are intrinsically unconstitutional, and morally unfair, because they challenge the principle of awarding merit. But if the *Plessy* decision and its effects teach us anything about the current social situation, it is surely that the existing distribution of economic and social power in America has a great deal to do with the persistence of discrimination. Equally important, American social policy is full of "exceptions" to the principle of meritocracy: from veterans' preferences in civil service exams (which often extend to the veteran's widow), to the preferences that college admissions offices often extend to the children of alumni, and even the legally sanctioned nepotism that limits membership in various trades and businesses (Skrentny 1996).

Critics of color conscious remedies may have a more compelling case when they raise concerns about the tendency of some such remedies to impose heavy costs on especially vulnerable individuals in the name of a social good. It may be argued, for instance, that affirmative action frequently imposes economic and social burdens on those who are least likely to have been responsible for, or even simply to have benefited from, the inequality of opportunity resulting from racial segregation – and who, as a result, may be least able to bear the burdens so imposed. This is a difficult challenge to meet, and even the most thoughtful proponents of (temporary) color conscious remedies seldom given enough attention to the moral difficulties of asking some individuals to bear disproportionate burden of the costs of remedying racial injustice (Moody-Adams 1999).

Unfortunately, *Plessy* promises few answers to important questions about how to strike the proper balance between compensating the morally weighty wrongs of discrimination and fairly distributing the burdens of compensation. Of course, *Plessy* did not explicitly raise the question of compensating the wrongs it sought to end, and the nature of segregation's wrongs would forever be altered by the *Plessy* decision itself. But perhaps it must also be asked whether efforts to look at the contemporary problem solely through *Plessy's* lens of individual rights are intrinsically unlikely to succeed. To be sure, the notions of collective responsibility which are frequently implicit in contemporary defenses of color conscious social policies do not promise unproblematic solutions to the disagreements that shape the national debate about equality. In recent debates, expressions of moral fatigue about race are frequently linked with assertions that efforts to compensate black Americans for segregation and discrimination unfairly saddle current generations with responsibility for the moral wrongs of the past. This tendency is likely to continue into the twenty-first century. Changing patterns of immigration will exacerbate this tendency, when increasing numbers of Americans may genuinely be able to say that their significant ancestors had no direct role in discriminating against black Americans. Even if those new Americans might be shown to derive significant benefits from social and economic structures created by that discrimination, it will become more and more difficult to draw them into the debate about racial equality on the same terms that might have compelled the assent of some past generations of immigrants.

Yet while *Plessy v. Ferguson* yields no easy solution to the moral complexity of contemporary debates about social equality in America, it will always provide a compelling reminder of what is at stake in these debates – for, in the words of Justice Harlan's dissent, the destinies of all Americans "are indissolubly linked together." If we can reinvigorate widespread commitment to that truth, the efforts of those who have "agitated" for social equality, in *Plessy* and elsewhere, will not have been in vain.

References

Bell, Derrick. *Faces at the Bottom of the Well. The Permanence of Racism* (New York: Basic Books, 1992).

——. "Property Rights in Whiteness – Their Legal Legacy, Their Economic Costs." *Critical Race Theory: The Cutting Edge.* Editor Richard Delgado (Philadelphia: Temple University Press, 1995), 75–83.

Blaustein, Albert and Robert L. Zangrando, eds. *Civil Rights and African Americans* (Evanston: Northwestern University Press, 1991).

Boxill, Bernard. *Blacks and Social Justice* (Rowman and Allenheld, 1988).

——. "Washington, DuBois, and *Plessy v. Ferguson*." *Law and Philosophy* (1997) 16: 299–330.

Brown, Henry Billings. "The Dissenting Opinions of Mr. Justice Harlan." *The American Law Review* (1912) 46: 321–52.

Crenshaw, Kimberlé Williams. "Race, Reform, and Retrenchment: Transformation and Legitimation in Anti-Discrimination Law." *Harvard Law Review* (1988) 101: 1331.

D'Souza, Dinesh. *The End of Racism: Principles for a Multi-racial Society* (New York: Free Press, 1995).

Freeman, Alan. "Legitimizing Racial Discrimination through Anti-Discrimination Law: A Critical Review of Supreme Court Doctrine." *Minnesota Law Review* (1978) 62: 1049.

Gutmann, Amy "Responding to Racial Injustice." In Amy Gutmann and Anthony Apppiah, eds. *Color Conscious: The Political Morality of Race* (Princeton: Princeton University Press, 1996).

Harris, Cheryl. "Whiteness as Property." *Harvard Law Review* (1993) 106: 1707–91.

Hart, H. L. A. *The Concept of Law* (Oxford: Oxford University Press, 1962).

Kull, Andrew. *The Color-Blind Constitution* (Cambridge, MA: Harvard University Press, 1992).

Lofgren, Charles A. *The Plessy Case. A Legal-Historical Interpretation* (New York: Oxford University Press, 1987).

Moody-Adams, Michele. "Race, Class and the Social Construction of Self-Respect." *Philosophical Forum* (1992–3) 24: 251–66.

——. "A Commentary on *Color Conscious: The Political Morality of Race*." *Ethics* (1999) 109: 408–23.

Oberst, Paul. "The Strange Career of *Plessy v. Ferguson*." *Arizona Law Review* (1973) 13: 389–418.

Plessy v. Ferguson. 163 U.S. 537 (1896).

Skretny, John David. *The Ironies of Affirmative Action* (Chicago: University of Chicago Press, 1996).

Sowell, Thomas. *Civil Rights: Rhetoric or Reality?* (New York: William Morrow, 1984).

Wilkins, Roy. "Emancipation and Militant Leadership." *One Hundred Years of Emancipation.* Ed. Robert A. Goldwin (Chicago: Rand McNally, 1963), 25–46.

Woodward, C. Vann. "The National Decision Against Equality." In Woodward, *American Counterpoint. Slavery and Racism in the North–South Dialogue* (Boston: Little Brown and Company, 1964), 212–33.

19

Some Reflections on the
Brown Decision and Its Aftermath

HOWARD McGARY

Brown v. Board of Education is one of the crucial legal cases regarding desegregation, educational opportunity, and race relations. The *Brown* decision is praised by some and criticized by others. The proponents praise *Brown* for eliminating *de jure* segregation in schools and for paving the way for bringing about equal opportunity for all people. The critics of *Brown*, on the other hand, claim that *Brown* was well intentioned, but legally unsound. They question the reasoning in *Brown* and oppose the political philosophy upon which it is based. To be more specific, they believe that the Court was wrong to conclude that all black schools necessarily caused inferiority and low black self-esteem. They also challenged the assumption that the Court was entitled to use its authority to achieve equity. They believe that Constitution does not give the state the authority to use its coercive powers to achieve equity.

The *Brown* decision also engendered the debate over *de jure* versus *de facto* segregation. *De jure* segregation is the intentional segregation of the races. *De facto* segregation is segregation that is unintentional. Much of the present debate concerns whether the courts can and should attempt to eliminate *de facto* segregation.

The *Brown* decision is divided into two parts: *Brown I* and *Brown II*. It is often said that *Brown I* declared *de jure* segregation in schools to be unconstitutional and *Brown II* fashioned the remedy to what was declared unconstitutional in *Brown I*. However, in reality, things are not this simple. The debate over *Brown II* revealed the ambiguous nature of what was declared unconstitutional in *Brown I*. There are at least four interpretations of *Brown I*. The first interpretation is championed by those who embrace a conservative reading of the Constitution. According to this reading, the Constitution is color-blind and, as such, individuals should be judged by their words and deeds and not by suspect characteristics like race or sex. Such characteristics should be used only after the most careful scrutiny. On this interpretation the Constitution requires the end of *de jure* segregation in the schools, but it does not justify the use of characteristics like race or sex to compensate for prior harm caused by the segregation or the lingering effects of the prior harm. On this reading, the state does not have the legal authority to bring about equity or better race relations; no matter how worthy these aims might be.

The second interpretation endorses the view that *de jure* segregation is unconstitutional, but it goes on to claim that the Constitution allows or demands the remediation of the injury caused by *de jure* segregation even if the outcome of segregation was not an inferior education for any group.

The third interpretation also supports the remediation of the injury caused by *de jure* segregation, but unlike the second interpretation, it support such remediation only if it will promote better educational outcomes. Some advocates of interpretations two and three believe race can used as legally relevant characteristics in the remediation process while others are weary of using race in this way.

The fourth interpretation says that *Brown I* outlawed *de jure* and *de facto* segregation in schools and other institutions that serve the public. According to this interpretation, state authority and resources can be used to remedy the injurious effects of both types of segregation.

An important difference between interpretation two and interpretations three and four concerns the scope of *Brown*. According to two, the scope only applies to educational institutions, while three and four believe that the harm and lingering effects of segregation should be eliminated beyond the boundaries of the school yard.

As a philosopher, the following question intrigues me: Does the declaration that *de jure* segregation is unconstitutional mean that all single race schools are unjust? In order to answer this question, I shall first spell-out what I take to be a clear line of reasoning in *Brown I*.

An obvious line of argument in *Brown I* proceeds as follows:

(1)   According to the 14th Amendment, all citizens regardless of their race should be regarded equal protection under the law and due process.
(2)   *De jure* legal segregation of school children by race violates (1).
(3)   Legal *de jure* segregation of school children by race is unconstitutional.

However, the decision in *Brown I* was not this straightforward. The Justices did not take the truth of premise two to be a priori and they also felt that their reasoning should be in line with past legal precedents. They believed that they needed to provide some empirical support for premise two and they felt their decision had to be consistent with a host of legal decisions going all the way back to *Plessy v. Ferguson*. Given these requirements, we find an underlying presumption in *Brown I*. The idea that blacks were incapacitated and made less than whole because of slavery and a system of racial discrimination. This idea permeates much of the thinking about race relations in the United States. In *Brown I*, the Justices appealed to a body of empirical research which claims to establish the damaging psychological effects of racial isolation and segregation. In footnote #11 in *Brown I*, the justices relied on the doll studies by the psychologist, Kenneth Clark, which purported to show that black school children have low self-esteem, and that this low self-esteem can be connected to their racial isolation in school. Even if you had two schools, one black and one white, with the same quality of services and resources, the black children would be harmed by this racial isolation.

Although this line of reasoning was clearly well intentioned, and it has produced some positive effects, it does so by enshrining in the public consciousness and in the law a general conception of black people as psychologically unhealthy human beings.

In order to avoid direct contradiction of the separate but equal decision in *Plessy v. Ferguson*, the Justices in *Brown* claimed that educational institutions were special and different because of the special role they played in the shaping of young minds and characters. And, as such, segregation in these settings, given the history of race relations in this country, always will harm the black children who experience such isolation. In *Brown I*, the separate, but equal proposal was rejected not because it was deemed to be conceptually incoherent, but because it was thought to be impractical given the present reality for blacks and whites in the middle of the twentieth century. The Justices were very skeptical about the possibility of lack schools receiving adequate funding given the way public schools were financed.

In reading the opinion in *Brown I*, and the supporting literature, I conclude that the Justices recognized that compensatory efforts would be necessary if desegregation of the public schools was to be successful. In other words, additional resources would have to be earmarked for black or predominantly black schools. However, history shows us that when public funds are earmarked for these schools, it breeds white resentment.

Some of this resentment can be traced to motives that are less than honorable, but some of it can be attributed to the belief that the Constitution requires that state actions be color-blind. This is the position taken by Clarence Thomas and many other conservatives. In any event, widespread white resentment to providing compensation to black schools has been significant enough to give most legislators pause when it comes to providing resources to remedy the effects of racial segregation.

I want to emphasize that the Court did not rule that the doctrine of separate but equal was logically or legally inconsistent. They outlawed *de jure* segregation in the schools, but they did not conclude that all single race institutions were necessarily unconstitutional. They attempted to frame a remedy for *de jure* segregation in the schools that did not require the total dismantling of *Plessy v. Ferguson* and one that was consistent with the rulings in other important legal cases regarding race and educational opportunity. These cases included: *Canada v. Gaines* in 1938, continuing through *Sipvel v. Board of Regent* (1948), *Sweat v. Painter* (1950), and *McLaurin v. Oklahoma State regents* also in 1950.

The Court wanted to rule-out *de jure* segregation in the schools, but not close down the possibility that some racially isolated institutions could be constitutional. Given this belief, the burden in *Brown I* shifted to making the case that racially segregated schools always cause serious harm. In fact, the Court said "We conclude that in the field of public education the doctrine of separate but equal has no place. Separate educational facilities are inherently unequal."

As I said earlier, in order to validate their categorical stance regarding the inherent inequality of separate educational facilities the Court turned to social science research. Citing this research they concluded that the separation of black children, because of their race, generated feelings of inferiority about their status in the community. The Court felt that these feelings of inferiority were so deep and far ranging that their effects would unlikely ever be undone.

The critics of the reasoning of *Brown I*, in my view, have rightfully argued that appeal to research about the black inferiority was not needed to conclude that state imposed segregation in public schools violated the equal protection clause of the 14th Amendment. School children should have equal protection under the law even

315

if denying this protection did not make them feel inferior. A straightforward interpretation of the equal protection clause rules out *de jure* segregation in public schools.

Given this more direct way to outlaw *de jure* segregation in the schools, why did the Court bring social science into its reasoning? I think you have to look to *Brown II* for the answer. One full year after *Brown I*, the Court decided in *Brown II* to remand the cases in question in *Brown I* back to the federal courts. These district courts, guided by the decision in *Brown I*, were to order local school authorities to use "all deliberate speed" in ending school segregation. Why the Justices used the words "all deliberate speed" has been the source of some controversy. In my opinion, the Justices used these words because they realized that any remedy at this point in history, if it were to be successful, must have a moral or a sentimental component. In a hostile and deeply divided racist society, the appeal to constitutionality alone was not seen to be sufficient for creating the political and social will that would be necessary to end legal segregation in the schools. Drawing on the insight by David Hume about the importance of moral sentiment, I don't think they felt that appeal to sound legal arguments alone would be enough to motivate people to make the kinds of changes that desegregation plans would require. The idea of protecting black school children from the harm of state imposed inferiority might provide the additional motivation.

II

The Court certainly had good intentions when it embraced the feelings of black inferiority rationale. However by maintaining that all racially isolated schools create feelings of inferiority in black students, no matter how good the all black schools might be, they unwittingly contributed to the idea of white supremacy.

Why do I say this? Remember the Court said that legally coercing black students to attend all black schools entails feeling of inferiority on the part of the black students. The court believed that giving legal sanctioning to segregated public schools stamps a badge of inferiority on the students. By doing so, we brand them as less than bonafide members of the community. However, reasonable people can disagree over whether black children will develop feelings of inferiority in racially segregated schools. But one thing is clear, when the state sanctions legal segregation of a group because it is a member of a particular racial group it defines the group in pejorative terms. What is not clear, however, is that racial isolation entails feelings of inferiority. In fact, it is clearly possible for a dominate group to isolate a group that it considers to be superior. They may do so because they fear the group's superior abilities. Neither the group that is isolated nor the group that is doing the isolation needs to view the group as inferior. This is not to say they will not describe the group in pejorative terms, but these terms need not include inferiority.

Over forty years after *Brown I* and *II*, there is still widespread racial isolation in our public and private schools. And, on most accounts, the educational quality of the public schools is worse now than it was forty years ago. Some claim that this failure points to the failure of *Brown* as a coherent legal decision. And others maintain that the *Brown* decision was fine, but that the federal district courts lacked the resolve to force local school districts to do what the Supreme Court mandated in *Brown I* and *II*. After all that has been said and done, we are still left with the *de facto* racial segregation in our schools. But more importantly, we find that predominantly black and latino schools are not on a par with their white counterparts. Is it the racial isolation or is it the lack of resources that causes the disparities? Some continue to argue that the lesson of *Brown* is that all black schools cause feelings of inferiority in black students, and as such, cause harm to these students. This argument has also been made in the majority opinion by the Federal District Court concerning the desegregation of Kansas City, Missouri schools by converting the school district into a "magnet district to reverse the white flight from the district caused by desegregation efforts. The court argued that black students suffer an unspecified psychological harm from segregation that retards their mental and educational development. In his concurring opinion in *Missouri v. Jenkins* (1995), Justice Clarence Thomas argues that it is a misunderstanding of *Brown* to conclude that *de facto* racial segregated schools must be desegregated because they cause black children to feel inferior. Thomas adopts the first of the three interpretations of Brown that I described at the beginning of my discussion. As a conservative, he believes that the Supreme Court should not use its power to achieve moral ends. Their job is simply to determine whether laws and policies are constitutional. For Thomas, the point of the Equal Protection Clause is to ensure that all citizens are treated as equals under the law, and not to give preferences to citizens because of their race, and certainly not to mandate race mixing.

I don't share Thomas's conservative reading of the Constitution, but I do share his reservation about relying on the premise of feelings of black inferiority to frame public policy. I don't think that we can or should conclude that all black schools create feelings of inferiority, and that these feelings constitute a harm that requires state action. All black schools don't cause black students to feel inferior. Schools of poor quality do. Instead of focusing on whether a school is predominantly white or black, we would be better served by focusing on the quality of the schools.

I am fully aware that in a society with a long history of racism that it is extremely difficult to address the needs of a long suffering people that have been designated as inferior. It makes perfect sense on a practical level to think that in a racist society all black schools are unlikely to receive the resources that will allow them to provide quality education to their students. Because American society has frequently devalued the interests of black people, efforts to improve the situation of blacks will often have to be placed in a context where it is extremely difficult to harm blacks without also harming whites. So one powerful argument for desegregating all black schools with poor resources is that this is the best way to ensure increased funding and thus a better education for black students. However, this is not the argument that is often given for ending *de facto* racial isolation.

The Brown decision itself provides us with good evidence for thinking that American society does not place the same value on the interests of black people. If black children were experiencing serious harm because of *de jure* segregation in the schools, and white children were not, then fairness would dictate that the interests of black children should be given some priority in the light of their past treatment. Unfortunately, this was not the ruling in *Brown II*. Black children were asked to continue to experience an inferior education and feelings of inferiority until a way could be devised that would eliminate these problems without jeopardizing white students. Over forty years later we are still waiting for such a solution.

If blacks have a right to equity under the law, and a right to be treated with equal concern and respect by the state, then the issue is not whether an institution is predominantly black or white, but rather whether this institution violates these rights. In the latter part of the twentieth century, we should be careful to avoid stereotypical attitudes that grew out of American slavery and a system of racial oppression. The myth of innate black inferiority is one of the most prevalent of these stereotypes.

Black people have been viewed by the dominate society as either naturally inferior to whites or as inferior because of social conditioning. In either case, this presumption of black inferiority has far reaching negative consequences. It bolsters the racist attitudes in many whites and it causes many blacks to struggle with feelings of self-doubt. In most areas in American life, blacks are assumed to be incompetent until they prove otherwise. Laws or policies that reinforce rather than challenge these stereotypes deny to blacks the right to be treated with equal concern and respect.

Given the history of the economic and social relationship between blacks and whites, many black people are poor. As we all know, poverty is often conjoined with things like crime and illiteracy, but we should not fall prey to the *non sequitur* that black institutions are necessarily conjoined with these things. In a society that is increasingly divided along racial lines, racial isolation is a fact of life in most large cities that must be confronted with courage and candor. Predominantly black institutions, like their white counterparts, don't inherently engender feelings of inferiority. The National Basketball Association is a good example of this. Racial balance is not a necessary condition for black self-esteem. A respect for rights rather than racial balance is necessary for good self-esteem.

Observing each citizen's right to be treated with equal concern and respect does not entail that we must strike some racial balance in all the institutions of our society nor does it forbid it. However, unlike some critics who have questioned the uncritical condemnation of predominantly black institutions, I think any such assessment must involve a realistic historical assessment of the origins and maintenance of these institutions. Such an assessment will vindicate the conclusion that we cannot be color-blind if we are to fashion a remedy for the failure by the state to ensure that each of its citizens were treated with equal concern and respect. Even the avid racial assimilationist, Frederick Douglass, believed that institutions of a complexional character would be needed for a time in order to overcome the vestiges of slavery and segregation. Recognizing this necessity does not force us to endorse the view that there should be two nations: one black and one white. But it does ask us to take a realistic look at what the requirements are for freedom and equal citizenship.

There are many people who believe that even if black and white schools are totally equal in regards to the quality of education, racially isolated schools are wrong or at least deeply offensive. They contend that this isolation is bad for the individuals involved and for the society as a whole. According to this view, one of the important goals of the civil rights movement was to breakdown the barriers that separated the races and to bring the races closer together in a spirit of harmony and equal citizenship.

The supporters of this way of thinking buttress their position by pointing out that racially isolated schools would not be so bad if the society was more integrated in other aspects. But given that people who attend predominantly black or white schools generally come from predominantly black or white neighborhoods, the isolation in schools further contributes to the strife and misunderstandings that results when groups have very little interaction with each other. So, on their view, racial isolation in schools would not be so bad if people from different racial groups lived in the same communities and attended the same churches and social functions. But since this is not the case, racial isolation in schools contributes to a bad situation and should not be tolerated.

I sympathize with those who find this isolation offensive, but in a liberal society the relevant question seems to be: Do such schools violate anyone's rights or violate or cause serious harm to innocent persons? The supporters of liberalism would say if they do not, then these schools must be tolerated.

III

But what does it mean to say that these schools must be tolerated? Does it mean that public funds can be used to finance such schools? Some would say no. But are they correct? I don't think so. As long as people are not prevented or discouraged from attending such schools because of their racial identities, public financing should be permissible.

Is this too quick? Don't we have to take a closer look at what might constitute discouragement before we conclude that racially isolated schools don't discourage members of a particular racial group from attending? One could argue that the very fact of a predominantly black or white school could discourage students from other racial groups from attending because they would feel left out. This is an argument that is similar to the argument made by some black parents who were against having their children bussed to all white schools for the purpose of racial integration. But if we accept this argument, we have to conclude that in any school setting where there is racial imbalance, those students who are in the minority and feel left out have a legitimate complaint. This would mean that in any schools where there is any substantial racial imbalance, the students in the minority would have legitimate complaints.

Clearly it does not seem appropriate to deny public funds to a school simply because there is racial imbalance. Especially in cases where the school is doing all that it can to make all students feel at home by promoting diversity in curricula and social activities. Only the most ardent advocate of racial integration as racial balance would think otherwise.

But having said this, I still recognize that there is a popular belief among today's intellectuals that anything that makes a person's race a relevant characteristic is inappropriate. These theorists have argued that races are real and that talk about them is meaningless. So, any policy or proposal that requires us to give credence to racial identity is seen as suspect. They argue that there is no naturalistic basis for making racial distinctions, and that any social definitions of races are incoherent.

Unlike fifty years ago, these intellectuals believe that the goal of the good society should be the elimination of racial distinctions altogether. This is in direct opposition to the major intellectual figures in the civil rights movement of the 1950s and '60s who accepted racial distinctions under conditions of fair equality of opportunity for all.

Armed with this strong assimilationist outlook, any advocation of racially defined institutions is viewed with much suspicion. In fact, one of the strong advocates of the racial assimilationist outlook has coined the term "racialism" to negatively describe making a person's race a relevant characteristic of persons.

Do we endorse racial essentialism or what Appiah has called "racialism" by allowing schools to be voluntarily populated by members of the same race? I think not. Even if we endorse a strong racial assimilationist ideal, this is not inconsistent with every single race school. My reading of the *Brown* decision does not commit me to the view that we should go about intentionally creating single race schools, but it does say that the state should not use its coercive power to integrate schools simply because most or all of the students are members of one racial group.

In a free society, we have to be willing to tolerate things that we don't like or even find offensive. This view has been championed by John Stuart Mill and other liberal thinkers. People who oppose all single race schools should use the power of persuasion to encourage people to voluntarily place their children in integrated environments, but they should not use state funds to abolish or discourage single race schools that don't violate anyone's rights.

I want to be clear and point out that people should not be forced to send their children to certain schools because of their race. The state has full authority to step in when this is the case. But where people's voluntary choices have the result of creating a single race school, these choices must be respected.

I recognize that determining when people are being forced to do something is not always a simple matter, but the place to begin is with the people who stand to be harmed by the choice. If they say that their choice is free, then it should be respected unless that there is overwhelming evidence that they are not of sound mind or that they are being misled. But the fact that their choices differ from the majority's choices is not reason in itself for thinking that these people are not of sound mind or that they are being misled. In saying this, I am not maintaining that legal paternalism is never justified. It can, under very strict conditions, be justified. However, we should be careful not to use this principle to force people to do what the majority or some powerful minority believes to be the appropriate thing to do.

Liberal political thought in the latter part of the last century was dominated by attempts to find ways to achieve consensus about what is right in an increasingly pluralistic world. The most recent proposals have not been totally persuasive, but perhaps they are the best hope for the liberal project. However, the critics of liberalism point out that the failed efforts to gain such a consensus just goes to show the limitations of the doctrine. These critics have argued the liberals cannot succeed in their efforts to derive a conception of right that does not presuppose a conception of what is good for the community. Communitarians and Marxists insist that there is no impartial or neutral conception of the right that can be deduced in some fair choice situation.

Communitarians and Marxists have had a difficult time convincing citizens that the common or community good is the good that they should endorse due to a strong commitment in Western democratic societies to individual liberty. In diverse pluralistic societies where people don't already have strong fraternal bonds because of common religious convictions or strongly held shared cultural beliefs, then it is doubtful that we can move them from an individualistic to a communal conception of good without the use of state coercion.

It seems clear that negative stereotypical beliefs about members of certain racial groups and bias acts committed against these groups flourish when these groups don't have much communication and contact, and that bringing them together where they can get to know one another through frank discourse would be useful in destroying these stereotypes and bias actions. However in a free society, how do we do this without violating our commitment to individual liberty?

Some would say that it is not a violation of individual liberty to force people to do things that would prevent significant societal harms, even when their own individual conduct does not cause harm to others. And they would add that preventing racially isolated schools (even in cases where no one is forced to attend or prevented from attending such schools) is such a societal harm. Supporters of this position adopt a broad interpretation of John Stuart Mill's harm principle. According to this interpretation, individuals can be coerced by the state to aid others when doing so prevents a collective harm that can be prevented. In the case of racially isolated schools, even those people who do not endorse legal segregation can be prevented from making choices hat result in single race schools. The idea is the state can prevent this harm by preventing citizens from making choices that in themselves cause no harm. It is only when a certain number of people make such choices that the behavior becomes harmful.

This case might be seen as analogous to the situation where everyone is prevented from cutting across a lawn because if we allow some people the freedom to do it, others will want to do it, and this would cause the destruction of the lawn. So, on general utilitarian ground, the greater good is served by preventing all from doing it. In a like manner, if some European Americans and African Americans choose to attend a particular school their choices will be honored. But if all or most members of these groups choose to segregate, then these choices will be deemed unacceptable.

This argument has been made with schools, but it is equally powerful in terms of other institutions, e.g., churches, social clubs. Why should the racial eliminativist be content with schools? If she is inconsistent, she should not stop with schools. But if the eliminativist goes this far, I doubt whether the state could achieve these ends without taking upon itself the kind of power that any liberal would find deeply objectionable.

In my judgment, the *Brown* decision forces us to focus on the meaning of racial equality and equal educational opportunity, but it also challenges us to come to grips with the value of racial identities in a pluralistic society. The latter concern is one of the pressing issues of the new millennium. At the end of the nineteenth century, W. E. B. Du Bois said that blacks would have to identify and develop as members of a group if they were to progress. He rejected the assimilationist goal of eliminating racial identities. According to Du Bois, this proposal would insure that blacks, as a group, would remain at the bottom rungs of society. Of course, he recognized that some black individuals would prosper. However, the masses of black people would be left out of the mainstream. Du Bois and his contemporary anti-assimilationist supporters believe that getting rid of racial identities in order to wipe out racism is to throw the baby out with the bath water.

Does the *Brown* decision give the state the legal authority to use its coercive powers to bring about racial assimilation? Or does *Brown* merely forbid forced segregation in public schools? I believe that it is the latter. I don't think that the mere fact that a school is comprised of one racial group implies that students are the victims of forced segregation. Nor does it imply that they are supporting racism or some form of racial essentialism.

But in today's political climate, there is little sympathy for those who believe that there can be some value in single race institutions. Such institutions are often quickly dismissed as racist. In fact, non-racists who support them often find themselves in the company of people who clearly hold racist views. The prevailing belief is that there must be some extremely compelling reason for the existence of these schools, and that in all or the overwhelming majority of cases, no such reasons exits. The received view is that such institutions, particularly in the case of schools, don't promote the greatest good of the people who attend them. Nor do they maximize the good of the communities of which they are a part.

Most of the focus is on whether this received view is true, but whether it is true or not is really beside the point. The relevant question is whether such schools violate anyone's rights. Clearly it is possible for a state of affairs to create less utility without violating anyone's rights. One does not have to adopt the view of the political libertarian in order to accept the principle that people should be free to associate with whom they choose, provided that their choices don't interfere with others rights to the same guarantees. Conservatives, like Justice Clarence Thomas, don't make a mistake in allowing some single race institutions, but in their failure to support the kinds of resources that will be necessary to insure that people are not compelled by their financial circumstances to attend such schools. If we are going to respect people's rights to make controversial decisions about sending their children to single race schools, then we must insure that the parents are not compelled to make these choices simply because they lack resources. For example, it is disingenuous to say that poor black families don't want to send their children to safe, well-funded schools in white areas unless the resources are available to make such a choice real. What too many conservatives and libertarians often fail to see is that racial injustice still exists, and that innocent children should not be held accountable for the bad choices of their parents, even when their parents are grossly irresponsible.

Bibliography

Appiah, Anthony, "Race, Culture, Identity; Misunderstood Connections," in Anthony Appiah and Amy Guttman, eds., *Color Consciousness: The Political Morality of Race* (Princeton: Princeton University Press, 1996): 30–105.

——. "Racisms," in David T. Goldberg, ed., *Anatomy of Racism* (Minneapolis: University of Minnesota Press, 1990): 3–17.

Brown v. Board of Education (*Brown I*), 347 U.S. 484 (1954).

Brown v. Board of Education (*Brown II*), 349 U.S. 297, 75 S. Ct. 753 (1955).

Clark, Kenneth, "The Effects of Segregation and the Consequences of Desegregation: A Social Science Statement." Reprinted in *Minnesota Law Review* 37 (1953): 457.

Du Bois, W. E. B., "The Conservation of Races," in Robert Bernaseoni and Tommy L. Lott, eds., *The Idea of Race* (Indianapolis: Hackett Publishing Company, 2000)

Feinberg, Joel, *The Moral Limits of the Criminal Law: Harm to Others* (Oxford: Oxford University Press, 1984).

Gralia, Lino A., *Disaster By Decree: The Supreme Court Decision on Race and the Schools* (Ithaca: Cornell University Press, 1997).

Hochschild, Jennifer L., *Thirty Years After Brown* (Washington, DC: Joint Center for Political Studies, 1985).

Hume, David, *An Inquiry Concerning the Principles of Morals*, ed. Charles W. Hendel (Indianapolis: Bobbs-Merrill, 1957): 104–12.

Jenkins v. Missouri, 639 F. Supp. 19, 24 (WD Mo. 1986).

Lyons, David, "Liberty and Harm to Others," in *Readings in Social and Political Philosophy*, ed. Robert N. Stewart (Oxford: Oxford University Press, 1996): 171–82.

McGary, Howard, "Douglass on Racial Assimilation and Racial Institutions," in Bill Lawson and Frank Kirkland, eds., *Frederick Douglass: A Critical Reader* (Oxford: Blackwell Publishers, 1999); 50–63.

——. *Race and Social Justice* (Oxford: Blackwell Publishers, 1999), ch. 11.

Mill, John Stuart, *On Liberty*, ed. Curvin v. Shields (Indianapolis: Bobbs-Merrill, 1956).

Missouri et al. Petitioners v. Kalima Jenkins et al., U.S. 93–1823 (1995).

Rawls, John, *Political Liberalism* (New York: Columbia University Press, 1992).

Sandel, Michael, *Liberalism and the Limits of Justice* (Cambridge: Cambridge University Press, 1982).

323

20

Contesting the Ambivalence and Hostility to Affirmative Action within the Black Community

LUKE C. HARRIS

Today I know they have this thing called Affirmative Action. I can see why they need it. There are some places where colored folks would never, not in a thousand years, get a job. But you know what? I really am philosophically against it. I say: "Let the best person get the job, period." Everybody's better off in the long run.
Bessie Delany (Hearth, 1993: 110)

In America many marginally competent or flatly incompetent whites are hired every day – some because their white skin suits the conscious or unconscious racial preference of their employer. The white children of alumni are often grand-fathered into elite universities in what can only be seen as the residual benefit of historic white privilege. Worse, white incompetence is always an individual matter, while for Blacks it is often confirmation of ugly stereotypes. . . . I think that one of the most troubling effects of *racial preferences* for Blacks is a kind of demoralization, or put another way, an enlargement of self-doubt. Under affirmative action the quality that earns us *preferential treatment* is an implied inferiority.
Shelby Steele (Steele, 1990: 112, 116)

[Black conservatives] simply want what most people want, to be judged by the quality of their skills, not the color of their skin. But the Black conservatives overlook the fact that affirmative action policies were political responses to the pervasive refusal of most white Americans to judge Black Americans on that basis. . . . If I had been old enough to join the fight for racial equality in the courts, the legislatures, and the board rooms in the 1960's . . . *I would have favored – as I do now – class-based affirmative action in principle.*
Cornel West (West, 1993: 52, 64)

Again and again, as I spoke with people who had every accouterment of success, I heard the same plaintive declaration . . . "I have done everything I was supposed to do. I have stayed out of trouble with the law, gone to the right schools, and worked myself nearly to death. *What* more do *they* want? . . . Why am I still not allowed to aspire to the same things every white person in America takes as a birthright?" [But] like many Black professionals, I find myself profoundly ambivalent on the question of affirmative action. I don't believe that it works very well, nor that it can be made to satisfy much of anyone. Moreover, I believe that programs based on *racial preferences are inherently riddled with the taint and the reality of unfairness.*
Ellis Cose (Cose, 1993: 1, 130–1)

324

The ideological diversity of the four African Americans quoted above is striking. Shelby Steele is regarded as conservative; Cornel West is thought to be on the radical left; Ellis Cose is considered liberal and the moderate political sensibilities of the late Bessie Delany, a woman more than one hundred years old, were honed throughout the entire twentieth century. Nonetheless, their views on affirmative action policies reflect common themes. They all begin by recognizing that, historically and today, to be an African American has meant being the target of pervasive and unwarranted patterns of institutional exclusion. But reflecting the backlash against affirmative action policies in contemporary America, they all end with either a rejection of, or a lack of enthusiasm for race based affirmative action programs which, in their view, offer preferences to black Americans.

In this article, I will examine the hostility and ambivalence that informs the perspectives on affirmative action that have emerged from within the black community. In my view, the rejection and misgivings that dominate the public debate over affirmative action are prompted and nourished, in part, by a series of understandings about these policies that distorts the terms of the current debate and that unwarrantedly predetermine a negative response to affirmative action programs. Those opposed to affirmative action often point to critics within the black community as evidence that affirmative action is a flawed social policy. But there is nothing exceptionally compelling about their critique once affirmative action is accurately portrayed (Harris and Narayan, 1994). My view, which I have developed in a series of previously published essays, is that, as a general rule, when properly administered, affirmative action does not afford preferences to its beneficiaries. Indeed, I argue that affirmative action is better represented as an attempt to offer its beneficiaries a greater equality of opportunity than they would otherwise experience in certain spheres of American life.

Challenging the Myth of "Preferential Treatment"

Many misperceptions about affirmative action in academia and in recruitment, hiring and promotion policies in the workplace, are a function of misunderstandings about the rationales for these programs. These misunderstandings are compounded because the national debate about affirmative action consists of a public discussion between foes who generally hold one of two widely shared perspectives. On the one hand, critics of these programs, within the black community and beyond, such as Justice Clarence Thomas, Shelby Steele, Thomas Sowell, and Antonin Scalia describe them as a form of reverse discrimination that bestows "undeserved privileges" on their beneficiaries (Mills, 1994: 37, 89; Sowell, 1984; and Scalia, 1989).

On the other hand, proponents of affirmative action programs such as Cornel West, Ellis Cose, Randall Kennedy, and Ronald Dworkin characterize them as a benign set of "preferential" programs that are justifiable either as "compensation" for past or present wrongs or on the grounds of short- and long-term goals such as diversity (Mills, 1994: 48, 83; Cose, 1995; and LaFollette, 1997). Only a few of affirmative action's advocates, such as Kimberlé Williams Crenshaw, Charles Lawrence III, Mari Matsuda and Uma Narayan, in work we have collaborated on together, question the assumption that affirmative action necessarily involves the "bestowal of preferences," and challenge the

325

widely shared premise that it represents a marked departure from a set of egalitarian standards that operate on the basis of a genuine meritocracy (Crenshaw, 1995; Lawrence and Matsuda, 1997; and Harris and Narayan, 1994). Even Ellis Cose and Iris Young, who write perceptively about the need to rethink and reenvision the traditional forms of meritocracy in many spheres of American life, equate the dismantling of discriminatory visions of meritocracy with the "preferential" treatment of the beneficiaries of affirmative action (Young, 1990).

I maintain that the lack of enthusiasm, and sometimes hostility, that pervades the perspectives on affirmative action embraced by many African Americans is inextricably linked to the idea that race-based programs give blacks a "leg up," an idea that suggests that these programs unfairly privilege people of color. The idea that affirmative action is tantamount to preferential treatment is deeply embedded in the writings by African Americans on this topic from a wide range of political perspectives, including critics and supporters alike. I think this shared idea of affirmative action seriously dampens the enthusiasm for it even amongst its adherents. In what follows, I will indicate the pervasive use of the language of "preference" amongst African Americans engaged in this debate. Thereafter, I will offer an alternative perspective on this debate, a perspective that affords us the opportunity to develop a richer vision of affirmative action that is unburdened with false moral dilemmas.

The idea of unjustified preference fuels the hostility to affirmative action on the part of its harshest critics within the Black community. Shelby Steele argues that affirmative action "nurtures a victim focused identity" which sends Blacks the message that there is more power in past suffering than in our present achievements. He contends that the preferences associated with affirmative action cause self-doubt among its recipients and resentment among the non-beneficiaries. He also maintains that affirmative action reinforces the belief in black inferiority, stigmatizes the already stigmatized, and focuses attention on group identities rather than on individuals while at the same time encouraging the lowering of standards to increase black representation. In Steele's view, affirmative action "has shown itself to be more bad than good" becaus such programs encourage dependency and an expectation of entitlement. Thus, he calls for a de-raced policy.

In *Reflections of an Affirmative Action Baby*, Stephen Carter recounts all of the indignities that he contends befall the beneficiaries of affirmative action, while at the same time arguing on behalf of these programs in some contexts. He contends that affirmative action is both patronizing, and demeaning, and that it was created in the belief that black people were unable to compete on the same playing field with whites. Anything that smacks of racial preference is anathema to Carter. In fact, in Carter's view, not only the recipient, but all blacks are tainted with the suspicion that they have not "earned their success on the basis of merit alone" by affirmative action programs. He calls into question the legitimacy and the values of affirmative action itself, even as he takes an equivocal position in support of it.

Because he is middle class, he suggests that he cannot know racism, at least not the same racism as a black person who is poor. Middle-class status, as he sees it, makes him immune from serious problems of racism. Indeed, he contends that racism is receding for the black middle class, but that "it continues to operate with awesome force in the lives of many of the worst off members of our community." How racism could operate with awesome force against one class of blacks and have limited impact on another is left unexplained. But what Carter is clear about is that, in some respects, affirmative action has done him an injustice. It has denied him the recognition of his merit because it represents a process that gives blacks a "leg up" in the competition with their white counterparts by circumventing or eradicating legitimate academic and professional standards (Carter, 1991).

In keeping with Steel and Carter, Thomas Sowell, one of the first blacks to attack affirmative action programs publicly, argues that these programs have failed to achieve their putative goals and that they undermine the legitimacy of black achievements by making them look like gifts from the government. Steele, Carter, and Sowell all applaud individual choice and self help and each is critical of the stigma associated with affirmative action. Each focuses on economic class differences within the black community. But individually and collectively they lose sight of the reality that to argue that affirmative action programs should be attentive to class differences amongst blacks does not mean that middle-class blacks are identically situated to their white counterparts or that the black poor are treated and perceived in the same way as poor whites.

William Julius Wilson, a self-described social democrat, agrees that affirmative action programs should not be race-based. He supports universal programs that apply to everyone (Wilson, 1978). Wilson argues that during the early stages of the Civil Rights Movement of the 1960s, the Movement's underlying principle was that individual merit should be the sole determining factor in choosing among candidates for positions in American institutions. But he contends that over time the focus of the Movement changed, and remedying the effects of past discrimination against blacks, through the use of "preferential" programs, became its ultimate goal. In the alternative, Wilson proposes a "hidden agenda" for blacks "because there are no political constituencies for policies targeted specifically for blacks." In his view, it is necessary to hide such programs behind universalistic policies that "more advantaged groups of all races and class backgrounds can relate to." He calls for universal programs out of political expediency. But the need for the hidden agenda that he proposes contradicts his claim that racism is "declining in significance." In fact, his underlying assumption appears to be that racism is such a force in American life that programs designed to focus on the legitimate concerns of Blacks must be camouflaged behind programs that benefit the white majority.

Wilson also objects to affirmative action programs because he contends that they disproportionately benefit the black middle class. But as William Taylor has pointed out, "the focus of most of the [affirmative action] effort has been not just white collar jobs, but also in law enforcement, construction work, and craft and production jobs in large companies, all areas in which the extension of new opportunities has provided upward mobility for less advantaged minority workers" (Taylor, 1986).

In suggesting that class is a bigger problem for blacks than race in his book *The Truly Disadvantaged*, Wilson defines racism as the "conscious refusal to accept Blacks as equal human beings and the willful systematic effort to deny Blacks equality of opportunity" (Wilson, 1987). It is precisely this definition of racism that ultimately links the perspectives of Steele, Carter, Sowell and Wilson. Their inability to conceptualize institutional forms of racial discrimination that are not rooted in conscious and willful acts makes it impossible for them to critique the limits of the traditional forms of meritocracy which operate in different domains of American life. Yet such a critique is essential if we are to clarify the full range of rationales for affirmative action because our normative evaluative processes in academia and the workplace are seriously flawed.

As a consequence of their narrow conception of racial discrimination the scholars I have cited are led to oppose affirmative action. Their vision of discrimination leads them to see affirmative action as unjustified benefits for a relatively privileged black middle class. This myopic understanding of affirmative action is compounded by a myopic understanding of racial power. One might infer from their perspective that affirmative action is illegitimate because it unwarrantedly empowers blacks. Some such critics even acknowledge that unfair exclusionary practices compromise equal opportunity. But they still oppose affirmative action because of a failure to comprehend who benefits from affirmative action. It's almost as if, in the critics view, the only people who have benefited from affirmative action were undeserving middle-class blacks. This is, of course, decidedly untrue.

First of all, it reflects a misconception about who benefits from affirmative action. Over the past thirty years, the idea of affirmative action has broadened to embrace the concerns of many groups of Americans who face discrimination and a lack of equal opportunity. Affirmative action has promoted the entrance of white women as well as women of color into an array of fields once closed to them. In institutions like the Rutgers Law School in Newark, New Jersey it has also promoted the entry of working-class white applicants, including working-class white men. But the scope of these programs is often ignored by critics who pit the interests of blacks and working-class whites against one another in the context of this debate.

Unfortunately, black critics such as Shelby Steele continue to harbor the misconception that affirmative action principally benefits blacks, even though affirmative action policies were created to confront the problems faced by a range of marginalized and culturally distinct groups. Consider, for example, the debate engendered by the landmark *Regents of the University of California v. Bakke* decision. There Allan Bakke had claimed that a large number of "lesser qualified" students of color had been granted admission over him. He argued that Davis's program had reserved up to 16 of the 100 places in the class for members of minority groups. He maintained that the large differences between the grade point averages and test scores of the white and the minority applicants, combined with the fact that the minority candidates were not directly compared to their white counterparts necessarily meant that students of color were preferred over their white counterparts. Yet the national debate that swirled around this decision tended to concentrate almost entirely on blacks and whites alone, although close to two-thirds of the actual participants in the program were Asian and Latino.

One other critique of race-based affirmative action policies that appears related to misperceptions about its actual scope is the objection that these programs do absolutely nothing for truly disadvantaged blacks. This argument appears to ignore completely the many autobiographical narratives that speak to the ways in which affirmative action has helped to carve out opportunities for many blacks at the bottom of American society (Harris, 1994; and Fair, 1997). In fact, the vast majority of blacks were poor, working-class, and marginally middle class prior to the Civil Rights era in the 1950s and 1960s; and the expanding black middle class that exists today was, in significant part, created by both the civil rights laws and the affirmative action policies that developed during that era (Blauner, 1989). From sanitation departments to University departments, from the construction industry to the corridors of corporate power, affirmative action programs have helped to knock down barriers that had closed opportunities for countless millions of Americans, including many Americans from the bottom of our society.

Another dimension of the class-based arguments against affirmative action assumes that middle-class blacks and Latinos neither need nor deserve affirmative action. For example, Shelby Steele assumes that middle-class blacks, allegedly shielded from racial bias by their middle-class status, should be treated exactly like their white counterparts. He assumes they are similarly situated. But the experiences of blacks and whites are still markedly different from one another. Tester studies conducted by the Fair Employment Council of Greater Washington between 1990 and 1992 demonstrated that blacks were treated worse than equally qualified whites 24 percent of the time. Latinos were treated worse 22 percent of the time. In the Urban Institute's Employment and Housing study in 1991, the white testers advanced further in the hiring process than equally qualified blacks 20 percent of the time. Moreover, the Urban Institute's research revealed that black and Latino testers faced discrimination in housing in roughly half of their contacts with real estate agents. The black to white ratio of median income has been stuck in the mid-50s to mid-60s percentage range for over two decades; and correllatively, according to the 1990 census, only 2.4 percent of the nation's businesses are owned by African Americans; and 85 percent of those businesses have no employees. Finally, white males hold 97 percent of the senior management positions in Fortune 1000 industrial and Fortune 500 service corporations. Only 0.6 percent of senior management is African American, only 0.4 percent is Hispanic, and only 0.3 percent is Asian (Edley, 1996).

Color-blind policies will not serve to combat the structural inequities and the forms of discrimination discussed above. Consequently, race-based affirmative action policies are just as appropriate in contemporary America as gender and class-based programs. We must recognize the interconnected ways in which factors such as class, race, gender, and sexual orientation conjoin to create and maintain unwarranted disparities between and within disparate groups across a range of occupational and institutional settings. Class, then, should not be pitted against race or gender or sexual orientation, for that matter, as the only legitimate rationale for affirmative action programs. Instead these programs should be sculpted to the contours of the institutional contexts in which they operate. When a number of factors jointly contribute to discrimination, as in the case of a working-class woman of color, we should consider each such factor. But if only one aspect of a person's identity adversely subjects him to discrimination – as in the case of a working-class white man – then we should take only that factor into account.

Kimberlé Williams Crenshaw offers an illuminating metaphor for the ways in which discriminatory intersecting factors can limit the opportunities of African Americans in the case of black women. She asks us to consider an analogy to traffic in an intersection, coming and going in all four directions. Discrimination, like traffic through an intersection, may flow in one direction, and it may flow in another. If an accident happens in an intersection, it can be caused by cars traveling from any number of directions and, sometimes, from all of them. Similarly, if a black woman is harmed because

329

she is in the intersection, her injury could result from sex discrimination or race discrimination or both (Crenshaw, 1989).

The critics assume that class is the only reason blacks and other minorities would need affirmative action. Thus, they fail to embrace a basic understanding that affirmative action should correct for all of the factors that contribute to the unwarranted exclusion of the members of marginalized groups. The factors considered by those who administer affirmative action programs should relate concretely to the institutional settings under consideration. Affirmative action policies in the bluecollar trades should target women of all races and minority men because they are the individuals who have confronted discriminatory obstacles in their attempts to enter these trades. Correspondingly, affirmative action policies at elite universities and colleges like Vassar should target both minority and working-class white students – including working-class white males – because they are the individuals who have faced discriminatory obstacles in these contexts.

Conclusion

If we are to foster equal opportunity and the rights of full citizenship for blacks, we must be able to focus our attention on the ways in which black people continue to face institutional obstacles to equal consideration and treatment in academia and in the workplace. We must challenge not only the continuing forms of blatant discrimination, but also a range of subtle institutional practices that circumscribe opportunities for many Americans. In so doing, we offset systematic "preferences" that unwarrantedly favor some Americans over others for reasons unattributable to a genuine conception of meritocracy. In such settings, affirmative action does not compensate blacks for injuries suffered in the past. Rather it allows institutions to promote equality by attempting to eradicate the problematic consequences of their unfair exclusionary practices.

Without question, the notion that affirmative action is merely a form of preferential treatment not only fails to contest the normative criteria of evaluation used within our institutions, it also fails to encourage us to reconsider the modes of assessment used to create these "qualifications" – fostering the view that affirmative action programs promote the entry of "less qualified" persons into an array of institutional settings once closed to them. This leaves unproblematized the idea that affirmative action "bestows preferences" on its beneficiaries, or the idea that it imposes "costs" on others.

I insist, however, that programs that seek to undo the effects of institutional practices and criteria that have a past history of granting unfair privileges to some Americans over others do not provide a preference for their beneficiaries. From this perspective, the problem of stigma often associated with affirmative action policies has to be rethought. Affirmative action opponents who use this line of criticism often presume that the beneficiaries of affirmative action are "preferred" over more competent applicants within the context of a genuinely meritocratic system. No stigma should rightly exist, however, just because someone participates in a program that treats him more fairly. The only "costs" to the nonbeneficiaries of such programs are the loss of privilege that grows out of the use of a variety of discriminatory institutional procedures and criteria. The departure from the use of such criteria may be experienced as a "loss" to those who would stand to gain most from the application of the old criteria. But what is lost are privileges that are the results of a lack of unfairness to, and equal opportunities for, others who are deserving of the rights of full membership in our community.

References

Abram, Morris B. "Affirmative Action: Fair Shakers and Social Engineers." *Harvard Law Review* 104 (1986).

Adarand Constructors, Inc. v. Pena, 515 U.S. 200 (1995).

Bell, Daniel "Meritocracy and Equality." *The Public Interest*. No. 29 (Fall 1972): 3.

Bell, Derrick. *Race, Racism and American Law*, 3rd edn. Boston: Little Brown and Company, 1992.

Bickel, Alexander M. *The Morality of Consent*. New Haven: Yale University Press, 1975.

Blauner, Robert. *Black Lives, White Lives: Three Decades of Race Relations in America*. 1989.

Carter, Stephen L. *Reflections of an Affirmative Action Baby*. New York: Basic Books, 1991.

Cohen, Carl. "Who Are Equals." In *Today's Moral Problems*. Richard Wasserstrom, ed. 1985.

Cose, Ellis. *The Rage of a Privileged Class*. New York, Harper Perennial, 1995.

Cross, Theodore and Robert Bruce Slater, "Why the End of Affirmative Action would Exclude all but a Very Few Blacks from America's Leading Universities and Graduate Schools." *Journal of Blacks in Higher Education* 17 (1997).

Crenshaw, Kimberlé. "A Black Feminist Critique of Antidiscrimination Law and Politics." *Chicago Legal Forum* 139 (1989).

Crenshaw, Kimberlé, Neil Gotanda, Gary Peller, and Kendall Thomas, eds., *Critical Race Theory*, New York: New Press, 1995.

D'souza, Dinesh. *Illiberal Education: The Politics of Race and Sex on Campus*. New York: Free Press, 1991.

Dworkin, Ronald. "The Rights of Allan Bakke." In *Ethics in Practice*. Hugh LaFollette, ed. Oxford: Blackwell Publishers, 1997.

Edley, Christopher. *Not All Black and White: Affirmative Action, Race and American Values*. New York: Hill and Wang, 1996.

Fair, Bryan K. *Notes of a Racial Caste Baby*. New York: New York University Press, 1997.

Feagin, Joe R. and Clarice Feagin. *Racial and Ethnic Relations*, 6th edn. Upper Saddle River, New Jersey, Prentice Hall, 1999.

Fineman, Howard and Andrew Muir "Rage and Race." *Newsweek*, April 3, 1995, pp. 22–5.

Fineman, Harvey. "Proposition 209 Shuts the Door." *The New York Times*, April 4, 1998, Saturday, Late Edition, Section A, page 23, Column 1.

Gotanda, Neil "A Critique of 'Our Constitution is Color-Blind,' " *Stanford Law Review* 44 (1991).

Graglia, Lino. "Racial Preferences in Admissions to Higher Education," *The Imperial Academy*. Howard Dickman, ed. New Brunswick, NJ: Transaction, 1993.

Harris, Cheryl, "Whiteness as Property," *Harvard Law Review* 106 (1993), 1707.

Harris, Luke Charles. "Affirmative Action and the White Backlash: Notes from a Child of Apartheid." In *Picturing Us: African American Identity in Photography*. Deborah Willis, ed. New York: the New Press, 1994.

Harris, Luke Charles and Uma Narrayan "Affirmative Action and the Myth of Preferential Treatment: A Transformative Critique of the Terms of the Affirmative Action Debate." *Harvard Black Letter Law Journal*, 11 (1994): 1.

——. "Affirmative Action as Equalizing Opportunity: Challenging the Myth of Preferential Treatment," *Practical Ethics: Classical and Contemporary Readings*. Hugh LaFollete, ed. Oxford: Blackwell Press, 1997.

Hearth, Amy Hill. *Having Our Say: The Delaney Sisters First 100 Years*. New York: Kudansha International, 1993.

Henderson, Donald H. and Alfonso G. Washington, "Cultural Differences and the Education of Black Children: An Alternative Model for Program Development." *The Journal of Negro Education* 44. Summer, 1997.

Hopwood v. State of Texas (1996).

Kahlenberg, Richard D. *The Remedy: Class, Race, and Affirmative Action*. New York: Basic Books, 1996.

Kull, Andrew. *The Color-Blind Constitution*. Cambridge, Mass.: Harvard University Press, 1992.

LaFollette, Hugh, ed. *Ethics in Practice*. Oxford: Blackwell Publishers, 1997.

Lawrence, Charles R. III, and Mari J. Matsuda, *We Won't Go Back*. Boston: Houghton Mifflin, 1997.

McClelland, David C. "Testing for Competence Rather than 'Intelligence.'" In *The IQ Controversy*. Black and Dworking, ed. The Anchor Press Ltd., 1974.

Mills, Nicolaus, ed. *Debating Affirmative Action*. New York: Delta, 1994.

Murray, Charles. "Affirmative Discrimination." *Debating Affirmative Action: Race, Gender, Ethnicity, and the Politics of Inclusion*. Nicolaus Mills, ed. New York: Delta, 1994.

Proposition 209, Article 1, Section 31 of the *California Constitution*.

City of Richard v. J.A. Croson Co., 488 U.S. 469 (1989).

Regents of the University of California v. Bakke 438 U£ 265, 1978.

Schwartz, Bernard. *Behind Bakke: Affirmative Action and the Supreme Court*. New York: New York University Press, 1988.

Scalia, Justice Antonin. *Richmond V. Croson*, concurring opinion 488 U.S. 469, 1989.

Steele, Shelby. *The Content of Our Character*. New York: St. Martin's Press, 1990.

Sowell, Thomas. *Civil Rights: Rhetoric or Reality*. New York: William Morrow, 1984.

Steinberg, Stephen. *Turning Back: The Retreat from Racial Justice in American Thought and Policy*. Boston: Beacon Press, 1995.

Taylor, William L. "Brown, Equal Protection, and the Isolation of the Poor." *Yale Law Journal* 95 (1986): 1714.

West, Cornel. *Race Matters*. New York, Vintage Books, 1993.

Wilson, William Julius. *The Declining Significance of Race*. Chicago: University of Chicago Press, 1978.

——. *The Truly Disadvantaged*. Chicago: University of Chicago Press, 1987.

Young, Iris Marion. *Justice and the Politics of Difference*. Princeton: Princeton University Press, 1990.

21

Subsistence Welfare Benefits as Property Interests: Legal Theories and Moral Considerations

RUDOLPH V. VANTERPOOL

The debate over the legitimacy of public assistance programs has had a long and turbulent history in American jurisprudence. A host of issues associated with the more basic question of whether beneficiaries of welfare have a *right* to receive the benefits have spawned a massive body of litigation. A careful review of the reasoning behind Supreme Court rulings on questions involving welfare "rights" is quite instructive in highlighting the complexity of the problem. Welfare litigation has led to judicial articulation of theories ranging from the treatment of programs such as Aid to Families with Dependent Children (AFDC) and other forms of public assistance as mere gratuities to the more expansive statutory entitlements doctrine.

With the recent passage of the *Personal Responsibility and Work Opportunity Reconciliation Act of 1996* (hereinafter referred to as, Reconciliation Act) the judiciary, amidst a resurgent libertarian social climate, suddenly faces new constitutional challenges. Justices of our highest court are human beings who have their own ideological preferences and must make informed, reasoned judgments consistent with their perceptions of fairness and prevailing social policies. There is support for the view that despite the expectation of neutrality, justices tend to be influenced by a particular political ideology even if they are understandably hesitant to make such an admission (Nowak 1980, 272; Miller and Howell 1960, 664, 671–83). Public policy preferences are not static; such policies frequently tend to shift in direct response to factors such as existing political and economic conditions, the legislative intention behind the enactment of laws, and the level of direct interest the body politic takes in the disputed area. A lesson to be learned here is that to a large extent law is indeterminate and is inseparable from politics. In moral philosophy the welfare debate has likewise been fueled by clashes arising out of disparate schools of thought. Of particular concern are the moral implications of welfare policies with regard to the desirable end welfare legislation seeks to accomplish (i.e., bettering the circumstances of the needy) and, correspondingly, the means used to achieve that valued goal. Much of the current national debate among ethicists centers increasingly around reform initiatives, a trend which is certain to alter our language and ways of thinking about public assistance.

My first task is to review and comment on the significance of legal theories insofar as these evolved with the rise of the so-called welfare state. I am particularly concerned with decisions involving categorical assistance programs (e.g., AFDC) and, to a lesser extent, aid to the medically needy (i.e., Medicaid). Secondly, I examine the treatment of the controversy in moral discourse and draw attention to applicable principles relied upon in assessing the objective of lessening harms germane to all such arguments. There are natural similarities between legal and moral discourse, particularly with respect to determining whether people have obligations to assist other persons in need.

Legal Theories

The right–privilege distinction

A doctrine that gained widespread popularity in the early history of welfare litigation was the characterization of welfare benefits as mere government gratuities or charitable contributions. Welfare interests, as such, were not regarded earned property entitlements but treated as privileges extended to designated classes of beneficiaries. This doctrine surfaces in Supreme Court rulings such as *Shapiro v. Thompson* (1969), *Goldberg v. Kelly* (1970), and *Wyman v. James* (1971). In each of these cases reference is made to a "right–privilege" distinction. In a much earlier case, *Flemming v. Nestor* (1966), the majority did not believe it was profitable to distinguish between "earned rights" and "gratuities" in holding that the interest of an eligible recipient of Old Age Social Disability Insurance (OASDI) is not equivalent to an accrued property right (610–11). Despite the fact that OASDI was a program of social insurance to which workers contributed through their earnings, no *accrued* property right can be said to result therefrom. Naturally, then, the simple denial of OASDI benefits could not be a "taking" of property. Justice Douglas, however, in his dissenting opinion made a persuasive appeal for acceptance of the rights theory. He reasoned that the kind of government benefits at stake here, intended in particular for members of the class of disabled elderly, were by no means mere gratuities or handouts. This type of social security benefit is the product of a contributory system, the funds having been accumulated through payments from both employees and employers (*Flemming* 1966, 628–34). Douglas's intellectual clash with the *Flemming* majority provided new impetus for making use of the distinction.

At issue in *Shapiro* was the constitutionality of statutory provisions in several states that denied welfare assistance to individuals who had not resided within the respective jurisdictions for at least one year preceding their applications for assistance. The claimants were all otherwise eligible for either assistance under the AFDC program or the program for Aid to the permanently and Totally Disabled. Justice Brennan, in a footnote to the opinion, cautioned that this constitutional challenge involving welfare aid to families to obtain the very means to subsist (e.g. food, shelter, and other necessities of life) could not be answered by the argument that public assistance benefits are a privilege rather than a right (627). According to the *Shapiro* majority, the one-year waiting-period provisions denied welfare benefits to eligible applicants on the sole ground that they were recent residents. The needy claimants had used their constitutional right to travel from one state to another and, as such, it was unjust to punish them for the exercise of that fundamental right. The Court could find no compelling governmental interests being served by the statutes. It was noted that we are one people belonging to one country and that "our constitutional concepts of personal liberty . . . require that all citizens be free to travel throughout the length and breadth of our land uninhibited by statutes, rules, or regulations which unreasonably burden or restrict this movement" (*Shapiro* 1969, 629).

The *Goldberg* case, by contrast, involved claimants receiving financial aid under the federally assisted AFDC program administered by the state of New York. The issue before the Court was whether a state could terminate public assistance payments to a particular recipient without affording the claimant an opportunity for an evidentiary hearing before the benefits were cut off. Justice Brennan once again revisited the right–privilege distinction and this time held unequivocally that since welfare benefits constitute statutory entitlements for individuals qualified to receive them, due process requires an adequate hearing before termination of benefits (*Goldberg* 1970, 262–70; Vanterpool 1988, 1985, 79–80, 83). The eligible recipient's property interest in the uninterrupted receipt of public assistance that provides for his or her essential needs to food, clothing, housing, and medical care is not outweighed by the government's competing interest in preventing any increase in its fiscal and/or administrative burdens. In a scathing dissent, Justice Black countered the statutory entitlements rationale. Black characterized state and federally funded public assistance programs as *allowances* or *gratuities*. In his own assessment, the *Goldberg* ruling simply facilitates the process of moving this nation in the direction of a welfare state (*Goldberg* 1970, 271–4). Everyone stands to lose when the nation taxes its most affluent citizens to help support, feed, clothe, and shelter the less fortunate in our midst. The ruling, in Black's words, "does not depend on the language of the Constitution itself or the principles of other decisions, but solely on the collective judgment of the majority as to what would be a fair and humane procedure in this case" (276).

Wyman v. James relied, in part at least, on the controversial right–privilege distinction to reach the holding that home visitations which are not forced are not criminal searches within the traditional meaning of fourth amendment guarantees. Justice Blackmun, addressing the issue whether a beneficiary of AFDC may refuse a home visit by a caseworker without risking termination of her benefits, found that the visitation as *statutorily* structured was a reasonable administrative tool. Such home visitations served valid and proper administrative purposes for the dispensation of the overall AFDC program. Social workers, as agents of the government, are in this way merely fulfilling a public trust in their efforts to maintain close contacts with the beneficiaries. Since the state and federal agencies involved are dispensing "purely private charity," the government dispensers have a justified concern, or more precisely a fiscal responsibility, in knowing how the taxpayers' charitable funds are being utilized (*Wyman* 1971, 318–24). The validity of the regulation is further reinforced by its *rehabilitative* objective – the home visit may allow caseworkers the opportunity to provide counsel to aid recipients. Such rehabilitative efforts are all geared toward restoring needy individuals to conditions of maximum self-support or personal independence. Justice Blackmun's characterization of AFDC welfare interests as charitable funds just one year after the

335

Goldberg statutory entitlements holding is a good illustration of how the Supreme Court was shifting back and forth in its attempt to characterize the property status of welfare interests.

The statutory entitlements doctrine and liberal and libertarian ideologies

The *right* to receive welfare, under a *statutory* entitlements construction, is acquired upon a determination that the claimant has met all stipulated conditions for eligibility under the applicable welfare laws. To determine *subsistence* needs, the applicant's present income and resources are carefully assessed. Of course, the ownership interest acquired at law in this subsistence domain is not to be equated with having a *fundamental* right to unconditioned receipt of benefits or continuance in specified programs. John Nowak argues that certain ideological preferences help explain the reasoning of the judiciary in the welfare cases. The earlier Warren Court was predominantly committed to liberalism whereas the later Burger Court was more closely aligned with libertarianism (Nowak 1980, 274–311). Proponents of the statutory entitlements doctrine found strong support in liberal political ideology. Generally speaking, modern liberals advocate the use of government intervention to enable individuals to engage in fair, open competition in the marketplace on roughly equal terms. The objective is, of course, not to abolish free market enterprise, but to harness government power in order to remedy *inequalities* of opportunity that an individualistically driven laissez-faire marketplace produces.

In *Goldberg*, Brennan cited Charles Reich approvingly for the latter's conceptualization of the changing nature of property in the emerging marketplace (262, footnote 8). According to Reich, modern society is built around entitlement and new marketplace realities make it necessary for government to allocate some resources as subsistence benefits. Indeed, all sorts of entitlements flow for example, as public largesse, from the government in the form of subsidies to farmers, businesses, and national defense contractors (Reich 1964, 733; Reich 1965, 1255). In effect the beneficiaries of such subsidies, though differently circumstanced, all have a share in reallocated public wealth.

Frank Michelman along similar lines contends that in order for all members of the body politic to be productive members of the society and to enjoy other basic rights, each of us is entitled to satisfaction of a minimum amount of subsistence needs. Taking his cue from John Rawls, Michelman argues that subsistence needs amount to "just wants," arising from an economic system of inequalities (Michelman 1969, 14–15). Inequalities of wealth and income are unjust unless they are supportive of mechanisms that better the circumstances of the least advantaged members of society. Accordingly, to ensure minimum protection against economic hazard, *eligible* individuals are entitled to have their just wants satisfied by government out of a general tax supported by public treasury.

Noted for his restrictive position on the original intent of the framers of the Constitution, Robert H. Bork takes issue with the theory of Michelman and others that welfare rights derive from the Constitution itself. He could find no scintilla of evidence supporting the argument that the framers and ratifiers of the Bill of Rights intended the judiciary to develop new individual rights such as the right to receive welfare benefits. The effect of Professor Michelman's argument is to allow the judiciary "to create rights by arguments from moral philosophy rather than from constitutional text, history, and structure" (Bork 1979, 695–6). In addition to its many other defects, Bork concludes that "the welfare-rights theory rests less on demonstrated fact than on a liberal shibboleth" (701).

John Rawls, with his theory of distributive justice that permits wealth reallocations, adds further support to the Reich–Michelman liberal political ideology. The Difference Principle in Rawls's second principle of justice as fairness has a remedial function, as it is designed to ameliorate economic inequalities. The Difference Principle states that "social and economic inequalities are to be arranged so that they are both (a) reasonably expected to be to everyone's advantage, and (b) attached to positions and offices open to all . . ." (Rawls 1971, p. 60). Inequalities of wealth are just only if they result in collective gain – that is, "in compensating benefits for everyone, and in particular for the least advantaged members of society" (pp. 14–15). To invoke the Difference Principle is to categorize welfare allocations, drawn from the public treasury, as equitable shares in redistributed wealth. However, neither Reich nor Michelman nor Rawls were envisioning a society free of all inequalities. What they each envisioned was a democratically governed society in which the rights of the needy could be thought of as requiring constitutionally guaranteed minimum protection (Nowak 1983, p. 822; Michelman 1979, 681–5).

At the other end of the continuum of the right–privilege debate, advocates of the charity doctrine found theoretical support in conservative libertarian ideology. Libertarians maintain that in a just society the primary purpose of government is to protect individuals against unwarranted interferences with the exercise of their fundamental rights to life, liberty, and property. For the libertarian, *individual* liberty is the ultimate moral-political ideal. This ideological preference for a government that is as limited as possible – that is, a "minimal state" under which free-market economics flourishes – has its advocates among theorists such as Ralph Winter, Robert Nozick and Milton Friedman (Nowak 1983, pp. 822–3; Levinson, 1996, pp. 553–4; Winter 1972, 61–73).

A common theme among these libertarians is that reallocations of wealth in a welfare state lead ultimately to greater injury to the society as a whole. Justice Black's criticism in *Goldberg* of the government's abusive use of power to unfairly tax the more affluent members of society so as to help support its less fortunate citizens echo similar libertarian sentiments. Actions of government whereby portions of other people's earnings are reallocated as welfare benefits are said to undermine the exercise of individual autonomy and to foster attitudes of dependency and helplessness on the recipients (Butler and Kondratas 1987, 13–15). Nozick's conservative doctrine of justice as entitlement within the framework of a minimal state shows where the line is to be drawn between coercive government interference and individual liberty. According to Nozick, a critic of liberalism, individuals are justly entitled to either (a) what they have originally acquired as holdings or (b) what they have acquired by rightful transfer (Nozick 1974, pp. 150–3). The first kind of entitlement is referred to as the principle of justice in acquisition and the second kind is identified as the principle of justice in transfer. Nozick accordingly sums up his justice-maxim to mean: "From each as they choose, to each as they are chosen" (p. 160).

The main thrust of Nozick's maxim is, of course, that private property is acquired by disciplined work habits and personal independence. Over such earned acquisitions the possessor is entitled to exercise dominion and control – that is, he or she may choose exclusive appropriation and use or voluntarily pass the title on to someone else. Any holding that has been voluntarily transferred to another becomes a rightful new acquisition of the inheritor. Hence, whenever the government takes property from entitled holders *involuntarily* and passes this on as benefit to others, one's government has in effect donated away stolen property. This is the net effect of public assistance programs in the welfare state. There are no *bargained*-for exchanges taking place here despite the original good intentions of the lawmakers. Forceful taking of property earmarked as charity to the needy violates the rightful holder's exercise of personal autonomy. Justice requires that it should be left to the holder to determine whether a voluntary transfer to needy persons is in order and to decide who he or she wishes to assist. It is not the role of government to intervene to redistribute income.

Welfare reform: a libertarian alternative?

The Personal Responsibility and Work Opportunity Reconciliation Act, passed by Congress in 1996 and signed by the President, is designed to radically transform our nation's welfare system. The new federal welfare law allows welfare systems to be reconstructed on a state-by-state basis. As states start implementing welfare reform policies, it is certain that a number of provisions in the Reconciliation Act will give rise to constitutional challenges. For example, in refashioning their welfare systems, states are permitted to employ residency conditions and devise alienage classifications as they deem reasonable. From all indications the statutory entitlements era will fade into oblivion with a corresponding swing of the pendulum in the direction of libertarian ideals of the common good. A few examples gleaned from case law on this reasonably foreseeable trend should suffice.

Under the new welfare regulations, states have the authority to treat interstate immigrants under the rules of the former state (Section $103.404_{(c)}$). That is, the state may apply to a new applicant the rules of the cash assistance program (including benefit amounts) in effect in the applicant's previous state of residence, if the applicant has resided in the current state for less than one year. This sort of residency condition is nothing new. As we already saw in *Shapiro*, distinctions based on length of residence violate an individual's constitutional guarantee of equal protection under the fourteenth amendment and the right to travel as one chooses.

A similar constitutional analysis was applied in *Zobel v. Williams* (1982), with the Court penetrating even deeper into a residence scheme that attempted to make permanent distinctions between residents based upon their duration of residency. In that case, the state of Alaska had devised a statutory dividend plan whereby it distributed income accrued from its natural resources to the adult citizens of the state in varying amounts, based upon the length of each citizen's residence. The longer the residency the greater the dividend share. The stated government objective of the dividend distribution plan was to create a financial incentive to establish and maintain residence in Alaska. The Court found the residency condition underlying the dividend plan violative of equal protection guarantees under the fourteenth amendment. In effect, any such residency qualifier is tantamount to the imposition of an unconstitutional condition on similarly situated persons (*Zobel* 1982, 61–4; O'Neil 1966, 447–50; Harvith 1966, 567–9, 640–1). Instead of invoking equal protection analysis, state welfare residency provisions now under construction will, once contested, in all probability be tested for their *reasonableness* in accomplishing legitimate governmental interests. The effect of such minimum scrutiny of residence conditions is that they will be upheld as fiscally feasible regulations unless they are patently irrational, arbitrary, or capricious.

There are troubling provisions under the Reconciliation Act that allow states to use their discretion to limit eligibility or deny welfare benefits to individuals who are not citizens of the United States (Sections 402, 403, and 412). To differentiate between citizens and resident aliens in this manner raises concerns about the constitutionality of the resulting alienage classification. This sort of classification scheme poses concerns reminiscent of matters already attended to by the Court in *Graham v. Richardson* (1971) and *Matthews v. Diaz* (1976).

The first of these cases, *Graham*, addressed the issue whether the equal protection clause of the fourteenth amendment prevented a state from conditioning welfare benefits either upon the applicant's possession of United States citizenship or, if the beneficiary is an alien, upon the beneficiary having resided in the United States continuously for a specified number of years. The Court found the alienage classification in violation of equal protection and an infringement on the federal government's plenary power over immigration policy. Like racial classifications, classifications based on alienage, were held to be inherently suspect (*Graham* 1971, 371–2). The state's objective in reducing welfare spending was accordingly not sufficiently compelling to justify the classification. The *Matthews* ruling had a unique twist in that while federal plenary power over immigration law was sufficiently broad to allow the *federal* government to distinguish citizens from aliens (and to distinguish between alien groupings), *states* were held to have no legitimate grounds for treating citizens and legal immigrants differently (*Matthews* 1976, 84–5). It will be interesting to see if the Supreme Court will make a daring shift in focus, away from suspect classification analysis, for newly designed *state*-alienage welfare provisions by delegating its plenary immigration authority to the states in the welfare arena.

These troublesome implications of the reform initiatives are not purely speculative. The Reconciliation Act itself seeks to relax the rigidity of scrutiny the judiciary may apply to test the constitutionality of welfare legislation. In fact, for some time now the prevailing standard of review employed by the courts has been the Rational Basis Test and there is every reason to believe that this method of review will be expanded. The Reconciliation Act now classifies the former categorical assistance programs as "temporary assistance for needy families" and stipulates that no individual entitlements accrue to the beneficiaries. One of the stated purposes of Section 401 is that "This part shall not be interpreted to entitle any individual or family to assistance under any State program funded under this part." Right in line with this state-autonomy trend, *Anderson v. Edwards* (1995) approved of California's method of factoring in all of the income and resources of everyone in the assistance unit in establishing the amount of the benefit payment (which could not exceed a fixed cap), even though this frequently results in disproportionate hardships on some family units due their large size. In its deferring posture the Court was giving due recognition to the great latitude states have in administering their AFDC programs. Similar results were arrived at in *Wilder v. Virginia* (1990) involving states Medicaid reimbursement schemes for health care providers, and quite recently in *Blessing v. Freestone* (1997) where individuals were held not to have an individual right to compel state agencies to "substantially comply" with their own child support program regulations, as provided for under Title IV-D of the Social Security Act. Justice O'Connor reasoned that Title IV-D guidelines were not intended to benefit individual children or their custodial parents, but functioned merely as a yardstick for the Secretary of Health and Human Services to measure system wide performance of the *state's* Title IV-D program (*Blessing* 1997, 1361).

A decided preference for libertarian personal responsibility expectations and a commitment to the return-to-work ethic seem pervasive in this emerging line of judicial reasoning. These interests in the 1996 Reconciliation Act in promoting self-sufficiency coupled with time limitations for benefits fall squarely in line with welfare reform objectives which began in the early eighties, culminating in the Family Support Act (FSA) of 1988. The FSA stressed work, child support and needs-based family support services aimed at helping beneficiaries obtain education, training and employment necessary to prevent long-term dependency on public assistance (Bane and Ellwoood 1994, pp. 1–27; Norris and Thompson 1985, pp. 1–18). In order to allow states to have more autonomy over their own legislation and individual freedoms to flourish to the maximum, it is unlikely that the judicial branch will probe very deeply into the "wisdom" of state welfare legislation.

Moral Considerations

Assuming the soundness of the proposition that the primary moral objective of public relief measures is to make bad life circumstances better for needy persons, I want to consider in this section the kinds of moral principles invoked in response to this desirable end. While it is true that it is not always easy to pinpoint the gravity of specific subsistence needs, it is apparent that welfare policies are generally intended to turn already bad social situations into better ones. However, as with legal theory, the ethical field in which the debate about the appropriateness of benevolence is carried out is a competitive intellectual arena, encompassing a diversity of visions of the good life and ways of rectifying social ills such as poverty and economic inequalities.

The lifeboat metaphor and conservative individualism

It has been argued that the rendition of aid to needy persons may, under certain circumstances, do more harm than good. However laudable the motive for helping others, the donor may worsen not only the aid recipient's condition, but the donor's circumstances as well. This sort of argument has been made in particular by Garrett Hardin in the context of rendering aid to the poor of the third world (Hardin 1974, 38; 1976, 120). Hardin likens the life circumstances of potential donors in the wealthier nations to existence on a lifeboat. All lifeboats have limited carrying capacities in terms of survival resources and habitable space allocations. Blinded by feelings of generosity,

340

as if we were duty-bound to be either "our brother's keeper" or to follow the Marxist "to each according to his needs" justice-maxim, we set suicidal policies of foreign aid in motion. The inevitable outcome is to swamp our own lifeboat, drowning everyone, including the recipients of our unprincipled aid and ourselves. For example, a "food only" assistance foreign policy leads to further population growth among starving peoples often without any accompanying improvement in the development of technologies and means of producing their own food supplies. Likewise, unrestricted immigration policies only move starving people to where the food is, in this way hastening the destruction of the environment and the depletion of natural resources of the wealthier host countries (Hardin 1974, 124–5; 1976, 130–1).

The lifeboat metaphor with all its harsh implications is, of course, of somewhat limited utility when applied to the life experiences of welfare recipients in the so-called welfare state. In the latter situation, beneficiaries of welfare have a more direct nexus to the sources of aid, either presumptively as members of a tax paying citizenry or on account of some other residency qualifier. In the case of rendition of foreign aid the link between donors and recipients is far more amorphous. Nevertheless, conservative individualists advance a parallel ethic of harm-producing consequences when critiquing welfare measures employed in the welfare state. Ayn Rand discovers the basic flaw in national welfare programs in the government's own abuse of its limited exercise of authority (Rand 1964 [1961], pp. 92–120; Hospers 1971). Our government has been only entrusted with specified police powers for the protection of the citizenry from unwarranted interferences with the exercise of basic individual rights, with the authority to arbitrate civil disputes, and with the protection of our national interests against foreign intruders. The government was not created to ensure minimum conditions of well-being for everyone within its national borders. According to Rand, the right to the pursuit of happiness is not the equivalent of the further proposition that there is a government-enforced right to be happy (Rand 1964 [1961], p. 97).

Rand and others, such as the libertarian John Hospers, argue that the interest in pursuing happiness should be understood to mean that each individual is entitled, with government protection if necessary, to undertake those actions deemed appropriate to achieve one's own happiness (Rand 1964 [1961], p. 94; Hospers 1974, pp. 5–7, 14). This is by no means the same as saying that *others* have an obligation to make *you* happy. While individuals have a right to support themselves through the earnings of their work, other people do not have to provide anyone with the necessities of life. A government that unreasonably interferes with how people live their lives and imposes unchosen obligations on some to give of their earnings to others in need is setting up a one-way relationship of unrewarded duty or involuntary servitude. This means of alleviating harm imposes unfair expectations on individuals. In a free society individuals must be left alone to decide the objects of their bounty. We must make these sacrifices or gratuitous services ourselves, motivated by our own feelings of benevolence. When one is forced to assist others, such aid amounts to theft. This sort of wealth "redistribution" plan makes everyone worse off in the long run. It discourages hard work and independence and instead rewards idleness and economic dependency. Undoubtedly, Justice Black's attack on abusive welfare state practices and related coercive wealth redistribution measures challenged by Robert Nozick and Ralph Winter resurface in the Rand-Hospers critique of public welfare as direct handouts to nonproducers.

341

It may be possible however, even on individualistic libertarian grounds, to make a modest case for a minimum duty to aid others in distress. I have argued elsewhere for some such "moral obligation" on grounds of supererogatory ideals (Vanterpool 1988, 101–6). My point is that while acts of benevolence toward strangers are exceptions to the general rule that we are prone to show generosity to parties within the narrow circle of immediate acquaintances, our larger benevolent actions may be said to flow from an exceptional sense of sympathy for others. While there is really no *prima facie* moral duty to render such extensive assistance in the first instance, to do so would nevertheless be in compliance with the pursuit of strongly felt *sacrificial* moral ideals of beneficence. In the strict sense, my sacrificial act of giving is purely supererogatory – that is, an act beyond the call of duty. When so motivated to engage in voluntary sacrifices of my earnings, I am properly carrying out a felt sense of "actual" duty, to be equated perhaps with the responsibility of a minimally decent Samaritan. Such a duty is a very weak one indeed. If I fail to respond on a particular occasion to a person in distress, I choose at that time not to intervene. My act of non-intervention, however, cannot be said to worsen an already bad situation – that is, I do not thereby *cause* further injury by deciding not to do or promote good. In such a situation I at least leave the option open for someone else to come along and act either as a minimally decent or perhaps a very good Samaritan would act.

Balancing of interests

Utilitarians such as Peter Singer tend to assess the appropriateness of public assistance subsidies in terms of the manner in which relevant interests are balanced. Singer's main focus, as was Hardin's, is on the giving of aid to people in famine-stricken nations. People in the more affluent nations have it within their power to at least reduce absolute poverty abroad, without sacrificing anything of comparable moral significance. To help in this manner is not to be "charitable" as we normally label such acts of giving; this sort of help is expected of everyone. The underlying principle supportive of any possible obligation owed to needy persons in general remains the same. Singer believes that more affluent people have a moral responsibility to *prevent* others from starving. He formulates the moral principle that establishes such a duty as follows: "if it is in our power to prevent something very bad from happening, without thereby sacrificing anything of comparable moral importance, we ought to do it" (Singer 1979, p. 167; 1972, 231). To follow this principle merely imposes a duty to prevent bad things from happening, not to aggressively promote what is good.

So how is Singer's principle applicable to welfare assistance intended for, say, the categorically needy and the medically needy in our own midst? To begin with, it doesn't make sense to argue against a duty to render aid in these contexts on the theory that there is no special relationship between the more affluent donors and their poorer counterparts. Singer's principle applies *across distances* in relationships – it is as applicable to strangers as it is to special kinship ties. Secondly, the principle is not framed in terms of a "duty–charity" distinction. To relieve suffering caused by lack of food, shelter, and medical care is something fellow-humans ought to participate in, so long as in doing so something of *comparable value* is not sacrificed. It would, for example, be a breach of moral duty to expend my earnings to help others in distress in the short run (say, by selling my rental property and using most of the proceeds for such aid), if by so doing I cause a comparable longer lasting worsening of harm to members of my own family. Singer's point is that the more affluent can normally afford to share a portion of their wealth with the less fortunate without worsening anything of value to their own lives. This outlook, however, is only possible if we regard poverty as a collective social problem requiring solutions from both private parties acting on their own volition as benefactors and the government serving in its representative role as a public dispenser of the national wealth. At the individual level, the more well-off members of a society have far more than they need to live comfortably. They do themselves no comparable harm by passing up the purchase of a big screen color television or not taking a pleasure trip to Europe or not indulging in an African safari, and allow the monies to be spent instead on food or medical supplies for others in need. It can be argued with similar force that since a democracy is a form of representative government, the interests of the represented in establishing a government sponsored public assistance program is the result of free citizens agreeing to have a portion of their tax set asides used as subsistence benefits for qualified persons.

All things considered, Singer's approach calls for a balancing of several competing interests, such as the interests of donors, the number of qualified donors involved, the number of intended beneficiaries, and the probability that the aid will actually be used to cushion the subsistence hardships. While calculations of the relative values of competing interests are of necessity inexact, *approximations* of harm reductions are enough to satisfy the moral principle of comparable worth. So whereas the Rand–Hospers categorization of welfare as charity terminates in a gloomy picture of *aggravation* of injuries attributable to coerced giving, the "interest balancing" means–ends test aims at *ameliorating* the harsh effects of human suffering. In this way, welfare policies are not cure-all programs. More properly assessed, they are temporary measures used to prevent or cushion economic hardships. Such benign measures are particularly valued when the sacrifices placed on donors have the best prospects of reducing poverty in the long run.

Imperfect moral duties

Dissatisfied with what some believe to be merely prudential reasons offered by utilitarians for aiding needy persons, nonconsequentialists often appeal to a Kantian moral justification as an alternative. Robert N. Van Wyk's position fits this latter line of thought, particularly his treatment of notions such as respect for persons and imperfect moral duties (Van Wyk 1988, 77–8). At a threshold level, it is Van Wyk's contention that former colonizing nations may owe duties of reparation in the form of rendering assistance now to poor and starving people in third world countries they previously exploited. A case can also be made that Henry Shue's inclusion of a right to welfare – broadly, a right to subsistence – in the category of basic rights is at least compatible with Immanuel Kant's justification for rendition of public aid (Shue, pp. 18–29). That is, both security and subsistence rights are minimum reasonable demands each person can make on the rest of humanity.

Kant himself in illustrating the operation of the categorical imperative placed the duty of benevolence alongside the prima facie duties of promise keeping, truth telling, and respect for the sanctity of human life (Kant 1959, 14, 39–41). He does, however, differentiate between the stringency in carrying out such prima facie duties. Since the prima facie duty not to take another human being's life with malice aforethought is unconditional, i.e., is a *perfect* duty, I am bound to carry out the duty at all times and to all persons. By contract, the prima facie duty to help others in need is *imperfect*, being prompted from a compelling interest to promote good. I must use my practical judgment, on a case by case basis, to determine when and to whom I owe a duty to render aid. Not everyone is under all circumstances entitled to my assistance, and so long as helping others is made part of my *considered* and steadfast moral habits I have placed myself in a position to render appropriate help when called for. A special advantage of Kant's duty ethic is that it makes the distinction between refraining from causing harm and promoting good practically insignificant. In the Kantian conceptual framework there is an asymmetrical relationship between duties to refrain from causing harm and duties to intervene to promote good (O'Neill 1985, 42). Kant's duty of beneficence has an inner source, the rational will itself. We can rest assured then that we are not being forced by anyone else to do good when the motive to do so is the product of practical, rational, self-legislation. To follow the dictates of reason allows me to value the quality (and extent) of human well-being I contribute to rather than to concentrate on the incidental, but often naturally accompanying harms of benevolent acts. In the overall Kantian scheme, it is the causing of the spread of good that makes the benevolent deed something of objective value in itself. Benevolence is a positive, meritorious duty to others that harmonizes with the principle of humanity, placing the benefactor in a position from which to "endeavor, so far as he can, to further the ends of others. For the ends of any person, who is an end in himself, must as far as possible also be my end, if that conception of an end in itself is to have its full effect on me" (Kant 1959, 49).

Van Wyk's ultimate source for a nonconsequential moral duty is found in the Kantian idea of respect for persons, a principle that requires us to value others as ends in themselves (Van Wyk 1988, 80). All of us, as members of the reference group humanity, have reciprocal responsibilities to each other to aid in the maximal realization of human potentials. Lacking the basic necessities of life often impairs our abilities to realize our human potentials. To come to the aid of another, out of a sense of duty, is hence motivated by the practical moral imperative to enhance another's self-respect as a valued person in his or her own right. From this underlying concept of respect for persons Van Wyk posits a strict minimum "duty of perfect obligation for an individual to give at least her fair share . . . toward seeing that all human beings are treated as ends in themselves, which involves seeing that they have the basic necessities of life in so far as that can depend on the actions of others" (81; Michelman 1979, 683–4). The main advantage of the "fair share" doctrine is that it diminishes any thought of overload-giving by drawing a practical line somewhere between doing nothing and sacrificing all our possessions to help relieve human distress. In order to help ensure a smooth operation of the individual fair share obligation principle, Van Wyk postulates a corollary "upward pressure" principle (83). By this he means that we can ensure protecting the vulnerable poor by putting pressure on government to enact policies aimed at providing aid for the needy. In this way, a collective tax funded structure is set in motion, thereby guaranteeing that minimum fair shares are systematically contributed more equitably from the populous generally. Such already acquiesced-in government financing of welfare needs could by no stretch of the imagination be equated with official theft.

Kant's principle of respect for persons is also implicit in John Rawls's Difference Principle. In a society governed by ideals of distributive justice, a natural expectation arises to alleviate the misery of those who lack basic subsistence necessities. The needs of the worst off members of society deserve to be given equality of consideration. The point is, each of us could be in need someday, and behind a veil of ignorance, as rational and mutually self-interested persons, we would agree to a system of redistribution whereby the hardships of need are lessened, making the lives of everyone better off. Inasmuch as distributive justice requires fair and equitable allocations of *benefits* the same ideal of distributed fairness calls for allocating *burdens* equitably. In this connection, a reasonable inference to draw from Henry Shue's account of the ethics of giving is that the worst off members of society, as encompassed by Rawls's Difference Principle, have needs that actually amount to subsistence rights. So-called subsistence rights are basic or fundamental in that their satisfaction is necessary for the subsequent enjoyment of all other rights such as security rights to life, liberty, and property (Shue 1980, pp. 24–5).

Needs, considerations and obligations

In a trend of discussion that gets away from talk about welfare recipients having rights to welfare, the focus is placed instead simply on the relationship between needs and moral obligation. Onara O'Neill's approach exemplifies this kind of response. O'Neill argues that the major problem with welfare rights accounts is that "rights" holders are placed in a passive position of *recipience* from which they make entitlement demands of others (O'Neill 1985, 31). However, this rights paradigm lacks objective criteria to adequately ascertain *who* exactly the corresponding bearers of obligation are who are required to act on behalf of the distressed claimants. If it is alleged for instance that former colonizers owe duties of reparations to exploited third world peoples, it would still have to be determined which colonizers actually brought economic ruin on current underdeveloped countries. Are the original government perpetrators of harm in the former colonies still around to be specifically identifiable? Are the living descendants of colonizers to be shouldered indefinitely with the blame of unconscionable past exploitation? Besides all this effort expended in assigning blame for lingering human suffering, there are third world countries in which their own histories of poverty precede imperial expansion and nation building. How would such economically vulnerable groups make their appeal for aid as *harmed* rights holders?

It makes far more sense to start off with fundamental moral obligations instead of entitlements to aid. Obligations or moral duties precede claims about having rights to be helped. From this vantage point Kant's way of grounding affirmative responses to human need in an imperfect duty of beneficence avoids the difficulty of assigning arbitrary duties of action on *unallocated* bearers of responsibility. From the perspective of obligations, benefactors accept it as their moral duty to take appropriate action to help relieve the hardships of their fellow men brought on by the lack of means whereby to live in minimum dignity. As O'Neill affirms, "Kantian benevolence is directed toward helping agents achieve *their* ends, and not simply at providing whatever they may desire. . . ." (1985, 44–5).

We are all vulnerable to the possibility of becoming needy at some point in our lives, and the lack of minimal standards of satisfying our subsistence needs invariably affect our capacities to function as free and responsible moral agents. We are all intertwined in the causes of poverty and justice demands that we share collectively in efforts at ameliorating the accompanying individual and social harms. Imagining the very possibility of *personal* deprivation of means whereby to exist in decency is argument enough to show that the rational will would not desire to be part of a world that followed a maxim that would legislate the neglect of other's subsistence needs. So as finite, mutually vulnerable human beings, we would find no offense with public policies to develop social institutions charged with obligations of helping individuals meet the basic needs of life, thereby enhancing their capacities of agency.

Postscript

Subsistence needs vulnerability is a universal phenomenon. There is, however, no uniformity in justifications available when it comes to dealing with solutions to the plights of the needy. It is also true that our world is not peopled by isolated, solitary individuals. As a global family we are all affected by both the pleasures and the pains, the happiness and the miseries of our fellow beings in some way. These realities all suggest that affirmative responses to promote human well-being are not *per se* without compelling justification. It is also true that existing resources necessary for rendering of help are becoming less abundant, leading to further frustration of positive efforts to facilitate the flourishing of human happiness. From a public policy perspective, an action-ethic must accordingly make strong appeals for intensified work on new solutions to welfare problems. On the theoretical frontier, there are groundbreaking opportunities for construction of creative, viable alternatives to limiting modes of welfare rights discourse.

It would benefit policy makers such as the framers of the new welfare reform initiatives not to downplay the complexity of problems of poverty and social inequalities. Similarly, the states have difficult times ahead in redesigning their public assistance programs in ways that will not unjustly impair the exercise of our individual liberties in a democracy or offend our sense of fair play. New lines of eligibility are sure to be drawn in the deliberative law making process, as should be expected. In my own estimate, the welfare entitlements era has been wisely made a thing of the past. But a naive return to charity discourse would be an unforgivable loss instead of a welcome gain. One is not automatically turned into a passive griever or a mere beggar of favors just because one is living on the very margin of subsistence. The inclusion of education incentives and employment training requirements in the Reconciliation Act is certainly a good constructive start to help recipients achieve income independence and overall life empowerment. These are objectives which go a long way in meeting the Kantian imperative that welfare subsidies enhance the well-being of persons to the point at which their abilities as agents can be exercised to the fullest. But it also behoves an impartial judiciary to rule on the new realities with open minds and with sensitivity to reasonable expectations of obligations of helpfulness, kindness, and sympathy for others. In this transitional phase in welfare litigation, justices must be cognizant of their own value orientation and take a neutral look at the constitutional implications of strict deference to libertarian principles (Nowak 1980, 312).

The upshot of my discussion of welfare distributions is that such government sponsored programs aid in the overall realization of the pursuit of happiness among an informed and free citizenry in modern democracies. Hence, any decision to dismantle the welfare system as we know it should proceed with extreme caution, absent a more viable (and equitable) alternative for assisting the less well-off members of society.

References

Anderson v. Edwards, 115 S. Ct. 1291 (1995).

Bane, Mary Jo and David T. Ellwood. 1994: *Welfare Realities: From Rhetoric to Reform*, Cambridge, Mass.: Harvard University Press.

Bork, Robert H. 1979: "The Impossibility of Finding Welfare Rights in the Constitution," *Washington University Law Quarterly*, 695–701.

Brudno, Barbara (ed.). 1976: *Poverty, Inequality, and the Law: Cases – Commentary – Analyses*, St. Paul, Minn.: West Publishing Co., pp. 1–39.

Butler, Stuart and Anna Kondratas. 1987: *Out of the Poverty Trap: A Conservative Strategy For Welfare Reform*, New York: The Free Press.

Blessing v. Freestone, 117 S. Ct. 1353 (1997).

Flemming v. Nestor, 363 U.S. 603 (1966).

Goldberg v. Kelly, 397 U.S. 254 (1970).

Graham v. Richardson, 403 U.S. 365 (1971).

Hardin, Garrett. 1976: "Carrying Capacity as an Ethical Concept," *Soundings: An Interdisciplinary Journal*, vol. 59, no. 1, 120–37.

——1974: "Lifeboat Ethics: The Case Against Helping the Poor," *Psychology Today*, 38–43, 123–6.

Harvith, Bernard Evans. 1966: "The Constitutionality of Residence Tests for General and Categorical Assistance Programs," *California Law Review*, 54, 567–641.

Hospers, John. 1971: *Libertarianism: A Political Philosophy for Tomorrow*, Los Angeles: Nash Publishing. See, "Welfare and Government," pp. 281–320.

——1974: "What Libertarianism Is." In Tibor R. Machan (ed.), *The Libertarian Alternative: Essays in Social and Political Philosophy*, Chicago: Nelson-Hall Company, pp. 3–20.

Kant, Immanuel. 1959: *Foundations of the Metaphysics of Morals*, Lewis White Beck (trans.), Indianapolis: The Bobbs-Merrill Company, Inc.

Levinson, Sanford. 1996: "The Welfare State," in *A Companion to Philosophy of Law and Legal Theory*, Cambridge, Mass.: Blackwell Publishers, pp. 553–61.

Matthews v. Diaz, 426 U.S. 67 (1976).

Michelman, Frank I. 1969: "On Protecting the Poor Through the Fourteenth Amendment," 83 *Harvard Law Review*, 7–59.

——1979: "Welfare Rights in a Constitutional Democracy," *Washington University Law Quarterly*, 659–93.

Miller, Arthur S. and Ronald F. Howell. 1960: "The Myth of Neutrality in Constitutional Adjudication," *The University of Chicago Law Review*, 27:661–95.

Norris, Donald F. and Thompson, Lyle (eds.). 1985: *The Politics of Welfare Reform*, Thousand Oaks, CA.: Sage Publications.

Nowak, John E. (ed.). 1983: *Constitutional Law: Hornbook Series, Student Edition*, St. Paul, Minn.: West Publishing Co., pp. 821–31.

—— 1980: "Evaluating the Work of the New Libertarian Supreme Court," *Hastings Constitutional Law Quarterly*, vol. 7:263.

Nozick, Robert. 1974: *Anarchy, State, and Utopia*, New York: Basic Books, Inc.

O'Neil, Robert M. 1966: "Unconstitutional Conditions: Welfare Benefits with Strings Attached," *California Law Review*, 54, 443–78.

O'Neill, Onora. 1985: "Rights, Obligations, and Needs," *LOGOS: Philosophic Issues in Christian Perspective*, vol. 6, 29–47.

Personal Responsibility and Work Opportunity Reconciliation Act of 1996 (U.S. Congress, 1996).

Rand, Ayn. 1964 [1961]: *The Virtue of Selfishness: A New Concept of Egoism*, New Jersey: A Signet Book, New American Library.

Rawls, John. 1971: *A Theory of Justice*, Cambridge Mass.: Harvard University Press.

Reich, Charles. 1965: "Individual Rights and Social Welfare: The Emerging Legal Issues," *Yale Law Journal*, 74, 1245

—— 1964: "The New Property," *Yale Law Journal*, 73, 733.

Shapiro v. Thompson, 394 U.S. 618 (1969).

Shue, Henry. 1980: *Basic Rights: Subsistence, Affluence, and U.S. Foreign Policy*, Princeton, NJ: Princeton University Press.

Singer, Peter. 1972: "Famine, Affluence, and Morality," *Philosophy & Public Affairs*, vol. 1, no. 3, 229–43.

—— 1979: *Practical Ethics*, Cambridge: Cambridge University Press, pp. 158–81.

Vanterpool, Rudolph V. 1988: "Hume on the 'Duty' of Benevolence," *Hume Studies*, vol. XIV, Number 1, 93–110.

—— 1985: "Welfare Rights and Procedural Due Process," *LOGOS: Philosophic Issues in Christian Perspective*, vol. 6, 79–89.

Van Wyk, Robert N. 1988: "Perspectives on World Hunger and the Extent of Our Positive Duties," *Public Affairs Quarterly*, vol. 2, 75–90.

Wilder v. Virginia, 496 U.S. 498 (1990).

Winter, Ralph. 1972: "Poverty, Economic Equality, and the Equal Protection Clause," *Sup. Ct. Rev.*, 41.

Wyman v. James, 400 U.S. 309 (1971).

Zobel v. Williams, 457 U.S. 55 (1982).

22

Racism and Health Care:
A Medical Ethics Issue

ANNETTE DULA

The field of medical ethics is largely concerned with the ethical problems associated with the technological advances of the last thirty years. Medical ethicists pay a great deal of attention to general principles like autonomy, beneficence, and justice. These principles form the background for addressing the ethics of genetic cloning, informed consent, multiple births, abortion, surrogate motherhood, advance directives, and the economics of health care. They are important and sexy ethical issues, to be sure. However, one important failing in medical ethics discourse is the omission of discussions of race. Race is not just another issue like cloning; rather it is a dimension in every ethical consideration from surrogate motherhood to violation of informed consent to access to health care. Race (as well as gender and class) is completely overlooked as a significant ethical issue in mainstream medical ethics. At most, it is dealt with as a "Oh, don't forget to include race" matter. The unfortunate result is that medical ethicists, whether intentional or unintentional, almost completely ignore considerations of difference (Dula and Goering 1994, Wolf 1996a) and how such issues play out for women and people of color. Because they ignore race, medical ethicists misrepresent the dilemmas.

In the United States, African Americans, other people of color, and women have historically been treated as different in almost every dimension of group and individual life. This different treatment has made a tremendous impact on our collective destinies, life opportunities, worldviews, conceptions of ourselves, perception of others, and particularly on health status. Race-based differential treatment is an ethical issue that has not been sufficiently addressed in medical ethics scholarship. In this essay, I focus on the relationship between the poor health of African Americans and racism. I argue that the poor health of African Americans is an ethical issue. I develop my argument by presenting factual evidence to demonstrate that poor health of African Americans is a consequence of institutionalized racism in the health care system and in our larger social and economic arrangements. Then I suggest how two concepts might be used in a non-dogmatic way to improve the health of not just African Americans, but of all US citizens.

After I briefly discuss the health status of African Americans, I turn to consider how different, and racist, treatment is a major factor in the health status gap. Finally, I explore how the concepts of universalism, difference, and affirmative action in health care might be applied to improve the poor health of African Americans and others disadvantaged in access to health care and healthy lives. Though this paper focuses on African Americans, similar trends and patterns apply to other people of color.

The gap in the health status of African Americans

There is a gap in the health status of African Americans and whites; that gap is getting wider because the health of African Americans continues to worsen. The gap is an ethical issue because it is in large part due to unequal and unfair treatment of one group of citizens – African Americans. African Americans have higher death rates due to cancers, diabetes, cirrhosis, homicide, AIDS, and cardiovascular diseases than whites. The infant mortality rate is more than twice that of whites (CDC 1996a); maternal death is between three and four times higher for black women than for white women (CDC 1996a, CDC 1997a). More white women have breast cancer, but the death rate for breast cancer is 19 percent higher in black women and is increasing (CDC 1996b, CDC 1994). The excessive rates of illness contribute to the high mortality rate of African Americans: the life expectancy for white women is 79.5 years; 73.7 years for black women; 73.1 years for white men; and for black men it is 64.6 years (CDC 1996a).

Several explanations for the gap in health status and mortality have been offered (Kreiger and Bassett 1993). Some observes attribute it to innateness, suggesting that excess infant deaths and homicides in blacks are due to genetics. Others attribute the high rate of sickness and death to "irresponsible lifestyles": African-American women and men refuse or neglect to get timely mammograms or be screened for prostate cancer. Or they prefer to smoke high-nicotine content cigarettes and drink high-alcohol content beers such as Colt 45 (Moore et al. 1996). Still others attribute the disparity in status to cultural attitudes and deficits that prevent health-seeking behaviors. This explanation asserts that patient preferences (i.e., African Americans prefer dialysis to a kidney transplant), lack of education, patient or family beliefs, suspicion of the health care system, and cultural attitudes toward health care providers prevent African Americans from taking advantage of available health services (Lozano et al. 1996).

Another explanation is now slowly gaining credence: the poor health of African Americans is due to racism in the delivery of health care services (Kreiger and Fee 1994). The term is grudgingly used. Researchers prefer using phrases like "racial bias," "race-related," or "structural and cultural barriers" to explain differences in treatment (King 1996). Regardless of what terms researchers prefer to use, there is increasing evidence that institutional and individual racism have a negative impact on the quality and quantity of services, procedures, and health care that people of color receive. That is, the racism that permeates US society is a contributor to disparities in health status and is itself a medical ethics issue that ethicists have been reluctant to address.

Racism and access to health care

Different treatment based on one's race or the group to which one belongs is an ethical problem because such treatment usually has a negative impact on life opportunities, health, education, and mental well-being. Although African Americans have always been sicker and died earlier than whites they have historically had – and continue to receive – different, unequal, and inferior access to health care. Even though heart disease is the number one killer of African Americans, whites get more aggressive treatment. Blacks with coronary heart disease are significantly less likely than whites to undergo bypass surgery, angioplasty, and a host of other procedures (Ayanian 1993, Blendon et al. 1989, Caralis et al. 1993, Council on Ethical and Judicial Affairs 1990, Gaston et al. 1993, Geronimus et al. 1996, Gornick et al. 1996, Krieger and Sidney 1996, Wenneker and Epstein 1989). Unfortunately, those predicted most likely to benefit from a treatment are those most likely not to receive the procedure (Peterson et al. 1997). Most race research in health has been done with regard to heart disease, but differential and racist treatment has also been documented regarding kidney transplants (Gaston et al. 1993, Sabatier 1988), intensive care unit (ICU) treatment (Williams et al. 1995), and even the kind of information provided to pregnant African-American women (Kogan et al. 1994). One might counter that differential treatment has nothing to do with race. However, studies that have adjusted for income, age, severity of disease, health insurance status, and demographic variables show that race is a significant variable in the health and health care of African Americans (Escarce et al. 1993, Geiger 1996, Whittle et al. 1993).

Differential treatment is dramatically illustrated in government programs that provide health insurance for three groups of citizens: war veterans, poor people, and the elderly. Under Medicare, the VA systems, and Medicaid, money is not passed between patient and provider; thus, one might assume that patient enrollees in these three programs would be treated fairly, regardless of race. This is not the case. Studies on the distribution of services under all three programs show that blacks do not get the same quality of care that whites receive. Gornick and her colleagues, for example, surveyed 26 million Medicare enrollees. They found that elderly whites received more hip replacements, more flu shots, and twice as many cardiac procedures as blacks. Even though mortality for breast cancer is higher in black women, white women received more mammograms. Elderly blacks, however, did receive more amputations of the legs and feet and black men received more castrations for prostate cancer (Gornick et al. 1996). In an editorial accompanying the Gornick article, the *New England Journal of Medicine* raised the specter of racism as an explanation for the differences in treatment (Geiger 1996).

The Veteran Administration systems is also guilty of racial discrimination (Peterson et al. 1994, Whittle et al. 1993). Peterson and colleagues found that African-American veterans get substantially fewer treatments for Acute Myocardial Infarction (AMI) than do white patients. Black men are one-third less likely to undergo cardiac catherization and less than one-half as likely to receive coronary bypass surgery (Peterson et al. 1994).

Medicaid ensures access to health care for poor people who meet certain criteria. Yet Medicaid too offers differential and substandard treatment to people of color. For instance, African-American children have a disproportional incidence of asthma; prevalence is twice that of whites, and death rates from asthma are between two and six times higher (CDC 1997b, National Institute of Allergy and Infectious Diseases 1996). Certainly poverty, substandard housing, exposure to certain indoor allergens, lack of education, and failure to take medications contribute to severe asthma attacks

351

and death. But Medicaid physicians also play a role in poor asthma outcomes. In 1991, NIH guidelines discouraged the use of the drug, theophylline, for asthma and recommended alternative more effective drugs. Yet asthmatic African-American children are 34 percent more likely to be prescribed theophylline than white children on Medicaid. One can only conclude that African-American children on Medicaid are less likely to receive state of the art drugs than white children on Medicaid (Lozano et al. 1996).

Government programs also perpetuate disparities in health status and access to services in other ways. Currently African Americans represent one-third of those on the national waiting list for kidney transplants (Starzl et al. 1997). Because of federal medical criteria, African Americans receive fewer kidneys and they wait twice as long for them as whites (Gaston et al. 1993). World renowned transplant surgeon, Thomas Starzl, and his colleagues report that the national kidney allocation system inherently favors white patients because of the heavy emphasis placed on donor-recipient compatibility. They argue that antigen matching should not weigh so heavily in deciding who gets a kidney since differences in survival rates (the justification for current donor allocation) are negligible (Starzl, et al. 1997).

Not only is there a gap in status and access, but there is also a gap in the way African Americans and whites think about the health of African Americans. In a survey about the government's role in improving the health of African Americans, researchers found that 80 percent of African Americans thought the government should do something to improve the health and lives of African Americans while 65 percent of whites thought the government was already doing enough for African Americans (Blendon et al. 1995). Whether intentional or not, government programs support discriminatory policies that treat African Americans as second-class citizens. Differential treatment in access to health care is clearly a medical ethics issue.

Informed consent and racism in research

Informed consent is an ethical principle that has particular relevance to African Americans and similarly oppressed and vulnerable populations. Although the Tuskegee Experiment (Jones 1981) is the most egregious violation of informed consent, other examples of research abuse abound from slavery times to the present. Enslaved women were used to conduct painful research on urine leaks into the vagina (Gamble 1997) and black women were used to perfect Cesarean-sections. More recently, President Clinton's Advisory Committee on Human Radiation Experiments observed that in several studies, subjects were disproportionately chosen from minority populations, again without consent (Advisory Committe on Human Radiation Experiments 1996). Questions have also been raised about an early 1990s measles vaccine trial that involved mostly minority children in several inner cities. Though presumably well-intentioned, researchers did not adequately inform parents of risks, that the drug was experimental, or that it had not been approved for use in the US (Marwick 1996). Although blacks have been overrepresented in unethical research, generally blacks and women have been excluded from ethical research that might benefit them. Hence, the NIH Revitalization Act of 1993 mandates that women and minorities be included in federally funded research.

Given the history of research abuse against vulnerable populations, why should African Americans even want to be included in research? There are several reasons: Women and minorities sometimes respond differently from white men to the same drug. For example, lithium, a drug tested and used successfully on white men with psychiatric problems, was found to be toxic in African-American men, increasing their already high risk of renal failure (Cotton 1990). In addition exclusion means that women and ethnic minorities will not have access to new and perhaps beneficial therapies not yet available commercially. Women and African Americans are underrepresented in AIDS trials for new drugs; yet most women who have AIDS are women of color. AIDS patients in research often receive better health care just because they are research subjects. Because black women have been excluded from AIDS research, they receive less care and less quality care than men with AIDS (DeBruin 1994). Of course there are the ethical problems of tying research to therapy. As Jay Katz points out, the line between therapy and research should not be blurred (Advisory Committe on Human Radiation Experiments 1996). Furthermore it is an ethical issue if access to care is determined by whether one is enrolled in a research protocol.

Despite possible benefits from research, it is well to remember that research still offers a potent possibility for continued abuse of informed consent. On November 1, 1996, federal regulations (21 CFR Parts 50 et al. and 45 CFR Part 46) became effective that permit medical experimentation in emergency or traumatic situations without informed consent of the subjects. The regulations allow researchers to use experimental drugs or devices on individuals who are in life-threatening emergency situations, unconscious, and therefore can not consent to participate in medical trials. Conceivably, the new rules could have a disproportionate effect on society's more vulnerable members – African Americans, Hispanics, and poor people. A large proportion of trauma centers are located in public hospitals in or near inner-cities. And as public hospitals are often associated with universities, they are also sites for teaching and medical research (Dula 1997). Emergency research will most likely take place in poor communities because that's where the hospitals with sophisticated and well-run trauma centers are located. Unethical research practices and policies, then, continue to have a disproportionate effect on the health of African Americans.

Racism, health, and living conditions

It is clear that racism in our health care systems powerfully affects the health of African Americans. But racism pervades all our institutions, and the practices of other societal institutions also endanger the well-being of African Americans. Unhealthy housing conditions, differential toxic dumping, and targeted advertising leave their marks on the health of African Americans. People of color have the most dangerous and the lowest paid jobs. They are more likely to suffer occupational injuries and disabilities, but are less likely to report injuries to their employers. Therefore they do not receive compensation for work related injuries and may not have been fully informed of the dire health consequences of their jobs (Davis and Rowland 1983).

Although all poor people are subjected to environmental discrimination, race determines where toxic materials are processed or dumped. In 1983, the Government Accounting Office (GAO) found a relationship between race and socioeconomic status and location of hazardous land fills. Ten years later, the situation had not changed. In EPA region IV (composed of eight southern states) three out of four federally designated hazardous waste sites are located in communities of color (Bullard 1990, 1994). Segregated cities and unhealthy housing conditions add their toll to sickness and death in minority communities. Racist mortgage underwriting policies help ensure racially segregated cities. Housing segregation patterns have been associated with poor health, lack of health insurance, high death rates, dilapidated housing, high blood lead levels, less medical services, and overcrowded emergency rooms (Lanphear et al. 1996, Northridge and Shepard 1997, Polednak 1996).

Industries and corporations contribute to the disparities in health status by targeting communities of color for tobacco and alcohol advertising. There are more and larger billboards advertising tobacco and alcohol in inner-city black and Latino communities and more money is spent for advertising (Moore et al. 1996). Tobacco has been implicated in circulatory, respiratory and cancer deaths – leading causes of deaths among African Americans. Deaths attributed to smoking is 20 percent higher for blacks than for whites (CDC 1997c).

Differential access to health care, research abuse, and unethical practices of societal institutions are clear and indefensible evidence that racism is a major culprit contributing to morbidity and mortality in black communities. The result has been a worsening of health and the construction of a health gap that is racist in nature and is fundamentally a medical ethics issue.

An ethical solution: What are we to do?

Over the last few years there has been heated intellectual discourse that pits a universalist or colorblind morality against a morality that promotes and values diversity, multiculturalism, and difference. The debate has also flowed over into the field of medical ethics (Dula 1994, Dula and Goering 1994, Flack and Pellegrino 1992, Wolf 1996a, 1996b). I want to consider these concepts in the context of the health status gap and unfair access to health care that is racial in nature.

The principle of universalism maintains that all humans are essentially the same and therefore ought to be treated the same way. Nobody should be treated better or worse than anybody else. A moral universalist emphasizes the equal dignity of all individuals. Differences like race, class, and gender are morally and ethically irrelevant; therefore, particular groups like women and minorities should not get preferential treatment. Each individual has the same rights, no more and no less than any other individuals. If all people are essentially the same, then special treatment for any individual or group regardless of gender or race is discriminatory and racist. Moreover, universalists argue that preferential treatment threatens the unity and stability of society, leading to chaos. Beyond that, preferential treatment is wicked and immoral. For the universalist, there is only one morality (Banner 1992).

Often those who advocate diversity and multiculturalism say that universalist morality is mere rhetoric. The principles of universalist moral theory have been unfairly applied to women and minorities. Universalist principles are supposed to be neutral, but in reality, they reflect the values of the dominant culture (Wolf 1996a). Colorblindness is discriminatory because it ignores peoples' histories and pays no attention to social and political contexts (Dula and Goering 1994). Denial of racism obscures the facts that created the need for the remedy in the first place (Wilkins 1995). Recognition of difference is the guiding force of advocates of diversity and multiculturalism. Not recognizing a group is harmful and causes damage to that group (Taylor 1992). Affirmative action is required because groups have experienced this country differently; affirmative action merely attempts to level the playing field (Wilkins 1995).

How might universalist and color-conscious approaches to health care improve the health status of African Americans? Under universalism all citizens would receive a decent minimum of health care and equal distribution of services regardless of lifestyle, sexual orientation, ethnicity, race, class, diagnosis, prognosis, social station, employment status, or ability to pay. Under universal health insurance, however, there would still be problems of access for African Americans, women, poor people, and other people of color. First, as discussed earlier, even when money is not an obstacle, access to procedures and services is not equally distributed. Second, African Americans would start with the handicap of poorer health, so it would take more to catch up to whites. A pure universalist application would not be able to give more because it does not believe in preferential treatment. Third, there would be problems because the colorblind or universalist approach "whites" out or minimizes the devastating effect of past discrimination, disadvantage, history, and racism (Jaggar 1996). Additionally, a universalist approach assumes that racism in health care would no longer be a problem once services are available on an equal basis. This ignores the cumulative impact that a history of intentional and unintentional discrimination and individual and institutional racism have had on the health of African Americans. Under a universalist system, poor health could still be explained as a consequence of genetic mishap, irresponsible lifestyle, poor education, poor personal choices, or individual misfortune (Jaggar 1996). A universalist approach could mask the impact of the decisions of individual providers who prescribe, refer, and provide information to patients unlike themselves. Fourth, there would still be problems because racism is not a phenomenon of the past. A universalist approach denies the stubborn persistence of racial discrimination in health care.

Certainly, a universalist approach to health care is a good starting point because it would ideally ensure that everyone would get some decent minimum; that no citizen would be excluded and all would benefit. That's certainly better than what we have now, where over forty million people have no health care coverage, forty million are underinsured, and millions of children have no access to basic preventive care. But a pure universalist approach is limited because it does not recognize the differences in histories and health experiences. It offers a clean slate, without context, where nothing has gone on before and all treatment is fair and just. Finally a universalist approach may keep the health gap from widening, but will it significantly narrow or eliminate the gap?

On the other hand, a color conscious approach insists that African Americans, other minority groups, and women have historically been – and continue to be – subjected to racist and sexist policies and actions that negatively affect health. This approach acknowledges that African Americans have been wronged by the health care system and compensation is in order. Compensation requires the establishment of programs and services that *explicitly* try to improve the health of African Americans and others disadvantaged in health and that ultimately eliminates disparities.

355

Is there a justification for giving some groups special treatment in health care? One justification for affirmative action programs in health is for the survival of the group. A disadvantaged health status threatens the well-being of a group and its ability to sustain itself as a community. A wise, caring, and fair society recognizes the worth of all its diverse groups and such a society allows that survival of the group is a legitimate goal. It realizes that the individual's well-being is tied up to the well-being of the group (Outlaw 1996). There are other justifications: Different treatment in health care has not only wronged African Americans, but it has also harmed them, contributing to excess sickness and deaths. Boxill argues that affirmative action or color-conscious policy can work in two ways: it can harm and it can help (Boxill 1992). Differential treatment in health has harmed because it contributes to the poor health of African Americans. Race-conscious policies could elevate a group by addressing harms caused by past and current discriminations and abuses. Color-conscious programs would help achieve greater equality in health status by elimiminating unjust distribution of health goods. Finally, affirmative action in health would benefit not only African Americans, but the nation as well. Improved health could mean better life opportunities, fewer health care costs, and a more just nation.

But color-consciousness raises other issues. Like affirmative action programs in education and hiring policies, color conscious programs might benefit those African Americans who have not been discriminated against in the health care system. Their poor health may indeed be a consequence of irresponsible lifestyles, and hence they do not "deserve" preferential treatment in health care. Also affirmative action programs based on race don't address the health care of the millions of poor whites who also do not receive adequate access to health care.

The concepts of universalism and pluralism are not going to go away. The notion of "equal treatment" and individualism are deeply rooted in intellectual, political, and social thought (Taylor 1992), so much so, that universalists may be unwilling to allow preferential treatment (at least preferential treatment for non-whites or non-males).

And multiculturalists are unwilling to give up identity with their own culture (Kymlicka 1995) or ignore the devastating effects that racism has had and continues to have on the destinies of people of color. For many who prefer a difference-based approach, the US has never been, and may never be a color-blind society (Blendon et al. 1995, Wilkins 1995).

Is there a way what we can achieve the goals of improving the health of African Americans and ultimately eliminating the gap in health care and status? In a good and wise society there ought to be a way to address both universal and group-specific needs. Universal health care would minimally require that all citizens be treated fairly, decently, and respectfully in the delivery of health care services. Preventive care, for example, would be available to all citizens from prenatal care through all stages of development, without regard to social station, gender, or cultural affiliation. Diagnoses, procedures, screening, drug prescriptions, and organ donations would be equally available to all citizens, regardless of ability to pay. But a wise society also recognizes and understands that some groups have different or more needs because they have been vulnerable to economic, political, social, racial, biological, and cultural pressures (Kymlicka 1994) that have affected their health. It would recognize that a history of institutional racism, sexism, and classism in the organization of medical care has

356

undermined the health of some groups. Applying both a universalist and a difference approach could improve the health of all Americans.

References

Advisory Committee on Human Radiation Experiments. *The Human Radiation Experiments*. New York: Oxford University Press, 1996.

Ayanian, John Z. "Heart Disease in Black and White." *New England Journal of Medicine* 329, no. 9 (1993): 656–7.

Banner, William A. "Is There an African-American Perspective on Biomedical Ethics? The View from Philosophy." In *African-American Perspectives on Biomedical Ethics*, edited by H. E. Flack and E. D. Pellegrino, 188–91. Washington DC: Georgetown University Press, 1992.

Blendon, Robert J., L. Aiken, H. Freeman, and C. Corey. "Access to Medical Care for Black and White Americans: A Matter of Continuing Concern." *Journal of the American Medical Association* 261 (1989): 278–81.

Blendon, Robert J., Ann C. Scheck, Karen Donelan, and Craig A. Hill. "How White and African Americans View Their Health and Social Problems: Different Experience, Different Expectations." *Journal of the American Medical Association* 273, no. 4 (1995): 341–6.

Boxill, Bernard R. *Blacks and Social Justice*. Revised edn. Totowa, NJ: Rowman and Littlefield Publishers, Inc., 1992.

Bullard, Robert D. *Dumping in Dixie: Race, Class, and Environmental Quality*. Boulder, CO: Westview Press, 1990.

——. "Environmental Justice for All." In *Unequal Protection: Environmental Justice & Communities of Color*, edited by Robert D. Bullard. San Francisco: Sierra Club Books, 1994.

Caralis, P. V., Bobbi Davis, Karen Wright, and Eileen Marcial. "The Influence of Ethnicity and Race on Attitudes toward Advance Directives, Life-Prolonging Treatment, and Euthanasia." *Journal of Clinical Ethics* 4, no. 2 (1993): 155–65.

Center for Disease Control (CDC). "Deaths from Breast Cancer – United States, 1991." *Morbidity and Mortality Weekly Report* 43, no. 15 (1994): 273–81.

——. "Mortality Patterns – United States, 1993." *Morbidity and Mortality Report* 45, no. 8 (1996a): 161–3.

——. "Breast Cancer Incidence and Mortality." *Morbidity and Mortality Weekly Report* 45, no. 39 (1996b): 833–7.

——. "Pregnancy Related Mortality Surveillance – United States, 1987–1990." *Morbidity and Mortality Report* 46, no. SS-4 (1997a): 17–36.

——. "Asthma Hospitalizations and Readmissions Among Children and Young Adults – Wisconsin, 1991–1995." *Morbidity and Mortality Weekly Report* 46, no. 31 (1997b): 726–8.

——. "Smoking-Attributable Mortality and Years of Potential Life Lost – United States, 1984," *Morbidity and Mortality Weekly Report* 45, no. 20 (1997c): 444–51.

Cotton, P. "Is There Still Too Much Extrapolation From Data on Middle-aged White Men." *Journal of the American Medical Association* 263, no. 8 (1990): 1049.

Council on Ethical and Judicial Affairs. "Black–White Disparities in Health Care." *JAMA* 263, no. 17 (1990): 2344–6.

Davis, M. E., and A. Rowland. "Problems Faced by Minority Workers." In *Occupational Health: Recognizing and Preventing Work-Related Disease*, edited by Barry S. Levy and D. H. Wegman. Boston: Little, Brown and Company, 1983.

DeBruin, Debra A. "Justice and the Inclusion of Women in Clinical Studies: An Argument for Further Reform." *Kennedy Institute of Ethics Journal* 4, no. 2 (1994): 117–64.

357

Dula, Annette. "Bearing the Brunt of the New Regulations: Minority Populations." *Hastings Center Report* 27, no. 1 (1997): 11–12.

Dula, Annette, and Sara Goering, eds. *"It Just Ain't Fair!": The Ethics of Health Care for African Americans.* Westport, CT: Praeger, 1994.

Dula, Annette. "The Life and Death of Miss Mildred; An Elderly Black Woman." *Clinics in Geriatric Medicine* 10, no. 3 (1994): 419–30.

Escarce, J. J., K. R. Epstein, D. C. Colby, and J. S. Schwartz. "Racial Differences in the Elderly's Use of Medical Procedures and Diagnostic Tests." *American Journal of Public Health* 83, no. 7 (1993): 948–54.

Flack, Harley E., and Edmund D. Pellegrino, eds. *African-American Perspectives on Biomedical Ethics.* Washington, DC: Georgetown University Press, 1992.

Gamble, Vanessa Northington, "Under the Shadow of Tuskegee: African Americans and Health Care," *American Journal of Public Health* 87, no. 11 (1997): 1773–8.

Gaston, Robert S., Ian Ayres, Laura G. Dooley, and Arnold G. Diethelm. "Racial Equity in Renal Transplantation: The Disparate Impact of HLA-Based Allocation." *Journal of the American Medical Association* 270, no. 11 (1993): 1352–6.

Geiger, H. Jack. "Race and Health – An American Dilemma." *New England Journal of Medicine* 335, no. 11 (1996).

Geronimus, Arline T., John Bound, and Timothy A. Waidman. "Excess Mortality Among Blacks and Whites in the United States." *New England Journal of Medicine* 335, no. 21 (1996): 152–5.

Gornick, Marian E., Paul W. Eggers, Thomas W. Reilly, Renee M. Mentnech, Lesley K. Fitterman, Lawrence E. Kucken, and Bruce C. Vladeck. "Effects of Race and Income on Mortality and Use of Services Among Medicare Beneficiaries." *New England Journal of Medicine* 335, no. 11 (1996): 791–9.

Jaggar, Alison M. "Gender, Race, and Difference: Individual Considerations vs. Group-Based Affirmative Action in Admissions to Higher Education." *The Southern Journal of Philosophy* XXXV, Supplement (1996): 21–51.

Jones, James H. *Bad Blood: The Tuskegee Syphilis Experiment: A Tragedy of Race and Medicine.* New York: The Free Press, 1981.

King, Gary. "Institutional Racism and the Medical/Health Complex: A Conceptual Analysis." *Ethnicity and Disease* 6, no. 1, 2 (1996): 30–46.

Kogan, Michael D., Milton Kotelchuck, and Greg Alexander. "Racial Disparities in Reported Prenatal Care Advice from Health Care Providers." *American Journal of Public Health* 84, no. 1 (1994): 82–8.

Kreiger, Nancy, and Mary Bassett. "The Health of Black Folk." In *The Racial Economy of Science*, edited by Sandra Harding, 161–9. Bloomington: Indiana University Press, 1993.

Kreiger, Nancy, and Elizabeth Fee. "Man-Made Medicine and Women's Health: The Biopolitics of Sex/Gender and Race/Ethnicity." In *Women's Health, Politics, and Power: Essays on Sex/Gender, Medicine, and Public Health*, edited by Elizabeth Fee and Nancy Kreiger, 9–11. Amityville, NY: Baywood Publishing Company, Inc., 1994.

Kreiger, Nancy, and Stephen Sidney. "Racial Discrimination and Blood Pressure: The CARDIA Study of Young Black and White Adults." *American Journal of Public Health* 86, no. 10 (1996): 1370–8.

Kymlicka, Will. "Individual and Community Rights." In *Group Rights*, edited by Judith Baker, 17–33. Toronto: University of Toronto Press, 1994.

——. *Multicultural Citizenships: A Liberal Theory of Minority Rights.* Oxford: Clarendon Press, 1995.

Lanphear, Bruce P., Michael Weitzman, Nancy L. Winter, and Shirley Eberly. "Lead-Contaminated House Dust and Urban Children's Blood Lead Levels." *American Journal of Public Health* 86, no. 10 (1996): 1416–21.

Lozano, Paul, Frederick A. Connell, and Thomas D. Koepsell. "Use of Health Services by African American Children with Asthma on Medicaid." *Journal of the American Medical Association* 274, no. 6 (1996): 469–73.

Marwick, Charles. "Questions Raised About Measles Vaccine Trial." *Journal of the American Medical Association* 276, no. 16 (1996): 1288–9.

Moore, David J., Jerome D. Williams, and William J. Qualls. "Target Marketing of Tobacco and Alcohol-Related Products to Ethnic Minority Groups in the United States." *Ethnicity and Disease* 6, no. 1, 2 (1996): 83–99.

National Institute of Allergy and Infectious Diseases. "Asthma: A Concern for Minority Populations." National Institutes of Health, 1996.

Northridge, Mary E., and Peggy M. Shepard. "Comment: Environmental Racism and Public Health." *American Journal of Public Health* 87, no. 5 (1997): 730–2.

Outlaw, Lucius T. *On Race and Philosophy.* New York: Routledge, 1996.

Peterson, Eric. D., Steven M. Wright, Jennifer Daley, and George E. Thibault. "Racial Variation in Cardiac Procedure Use and Survival Following Acute Myocardial Infarction in the Department of Veterans Affairs." *Journal of the American Medical Association* 271, no. 15 (1994): 1175–80.

Peterson, Eric D., Linda K. Shaw, Elizabeth R. DeLong, and David B. Pryor. "Racial Variation in the Use of Coronary-Revascularization Procedures – Are the Differences Real? Do They Matter?" *New England Journal of Medicine* 336, no. 7 (1997): 480–6.

Polednak, Anthony P. "Segregation, Discrimination and Mortality in U.S. Blacks." *Ethnicity and Disease* 6, no. 1, 2 (1996): 99–108.

Sabatier, R. *Blaming Others.* London: Panos Publications, 1988.

Starzl, Thomas E., M. E. Aliasziw, and D. Gjertson. "HLA and Cross-Reactive Antigen Group Matching for Cadaver Kidney Allocation." *Transplantation* 64, no. 7 (1997): 983–91.

Taylor, Charles. *Multiculturalism and "The Politics of Recognition."* Princeton: Princeton University Press, 1992.

Wenneker, M. B., and A. M. Epstein. "Racial Inequalities in the Use of Procedures for Patients with Ischemic Heart Disease in Massachusetts." *Journal of American Medical Association* 261 (1989): 253–7.

Whittle, Jeff, Joseph Conigliaro, C. B. Good, and Richard P. Lofgren. "Racial Differences in the Use of Invasive Cardiovascular Procedures in the Department of Veterans Affairs Medical System." *New England Journal of Medicine* 329, no. 9 (1993): 621–7.

Wilkins, Roger. "The Case for Affirmative Action: Racism has its Privileges." *The Nation*, March 27, 1995, 409–16.

Williams, John F., Jack E. Zimmerman, and Douglas P. Wagner. "African American and White Patients Admitted to the Intensive Care Unit: Is There a Difference in Therapy and Outcome?" *Critical Care Medicine* 23, no. 4 (1995): 626–36.

Wolf, Susan M., ed. *Feminism & Bioethics.* New York: Oxford University Press, 1996.

Wolf, Susan M. "Introduction: Gender and Feminism in Bioethics." In *Feminism & Bioethics: Beyond Reproduction*, edited by Susan M. Wolf. New York: Oxford University Press, 1996.

359

23

Racialized Punishment and
Prison Abolition

ANGELA Y. DAVIS

Michel Foucault's *Discipline and Punish* is arguably the most influential text in contemporary studies of the prison system. Although its subtitle is *The Birth of the Prison System*, Foucault was not so much interested in the prison *per se* as in the disciplinary technologies perfected within this institution. He attempted to explain the production of manipulable bodies within the context of a panoptic carceral network that reaches far beyond the prison. While the category of class plays a pivotal role in his analysis – though his reconceptualization of power leads to critical revisions of class as a Marxist category – gender and race are virtually absent. Feminist critiques of Foucault have led to a proliferating body of Foucauldian literature on gender discipline, including an extended study on women in prison by Dobash, Dobash, and Gutteridge (1986). However, few scholars have seriously examined the racial implications of Foucault's theory of power and his history of the prison. Joy James's assertion that "Foucault's elision of racial bias in historical lynching and contemporary policing predicts his silence on the racialization of prisons" points to the need to move beyond a strictly Foucauldian genealogy in examining histories of punishment (James, 1996).

Foucault revises the penal historiography that privileges the development of the penitentiary in the United States, arguing that the oldest model of imprisonment as punishment rather than detention is the Raspuis of Amsterdam, which opened in 1596 and originally "was intended for beggars or young malefactors (Foucault, 1979)." The eighteenth-century *mason de force* in Ghent, in which idlers were imprisoned and subjected to "a universal pedagogy of work," and the penitentiary built in Gloucester to implement Blackstone and Howard's principles of imprisonment, served as the models for the Walnut Street Jail in Philadelphia, which opened its doors in 1790 (ibid., 121–2).

As interesting as it may be, however, to examine the influences of the earlier European models on the emergent US prison system, what may help us to understand the way in which this system would eventually incorporate, sustain and transform structures and ideologies of racism is an examination of the impact of the institution of slavery on US systems of punishment. Beyond slavery, which is the focus of this paper, a more expansive analysis of US historical specificities might serve as the basis for a genealogy of imprisonment that would differ significantly from Foucault's. Such a genealogy would accentuate the links between confinement, punishment and race. At least four great systems of incarceration could be identified: the reservation system, slavery, the mission system, and the internment camps of World War II. Within the US incarceration has thus played a pivotal role in the histories of Native Americans and people of African, Mexican, and Asian descent. In all of these cases, people were involuntarily confined and punished for no reason other than their race or ethnicity.

As Foucault points out, soon after the establishment of imprisonment as the dominant mode of punishment, prison acquired a "self-evident character." "[O]ne cannot 'see' how to replace it. It is the detestable solution, which one seems unable to do without."

> This "self-evident" character of the prison, which we find so difficult to abandon, is based first of all on the simple form of "deprivation of liberty". How could prison not be the penalty *par excellence* in a society in which liberty is a good that belongs to all in the same way and to which each individually is attached, as Duport put it, by a "universal and constant" feeling? Its loss has therefore the same value for all; unlike the fine, it is an "egalitarian" punishment. The prison is the clearest, simplest, most equitable of penalties. Moreover, it makes possible to quantify the penalty exactly according to the variable of time. There is a wages-form of imprisonment that constitutes, in industrial societies, its economic "self-evidence" – and enables it to appear as a reparation. (ibid., 232)

The modes of punishment associated with the two dominant models of imprisonment developed at the beginning of the nineteenth century in the US – the Philadelphia and Auburn models – were based on a construction of the individual that did not apply to people excluded from citizenship by virtue of their race and thus from a recognition of their communities as composed of individuals possessing rights and liberties. These prisons were thus largely designed to punish and reform white wage-earning individuals who violated the social contract of the new industrial capitalist order by allegedly committing crimes. The gendering of these institutions as male reflected the marginalization of women within a domestic, rather than public, economy. In fact the history and specific architecture of women's prisons reveal a quite different penal function: that of restoring white women to their place as wives and mothers, rather than as right-bearing public individuals.

Within the US – and increasingly in postcolonial Europe – the disproportionate presence of people of color among incarcerated populations has also acquired a "self-evident" character. But this reification is not based on the reasoning proposed by Foucault in *Discipline and Punish*. In an analysis that predates the publication of *Discipline and Punish*, Foucault allows for the possibility that the prison's purpose is not so much to transform, but to concentrate and eliminate politically dissident and racialized populations. After an April 1972 visit to Attica – the very first visit Foucault made to a prison, which occurred just eight months after the Attica uprising and massacre – he commented in an interview:

> At the time of the creation of Auburn and the Philadelphia prison, which served as models (with very little change until now) for the great machines of incarceration, it was believed that something indeed was produced: "virtuous" men. Now we know, and the

administration is perfectly aware, that no such thing is produced. That nothing at all is produced. That it is a question simply of a great sleight of hand, a curious mechanism of circular elimination: society eliminates by sending to prison people whom prison breaks up, crushes, physically eliminates; . . . the prison eliminates them by "freeing" them and sending them back to society; the state in which they come out insures that society will eliminate them once again, sending them to prison . . . Attica is a machine for elimination, a form of prodigious stomach, a kidney that consumes, destroys, breaks up and then rejects, and that consumes in order to eliminate what it has already eliminated. (Simon, 1991: 27)

Foucault was especially struck by the disproportionately large population of black men and commented that "in the United States, there must be one out of 30 or 40 Black men in prison: it is here that one can see the function of massive elimination in the American prison (ibid., 29). One wonders how Foucault might have responded in the 1990s to the fact that one of out three young black men was incarcerated or under the direct control of the criminal justice system (Mauer, 1995).

Historically, people of African descent consigned to slavery in the US were certainly not treated as rights-bearing individuals and therefore were not considered worthy of the moral reeducation that was the announced philosophical goal of the penitentiary. Indeed, the slave system had its own forms of punishment, which remained primarily corporal and of the sort that predated the emergence of incarceration as punishment. In her slave narrative, Harriet Jacobs described a neighboring planter whose plantation included six hundred slaves, a jail, and a whipping post. The jail, however, did not serve as a means of depriving the slave of his/her time and rights, but rather as a means of torture, for "[i]f a slave stole from him even a pound of meat or a peck of corn, if detection followed, he was put in chains and imprisoned, and so kept till his form was attenuated by hunger and suffering." One of the planter's favorite punishments "was to tie a rope round a man's body, and suspend him from the ground. A fire was kindled over him, from which was suspended a piece of fat pork. As this cooked, the scalding drops of fat continually fell on the bare flesh (Jacobs, 1987)."

If, as Foucault insists, the locus of the new European mode of punishment shifted from the body to the soul, black slaves in the US were largely perceived as lacking in the soul that might be shaped and transformed by punishment. Within the institution of slavery, itself a form of incarceration, racialized forms of punishment developed alongside the emergence of the prison system within and as a negative affirmation of the "free world," from which slavery was twice removed. Thus the deprivation of white freedom tended to affirm the whiteness of democratic rights and liberties. As white men acquired the privilege to be punished in ways that acknowledged their equality and the racialized universality of liberty, the punishment of black slaves was corporal, concrete, and particular.

It is also instructive to consider the role labor played in these different systems of incarceration. In the philosophical conception of the penitentiary, labor was a reforming activity. It was supposed to assist the imprisoned individual in his (and on occasion her) putative quest for religious penitence and moral reeducation. Labor was a means toward a moral end. In the case of slavery, labor was the only thing that mattered: the individual slaves were constructed essentially as labor units. Thus punishment was

362

designed to maximize labor. And in a larger sense, labor was punishment attached not to crime, but to race.

Even if the forms of punishment inherent in and associated with slavery had been entirely revoked with the abolition of slavery, the persistent second-class citizenship status to which former slaves were relegated would have had an implicit impact on punishment practices. However, an explicit linkage between slavery and punishment was written into the constitution precisely at the moment of the abolition of slavery. In fact, there was no reference to slavery in the US constitution until the passage of the Thirteenth Amendment declared chattel slavery unconstitutional: "Neither slavery nor involuntary servitude, except as a punishment for crime whereof the party shall have been duly convicted, shall exist within the United States, or any place subject to their jurisdiction." The abolition of slavery thus corresponded to the authorization of slavery as punishment. In actual practice, both Emancipation and the authorization of penal servitude combined to create an immense black presence within southern prisons and to transform the character of punishment into a means of managing former slaves as opposed to addressing problems of serious crime.

The incarceration of former slaves served not so much to affirm the rights and liberties of the freed men and women (i.e., as rights and liberties of which they could be deprived), nor to discipline, in the Foucauldian sense, a potential labor force; rather it symbolically emphasized black people's social status continued to be that of slaves, even though the institution of slavery had been disestablished. In constructing prisoners as human beings who deserved subjection to slavery, the Constitution allowed for a further, more elusive linkage of prison and slavery, namely the criminalization of former slaves. This criminalization process became evident in the rapid transformation of prison populations in the southern state, where the majority of black Americans resided. Prior to Emancipation, prisoners were primarily white, but "[d]uring the post Civil War period, the percentages of Black convicts in relation to white was often higher than 90%. In Alabama, the prison population tripled between 1874 and 1877 – and the increase consisted almost entirely of Blacks" (Fierce, 1994).

The swift racial transformation of imprisoned southern populations was largely due to the passage of Black Codes which criminalized such behaviour as vagrancy, breech of job contracts, absence from work, the possession of firearms, insulting gestures or acts (Franklin, 1967). The Mississippi Black Codes, for example, defined a vagrant "as anyone/who was guilty of theft, had run away [from a job, apparently], was drunk, was wanton in conduct or speech, had neglected job or family, handled money carelessly, and . . . all other idle and disorderly persons." (Fierce, 1994: 85–6). In other words, white behavior that was tolerated and thus went unnoticed by the criminal justice system could lead to the conviction of black individuals and to the ideological criminalization of black communities. "Arguing or even questioning a white man could result in a criminal charge" (Mancini, 1996: 41–2). Moreover, as many slave narratives confirm, many of these acts – for example theft and escape – had been considered effective forms of resistance to slavery. Now they were defined as crimes and what during slavery had been the particular repressive power of the master, became the far more devastating universal power of the state. "Free" black people entered into a relationship with the state unmediated by a master, they were divested of their status as slaves in order to be accorded a new status as criminals. "Throughout the South, thousands of ex-slaves were being arrested, and convicted for acts that in the past had been dealt with by the master alone. . . . An offense against [the master] had become an offense against the state" (Oshinsky, 1996: 28). Thus, the criminal justice system played a significant role in constructing the new social status of former slaves as human beings whose citizenship status was acknowledged precisely in order to be denied.

Southern prison populations not only became predominantly black in the aftermath of slavery, penitentiaries were either replaced by convict leasing or they were restricted to white convicts. According to Matthew Mancini,

> for a half-century after the Civil War, the Southern states had no prisons to speak of and those they did have played a peripheral role in those states' criminal justices system. Instead, persons convicted of criminal offenses were sent to sugar and cotton plantations, as well as to coal mines, turpentine farms, phosphate beds, brickyards [and] sawmills. (Mancini, 1996)

This racialization of punishment practices determined that black people were to be socially defined in large part by recreated conditions of slavery. In fact, as historian David Oshinsky has documented, convict leasing in institutions like Mississippi's Parchman Farm created conditions "worse than slavery" (Mancini, 1996: 37). When Arkansas governor George Donaghey called for the abolition of convict leasing in 1912, he argued that leasing was "a form of legalized murder that sentenced thousands of faceless victims to a 'death by oppression' for often trivial acts. Under no other system, he believed, did the punishment so poorly fit the crime" (ibid., 67). His list of abuses included:

> Instance No. 1. In Phillips County . . . two negroes jointly forged nine orders for one quart of whiskey each. For this offense one of them was convicted for eighteen years and the other for thirty-six years . . .
> Instance No. 10. In Miller County a negro convicted in a justice of the peace court was . . . sentenced [to] over three years for stealing a few articles of clothing off a clothes-line. (ibid., 69)

During the last three decades of the nineteenth century, southern criminal justice systems were profoundly transformed by their role as a totalitarian means of controlling black labor in the post-Emancipation era. Because so many of the particular crimes with which black people were charged served more as pretexts than as causal factors for arrest, these punishment strategies were explicitly directed at black communities, rather than at black individuals and they eventually informed the history of imprisonment outside the South as well. In the process, white prisoners, along with the black people this system specifically targeted, were affected by its cruelty as well.

> Southern Blacks were trapped in [a] penal quagmire in excessive numbers and percentages of the total prison population of each southern state. For the victims, many of whom were ex-slaves, this predicament represented nothing short of a revisit to slavery. Those Blacks who were former slaves, and became victims of the convict lease system – especially those convicted and incarcerated on trumped up charges, or otherwise innocent of crimes for which they were imprisoned – must have imagined themselves in a time warp. (Fierce, 1994: 88)

364

The widespread use of torture in connection with convict leasing consolidated forms of punishment that Foucault periodizes as pre-capitalist, inextricably linking them with incarceration itself. As Mancini has pointed out, Foucault's assumption that torture had become historically obsolete in the industrial capitalist countries "misses a fundamental aspect of convict leasing – namely the license it gave for the display not of a sovereign's but of a petty camp boss's power. Leasing allowed the accumulated reservoirs of human cruelty to overflow in the isolated camps and stockades" (Mancini, 1996: 75). As flogging was the primary mode of punishment during slavery, "the lash, along with the chain, became the very emblem of servitude for slaves and prisoners" (ibid.). Mancini points out that as late as 1941, the state of Texas still relied principally on the whip.

I have devoted a considerable portion of this article to an exploration of some of the ways slavery's underlying philosophy of punishment insinuated itself into the history of imprisonment. In this concluding section, I want to argue that the tendency to treat racism as a contingent element of the criminal justice system in research, advocacy and activism associated with the prison abolition movement results in part from its marginalization in histories and theories of punishment. If the category of race rarely appears in Foucault's analyses, so it is also generally absent in the leading contemporary abolitionist texts. Although racism has often been evoked in activist campaigns, the absence of race as an analytical category in the diverse literature associated with prison abolitionism points to problems of the same order as those Joy James detects in Foucault.

Like Foucault, the major theorists of prison abolition have worked within European contexts, and in a large measure in those European countries that can claim historically less repressive penal systems – the Scandinavian countries and the Netherlands. Academics in Norway and the Netherlands began to produce abolitionist theories during the 1960s (Bianchi and van Swaaningen, 1986: 9). Thomas Mathieson, author of *The Politics of Abolition* grounded his analysis in the work of the Norwegian prisoners movement, KROM, in which he actively participated during the sixties and seventies (Mathiesen, 1974). Mathieson's formal approach calls for abolitionist activism that attempts strategically to avoid demands for reform that might further strengthen the prison system, as prison reform has historically tended to do. The local and tactical emphasis of his analysis, first published in 1974 militates against a substantive engagement with issues of race. While Dutch criminologist Willem de Haan, author of a recent work entitled *The Politics of Redress: Crime, Punishment and Penal Abolition*, explores the implications of prison reform in North America and Cuba as well as in Western Europe, his interests do not include an analysis of the close links between punishment practices and structures of racism. It should be pointed out, however, that as postcolonial immigration has radically transformed the racial composition of European populations in general, the prison population in the Netherlands approaches the US in its disproportionate numbers of people of color.

Since an extensive review of the literature on abolitionism is beyond the scope of this article, I will simply point out that while the works of other leading European criminologists and philosophers associated with the international movement for penal abolition – such as René van Swaaningen, Herman Bianchi, Nils Christie, Stanley Cohen, Louk Hulsman and Rolf de Folter – contain many important insights, there is no sustained analysis of the part antiracism might play in the theory and practice of abolitionism.

In the US, abolitionists can discover a historical relationship of prison activism and antiracism. During the late eighteenth and early nineteenth centuries, Quaker reformers played a pivotal role in developing the US penitentiary. Indeed, the penitentiary system emerged from an abolitionist movement of sorts – a campaign to abolish medieval corporal punishment. The campaign to replace corporal punishment with the penitentiary and the abolitionist movement against slavery invoked similar philosophical arguments based on the Enlightenment belief in a universal humanity and in the moral perfectibility of every human being. If the inherent humanity of African slaves required their release from bondage, then the humanity of "criminals," demanded that they be given the opportunity to repent and perfect their characters.

It is therefore understandable that in North America, the dominant abolitionist trend in scholarship and activism is peacemaking. Harold Pepinksy has observed that as he organized the Fifth International Conference on Penal Abolition,

> I discovered that by far the strongest contingent among the hundreds of correspondents are workers and activists with religious affiliations, notably the peace churches and ecumenical peace groups. Religiously self-identified people cross all eight intellectual traditions which have emerged: academicians and theorists, activists and reformers, feminists, lawmakers, mediators, native traditionalists, peoples of color, and prisoners. (Pepinsky and Quinney, 1991: 300)

Nevertheless, it seems that no sustained analysis has emerged of the role antiracism might play in effective abolitionist theories and practices.

One of the major critiques proposed by abolitionists in Europe and North America is directed at social scientific and popular discourses that assume a necessary conjunction between crime and punishment. Likewise, in the philosophical literature on imprisonment, the prevailing assumption is that individuals are punished because of the crimes they commit. The literature in the field of philosophy of punishment rarely goes further than exploring what Adrian Howe refers to as "relentless repetitions of the unholy trinity of retribution, deterrence and reform" (Howe, 1994: 3). The problems these literatures address largely have to do with the justification and function of punishment. Thus a major theoretical and practical challenge of penal abolitionism is to disarticulate crime and punishment. In fact, many abolitionists deploy statistics that demonstrate how few people who have broken a law are actually called upon by criminal justice systems to answer for their crimes. Sociologists Jim Thomas and Sharon Boehlefield, for example, who are both critics and advocates of abolitionism, use US Bureau of Justice statistics to demonstrate that "only three persons are incarcerated (in prisons or jails) for every 100 crimes committed (Thomas and Boehlefeld, 1991: 18)."

The Institute for Social Research published Rusche and Kirchheimer's groundbreaking study, *Punishment and Social Structure* in 1939, which would later have a significant influence on the critical sociology of punishment. Kirchheimer wrote in the introduction that it was

> necessary to strip from the social institution of punishment its ideological veils and juristic appearance and to describe it in its real relationships. The bond, transparent or not, that

is supposed to exist between crime and punishment prevents any insight into the independent significance of the history of penal systems. It must be broken. Punishment is neither a simple consequence of crime, nor the reverse side of crime, nor a mere means which is determined by the end to be achieved. Punishment must be understood as a social phenomenon freed from both its juristic concept and its social ends. We do not deny that punishment has specific ends, but we do deny that it can be understood from its ends alone. (Rusche and Kirchheimer, 1939: 5)

Rusche and Kirchheimer, as well as others influenced by their attempt to develop a political economy of punishment, examine the influence of the capitalist market and bourgeois ideology in shaping punishment practices. According to legal scholar Adrian Howe,

Ruschean-inspired studies . . . made a crucial break with the analytically restricting "legal syllogism" – the common-sense idea that punishment is simply the consequence of crime and that, if there is a need for sociological explanation, "social structure explains crime and crime explains punishment." (Howe, 1994: 37)

However, they, too, do not explore the extent to which the penitentiary system and its attendant forms of labor were heavily influenced by the prevailing ideologies and economic structures of racism, nor, as Howe points out, do they give serious consideration to gender. Nevertheless, their insistence on disarticulating punishment from crime can be seen as opening the way for a consideration of the relationship between race and punishment, a much-needed dimension in the scholarship and activism associated with the abolitionist movement today.

In the contemporary era, the tendency toward more prisons and harsher punishment leads to gross violations of prisoners' human rights and, within the US context, it summons up new perils of racism. The rising numbers of imprisoned black and Latino men and women tell a compelling story of an increasingly intimate link between race and criminalization. While academic and popular discourses assume a necessary conjunction between crime and punishment, it is the conjunction between race, class, and punishment that is most consistent.

In 1926, the first year in which there was a national recording, 21 percent of prison admissions were black. By 1970, black people constituted 39 percent of admissions and in 1992 54 percent (Irwin and Austin, 1997: 7). In 1995, almost one-third of young black men were either in prison or directly under the control of a correctional system. If we consider that "[m]ost people have been involved in delinquent behavior at some point of their lives, and only a small fraction of overall criminal activities are touched by the criminal justice system," against the backdrop of the increasing proportion of black people entering the ranks of the imprisoned, we are faced with a startling implication (Rotman, 1990: 115). One has a greater chance of going to jail or prison if one is a young black man than if one is actually a law-breaker. While most imprisoned young black men may have broken a law, it is the fact that they are young black men rather than the fact that they are law-breakers which brings them into contact with the criminal justice system.

In this paper, I am specially concerned with the way the prison system in the US took up and was bolstered by historical forms of racism and how it continues to play a

367

critical role in the racialization of punishment. An effective abolitionist campaign will have to directly address the role of race in the criminalization process. I emphasize the need to disarticulate notions of punishment from crime because I want to argue for a serious consideration of abolitionist strategies to dismantle the prison system in its present role as an institution which preserves existing structures of racism as well as creates more complicated modes of racism in US society. This strategy, I argue, is no more outlandish than is the fact that race and economic status play more prominent roles in shaping the practices of social punishment that does crime, which is always assumed to be the basis for punishment in this society.

References

Bianchi, Herman and René van Swaaningen, eds. *Abolitionism: Toward a Non-Repressive Approach to Crime*. Amsterdam: Free University Press, 1986.

Dobash, Russel P., R. Emerson Dobash and Sue Gutteridge. *The Imprisonment of Women*. London: Basil Blackwell, 1986.

Fierce, Milfred. *Slavery Revisited: Blacks and the Southern Convict Lease System, 1865–1933*. New York: Brooklyn College, CUNY, Africana Studies Research Center, 1994.

Foucault, Michel. *Discipline and Punish: The Birth of the Prison*. New York: Vintage, 1979.

Franklin, John Hope. *From Slavery to Freedom*. 3rd edn. New York: Alfred A. Knopf., 1967.

Howe, Adrian. *Punish and Critique: Toward a Feminist Analysis of Penality*. New York: Routledge, 1994.

Irwin, John and James Austin. *It's About Time: America's Imprisonment Binge*. Belmont, California: Wadsworth Publishing Company, 1997.

Jacobs, Harriet A. *Incidents in the Life of A Slave Girl*. Cambridge, MA: Harvard University Press, 1987.

James, Joy. *Resisting State Violence: Radicalism, Gender and Race in U.S. Culture*. Minneapolis: University of Minnesota Press, 1996.

Mancini, Matthew. *One Dies, Get Another: Convict Leasing in the American South, 1866–1928*. Columbia, South Carolina: University of South Carolina Press, 1996.

Mathiesen, Thomas. *The Politics of Abolition*. (Published under the Auspices of the Scandinavian Research Council for Criminology. *Scandinavian Studies in Criminology Law* in Society Series) New York: John Wiley and Sons, 1974.

Mauer, Marc. *Young Black Men and the Criminal Justice System: Five Years Later*. Washington, D.C.: The Sentencing Project, 1995.

Oshinsky, David. *"Worse Than Slavery": Parchman Farm and the Ordeal of Jim Crow Justice*, New York: The Free Press, 1996.

Pepinsky, Harold and Richard Quinney, ed. *Criminology as Peacemaking*. Bloomington and Indianapolis: Indiana University Press, 1991.

Rotman, Edgardo. *Beyond Punishment: A New View on the Rehabilitation of Criminal Offenders* (New York: Greenwood Press, 1990).

Rusche, George and Otto Kirchheimer. *Punishment and Social Structure*. New York: Morningside Heights, Columbia University Press, 1939.

Simon, John K. "Michel Foucault on Attica: An Interview" in *Social Justice*, Vol. 18, No. 3 (Fall 1991).

Swaaningen, René van. "What is Abolitionism: An Introduction" in *Abolitionism: Toward a Non-Repressive Approach to Crime*. Proceedings of the Second International Conference on Prison

Abolition. Amsterdam, 1985. Edited by Herman Bianchi and René van Swaaningen. Amsterdam: Free University Press, 1986.

Thomas, Jim and Sharon Boehlefeld. "Rethinking Abolitionism: 'What Do We Do With Henry?'" *Social Justice*, 1991. 18 (Fall).

Part VI

AESTHETIC AND CULTURAL VALUES

Introduction to Part VI

The politics of representation and black cultural production are sources of reflection that have generated a great deal of discussion in African-American philosophy. Hortense Spillers's observation that the Harlem Renaissance followed a prior history of resistance in the nineteenth century that was organized around culture is a reminder that this legacy has a contemporary cultural manifestation – particularly in music, film, literature, and sports. Leonard Harris discusses the social context from which the so-called "New Negro" emerged. Lorenzo Simpson and Clyde Taylor challenge the claims of Eurocentric aesthetic theory regarding the status of jazz and black cinema as art forms. T. Denean Sharpley-Whiting and Trudier Harris-Lopez critically examine the ideological function of narratives dealing with interracial rape and lynching. Richard Shusterman discusses the pragmatic orientation of rap music as an art form, while Bill Lawson discusses the political implications of the ideology expressed in rap lyrics. Gerald Early explores the history of race and sport in America to show the influence of a new kind of "romantic racialism" on certain cultural values that have been internalized by black youth. Many of the questions arising from their reflections on African-American aesthetic and cultural practices have political implications that illuminate a relationship between subordination and values.

Leonard Harris addresses an important theme discussed earlier by Hortense Spillers; namely, the nationalist-Marxist dilemma faced by black intellectuals at the time of the Harlem Renaissance. He poses the question, "Which is more compelling – the fight to liberate an oppressed racial group, or the fight to liberate the working class?" to indicate that Marcus Garvey's nationalist movement, Du Bois's NAACP, and Henry Harrison's socialist party all contended for moral commitment. Harris situates the Harlem Renaissance in the era of mass migration to industrial cities in the North. The emergence of cultural centers for previously itinerant musicians, artists, and journalists was a by-product of this new social formation. He highlights the conflicting aesthetic views of Alain Locke and Du Bois to indicate what he calls "the metropolis of competing philosophies." With regard to the question of how to achieve liberation for African Americans, Du Bois advocated the use of art as propaganda, whereas Locke proposed an aesthetic strategy involving the transformation of black popular culture into an American high culture.

Harris also notes that there were conflicting "background assumptions" regarding commitments to community and visions of the future characterizing these disparate orientations to the question of liberation. These assumptions became foregrounded when irreconcilable issues had to be faced. He refers to the "Garvey Must Go" campaign as an example of this. Randolph and Du Bois cooperated with the State Department for the purpose of subverting and destroying Garvey's Universal Negro Improvement Association. According to Harris, this alliance with the government against Garvey was prompted by Garvey's willingness to affiliate with the Ku Klux Klan to help blacks emigrate to Africa. Harris claims that, by pushing the question of the national status of African Americans, Garvey raised the issue of what is the most viable concept of the future for African Americans.

The creation of jazz as an art form is one of the greatest achievements of African-Americans. Lorenzo Simpson critically examines Theodor Adorno's treatment of jazz as an application of a critical theory of popular culture he and Max Horkheimer presented in *Dialectic of Enlightenment* (1972). Adorno views cultural institutions in terms of capitalistic social relations that govern the production of commodities, including even the commodification of social distinctions between high art and low art. Simpson discusses Adorno's twofold account, observing that, on the one hand, aesthetic practices function ideologically to neutralize political opposition. Needs that might foster resistance to the economic system are suppressed, while needs necessary to justify capitalist production are themselves manufactured by the system. On the other hand, although Adorno believed works of art are commodity fetishes, he also maintained that autonomous works are fetishes that call into question the system of commodification itself. In this manner he viewed the ideological status of autonomous art as a "critical status."

Simpson attributes to Adorno a view that allows for the "redemptive power" of art, to the extent that "genuine" art expresses the contradictions inherent in the society from which it emerges. He tells us, for example, that Adorno viewed Schoenberg's atonal compositions as an acknowledgement of alienation that represents the negative as negative. This prevents us from being seduced into "prizing our chains." In 1936 Adorno criticized jazz, claiming that it was a kind of dance music which presumed to be modern by articulating "a putative oppositional stance" in terms of a characteristic sound and rhythmic principle that were transgressive. According to Adorno, jazz was not really a product of immediacy and "instinctual liberation," but only "a commercialized ersatz" of this. Jazz fails to live up to its own criteria of "primitivism," instead it is "a thoroughly domesticated and packaged product" of the culture industry.

Simpson responds to Adorno's criticism by pointing out that there is a manifest "hermeneutic inadequacy" in Adorno's discussion of black aesthetic practice that renders his view "exaggerated, ahistorical and regressive." To address Adorno's charges regarding jazz's atemporality, lack of organic integrity, and mechanical nature, along with his view that syncopation is "mechanical contrivance" and that improvisation only "masquerades" as individual expression, Simpson appeals to criteria that jazz practitioners themselves take to be salient for the evaluation of a jazz performance. For example, Simpson compares Count Basie's *One O'Clock Jump* with Stravinsky's ostinati in *Rite of Spring* to illustrate the manner in which repetition in jazz is often a means to impart movement. Adorno maintains that spontaneity is compromised by the rigid adherence to bar lines and slavish restriction to the chord structure of popular songs. Simpson argues against this by pointing out that harmonic structure need not be seen as a restriction on the genuineness of improvisation. It is "an enabling condition of intelligibility," providing "a metalinguistic frame" that enables members of an ensemble to communicate with each other and participate in a common project.

Simpson believes Adorno was right to be concerned about the vulnerablity of jazz to the culture industry, although this is also true to a lesser degree of concert music. Adorno's emphasis on composition alone prevented him from viewing jazz as having a tradition with "a developmental history given shape by progressive resolutions of aesthetic problems." According to Simpson, Adorno's compositional paradigm forces what is central to jazz to the aesthetic periphery. Simpson points out that Adorno failed to understand that "timbral individuality" is a prominent musical value in the African-American tradition. Adorno commits a category error of applying classical music criteria regarding instrumentation to jazz practice and subordinates what is distinctive about jazz to composition. Simpson compares jazz compositions with cubist paintings. The original melodic and harmonic structure is treated as "raw material" that the artist decomposes and reconfigures with new meanings. Simpson concludes that Adorno's aesthetic view lapses into "a dialectics of blindness and insight."

Clyde Taylor's discussion of black cinema highlights the importance of the Harlem Renaissance for subsequent cultural movements by black artists and intellectuals. He argues that the rationale of the Black Aesthetics movement in literature, poetry, and criticism was extended to cinema by independent African-American filmmakers who brought "a new, theoretical self-consciousness" to filmmaking during the Civil Rights era. With regard to identifying criteria by which to assess the success of black cinema, Taylor points out that the expression "black cinema aesthetics" carries baggage that illustrates a crisis of knowledge. When it demands a definition, the question "What is black cinema?" poses a challenge to the concept of aesthetics. He proposes instead to pursue the question "What is aesthetics?" from a ground in black cinema. This reversal is important because historically the "path" of intellectual and material development of black cinema has been consistently "colonized, frustrated, and deterred by a preemptive line of aesthetic reasoning." He cites Pierre Bourdieu's claim that aesthetic reasoning is little more than the rationalization of the taste of the more influential classes.

According to Taylor, avant-garde art and anti-art movements influenced by postmodernism have generated a need for a critique of "the congruence of aesthetic discourse with Eurocentrism and racism." He observes that nothing in the discipline's claims to disinterestedness, or objectivity, impeded "the barrage of animalization and deformation of black people" in classical Hollywood cinema, and that there was an entrenched precept of aesthetics that "white is equal to beauty and black to ugliness." He maintains that this "aestheticism" in cinema production and interpretation has generally functioned to serve the interests of white supremacy.

Another function of aesthetic discourse has been to *marginalize* black cinema. Taylor points out that this marginalization has had a profoundly negative influence on the production and reception of black films – affecting the judgments of reviewers, distributors, and funding agendas. He discusses the "aesthetic rationales" frequently employed to discount, or dismiss black cinema, according to which black film are deemed to suffer various shortcomings. Taylor claims that it was this "cultural miscognition" that justified the need for a black film aesthetic similar to what was called for in the case of the misperception of African-American literary values – the development of a "self-determining outlook." Because of a discrepancy of power, black cinema is confined to a subordinated stratum of the dominant film industry. Hence, black cinema has profited more from what he calls "the politics of representation" than from theories of aesthetics.

Taylor claims that it would be just as fruitless to look for some essentialized quality in the case of a black aesthetic as it would be in the case of a feminine aesthetic, or a gay aesthetic. Nonetheless, he believes a group can share collective values and a common historical outlook and create art out of shared assumptions and, hence, a recognizable style might emerge from that collective expression. On this basis he maintains that a black film "ethos" can be imagined. The thrust of the independent movement, led by a group of radical black filmmakers at UCLA, was to create an alternative to Hollywood's representation of black people. According to Taylor, this resistance demanded a rejection of the master narrative promoted by Hollywood movies and requires a recognition of the primacy of political interpretation over aesthetic analysis. He insists that the indeterminacy surrounding the concept of black cinema is intrinsic to its situation in a society that exploits blackness in films.

The major thrust of Taylor's critique of aestheticism is that it has been used to legitimate white supremacy in terms of mainstream cultural values. Reiterating the account given by Charles Mills, he recognizes that the logic of Western aesthetics is hardly ever associated with the antiblack racism that informs lynchings and other Klan activity. Denean Sharpley-Whiting discusses the emergence of a "postmodern" Klan that has been "repackaged to fit in with mainstream conservative thought. She aims to show that behind the new media image stands the same old racism. Her reflections on the political significance of a joke card with a pornographic depiction of a black woman situates this image at the very core of the Klan's anti-interracial sex ideology. With the focus on sex between white women and black men, the most common form of coercive sex between white men and black women never appears as a point of contention in the Klan's antimiscegenation discourse. The interracial rape of black women is the "unspeakable act" in contemporary Klan culture. According to Sharpley-Whiting, given the profuse testimony by black women victims of interracial rape, the Klan's silence must be understood within "the framework of power and desire in practice and theory." The Klan ideology fosters a practice of rape while simultaneously never addressing its existence. Such an acknowledgment would contradict the antimiscegenation teachings that are so critical to the Klan's ideological cohesion.

While Sharpley-Whiting explores the Freudian implications of the pornography depicted on the Klan's joke card to show how such images are related to racially motivated lynchings, Trudier Harris-Lopez cites a 1997 burning and lynching incident to indicate that the practice continues. She refers to the fact that the Dyer antilynching bill presented to Congress on repeated occasions was never made into law because it was believed that lynching could not be outlawed when black men were still prone to rape white women. In response to this overtly racist practice, there has developed an important strand of African-American thought by writers who joined with political activists in the struggle to end lynchings by depicting this form of "summary justice" in their work.

376

Harris-Lopez surveys the depictions of lynchings in the work of African-American writers from William Wells Brown in the mid-nineteenth century to David Bradley as recent as 1981. She claims that, because almost always the black male is accused of sexual impropriety with a white woman, lynching has influenced every generation of black male writers, who far outnumber black women who have written about this topic. According to Harris-Lopez, there is an important difference, related to gender, between works that deal with lynching. Black male writers depict graphic lynching scenes more than black female writers. Citing several black women playwrights who employed the theme of lynching, Harris-Lopez points out that, in these works, all the lynchings take place offstage. She notes that men and women writers have employed lynchings contemporaneously with the occurrence of a lynching, and were aware of it as a constant threat to black people.

As in the case of film and literature, music also has been employed to address political issues. Rap music is one of the most politically engaged forms of African-American cultural expression. Richard Shusterman discusses the manner in which rap music addresses matters pertaining to ethics, race, gender, multiculturalism, diaspora identity, and African-American philosophy. Bill Lawson discusses the political ideology expressed in rap lyrics to highlight its radical implications for liberal democratic theory. These authors agree that certain forms of rap music constitute a thoroughly pragmatic art form that operates at levels of political theory and social practice with the aim of fostering change.

Some aspects of rap have important implications for the prevailing view of aesthetics and art. Shusterman views the aesthetic significance of the DJ appropriating disco sounds and techniques in terms of the challenge it poses for the traditional ideal of "unique originality" in art. By deploying its appropriation in a new form, rap shows that borrowing and creation are not at all incompatible. What he refers to as "transfigurative sampling" supersedes old works and "dialectically recalls," and so preserves, the sampled works in lived experience. He claims that rap can be viewed as an "aural museum," one devoted to the works of its own tradition.

Rap's militant insistence on politics also challenges the modern dogma of aesthetic autonomy. Noting that art has been divorced from the practical activity of ethics and politics and consigned to a disinterested, imaginative realm, Shusterman cites, as evidence of rap's praxis, its functioning to develop linguistic skills and communicate cultural tradition and history, while raising political consciousness and ethnic pride. Shusterman adopts an attitude of "pragmatic meliorism" towards the negative aspects of rap, affirming knowledge (message) rap, which is devoted to the integration of art with "the pursuit of knowledge, ethical growth, and sociopolitical emancipation." He argues that the concept of truth in rap is closer to that espoused by William James and John Dewey. Some rap with a criminally violent style often is educational, aiming to promote values quite remote from crime. According to Shusterman, these street-smart moral fables are cautionary narratives that offer practical advice on the problematic seductions of crime, drugs, sex, and money. Rap often conveys the crucial message that better living can be found in the proper practice of a hip-hop lifestyle, as a means of overcoming conditions of crime and poverty.

Shusterman compares rap as philosophy with stoicism, Epicureanism and Cynicism in the ancient world. Rap embraces a philosophy that is more about a style of life than technical doctrines of metaphysics and logic. Knowledge rappers insist on the actual practice of theory. In response to the question of whether the emphasis on passionate movement is inconsistent with rap's cognitive role as philosophy, Shusterman points out that pragmatism challenges the mind–body opposition on which the apparent inconsistency rests. Rap recognizes "that bodily movement and impassioned feeling are often necessary to aid cognition," where cognition is understood to include more than what is conveyed by propositional content.

Shusterman's discussion of the political orientation of rap is supported by many scholars – all of whom have articulated a view of rap as political resistance. Lawson maintains that rap poses a challenge to deeper and more basic assumptions about the political order – and, hence, it poses a more fundamental challenge to the meaning of citizenship. Some rappers have questioned the fundamental relationship between the state and African Americans. While acknowledging that not all rap is overtly political, Lawson points out that rap artists often contend that the social contract of liberal democratic theory has been broken.

Lawson cites John Locke's *Second Treatise* to present the basic tenets of liberal democratic theory. According to Locke, governments are established to protect the rights of individuals, including personal well-being. By consenting to join with others in civil society each individual is to be protected from "invaders" and "unsavory characters" within the state who infringe on basic rights by stealing, defrauding, or destroying property. Lawson uses the notion of citizenship in a broad sense to specify the status of an individual in a modern nation-state, who has responsibilities to the government and who is entitled to certain protection and rights. There are two components of citizenship: (1) the feeling of being a vital part of a society and (2) having legal rights and political responsibilities as a member of a society. In a quote from *Corfield v. Coryell*, Lawson identifies protection by the government, enjoyment of life and liberty, property, trade and profession, habeas corpus and other court actions, exemption from higher taxes, elective franchise, as some of the basic rights denied to African Americans. Using rap lyrics to show that this claim regarding political oppression is made by rap artists, he argues that political oppression lessens the political obligations of African Americans to the state.

According to social contract theory, one of the basic reasons for joining the state is protection. Lawson points out that rap artists cite racist police practices to show how the state has failed to provide physical protection for black residents, who are often the victims twice – by criminals and by the police. The behavior of the police toward black communities draws the obligations of blacks to the state in question. Lawson cites the case of the Nation of Islam being harassed by Los Angeles police while protecting the community from drug dealers – a function the state has failed to provide. This case is an illustration of the meaning of KRS-ONE's question "Who Protects Us from You?" and Ice Cube's angry statement "I want to kill Sam."

The idea of revolution and rebellion is a prominent element in rap and black urban youth culture, but the view that black men are even capable of revolt involves a complicated history of ideas that can be traced to the nineteenth century. Gerald Early notes that blacks were referred to by whites as the "lady of the races" and that African Americans as a group were seen as exhibiting qualities that were considered feminine – or associated with women – e.g., deeply religious, tending towards the arts and oratory, more musical, more emotional, and more attracted to colors and physical sensations rather than abstract ideas. Like women, blacks *feel*, but cannot *think* deeply.

Harriet Beecher Stowe popularized this idea in her novel, *Uncle Tom's Cabin* (1852) in which a picture of the African is presented as "the epitome of non-aggression" in the person of Uncle Tom. Although Tom is described as having the physique of an athlete, Early points out that athletics for a black person, except prizefighting and horseracing, did not exist prior to the Civil War. Tom is maternal, gentle, patient, and willing to sacrifice. According to Early, Stowe suggests that "the only way a black man could be a father was by being in effect a mother." Hence, the novel is called *Uncle Tom's Cabin* to represent "a peaceable kingdom of family relations." In stage versions, Tom is portrayed as an old man, well beyond the age of an active sex life, not as the strong-limbed black man in the prime of life that he actually is. According to Early, this "unmanning" of the black man may have led African Americans to use Uncle Tom as a "vituperative epithet."

The philosophical and political issues surrounding the muscular black man were to achieve their highest resonance in the realm of sports. Early views sports as a form of "white hegemonic ideology." He argues that Stowe transformed the muscular black man "by dressing him up in sentimental clothing to make him more palatable" to whites. In her other novel *Dred* (1856) she presents another muscular black man, the son of Denmark Vesey, the slave rebel, only Dred is an emasculated romantic hero who dies without rebelling. Sports accomplishes a similar transformation with what Early, following George Fredrickson, refers to as "romantic racialism," an important variety of racist ideology that has gone largely unremarked.

Early maintains that the physicality of blacks has been interpreted by whites through the haze of romantic racialism. He is concerned with the fact that blacks have found it difficult to overcome this view of themselves, citing its persistence in earlier Negritude and Black Aesthetics movements, and, more recently, in Afrocentrism. All have employed a verison of romantic racialism that claims blacks are more caring, spiritual, musical, family-oriented, emotional and less interested in abstract concepts than whites. Early believes that this view of blacks buys into the idea of blacks as the "lady of the races."

The success blacks have achieved in music and sports – both perceived in American culture as charismatic and anti-intellectual – supports and contests this notion. As sources of pride for blacks these areas stress physical superiority, which whites have granted as a sign of black mental inferiority. Early draws attention to the African-American body as the subject of certain philosophical and political beliefs. As blacks began to excel in athletics, they became associated with aggression, enterprise, inge-nuity and improvisation, but not in a way that freed them from the assumptions of romantic racialism. By the twentieth century blacks were no longer the "lady," but the opposite – a romantic version of an exaggerated masculinity. Early points out that, just as in the case of Stowe's romantic racialism, the black man's superlative performances in sports is seen as evidence of his status as a primitive noble savage.

Early attributes the shift in romantic racialism toward this meaning to the growth of the entertainment industry and mass culture. Athletics were initially considered a sign of white male superiority. Sports were used symbolically to show the world that whites were the better race, more aggressive, and masculine. According to Early, blacks were thought to lack the nerve and skill to beat whites in head to head competition until, in 1908, Jack Johnson became heavyweight champion. This marked another important shift whereby black men became associated with being superior athletes and "the idea of black ultramasculinity became even more lurid." As other blacks achieved in sports, a new twist on the old romantic racialism of the nineteenth century was introduced. Whites began to promote the idea of a "natural" black athletic superiority. Early argues that this idea was fostered by the mainstream view of blacks as intellectually inferior, and the fact that athletes lack political power. He points out that "athletic achievement by blacks did not threaten white hegemonic assumptions."

Early acknowledges that African Americans have expressed ambivalence toward sports. While, on the one hand, there is a fierce opposition based on the perception of sports as "unenterprising" and a form of racial degradation. On the other hand, African Americans have seen sports as a means of access, a way to social and economic mobility. For Early, this raises the question of whether the hegemonic power of sport is a function of its representation, or a function of its relation to the corporate structure. With regard to the issue of race and sports, Early thinks there is a twofold problem that revolves around the political and social meaning attached to the idea of black athletic superiority. He claims that the promotion of this general perception inclines blacks themselves to pursue athletics, "because no one questions their ability." He cites the "overdetermined" aspiration of young black men to be athletes and their "intense anti-intellectualism." Early attributes such thinking to the effects of the romantic racialism that has shaped American culture.

Early refuses to go so far as to endorse the claim that in American Society black men represent the body in the American mind. He believes women, white women in particular, serve that purpose. He insists on "a greater precision" in the matter of determining what type of physical presence blacks actually are in the white mind. He points out that both black and white college athletes are recruited for their athletic abilities, not their academic abilities. Rejecting Marxist views, he insists that athletes are no more exploited than Ph.D. students, and, following Thomas Sowell, he dismisses the analogy with colonialism. To those who argue that black participation in high-level sports is an act of degradation because of the fixation by the white public on the physicality of the black body, Early points out that "this is not the affirmation of a fact about sports, but an attitude toward the value of sports." He concludes that the romantic racialist assumptions about blacks being natural athletes have made it very difficult for blacks to be seen as equals and having equal merit with whites in areas other than sport. He acknowledges, on the other hand, that sport may have widened the concept of democracy and given blacks greater visibility and more access than they might otherwise have had.

24

The Harlem Renaissance and Philosophy

LEONARD HARRIS

Which moral commitment is more compelling: fighting for the liberation of a raciated ethnicity in a racist society or fighting for the liberation of the working class in that same society? African Americans are a race in the sense that they are perceived as a biological kind and treated as if each member, in a racist society, has identical intrinsic traits. As an ethnic group, African Americans, or at least a sector of African Americans, are tied to Africa because of family links, language inheritances, religious forms of expression, and common experiences. If the liberation of the working class will end racism, then it would seem that a strong moral commitment, if liberation is the objective, has appeal. However, if no such prediction is warranted, then it would seem that commitment to the liberation of a raciated ethnicity gains warrant if that commitment would be more instrumental in ending racism.

Intellectuals and working-class African Americans often faced this somewhat contrived choice. Marcus Garvey's Universal Negro Improvement Association (UNIA), the largest nationalist movement in the history of African Americans; W. E. B. Du Bois's National Association for the Advancement of Colored Peoples (NAACP), the nascent organization that promoted legal changes to segregation as well as non-violent direct action protests, and directed boycotts; and Hubert Henry Harrison's Socialist Party, a party that exemplified the largest alligiance of African Americans to socialism, all vied for the loyalty of African Americans. Each individual and group contended that the root to liberation from racism was dependent on their approach. Moral commitment was demanded by each group and opposing approaches decried as fundamentally harmful and indicative of approaches that created self-deprecation or inclined persons to be self-deprecators.

The tremendous migration of African Americans from declining agricultural and rural locations to the growing industrial and urban centers in the late nineteenth and early twentieth centuries provided a new material situation. Increased incomes and effective mass communications enhanced the process of ethnogenesis. Progressively, African Americans saw themselves as a race and an ethnic group, counterdistinct from, and oppressed by, other groups. Kansas City, Kansas, Chicago, Illinois, Cleveland, Ohio, Philadelphia, Pennsylvania, and New York, New York became not only important industrial centers employing African Americans but also cultural centers where previously itinerant musicians, artists, and journalists could find regular employment and maintain stable families. American slavery had already accomplished the destruction of all native African religions and thus African Americans were a homogenous religious population. At most, there were competing denominations and sub-practices that were African survivals or new adaptations, but no named Gods or coherent faiths of the Mende, Fulani or Asante. Even Voodum, surviving especially in the Caribbean and South America, survived in America as only a practice within Christianized communities. Civic religious orientations were divided, in the same way that humanist traditions were divided: along competing conceptions of moral commitment, self conceptions, justifiable methods of change, visions of possible futures, explanations, predictions, and conceptions of instrumental strategies to effect change.

One way to appreciate the metropolis of competing philosophies is by considering the conflicting views between Alain L. Locke and W. E. B. Du Bois regarding the aesthetic. Du Bois, the Harvard educated sociologist and leading scholar of the period, argued that the role of art was to be a form of propaganda. That propaganda should have, for its intended objective, motivating persons to improve their living conditions, providing a sense of self worth, condemning degrading images, and providing a sense of hope. The evaluation of literature, sculpture, painting, or music was thus a function of how well or poorly it performed these roles. Such features as form, internal coherency, style and idiom would be considered in relationship to their utility for message and motivation conveyance.

Locke, first black Rhodes Scholar and Harvard educated philosopher, was a close associate of Du Bois. Locke provided young artists and intellectuals with publishing opportunities, intellectual guidance, and introductions to patrons. Locke, in disagreement with Du Bois, believed that art could form a propaganda role, but that there were other criteria, associated with notions of beauty as a pragmatic good, due consideration as criteria of evaluation. Moreover, for Locke, the artist should be free to conceive of the world in unique ways – ways that are not subject to appreciation only if they fit an algorithm of what is instrumentally needed for the purpose of conveying a message and creating appropriate motivation.

Locke argues for a pragmatic conception of the beautiful. That is, the beautiful is always encoded in useful, enriching, and context laden values. Yet, those values are at their best when they express, depict, convey, show and elevate what is universal – universal within the species. Locke argues for transforming lowbrow culture into high culture; claiming the universalizable from folk idioms; seeing the magnanimous in untutored performances of the spirituals; and presenting African religious artifacts as tokens of expressivity. The instrumentality of Locke's *The New Negro*, 1925, the anthology that announced the existence of the Harlem Renaissance and a "new Negro," was expository – as a presenting of high culture which was wrongly thought to be only folk idioms without universal appeal – and simultaneously a message and a source of motivation. As Locke contended in his "Introduction" to *The New Negro*, "So for generations in the mind of America, the Negro has been more of a formula than a human being – a something to be argued about, condemned or defended, to be 'kept down,' or 'in his place,' or 'helped up,' to be worried with or worried over, harassed or patronized, a social bogey or a social burden. . . . By shedding the old chrysalis of the Negro problem we are achieving something like a spiritual emancipation. . . . With this renewed self-respect and self-dependency, the life of the Negro community is bound to enter a new dynamic phase. . . ." Neither the message nor motivation was an algorithm. Rather, there is an openness to the future. If art was, or should be, fundamentally orchestrated as propaganda its utility and result would need to be much more controlled. And social control of artistic creation is one feature that Locke decries.

The distance between Locke, a critical pragmatist, and Du Bois, a critical and unique sociologist, was far less broad than the distance between the nationalism of Marcus Garvey and the Marxism of Hubert H. Harrison. The working class for socialists and communists, whether Richard Wright, Hubert H. Harrison or A. Philip Randolph, is the instrument for universal human liberation. The possibility of the negation of racism is contingent for socialists and communists on the ascendancy of the working class to power. The "African-American community" is not, *mutatus mutandis*, the source of its own liberation. Rather, the empowerment of the working class, of which African Americans as a central component (but only a component) are within its historical course, holds to the key to liberation of all African Americans. That liberation is not as a separate community but as a community of workers in pursuit of the destruction of substantive class, status, racial, and ethnic distinctions. What counts as liberation is not equity in the sense that African Americans would have similar incomes, rights, powers, and privileges as whites as per their class and status positions, but the destruction of significant class and status distinctions as well as the destruction of divisive racial and ethnic distinctions.

How the question, "What is liberation?" was answered deeply divided nationalists and the left. The Harlem Renaissance provided a stage that made obvious competing views, strategies, and commitments that were in conflict throughout the country. African-American workers in Mississippi and black nationalists in Omaha, Nebraska, were engaged in the pursuit of liberation along radically different lines. The urbanization of the African American, and the centrality of numerous publications and offices, made these orientations readily public. Thus, for example, the headquarters of the NAACP, the UNIA, and the African Blood Brotherhood was located in New York. Kansas City, Kansas hosted a tremendous number of theaters, Chicago was often the center of African American industrial labor organizations, and Washington, D.C. maintained an impressive number of "salons" in which literary artists would entertain, through poetry readings and pithy literary conversations, members of high society.

In the late nineteenth and the twentieth century, tremendous numbers of nearly every ethnic and racial population in the world became urbanized, compelled to join the industrial working class, and watched folk cultures transformed by commercialism and commodification. What helps make the Harlem Renaissance unique is that African Americans were confronting universal issues as both a race and ethnic, and doing so as members of the most advanced capitalist country in the world. "What is liberation?" had to be answered in terms of what it is to be liberated for a race, an ethnic group, and every class and status shared with all other Americans. Approaches to the question "What is liberation?" was thus peppered with numerous background assumptions about moral commitments to community and visions of the future. These background assumptions were foregrounded when irreconcilable issues had to be faced.

The "Garvey Must Go" campaign was an example of irreconcilable commitments that became foregrounded within the Harlem Renaissance. A. Philip Randolph, a member of the Socialist party, and numerous liberals such as W. E. B. Du Bois, co-operated with the State Department for the purpose of subverting and destroying the UNIA. One reason African-American liberals and socialists found common cause was that they strenuously objected to the common cause Garvey seems to have found with his overtures to the Ku Klux Klan to help recolonize blacks to Africa. The Ku Klux Klan was, on all accounts, a major initiator of the cruel lynchings of blacks and racial seg-regation. In addition to complete disagreement on strategies and goals for liberation, Garvey's initiatives seemed an ultimate insult to the integrity of African people, i.e., cooperating with the worst possible enemy for a most heinous, if not the worst possi-ble, objective of intentionally disenfranchising the Negro of ownership and entitlement of American status. The nuances of how "community" should be defined and what moral and non-moral commitments are due was thus foregrounded; the question of what concept of the future to embrace, including the question of national status of African Americans, was deftly confronted when the "Garvey Must Go" campaign removed subtle differences in favor of direct, and unabashed confrontation of compet-ing philosophies.

The reality of World War I and a depression changed the material status of Africa Americans. Moreover, there was an increasing acceptance of African-American culture as not a marginal reality or an exotic feature of American life but a com-mercially viable and salable product. That product was marketed by almost exclusively white owners of record companies, art studios, publishing houses, and white domi-nated labor unions and pension funds. Such changes rendered the romantic moments of the renaissance progressively less appealing. The sort of messianic hope that engines radical movements was lost to the sobering effect of powerlessness and marginalization as well as the conservatism that accompanies the success of heroic struggles for inclu-sion into established institutions. By the late 1930s the Harlem Renaissance was history. It provided a tremendous social context within which universal issues were addressed, and addressed with deep appreciation for the complexities of possible answers.

Bibliography

Alain L. Locke, ed., *The New Negro*, New York: Maxwell Macmillan, 1992, ca. 1925, "Introduction," Arnold Rampersed.

Alain L. Locke and Bernhard J. Stern, eds., *When Peoples Meet*, New York: Progressive Education Association, 1942.

Houston A. Baker, Jr., *Modernism and the Harlem Renaissance*, Chicago: The University of Chicago Press, 1987.

Philip S. Foner, *American Socialism and Black Americans*, Connecticut: Greenwood Press, 1977.

Leonard Harris, *Philosophy Born of Struggle*, Iowa: Kendall Hunt Publishing Co., 1983.

George Hutchinson, *The Harlem Renaissance in Black and White*, Mass.: The Belknap Press of Harvard University Press, 1995.

David Levering Lewis, *When Harlem Was in Vogue*, New York: Alfred A. Knopt, 1981.

——. *W. E. B. Du Bois: Biography of a Race*, New York: Henry Hold and Company, 1993.

Russell J. Linnemann, ed., *Alain Locke: Reflections on a Modern Renaissance Man*, Baton Rouge: Louisiana State University, 1982.

Tony Martin, *Race First*, Connecticut: Greenwood Press, 1976.

Jeffrey C. Stewart, *Race Contacts and Interracial Relations*, Washington, DC: Howard University Press, 1992.

Johnny Washington, *A Journey Into the Philosophy of Alain Locke*, Connecticut: Greenwood Press, 1994.

25

Critical Theory, Aesthetics, and Black Modernity

LORENZO C. SIMPSON

Theodor Adorno's writings on jazz, black America's major contribution to aesthetic modernism, represent Critical Theory's most extensive engagement to date with black artistic practice. Though many find his conclusions regarding jazz music hard to swallow, his treatment of jazz is an extension and application of a theory of popular culture that has continuing relevance. Moreover, there are not a few who, even now, think Adorno "got jazz right." These considerations suggest that a renewed interrogation of Adorno on the "jazz question" remains of moment for those who believe it is possible to reconcile progressive political hope with an appreciation of the aesthetic delights of jazz music.

Critical Theory, Aesthetic Theory, and the Culture Industry

"Critical Theory" refers to a rather heterogeneous tradition of social theory that traces its origin to the Institute of Social Research, established at Frankfurt, Germany in 1923. Its central figures are Max Horkheimer (1895–1973), Theodor Adorno (1903–69), Herbert Marcuse (1898–1980) and Jürgen Habermas (1929–   ). It is generally acknowledged that Habermas's work represents a decisive recasting of the research program of such earlier "Frankfurt School" theorists as Adorno and Marcuse. Accordingly, his work represents a new departure. However, what arguably unites Critical Theorists is the ongoing attempt to forge intellectual syntheses that are productive for a critical analysis of late capitalist societies, an analysis that is undertaken with an eye to possibilities for human emancipation from historically contingent social fetters. Key ingredients in their syntheses, though with inflections characteristic of the various thinkers comprising the tradition, are Hegel's historicist sensibility, Marx's conception of the critique of ideology, Weber's analysis of modernity, and Freud's psychoanalysis.

The classic articulation of critical theory's position on the culture industry is contained in Adorno's and Horkheimer's *Dialectic of Enlightenment* (Adorno and Horkheimer, 1972). They speak there of cultural institutions so seamlessly wed to the forces of capital that cultural products become commodities pure and simple. In terms

386

to be given perhaps greater currency by Marcuse's famous one-dimensional society thesis, Horkheimer and Adorno hold that under such conditions aesthetic practices and their products comprise a thoroughly uniform system, a cultural and aesthetic ether fully obedient to the iron laws of capitalism that neutralize political opposition. It is a system in which the needs necessary to justify cultural production are themselves manufactured by the system, a circle in which needs that might resist the system are suppressed at the level of the individual's consciousness. As Adorno claims, "[t]he liquidation of the individual is the real signature of the new musical situation" (Adorno, 1988, p. 276). In such a society, the high art/low art contrast takes on the fetishized form of pure distinction for distinction's sake. Well before Bourdieu's work, Horkheimer and Adorno pointed out that aesthetic taste has become a matter of distinction that is itself a salable commodity, that, for example, being able to purchase tickets for the symphony was the mark of a social difference that was itself the object of enjoyment, as opposed to the actual symphony. And the culture industry reinforces and cynically capitalizes on this situation, ruthlessly commodifying social distinctions. Its hegemony transforms genuine aesthetic differences into simulacra and leaves no space for critical reflection as it reproduces individuals who come to believe that their needs can be harmonized with the existing state of affairs. As a consequence, popular cultural forms, particularly those of movies and music, are most adequately understood as being essentially media of manipulation, and even the reception of "serious" art has fallen victim to the iron laws of commodification. As Adorno summarizes it in a more recent reconsideration of their analysis of the culture industry:

> The total effect of the culture industry is one . . . in which . . . enlightenment . . . becomes mass deception and is turned into a means for fettering consciousness. It impedes the development of autonomous, independent individuals who judge and decide consciously for themselves. (Adorno, 1989, pp. 134–5)

Adorno's critique of the culture industry can be given greater definition by a brief consideration of that to which it stands in contrast, namely, the associated practices of autonomous art. As I suggested above, Adorno is highly critical of the high art/low art distinction as it is typically deployed in bourgeois-capitalist culture. What is useful in this distinction for him, and what he wants to retain, is captured by the contrast between autonomous art and commercial art, a contrast which is not for him isomorphic to the anti-democratic opposition of elite art to folk art. But, advanced capitalism, and were he alive today he would no doubt include postmodernism as a co-conspirator, has leveled this distinction in all of its substantive forms.

The autonomy of *genuine* art consists in its serving needs which are "orthogonal" to those which reinforce existing social relations. Art's autonomy, won through its gradual emancipation from magic, the court and religion, secures for art its own inner logic of development and of evaluation (Adorno, 1984). Ringing a change on Kant's description of aesthetic phenomena as exhibiting a purposiveness without purpose, Adorno claims that "[i]f any social function can be ascribed to art at all, it is the function to have no function" (ibid., p. 322).

While art's autonomy *vis-à-vis* society means that it has no function in any straightforward sense, such an independence does endow art with a distinctive social *signifi-*

cance for Adorno. Because art's autonomy as a separate sphere of value was the outcome of a development within bourgeois society, art's independence is predicated upon arrangements within that very society. The institution of autonomous art is an institution of bourgeois society – it is a bourgeois institution. Works of autonomous art, then, belong to a society where the principle of exchange has achieved hegemony in regulating social relationships, and such works circulate in accordance with this principle. Works of art, even autonomous works, are therefore commodity fetishes (Adorno, 1984, 323–4). But, autonomous works are fetishes that call into question the system of commodification and reification itself. The "ideological" status of autonomous art is at the same time a *critical* status. Like so many of his philosophical predecessors, Plato being perhaps the notable exception, Adorno pins his hopes on the redemptive power of art, claiming that "[w]orks of art are plenipotentiaries of things beyond the mutilating sway of exchange, profit and false human needs" (ibid., p. 323).

Autonomous art voices a "promise of happiness, a promise that is constantly being broken" (Adorno, 1984, p. 196). As such, it is ineluctably the "language of suffering," and in this lies its claim to truth. Genuine art is expressive of the contradictions inherent in the society from which it emerges. The atonality of Schoenberg, for instance, is an acknowledgment of social alienation, of the problematic relationship of the individual to the community, in contrast to the less uneasy insertion of the individual into the social nexus expressed in the tonality of earlier classical forms. By refusing to "sugar coat" deprivations and by representing fulfillment as a broken promise, genuine works represent the negative *as* negative and prevent us from being seduced into prizing our chains. The culture industry claims to procure for us the object of desire and thus desublimates it, but it is a repressive desublimation which presents the object only as a simulacrum with no *real* relation to instinctual gratification.

Adorno's Jazz Critique

For Adorno, writing in 1936, jazz was a kind of dance music which *presumed* to be modern, its presumed modernity grounded in its putatively oppositional stance, a stance that was articulated musically in terms of a characteristic sound and rhythmic principle that feigned transgression in their mechanical soullessness and licentious decadence (Adorno, 1989–90, 45). He designates syncopation as the central rhythmic principle.

The terms of Adorno's jazz critique are interesting in that he criticizes jazz for *not really* being a product of immediacy, of the primitive, the archaic, the "raw," and for being only a commercialized ersatz of this. The very criteria which jazz presumably *fails* to satisfy are themselves the warp and woof of the primitivist myth of black creativity. In his claim that, because of its prior colonization by the culture industry, the jazz subject is *not* the vehicle for the presentation of unmediated sexuality, "original, untrammeled nature," and instinctual liberation, Adorno implicitly criticizes exoticism and the implicitly racializing fetishization of black performers by the white intelligentsia, both American and European. Representative of this reaction were Gertrude Stein's and Picasso's responses to their first encounter with Duke Ellington's orchestra, where they marveled at what they took to be Ellington's ability to access the instinctual and unconscious layers of the psyche. But in Adorno's salutary critique of primitivism, of the fetishization of the "jungle," the archaic and the natural, there are two problematic moments. First, black creativity is saved from being viewed as the purely instinctual, unreflective, and artless expression of undomesticated animality only at the cost of its being understood as the thoroughly domesticated and packaged product of the culture industry. Such a rescuing strategy implies that the possibilities for black creative expression are exhausted, one might say, by the "jingle and the jungle." I shall suggest presently that this predicament is indicative of a manifest hermeneutic inadequacy in Adorno's encounter with black aesthetic practice. Moreover, Adorno was greatly suspicious of the primitive *per se*, even as and perhaps especially as it is invoked in Western "art music," as his critical response to Stravinsky's "Rite of Spring" clearly demonstrates. For Adorno, any such invocation is ahistorical and thus necessarily regressive. He thus constructs a box in which black creative expression has no place to turn.

Adorno criticizes jazz for being mechanical, static, repetitive music which only *feigns* democratic and individual self-expression, for being music which only *appears* to be reflective of the autonomy of instinctual liberation, and psychic integration. Its merely illusory status in this regard leaves it fit only for the ideological job of providing an ersatz for true liberation and thus for beguiling an already mutilated public into feeling that prevailing social and economic arrangements are "delivering the goods." And it is an agent of that mutilation, part of the apparatus facilitating the introjection of the administered society and its controls, an introjection that fashions a brutalized subjectivity. As he famously said in his first extensive treatment of the subject in 1936, in an essay responding to Walter Benjamin's "The Work of Art in the Age of Mechanical Reproduction," "jazz is not what it 'is': its aesthetic articulation is sparing and can be understood at a glance. Rather, *it is what it is used for . . .*" (Adorno, 1989–90, p. 47; italics mine).

The elements of jazz in which immediacy and spontaneity seem to be most conspicuous are improvisation and syncopation. But Adorno holds that these features are mere ornaments, "add-ons" to the standardized commercial product that he thinks is the essence of jazz, and they are added on for the ideological purpose of masking its naked commodity structure (ibid.). Jazz is social authority packaged to appear as libidinal freedom. Blackness itself presences as an absence in jazz; it too is a mere commodity fetish, indicating all the more the black person's colonization by the very context within which s/he deludedly asserts his/her individuality: "the skin of the black man functions as much as a coloristic effect as does the silver of the saxophone" (ibid., p. 53). Since jazz offers only the deceptive semblance of liberation, the pleasure taken in it by both producers and consumers is *au fond* a masochistic and sadistic pleasure in one's own alienation from oneself, in the "othering" of one's own instincts, and in the "othering" by others of theirs (ibid.). For Adorno, jazz is thoroughly modern, then, not in its aesthetic, but in its having been engendered by the dialectic of Enlightenment through the mechanism of suppression. Recalling in some ways Marcuse's idea of "repressive desublimation," Adorno holds that the "jazz subject" is not quickened by the liberation of old and repressed instincts; instead it presents only a static, standardized and petrified mask that testifies to its domesticated, controlled, and mutilated instinctual structure.

And as for jazz's supposed "progressiveness," its genuine *aesthetic* modernity, Adorno takes what is musically progressive in it to be plagiarized from European impressionism and to be simply pasted on, rather than developing organically from out of the musical material itself as it did for Debussy, Ravel et al. So jazz makes false claims both to the Dionysian archaic and to that which is truly modern (Adorno, 1989–90, 6).

Locating jazz's origin, and just as speciously, its essence, in a combination of salon dance music and military march music, Adorno sees jazz as inextricably circumscribed by the authoritarian control of the eight-bar cycle and the machine-like steady beat. Even jazz at its best, the so-called "hot music" of, say, Louis Armstrong, music in which it appeared that the lyrically self-asserting individual soloist willingly and autonomously engaged with the collective, is really a music in which the individual is sacrificed to the mechanistically contrived collective. Adorno finds it no accident that the Western composer whom he took to be most sympathetic to jazz, Stravinsky, placed human sacrifice at the center of his principal work, "The Rite of Spring" (Adorno, 1989–90, 64).

Adorno maintains that the social authority of the prescribed metric law, manifested by a rigidly maintained basic beat, is never effectively challenged by jazz syncopation. Indeed he likens jazz syncopation to sexual dysfunction and *impotence*, to premature and incomplete orgasm, to what is at best a gesture without a meaningful purpose. Like Benjamin's bourgeoisie taking pleasure in its own alienation and *presumably* like black Vaudeville performers taking pleasure in their own clownishness and in "acting the fool," the jazz subject takes pleasure precisely, for Adorno, in its own weakness (Adorno, 1989–90, 66). As a sort of pre-emptive strike, and to the tune of the superego's sado-masochistic dance, the jazz subject enacts a moment of self-castration, achieving its power through an internal split whereby it identifies with a repressive social authority over itself. But this is all the latent content of the dream that is jazz; its manifest content, the text on which we are encouraged to enact a hermeneutic of suspicion, is the myth of the empowered individual democratically engaged with the collective and uncon-strained by social authority. But this text enacts the symptoms of the neurotic; the non-spontaneous, ritualized and mechanical behavior of the neurotic has for Adorno a musical parallel in the thoroughly conventional nature of jazz music. Jazz expresses the thoroughly mutilated status of oppressed black humanity (ibid., 67).

Inspired both by Marx's analysis of the commodity and no doubt also by the cen-trality to industrial production of the Fordist principle of interchangeable parts, Adorno avers that the formal elements of jazz have been pre-fabricated in accordance with the capitalist requirement that they be exchangeable and interchangeable (Adorno, 1989–90, 52–3). With this thesis of what I shall call the "detachability" of jazz's char-acteristic features, Adorno implies that a jazz performance cannot have the organic integrity of a genuine work of art, for it will always be a whole fully reducible to its arbitrarily arranged interchangeable parts.

Further, since for Adorno the details of a jazz performance are interchangeable in *time*, jazz cannot be governed by an imperative of temporal articulation and develop-ment. Since its elements are arbitrarily fungible, its progression in time lacks the organic developmental inevitability of concert music; its essential temporal nature is stasis (Adorno, 1941, 173).

The reader will be forgiven for feeling at this point compelled to interject something on the order of, "Given what is at issue in a genuine jazz performance, actual jazz prac-tice is virtually unrecognizable in Adorno's descriptions." Today it is argued increas-ingly that the object of Adorno's ire was not what we refer to today as "jazz," but rather

390

what was the popular music of his time, which was not necessarily even American music (Robinson, 1994). So we should attend to what was in Adorno's "ear" when evaluating his jazz essays, and, given the musical context of 1920s Germany, that was a peculiarly German interpretation of commercial dance music (*Tanzjazz*). No American jazz band visited Germany prior to 1924, and virtually no recordings of the major black American jazz artists were available at any time during the Weimar Republic (ibid.). Among the white bandleaders, Paul Whiteman was especially important, and if, as one writer suggests, we listen to a typical Whiteman performance, much of what Adorno says in "On Jazz" hits home (Cooper, 1996). But, as late as 1953, when what is translated as "Perennial Fashion – Jazz" was published and he had spent over eleven years in the US, Adorno's critique remained virtually unchanged. Moreover, he insisted to the end on the underlying unity between the "hot" jazz characteristic of the first rank of African-American practitioners and the "sweet" jazz or dance music of the '20s.

"Talking Back" to Adorno

Perhaps most significant are Adorno's charges of jazz's atemporality, its lack of organic integrity and its thoroughly mechanical nature. I wish to respond to these charges by briefly taking up in turn his critique of jazz's temporality, his assertion that jazz syncopation is a mechanical contrivance that gives the lie to its claim to rhythmic freedom, and his claim that improvisation is a similarly mechanical practice masquerading as individual expression. I shall then turn to a brief account of the criteria that jazz practitioners *themselves* take to be salient for the evaluation of a jazz performance.

On the issue of temporality, repetition in jazz is often a means to impart movement. One need only listen to the deployment of riffs (repeated background melodic phrases that are rhythmically oriented) in the work of Count Basie (for example, his "One O'Clock Jump," *Count Basie: The Complete Decca Recordings* Decca GRD-3-611). As opposed to this, repetition in Stravinsky, for example, *does* impart a sense of stasis, of having suspended time, of a musical "meanwhile" (for example, in "Rite of Spring," the *ostinati* in "Danses des Adolescentes"). While repetition is arguably an important strategy in black culture, one should be attentive to the various uses to which it can be put.

As far as Adorno's critique of syncopation (his insistence on the performer's submission to the domination of a uniform basic beat) is concerned, he seems unable to acknowledge that the regular beat is the condition of the possibility of syncopation. Such a beat provides the coordinate system or context within which rhythmic experimentation can intelligibly take place. As Kierkegaard pointed out in his discussion of the interesting, it is precisely our expectations that form the ground for the unexpected (Kierkegaard, 1959, 364). The established and recurring beat configures or articulates the very temporal horizon that allows syncopated rhythms to have *meaning*. In fact, it is the recognition of this that allowed one critic to *fault* Ellington for variations in tempo in his "Black, Brown and Beige," for those variations undermined the possibility of syncopation (Tucker, 1993, 166). And, unless one claims that such musical intelligibility is necessarily equivalent to the utterly undemanding accessibility required by the market, as Adorno implausibly does, then the case that Adorno wishes to make for jazz syncopation's necessarily authoritarian character cannot be made.

391

Adorno further alleges that jazz's musical spontaneity is fatally compromised by its rigid adherence to bar lines and its slavish restriction to the chord structure of the popular songs that form its basis. While it is true that excessive intelligibility flirts dangerously with cliché and that genuine art is ambiguous, we obviously cannot dispense with intelligibility altogether, and there are a number of important enabling conditions of musical intelligibility. Chord progressions in a jazz performance constitute one of those enabling conditions. So it is not the case that the harmonic structure need be seen as a restriction on the genuineness of improvisation; it is rather an enabling condition of the intelligibility of the improvisation, of its being recognized as a move in the game that makes sense as opposed to an arbitrary gesture. Further, the chord structure provides a metalinguistic frame that enables members of an ensemble to communicate with each other, to respond to one another and to participate in a common project. The touchstone of harmonic structure is one of the conditions of jazz's being the "sound of surprise," to adopt Whitney Balliett's suggestive phrase, without its degenerating into the arbitrariness of noise. Originality is to be sought, at least in the first instance, in what the musician fashions within the "constraints" of form and material, in the distinctiveness of the story s/he is able to articulate using the vocabulary of the tradition. Does adherence to the sonata form render all Western concert music of the Classical period interchangeable?

We recall Adorno's account of the relationship between the individual and the collective in jazz performance, his conviction that in such contexts genuine individuality is sacrificed to the collective. But certainly what is *sought* is a genuine dialogical or conversational interaction, featuring antiphony (call and response), signifying (humorous and ironic dueling) and so on, an interaction that places a premium on attentive listening (Berliner, 1994, 389, 399). In this way, at least ideally, the dialectic of the individual and the collective is not collapsed, and a genuine communal creation is forged. The soloist speaks the language of the collective, but a language that enables the formulation of one's own statement. Max Roach and Wynton Marsalis confidently assert that jazz is a democratic form of music in that, as Roach puts it, "[w]hen a piece is performed, everybody in the group has the opportunity to speak on it, to comment on it through their performance" (Berliner, 1994, p. 417; Scherman, 1995).

For a critical response to jazz, we can easily avoid critiques that, like Adorno's, flirt with insinuating musical unintelligibility as a critical counterpoint. By attending to the criteria that jazz musicians themselves employ in evaluating performances, a recent major study provides strong evidence both against Adorno's charge that jazz improvisation is largely a matter of the mechanical or arbitrary application of clichés and for the claim that there is a language of criticism and evaluation that is internal to jazz musical practice. By attending to the criteria that those who engage in the practice themselves employ, Adorno's manifest hermeneutic failure is underscored. Discussing jazz musical values, the author of that study, Paul Berliner (Berliner, 1994, 244–76), mentions nine criteria that are implicitly or explicitly brought to bear in musical evaluations. First, there is an emphasis upon the degree to which a performance "swings," i.e., the degree to which the variety of an artist's rhythmic conceptions and the stylistic manner in which they are articulated or phrased contributes to giving them qualities of syncopation and forward motion. Adorno claims that a jazz performance is rigidly governed by bar lines. However, in a competent improvisation there is no such rigid observance. The intentional anticipation of chord changes is one way in which bar lines are blurred. Listen, for instance, to Coleman Hawkins' solo on Ellington's "Mood Indigo" (*Duke Ellington Meets Coleman Hawkins* MCA/Impulse MCAD-5650 JVC-461). This anticipation is itself an instance of syncopation. Phrasing across bar lines was something that Louis Armstrong and Charlie Parker commonly did. Further, the jazz solo typically eschews the repetition of four- and eight-bar phrases characteristic of the AABA song form. In general, mature performers obscure the formal elements that guide their inventions. Second, there is the matter of the melodic substance of ideas, as evaluated in terms of the economy of expression and of lyricism. Third, one seeks evidence of the artful handling of harmonic dissonance to achieve the appropriate mixture of pitches inside and outside indicated chords for creating interesting melodies. Fourth, it is important that there be a balance between originality, on the one hand, and taste or discretion, on the other, where the emphasis is upon avoiding the overuse of conventional jazz vocabulary while respecting the conventions of a given repertory. Fifth, there is an eye to the emotional coherence or integrity of expression displayed in a performance, embodying such qualities as pathos, intensity, urgency, fire, energy, and humor of the ironic, "signifying," sort. Sixth, but always in the context of emotional expressiveness and the distinctiveness of the performer's sound, one evaluates instrumental virtuosity and the technical features of musical ideas. Seventh, there is a central concern about the ability of a soloist to shape, and thereby tell, coherent, "organic," and unified narratives through the suspenseful development of ideas and the dramatic shaping of sound, with the effect that the solo moves forward in time with such logic that its "direction seems inevitable" (recall Adorno's invidious comparison of jazz and classical music in this regard), its narrative compelling. Eighth, one looks for spontaneity of musical invention, where here is meant the extemporaneity of the performance. "Premeditated" and "conventional" are often terms of derision in the evaluation of a jazz performance. To describe an improvisation as cliché ridden or as relying upon patterns is to *criticize* it. So, I would argue, the very language game of jazz practice draws distinctions between the derivative and the original which are important to the jazz community itself. Last, and the most rarely achieved of the desiderata Berliner adduces, is innovation in the sense of the creation of a new performance idiom. This refers to the sort of extra-paradigmatic accomplishment achieved by the likes of Louis Armstrong, Charlie Parker, Miles Davis, John Coltrane and Ornette Coleman. The evolution of jazz practice and the coexistence of different performance idioms or performance schools contributes to there being competing musical values *within* the jazz community and a contest of interpretations that insures the vitality of the tradition and the viability of the music.

It is true that jazz is in some ways more vulnerable to colonization by the culture industry than is Western concert music (though current responses to the growing concern about the graying of the audience for classical music, as well as Adorno's own acknowledgment of the fetish character of this music, make even this a distinction in degree rather than kind). In many ways, the constraining, overly arranged character of some swing bands, the clichés of the hard bop or "soul jazz" movement, some of the banalities of the fusion movement and, today, what is called "smooth jazz" are testimony to jazz's distinctive vulnerability. Indeed, in the ever more prevalent smooth jazz format, the saxophones *do* simulate sexual ecstasy (and they are almost always soprano saxophones, à la Kenny G), and do so to the rhythm of the drum machine. Here we truly have an example of music in the age of (electro)mechanical reproduction and of a music that is a virtually unalloyed product of the culture industry. But the distinction between what, say, Ellington was doing, on the one hand, and the "machine-products of Tin Pan Alley," on the other, was well-known and perceived circa 1936, the time of Adorno's first entry into the fray (Tucker, 1993, 127). Already in 1954, André Hodeir offers an implicit critique of Adorno's claim that a jazz treatment can have only a merely decorative, artificial, or gratuitous effect (ibid., 284). Moreover, with respect to composers in the classical tradition such as Ravel, Delius and Debussy, whose works have harmonic affinities to jazz and who no doubt either directly or indirectly influenced Ellington's compositions, *pace* Adorno, a strong case can be made for Ellington's harmonic and timbral originality *vis-à-vis* the impressionists (ibid., 414–17).

I can compress my argument by claiming that Adorno lacks the vocabulary or spectacles requisite to bringing jazz into proper focus; he reads it as *lacking* a taken for granted good, rather than as *possessing* an alternative good, where the latter can be demonstrated to be an acknowledged musical value. He is thus unable to render a perspicuous and noninvidious comparison between jazz and traditional concert music. For example, jazz and classical music arguably embody competing conceptions of sound, of what are musically appropriate tonal criteria. It is not here a case of one being correct and the other not, but of competing conceptions of the good. One of the central points that I should like to highlight now is that, by emphasizing *composition* alone, Adorno commits category errors in assessing the tradition of jazz practice (Adorno, 1941; 1984, 146–7). In fact, because of these category errors he cannot even see this tradition *as a tradition*, as a set of practices with a developmental history given shape by progressive resolutions of aesthetic problems. His compositionalist bias along with what I earlier referred to as his embrace of the "detachability thesis" conspire to force him to see jazz structure as, to borrow a phrase from the architect Robert Venturi, a "decorated shed," with the consequence that all that can count for Adorno musically is the shed, which is to him a shack. The compositionalist paradigm that informs his "way of hearing" forces what is central to jazz to the aesthetic periphery. His rhetorical strategy is to effect an inversion by prefixing "mere" to what is essential to jazz's aesthetic nature, to what is distinctive about it, thereby relegating what is essential to it to the artistically superficial and making what is only an occasion for it, e.g., the popular song, its essential nature.

From this follow the blind spots that prevent him from seeing, for example, timbral individuality (a performer's "sound") as a legitimate element of musical spontaneity. The frequently made observation that he largely ignores musical instrumentation *per se* (Zuidervaart, 1991, 107) points to a lacuna in Adorno's analysis of music in general, but it is perhaps even more fatal to his jazz analysis than to his account of Western concert music. For in jazz practice, musical spontaneity is often constitutively mediated through idiosyncratic instrumental timbre or sound. In Ellington's classic "Concerto for Cootie" (*The Blanton-Webster Band* RCA 5659-2-RB), the improvisation within this thoroughly composed piece is almost exclusively timbral, with Cootie Williams deploying a broad spectrum of tone colors (Tucker, 1993, 276–88; Rattenbury, 1990, 199). To focus upon composition alone here is to thoroughly miss the point. More generally, a varied timbral palette and an expectation that soloists will develop a unique personal sound are acknowledged to be prominent among African-American musical values.

(Within a couple of bars, one can fairly easily distinguish the light and fluid sound of a Johnny Hodges on the alto saxophone from the tartness of a Jackie MacLean, or from the heavily blues inflected sound of a Cannonball Adderly; or, on the tenor, the breathiness of a Ben Webster from the hardness at the center of the tone of a John Coltrane; or the lyricism of a Miles Davis on the trumpet from the jagged rhythmic sensibility of a Dizzy Gillespie, and so on.) Moreover, vocalized tonal qualities and pitch inflections are staples of jazz practice (Berliner, 1994, 108, 126–7). Adorno can see such modifications of "objective" sound as at most a "whimpering which is helplessly testing itself" (Adorno, 1989–90, p. 67). Given that criteria for tone production tend to be (at least relative to jazz) standardized in the *classical* repertoire, less is lost if in *its* analysis musical instrumentation itself is not thematized. But such an elision is fatal to jazz analysis. This category error or failure to fuse horizons takes the form of not understanding *performance* and the evaluative categories relevant to it as the appropriate rubric for responding to jazz (Locke, 1936; Gioia, 1988, 15–16). Adorno quite explicitly refused to acknowledge that the categories of performance and sound were those that were best suited for bringing into focus what is most distinctive about jazz and, in his graphocentrism, continued to subordinate them to that of composition.

A Path Not Taken

Jazz retains and foregrounds the improvisatory character of the social, economic, and cultural strategies of a people who, at critical junctures in their history, were forced to "make themselves up" as they went along. The tunes that Adorno maligns, that form the basis of much jazz performance, are often only *occasions* for improvisation. And those improvisations sometimes constitute a parodic *response* to the banality of those very tunes (Monson, 1994). The relationship of a jazz treatment to the original tune is more analogous to the relationship of an analytical cubist painting to its subject matter than it is to the relationship of a "detachable" decorative overlay to an unadorned structure. The jazz improvisation treats the original's melodic and harmonic structure as raw material that it decomposes and reconfigures in novel and, if successful, *meaningful* ways. This bears deep affinities with what the critic Albert Murray discusses as the "riff style" of African Americans (Murray, 1970, 58–9). (There are also undoubtedly ties to the African aesthetic of creation for the moment, wherein masks are created to be "danced" in significant rituals and then not infrequently tossed aside.) Jazz's spontaneity and hence critical negativity must be sought here. Adorno's Frankfurt School colleague Herbert Marcuse was much more sanguine about jazz's potential for critically negating "affirmative culture." Through its possibilities for revolutionizing perception, Marcuse includes it, along with the twelve tone composition of Schoenberg's school, as a vehicle for the dissolution of the prevailing mode of perception (Marcuse, 1969, 36–8).

In "conceding" jazz's origins in the African-American folk tradition, Adorno goes on to say that "[t]he Negro spirituals . . . were slave songs and *as such* combined the lament of unfreedom with its oppressed confirmation" (Adorno, 1981, p. 122; emphasis mine). But are the songs of slaves necessarily slavish songs? Espousing a different basis for an aesthetic, Ralph Ellison insists that it is not the case that a slave cannot be a man but that "the enslaved really thought of themselves as *men* [sic] who had been unjustly enslaved" (Ellison, 1964, p. 254). For Adorno, art's truth registers the unhappy consciousness of a utopia denied. Autonomous music expresses the suffering attendant upon the recognition of the impossibility of the achievement of true individuality. For Ellison and Murray, art's truth lies in its heroic affirmation of individuality *in spite of* the chaos that threatens to swallow it. Referring to jazz musicians he knew as a boy, Ellison writes:

> The delicate balance struck between strong individual personality and the group . . . was a marvel . . . [T]he end of all this discipline and technical mastery was the desire to express an affirmative way of life . . . Life could be harsh, loud and wrong if it wished, but they lived it fully, and when they expressed their attitude toward the world it was with a fluid style that reduced the chaos of living to form. (Ellison, 1964, pp. 189–90)

And Murray suggests that "the nature of the creative process [is realized in an exemplary way in] the affirmative disposition toward the harsh actuality of human existence that is characteristic of the fully orchestrated blues statement" (Murray, 1996, p. 7). But its affirmation is not the affirmation of which Adorno accuses it. It is not that the "jazz subject," in Murray's and Ellison's estimation, is engaged in practices of self-deception, leading it to think that the social dialectic of the individual and the collective has finally reached a satisfactory resolution. For Murray's and Ellison's jazz subject, there are no illusions about having achieved utopia. The idea of satisfactory resolution has little purchase for it – life is "always wrong." It faces with utmost clarity utopia's perpetual postponement. The struggle to wrest individuality, and hence meaning, from the chaos is never ending. And if life is always wrong, the incessant registering of suffering becomes a kind of "false utopianism" bereft of a true tragic sense of life, like deconstruction's ceaselessly repeated refrain of meaning's indeterminacy.

While it is beyond the scope of this essay to stage a full fledged confrontation between these contrasting aesthetics, the Murray-Ellison position does have a hermeneutic advantage in this case. Something akin to the methodological role played by the principle of interpretive or hermeneutic charity is very much to the point here. I refer to the idea that, as a regulative principle, a field linguist has to assume that most of the assertions made in a yet to be translated language are true, and a student of culture has to assume that most of the behavior in a culture of interest is, at least minimally, rational. Just as we should be skeptical of a translation procedure that renders most of the utterances in a target language false, or most of the behavior irrational, we should be suspicious of a cultural-aesthetic account that makes of an entire artistic tradition an aesthetic dysvalue, that renders it meaningless in the sense that its significance is exhausted by its systemic function. It redounds to the credit of the Murray-Ellison position that it allows the richness, integrity and, dare I say it in these postmodern times, humanity of the jazz tradition to come to the fore and into focus, and to do so without our sacrificing critical standards. In making this claim I do not intend to give their position a blanket endorsement, for in its existential and ahistorical resignation before the absurdity of human existence, it has the potential to encourage social and political quietism. Moreover, and though this is by no means a necessary consequence of the position, I question some of Murray's judgments about which musical practices ought to be allowed into the "jazz canon." And Adorno's unwavering focus on sources of manipulation in late capitalist societies is all to the good, despite the questionably totalizing nature of his claims about the "liquidation of the individual." But, like all theories, Adorno's aesthetic theory is implicated in a dialectics of blindness and insight. And when it comes to jazz, its blindness is all too apparent.

It is perhaps a genuine question whether jazz and Western classical music can be brought into focus at the same time. Nonetheless, if we are not prejudiced by narrowly compositionalist blinders, the demonstrable overlap in musical values between the two traditions – an intersection to which Adorno was not attentive and that is insured in part by jazz's hybrid status and perhaps to some extent by its Du Boisian "doubleness" – would enable a mediated transition from one focus to the other, and thus a fusion of hermeneutic horizons in the sense I would advocate. One element of the set of intersections would no doubt be the idea of *rubato*, or of taking liberties with tempo without changing the basic pulse. This is an acknowledged interpretive practice of classical musicians and is obviously a feature of the jazz repertoire. Another would be sonority. Indeed, if Adorno had not concentrated so single-mindedly on composition, he might have had a fuller appreciation not only of jazz but of the classical tradition as well.

References and Further Reading

Adorno, Theodor. *Philosophy of Modern Music*, trans. Anne Mitchell and Wesley Blomster (New York: Continuum, 1994).
——. "On Jazz," trans. Jamie Owen Daniel *Discourse* 12.1 (Fall–Winter 1989–90).
——. "The Culture Industry Reconsidered," in *Critical Theory and Society: A Reader*, eds. Stephen Bronner and Douglas Kellner (New York: Routledge, 1989).
——. "On the Fetish-Character in Music and the Regression of Listening," in *The Essential Frankfurt School Reader*, eds., Andrew Arato and Eike Gebhardt (New York: Continuum, 1988).
——. *Aesthetic Theory*, trans. C. Lenhardt (New York: Routledge, 1984).
——. "Perennial Fashion – Jazz," in *Prisms*, trans. Samuel and Shierry Weber (Cambridge, MA: The MIT Press, 1981).
——. Review of Wilder Hobson, *American Jazz Music* and Winthrop Sargeant, *Jazz: Hot and Hybrid*, *Studies in Philosophy and Social Science* IX, no. 1 (1941).
Adorno, Theodor, and Horkheimer, Max. *Dialectic of Enlightenment*, trans. John Cumming (New York: The Seabury Press, 1972).
Bayles, Martha. *Hole in Our Soul: The Loss of Beauty and Meaning in American Popular Music* (New York: The Free Press, 1994).
Berliner, Paul. *Thinking in Jazz: the Infinite Art of Improvisation* (Chicago: University of Chicago Press, 1994).
Bernotas, Robert. "Critical Theory, Jazz, and Politics: A Critique of the Frankfurt School," Ph.D. Dissertation, Johns Hopkins University, Baltimore, 1987.
Cooper, Harry. "On *Uber Jazz*: Replaying Adorno With the Grain," *October* 75, Winter (1996).
DeVaux, Scott. "Constructing the Jazz Tradition: Jazz Historiography," *Black American Literature Forum*, vol. 25, no. 3 (Fall 1991).
Ellison, Ralph. *Shadow and Act* (New York: Vintage Books, 1964).
Gilroy, Paul. *The Black Atlantic: Modernity and Double Consciousness* (Cambridge, MA: Harvard University Press, 1993).
Gioia, Ted. *The Imperfect Art: Reflections on Jazz and Modern Culture* (Oxford: Oxford University Press, 1988).

Jay, Martin. *The Dialectical Imagination: A History of the Frankfurt School and the Institute of Social Research, 1923–1950* (Boston: Little, Brown, 1973).

Kierkegaard, Soren. *Either/Or*, vol. I, trans. David F. Swenson and Lillian M. Swenson, revised by Howard A. Johnson (Princeton: Princeton University Press, 1959).

Lewandowski, Joseph D. "Adorno on jazz and society," *Philosophy and Social Criticism* 22 (1996).

Locke, Alain. *The Negro and His Music* (Washington, D.C.: The Associates in Negro Folk Education, 1936).

Marcuse, Herbert. *An Essay on Liberation* (Boston: Beacon Press, 1969).

Monson, Ingrid. "Doubleness and Jazz Improvisation: Irony, Parody, and Ethnomusicology," *Critical Inquiry* 20 (Winter 1994).

Murray, Albert. *The Blue Devils of Nada: A Contemporary American Approach to Aesthetic Statement* (New York: Pantheon Books, 1996).

——. *The Omni-Americans* (New York: Da Capo Press, 1970).

Nye, William P. "Theodor Adorno on Jazz: A Critique of Critical Theory," *Popular Music and Society* 12 (1988).

Rattenbury, Ken. *Duke Ellington: Jazz Composer* (New Haven: Yale University Press, 1990).

Robinson, J. Bradford. "The jazz essays of Theodor Adorno: some thoughts on jazz reception in Weimar Germany," *Popular Music*, Vol. 13/1 (1994).

Robinson, Joseph. "What I Learned in the Lenoir High School Band," *The Wilson Quarterly*, vol. XIX (Autumn 1995).

Roblin, Ronald, ed., *The Aesthetics of the Critical Theorists: Studies on Benjamin, Adorno, Marcuse, and Habermas* (Lewiston, NY: Edwin Mellen Press, 1990).

Scherman, Tony. Interview of Wynton Marsalis, *American Heritage*, October 1995.

Snead, James H. "Repetition as a Figure of Black Culture," in *Black Literature and Literary Theory*, ed. Henry Louis Gates, Jr. (New York: Methuen, 1984).

Southern, Eileen. *The Music of Black Americans: A History* (New York: W. W. Norton, 1971).

Taylor, Charles. *Philosophical Arguments* (Cambridge, MA: Harvard University Press, 1995).

Tucker, Mark, ed. *The Duke Ellington Reader* (Oxford: Oxford University Press, 1993).

Zuidervaart, Lambert. *Adorno's Aesthetic Theory: The Redemption of Illusion* (Cambridge, MA: The MIT Press, 1991).

26

Black Cinema and Aesthetics

CLYDE R. TAYLOR

Independent African-American filmmakers brought a new, theoretical self-consciousness to film production and reception during the Civil Rights/Black Power era. They sought to extend to cinema the rationales of the black aesthetic, whose revisionary doctrine first arose in the arena of literary criticism. Many efforts have since been made to establish criteria by which the success or rewards of black cinema might be calculated, apart from those of a more general and supposedly race-free interpretation. Before those criteria are looked at, some questions of definition arise.

The phrase "black cinema aesthetics" carries baggage that illustrates contemporary crises of knowledge. Which of the two elements in this couplet should be interrogated first? Here, it is useful to reverse the anticipated order and ask, not "what is black cinema?" but "what is aesthetics?" and then pursue that question from a ground in black cinema, understanding that this order upends the way knowledge is usually formulated, from the familiar, Western standpoint to the less familiar, exotic phenomena. If in fact one were to make an archaeology of these two constructs, tracing them back historically, we would find the path of intellectual and material development of black cinema to have been consistently colonized, frustrated, and deterred by the preemptive development of aesthetic reasoning.

Mystification around the notion of the aesthetic has been evaporating in recent decades, leaving a less self-evidential reception of this "science of beauty." It is increasingly understood that aesthetic reasoning is historical, i.e., constructed in the seventeenth and eighteenth centuries, and therefore not some inevitable, eternal fixture of human thought; class-serving, i.e., made to reflect the interests of the dominant social stratas; and culture-bound, i.e., arising in Western Europe and determined by its historical and cultural experience. The cogno-political problem emerges from the masking of these origins and interests behind claims of universal application. On the basis of these claims an art-culture system has been established, composed of cultural gatekeeping institutions, museums, libraries, university departments and disciplines, newspapers and journals, galleries, and associations like the Academy of Motion Picture Arts and Sciences that distributes the Academy Awards, all heavily invested in the rhetoric and rationales of aestheticism.

Among recent rejections of the claims of aesthetic science has been Pierre Bourdieu's *Distinction: A Social Critique of the Judgement of Taste*. Armed with questionnaires, polls, graphs, statistics, Bourdieu masses considerable evidence that aesthetic reasoning is little more than the rationalization of the taste of the more influential classes. He strengthens his earlier argument that educational credentials largely rely on the unequal possession and transference of "cultural capital," the stock of cultural knowledge and practice that the elite impose on curricula as minimal information for educational advancement.

The dubious credentials of aesthetic discourse have been further picked apart from all sides, subjected to internal and external interrogations. Philosopher George Dickie's 1964 article "All Aesthetic Attitude Theories Fail: The Myth of the Aesthetic Attitude" had been followed by a variety of theoretical and ideological re-examinations, including Tony Bennett's analysis of aesthetics as "Useless Knowledge," on his way to developing a post-Marxist theory located Outside Literature. Laura Kipnis called for a "post-aesthetic theory" in her essay "Aesthetics and Foreign Policy." And Susan Kappeller, in *The Pornography of Representation* derides the use of concepts like aesthetic disinterestedness to protect work framed as fine art from the charge of obscenity. Meanwhile, avant garde art camps from Dada and Duchamps, through the Situation International of the 1960s in Paris and various other anti-art movements associated with postmodernism, have left few aspects of aestheticism digestible in their original formulations. But, except for some important passing shots from the Black Aesthetic movement in the 1960s US, little organized critique of the congruence of aestheticism with Eurocentrism and racism has appeared (but see Kipnis, 1986 and Taylor, 1985 and 1998).

The interplay between aestheticism and the representations of people of color in cinema is a prime location for the excavation of the ethnocentrism of aesthetic discourse. Nothing in the discipline's claims to disinterestedness or objectivity impeded the barrage of animalization and deformation of black people in Hollywood's era of classic cinema. The quantity and intensity of this imagery of debasement approached the venom of a wartime propaganda campaign. The entrenched precept of aesthetic reasoning that white is equatable with beauty and black with ugliness worked to support this monumental dehumanization. The resistance of some theorists to technicolor in favor of the more "classical" black and white movies may owe something to this racialized reading of the earliest cinema.

The distance from useless to destructive effect is a short step for aestheticism in the arena of black screen representation. While the aesthetic has principally framed its values above films as a popular, commercial entertainment medium, when aestheticism has been evoked in cinema production or interpretation, it has generally been in the service of white supremacy. The most powerful case in point is D. W. Griffith's *The Birth of a Nation* (1915). A full arsenal of aesthetic interpretation arose surrounding this film, to the extent that the vocabulary of aesthetic cinema studies finds this film foundational and canonical. At the same time cinema aestheticism has worked to soften or obscure the film's heavy commitment to racism and fascism. The assertion that Leni Riefenstahl's *Triumph of the Will* (1935) is the most powerful example of screen propaganda does injustice to Griffith's epic of bigotry. In instances such as this, the discipline of US cinema studies has shown a firmer commitment to the aestheticization of its field than to humanist pedagogy. Aesthetic discourse, we may conclude, composes an ideological screen of apology and glorification for a cultural regime that has remained indifferent or inimical to the rewarding development of non-white cinema.

The function of aesthetic discourse in marginalizing black cinema is supplemental to its major role as validator of dominant values. But the impact of this marginalization can be decisive within the sphere of production and reception of black films. Were all things equal, the judgments of reviewers, distributors, funding agencies about the projects of black cinema would be as accurate or unreliable as they are for the general population of American film culture. But all things are never equal. The initiatives of black cinema are frequently discounted, dismissed or smothered under aesthetic rationales: the lack of a story, too narrow an appeal, the content is too political, the theme is outdated, the practitioners lack a track record.

The cultural miscognition behind such judgments, when they are not mere excuses for other motives, goes far toward justifying the need for a "black film aesthetic," just as the misperception of African-American literary values earlier provoked the creation of a self-determining cultural outlook. But the differences between African-American and Euro-American possibilities in cinema ultimately rest in discrepancies of power for which aestheticism merely provides cosmetic cover. To develop and subscribe to a black cinema aesthetic may merely confine such designated work to the category of an ethno-aesthetic, a subordinated stratum of the controlling art-culture system, minimally granted the freedom of expression needed to achieve self-identity.

For that project, black cinema has profited more from the politics of representation than from the theories of aesthetics. The most refined models and theories of aesthetics would remain useless in a climate where films made in the interest of a developing African American film culture are not supported through production, or where the lingua franca of movie screens remains exploitive images of black people filtered through a prism of cultural colonization. The principal contribution to knowledge from the experience of African Americans with cinema lies in this arena of the politics of representation, both in the examples of ethnocentric distortion that American cinema generously provides, and through the counter-efforts of black people to challenge the imbalance of screen power. The contribution to these "culture wars" from disciplines thought to be "aesthetic," i.e., rhetoric, stylistics, cultural symbolism and critical judgment, may be important but secondary. Black cinema may be thought of as cinema made with the interests of blacks, as expressive and authenticating community, given a priority. To serve those interests the goals of black cinema have included other imperatives besides entertainment or art. A subtextual agenda of many black-directed films is to redress the imbalance between black and white screen power by challenging or deconstructing stereotypes, a motive seen in *Sweet Sweetback* (1970), *Child of Resistance* (1974), *Hollywood Shuffle* (1987), and *Do the Right Thing* (1988), among several others. Mainstream reluctance to accept this agenda pushes its most serious supporters into the precarious circumstances of independent film-making.

The relation between an "aesthetic" or cultural style and a social identity group is confused if that relation is thought of as genetic. The search for a feminine aesthetic in literature or painting, or a gay aesthetic in classical music, is bound to be fruitless if one is looking for some essentialized quality that emerges form an inherent source within the group. On the other hand, if a group shares collective values and a historical

401

outlook and creates out of shared assumptions, a recognizable style might emerge from that collective expression, like romantic orchestral music of Europe's nineteenth century, or like jazz, reflecting the signature of cultural identification, a common history and the will to pass the learning from that history down to identified sharers. The resulting expressive form can never be the exclusive iconology of the group because of the routine behaviors of cultural forms, i.e., that they are seldom if ever "pure" and are subject to much cross-breeding, and that however insularly developed a cultural form may be, like a language, it can be learned and practiced by outsiders, at least well enough to deceive insiders asked to separate the "authentic" from the learned in blind-fold tests. The originating group may nevertheless exert a determining influence on the development, circulation, and reception of this form as the core location of the values and experience from which it has been generated.

On this basis, a black film ethos can be imagined. But such an ethos has not acquired recognizable, stabilized form, as it has in black music. Nevertheless, the discussions of a "black film aesthetic" argue the desire for such a construction among some film-makers. The pursuers of such a goal have understandably been independent film directors. The corresponding negative position has been the argument that there can be no such thing as a "black film aesthetic," because there can be no separate Black film language, since the language of cinema is held to be unitary and universal. The holders of this view are likely to support ventures where the primary motivation is commercialization of the commodifiable.

A black cultural film style which, again, would be neither inimitable, nor essential, i.e., isolated from all other cultural practice, can be located only in an inchoate, formative stage. Putting aside the lineaments of such a stylistic among the "race movies" of the 1920s to 1950s, the emergence of this vocabulary of cultural signs might be traced to Melvin Van Peebles's *Sweetback*, and to the innovations of such independents as Haile Gerima, Charles Burnett, Julie Dash, Ben Caldwell, Larry Clark and Zeinabu Davis, all former students at UCLA's film school and often identified as the "LA Rebellion" for their efforts to forge alternative visual framing for black representation, as well as Kathleen Collins, Ayoka Chinzera, Bill Gunn, and Spike Lee.

Resistance to the aesthetics of assimilation may demand rejection of the master narrative promoted by Hollywood movies, which routinely presents a white male adventurer encountering and overcoming obstacles in a narrative trope that signifies the inevitable triumph of the established Western social-political order. The alternative of constructing a black version of the same narrative pattern has been explored, frequently around some marquee actor (and possibly former athlete), like Jim Brown, Fred Williams, Bernie Casey, Wesley Snipes, or occasionally an actress like Pam Grier or Tamara Dobson. This formula accounts for most of the black exploitation movies of the 1970s. But even in 1970s black exploitation films or subsequent spin-offs in later decades, the master narrative of inevitable Western patriarchal triumph is frequently adopted with tongue in cheek. This self-ironized miming of the master narrative is curiously also found in the race movies of the earlier decades of the century, but there, the manners of the majority are taken very seriously instead of being satirized as in the later films.

As philosopher Tommy Lott has pointed out in his analysis of theories of black cinema, black exploitation complicates definitions for those who wish to define the genre by only its intellectually and culturally sanctioned efforts, generally connected to a search for a black film aesthetic. Recognizing the value of deferring analysis on the basis of aesthetic interests, in favor of the primacy of political intepretation, he arrives at a "no-theory theory, because I see no need to resolve, on aesthetic grounds, the dispute over what counts as blaxpoitation."

Efforts to define black cinema according to some desired set of meritorious expressive features, to the exclusion of black exploitation movies, ignore the politics of representation, which isolates essentialization, either of culture or rhetorical methodology. There is no reason to suppose that a black film stylistic is the only or even dominant criterion for defining black cinema, which should be defined by its socio-linguistic or representational-political features. The features of black film style are relevant because they reflect a self-conscious practice that may have more impact on the definition of such a described body of work than films indifferent to issues of identity and cultural integrity. These stylistics are significant for likely being more consistent with Black cultural values than movies willing to compromise these values in favor of commercial success.

The features of an emergent black film cultural stylistic deliberately confront and recode the formulas of the master narrative and challenge the restricted, instrumental roles confining minorities and women in that narrative. The disruption of conventional ethnic representation may take the form of films like *Ganga and Hess* (1973), *Losing Ground* (1982) and *Daughters of the Dust* (1991), all films that aroused resentment from quarters within the art-culture establishment for depicting black people who were educated, beautiful, sophisticated, and independent of white sponsorship.

Given the burden of overturning existing misconceptions and the need not to repeat the social mythologies of the master narrative, black film rhetoric veers toward greater social reality, even when using non-figurative, unconventional, or highly symbolic iconology. Importantly, black films made with the mission of identity-configuration tend to vary structurally from classical Hollywood patterns, eschewing well-made plots where the motivations for the movement between scenes is psycho-heroical, i.e., determined by the need to advance the destiny of a heroic figure framed for audience identification. Instead, the films are often organized thematically, in episodes ordered to illustrate an idea central to the films' meditation. As in many other Hollywood-resisting films, tight closure at the end, resolving all loose narrative threads, is avoided.

This looser, thematic structural organization often approximates musical development, as though the scenes were passages making variations on a theme. This organization is apparent in Spike Lee's musical satire, *School Daze*. Connections with black musical forms like jazz and the blues are strengthened by an appearance of improvisation in both narrative progression and acting style, often with non-actors involved in the performance. Searches for a culturally-based film structural style founded on black music has been deliberately pursued, strikingly by Larry Clark in *Passing Through* (1977), which catches some of the urban hip sensibility of jazz, and more casually in films of Charles Burnett such as *Killer of Sheep* (1977) and *To Sleep With Anger* (1990) where a blues sensibility lays a basis for understanding, or *Ganga and Hess*, where a fusion between African spirituality and gospel music provides the dominant film-tone, or *Daughters of the Dust* which takes its scenic pulse from traditional African music. Generally, music in black film stylistics provides a cognitive grounding for exploration of thematic issues, while also serving as aural icon of ethnic identity, rather than offering enhancement for emotional moods, as in Hollywood movies.

These and other features of emerging black film stylistics draw on African-American oral tradition, or "orature," as a means of distinguishing films from the formulaic "literacy" of Hollywood. This tradition involves a respect and use for black vernacular speech, but extends to all the characteristics so far noted, including the thematic-episodic narrative organization, the reliance on music as organizing principle, the use of non-actors or naturalistic styles of acting, the suggestion of improvisation, and in the case of some films like those of Spike Lee, an attraction to popular cultural forms of expression approaching the carnivalesque.

One sign of the influence of oral tradition is the wide use of off-screen, vernacular narrators in such films as *Cameleon Street* (1989), *Child of Resistance, Daughters of the Dust, Bush Mama* (1976), and *Just Another Girl on the IRT* (1993). These narrators evoke a mood of storytelling which supports not only the needs of orature, including the openness to audience participation, but also invites departure from invisibly sutured, illusionist Hollywood narrative style. Such off-screen voices justify a degree of idiosyncrasy in narrative development.

Yet another feature of black film stylistics, shared with African and other marginalized screens, is an implicit philosophy of history characterized by prophecy, looking toward the past as a body of crucial experiences with decisive contemporary significance rather than vignettes of the past captured in cameo celebrations, and toward the present as a barely tolerable situation which waits to be transcended toward an improving future. This temporal/mental orientation differs from the master narrative where past, present, and future all commemorate the implausibility of any design of history or knowledge other than that proposed by "the explanation industry," as Toni Cade Bambara describes dominant media and its in-house ideological shapers. This different sense of time/history accounts for the refusal of formal, symmetrical closure as a narrative ideal. For all the contempt heaped upon the ending of Spike Lee's musical satire *School Daze*, the ultimate scream from the lead character to the assembled population, "Wake up!" perfectly illustrates the prophetic mode of narrative that often more subtly underlies black film rhetoric.

The most basic understanding of the politics of difference ought to perceive the conflicts of interpretation likely to arise from this assemblage of values when encountering the entrenched art-culture system. The various stylistics mentioned such as those attached to oral tradition, the preference for thematic narrative development, the attraction to musical forms of narrative organization, the interpretation of time and the social/historical moment from an impassioned, prophetic stance, as opposed to a complacent acceptance of the idea of bourgeois progress, have all been the point of unsympathetic criticism from culture gate-keepers who read such differences as failures to grasp the vocabulary of cinema literacy, misconceived introduction of sociology into art, indulgence in narrow, ethnic self-celebration, in short, failure to conform to the cultural inheritance embodied in the aesthetic.

The struggle to establish a self-determining hierarchy of cultural cinema values is further complicated for blacks by the attractions of black culture for those who turn there for entertainment, psychic reassurance, confirmations of superiority, rituals of guilt-atonement, titillating erotic displacements, self-defensive projections of rage, and other touristic fascinations. With their relative numbers, wealth and power, these cultural browsers and their interests often push black cultural identity into crisis, where internal control is threatened. Between this external interest and the impulse behind exploitation cinema to cater to it, the attempt at an internally defining black film culture remains precarious.

The quest for culturally-identifying black film stylistics and rhetorical principles, often rewarding as spectacle of heroic and artistic achievement, retains a greater importance in the larger context of its struggle between these internal and external pressures. The effort to exert such a stylistic identity and the resistance it encounters unfolds like an allegory of modern American identity, an allegory with the most serious consequences, since it relates to fundamental issues of cultural identification, to the effort of white Americans to define themselves and their culture negatively or oppositionally in relation to blacks and their cultural expression.

On scrutiny, the indeterminacy around concepts of black cinema is readable as intrinsic to its situation. This instability of definitions and theoretical paradigms reflects the political instability of African-American society. The multiple overlaps and loose ends of its parameters are little different than the contradictions quietly overlooked in the case of national definitions like "American cinema." The tension between those who feel empowered to articulate and practice "black cinema" as opposed to those who exploit blackness in films merely rehearses an internal dialectic likely to occur among minority or marginalized groups anywhere. Thus is repeated the circumstance that the target of discrimination must carry the burden of representation. One mark of success for black cinema would be release from the need to place such issues in the foreground. In a humanist reading of history, however, this effort to establish a cultural identity in a hostile media environment may disclose large contributions to evolving possibilities of human and societal development other than the supposedly unpolitical pursuits of "pure" entertainment of Hollywood. But this conclusion can only be reached by understanding the politics of representation as more productive than aesthetics in understanding the form, substance, and significance of cinema as an institution.

Bibliography

Bennett, Tony. 1990. *Outside Literature*. London: Routledge.

Bogle, Donald. 1974. *Toms, Coons, Mulattoes, Mammies and Bucks: An Interpretive History of Blacks in American Films*. New York: Bantam Books.

Bourdieu, Pierre. 1984. *Distinction: A Social Critique of the Judgement of Taste*. Cambridge, MA: Harvard University Press.

Cripps, Thomas. 1978. *Black Film as Genre*. Bloomington: Indiana University Press.

Diawara, Manthia. "Black Spectatorship: Problems of Identification and Resistance." In Manthia Diawara, ed., 1993. *Black American Cinema*. New York: Routledge.

Dickie, George. 1977. "All Aesthetic Attitude Theories Fail: The Myth of the Aesthetic Attitude." In George Dickie, ed., *Aesthetics: A Critical Anthology*. New York: St. Martins Press.

Guerrero, Ed. 1993. *Framing Blackness: The African American Image in Film*. Philadelphia: Temple University Press.

Kappeller, Susan. 1986. *The Pornography of Representation*. Minneapolis: University of Minnesota Press.

Kipnis, Laura. 1986. "Aesthetics and Foreign Policy." *Social Texts* (Fall): 89–98.

Lott, Tommy. 1991. "A No-Theory Theory of Contemporary Black Cinema." *Black American Literature Forum* 25.2 (Summer): 221–36.

Reid, Mark. 1994. *Redefining Black Cinema.* Berkeley: University of California Press.

Taylor, Clyde. 1985. "Decolonizing the Image: New U.S. Black Cinema." In Peter Steven, ed., *Jumpcut: Hollywood, Politics and Counter Cinema.* Toronto: Between the Lines.

——. 1998. *The Mask of Art: Breaking the Aesthetic Contract: Film and Literature.* Bloomington: Indiana University Press.

27

Thanatic Pornography, Interracial Rape, and the Ku Klux Klan

T. DENEAN SHARPLEY-WHITING

With the onslaught of tele-news magazines, television talk shows, and newspaper articles detailing the rise in paramilitary organizations and politically extreme activities across America and abroad, I was not at all surprised one evening to tune my television set into segment devoted to the new Knights of the Ku Klux Klan (KKK) (*Burrell's Transcripts*, 1994). In these racially-divided, heterosexist, and gender discriminating times, the KKK is attempting a revival of sorts, recruiting those whites who are weary of affirmative action, black, women's and gay rights organizations, multiculturalism, big government and, despite broad sweeping claims by Wall Street pundits and market signifiers of American fiscal prosperity, those harboring feelings of economic marginalization and entitlement. Notwithstanding the particularly obvious markers of my being – race and gender – that would lead to a heightened stake in such subject matter, my interest was especially piqued, for I was on my way to Indiana, a state where the Klan held the most political clout and highest level of membership – one half million – of any state in the US in the 1920s; a state that was home to the infamous Klan Grand Dragon and Republican party boss D. C. Stephenson (Moore, 1991: 2). Stephenson, who was primarily responsible for the Klan's dominance in Indiana's state and local political machine, was arrested and convicted of the murder of Madge Oberholzter in a highly sensationalized 1925 murder trial. Stephenson sexually assaulted Oberholzter during an overnight train ride to Chicago; she poisoned herself in the aftermath of the assault, while Stephenson kept her sequestered without medical attention. Her slow and agonizing death was exacerbated by infections from bite wounds inflicted by Stephenson (ibid., 46).

Not since its founding during Reconstruction, revivals in every corner of the nation in the 1920s due to the popularity of Thomas Dixon's novels and D. W. Griffith's *Birth of a Nation*, and in the 1960s due to the Civil Rights Movement, has the fractious organization's national member roster reached the three to six million membership of its 1920s heyday (ibid., 1). The "Kuklos Klan," a neologism of Greek and Scottish origin that means "family circle," was brought into existence by Confederate General Nathan Bedford Forrest in Pulaski, Tennessee; its original covenant was to protect the women and children of dead Confederate soldiers. Feeling aggrieved by the presence in the

South of Northern Carpetbaggers, the Freedman's Bureau, and more specifically, Reconstruction's goals to afford newly freed blacks basic civil rights, the Ku Klux Klan took on its second mission in the words of nineteenth-century radical black feminist Ida B. Wells: "To keep the nigger down."

Renouncing its violent past and capitalizing on the beleaguered mood of the times, a repackaged, postmodern Klan has emerged with propaganda that reads much like the "hot button" issues articulated by mainstream Republican strategists: family values, sexual conservatism, opposition to abortion, anti-immigration legislation, antipathy towards welfare recipients and required drug testing of those recipients, and hostility towards liberal and radically progressive politics and organized labor. The organization's cause célèbre is "white pride" instead of "pure American values" and its primary goal is Political Power for White Christians. Ominous titles such as Grand Dragon and Imperial Wizard have been replaced by the more palatable National Director, President, and Chairman. And membership has even opened to include Catholics and women in key positions in the Knights organizational schema (Davis, 1998). Gone are the pointy hoods and white robes – replaced in these attempts to professionalize the Klan with insignia embroidered military-style uniforms. Indeed, the Knights of the Ku Klux Klan, founded in 1956 in Louisiana, is one of largest Klan organizations with fourteen chapters in places as diverse as Waco, Texas and Farmington, New Hampshire, and boasts the Republican David Duke, as its first National Director.

But for all of the organization's revamping efforts, the exposé revealed unsurprisingly not a new Klan, but a more savvy, media-friendly Klan. What I found most compelling during this roughly ten minutes of news coverage was a "humorous, surprise" card presented with cunning to the reporter and camera crew by the Knights's then National Director Pastor Thomas Robb. The card featured several hooded Klansmen surrounding a white tiered cake. The assembled Klansmen are drawn with shocked expressions – symbolized by wide white eyes piercing through holed robes – as a semi-nude, busty black woman, with an equally shocked expression, pops out of the cake. The grinning Pastor Robb offered something to the effect of "You see they are surprised . . . It's a joke."

In light of the fact that Klan lexicon is and has been historically inundated with catch phrases such as "racial purity," "proper blending of blood . . . pure and undefiled blood," the joke card strikes at the very core of the Klan's anti-interracial sex ideology, in effect providing a lens through which to explore the relationship between humor, pornography, rape, and miscegenation in contemporary Klan culture (MacLean, 1994: 141).

In an organization like the Klan, whose white supremacist political and economic agendas are so closely fused with sex, interracial sex, specifically sex between white women and black men, remains a conundrum to the Klan psyche. This particular sexual formation is perceived as a means through which social leveling and compatibility occur. Hence Klan responses to black male–white female coupling holds an acutely horrific place in US cultural and historical memory. As icons of white barbarity and depravity, images of black male bodies quartered and suspended from trees or burned alive at the stake surrounded by crazed and gleeful mobs instigated to such violent frenzies by the simplest intimation of interracial sex fill the pages of America's past – distant and not so distant. The protection of the purity of white womanhood, which translated into the punishment of offenses against the honor of "red-blooded" white men, was and remains the Ku Klux Klan's calling, their most chivalric duty (ibid., 128). In much of the Klan's journalistic propaganda from the early twentieth century such as the *Searchlight*, the *Fiery Cross*, and the *Kourier*, lamentations of "black men's yearning for . . . the fair women of their masters" or motivational battle cries of "Our PRICELESS white girls would in no time be bearing the children of black men" abound (ibid., 140). Bound up with this chivalric task and germane to an understanding of its urgency was its ability to garner race and class allegiances along a gender hierarchy that relegated white women to the status of private property in need of protection. Historian Nell Irvin Painter writes:

> Sex was the whip that white supremacists used to reinforce white solidarity . . . nearly all white men could claim to hold a certain sort of property in wives, sisters, and daughters. . . . [The threat] of [black] social equality invited all white men to protect their property in women and share in the maintenance of all sorts of power. (cited in McKay, 1992: 249)

White women's release from being the property of one man could only result in their becoming the property of an(O)ther: Black, Jew, Catholic. The "pedestal syndrome" and lynching, cultural affects of the Klan's strident regulation of gender/protection of white womanhood, functioned to shore up white male domination, as white women were constantly forced to confront their subordinate and asexual roles within the family and Klan social world. While white women's bodies represented borders in need of constant policing in the form of random lynching to ward off darker and non-Protestant interlopers, the most common form of coercive sex, that is, (k)landestine race mixing between white men and black women, never presented itself as a point of contention in the anti-miscegenation discourse espoused by Klan politicos, rank and file members, and sympathizers. If white women were deemed private property, black women were imagined, and indeed treated, as communal property to be shared among black and white males.

In fact, against the backdrop of scores of testimonies from black female victims of Klan sexual violence, on the question of the interracial rape of black women, the Klan has been and is virtually silent. This silence must be understood within the frameworks of power and desire – in practice and theory. The practice of raping black females emphasized white male power over women and blacks. Moreover, in practice, the rape of black females posed no threat to white racial hegemony, for the US "one drop rule" effectively racially circumscribed black female reproductive capabilities. That is, black females could only have black babies, while white women could birth white and black children. In theory, Klan silence on the interracial rape of black women relates to desire. As we have briefly discussed, metaphors of sex permeate Klan race ideologies. If black males possess voracious sexual appetites, resulting in their "lusting after fair women," then their black female counterparts were, by extension, hypersexual in order to meet such voracious needs, hence denied the sexual respect accorded their white female counterparts regardless of social class. As Gerda Lerner notes:

> By assuming a different level of sexuality for all Blacks than that of whites and mythifying their greater sexual potency, the black woman could be made to personify

sexual freedom and abandon. A myth was created that all black women were eager for sexual exploits, voluntarily "loose" in their morals. . . . Every black woman was by definition, a slut according to this racist mythology; therefore to assault her and exploit her sexually was not reprehensible and carried with it none of the normal communal sanctions against such behavior. (Lerner, 1972: 163)

The projection of the sexualized narrative onto black females represents desire: an investment of sexual desire into the body as well as a desire that the body be that which the Klan desires: hypersexual, thus different from white women's socially constructed asexuality. Epitomizing hypersexuality, driven by some racially coded instinct, the black female renders herself available, even assailable, yet simultaneously unassailable, sexually invulnerable, in effect, unrapeable, because of her "licentiousness." If the white female must be taken, specifically by the black male, then the black female theoretically never has to be taken, making the possibility of a white-on-black rape negligible. To deem the black female body unrapeable, encourages the practice of rape, while simultaneously never addressing the existence of such a practice all together. Such an acknowledgment of past or present practices of white-on-black sexual violence would contradict – theoretically – the anti-miscegenation discourse critical to the organization's ideological cohesion. Rape, more specifically, the interracial rape of black women, is the unspeakable act in contemporary Klan culture.

In his *Jokes and Their Relation to the Unconscious*, the father of psychoanalysis Sigmund Freud writes:

Joking . . . is an activity which aims at deriving pleasure from mental processes whether intellectual or otherwise. . . . The purpose of jokes can be easily be reviewed. Where a joke is not an aim in itself – that is, where it is not an innocent one – there are only two purposes that it may serve, and these two can themselves be subsumed under a single heading. It is either a hostile joke (serving the purpose of aggressiveness, satire, or defence) or an obscene joke (serving the purpose of exposure). (Freud, 1963: 96–7)

In following this Freudian analysis, at least two ideas emerge with respect to the nature of Klan humor: the joke is bound up with production of pleasure and necessarily power, and the joke card presented is at once hostile, serving the purpose of aggression, and obscene. Subsuming them under a single heading, the card represents a hostile, obscene joke. Obscene, on the one hand, as the body's sexual difference is literally laid bare through the exposing of black breasts, and hostile, on the other, given the history of antiblack racism and sexism of the card's target audience – Klansmen. Hostility is further invoked by the marginalized socioeconomic status of the black female as sex worker. The attendant results are necessarily the reduction of that body to its Klan-imagined functions – sex and the satiation of white male desire. Increments of pleasure are derived at both moments of objectification by the white male viewers: superiority, as the racially-gendered body itself represents degradation and inferiority of black females specifically and blacks generally, and excitement at the thought of an act of aggression on that body. As such, the joke card can be read within the framework of thanatic pornography. Derived from the Greek word, *thanotos*, which means death or a destructive principle, thanatic pornography, according to feminist anti-pornographers, "shows sexual relationships that fall woefully short in terms of full consent, real equality, and emotional identification . . . thanatica encourages men in particular to treat women as mere objects (Tong, 1991: 302). What lurks behind the mask of humor comes then slowly to the fore as we again turn to Freud:

> We shall be obliged to take a special view of certain groups of jokes which seem to be concerned with inferior or powerless people. . . . Are they worthy opponents of the jokes? . . . Is it not a case of [showing] one thing and meaning another? . . . But if a joke admits of this doubt, the reason can only be that it is a façade – in these instances a comic one – in the contemplation of which one person is satiated while another may try to peer behind it. . . . A suspicion may arise, moreover that this façade is intended to dazzle the examining eye and that there is something therefore to conceal . . . thanks to their façade, they are in the position to conceal not only what they have to say, but also the fact that they have something forbidden to say . . . anyone who has allowed the truth to slip out in an unguarded moment is in fact glad to be free of pretence. This is a correct and profound piece of psychological insight. (Freud, 1963: 105–6)

The caricatured black woman is certainly powerless/defenseless and undeniably deemed inferior. Is she thus the worthy opponent of the joke? Is the humorous surprise with its dazzling pornographic cover to the examining eye, a façade used merely as a means through which to show one thing and mean another? And what "something forbidden to say" – truth – slipped out in this "unguarded moment"?

In her essay, "Theory and Practice: Pornography and Rape," feminist anti-pornographer Robin Morgan hypothesizes that "pornography is the theory, rape is the practice" (Morgan, 1980: 134–40). While debates – philosophical, legal, feminist, scientific – rage on about the causal and/or analogous relationship between porn and rape in terms of their fulfillment of the need "to humiliate, control, and degrade women," Morgan's thesis has direct relevance to our understanding of the veritable nature of the humorous surprise card (Soble, 1981: 16–17). Using Freud, we have already determined that the joke was not an innocent one, but hostile and obscene. Using Morgan, we shall now peer behind it into the nature of the Klansmens' satiation.

Scantily-clad female sex workers popping out of human-sized cakes are common scenes at certain sorts of festivities. Like the cake, the women are imagined as sweet dishes for the tasting – visually, that is, and sometimes physically. The representational black female body will equally be served up and tasted; its abundance, visually highlighted by the voluminous breasts and compared to the human-sized tiered cake, provides for everyone. Every Klansmen will get a piece.

Pictures function like speech acts, communicating words, ideas, deeds visually. In decoding Klan visual and verbal signifiers, the sexually-laden, humorous surprise card reveals itself as a façade for violence, group sex, more specifically, gang rape, where the Klansmen will bond over the body of the black female in the satiation of their mutual anti-black racism and anti-black femaleness. Unable to commit interracial rape with the same near legal impunity of its heydays, although sentences for white-on-black rape remain disproportionately lower than black-on-white sexual violence, thanatic porn – the theory – allows for its metaphoric practice by the new Knights of the Ku Klux Klan, as such unspeakable acts are cryptically spoken.

References

Burrell's Transcripts, Summer 1994.

Davis, Daryl. *Klan-destine Relationships: A Black Man's Odyssey in the Ku Klux Klan*. Far Hills, NJ: New Horizon Press, 1998.

Freud, Sigmund. *Jokes and Their Relation to the Unconscious*. Trans. James Strachey. New York: W. W. Norton, 1963.

Lerner, Gerda, ed. *Black Women in White America: A Documentary History*. New York: Vintage, 1972.

MacLean, Nancy. *Behind the Mask of Chivalry: The Making of the Second Ku Klux Klan*. Oxford: Oxford University Press, 1994.

McKay, Nellie. " 'Advancing Luna – and Ida B. Wells': A Struggle Towards Sisterhood" in *Rape and Representation*. Lynn Higgins and Brenda Silver, eds. New York: Columbia University Press, 1992.

Moore, Leonard J. *Citizen Klansmen: The Ku Klux Klan in Indiana, 1921–1928*. Chapel Hill: University of North Carolina Press, 1991.

Morgan, Robin "Theory and Practice: Pornography and Rape," in *Take Back the Night*. Laura Lederer, ed. New York: Morrow, 1980.

Soble, Alan. *Pornography*. New Haven: Yale University Press, 1981.

Tong, Rosemarie. "Women, Pornography, and the Law," in *The Philosophy of Sex: Contemporary Reading*, 2nd edn., Alan Soble, ed. Savage, Lanham, MD: Rowman & Littlefield, 1991.

28

Lynching and Burning Rituals in African-American Literature

TRUDIER HARRIS-LOPEZ

In August of 1997, three white men in Elk Creek, Virginia, poured gasoline on a black man and burned him to death. That summary justice, or lynching, along with the dragging death of James Byrd in June 1998 in Jasper, Texas, are the most recent in almost two hundred years of such violence against persons of African descent upon American soil. For observers who believed the practice had ended in the United States, the 1997 incident brought back thoughts of the 1890s, the peak years for lynching in this country. In 1892, 1893 and 1894, an average of two hundred black people were lynched each year. Indeed, it could be argued that lynching almost became a nationally sanctioned pastime, for even in the years in which most deaths occurred, it was impossible to get national legislation passed to condemn or terminate the practice. The Dyer Anti-Lynching bill, which had several sponsors and was presented in Congress on repeated occasions, was never made into law. How could lynching be outlawed, so the logic ran, when black men were still prone to rape white women? Accusations of rape, which were the most emotional cause of mob-inspired lynchings (though other presumed crimes were more numerous), were frequently the incentive that creative artists used to shape their depictions of lynchings. As creators who drew their subject matter from the substance of the lives of the people about whom they wrote, African-American writers throughout their history in America have depicted occurrences in which black characters have been lynched, burned, shot, and otherwise executed in whatever version of summary justice was operative at the time. They joined with political activists from the mid-nineteenth century through the mid-twentieth century in waging a battle of public opinion against such barbarian acts directed toward African Americans.

"Lynch" and "lynching" have undergone a series of meanings in American history. Both refer to summary justice, that is, regular citizens taking the law into their own hands, which in the early development of the country occurred in the frontier states, but definitions of summary justice varied. Trudier Harris indicates that

> Summary justice in the frontier and border states did not always end in death. It usually consisted of whipping, or tarring and feathering, or being ridden out of town on a rail. To

413

be lynched, or to be a victim of Lynch's law, meant, at that time, that punishment for a crime had been meted out without a court hearing, or by a self-constituted court. To be 'severely lynched' could mean an individual had received one hundred lashes. Or that he had been whipped, then tarred and feathered. A man could be lynched, then hanged. Or lynched, then run out of town. (Harris, 1984: 6)

James E. Cutler, one of the prominent scholars of lynching history, points out that "previous to 1840 the verb lynch was occasionally used to include capital punishment, but the common and general use was to indicate a personal castigation of some sort. 'To lynch' had not then undergone a change in meaning and acquired the sense of 'to put to death.' . . . It was not until a time subsequent to the Civil War that the verb lynch came to carry the idea of putting to death" (Cutler, 1905: 116). In decades following the Civil War, lynching came to include a range of activities that always resulted in death. These included tarring and feathering, burning, shooting, and other tortures in addition to and in combination with "hanging by the neck until dead." Equally noticeable, these atrocious additions were more often than not applied when the victims were African American.

Early advocates of legislation to end lynching combined the literary and the political. Ida B. Wells-Barnett, who wrote newspaper columns as early as the 1880s admonishing black people to leave Memphis, Tennessee – where a grocer friend of hers had been lynched for owning a store that was too profitable for his white competition – also wrote pamphlets itemizing the atrocities. In works such as *Southern Horrors: Lynch Law in all Its Phases* (1892), *A Red Record: Tabulated Statistics and Alleged Causes of Lynchings in the United States, 1892–1893–1894* (1895), and *Mob Rule in Old New Orleans* (1900), she offered disclaimers that lynching occurred as a result of black men raping white women. Instead, she asserted that clandestine, voluntary transracial liaisons between black men and white women ended in lynching when the affairs were discovered and the white women cried rape. She further asserted, as with the Memphis case, that lynchings also occurred for economic reasons. This violent brutality was therefore not only a means of psychological control, but a political device of social control as well.

Lynching was not always targeted to African Americans. Initially, it was the preferred form of punishment on the American frontier. After the Civil War, when it came back into the eastern states, it became a means of keeping newly freed blacks, especially black males, in line. Researchers of lynching history, including Cutler and Robert L. Zangrando, maintain that nearly four thousand black people were lynched between 1880 and 1927. Women made up a small percentage of that number (Cutler asserts that 76 women were lynched). These numbers reflect recorded statistics, which means that it will never be possible to determine the exact number of black persons lynched in America. Many of these executions were ritualized, in that they evolved to contain features that were repeated again and again. A white mob gathered to punish an offender by lynching or burning. Total community sanction – if not direct involvement – characterized the gathering. Frequently, white people brought food and drink to the place of execution, and announcements of the execution often preceded the event. For the famous Henry Smith lynching in Paris, Texas, in 1895, for example, flyers were printed and announcements were made in local newspapers; excursion trains were run to the site of the lynching to accommodate the crowds (Smith was accused of rape and murder). The ritual often included a castration or a gathering of souvenirs (ears, toes, fingers) from the body of the black victim. These occasions were used as rites of initiation for young white children. White women, even pregnant ones, were also at times in attendance at such gatherings.

W. E. B. Du Bois made the recording of lynching statistics a regular part of *The Crisis* magazine agenda. Years later, Zangrando would publish *The NAACP Crusade Against Lynching, 1909–1950* (1980). Walter White, who became Executive Director of the NAACP, was a soldier in the war against lynching before his administrative duty. Blond hair, pale skin, and blue eyes allowed this "white" black man into company of many lynchers in small southern towns and enabled him to publish "I Investigate Lynching," an "insider's" view of the practice. Lynching was constantly before the African-American public, and in the early 1930s a group of white women joined the anti-lynching efforts. Jessie Daniel Ames and other white women organized to protest the assertion by white southern males that lynchings took place to save the honor of white women. Ames and her colleagues pledged to descend upon any town where a black man was accused of white rape and put their bodies in the way of summary justice; they also wrote to sheriffs and governors, met with black organizations, and gathered evidence about the real reasons for lynching.

As much a political construct as a social one, African-American literature took as one of its primary subjects the depictions of lynchings of black people, and lynchings portrayed in the literature were frequently as ritualized as those that occurred historically. William Wells Brown, who published the first novel written by an African American, portrayed a lynching in *Clotel* (1853); the "impudent" black man is executed for striking his master. While Brown passes rather quickly over the incident, his successors would linger over such atrocities. Sutton E. Griggs, writing at the turn of the twentieth century, depicts a lynching in *The Hindered Hand* (1905) in which a black man and his wife are lynched – but not before they have huge pieces of quivering flesh drilled from their bodies in a torturing ritual that goes on for more than three hours. Griggs's contemporary, Paul Laurence Dunbar, who is often thought to be anything but a protest writer, nonetheless focuses on lynching in "The Lynching of Jube Benson" (1900), in which a white narrator, Dr. Melville, relates his involvement in the lynching of the black man accused of raping and murdering the narrator's fiancée. The man is only proven innocent after he is lynched. In commenting on his inability to resist mob violence against his former black friend, Dr. Melville explains: "It's tradition." Charles W. Chesnutt discusses the topic without the ritual overtones in *The Marrow of Tradition* (1901). Chesnutt makes clear the social purpose of lynching rituals when one of his characters asserts: "'Burn the nigger,' reiterated McBane. 'We seem to have the right nigger, but whether we have or not, burn a nigger. It is an assault upon the white race, in the person of old Mrs. Ochiltree, committed by the black race, in the person of some nigger. It would justify the white people in burning *any* nigger. The example would be all the more powerful if we got the wrong one. It would serve notice on the niggers that we shall hold the whole race responsible for the misdeeds of each individual.'" (Chesnutt 1901: 85)

The Harlem Renaissance also brought its share of writers interested in lynching; some published their works in the 1920s, the decade identified with that movement, and others would publish their works later. Jean Toomer, in his experimental work *Cane*

(1923), includes a burning as a direct result of a conflict between a black man and a white man over a black woman. Mild-mannered Langston Hughes, lover of the blues, depicts a black man who is lynched in "Home," a selection from *The Ways of White Folks* (1933). The black man is too well dressed for the local whites, and he dares to talk to his former music teacher, a white woman, on the streets; they heighten this encounter into the mythical rape. James Weldon Johnson uses a lynching/burning in *The Autobiography of An Ex-Colored Man* (1912; 1927) as the incentive for his protagonist to pass from being a light-skinned black man to being a white man; the irony is that, in choosing not to be identified with people who can be lynched, the narrator elects to identify with the lynchers. Claude McKay, in "The Lynching" (1922), focuses on the initiatory quality of that practice, while Johnson in "Brothers – American Drama" (1935) depicts lynching from the point of view of the leader of the mob.

The fact that lynching has captured the imaginations of every generation of African-American writers attests to its psychological and creative impacts. There is almost an unstated agenda that any black person writing in America, especially any black male, would eventually get around to actually depicting a lynching or dealing with the implications of it. In practically every instance, the black male is accused of sexual impropriety with a white woman. Perhaps Richard Wright more than any other writer captured the intensity of these tabooed encounters. From "Between the World and Me," the poem he published in 1935, through "Big Boy Leaves Home" (1938), and ending with *The Long Dream* (1958), the last novel he published before his death, Wright was concerned about the negative consequences of interactions between black men and white women. No explanation can satisfy the white soldier who sees four nude black boys in the presence of his fiancée in "Big Boy Leaves Home." They could not possibly have been swimming; they could only have had raping sexual intentions, so he shoots two of them dead before the other two overpower him. A ritualized lynching occurs with one of the remaining boys, and only Big Boy escapes. For Wright, as for James Baldwin, the psychological dimensions of racial interactions in America are bound up with sexuality; the two cannot be separated.

Baldwin's powerful depiction of this thesis occurs in "Going to Meet the Man" (1965) and is implied in almost all of his work. In the story named, a white sheriff uses the memory of a lynching to overcome his impotence with his wife. As he relives his initiation at the lynching, he is inspired by the implied transfer of sexual potency from the black victim to himself as the black man is castrated. Baldwin's story is perhaps the last in the literature in which excruciatingly graphic details of torture and castration are inclusive features of the lynching/burning rituals, but other writers nonetheless continue to focus on the implications of the consequences of black male/white female interactions (an example preceding Baldwin is Chester Himes's *If He Hollers Let Him Go* [1945]). Where no ritual occurs, or where no physical lynching takes place, there is still an overwhelming sense of the possibility of such an occurrence, as in John Wideman's *The Lynchers* (1974) and David Bradley's *The Chaneysville Incident* (1981).

Male writers in far greater numbers than black women writers have been drawn to depicting lynchings in their works. Historical statistics would certainly suggest that black men have been more vulnerable than black women. Whether it was Wells-Barnett's male friend being too successful as a grocer in Memphis, or Richard

Wright's uncle being lynched for owning a prosperous saloon in Elaine, Arkansas, the possibility of black men losing their lives through lynching was ever constant. The threat of death, combined with the more psychologically wearing fear of castration, perhaps led black male writers to identify with their historical counterparts much more intensely.

While African-American male writers are the primary depictors of graphic lynching scenes, black women writers nonetheless treat the subject. In the first three decades of the twentieth century, several black women playwrights claimed the lynching theme as their special focus, sometimes in plays as short as five or six pages. These include Angelina Grimke's *Rachel* (1916 – full length play), Georgia Douglas Johnson's "A Sunday Morning in the South" (1925) and "Blue-Eyed Black Boy" (1935?), and Mary P. Burrill's "Aftermath" (1928). It is striking in these works that all the lynchings take place before the current action or offstage; that way, these women writers can treat lynching minus the graphic depictions so characteristic of black male writers. More contemporarily, Margaret Walker portrays the lynching of two black women accused of having poisoned their masters in *Jubilee* (1966); the occasion is used as an object lesson for other enslaved persons. Alice Walker uses the discovery of a lynching rope in "The Flowers" (1973) as the moment when a young black girl is initiated into the harsh realities of her segregated world. The threat of lynching pervades Sherley Anne Williams's *Dessa Rose* (1986), and Toni Morrison actually depicts the burning of Sixo, one of the black men on the Sweet Home plantation, in *Beloved* (1987). Where lynching is not portrayed, it is frequently metaphor, as in the case of Gwendolyn Brooks's "The Chicago Defender Sends a Man to Little Rock," in which she declares in the last line, "The loveliest lynchee was our Lord."

With all of these writers, lynching has saturated their works as thoroughly as the process by which they have claimed their space to be as black writers in America. Every one of them has written contemporarily with the occurrence of a lynching or some other form of summary justice. Every one of them has been aware of this constant threat to African-American existence. And every one has recognized that, though lynching could certainly end the lives of its victims, it could not kill the creative imagination determined to bring change to the American landscape.

Select Bibliography

Aptheker, Bettina, ed.: *Lynching and Rape: An Exchange of Views by Jane Addams and Ida B. Wells* (New York: The American Institute for Marxist Studies, Inc., 1977).

Bryant, Jerry H.: *Victims and Heroes: Racial Violence in the African American Novel* (Amherst: University of Massachusetts Press, 1997).

Cutler, James E.: *Lynch-Law: An Investigation into the History of Lynching in the United States* (New York: Longmans, Green and Co., 1905).

Hall, Jacquelyn Dowd: *Revolt Against Chivalry: Jessie Daniel Ames and the Women's Campaign Against Lynching* (New York: Columbia University Press, 1979).

Harris, Trudier: *Exorcising Blackness: Historical and Literary Lynching and Burning Rituals* (Bloomington: Indiana University Press, 1984).

Jordan, Winthrop D.: *White Over Black: American Attitudes Toward the Negro: 1550–1812* (New York: Penguin, 1969).

McGovern, James R.: *Anatomy of a Lynching: The Killing of Claude Neal* (Baton Rouge: Louisiana State University Press, 1982).

NAACP: *Thirty Years of Lynching in the United States, 1889–1918* (New York: Arno Press and *The New York Times*, 1969).

Zangrando, Robert L.: *The NAACP Crusade Against Lynching, 1909–1950* (Philadelphia: Temple University Press, 1980).

29

Rap as Art and Philosophy

RICHARD SHUSTERMAN

Aesthetics

The media hype of crime and violence has fueled rap's fame but obscured its deep philosophical import. The meaning of rap music and its "hip hop culture" extends into many areas of philosophy: ethics, political and social theory, theories of race and gender, multiculturalism and diasporic theory, and, more particularly, African-American philosophy. Rap's deepest philosophical message is the claim that it itself can be practiced as philosophy in reviving philosophy's ancient meaning as a critical, unconventional art of living. But to grasp rap's role as a philosophical life one must first grasp its aesthetics.

Artistic appropriation is the historical source of rap's sound and (despite an increased use of live music) remains central to its aesthetic. Through " sampling" (i.e., selecting and combining parts of prerecorded songs to produce a new soundtrack), the DJ produces the musical background for rap's lyrics. These in turn may praise the DJ's virtuousity in sampling but are most often devoted to boasting of the lyrical, rhyming power and skillfully phrased delivery of the rapper vocalist (called the MC). While the rapper's vaunting self-praise often highlights his (or her) sexual desirability, fame and material success, these signs of status are all presented as secondary to and derivative from the rapper's verbal power. Even the image of hard-core invincibility centers here – mind, mouth, and microphone being typically touted as the rapper's most trusted lethal weapons.

This valorization of language should not surprise us. Sociological and anthropological studies show that verbal virtuosity is highly appreciated in black ghetto life, while the assertion of superior social status through verbal prowess (rather than brute physical strength or violence) remains a deeply entrenched black tradition that goes back to the griots in West Africa and was long sustained in the New World through traditional contestatory verbal play such as "signifying" or "the dozens." Conscious of this heritage, rappers such as Guru proudly claim, "Deeply rooted is my rhymin'/Like ancient African griots/precise is my timin'."

Like its stylized boasting language, rap's other most salient feature – its dominant funky beat – can be traced back to African roots. But rap is unquestionably a diasporic product, emerging only through the disco era of the mid-seventies in the grim ghettos of New York (first the Bronx, then Harlem and Brooklyn) and not releasing its first records until 1979.

While appropriating disco sounds and techniques, rap provocatively transformed them – much as jazz (an earlier and previously scorned) black art of appropriation, had done with the melodies of popular songs. Proudly linking itself to the culturally respected art of jazz, rap sampled frequently from its tracks (and later collaborated with its musicians). But in contrast to jazz appropriations, rap's sampling did not take mere melodies or musical phrases – that is, abstract musical patterns exemplifiable in different performances and thus bearing the ontological status of "type" entities. Instead it snatched concrete sound-events, prerecorded "token" performances of such musical patterns. Thus, unlike jazz, its borrowing and transfiguration did not demand skill in playing musical instruments, but rather in manipulating records and other forms of audio technology.

Building on methods of cutting and blending between records on multiple turntables that disco club DJs had used for making smooth transitions between records to sustain the flow of dance, rap's street DJ's creatively revised these techniques to highlight those parts of records that seemed best for more rhythmic dancing. From the basic technique of cutting between sampled records, rap developed three other formal devices that contribute significantly to its sound and aesthetic: "scratch mixing," "punch phrasing," and simple scratching. The first is simply overlaying or mixing sounds from one record to those of another already playing. Punch phrasing is a refinement of such mixing, where the DJ moves the needle back and forth over a specific phrase of chords or drum slaps of a record so as to add a powerful percussive effect to the sound of the other record playing all the while on the other turntable. The third device is very rapid back and forth scratching of the record, too fast for the recorded music to be recognized but productive of a dramatic scratching sound which has its own intense musical quality and crazed beat. All three techniques are skillfully displayed in the rap classic "The Adventures of Grandmaster Flash on the Wheels of Steel."

Rap is also rich in appropriated content: popular and classical music, TV theme songs and advertising jingles, electronic music of arcade games. It even uses non-musical content: police sirens, gunshots, baby-cries, bits of media news reports, fragments of political speeches, and snatches of TV or movie dialogues. Though sometimes concealing (for fear of competition) the exact records they sampled, rap DJs never hid the fact that they were working from prerecorded sounds rather than composing their own original music. On the contrary, they openly celebrated their sampling method. What is the aesthetic significance of this proud art of appropriation?

First it challenges the traditional ideal of unique originality that long enslaved art. Though artists have always borrowed from each other's works, the romantic ideology of genius obscured this fact, posing a sharp distinction between original creation and derivative borrowing. By creatively deploying and thematizing its appropriation, rap shows that borrowing and creation are not at all incompatible. Originality thus loses its absolute "originary" status and is more freely reconceived to include the transfigurative remaking of the old; so creative energy can be liberated to play with familiar creations without fear of denying its own artistry by not producing a totally original work.

420

Rap's sampling also questions old ideals of artistic unity. Since Aristotle, the artwork was seen as an organic whole so perfectly unified that any tampering with its parts would aesthetically destroy it. Later ideologies of romanticism and "art for art's sake" reinforced the notion that artworks are transcendent, sacred ends in themselves, whose integrity must never be violated. Opposing this rigidity, rap's cutting and sampling offers the pluralistic pleasures of dismantling old works to create new ones that may achieve their own fragile unity.

But rap does this without the pretense that its own works are ever inviolable, that the artistic process is ever final, that there is ever a product which should be so fetishized as to prohibit appropriative transfiguration. Instead, rap's sampling implies that an artwork's integrity as object should never outweigh the possibilities for continuing creation through that object's use. Appropriating and remixing its favorite tracks, rap suggests the message that art is more essentially process than finished product – an important message in our culture whose drive to commodify artistic expression is so strong that rap itself is victimized by it even while protesting it.

In defying the fetishized integrity of artworks, rap also challenges the traditional demands for monumental permanence and universality – that an artwork should be forever and for everyone. Rap highlights the artwork's temporality not only by its sampling and remixing, but by thematizing the work's temporal context in the self-referential dating of its lyrics. Declarations of date (like KRS-One's "Fresh for '88, you suckers!", "Fresh for '89, you suckers!", "Fresh for 1995, you suckers!") suggest the likelihood of datedness in future years. But the transience of a work's "freshness" or power does not preclude the reality of its value; no more than the ephemeral freshness of cream renders its sweet taste unreal.

Nor does the temporality of rap's works preclude the genre's survival, just as the mortality of each individual does not mean the death of our species. Transfigurative sampling not only supersedes old works with new creations but also dialectically recalls and so preserves the sampled works in lived experience. Through the rich intertextuality thereby produced, rap can be seen not as a mere junk-pile of throw-away sounds but as an aural museum, one particularly devoted to the works of its own tradition.

Rap thematizes contextualities of place and public as well as time. Neighborhood identity has always been important to rap's street sound, not only engendering stylistic differences in music and lyrics, but contributing to aggressive duelling between west and east coast rappers that sometimes seemed to threaten hip-hop solidarity. Rap's impressive international success depends on neither a standard sound nor a monolithic message (the target issues, cultural allusions, and even musical mix often differ sharply in different nations); it instead bespeaks the imbrications and affinities of today's cosmopolitan diasporic cultures, as well as the fruitful flexibility of rap's form. By highlighting changing contextuality, rap underscores the pragmatist point that art's meaning and value are defined more by contextual functioning than by the fixed art object.

Knowledge and Praxis

As rap's eclectic sampling questions the traditional ideals of aesthetic purity and integrity, so its militant insistence on politics challenges the modern dogma of aesthetic autonomy. In modernity's division of cultural spheres, art was distinguished from science as not being truly concerned with knowledge, since its aesthetic judgment was essentially subjective. It was also sharply differentiated from the practical activity of ethics and politics, which involved real interests and appetitive will. Instead, art was consigned to a disinterested, imaginative realm that Schiller described as the realm of play and semblance and that logical positivism later dismissed as mere emotion.

More than any other aesthetic form today, rap forcefully demonstrates art's important political and ethical dimensions. Through its anti-establishment message and public, rap quickly earned the acute critical attention of institutions not typically associated with art's free realm of semblance. Police and law courts have always been busy with its censorship and surveillance. Even Presidents have condemned rap for fomenting divisive racial enmity and anti-American thinking while destroying the nation's social fabric through the celebration of crime and gangster values.

Rap's power for praxis is thus recognized, but only by demonizing it as the incarnation and cause of all ghetto crime. This demonization is achieved by blindly conflating *all* rap with the much publicized genre of "gangsta rap," whose notorious works are often not only morally detestable (glorifying greed, sexism, and violent crime) but also brutishly unimaginative and boringly preprogrammed. Though obviously false (there being not only non-gangsta rap but also militantly *anti*-gansta rap), the gangsta-rap conflation is increasingly reinforced by serving a most potent constellation of political and economic interests.

Making rap the general scapegoat for black criminality, the gangsta image provides an effective symbolic target that can unite very different political groups of often conflicting agendas, while at the same time obscuring the real socioeconomic and political causes of ghetto poverty and violence. Moreover, since this image panders (in both ghetto and suburb) to juvenile instincts of rebellion through vicarious criminality, the gangster–rap connection becomes economically most lucrative. Experience shows that public condemnations and threats of censorship give the greatest marketing hype, while the news media – always interested in facile sensationalism – likewise prefer to focus on rap's flashy criminal image. Ignored are its everyday positive uses: developing linguistic skills, communicating cultural tradition and history while raising political consciousness and ethnic pride, offering a symbolic yet powerfully audible form of protest, providing fruitful new means of employment and wealth for the ghetto community.

My position of "pragmatic meliorism" recognizes rap's flaws and consequent need for improvement, but equally argues that rap deserves meliorative care because of its proved potential for aesthetic merit while serving worthy praxis. Philosophers can help rap develop its better aspects by affirming one of rap's founding and still most central genres – "knowledge rap" or "message rap." Identifying itself with philosophy, this genre is self-consciously devoted to the integration of art with the pursuit of knowledge in the aim of ethical growth and sociopolitical emancipation. Ever since Grandmaster Flash's early hits "The Message" and "Message II (Survival)," knowledge rappers have been insisting that their role as artists and poets is inseparable from their philosophical function as inquirers of reality and teachers of truth, particularly those aspects of reality and truth which get neglected or distorted by establishment history books, institutional religion, and contemporary news coverage.

KRS-One (whose moniker stands for "Knowledge Reigns Supreme Over Nearly Everyone) presents himself, for example, not simply as "a teacher and artist, startin' new concepts at their hardest," but preeminently as a *philosopher*, a critical purveyor of truth in such raps as "My Philosophy," "R. E. A. L. I. T. Y," and "The Truth." Seeing his poetic-musical art as philosophy, he even signs his albums "KRS-One Metaphysician" and advocates (both on and off vinyl) a naturalistic, historicist metaphysics to support the radically militant critical humanism of his ethics and politics. In "The Real Holy Place," he raps that the sacred focus of progressive faith should not be a supernatural god, but the spiritual potential of the embodied mind that can question accepted dogmas and so change reality. "The real holy place is mental" yet embodied; for reality is "mental–physical, metaphysical," though not divisively dualistic or foundationally fixed or extrahistorical.

On this basis of historicist naturalism with its faith in critical intelligence, KRS-One develops a toughly critical humanism that rejects the supernatural opiates and fixities of traditional religions. Since reality is largely made and unmade through the struggles of human history, KRS-One urges a combination of critical revisionist history and revolutionary practice. In contrast to quiescent Christianity ("no answers, . . . [but] hand clappers and whole lot of dancers"), Christ's role as a revolutionary teacher is stressed and linked to KRS-One's own self-image as teacher of progressive revolution. Since establishment media and education likewise breed uncritical quiesence, they too are frequently targeted for critique. In contrast to the media's whitewashing lies, stereotypes, and escapist entertainment, he proudly claims of himself and his rap crew (BDP): "I'm tryin' not to escape, but hit the problem head on/By bringin' out the truth in a song/ . . . BDP will teach reality/No beatin around the bush, straight up/Just like the 'P' is free."

Of course, the realities and truths that rap reveals are less the transcendental, eternal verities of traditional philosophy than the mutable but coercive facts of the material, sociohistorical world. Yet this emphasis on the temporally changing and malleable nature of the real (reflected in rap's frequent time-tags and its popular idiom of knowing "what time it is") conveys a very tenable metaphysical position defended by pragmatists like James and Dewey. Rap philosophers continue the pragmatist tradition not merely in their metaphysics of material, historical flux, but in their noncompartmentalized aesthetics that highlight cognitive function and embodied process in the pursuit of productive, practical reform. Defining "rap music as a revolutionary tool in changing the structure of racist America," knowledge rappers like KRS-One not only link aesthetics with politics but blend monistic metaphysics with an ethical art of living whose ultimate aim is health and peace: "Metaphysics, the science of life/And how to live, free from strife. /Walk with ease and no disease. /Understand that I am the breeze and the trees, oceans and seas."

Identifying himself as a "knowledge seeker" and "soldier of truth [to] protect the lives of our youth," New York rapper Guru advocates a "New Reality Style," "a mind revolution" aimed not simply at facing the problematic new realities already in place but more importantly at creating new positive realities: "a mind revolution [for] redefining our purpose, organizing and utilizing our resources to gain focus so that we can produce positive change."

Knowledge rap serves a variety of messages and practical ends. Many are explicitly devoted to raising African-American political consciousness and cultural pride, often through revisionary historical narratives ranging from biblical history, to the history of African-American music, to the Afrocentric genealogy of philosophy itself (as in KRS-One's "The Blackman's in Effect": "So people that believe in Greek philosophy/ Know your facts; Egypt was a monopoly/Greeks had learned from Egyptian masters"). Other songs inculcate values of family life, hard work, and neighborly respect, depicting ideals of sensitive caring and stability while critiquing the stereotype ghetto life of drugs, violence, promiscuity, and sexism celebrated by gangsta rap. We find this not only in soft, commercial "candy-rap" like Arrested Development, but in positive hardcore rappers like KRS-One and Guru. An entire subgenre of knowledge rap aims at ending violence in hip hop and the wider black community; it can be traced from KRS-One's 1988 hit "Stop the Violence" through to Guru's (1995) "Watch What You Say" and Wu-Tang Clan's "Wu-Revolution" (1997).

Even rap with a criminally violent style often aims at educating its public toward values quite remote from crime, precisely by luridly depicting its dangers. Functioning as street-smart moral fables, such songs offer cautionary narratives and practical advice on the problematic seductions of crime, drugs, sex, and money. Unfortunately, vivid depiction of such seductions can reinforce them. Hence knowledge rappers like Guru insist on a onesidedly clear message advocating the positivities of self-disciplined self-improvement and respect for others while denouncing the evils of violence, greed, and despair. "So many misconceptions/ So many evil deceptions/ I come to bring direction./ For I am the Life Saver."

Rap as a Philosophical Life

Knowledge rap's most crucial message is that the needed resources for self-improvement and better living can be found in the proper practice of rap itself. So urgent is this message that its argument can be literally read off Guru's *Jazzmatazz II* song titles. Rap here is a means of "Looking Through the Darkness," "Defining Purpose," and "Maintaining Focus," thus serving as a "Medicine," "Revelation," and "Lifesaver" for "Lost Souls," and as the best "Choice of Weapons" for "Living in This World." Rap does more than "educate and elevate your mind." By "turning the anger and frustration straight into energy" (of poetry, music, and dance) it helps "maintain self-control" and "channel rage," providing joyful "stress-relief [through] the hip hop beats" while communicating the therapeutic light of this very message: "I rock from East New York to the suburbs./ The light keeper, knowledge seeker,/ I switch the stress that's on my mind into the voice that rocks your speaker."

Rap is thus urged as a superior, symbolic form of combat that can overcome not only criminal violence, but also the poverty that spawns it. Pragmatically alive to capitalist reality, rappers have always recognized the economic power of their art, once again portrayed as a better, poetic alternative to crime (the idea aptly captured in the very title of Ice-T's early "Rhyme Pays"). But money, though undeniably central and thematized, is only a tool in knowledge rap's fuller quest for improved existence. (Guru: "The game is money, but what about inner wealth/ The mental, the spiritual, and physical health?"; KRS-One: "It's not about a salary, it's all about reality").

More than a means of livelihood, rap recommends itself as a complete art of living, a comprehensive way of life designated more globally by the term "hip hop culture" and including not only rap music but break-dancing, graffiti, and a distinctive style of dress, speech, gesture, etc. that is as easily recognizable as misunderstood. This pragmatic message makes rap particularly attractive to youth who, malcontent with the establishment ethos, are seeking an alternative cultural style to help them shape their lives aesthetically. Rap's rich diversity allows the individual exercise of creative taste within a distinctive taste-community. That hip hop's distinctive style requires neither much cash nor an Ivy-league diploma makes it still more appealing, while proving that aesthetic self-stylization is not a project confined to an economic or intellectual elite. For its deepest devotees, rap thus becomes an all absorbing, comprehensive art of life, in the vernacular – *a philosophy*.

Stoicism, Epicureanism, and Cynicism were such philosophies in the ancient world, winning their followers less for their technical doctrines of metaphysics and logic than for the different styles of living they prescribed and practiced. Such lived philosophies covered not only matters of mind, but bodily practice, often specifying particular modes of exercise, diet, or even dress that might improve mental and moral functioning. The case is similar in Asian traditions. Considered in this context, KRS-One's advocacy of style and vegetarianism in "My Philosophy" is not an outrageous irrelevance but a reminder of philosophical forms disenfranchised by Western modernity but still deeply demanded by the many who are seeking the best, most attractive way to live.

In such philosophies, instruction was as much by the teacher's lived example as by words of formulated doctrine. Hence knowledge rap's insistence on the actual practice of its theory, the importance of being a good "role model" by living up to a positive musical message. "Quand je dis, je fais, pratique ma théorie" raps France's premier rapper MC Solaar; for, as Wu-Tang Clan insists, the MC should "be livin' proof, to kick the truth, to the young black youth." Recognizing his responsibility as exemplar ("eyes are watchin' me, every single-step I take"), Guru thematizes the need for self-mastery not only in eschewing crime but with regard to sexual temptations and the exploitation of groupies ("Young Ladies"). Likewise linking sexual self-control with the quest for self-perfection through self-knowledges, KRS-One concludes his 1995 album not only with the refrain "Monagamy, nothing else, but health wealth, and knowledge of myself," but by an exemplary act of tribute to his long-time wife, surrendering to her the mike so she can have the last words on the album.

Ameliorative self-mastery for better living is indeed what knowledge rappers want most to be imitated – not the mimicking of their clothes or the worship of their persons. "Please don't worship Sister Souljah," she herself raps, "Take what is useful and prove your belief/ In the ideas and values through your own deeds." The goal is not conformist copying but what MC Solaar (calls "la recherche de la perfection" through one's "sens critique." Confirming rap's commitment to the ancient philosophical message of disciplined care for the self, Guru urges: "Realize that the key is for each to master his own destiny/Deal with reality and keep a tight focus/Cause there's a lot we gotta cope with."

Conquering one's own negativity is thus the first step to conquering it in the world. Though clearly committed to active political engagement, rap philosophers reformulate the classic argument traceable from Socrates through Cynicism and Stoicism to the self-perfectionism of Emerson, Wittgenstein, and the later Foucault: that the transformational perfection of society can be achieved only (though not exclusively) through the ameliorative self-mastery of its individual constitutive members. As New York rapper Jeru the Damaja argues, the social body like the human organism is a collective whose individual parts must take care to perform their own special functions: "That's why each person is supposed to get with their own individual self. Because the way you destroy any negativity in the world is to destroy it first within yourself" (Dawsey 1994, 58).

In treating rap as philosophy, I have often been charged with falsely imposing my own philosophical meanings on rap's alleged mindless content. Do rappers themselves see their art as a comprehensive life-philosophy of stylization? Guru's "Hip Hop as a Way of Life" (rhythmically delivered in unrhymed earnestness over a jazz-inspired background) is an unequivocally clear affirmation.

> Yo, hip hop is a way of life. It ain't a fad; it ain't a trend. Not for those who are true to it. It's reflected in our style, in our walk, and in our stance, in our dress and in our attitudes. Hip hop has a history, an origin, and a set of principles, including rules and regulations that a lot of kids overlook nowadays. . . .
>
> Over the years, hip hop has evolved to represent what is happening now, the reality of street life. Rap is the oral expression of this, the tool, the literature. Hip hop is the life style, the philosophy, even the religion, if I may. . . . Although the music and life style is now propagandized by the media, and is now exploited by business, it will still remain for some of us as the raw essence of life. Peace.

Although long stifled by modernity's academic ideal of philosophy as impersonal theory, the notion of philosophy as an embodied, comprehensive art of living retains a popular power, since serving an undeniable existential need. In trying to revive this venerable practice, rap challenges not only modernity's aesthetics but its very conception of philosophy.

Modernity's purism of aesthetic autonomy had another limiting side. Just as the aesthetic was distinguished from the more rational realms of knowledge and action, it was also sharply separated from the more sensate and appetitive gratifications of embodied human nature – aesthetic pleasure instead was confined to distanced, disinterested contemplation of formal properties. Repudiating such purity, rappers want to be appreciated through energetic movement and impassioned dance, not mere immobile, dispassionate contemplation. Queen Latifah commands her listeners, "I order you to dance for me." For, as Ice-T explains, the rapper "won't be happy till the dancers are wet with sweat, "out of control" and wildly "possessed" by the beat, as indeed the captivating rapper should himself be possessed so as to rock his audience with his God-given gift to rhyme.

Is this emphasis on passionate movement inconsistent with rap's cognitive role as philosophy? If we are bodily possessed by the beat, how can we process the often subtle, complex messages of rap's texts? Pragmatism provides at least two kinds of answers. The first challenges the whole mind/body opposition on which the apparent inconsistency rests. Bodily movement and impassioned feeling are not the enemies of cognition but often necessary aids to it. Cognition includes more than what is conveyed by propositional content; and non-propositional forms of cognition can often create the context necessary for properly understanding certain claims of propositional knowledge. Dancing and thinking are simply not incompatible activities.

Contradictions

More troubling contradictions haunt hip hop. Most striking are its equivocal take on violence (as often celebrated in gangsta rap as denounced in its "Stop the Violence" tradition) and its concern for liberation yet its frequent use of a viciously sexist "pimpin' style." Rap's view of the ghetto is equally conflicted, affirming its rugged, hard-knocks training and artistic inspiration, while fiercely depicting its miserable woes. Though proud of its core identity as ghetto music, rap also aims its "penetration to the heart of the nation" (Ice-T) so as "to teach the bourgeois" (Public Enemy). There is, moreover, rap's ambivalent relation toward technology and the mass-media (which it both condemns and supports), as well as a similarly divided attitude toward capitalist wealth and commercialism. Rappers often extol their own achievement of consumerist luxury while simultaneously condemning its uncritical quest as dangerously wrong for their ghetto audience with which they identify. In the same way, underground rappers at once denigrate commercialism as an artistic and political sell-out, but nonetheless celebrate their own commercial success, often regarding it as indicative of their artistic power.

Such contradictions are not merely a product of rap's rich plurality of styles. They are expressive of more fundamental contradictions in the sociocultural fields of ghetto life (where one must fight for peace) and so-called noncommercial art that must be somehow commercially effective in order to survive. In African-American culture, there is surely a connection between independent expression and economic achievement that would impel even noncommercial rappers to tout their commercial success and property. As slaves were converted from free men to property, their way to regain independence was to achieve sufficient property of their own in order to buy their manumission (as in the liberation narrative of Frederick Douglass). Having long been denied a voice because they were property, African-Americans could reasonably conclude that only the economic power of property can ensure full expression. For underground rappers, then, commercial success and luxury trappings may function as a symbol of economic independence that enables free artistic and political expression, and that is conversely further enabled by such expression.

One useful strategy for handling contradictions is what Nelson Goodman calls "judicious vacillation." Even "the physicist flits back and forth between a world of waves and a world of particles as suits his purpose" (Goodman 1984, 32). In the same way, the underground rapper will vacillate between talk of his ghetto hunger and of his Gucci luxury, condemnation of his media censorship and celebration of his media success – in different contexts and for different purposes of legitimation. Sometimes he deploys the gangsta and pimpin' styles so as to convince his listeners that he knows the hardcore ghetto realities of sex, violence, and drugs. Other times, to highlight hip hop's Utopian message, he instead adopts the style of philosopher of peace. But even here a violent tone can suddenly return to insist that ideals of peace and love are not mere

427

products of weakness but instead demand tough strength and struggle. The MC and rap fan can likewise vacillate between intellectual scrutiny of the lyrics and wild dancing to the beat – often a complex message in its own right.

The key in all such cases is to preserve enough coherence between contextual points of view so that their plurality enriches rather than annuls each other, enabling and not merely confusing the person who alternatively adopts them. Such practical coherence, implied in the very notion of *judicious* vacillation, does not entail the existence of a supercontext where all conflicting contexts are made to cohere through resolution of all their tensions. Nor does the notion of judicious vacillation imply that a general formula for coherent combination can be articulated in advance. Achieving coherence becomes a challenging part of that difficult genre of aesthetic living which aims at pushing the values of pluralistic richness and complexity toward the very limits of unity. Though philosophical ideals of simple living once held sway, the life of hectic complexity today seems more attractive (or more necessary), not only to rap's audience in the ghettos but also to wealthier suburbanites, cosmopolitans, and even academic philosophers.

Bibliography

Baker, Houston A.: *Black Studies, Rap, and the Academy* (Chicago: Chicago University press, 1993).

Brenan, Tim: "Off the Gangsta Tip: A Rap Appreciaton, or Forgetting About Los Angeles," *Critical Inquiry*, 20 (1994), 663–93.

Dawsey, K. M., "It's all in the Mind: Philosophies of Jeru the Damaja," *The Source*, September, 1994, 58.

Decker, Jeffrey, "The State of Rap: Time and Place in Hip Hop Nationalism," in *Microphone Fiends; Youth Music and Youth Culture*, eds. Andrew Ross and Tricia Rose (New York: Routledge, 1994), 99–121.

Gates, Henry Louis, Jr.: *The Signifying Monkey: A Theory of African-American Literary Criticism* (New York: Oxford University Press, 1988).

Goodman, Nelson: *Of Mind and Other Matters* (Cambridge, MA: Harvard University Press, 1984).

Kochman, Thomas (ed.), *Rappin' and Stylin' Out* (Urbana: University of Illinois Press, 1972).

Lipscomb, Michael.: "Can the Teacher Be Taught?," *Transition*, 57 (1993), 168–9.

Perkins, Eric, ed.: *Droppin' Science: Critical Essays on Rap Music and Hip-Hop Culture* (Philadelphia: Temple University Press, 1995).

Rose, Tricia.: *Black Noise: Rap Music and Black Culture in Contemporary America* (Hanover: Wesleyan University Press, 1994).

Rose, Tricia and Ross, Andrew, eds.: *Microphone Fiends: Youth Music and Youth Culture* (Routledge: New York, 1994).

Shusterman, Richard. "The Fine Art of Rap," in *Pragmatist Aesthetics: Living Beauty, Rethinking Art* (Oxford: Blackwell, 1992). Precise references for all quotations whose sources do not appear in the body of the article can be found in this book or in the entry *Practicing Philosophy*.

——. "Rap Remix: Pragmatism, Postmodernism, and Other Issues in the House," *Critical Inquiry*, 22 (1995), 150–8.

——. "Art in Action, Art Infraction: Goodman, Rap, Pragmatism (New Reality Mix)," in *Practicing Philosophy: Pragmatism and the Philosophical Life* (New York: Routledge, 1997).

——. "Pragmatism, Art, and Violence: The Case of Rap," in T. Yamamoto (ed.), *Philosophical Designs for a Sociocultural Transformation* (Boulder: Rowman Littlefield, 1998), 667–74.

Toop, David. *Rap Attack 2: African Rap to Global Hip Hop* (London: Serpent's Tail, 1991).

30

Microphone Commandos:
Rap Music and Political Ideology

BILL E. LAWSON

Philosopher Tommy Lott in his insightful discussion of urban youth culture claims:

> As a dominant influence on black urban youth, rap music articulates the perspective of a black *lumpen proletariat*. For this reason, class lines have been drawn around it within the black community. This "underclass" status of rap, however tends to conceal the fact that it has certain social and political dimensions that suggest something other than pathology is occurring in black youth culture. (Lott, 1992: 79.)

According to Lott, because of the media portrayal of rap music, rap is often viewed by middle-class blacks and whites as noise emanating from the out-of-control-young-blacks, most often males. Lott thinks that there is an important element of resistance in rap music. That is, black youths realize that they are trapped under American apartheid and have used rap as a way to resist the racial assault on their physical and mental well-being in particular and on the black community in general. Lott sees this use of rap as giving rap music importance as a reflection of a culture of resistance. Lott, of course, is not the only person who has pointed out this element in rap and hip-hop culture. Such writers as Houston Baker, Tricia Rose and Theresa A. Martinez have articulated this view of rap. I agree with these writers. But what I want to argue here is that rap music to those who listen closely can be heard as challenging deeper and more basic assumptions about the political order. Rap music on this reading represents a fundamental challenge to our understanding of liberal democratic political ideology.

In rap music we hear a call for blacks to reassess their understanding of what it means to be an American citizen. Rap music calls in to question the nature of the political relationship between blacks and the state. By questioning the fundamental relationship between the state and blacks, rap music has a definite political perspective and one that political theorists, urban social workers, and urban specialists need to understand and assess if programs to reach urban youths are to be successful.

What I want to explore here is a particular view of the relationship between African Americans and the United States as articulated in rap music. I am, of course, not claiming that all rap music has an overtly political content. I do, however, think that there is a political perspective stated in much of the music.

I want to use as an ideological backdrop the concept of the social contract (Lawson, 1990). The view that the relationship between citizen and state is one of a contract has a long history in American political thought. It is my contention that certain rap songs and the stance rappers take suggests that the social contract, if any ever existed, between blacks and the United States has been broken.

The Social Contract

The book that has had the greatest impact on American political theory is John Locke's *Second Treatise of Government* (Locke, 1952). Locke argues that governments are established to protect the property rights of individuals, including their personal well-being. It is clear that the one of the most important benefits that the state can provide is protection. This protection can either be from outside invaders or from unsavory characters within the state, that is, those individuals who want to infringe on property rights by stealing, defrauding, or destroying property.

It was clear, according to Locke, that not all men were equally suited to press their property claims against others. Some civil mechanism was needed to adjudicate property claims. Thus, free, equal, and autonomous individuals come together to form a compact in which they agreed to give up to the state certain rights they naturally possess. These rights include the right to be their own judge, jury, and executioner. By freely consenting to join with others in civil society, each is thought to be politically obligated to obey the dictates of the state.

The state is to ensure protection of their property, which includes their lives, by providing known laws, impartial judges, and swift and certain punishment for property violations. Individuals should then be able to live peaceful and secure lives with the knowledge that their property rights are respected and protected. In this manner their chances of a life free of the inconveniences of the state of nature are ensured.

The Idea of Citizenship

These free autonomous beings are citizens in the full sense of the word. They identify with the state and see the state as the focal point of their social existence. It is here that rap music challenges our understanding of the meaning of citizenship. Generally, citizenship is used in a very broad sense to specify the status of an individual in an organized state. The status of citizen provides us with a guide for the rights and responsibilities of the individual in an organized state. I cannot deal fully with the perplexing issue of citizenship in this talk. Still, I believe that it is possible to give a definition of citizenship which will help clarify questions about how urban youth view the attempts by America's power elites to deny full citizenship status to blacks.

It is generally thought that citizenship is that status of being a member of a state, native or naturalized, who has responsibilities to the government of the state and who

430

is entitled to certain protection and rights within it. There are two important components of citizenship – the social and the political/legal. The social component of citizenship suggests that one is a member of a specific political community. Citizenship
encompasses a feeling of being a vital part of the state; it gives an individual a social
reference point to gauge his place in world history, world geography and world society.
The individual feels that his actions are part of the history and development of the state.
Citizenship is therefore a crucial aspect of an individual's identity. In rap music, we find
challenges to our understanding of blacks as full citizens. These challenges can be seen
in songs that subscribe to the proposition that blacks are Africans first and foremost.
We find this view articulated in the music of groups such as XCLAN and Brand
Nubians.

The second aspect of citizenship concerns the legal rights and political responsibilities that accrue to all members of a society. There may be members of the state whose
status may be somewhat ambiguous, e.g., aliens. Still, it is usually the case that each
state defines these rights and responsibilities in terms of its own system of beliefs and
values. No attempt has been made to specify all the rights and responsibilities of
American citizenship, but legislation and court decisions over the years provide a fairly
clear idea of what is involved. As early as 1824 Justice Bushrod Washington in the case
of *Corfield vs. Coryell* identified some of the rights of citizenship as:

> protection by the government; enjoyment of life and liberty; the right to acquire and
> possess property; the right of a citizen of one state to pass through or reside in other states
> for purpose of trade or profession; protection by writ of habeas corpus; the right to insti-
> tute and maintain court actions; exemption from higher taxes than are paid by other citi-
> zens of the state; the elective franchise, as regulated by the laws of the particular state in
> which it is exercised. (Morris, 1975: 71)

These are still considered to be among the basic elements of citizenship in the United
States. Yet, in rap music we find the claims that many of these basic rights are still
denied to African Americans. Blacks accordingly are politically oppressed.

It is the contention of political rappers that political oppression lessens the political
obligations of African Americans to the state. Racial and political oppression undermines the status of blacks as citizens of the state. Some rappers have claimed that the
oppression of blacks is total oppression and hence there is no question of obligation.
Blacks according to this position are still in slavery; the slave has no obligation to the
body politic of his master, for the slave is not even recognized as a citizen.

Although blacks were made citizens by the post-Civil War amendments, they have
been denied two of the most precious benefits of state membership, economic and
physical protection. Many urban youths view the United States government as working
against blacks when it comes to economic advancement in America.

The lack of economic protection constitutes a major charge against the United
States. Discrimination in the economic sphere affects the amount of income one can
earn and affects one's ability to secure the necessities of life. On his first solo album, the
rapper Tupac noted that blacks are "trapped," living in neighborhoods with few job
prospects and an oppressive police army watching them. Rappers understand how one's

income will to a large measure determine how one is treated in other spheres of the society, i.e., under the law, in the political arena, and in social relations. The rap group Naughty by Nature in "Everything is Gonna be All-right" notes that people want black youth to be positive, questions whether they can be positive when they view the economic system as stacked against them.

Closely related to economic discrimination is discrimination in education, since education is a means of economic advancement, whether directly through vocational courses or indirectly through academic courses. It is also argued that the educational systems has mis-educated blacks about their place in history and thus has undermined the self-respect that would come from such knowledge.

Because one's economic position is so basic to the amount of political power one may have, economic discrimination has often been thought to be an important obstacle created by racism. Lack of power to affect social policy can make one feel devalued. Economic discrimination lessens a group's access to the means of swaying public policy. For many young urban dwellers, rap has become their way to get their message across. In this regard, rap music serves a political function and is the best method to get news and information to other urban communities. The one message that comes across very clearly is that black urban neighborhoods are under siege. The attack is directed by whites in power and the goal is to destroy the black race. As the rapper Gangstar notes, the condition of blacks in America is not an accident, there is a white conspiracy.

The Police as Protectors

As noted, one of the basic reasons for joining the state, in social contract theory, is protection. Citizens must receive physical protection. It is the view of many rappers that the racist behavior of law enforcement officers clearly shows how the state has failed to protect blacks. Particularly distressing is the relationship between the police and the black community. In many urban areas, the residents believe that the efforts of the police are ineffective in protecting them from crime. These citizens complain that the police come late or not at all to calls for assistance. Many urban residents think that they are victims twice. First, they have to contend with crime in their communities, and then they have to contend with lack of protection from the state coupled with police brutality when they try to protect themselves.

In Los Angeles, for example, the Nation of Islam has been active in the battle against drugs in black communities. These individuals who patrol communities unarmed, have had run-ins with the police. One such account of an altercation between thirteen young Muslims and twenty-four Los Angeles police officers is indicative of the problem:

> Although accounts differ, Nation of Islam spokespersons say the Muslims objected to being ordered to assume a prone position on the ground. "Why do you want us to bow down to you – bow in the streets, face down, as though you were God?" a Farrakhan aide, Khallid Muhammad, said later. "You don't make the white folks of Beverly Hills bow down. . . . We bow down to God and God alone." All 13 of the Muslims were charged in the episode, and

the controversy fueled mounting tensions in predominantly black south-central Los Angeles over what many residents see as harassment and the overuse of force by city policy and sheriff's deputies. (Newsweek, 1990: 25)

Here it is important to note that the actions of the state are crucial in residents' decisions as to whether their own acts of protection are supplemental, or are essential because the government has abrogated its role as protector of the lives and property of African Americans.

The residents of this community believed they were justified in having patrols. The political powers in many cities believe that the patrols were unjustified, not unnecessary, but unjustified. When the state fails to allow citizens to perform those actions that they believe are within the legal parameters of the law to protect themselves, confidence that the state takes the welfare of these citizens seriously is eroded. KRS-One asks about the role of the police: "Who protects us from you?"

One of the fundamental reasons for continued allegiance to a government is the knowledge that the government can and will protect the individual more effectively than he could in the state of nature (or some alternative political structure). The question of whether the state has failed to uphold its obligation to protect citizens that comes to the fore in many urban areas.

In America, we consider sanctions in criminal law as being deterrents and look upon law enforcement agencies as being protective agencies. I believe that the purpose of a legal system is to ensure that an individual may go peacefully about her business without coercive interference. Many African Americans living in urban areas cannot go peacefully about their business. They live in fear based on personal victimization or the victimization of friends, neighbors or relatives. It is the same fear that has caused the residents of these areas to turn their houses into prisons in which they attempt to lock themselves from crime. The majority of these citizens are neither criminal nor involved in crime, yet they find themselves often at the mercy of the criminal element. Members of these black communities cannot feel that the state is protecting them.

One might object that there is too much police presence in black neighborhoods. The extraordinarily high lifetime arrest probabilities of young, male, urban blacks suggest that law enforcement agents have a very high profile in black urban neighborhoods. Many urban residents think that the police are there to contain rather than to protect.

Citizens have to believe that the state places importance on their lives as members of the state. When many young blacks review their social history, can they be sure that the state will protect them or values them? Locke and later contract theorists tacitly assumed that the state would provide equal physical protection for all members of the state. Blacks realize that the state has been slow to protect their constitutionally guaranteed rights. How can they be expected to believe that the government will protect them not only from crime, but the police?

I can at least say that if physical protection is one of the basic benefits of being a member of the social contract, then black urban residents are left to question the value of contract membership. The behavior of the police forces us to reassess our obligations to the state and our understanding of the value of the social order. To many urban youths, the behavior of the state indicates a broken contract and as a result there is no

433

obligation on the part of blacks to support the United States. This antagonism is expressed by Ice-Cube when he exclaims, "I want to kill Sam."

Romanticizing Rap and Revolution

There are a number of interrelated objections to our interpretation of rap music. First, am I romanticizing rap? Many middle-class blacks and whites think that rap is the music of young criminals. Why should we think that the concept of the social contract is applicable in this situation?

The impact of rap music and rap artists was clearly shown in the aftermath of the Rodney King verdict. In surveys of urban youth, rappers were seen as the only group that understands their plight and that spoke the truth about conditions in America. To many urban youth, rap and rappers represent the only means of expressing their concerns. This attitude toward rap gives rap and rappers a great deal of influence in shaping the attitudes of urban youth. But it might be claimed: "Its only music!" Youthful supporters view rap as their own communication device. When blacks are victimized in the United States, the event is retold in rap songs spreading the "news." Rap is a method keeping the struggle alive.

My point here is that rappers have a political ideology and that, from Grandmaster Flash's "Message" to the present, this message has been increasingly negative about the treatment of blacks in America. Rap is now more than twenty years old and has spread from US urban centers to countries around the world. There are rappers in Russia, China, and France. These young people are using rap to express their dissatisfaction with the "powers that be." Here it might be asked, why should we look for some political ideology underpinning rap? And why the social contract?

The social contract idea is an important ideological element of our conception of political authority. One aspect of this ideology is the role of the state in protecting the lives of its citizens. Rappers, as do many Americans, understand the relationship between the state and its members as one of reciprocal obligations. Many political rappers maintain that the United States has never lived up to its obligations to ensure justice for African Americans. It is this state-against-black-America perception that defines rap music's political stance.

My efforts are not directed toward giving an extensive overview of all attempts by rappers to express political themes in their music. Rap should be viewed as a post-civil rights music. Although rap has roots in the slave songs, freedom songs, and artists such as The Last Poets, Watts Prophets, and Gil Scot-Heron. Still, I contend that rap represents a break with these forms of expression in that it is the sound of young people who came of age in a period of great racial change in the social and political texture of the United States. These are young persons who were never denied entrance to places of public accommodation, persons who have seen more black images on television and in the movies than at any other time in American history. Their frustration with America is in essence a different type of frustration than that of previous generations of African Americans. Many urban youths see themselves in a battle for the social and political life of African peoples in a manner that older Americans, black and white, do not and can not. This may explain the reason that old-style messages of social responsibility are not effective in reaching many young urban black teenagers.

References

Cypress Hill. "Pigs." Ruff House/Sony Entertainment.

ED O. G. & Da Bulldogs. "Speak Upon It." *Life of a Kid in the Ghetto.* America/Mercury.

Granddaddy IU. "This is a Recording." Cold Chillin' Records.

Ice Cube. "I Wanna Kill Sam." *Death Certificate.* Priority Records.

Joe The Butcher. "Decade." Wumpy Music.

King Sun. "Be Black." *Righteous But Ruthless.* Profile Records.

KRS-One. "Who Protects Us from You." *Ghetto Music: The Blueprint of Hip-Hop.* Boogie Down Productions Jive.

L. L. Cool J. "Illegal Search." Def Jam.

Lawson, Bill E. 1989. "Locke and the Legal Obligations of Black Americans." *Public Affairs Quarterly* 49.

—— 1990. "Crime, Minorities and the Social Contract." *Criminal Justice Ethics* 9.2. Summer/Fall.

—— 1992. "Uplifting the Race: Middle-Class Blacks and the Truly Disadvantaged." In *The Underclass Question,* ed. by Bill E. Lawson. Philadelphia: Temple University Press.

Locke, John. 1952. *The Second Treatise of Government,* ed. Thomas P. Peardon. New York: Bobbs-Merrill.

Lott, Tommy L. 1992. "Marooned in America: Black Urban Youth Culture and Social Pathology." In *The Underclass Question,* ed. Bill E. Lawson. Philadelphia: Temple University Press.

Main Source. *Breaking Atoms.* Wild Pitch.

Morris, Milton D. 1975. *The Politics of Black America.* New York: Harper and Row.

Naughty By Nature. "Everything's Gonna be Alright." Tommy Boy Records.

Newsweek. "Farrakhan's Mission." March 19, 1990, p. 25.

Paris. "The Hate That Hate Made." Tommy Boy Records.

Sir Mix-a-lot. "One Times Got No Case." Polygram International.

The Gallup Report 8. March/April 1989.

Tupac. "Trapped." Interscope Records.

U.S. News & World Report. "This is Beirut, U.S.A." April 10, 1989, p. 20.

U.S. News & World Report. "Victims of Crime." July 31, 1989, p. 16.

W.C. and the Madd Circle. "Behind Closed Doors." Base Pipe Music.

31

Sports, Political Philosophy, and the African American

GERALD EARLY

There was a time in the United States, particularly in the nineteenth century, but not exclusively so, for the idea persisted in some sociological and anthropological circles well into the twentieth century, when blacks were referred to by whites as the "lady of the races." That is to say, blacks or African Americans, were seen as exhibiting qualities as a group that were considered feminine or associated with the female side of nature. Blacks, like women, were seen as being deeply religious, much more naturally religious than whites; tending more towards the arts and oratory; more musical than whites; more emotional than whites; more attracted to colors; to physical sensations rather than to abstract ideas. In short, blacks, like women, couldn't think but they could feel deeply. While this idea of blacks as the lady of the races was pervasive in some nineteenth century white intellectual circles, no one popularized it more than Harriet Beecher Stowe in her 1852 novel, *Uncle Tom's Cabin*, one of the best-selling novels of the nineteenth century, although now neglected, if not a book that has fallen into disfavor except among a group of feminist scholars who argue about whether the feminist vision of the novel is truly radical. And the novel that has given us the epithet, "Uncle Tom." The impact of this novel, despite the fact that few people read it now, cannot be overstated.

In this novel, we are given the picture of the African as the epitome of non-aggression, the African as the sacrificial saint, in the person of Uncle Tom himself. Tom is described as "a large, broad-chested, powerfully-made man, of a full glossy black, and a face whose truly African features were characterized by an expression of grave and steady good sense, united with much kindliness and benevolence." In short, Tom is described as having the physique of, well, an athlete. He is, of course, no athlete, although his appearance might bring to mind the legendary African-American boxer, former slave, Tom Molineaux, who fought British open-weight champion Tom Cribb for the world championship in 1810 and 1811, losing both times and who died a lonely and dissipated death a short time after his defeats. Professional athletics for a black person, with the exception of prizefighting and horse-racing, scarcely existed in the United States before the Civil War. (Indeed, professional and amateur sports as we understand them today are largely the result of industrialization and urbanization that occurred after the Civil War, in the later third of the nineteenth century.) Uncle Tom is not only a top field supervisor and clerk; he is a minister, a deeply religious man who believes whole-heartedly in his Bible. He is, moreover, looked up to on the various plantations where he works during the course of the novel by both the whites and the blacks. He is a leader, although he does not seem to comprehend clearly how much of a leader he is. And while his religious beliefs give him authority; it is his physical presence that gives him stature and brings him to the notice of others. Simon Legree, for instance, wishes to make Tom a slave driver on the basis of Tom's appearance. He is a big man whom other slaves will obey without questions, is how Legree thinks.

Yet, Tom is suitably humble to his station. He wants to be free but not in assertive or daring way. He is far different from George Harris, the other black man who is described at length and featured prominently in the novel. Harris is described in a fugitive slave poster as "six feet in height, a very light mulatto, brown curly hair; is very intelligent, speaks handsomely, can read and write; will probably try to pass for a white man." Harris is naturally aggressive and outgoing as Tom is "naturally patient, timid, and unenterprising." Harris flees from slavery to escape a cruel master and to rescue his family. Tom does not. Harris stands up to white slave hunters and even shoots one of his pursuers. Tom is beaten to death by Simon Legree's slaves and forgives them before he dies. The difference between the two men is that George Harris has hot, hasty Saxon blood. After all, as James Baldwin remarked about the character in his famous essay on the novel, "Everybody's Protest Novel," we have only the author's word that Harris is black. In no way does he seem different from the standard white fictional male hero of the mass-market literature of this period. Tom, on the other hand, is a full-blooded African. Alas, that difference is the only difference that matters. In an odd paradox in the novel, Tom is referred as "Father Tom" and seems a father figure to everyone, white and black. Yet, in this novel that is a celebration of motherhood, Tom is the grandest mother of them all. He is maternal with everyone, including, most famously, Little Eva, the doomed daughter of the paternal, effeminate planter, Augustine St. Clair. This is why Baldwin called Tom "de-sexed," despite the fact that Tom has a wife and children. Everything about him glows with the aura of the feminine: his gentleness, his patience, his willingness to sacrifice. It seemed that Harriet Beecher Stowe was saying that the only way a black man could be a father was by being, in effect, a mother. It might be said, of course, that Tom is meant to be a Christ figure which is simply saying the obvious. What we have in Tom is the feminization of Christ himself as a savior figure, much in keeping with the nineteenth-century view, the Victorian view of Christ. It is also much in keeping with the rampant feminization of Christianity that is taking place in the nineteenth century that Ann Douglas wrote about so incisively in her book, *The Feminization of American Culture*. Religion is no longer complex theology but simply speaking from the heart; in the womanly sphere of domesticity is where true religious virtue lives because it was in the sphere of domesticity and the hearth and home that one found refuge from the money values of the marketplace and from the corruption of outside world of politics. Remember the novel is called *Uncle Tom's Cabin*, the scene in which we are given this domicile in the novel is not a picture of masculine asceticism but womanly domesticity, a peaceable kingdom of family relations. In the stage shows and films that have been made based on *Uncle Tom's Cabin*, Tom is so "de-sexed" that he is usually portrayed as an old man, well beyond the age of an active sex life, not as the strong-limbed black man in the prime of life that he actually is.

This un-manning of the black man in what became not merely a popular novel but a virtually unstoppable force in American popular culture may have led to blacks using "Uncle Tom" as a vituperative epithet. Baldwin was right that the book seemed to give the black man his humanity by denying his human nature, by making him the personification of moral good while being completely non-threatening. Tom never said he hated the conditions he had to endure, the unfairness of his life. For some like Baldwin, this seemed to be asking a bit too much of the victims of oppression, particularly oppressed men who always had to bear the burden of being non-threatening and non-aggressive in order to gain the sympathy of their oppressors. The feminization of Uncle Tom was not the only factor that led to "Uncle Tom," the term, being used in the way that it currently is but I believe it is one of them.

What we realize right away with *Uncle Tom's Cabin* is that the muscular black man was an icon in American popular culture before the Civil War, who, even in the guise of being meek and mild, evolved as popular culture representations into an old man without virility. In this regard, he was a man whose presence generated a specific need to confine him, indeed, the presence seemed to have been evoked in order to confine it. The philosophical and political issues surrounding the muscular black man, and, in turn, the assertive black man, for the muscularity became an outward symbol of an assertiveness that had to be placed under white social control, were to achieve their highest resonance in the realm of sports.

In his controversial study of the intersection of race and sports, John Hoberman, in *Darwin's Athletes: How Sport has Damaged Black America and Preserved the Myth of Race*, writes: "The muscular black male for whom certain white men felt a kind of nostalgia long after Emancipation can thus be seen as a kind of domesticated noble savage, and it is likely that our own culture's taste for *Mandingo* style images of the black man is to some degree a legacy of this: an idealized black muscularity that was once safely confined by whips and chains is now financially controlled by the white businessmen who own and operate the professional sports leagues" (italics Hoberman). Here Hoberman is openly suggesting that sports exist as a form of white hegemonic ideology, a representation within the sphere of entertainment and popular culture of the same political arrangement that exists elsewhere and everywhere in American society. If this muscularity is no longer confined by religion, as we now live in more secular age, then it is dominated by, what some scholars have argued is, one of the major mass cultural activities that have replaced religion by taking on the characteristics of a religion: namely high-performance athletics.

What Stowe did in her novel, this transformation of the muscular black man to Jesus Christ, is called romantic racialism or romantic racism, dressing up blacks in sentimental clothing to make them more palatable, more acceptable to whites. (Stowe's novel, *Dred: A Tale of the Great Dismal Swamp* (1856), gives us another muscular black man, Dred, the son of Denmark Vesey, a slave who fomented rebellion in South Carolina. Unfortunately, despite Dred's long, Biblical speeches about vengeance, he is largely an emasculated, romantic hero who dies at novel's end having effected no rebellion at all. A poorly and hastily written novel, *Dred*, in any case, never gave the public the indelible image of the slave that *Uncle Tom's Cabin* did.) Historian George M.

438

Fredrickson provides a detailed historical overview of romantic racialism in his book on nineteenth-century American racial attitudes called *The Black Image in the White Mind*. The impact of this concept of romantic racialism has been wide and deep in this society and for the most part very pernicious. Although there have been subtle changes in the idea of romantic racialism, it has largely remained the same over the years and the major racial trait it emphasizes is the physicality of blacks. While perhaps not apparent at first blush, it would seem inevitable that blacks as slaves in the United States who were largely manual agrarian laborers, "primitives," if you will, in a country that was rapidly transforming itself from something agrarian to a highly complex industrial society would be seen through the haze of romantic racialism, a view reflecting its own anti-intellectualism and fear of modernity while emphasizing the lack of black intellectual capacity.

Blacks themselves have found it difficult to overcome this view of themselves. Its persistence has been intense. First, many blacks have adopted a version of romantic racialism where they themselves believe that blacks or Africans are more caring, more spiritual, more musical, more family-oriented, more emotional, less interested in abstract concepts than whites. At one time this was called Negritude. At another, it was called the Black Aesthetic. Now, it is called Afrocentrism. All of these racial orthodoxies suggests, in some of their aspects, that blacks are "the lady of the races," that they are somehow more "humane" than aggressive, competitive whites. Second, the enormous presence and success that blacks have achieved in two fields that are perceived in our culture as being both "charismatic" and "anti-intellectual" – popular music and sports – has further intensified the idea of blacks as primitives, as somehow more in tune with their bodies and more in tune with their feelings and their intuitions, their instincts, than whites. Many blacks, seizing these areas of achievement as sources of pride, have stressed their physical superiority. Many whites have granted blacks this physical superiority as a sign of their mental inferiority. Perhaps one of the most famous exchanges in the matter of black physical superiority was black sociologist Harry Edwards's "The Sources of the Black Athlete's Superiority," written in 1971 in response to another *Sports Illustrated* article by Martin Kane called "An Assessment of 'Black is Best'" (January 18, 1971). But this has been an ongoing discussion since the nineteenth century (Frederick Douglass's 1854 "The Negro Ethnologically Considered" as a response to the racist assessment of the black body and black mind by such racist intellectuals of the day as Josiah Nott, Louis Agassiz, Samuel Morton, and others). The most recent subtle but elaborate assertion of a black physical superiority as an explanation for a lower black IQ is Murray and Herrnstein's *The Bell Curve*, which has received numerous critical responses from blacks. There can be no real understanding of African Americans and sports or how African Americans see sports without a fundamental understanding of how the body of the African American has become the subject of racist philosophical and political beliefs, of romantic racialism.

Whites of course adopted these beliefs in romantic racialism for other reasons as well, in large measure, because they saw blacks as a kind of alter ego to themselves. Black faced-minstrelsy, the most popular and powerful theater in nineteenth century American, is proof of that. It gave whites a great deal of pleasure and psychic relief to pretend to be blacks and from this form of grotesque impersonation, rooted in European

439

mummery, emerged a form of mass entertainment. If whites saw blacks, on the one hand, as beasts, rapists, murderers, and potential rebels against the slave order who must be put down at all costs, this could be disguised by seeing them as child-like, emotional beings, full of Christian grace. Moreover, if whites, especially white males, felt that they lived in a super competitive society that demanded aggression and shrewdness to survive, that was so fluid as to produce acute anxiety and a deep sense of insecurity, blacks, especially slaves, became for them a kind of psychological escape. Here whites could fantasize about a group of people who did not need aggression to survive, who did not suffer anxiety and a sense of insecurity, who were timid, peaceful, and unenterprising in a land that was obsessed with enterprise, a land where aggression was highly valued because the United States, until the twentieth century, was largely a frontier society, rapidly expanding its space in hostile encounters against the indigenous peoples who lived here. In eighteenth- and nineteenth-century America, and the same remains true today, the main obsession was "making it." In some ways, the creation of high-level professional and amateur athletics in the latter-part of the nineteenth century was a dramatization and representation of the very values of aggression, enterprise, ingenuity, and improvisation that American society prized. Of course, as blacks began more and more to excel in athletics, they became associated with these values but in a somewhat perverse way, certainly not in a way that freed them from romantic racialist assumptions.

Eldridge Cleaver, in *Soul on Ice*, was to make much of this idea of romantic racialism as a primary force in American social thinking when it comes to sex and the physicality of blacks and whites. The twist was that, by the twentieth century, the black man was no longer quite "the lady" but a kind of romantic version of an exaggerated masculinity, a version of American machismo. This idea of the black man as exaggerated masculinity intensified as black men achieved fame in popular music and athletics that both, in their unique ways, sold, among other things, sex and sexual taboos to the American public. The black male as a superior form of masculinity to the white man was certainly an idea that Norman Mailer was trying to sell in his famous 1957 essay, "The White Negro," which was just a new expression of romantic racialism. But this was all still rooted in the old nineteenth-century idea of romantic racialism: for Norman Mailer and other like him, the African-American male was less repressed, more intuitive, more natural, more rhythmic, more in touch with his sexuality than the white man. And of course he was still less intellectual than the white man. Blacks don't deal with abstractions and highly complex ideas: the burden of the over-civilized white man. One can easily see the connection to Stowe's romantic racialism: in each instance, the black man is seen as a primitive, a kind of noble savage, as Hoberman suggested. The biggest difference is that with the rise of hipsterism and the cool, it was no longer necessary to see the black man as virtuous in Victorian terms, that is to say, in bourgeois Christian terms. Indeed, now the black man as an iconic symbol of masculinity, through his superlative performances in sports, was reified in even starker terms than before as something decidedly pagan and anti-bourgeois.

The shift in romantic racialism that changed a popular view of black men from naturally humble Christians to, using Eldridge Cleaver's phrase, super-masculine menials was largely the result of the creation of the huge entertainment machinery that was erected in the United States starting in the late nineteenth century. Today, we call this conglomerate, popular culture or mass culture. This machinery was created as America became a more urban society in the late nineteenth and early twentieth centuries, as it became a society with more leisure time that needed to be filled, and more consumer-oriented. The creation of popular culture as we understand it today occurred at the same time that black men were encouraged to exercise authority as heads of their own households in order to bring stability to the black family, that is, during Reconstruction. It must be remembered that black men, even though they may not have been able to exercise it as much as they would have liked, were able to vote and hold elective office, a good fifty years before black women could. In other words, black men had a kind of civic authority in their communities that black women lacked. Moreover, the Freedmen's Bureau and the white philanthropic foundations that financed black education in the south were very much interested in having black men hold authority in their communities. Finally, because the black church was, by far, the most powerful, most autocratic institution in the black community, the ascendancy of black men was assured as the black church is a deeply patriarchal institution. All of this effort to raise the black man as an authority figure in his own community helped produce, by way of cultural and political paradox, the many terrible lynchings and acts of terrorism that occurred during Reconstruction and after, most of these being crimes committed against black men. These lynchings were, of course, acts of political intimidation and social control.

So, what was this popular culture that came into existence. By the early twentieth century, the film industry was firmly established. Recordings made their appearance by the very early twentieth century (Enrico Caruso made records at the turn of the century, for instance) and this changed forever how popular music was packaged and sold in the United States and eventually the world. Another major component of popular culture was the rise of professional and collegiate sports. Black men were by and large shut out of most team sports. Organized baseball, the most popular sport in America, banned interracial play in the early 1880s and hardly encouraged it before. Scarcely any blacks played collegiate football because hardly any blacks were admitted to white colleges at this time. Blacks had a huge presence as jockeys in horse-racing but were driven from the profession in the early twentieth century by angry whites who wanted the jobs. As a result of this discrimination, the one sport where blacks were disproportionately represented was professional boxing. Blacks generally were able to fight for championships in boxing. George Dixon, Joe Gans, and Joe Walcott were all famous black champions at the turn of the century in the lighter weight divisions. The heavyweight title was considered the supreme title in sports by those who followed sports even casually. Blacks were largely banned from fighting for the heavyweight title for the same reason they were banned from other sports. Athletics were considered a sign of white male superiority. Sports existed symbolically, politically, to show the world that whites were the better race, the more aggressive race, the conquering, imperial, more masculine race. In other words, it was whites, not blacks, who first attached political significance to sports by banning blacks from competition. (Blacks were to interpret sports politically and symbolically in the years to come, especially as more blacks began to write on the subject.) In these days, African Americans were thought to lack the nerve and skill to beat whites in head-to-head competition.

The color line was drawn in heavyweight boxing until 1908 when Jack Johnson defeated Tommy Burns and became the first black heavyweight champion. Johnson's winning the title and the controversy that ensued is very important in understanding the shift that eventually occurred where black men became more associated with being superior athletes. Johnson not only beat the best white fighters of this day but he had white girlfriends. This did not make him unique among black public figures of the day. George Walker, for instance, of the successful black comedy team, Williams and Walker, had many white girlfriends. George Dixon, the famous black boxer, had a white wife. What made Johnson unique was that he flaunted his attraction to white women and their attraction to him. This tied together in our popular culture the idea of the black man as superior athlete and superior sexual competitor to the white man. It was the actualization of a secret fear that had played at the edges of white entertainment and American popular culture for years, the white hegemonic implications of this secret fear were to reach a new level of intensity with the emergence of the modern black athlete.

These ideas of black athletic superiority and black ultra-masculinity have remained with us ever since with an ever-growing luridness. As blacks like Joe Louis, Jesse Owens, Fritz Pollard, Jackie Robinson, and others continued to demonstrate great black athletic ability, whites began more and more to promote the idea of a natural black athletic superiority, that blacks were physically superior to whites. Most whites were willing to accept this because they always thought blacks were their intellectual inferiors. Black supremacy in sports proved black intellectual inferiority in the eyes of many whites. Besides, since big-time, high level sports are nothing more than a form of entertainment in our society, to be a sports performer is certainly not an expression of power; it was nothing more than a part of the mass culture machine, many whites thought that black sports prowess simply confirmed the idea that blacks were natural, showy entertainers. Thus, blacks as sports performers did not threaten white hegemonic assumptions embedded in the symbolism of sports themselves. Sport was the African American niche in American life, to show themselves off as flamboyant physical presences.

This was the new twist on the old romantic radicalism of the nineteenth century. As blacks became a more and more dominant presence in American's most popular sports, the idea that they were natural athletes gained more currency, as did the idea that the sports black dominated, and the positions they dominated in those sports (a practice known as stacking), required no particular intellect to play. This idea even now has a powerfully and complex hold in our society. Here is a recent example. The stories in the *New York Times* (July 7, 1997, page C9) and the *St. Louis Post-Dispatch* (July 7, 1997, page C5) that covered young black golfer Tiger Wood's recent win at the Motorola Western Open had these headlines, respectively: "Woods Wins in Triumph of Mind Over Matter" and "Brain, not Brawn, Captures Western Open for Woods." There are two important points being made here: first, golf, as a game dominated by white men who do not have to demonstrate spectacular physical gifts is implicitly more intellectual than most sports. Certainly, most people probably believe that although there is not a shred of objective evidence that says playing eighteen holes of golf in a professional tournament is more mentally taxing than being a major league catcher or a major league centerfielder or a wide receiver in pro football. Second, the newspapers as well as Woods himself seem to be stressing the fact that he has great mental abilities that explain why he is able to play this game well. Both the newspapers and Woods seem very aware of the dumb black jock stereotype and seem to be think that Woods, as the brainy champion in the white man's game, can counter-act it. This is all implicit in the headlines. Once again, there is not a shred of evidence that the considerable mental toughness and competitive spirit that Woods exhibits differ in either kind or degree from the mental toughness and competitive spirit necessary for a high-performance athlete to succeed in any sport where the pressure is intense and the risk of failure high. In other words, it might be said that a certain mentality, if not intelligence, wins any athletic contest (if not, luck). One must strategize to win any sports competition. It might also be said that brawn, physical ability, wins golfing matches as it does any sporting endeavor. After all, the pro golfer, like the centerfielder or the wide receiver, or the concert pianist, for that matter, is relying on muscle memory, on rote training, on automatic responses, as much as anything else. Naturally, there are many Hispanics and some Asians who are famous in American sports but the issue of race and sports in America is not a "minority" issue but a black and white one, which is why Woods's half-Asian ancestry is a political irrelevancy.

Broadly speaking, the main attitudes of blacks themselves towards sports might be seen, predictably enough, as, on the one had, a fierce opposition to sports and play as both a waste of time, unenterprising and unproductive, and a form of racial degradation, as, in most instances, sports competition between blacks was being performed for a white audience or at the behest of whites. Such an attitude was expressed by Frederick Douglass in his 1845 *Narrative*, and generally so in most anti-slavery literature written by blacks. If one were to interpret the Battle Royal scene in Ralph Ellison's *Invisible Man* (1952) as, in part, a representation, both politically and aesthetically, of blacks in athletic competition in this country, one finds, in a much more sophisticated and intellectually complex way, the same concerns about sports as a form of race degradation that the slave narrators like Douglass expressed in the nineteenth century. This anti-sports attitude is not uncommon among many blacks today largely fueled by a strict sense of Protestant or religious sobriety and propriety (many black religious denominations – including Baptists, on the one hand, and the Holiness Church, Black Muslims, Moorish Americans, on the other, discourage or prohibit their members from attending or watching sporting events) as well as a strong sense of race mission and race dignity.

On the other hand, blacks have seen sports as a means of access, a way to or route for social and economic mobility or they have seen it as a way of widening democracy, of spreading democratic values and ideals. The first view, studied as a sociological phenomenon in Othello Harris's "Race, Sport, and Future Orientation?" in the *Journal of African American Men*, largely supports sports as a way of giving black men, who have limited occupational opportunities in this country a chance not only to succeed in a high-paying, high visibility career but also to get a college education. Indeed, according to this view, many black men finish high school only because of the sports option and would exhibit very little interest in school if it were not there. The second view, championed most famously by long-time black sportswriter A. S. "Doc" Young in *Negro Firsts in Sports* (1963), sees sports as an arena where blacks compete with whites as equals, thus providing the country, through daily coverage of sporting events in the local papers, an opportunity to see, in action, the ideal of blacks and whites working together. Moreover, not only does the opening of sports to the black athlete, particularly after World War II, show the triumph of democratic ideals of fair play and the like but sports themselves are a representation of democratic ideals, the individual's interest balanced against that of the team, the same application of rules for both sides, the ultimate rewarding of superior merit, and so forth. This set of arguments was used by black and white sportswriters in support of the integration of major league baseball, a major cause for both the left and black sportswriters of the 1930s and they were to be used to interpret the significance of Jackie Robinson and baseball as symbols of American democratic values once baseball was integrated on the minor league level in 1946 and the major league level in 1947. This was an argument that saw no real hegemonic expression of white power in sports as a representation but rather located all hegemonic expression in its corporate structure of ownership which could be, by public pressure forcing the corporation to redefine its self-interest, made to change.

A new note was sounded in the African-American view of sports with the emergence of the civil disobedience phase of the civil rights movement. Famed black sportswriter Wendell Smith, who had campaigned hard for the integration of professional baseball and served as Jackie Robinson's companion during the first year of Robinson's career as Brooklyn Dodger, wrote in the *Pittsburgh Courier* on March 14, 1964 that "the Negro athlete in this country has, with a few exceptions, been conspicuously silent in the fight for civil rights. . . . most of them seem to hold themselves above the Negro masses with respect to civil rights and do nothing to help correct existing evils." If, at one time, the black athlete was a political and folk hero simply by virtue of his professional accomplishments or because he competed head-to-head against whites, by the 1960s, this was no longer a sufficient sign that he was committed to his people or a representation of the virtue of their struggle. In his article, Smith particularly criticizes baseball players: "on the whole, the Negro baseball player has been remiss in his responsibilities in the area of civil rights, even to the extent that he was voluntarily acquiesced to racial segregation and discrimination in certain instances." Smith is the black boxer as the political vanguard: "When Floyd Patterson was the champion, he went to Alabama with Jackie Robinson to march and demonstrate against racial bigotry. Joe Louis, Ray Robinson, and other Negro boxers contributed similarly toward the cause when they were in their prime. Cassius Clay has, unfortunately chosen the 'Muslim Way' to fight bigotry. But that does not obliterate the fact that he has had the fortitude to take a position. While you may not agree with his form of protest, you have to agree that Cassius is at last (sic) protesting."

It was, without question, the emergence of heavyweight boxer Muhammad Ali, known before 1964 as Cassius Clay, that generated the entire issue of how publicly political any black athlete should be. One month earlier, in February 1964, Clay, a huge underdog, defeated Sonny Liston and won the heavyweight boxing title. Immediately after the fight, Clay announced that he was a member of the Nation of Islam, a militant, separatist black group whose leading spokesman was Malcolm X. By 1967, Ali had taken a stance against the Vietnam War and refused to be inducted in the US Army. He was convicted of violation of the Selective Service Act and sentenced to five years in prison. Arguably, the famous athlete and probably the most famous black person in the world by this time, Ali had become also the world's most famous political dissident. As the civil rights movement grew increasingly more militant and disruptive as the

decade of the 1960s progressed, with the rise of Black Power and an increasing number
of urban race riots and political assassinations, there was, as a result of the example of
Ali, more and more pressure on the black athlete to take public political stances that
identified him clearly with the mood of black people at this time. Most of these athletes
were young and more inclined to identify with this more pronounced expression of militancy as largely the black freedom struggle in the United States at this time was dominated or at least very much energized by young people. Indeed, many began to look at
earlier black athletes such as Jackie Robinson, Jesse Owens, and Joe Louis as Uncle Toms
or decided compromised heroes. One culmination of this was at the 1968 Olympic
Games when sprinters Tommie Smith and John Carlos gave clenched fist salutes during
the playing of the Star Spangled Banner when they were awarded their medals. A full
account of this overt politicization of the black athlete in the 1960s is given in Harry
Edwards's *The Revolt of the Black Athlete* (1969). Since this period of the 1960s, black
athletes have never been openly political again. There remains some who think that the
black athlete should be more blatantly political (which generally among those who
espouse this position means more blatantly left-wing or anti-establishment) because he
is a role-model, a highly influential and publicized person, who can do much to bring
together what some see as a fractured black community or who could publicly
advocate for the black community. Basketball stars are most commonly criticized by
those who take this position for not being more publicly political. For instance, some
bitterly complained when Michael Jordan, from North Carolina, refused to publicly
support Harvey Gant, a black who ran for the Senate twice in the 1990s, feeling that
someone of the stature of Jordan not only had a responsibility to do so but could
have made a difference as Gant lost both times. Black sports historian Jeffrey Sammons
is one of the most ardent supporters of this view of the political engagement of
the black athlete. The representation of the black athlete as a political figure or, more
accurately, because he comes from an oppressed group, a political rebel or dissident,
leads to questions about whether sports themselves are the expression or representation of a political ideology or white corporate hegemony which the black athlete must
both conform to as a public performer while he criticizes it as a public citizen. The inherent contradictions and difficulties of such a position rarely dawn on those who espouse
the political engagement of the black athlete. There would seem to be nothing inherent in the performance of any sport that would be considered the expression of
an explicit political ideology. As a performance, sports seem to transcend any given
political system or political ideas. Free market democracies, Communist regimes,
right-wing dictatorships have all supported professional sports and have all lionized star
athletes. This, of course, does not mean in the act of attaching immediate or transcendent meaning or values to sports or in the structure created to support sports or
the athlete, there is not a great deal of political ideology or at least some number of
political issues.

Currently, the issue of race and sports revolves around the political and social
meaning attached to the issue of black athletic superiority or the general perception of
such supposed superiority. The cover story of the March 24, 1997 issue of *U.S. News
and World Report* was "Are Pro Sports Bad for Black America?" which dealt with the
preoccupation with sports in the black community. According to the story, "66 percent
of all African-American males between the ages of 13 and 18 believe they can earn

a living playing professional sports," while only 33 percent of white boys in the same age bracket think this. Doubtless, the over-representation of blacks in the major team sports (80 percent of all NBA players, 6 percent of all NFL players, and 20 percent of all baseball players) contributes to this. Moreover, as our society continues to debate heatedly the need for Affirmative Action, sports offers a curious dimension to the subject for it is the only competitive field where merit unquestioningly determines one's fate. And it is one of the few fields of endeavor in American life, in its performance aspect, where no one, especially no one white, questions the ability of blacks. Blacks themselves may feel less pressure pursuing athletics because of this: no one questions their ability; indeed, many are willing to grant their superiority.

To understand why our society is having this problem with young black males' over-determined aspiration to be athletes, one must, of course link this to the equally difficult battle to fight their intense anti-intellectualism. These boys generally think intellectualism and mental accomplishment are white, such thinking being largely the result of the romantic racialism that has shaped our culture. Oddly, the young black boys who think that being intellectual, that being literate and learned is "white," actually are right, for our society has promoted that every image, that very idea, that very concept, since, at least, the early days of colonial America.

An examination of two recent articles should put this issue of blacks over-pursuit of sports in perspective. "Great Black Hopes," written by Steve Sailor, a Chicago business-man was published in the August 12, 1996 issue of the famous conservative magazine, *National Review*. Sailor had, in the April 8, 1996 issue of the same magazine, written a piece called "How Jackie Robinson Integrated America" that argued that Robinson's integration of baseball was a victory for free market principles. In the piece entitled "Great Black Hopes," Sailor argues that "equality of opportunity in America's top team sports has led not to equality of results but to black superiority. For example, a random American black is currently 10 times more likely to reach the National Football League and 25 times more likely to reach the National Basketball Association that a random non-black." Sailor argues that sports is, in essence, black people's market niche in American society and that they should exploit their "natural edges" and "sizable cultural advantages." He further argues that in a multi-racial society such as the United States, it is no surprise that certain professions will become the specialties of certain ethnic or racial groups. He cites the fact that Asian Indians manage about half of America's hotels. He is cognizant of the fact that many believe that a black superiority in sports indicates or implies a general intellectual inferiority for the group. He counters this by asserting that "much of black sports success seems to originate above the neck, in certain common mental advantages blacks tend to have over whites." This superior intelligence that blacks have is for "creative improvisation and on-the-fly interpersonal decision-making." Blacks seem to be able to respond to situations quicker than whites. "These black cerebral superiorities in 'real time' responsiveness also contribute to black dominance in jazz, running with the football, rap, dance, trash talking, preaching, and oratory." These are, of course, the very "intelligences" that whites have granted to blacks since the days of Harriet Beecher Stowe's *Uncle Tom's Cabin*. In short, blacks are good at entertaining. Sailor is doing nothing more but giving us the old romantic racialist line but calling these so-called black or African qualities by the euphemism, intelligence. He ultimately suggests that black men, charismatic by nature,

446

ought to go into sales. Black men are generally ill-suited for paper-pushing bureaucratic jobs. "Natural leadership," writes Sailor, "is practically synonymous with something black guys have in abundance: masculine charisma." This sounds a great deal like the view of black men in Mailer's "The White Negro," the modern hipster's version of romantic racialism.

Sailor argues that because black men are so over-represented in certain sports, they should exploit this advantage by steering themselves toward these sports. This is tantamount to saying that because there are several prominent Hollywood filmmakers who happen to be Jewish, Jewish boys should be pushed toward filmmaking in school. Because an ethnic or racial group dominates a particularly small industry really says nothing about what the majority of people in the group should do, especially as the majority clearly will have insufficient talent to go into that industry for a living. Asian Indians may manage half the hotels in the United States but what that means is that the vast majority of Asian Indians have nothing to do with hotel management and are not especially helped by the fact that Asian Indians dominate that field, any more so than the average African American is in any way much affected by the fact that the NBA teams are 80 percent black. The reasoning may be less than persuasive here. Sailor's essay, nevertheless, is a common white conservative view. It was espoused, for instance, by Murray and Herrnstein in *The Bell Curve*.

Neither Sailor, Herrnstein, or Murray understand the implications of what they are suggesting. Blacks do not wish to be seen merely as America's entertainers or merely as people who are good at athletics. They want to explore the whole range of career possibilities. This is especially important because they have been denied access to so many careers for so long. In other words, it will not solve the race problem or ease it simply to tell blacks to exploit their natural "charisma" and go into sports and sales because such a solution does not address fundamentally the frustration and unhappiness many black people feel about their lives and the nature of the opportunities open to them in America. Black people have already proven to themselves and to the world that they can play sports. They feel a need to prove to themselves and to the world that they can do other things just as well. This is why the fact that so many black boys wish to play sports constitutes a serious problem in the black community.

The Winter 1995/96 issue of *Journal of African American Men*, a new academic publication, featured an article by Billy Hawkins entitled "The Black Student Athlete: The Colonized Black Body." In this piece, which, whether consciously intended or not, is a real counterpoint to the Sailor essay, Hawkins argues that black men historically have existed as a colonized presence, to be exploited like a physical resource. "The Black Body is the source of revenue for many Division I NCAA athletic departments," writes the author. They themselves cannot exploit being athletes for their own benefit in this society because they have virtually no power. To be a high-level college athlete, Hawkins asserts, by its very nature, is to be exploited. "Though the exploitation is disguised at the professional level by designer clothes and multi-million-dollar contracts the exploitation is even greater at the collegiate level where black athletes are only granted year-to-year scholarships that cover tuition, books, room and board while these institutions are benefiting to a far greater extent than the athletes." He says this is particularly true of black athletes at predominantly white, Division I NCAA schools where they rarely get a decent education, nor are they adequately compensated for the labor they provide as athletes. He goes into some lengthy discussion of the black man as the Body in the American mind, a truncated and somewhat distorted historical account. This discussion of the issue it seems to me is very flawed, equally as flawed as the white conservative view of Sailor's.

First, while black people are seen largely as physical presences in the United States, they are not really the Body in the American mind. Women, particularly white women, serve that purpose. It is their physical beauty that is central to American advertising and to the entertainment world. This is why women's dieting and women's beauty culture are such multi-billion dollar industries in this country. It is because of this emphasis on women as the body that women are generally so insecure about their looks and suffer a great deal from low self-esteem and depression. There is a need for greater precision in the matter of what type of physical presences blacks actually are in the white mind and in their own. Moreover, was the NCAA a colonizing/regulation body when white colleges exclusively recruited white student-athletes? Is it a form of exploitation when white student-athletes are recruited today? If not, why so? "Black student athletes are, in most cases, heavily recruited because of their athletic abilities; token interest, if any, is given to their academic abilities." But is not the same true for white student-athletes who are recruited by these schools? If this is not so, the author should explain as the difference is crucial to his argument.

Hawkins's discussion is further flawed by his attempt to make analogy between being a college athlete and colonialism. Colleges exploit the labor of many other students including, most notably, their Ph.D. and their post-doctoral students. One might argue that the Ph.D. students' exploitation is, after all, related to education, whereas the athlete is brought to the college to do something which is not really part of the primary mission or purpose of any college or university. But this is to suggest that intercollegiate competition cannot be a legitimate part of a college education and this would be incorrect. Only certain college athletics, such as football and basketball, are much the cause of the problem. Colleges almost never go on probation for recruitment violations in fencing, volleyball, women's gymnastics, or tennis. Athletics might, on the whole, be helpful to a university's mission. Certainly, sports are not a priori harmful or inimical to such a mission. Thomas Sowell makes this clear in his argument about sports and education in his book on American education. The existence of athletics at the university is not a self-evident case of exploitation. And exploitation of labor, as in the case of Ph.D. student, in and of itself, is not prima facie evidence of colonialism; for "colonialism," as understood as a policy of one nation dominating the indigenous people of another in the latter's own nation, is a philosophical and cultural system of social control and degradation. "Exploitation," a leftist cant word, does not even mean that those who are being exploited are suffering because of it. Hawkins's argument works only if we accept the premise that black participation in high-level sports is, in and of itself, an act of degradation which he seems to suggest because of the fixation by the white public on the physicality of the black body. To believe this is not the affirmation of a fact about sports but the acceptance of an attitude or stance toward the value of sports.

The explosive expansion of professional and high-level amateur sports may have intensified racism in this country through its romantic racialist assumptions about blacks being natural athletes and it may have made it very difficult for blacks to be seen as equals, having equal merit with whites, in other arenas of human endeavor. On the other hand, sports may have widened the concept of democracy in America and given blacks greater visibility and more access than they might otherwise have had. How the issue of race and sports will be resolved is nearly impossible to say. John Hoberman's controversial *Darwin's Athletes* has sparked considerable debate among black scholars, even outrage in some quarters. Whether such response is justified is not as important a concern as that a full engagement of this issue by black thinkers may not lead to a solution but it may lead to a fuller understanding of why things are the way they are and how the black community might intelligently be able to make changes.

References

Baldwin, James. 1955. "Everybody's Protest Novel." In James Baldwin, *Notes of A Native Son*. Boston: Beacon Press.

Cleaver, Eldridge. 1968. *Soul on Ice*. New York: Dell Publishing Co.

Douglas, Ann. 1997. The Feminization of American Culture. New York: Knopf.

Douglass, Frederick. 1848. *Narrative of the Life of Frederick Douglass, an American Slave*. New York: Penguin, 1982 rpt.

——. 1854. "The Claims of the Negro Ethnologiclly Considered." Rochester: n. p.

Edwards, Harry. 1969. *The Revolt of the Black Athlete*. New York: The Free Press.

——. 1971. "The Sources of the Black Athlete's Superiority." *Black Scholar*. November.

Ellison, Ralph. 1952. *Invisible Man*. 1948/75. New York: Vintage Books.

Fredrickson, George M. 1971. *The Black Image in the White Mind*. New York: Harper & Row.

Harris, Othello. 1996/97. "Race, Sport, and Future Orientation." *Journal of African American Men* 2.2/3. Fall–Winter.

Hawkins, Billy. 1995/96. "The Black Student Athlete: The Colonized Black Body." *Journal of African American Men* 1.3. Winter.

Hoberman, John M. 1997. *Darwin's Athletes: How Sport Has Damaged Black America and Preserved the Myth of Race*. Boston: Houghton Mifflin Co.

——. 1984. *Sports and Political Ideology*. Austin: University of Texas Press.

Kane, Morton. 1971. "An Assessment of 'Black is Best'." *Sports Illustrated*, January 13.

Mailer, Norman. 1956. "The White Negro: Superficial Reflections on the Hipster." In Norman Mailer, *Advertisements for Myself*. New York: Putnam, 1959.

Murray, Charles and Richard Herrnstein. 1994. *The Bell Curve: Intelligence and Class Structure in American Life*. New York: The Free Press.

Sailor, Steve. 1996. "Great Black Hopes." *National Review*. August 12.

Smith, Wendell. 1964. *Pittsburg Courier*. March 14.

Sowell, Thomas. 1993. *Inside American Education: The Decline, The Deception, The Dogmas*. New York: Free Press.

Stowe, Harriet Beecher. 1852. *Uncle Tom's Cabin; or Life Among the Lowly*. New York: Collier Books, 1962 rpt.

——. 1856. *Dred: A Tale of the Great Dismal Swamp*. Boston: Phillips, Sampson.

Young, A. S. 1963. *Negro Firsts in Sports*. Chicago: Johnson Publishing Co.

Index

Adderly, Cannonball, 395

Adorno, Theodor, 80, 97; critique of jazz, 374–5, 388–91; and cultural institutions, 374, 386–7

aesthetics, 5, 161, 373; and African retentions in culture, 184; and the beautiful, 382–3; and black cinema, 375–6, 399, 400–5; credentials of, 400; critique of, 376; and the culture industry, 387; and jazz, 374–5, 394, 397; and modernity, 426; and musical authenticity, 180–2; and Negritude, 439; notion of, 399; of rap music, 419–21; science, 400

affirmative action, 288–9, 446; attacks on, 327; beneficiaries of, 326, 330–1; as benign, 325–6; and color-blind policies, 329; common themes, 325; diverse views on, 324; hostility toward, 326; misconceptions concerning, 325, 328–30; and myth of preferential treatment, 325–30; objections to, 327–8; as race-based, 327; as reverse discrimination, 325; and welfare, 345, 346

Africa, colonizing as means of civilizing, 171–2; and cultural influences from diaspora, 172–3; European visions of, 193; and fusion of tradition/modern, 193–4; links with, 170, 381; positive image of, 172; and return to source theme, 193; and technology, 193

Africalogical inquiry, 151–2; concept of, 162, 165–6; epistemological issues, 161–3; and Eurocentrism, 163; identifying/querying, 162; methodology, 163–5; and objectivity, 162–3; as partisan, 164, 166; self-contradictory approach, 163; sources of, 161; strengths/weaknesses, 166

African Blood Brotherhood, 383

African diaspora, black nationalist impulse derived from, 90; and cultural heritage/ patriotism, 72, 74–5, 77, 81; cultural influences of, 172–3; and ethnic nationalism, 72; and European humanities, 74–5; functionalist modernism, 69, 71, 72–3; historical experience of, 70, 79; nationalist modernism, 74–7, 79; philosophies of, 63–5; and pre-generic myth of literacy, 97; and race, 74, 75; and racial enslavement, 69; relation with modernism, 67, 78; and sense of the past, 72; sociopolitical backdrop, 88–9

African-American philosophy, Africana perspective, 4–5, 48, 50–1; Africanisms in, 151; Americana perspective, 48, 49–50; assimilation vs. separation, 6; central notion of, 12; challenges confronting, 11; cultural perspective, 5; definition of, 3, 11, 29n, 49; development of, 58; double consciousness of, 60, 61; ethnophilosophical component, 63; European influences on, 3; historical traditions, 3–4; as hybrid discourse, 48; identity of, 58; impact of religion on, 58–60; integration vs. nationalism, 6; intertextual connections, 62; major function of, 11; and Marxism, 6; and modernity, 5, 12; outside of mainstream institutions, 48; politico-ideological orientation, 61; pragmatic conception of, 49; secular/ideological phase, 60–1; and self-image/self-determination, 11; stress on cultural/social practices, 10; suicidal tendencies, 6; theoretical constructs of, 12–27, 29–30n; and understanding of African-American experience, 3; widening scope of, 62–3, *see also* philosophy

African Americans, and black reactionaries, 235; and class, 26; cultural development of, 175–7; diachronic study of, 7, 27n; distinctiveness of, 13; and encounters with the past, 25–7; gap in health status of, 350; inferiority of, 18–19; liberation of, 383; links with Africa, 381; nationalist perspectives, 90; as passive objects of history, 12; pathological aspects, 13; and political extremism, 236; racial genius of, 15; restrictive, constraining, confining aspects, 13; in rural setting, 24–5; and segregated space, 211; uniqueness of, 12–13; in urban setting, 25; urbanization of, 381–2, 383, *see also* blacks

African-Caribbean philosophy, 54, 56, 57, 58; development of, 58; double consciousness of, 60, 61; ethnophilosophical component, 63; impact of religion on, 58–60; politico-ideological orientation, 61; secular/ideological phase, 60–1; widening scope of, 62–3, *see also* philosophy

Africana philosophy, 33, 48, 49–51, 151; and common identity, 50–1; and commonality, 50–1; and conceptual decolonization, 154; contact with Euro-American/European pragmatism/philosophy, 62–3; and cultural/economic imperialism, 154; and diasporic African philosophies, 63–5; and difference, 194–5; formation of, 57–8; invisibility of, 58, 60; and mythic discourse, 64–5; and reconstitution of racialized self, 51–3; and religion, 58–61; requirements for, 153–4; and scientism, 65; and shared writers, 62; three strands, 190–5; and traditions of activism, 64; western sources of, 154; widening scope of, 62–3, *see also* philosophy

Africana Studies, 164–5
Afrocentrism, 152, 195, 439; concept of, 160, 162; criticism of, 172; and focus on preslave past, 174; and knowledge production *see* Africalogical inquiry; orientation/agenda, 161; viability of, 164
Agassiz, Louis, 439
Aid to Families with Dependent Children (AFDC), 333, 334, 335, 340
Aid to the Permanently and Totally Disabled, 334
Alcoff, Linda Martin, 277
Allen, Richard, 59
A. M. E. Church, 15
American Baptist Home Missionary Society (ABHMS), 231
American Ethnological Society, 112, 113
American Negro Academy, 91, 92–4, 95
American Statistical Association, 261
Ames, Jessie Daniel, 415
Amin, Samir, 62, 157
Amish, 298
Ansley, Frances Lee, 269
Anthias, Floya, 208
Appadurai, Arjun, 257
Appiah, Anthony, 40, 42, 55, 62, 191, 194, 320
Aristotle, 293, 295, 421
Armstrong, Louis, 393
art forms, Africanisms in, 175–7; autonomy of, 387–8; avant garde, 400; and creative powers, 15; cultural centers for, 373, 382, 383; dance, 161; and propaganda, 373, 382–3; redemptive power of, 374, *see also* jazz; music; rap music
articulation, 225–6n
Asante, Molefi Kete, 39, 50, 159, 160–4, 172, 174
Asian Pacific Islanders (API), 260
assistance programs, 289
autonomy, individual, 337; state, 340

Baker, Ella, 230, 231, 234
Baldwin, James, 22–3, 41, 42, 57, 102, 278, 416, 437
Baltazar, Eulalio, 36
Baraka, Imamu, 15, 26
Basie, Count, 391
Beale, Frances, 222